Intro to FORENSIC SCIENCE

FROM A BIBLICAL WORLDVIEW

MasterBooks® CURRICULUM

MasterBooks® Curriculum

Curriculum Development:
Kristen Pratt

Editor-in-Chief:
Laura Welch

Editorial Team:
Craig Froman
Willow Meek
Judy Lewis

Art Director:
Diana Bogardus

Design Team:
Diana Bogardus
Terry White
Jennifer Bauer

Content Review:
Ron Smith and Associates, Inc.

First printing: May 2023
Second printing: February 2024

Copyright © 2023 by Jennifer Rivera and Master Books®. All rights reserved. No part of this book may be reproduced, copied, broadcast, stored, or shared in any form whatsoever without written permission from the publisher, except in the case of brief quotations in articles and reviews. For information write:

Master Books, P.O. Box 726, Green Forest, AR 72638
Master Books® is a division of the New Leaf Publishing Group, LLC.

ISBN: 978-1-68344-241-7
ISBN: 978-1-61458-802-3 (digital)
LOC: 2023933564

Unless otherwise noted, Scripture quotations are from the ESV® Bible (The Holy Bible, English Standard Version®), copyright © 2001 by Crossway, a publishing ministry of Good News Publishers. Used by permission. All rights reserved.

All Scriptures marked (KJV) are from the King James Version.

Printed in the United States of America.

Please visit our website for other great titles:
www.masterbooks.com

For information regarding promotional opportunities, please contact the publicity department at pr@nlpg.com.

Permission is granted for copies of reproducible pages from this text to be made for use with immediate family members living in the same household. However, no part of this book may be reproduced, copied, broadcast, stored, or shared in any form beyond this use. Permission for any other use of the material must be requested by email from the publisher at info@nlpg.com.

About the Author

Jennifer Hall Rivera EdD is the Director of Educational Programs for Answers in Genesis, where she oversees and presents in daily workshops and is involved in educational outreach and the high school lab programs. Her interest in the forensic sciences started at an early age and is credited to the godly instruction of her father, a renowned fingerprint expert. Her experience in the field of forensic science includes employment in a crime scene unit, over a decade of teaching, journal publications, and numerous speaking events.

TABLE OF CONTENTS

Foreword 5

Unit 1: Introduction

Lesson 1: What is Forensic Science? 8

Lesson 2: The Two Types of Science 16

Unit 2: The Crime Scene

Lesson 3: The Crime Scene 26

Lesson 4: Evidence Collection and Documentation 36

Unit 3: Physical Evidence

Lesson 5: Drugs 46

Lesson 6: Toolmarks 62

Lesson 7: Weapons 70

Lesson 8: Documents 84

Lesson 9: Computer Forensics 96

Unit 4: Biological Evidence

Lesson 10: DNA 112

Lesson 11: Serology 126

Lesson 12: Toxicology 140

Lesson 13: Anthropology 154

Lesson 14: Entomology 166

Lesson 15: Death Scenes 176

Unit 5: Transitory Evidence

Lesson 16: Human Fingerprints 186

Lesson 17: Animal Fingerprints 204

Lesson 18: Fingerprint Processing 214

Lesson 19: Trace Evidence Part I: Hair vs. Fur 228

Lesson 20: Trace Evidence Part II: Fibers 240

Lesson 21: Trace Evidence Part III: Glass and Paint 254

Lesson 22: Trace Evidence Part IV: Pollen and Soil 268

Lesson 23: Impressions 282

Lesson 24: Arson and Explosive Investigation 296

Lesson 25: Residues and Patterns 308

Unit 6: Forensic Tools

Lesson 26: Microscopes 320

Lesson 27: Crime Labs 334

Lesson 28: Mobile Forensics 342

Lesson 29: Facial Reconstruction 352

Unit 7: Forensic Specialties

Lesson 30: Forensic Odontology 364

Lesson 31: Forensic Psychiatry 378

Unit 8: The Judicial System

Lesson 32: The Judicial System 390

Lesson 33: Chain of Custody 404

Lesson 34: Courtroom Testimony 412

Glossary 427

Endnotes 439

DEDICATION AND THANK YOU

This book is dedicated to my hundreds of students who, over the years, have wished there was a forensic science textbook from a biblical worldview; and to all future students who are interested in pursuing this fascinating career. Science confirms the Bible, and this is clearly seen in the study of forensic science (Romans 1:20).

Thank you to my husband Michael, Dr. Dana Sneed, Dr. Georgia Purdom, Mr. P (Roger Patterson), and Ron Smith and Associates, Inc., who assisted in reviewing content, capturing images, editing, and so much more. Your support and prayers are greatly appreciated.

FOREWORD

Forensics is a scientific discipline that captures the attention of many young people. It's been made popular by a plethora of TV shows (some more based in reality than others!). My own daughter, while not very interested in science, enjoyed taking forensic science in high school. I homeschooled her and I remember the frustration of choosing a textbook because at that time one didn't exist that taught forensics from a biblical worldview. I was thankful she was able to attend the forensic science high school labs taught by Dr. Jennifer Rivera at the Creation Museum in Petersburg, Kentucky. Dr. Rivera has drawn on her extensive knowledge and experience as both a forensic scientist and educator to develop and write a forensic science textbook that is both factual and practical.

One of the things that makes forensic science unique is its very observable application to real life. Students don't have to wonder how this science would ever be something that's important because it's used every day by police officers and investigators to solve crimes. As God's image bearers, we desire justice and for wrongs to be made right, and forensic science helps accomplish that. I also appreciate that forensic science encompasses many sub-disciplines like chemistry, entomology, botany, genetics, etc., and students can see how all the sciences work together and build on each other.

I'm thrilled that students and teachers alike will now have this tremendous resource to learn forensic science from a biblical worldview. It's filled with not only the facts of forensic science but also real-life case studies and labs that help students apply what they've learned. It's a great opportunity to get students engaged in science!

Georgia Purdom, PhD
Vice President of Educational Content
Answers in Genesis

IMAGE CREDITS

L = left, T= top, TL = top left, B=bottom, BL = bottom left, C = center, CR = center right, CL = center left, R = right, TR = top right, BR = bottom right, BC = bottom center

Getty.com: p 7, p 26 (2), p 28, p 29 B, p 30 (2), p 31 T, p 32 B, p 33 (5), p 34, p 54

Shutterstock.com: p 5, p 8 (2), p 9, p 11, p 14 (2), p 15 B, p 16 (3), p 17, p 20 T, p 21 (2), p 22 (2), p 23 T, p 24 (2), p 29 T, p 30 C, p 35, p 36 (2), p 38 (2), p 39, p 40 (2), p 41, p 42 (2), p 43 B, p 44 (3), p 46 T, p 49 (2), p 50 B, p 51, p 53 (2), p 55 (2), p 56 (2), p 57, p 59, p 60, p 61, p 62 (3), p 63, p 65, p 67 (5), p 72 (2), p 73 (2), p 77, p 78 (2), p 79 (3), p 80 (3), p 81 (2), p 82 T, p 83, p 89 B, p 92 (2), p 93 (2), p 94 B, p 95, p 96, p 98, p 99 T, p 100 T, p 101, p 102 (2), p 103, p 104, p 105, p 106 (2), p 107 (2), p 108, p 109, p 110, p 112 (2), p 113, p 114, p 115 B, p 117 C, p 118 (2), p 119 C, p 120 B, p 121 (2), p 122 (3), p 123 (2), p 124 (2), p 125 (2), p 126 (2), p 127, p 129 (2), p 130 T, p 132, p 133 (3), p 134 (2), p 135 T, p 136 (2), p 137 B, p 138 (2), p 140 B, p 141, p 143 (2), p 144 (2), p 145, p 146 (2), p 147, p 148 (2), p 149 T, p 150, p 151 (2), p 152, p 153, p 154, p 155, p 157 (2), p 158, p 159 (2), p 160 (6), p 161 (4), p 162 (2), p 163 (4), p 164, p 166 R, p 168, p 169 (2), p 170 (4), p 171 (5), p 173, p 174, p 175, p 176, p 179, p 180, p 181 B, p 182, p 186 (2), p 187, p 188, p 189 (2), p 190 (2), p 192 T, p 193 (3), p 194 T, p 196, p 200 L, p 201 L, p 202 T, p 203, p 204, p 205, p 206 (2), p 207 BR, p 208, p 209 B, p 210 C, p 213, p 214, p 215, p 216, p 218 (2), p 219 (3), p 220, p 221 (2), p 222, p 223 (2), p 224, p 225 T, p 226, p 228, p 229, p 231, p 233 (2), p 234 (5), p 235 (6), p 236 (4), p 237 (3), p 238, p 239 (4), p 240, p 241, p 243, p 244 (2), p 245 (2), p 246 B, p 247 (2), p 249 (2), p 254 (2), p 255, p 257 (2), p 259 (2), p 262 (3), p 263 (2), p 264 (2), p 265 (2), p 266 T, p 267 B, p 268, p 269, p 270 BL, p 271 B, p 272, p 273 (3), p 274 (7), p 275 (2), p 276 T, p 277 B, p 279 (2), p 280 (2), p 281 (T), p 282 (2), p 283, p 285, p 286 (9), p 287, p 288 (2), p 290 (2), p 291 (2), p 292 T, p 293 (5), p 294 (2), p 295 B, p 296, p 297, p 298, p 299 B, p 300, p 301, p 302 (2), p 303 (5), p 304 (2), p 305 B, p 306 (2), p 307, p 309, p 312, p 313 C, p 314 (3), p 315 (4), p 316 (4), p 317 (2), p 318 (2), p320 R, p 321, p 324, p 325, p 328 T, p 330 (2), p 331 (2), p 333 B, p 334 (2), p 335, p 337, p 338 B, p 343, p 344, p 345, p 347, p 348 (2), p 349 B, p 351, p 354, p 355 (2), p 357 (4), p 358 T, p 359, p 360 L, p 361 (2), p 362, p 365, p 367 B, p 368, p 369 T, p 371, p 372, p 373 (2), p 374 (2), p 375, p 376, p 377, p 378, p 379, p 381, p 382 (2), p 383, p 384, p 386, p 388, p 390, p 392, p 393 (2), p 395, p 397, p 398 T, p 399, p 401, p 402, p 405, p 406, p 407, p 409, p 410, p 411, p 412, p 413, p 415, p 416, p 417, p 418, p 420, p 421, p 422, p 424 (2), p 425

FBI Multimedia: p 192 (2), p 225 (2), p 227, p 241, p 340 C, p 341, p 358 B, p 360 R, p 364 T

iStock.com: p 262 CR, p 268, p 291 (2), p 326

Colourbox.com: p 131 B

Science Photo Library: p 117 B, p 183, p. 267 T, p 278 T

NLPG Staff: p 20 B, p 44 T, p 107 T, p 123 TR, p 246 (2), p 261 (2), p 273 (6), p 292 B, p 313 B, p 317 (3), p 419

J. Rivera: p 19, p 23 B, p 31 (2), p 32 (2), p 50 T, p 66 (2), p 67 TL, p 68 (2), p 69, p 76 R, p 80 (2), p 82 (3), p 87, p 91 (3), p 92 B, p 94 T, p 119 B, p 120 T, p 124 C, p 137 T, p 149 B, p 161 B, p 165, p 170 (4), p 171 (3), p 172 (2), p 181 T, p 184, p 193 T, p 194 B, p 195 (2), p 196 (4), p 197, p 198 (6), p 199, p 200, p 201, p 202 (2), p 207 (3), p 209, p 210 (3), p 211 (2), p 212 (5), p 215 (2), 232 (4), p 237 (3), p 248 (8), p 271 T, p 295 (2), p 312, p 369 (2), p 396, p 398 B, p 404, p 412

Answers in Genesis: p 20 B, p 74 (2), p 89 T, p 299 T, p 367 T

Library of Congress: p 340 T

Wikimedia Commons: p 12, p 13, p 15 T, p 26 T, p 27, p 36 C, p 37, p 43 T, p 46 B, p 47, p 52, p 67 TR, p 70 (2), p 71, p 75 (3), p 76 L, p 84 (2), p 85, p 88 (2), p 96 T, p 97, p 99 B, p 100 B, p 115 T, p 116 (3), p 117 T, p 118 (2), p 119 T, p 130 (2), p 131 T, p 135 B, p 139, p 140 T, p 154 (2), p 166 L, p 167, p 170, p 176 (2), p 177, p 190 C, p 191 (2), p 195 T, p 196 B, p 207 (4), p 209 T, p 210 (3), p 217, p 232 B, p 255, p 258 (3), p 264 TR, p 266 B, p 270 (2), p 273 C, p 276 B, p 277 (2), p 278 B, p 281 (B), p 288 B, p 289, p 290 T, p 291 B, p 294 B, p 299 T, p 305 T, p 308, p 313 T, p 316 BR, p 320 L, p 322, p 323, p 327, p 328 B, p 329 (2), p 332 (2), p 333 T, p 334, p 335, p 338 T, p 339, p 340 (2), p 342, p 346 (3), p 349 T, p 352, p 353, p 356 (3), p 360 TR, p 361 T (Karen T. Taylor, KTT), p 364, p 365, p 369 (2), p 370 (2), p 391, p 396, p 398 B, p 404

Images from Wikimedia Commons are used under the (PD-US), CC0 1.0, CC BY-SA 2.0, CC BY-SA 2.5, CC BY-SA 2.0 DE, CC-BY-SA-3.0, CC By SA 4.0, CC By SA 4.0 International, CC By SA Spain, license or the GNU Free Documentation License, Version 1.3.

INTRODUCTION

UNIT 1

Lesson 1
What is Forensic Science?

*Great are the works of the L*ORD*, studied by all who delight in them* (Psalm 111:2).

A period of unrest in a culture can often result in violent, and often unjust, measures to pacify disorderly mobs. Disturbances like these have occurred multiple times throughout criminal justice history. The following case is not only the most famous in history, but the effect of the unjust conviction brought upon necessary consequences that are still felt today.

An innocent man was convicted and executed in an attempt to prevent possible rioting. The populace at the time was supportive of the execution, and hundreds observed his death. Guards assigned to the execution verified the man was deceased. The burial site of the executed man was public knowledge. Once the body was laid to rest, it was officially sealed by the government. If anyone were to break the seal, the punishment would be immediate death. Due to the man's notoriety and the controversy surrounding his execution, the government was concerned the man's supporters would attempt to extract his body. A group of armed guards were assigned to secure the location of burial. The armed guards were a well-trained "military machine" with extensive combat training and loyal allegiance to the government.[1]

Within three days of the burial, the guards would flee for their lives and the body would disappear. According to historian Tacitus, the disappearance of the executed man's body was a "most mischievous superstition."[2]

Three basic theories exist for the disappearance of the body:

1. The man was not really dead and escaped.
2. The body was stolen by his supporters.
3. The man resurrected from the dead.

Sir Arthur Conan Doyle, the author of the Sherlock Holmes mysteries, stated in one of his short stories, "Once you eliminate the impossible, whatever remains, no matter how improbable, must be the truth."[3]

Therefore, consider these facts:

1. The death was verified by the guards assigned to the execution.
2. The burial site was sealed by government professionals.
3. Due to the skilled military machine guarding the burial site, it is improbable the man's supporters would have been physically able to overcome the guards and steal the body.
4. Multiple independent sources attested to the fact that the burial site was empty.
5. The guards disappeared during the night, fearing the repercussions of their failure to secure the burial site.
6. Over 500 eyewitnesses verified through oral and written documents that the executed man was, in fact, alive.

Though a mystery to many individuals during this time period, for others it is a fulfillment of prophecy. Have you determined what famous case this is referring to?

Each case study in this book will correlate to the lesson material. It is important to learn about how the information learned applies to real case work. This case study is referring to the most horrific murder in history, the death of the Creator of Universe, the Lamb of God, the I Am, Jesus Christ. Jesus Christ is the author of knowledge and the study of science. Enjoy this lesson as you learn more about the Savior and how He relates to forensic science.

CASE STUDY

The discipline of forensic science produces iconic images in the minds of students: investigators probing with flashlights in the night, heroic discoveries of key evidence, and the opportunity to be an adventurous participant in the investigation of a famous crime scene mystery. These images are largely fueled by fictional crime scene television shows, which have popularized the profession of forensic investigation. Fundamentally, forensic science is the application of scientific investigation to the judicial system. There are over twenty forensic disciplines that exist in the field today, and crime scene personnel specialize within this realm of expertise. Regardless of the area of focus for an investigator, there is the opportunity to delight in the works of the Lord (Psalm 111:2). God is the Creator, Designer, and Author of science.

Forensic science experts, or criminalists, require extensive training and must be willing to use a multidisciplinary approach, meaning a forensic investigator works closely with police officers, detectives, coroners, and lab personnel toward a resolution. The American Academy of Forensic Sciences (AAFS) outlines the roles of a forensic scientist as having the ability to distinguish relevant facts from random ones, conduct appropriate testing measures, develop hypotheses, and interpret these results in an attempt to "reach a conclusion or opinion" regarding the evidence's relationship to the crime.[4] This approach will utilize the expertise of several individuals and departments within an agency for the sole purpose of finding evidence that directly links a suspect to a crime or absolves a suspect of a crime.

WHAT IS FORENSIC SCIENCE?

Merriam-Webster defines forensic science as "the application of scientific principles and techniques to matters of criminal justice especially as relating to the collection, examination, and analysis of physical evidence."[5] The Latin root for forensic is *forensis*, which means "of or before the forum," and the root of the word *science* means knowledge. Therefore, the term "forensic science" refers to the acquisition of knowledge gained from the evidence, analysis, and investigator interpretations, with the goal of presenting this knowledge before individuals in the judicial system (the forum).

Psalm 111:2:

"Great are the works of the Lord, studied by all who delight in them."

Forensic investigation includes:
- Preservation of the crime scene
- Collection and examination of physical evidence
- Selection and administration of appropriate testing
- Interpretation of data
- Drawing conclusions
- Clear and concise reporting
- Cooperation amongst the investigative team
- Truthful articulation of the facts through the testimony of forensic scientists

The requirements to be a forensic science expert often include hundreds of hours of training, keen observational techniques, rigorous certification testing, the ability to engage in the tedious examination of evidence, and the clear articulation of the facts in courtroom testimony. Once a scientist has prepared themselves with these tools, they are ready for the challenges waiting in forensic field work.

WHAT IS SCIENCE?

The Latin root for the word science is *scientia*, which means knowledge. The word knowledge originated from the Greek word *gnosis* and means to have the capacity to know or understand through observation.[6] But where did knowledge come from? The Bible provides clear answers to this question and tells us that science (knowledge) cannot exist apart from God. Since the Bible is the perfect Word of God, we can trust the authenticity and reliability of this historical record from the very first verse (see **Table 1**).

Table 1

The Beginning of Knowledge	Reference
In the beginning, God created everything from nothing.	Genesis 1
God created man in His image with an inborn knowledge of Him.	Genesis 1:26–27 Romans 1:21 Romans 2:15
At the end of the creation week, knowledge was perfect and "very good."	Genesis 1:31
Man's sin against God corrupted knowledge.	Genesis 3:6
Humans sinfully desire knowledge for self-glorification.	Genesis 11:4
Jesus Christ is the only source of knowledge.	Colossians 2:2–3 Luke 24:25
Salvation through the Cross is the only path to true knowledge.	1 Corinthians 1:18
One day, God will restore the perfect knowledge of Him.	1 John 3:2

The Knowledge of God[7]	Reference
He is the God of knowledge.	Psalm 139:1–6
He has infinite knowledge.	Psalm 147:5
His knowledge is separate from human knowledge.	Isaiah 55:8
His knowledge is perfect.	Job 37:16
His knowledge is denied by the wicked.	Psalm 73:11–12
The believer is secure in this knowledge.	1 John 3:20

Based on the Bible's explanation of knowledge, it is clear that science cannot exist without God as the foundation upon which creation is studied (Proverbs 2:6). And, for centuries, scientific study was attributed to the pursuit of learning about God's creation. The majority of pioneers in science were Bible-believing Christians (see **Table 2**).

Table 2: Timeline of Christian Scientists

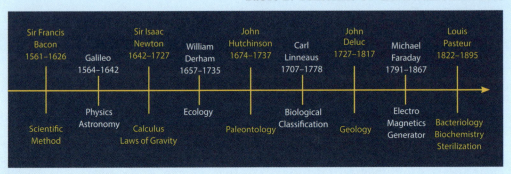

After the publication of Charles Darwin's *Origin of Species* in 1859, there was a significant abandonment of scientific endeavors dedicated to the glory of God. The entrance of naturalism (origins without the need for a Creator God) into science academia started a snowball effect away from biblical authority that continues to this day. On the most fundamental level, we can see this change in the very definition of science. Observe how *Webster's Dictionary* has modified the definition of science over time (see **Table 3**). The Webster's 2023 definition of science states it is "knowledge … tested through scientific method."

Table 3: Webster's Chronological Definitions of Science

1828	Science: "knowledge; the comprehension or understanding of truth or facts by the mind. **The science of God must be perfect** [emphasis added]."[8]
1913	Science: "knowledge as it relates to the physical world, the nature, constitution, and forces of matter, **called also natural science** [emphasis added]."[9]
2020	Science: "knowledge or system of knowledge covering general truths or the operation of general laws especially as obtained and tested through scientific method."[10]

THE HISTORY OF FORENSIC SCIENCE

When we start with God's Word, we can see evidence of investigation and judgment for criminal behavior as early as 6,000 years ago with the very first murder involving Cain and his brother Abel. God, the all-knowing, all-powerful, and final Judge, punished Cain for his crime. The Bible tells us in Genesis 4:11–12, "And now you are cursed from the ground, which has opened its mouth to receive your brother's blood from your hand. When you work the ground, it shall no longer yield to you its strength. You shall be a fugitive and a wanderer on the earth."

All throughout history, there are traces of investigative techniques used in disappearances, deaths, thefts, and related crimes, but the earliest beginnings of the techniques we associate with forensic science can be traced to approximately 300 B.C. Archaeology has provided evidence that the Chinese used fingerprints and handprints as a form of identification.[11] In the early 1200s, forensic entomology (study of bugs) was used to solve a murder case,[12] and the 1600s revealed observations and writings on the unique characteristics in friction ridge skin, but it was not until the late 1800s that we see the

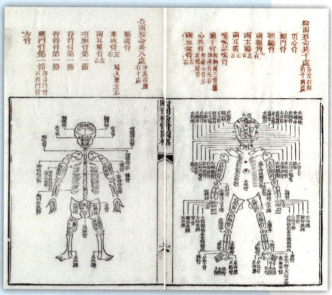

Xĭ-yuān lù jí-zhèng, 1843 edition

beginnings of early crime scene analysis. This was largely due to a book published in 1887 titled *A Study in Scarlet*, written by Sir Arthur Conan Doyle. This fictional book introduced a new character to the world, Sherlock Holmes. Holmes utilized reason, innovative techniques, and investigation to solve crimes.[13] Many of the techniques Sherlock Holmes used were not even practiced or implemented in police work. Interestingly, this is a case where a fictional character sparked innovation in the physical world.

Edmond Locard, a French criminologist known as the Sherlock Holmes of France, started the very first crime lab in 1910. As a pioneer in early investigative practices, Locard initiated many practices still used today. He also worked closely with Alphonse Bertillon on one of the first systems of classification based on body measurements, called anthropometry.[14] He is also considered the father of poroscopy, or the study of pore patterns on friction ridge skin.

Locard's best known contribution to forensic science is Locard's Exchange Principle, which states that when two items come into contact with one another, there is an exchange of material between them. Locard's Exchange Principle is the foundation for forensic science.

Forensic science techniques continued to develop well into the mid-1900s. Sir Edward Henry created a fingerprint classification system in 1896 that is still used today in English-speaking countries. In 1910, the first book examining questioned documents was written by the father of document examination, Sherman Osborne. World War II and the Korean War provided the anatomical bone database for forensic anthropology investigation. But the most important discovery of the last 100 years was the discovery of the DNA double helix in the 1950s by Rosalind Franklin, Maurice Wilkins, James Watson, and Francis Crick. Further advancement by Alec Jeffreys in the 1980s included the development of the testing necessary to process an individual's DNA and create a DNA fingerprint. This technique was integral for DNA comparison between crime scene samples, victims, and suspects. The future of forensic science continues to be on the cusp of innovation within the fields of mitochondrial DNA, computer forensics, and evidence processing techniques.

FORENSIC SCIENCE CAREERS

As stated earlier, there are over twenty disciplines, or specialties, in the field of forensic science. Employment within this field ranges from civilian personnel and sworn deputies to Ph.D. scientists working in laboratories and medical doctors performing autopsies. The American Academy of Forensic Scientists (AAFS) is the largest governing body in the field of forensic science and is composed of over 7,000 scientists. Though the AAFS only distinguishes eleven forensic distinctions on their official list, there are many more areas where experts are needed. According to the AAFS, forensic science career choices include:[15]

- Anthropology
- Criminalistics
- Digital & Multimedia Sciences
- Engineering & Applied Sciences
- General
- Jurisprudence
- Odontology
- Pathology/Biology
- Psychiatry & Behavioral Science
- Questioned Documents
- Toxicology

Early forensic scientists (left) who assisted in solving the Lindberg kidnapping case and began the FBI crime laboratory. The numbers indicate the area the employee worked in.

The FBI crime laboratory started in 1932 is one of the largest in the world and employs a variety of forensic experts. In addition to the fields already mentioned, the FBI employs:[16]

- Chemists
- Cryptanalyst-Forensic Examiner
- Forensics Operation Specialist
- Geologist-Forensic Examiner
- Management & Programs Analyst
- Metallurgist Forensic Examiner
- Photographer
- Physical Scientist
- Forensic Accountant
- Fingerprints & Biometric Examiners

Qualifications for employment vary between local, state, and national agencies, but a minimum of a bachelor's or master's degree is required for most forensic fields. Prior to career selection or college coursework, it is recommended that you research the requirements in your field of interest. Many of the specializations mentioned above will require training and additional certifications after employment. Regardless of the forensic field, each one provides the opportunity to give honor to the Creator and Designer of all scientific disciplines, our Lord and Savior Jesus Christ.

What is Forensic Science?   Lesson 1   15

Lesson 2
The Two Types of Science

For by him all things were created, in heaven and on earth, visible and invisible, whether thrones or dominions or rulers or authorities—all things were created through him and for him (Colossians 1:16).

Cold Case: JonBenét Ramsey

JonBenét Ramsey was a six-year-old beauty queen from Boulder, Colorado. Her parents, multi-millionaires John and Patsy Ramsey, were considered part of the elite class in Boulder. Patsy Ramsey was a former beauty queen herself when she was Miss West Virginia in 1977.

It was the day after Christmas, December 26, 1996. John and Patsy Ramsey woke early to prepare for a trip. Patsy was walking down the stairs from her bedroom to the kitchen when she found a note at the foot of the stairs. The note stated that her six-year-old daughter, JonBenét, had been kidnapped and the ransom was $118,000. The police were called and arrived at the home at 5:55 a.m. The police determined there was no forced entry and searched the house, but they did not search the basement or secure the house to protect the evidence. The only room in the house that was secured was JonBenét's bedroom. JonBenét was not found during this initial search. Due to this major investigative oversight, evidence was contaminated as family and friends, frantic to find JonBenét, touched items all over the house. At 1:00 p.m., the police asked John Ramsey to search the house for things out of place. When John entered the basement, he found the lifeless body of his daughter. John Ramsey picked up the body of his daughter and carried her upstairs, destroying potential evidence. The autopsy of JonBenét revealed she died of asphyxiation by strangulation and a skull fracture.

There were two overarching theories in the investigation: JonBenét was murdered by a family member (John, Patsy, and/or 9-year-old brother Burke) or an intruder to the home. The police immediately focused on the family for a number of factors. Evidence for this theory included:

- The ransom note appeared staged since it was written using paper and a pen from within the Ramsey house.
- The ransom note was unusually long in comparison to traditional ransom notes.
- The ransom note showed intentional forging.
- John Ramsey had received a work bonus for almost the exact amount requested in the ransom note.

The family members were considered possible suspects in the crime for many years, though the parents were never "officially" named suspects of the crime and the DNA at the crime scene was never directly linked to the Ramsey family. Patsy Ramsey died in 2006 from ovarian cancer. In 2008, advances in touch DNA exonerated the Ramsey family from suspicion. The DNA sample was entered into CODIS (the national storehouse for DNA samples), but there has never been a match.

The second theory was an intruder. Evidence for this theory included:

- The house had thick, plush carpet, which would have hidden the footsteps of an intruder.
- A boot print was found next to the body that did not match anyone's shoes in the house.

- There was evidence of a point of entry in the basement where a broken window was discovered.
- DNA found on JonBenét's clothing, after technological advances in DNA analysis, showed an unknown male was present at the scene.
- Handwriting samples were taken from John, Patsy, and JonBenét's 9-year-old brother living in the house. After analysis, it was determined that the family members did not write the ransom note.

Technology surrounding DNA profiling continues to improve, and new information is still being developed in this case. In 2016, experts released information stating that the DNA sample was from two different individuals. Varying individuals have claimed they were responsible for the murder, but after investigation, these claims could not be verified by police.

This case remains in the spotlight due to the very nature of the crime and the number of TV specials about the case. It also threatened the idea that people are safe within their own home. As Sherlock Holmes stated, "Life is infinitely stranger than anything which the mind of man could invent."[17]

This case remains unsolved and open for investigation. Who do you think is responsible for this crime?

Forensic science involves the study of events in the past, events that are unobservable. This has largely been the issue with the JonBenét Ramsey case. This lesson will dive deep into the important difference between historical and observational science.

WHAT ARE THE TWO TYPES OF SCIENCE?

Historical (origins) vs. Observational (operational): The root of the word science means knowledge, and there are two types of science: historical (also called origins) and observational (also called operational). Basically, historical science analyzes things of the past that are no longer observable in their original form, like fossils. Observation science requires the use of the scientific method and our five senses and allows us to study processes in real time. Therefore, forensic science is inherently a historical science.

This is often a difficult concept for students to understand because we use observational techniques to solve crimes, like DNA analysis or fingerprints. The distinction between historical and observational science is rooted in the idea of direct observation. In forensic science, investigators were not there to observe the crime occurring in real time but are left with clues about events that occurred in the past. Therefore, assumptions must be made, theories proposed, and conclusions developed from the evidence left behind. Let's explore this topic in more detail in this excerpt from the following article:

Recommended Resource:

Read *Glass House: Shattering the Myth of Evolution*, chapter two, "What Is and Isn't Science?" This chapter provides a discussion on historical and observational science through the lens of forensic science. Available through Master Books.

Can Forensic Science Trace the World's Origins?[18]

To assist researchers in organizing the knowledge gained through scientific study, it is helpful to categorize science into one of two areas: historical science (a type of which is origins science) and operational science (also called observational or experimental science).[19] Scientific disciplines categorized as historical science involve the study of current processes to interpret past events. The term *interpret* is used primarily because the scientist was not privy to a firsthand, observable account of the event being investigated. Since the incident already occurred, the scientist is relying upon a predisposed set of ideas or assumptions defined by the investigating scientist's personal bias and belief system.[20] In contrast, operational science involves the use of the scientific method through direct observation and application of ongoing events, though there is still interpretation of results and bias of the investigator.[21] Operational science has led to numerous inventions and technological advances. In forensics, examination of DNA for individual identity, the development of the forensic facial reconstruction software programs, and the use of fluorescence to highlight latent fingerprints are all considered the practice of operational science, particularly when the samples are recent and in situ [in the original position].

> **Cold case:**
> A cold case is an unsolved criminal investigation that remains open, pending the discovery of new evidence. Simply, it has never been solved.

However, historical science relates to describing events and conditions that are not observable in their original form and often not in their original location. The very definition of historical science reflects the nature of forensic science investigation, considering the investigator studies the remnants of an event that has occurred in the past. Forensic science is a science that focuses on the reconstruction of past events, as investigators present clues and make educated guesses about what may have occurred at a previous point in time.

facial recognition

The ability of forensic scientists to interpret the evidence and construct probable explanations for past events necessarily involves assumptions about past events since CSI personnel were not present when the crime occurred. The forensic investigator is not able to apply a firsthand, observable account of what occurred during the criminal act. Therefore, their assumptions rely on historical evidence to support their forensic identifications. Considering mankind is fallible, their assumptions are subject to human error and misinterpretation. Doyle, in his article "CSI and Evolution," clarifies this distinction between historical and observational science when he states, "Between the science of present processes and the 'science' of figuring out what happened in the past . . . there is generally a

greater potential for uncertainty in the science of past events than there is in the science of present processes."[22] This is further supported by Young, who provides four distinct reasons why forensic science is inherently a historical science in practice, despite using some methods and procedures considered observational science:

1. The past is not observable: it "cannot be seen, smelled, heard, tasted, or sensed in any way."
2. The past is not predictable and is therefore retrodiction (or stating inferences about the past).
3. It is impossible to recreate the past in the present: "one cannot design an experiment that will replicate the complex variety of conditions that existed in the past—conditions that are often not known in full detail."
4. Forensic science incorporates the use of existing theories but does not form new theories.[23]

ASSUMPTIONS OR SCIENCE?

Influencing a forensic investigator's educated assumptions is a certain level of personal and systematic bias. Psychology professors Scott and Manzanero discussed the philosophy existing within the criminal justice system by recognizing the process is "essentially human act and as such is not without bias."[24] Assumptions and bias affect the application of the scientific method to the use of observational science. Further, they affect how an investigator interprets the historical evidence at crime scenes. In the famous 2014 creation vs. evolution debate, Bill Nye and Ken Ham focused on the question, "Is creation a viable model of origins?" Nye (an evolutionist) attempted to validate the use of historical science as equivalent to observational science. Nye supports the theory that current scientific processes are sufficient to explain events of the past (unobservable) with absolute certainty. Nye discussed this belief during the debate when he stated,

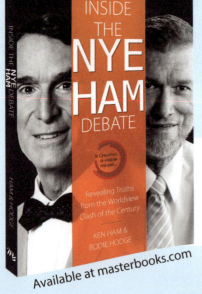

Available at masterbooks.com

I say this is something that we in science want, we want the ability to predict. And your assertion that there's some difference between the natural laws that I use to observe the world today and the natural laws that existed 4,000 years ago is extraordinary and unsettling.[25]

This is not an unsettling concept for young-earth creation researchers, since new scientific evidence clearly shows that some natural processes may have been accelerated in the past. . . . Therefore, it is imperative a scientist evaluate the evidence in context, while considering the effect of past (historical) processes on current observable findings.

The equivalency of historical science to operational science is foundational to evolutionary ideas, considering there is no evidence for molecules-to-man evolution, though this is often conflated with natural selection and change in general, for which there is evidence. For example, evolutionary scientists have never observed a species changing from one taxonomic kind (or family) to another (e.g., a dog to a cat) or identified a species gaining new genetic information of the type needed for molecules-to-man evolution. However, when Nye attempted to relate the use of forensic investigation (historical science) to operational science, he clearly recognizes it as the study of past events. Nye stated, "When you go to a crime scene and find evidence, you have clues about the past, and you trust those clues."[26] Even Nye admits that studying events of the past demands a level of trust to develop assumptions about the evidence. It is within this context that Nye and other evolutionists apply the current nature of scientific processes to unobservable events in the past. They assume the present is the key to the past, a method that primarily relies on uniformitarianism.[27] Further examination of the validity of historical science has the potential to lead to misinterpretation, misidentification, and erroneous conclusions that lie outside the realm of observable, operational science. Misinterpretation and misidentification have become a concern within the judicial system and forensic science community.

THE SCIENTIFIC METHOD

As stated in the previous section, forensic science uses observational science techniques (such as observation, collection, and testing) to make assumptions about past events. The forensic investigator was not present when the crime occurred. Therefore, they use the evidence gathered, by utilizing the scientific method, to make an educated guess on what may have happened in the past.

Imagine a wallet has been stolen from a coffee shop. Eyewitnesses' testimonies provide police with clues to the location of the suspect in the restaurant, and on the table is an empty coffee cup.

When the forensic investigator arrives on the scene, they will begin by analyzing the problem to uncover evidence to aid in the identification of the person who stole the wallet. Once the problem is identified, a forensic scientist is able to develop a set of ideas or hypotheses to solve the problem. Many important scientific advances were discovered because someone asked a simple question like "how" or "why."

But it is important to remember that for observational science to be effective, the question must be testable through an observable, measurable, and repeatable process. A scientist cannot use the scientific method to answer the question, "What is moral or good?" Nor can they use this (experimental) scientific method to answer the question, "What happened in the unobservable, unrepeatable past to produce the Grand Canyon or the first dog or Saturn?" This requires a different method.

Secondly, the investigator develops a hypothesis. A standard hypothesis includes an if-then statement. For example, "If I process the coffee cup for fingerprints, then I will uncover a latent print for comparison." A hypothesis is fundamentally an educated guess developed by the scientist. A hypothesis is not required to be accurate; it just needs to be testable.

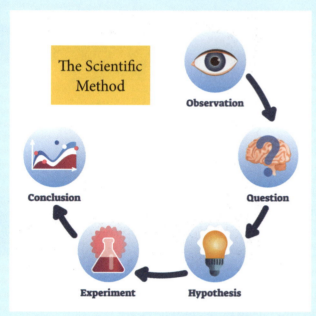

The hypothesis is influenced by the expertise, viewpoint, and bias of the scientist. It is impossible to eliminate bias in scientific research. Every scientist begins with a preconceived set of ideals, or starting points, which influence their experimental process. If a scientist believes there is no God, their hypotheses, observations, and analyses will reflect this starting point. The same is true of a scientist who starts with God's Word. This scientist recognizes that the inerrant truth of God's Word is superior to man's imperfect ideas.

The third step in the scientific method is a form of experimentation or measurable observation. This involves using one or more of the five senses for direct observations. The scientist will also try to eliminate extraneous variables by creating a controlled environment. In this case, the investigator attempts to control the environment from contaminants by sectioning off the area to be examined with crime scene tape. This allows the forensic scientist time to process the area for fingerprints in an environment where careful, methodical forensic procedures can be performed on the crime scene while limiting the influence of extraneous variables.

Theoretically, a controlled experiment reduces the possibility of outside variables influencing or contaminating the research, but not every experiment is examined within a controlled environment. A true controlled environment or experiment is very difficult to achieve and should always be scrutinized due to the difficulty in effectively attaining a 100% controlled environment.

The fourth step is collection of experimental results. Once the investigator has retrieved viable latent fingerprints, they will submit the prints to the database for comparison. Once the computer completes a search, the investigator will gather the results and form an analysis. The goal of gathering results is to compare them to the original hypothesis for confirmation.

Subsequently, scientific results are only as accurate as the experimental data. Results are also influenced by the scientist's starting assumptions, which can lead to errors. These errors occur in crime scene investigation. The National Registry of Exonerations has been tracking individuals who were found guilty at trial but were later exonerated due to advances in technology or the discovery of investigator error. Currently, they have documented over 2,263 exonerations. This is just one example of how assumptions influence interpretations of evidence.

Since the forensic scientist was not an eyewitness to the crime and has only the evidence left behind at a crime scene, their assumptions about what may have occurred in the past have the potential to be flawed and may result in an inaccurate analysis.

The investigator now completes the final step in the scientific method by analyzing and interpreting the results and applying the results to the criminal act. Their analysis should include the rejection or acceptance of the original hypothesis. Often in scientific discovery, rejection of the hypothesis is just as important as the acceptance of it because it leads the scientist in a new direction or area needing further study.

Ideally, the forensic investigator identifies the suspect, but ultimately the interpretation of experimental results lies in the value of the evidence and the bias of the scientist conducting the research.

Geddes, in her article about flaws in forensic science, stated, "Research has shown that the same fingerprint expert can reach a different conclusion about the same fingerprints depending on the context they're given about a case."[28] It is important to point out that the forensic investigator did not directly observe the criminal act; therefore, their analysis applies to a historical event. This means that the investigator cannot prove anything but can only establish facts.

FORENSIC SCIENCE FROM A BIBLICAL WORLDVIEW

How does a scientist analyze and view evidence through the lens of a biblical worldview in light of these two types of science? A biblical worldview requires a scientist to start with God's Word to interpret historical science. Remember, historical science refers to events that occurred in the past. This could include the historical account of origins (creation by God in six days) provided in the Bible versus man's evolutionary ideas (goo to the zoo to you). A secular worldview starts with man's ideas regarding past events. Both worldviews examine the same evidence but come to very different, and often conflicting, conclusions because the starting point is different.

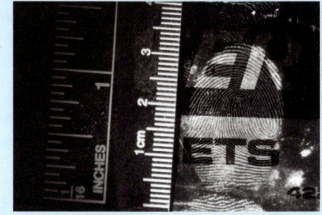

In the world of forensic science, investigators operating from a biblical worldview must recognize that they are not "good" people sending "bad" people to prison. In the Bible, Romans 3:10 is clear that no one is good: "None is righteous, no, not one." This goes back to the original sin described in the book of Genesis. At the end of creation week in Genesis chapter one, God tells us it was "very good" (1:31). The earth — including the land, weather, plants, animals, humans, the solar system, and the galaxies — was perfect. There was no suffering, disease, death, or crime. But in Genesis 3:1, we see the very first attack on a governing authority:

> **Romans 8:22:**
> "For we know that the whole creation has been groaning together in the pains of childbirth until now."

> **Romans 5:12:**
> "Therefore, just as sin came into the world through one man, and death through sin, and so death spread to all men because all sinned."

> Now the serpent was more crafty than any other beast of the field that the Lord God had made. He said to the woman, "*Did God actually say*, 'You shall not eat of any tree in the garden'?" [emphasis added].

Satan directly questioned the authority of the all-powerful God. Adam and Eve listened to the serpent and sinned against God that day, and everything changed. Their sin cursed God's perfect world, resulting in the effects we still observe on a daily basis. The world continues to groan under the effect of sin (Romans 8:22). Every individual born enters this world with sin (Romans 5:12) and is in need of redemption. It is very humbling to realize that a forensic investigator (and yourself) is no better in the eyes of a perfect God than the criminals they are investigating.

As a result, the role of a forensic scientist operating through a biblical lens should reflect certain traits and a work ethic that distinguish them from other investigators. A few characteristics might be honesty, integrity, and servanthood. Proverbs 10:9 reminds us, "Whoever walks in integrity walks securely, but he who makes his ways crooked will be found out." This involves following the policies and procedures outlined by the employing agency and maintaining high levels of excellence throughout the entire investigative process from the crime scene to the courtroom. Additionally, a forensic scientist must provide truthful testimony regarding their technique and analysis throughout the investigation. Exodus 23:1 states, "You shall not spread a false report."

By following biblical principles, a forensic scientist has the opportunity to stand out from other investigators by providing a model of godly leadership and the servant heart of Christ. Ultimately, the work of a forensic scientist should glorify the God they serve in every decision, action, and reaction that occurs in the field of investigation.

THE CRIME SCENE

UNIT 2

Lesson 3
The Crime Scene

. . . *teaching them to observe all that I have commanded you. And behold, I am with you always, to the end of the age* (Matthew 28:20).

Cold Case: Caylee Anthony[29]

On July 15, 2008, Caylee Anthony, a two-year-old toddler from Orlando, Florida, was reported missing to authorities by her grandmother, Cindy Anthony, 31 days after she disappeared. During the 911 phone call to police, Caylee's mother, Casey Anthony, told the police the last time she had seen her daughter Caylee was on June 15, 2008, when she dropped her off at the babysitter's house. Casey claims that when she returned to pick up Caylee, neither the babysitter nor Caylee were home.

The grandmother became alerted after she received a phone call on June 30, 2008, from a car impound informing her that her car had been towed from the front of a cash advance store in Orlando. This was after her daughter, Casey, told her she was taking the car on a mini vacation to Jacksonville, Florida. It was later discovered this was not true and that Casey had been with a boyfriend and seen partying at several locations. After pressing Casey about the whereabouts of Caylee, the grandmother notified authorities that her daughter Casey had stolen her car, and she told police, "I told you my daughter has been missing for a month and I just found her today. But I can't find my granddaughter. She [Casey] just admitted to me [Cindy] that she's been trying to find her by herself. There is something wrong. I found my daughter's car today and it smells like there's been a dead body."[30] The grandmother later retracted this statement.

Police immediately launched an investigation, arresting Casey Anthony on July 16, 2008. Sherlock Holmes postulated, "It is a capital mistake to theorize before one has data. Insensibly one begins to twist facts to suit theories, instead of theories to suit facts." But often, the gathering of the "truth" is the real challenge.

During questioning, there were multiple lies, discrepancies, and red flags with Casey Anthony's account. Below are just a few examples:

- When the police asked Casey why she did not report the disappearance 31 days prior, she stated, "I've been looking for her and have gone through other resources to try to find her — which is stupid."[31]
- Upon searching the location of the babysitter, the police discovered the residence had been vacant for 140 days. The "babysitter" did not exist.
- Casey lied about her place of employment, her friends, and many other facts.
- Casey was seen drinking and partying four days after Caylee's disappearance, in addition to visiting a tattoo parlor.
- Evidence of human decomposition and chloroform were found in the trunk of the family car.
- Casey told police she had spoken to Caylee on the phone July 15, but Caylee would have been deceased by that date.
- Computer forensics revealed searches on the home computer accessed by Casey for terminology related to the criminal act and how to make chloroform.

More than five months after Caylee was reported missing, decomposed remains were found by a meter reader working not far from her home. Caylee had been found. There was evidence of duct tape on the girl's mouth. After a lengthy trial, 400 pieces of evidence, and over 90 witnesses, Casey Anthony (Caylee's mother) was found not guilty for the murder of her daughter.

Theories surrounding this case:

- Casey Anthony's defense team claims that Caylee accidentally drowned in the family pool and was covered up by George, Casey's father.
- The prosecution claimed that Casey Anthony chloroformed her daughter, duct taped her mouth and nose, and the child suffocated.
- The grandmother, Cindy, originally accused her daughter of the disappearance of Caylee on the 911 call, but later retracted her statements.
- Caylee's body was intentionally put in two plastic bags and a canvas bag, hidden behind a log, and placed under leaves not far from her home. Therefore, this case is undoubtedly a murder.
- The jurors on the case claimed there was lack of evidence on how Caylee died, and the prosecution did not prove Casey Anthony's guilt beyond a reasonable doubt.
- Medical examiners have stated there is no sign of accidental death.

The truth of what happened to Caylee is still a mystery today, and until the truth is revealed, it will continue to be a prominent case in criminal investigation discussions.

There were multiple forensic disciplines used in this case. It's also important to understand the critical importance of securing and documenting the crime scene and understanding this information from a biblical worldview.

When you hear the words "crime scene," certain images immediately come to your mind. One might be a mysterious, glamorous world where forensic scientists save the day with their brilliant investigative work in just 45 minutes. These images have been largely influenced by he *CSI* effect, a phenomenon that has resulted from a rise in jurors' viewing of forensic television in the mid-2000s, influencing their perception of how criminal investigation works. Glamorized forensic TV shows showing rapid testing in seconds, case resolution within 45 minutes, and many other factors are believed to have influenced juror expectation surrounding evidence. District Attorney Andrew Thomas, who coined the term, noticed a trend in juries failing to convict. The Oxford Research Dictionary (2017) explains,

> District Attorney Andrew Thomas complained that juries had become less likely to convict, because *CSI* had improperly heightened their evidentiary expectations of the prosecution (requiring proof to a near certainty), and, in turn, was causing an epidemic of wrongful acquittals. He asserted that since forensic tests are always conducted on *CSI*, it creates in jurors an unreasonable expectation that forensic evidence of guilt always exists, and that the prosecution will introduce such proof. Consequently, if the prosecution does not introduce such evidence—even if it is irrelevant or unavailable—jurors will refuse to convict or deem it "reasonable doubt" warranting an acquittal. Because this effectively imposes on the prosecution a prerequisite of forensic proof (regardless of its relevance) for conviction, it functionally increases the prosecution's burden of proof to a near certainty.[32]

The reality is that investigating a crime scene requires the art of observation, along with preservation, methodical procedures, and thorough documentation. Once evidence is gathered from the scene, the time from the analysis in the lab to the presentation in the courtroom is often months if not years. The ultimate goal of any crime scene investigation is to document the scene in an unaltered form and to preserve the evidence for analysis.

THE CRIME SCENE FROM A BIBLICAL WORLDVIEW

As we begin to explore the world of crime scene investigation, it is important to realize that these processes, techniques, and procedures are only possible because God created the world with order. Without an underlying orderly framework, there is chaos, but that is not what we see in scientific study. What we find is an organized method to study scientific phenomena called the scientific method. We find exact mathematical measurements and quantities that testify to order. Al Mohler said it best in his podcast called *The Briefing* from Friday, April 3, 2020, titled "The World is Real":[33]

> As we look at the rise of modern science, of modern empirical observation, and the scientific method as a way of knowing, we have to recognize that those particular forms of thought are only possible if you come with the prior affirmation that the universe is intelligible. Where does that come from? It comes from the basic Christian worldview that tells us not only did the Creator make the cosmos, but that He embedded the knowledge of Himself in the cosmos. He made it intelligible. He gave us an orderly universe. Modern science is based upon that presupposition. It is looking for order, it is looking for explanation. It is understanding that there is a basic intelligibility. What does that mean? It means that God created the cosmos in such a way that it can be known. Many of its secrets can be unlocked. And this takes us to another presupposition of a biblical worldview, and that is realism, metaphysical realism, there is a real world. There really is matter. There really is stuff. Matter is not an illusion. A very real God created a very real world.

SECURING THE CRIME SCENE

Securing the crime scene in its original form is often the most challenging issue facing investigators. Once an officer arrives on the scene, it is their duty to assess any injuries and secure the scene from possible contamination. Contamination can come from the families of victims, emergency services, the media, other officers, and even from crime scene personnel. Sadly, a violent crime scene quickly becomes a hub of activity, which often disrupts the security and integrity of the scene. It is therefore of utmost importance that investigators prohibit any unauthorized personnel and begin photographing and processing the scene immediately. It is also important to remember that some types of evidence may need to be collected quickly to ensure their viability. Once the boundaries of the scene are confirmed, officers will often secure the scene with yellow barricade tape and remain stationed outside the perimeter to prohibit observers from entering the scene. The crime scene personnel will now begin the tedious process of recording the scene and the search for evidence.

RECORDING THE CRIME SCENE

The primary goal when processing a crime scene is to document the details of the scene in its unaltered form. Time is of the essence, and investigators must often work quickly to preserve fragile evidence. The lead investigator will begin the record of the scene with a walkthrough of the entire scene to determine how many investigators are required, confirm the key features that require some form of documentation, and assign roles to the team.

There are three key components in the recording process:
- Photography and/or videography
- Sketches
- Notes

It is important to note that each of these components are not independent of each other but join in together, like instruments in a symphony, to provide a complete account of the events that occurred at the crime scene.

Photography and Videography. Photography of the crime scene is one of the most important components in preserving a record of what occurred at the scene. Once the investigator concludes their investigation of the scene, they can never go back and see it in the original, unaltered form. Photography and videography provide a record of these details for future reference. Crime scene photography falls within three types: overview photographs, midrange photographs, and close-up photographs.[34] It begins with a complete overview of the exterior of the scene by including location markers, point of entry and exit, surrounding areas, occasionally bystanders, and any other relevant information. The crime scene personnel will often shoot these features from various angles and with various lighting sources. Once the exterior has been adequately captured, the investigator will move into the physical crime scene and begin the midrange photographs. These set perspective by including evidence in relation to fixed objects or features in the crime scene.

Whether the scene is inside or outside, a methodical step-by-step, close-up photographic record of all key evidence is required. Every piece of evidence must have a numbered marker and be photographed with and without scale measurements prior to collection. This includes every wall of every room involved in the scene, every cabinet, close-ups of weapons, blood spatter, injuries, bodies, any physical evidence of struggles, and other important details. This process may take several hours to a few days depending on the extent and severity of the crime. The following example from *Principles of Crime Scene Photography* demonstrates the importance of photography:

> A photographer in Florida shot the inside of every cabinet and the refrigerator at a homicide scene in a home, just as a matter of procedure. It was later discovered that the victim had a receipt for a six-pack of beer, matching the beer shown in the photograph of the refrigerator. Relatives noted that the victim did not drink beer. Further investigation led the team to the convenience store where the beer was purchased, and the surveillance tape showed the victim with an unknown person purchasing the beer. It turns out that the victim had picked up a hitchhiker, purchased beer for that person and come back to the house. The photograph of the refrigerator contents had created the link enabling the investigators to find the suspect.[35]

Outdoor crime scenes present a number of challenges. A few of these include the weather, time of day, and temperature factors. Photographing outdoor scenes at night requires a skilled photographer. These experts have learned how to "paint with light"[36] by lighting up the night and allowing investigators to observe details that otherwise may have gone unnoticed. This specialized technique requires multiple light sources and the use of a camera with a "B" bulb and manual setting, which can hold the shutter open for a specified length of time.

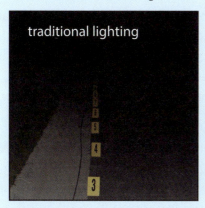

There are multiple reasons investigators choose to use videography along with photography. Scenes of mass casualty, similar to an airline crash, bombing, or terrorist attack, will require multiple investigators and several days if not weeks to process the scene. This could encompass the examination of a large area and is often better recorded with the addition of videography. Videography also allows the investigator to make a verbal recording, or notes, while they are videotaping the scene, preserving important details for future reference.

Sketches. There are two types of sketches that investigators utilize, each with a unique purpose. The first is the rough sketch. This sketch is completed while investigators are at the scene and prior to the collection of evidence. The difficulty with a rough sketch is deciding what should and should not be included because it is impossible to include every detail. Additionally, the investigator must decide whether the sketch should be from an overhead view or side view, both of which provide unique perspectives. It does not need to be to scale and will pinpoint the exact location of all the evidence to be collected through measurement and the triangulation to fixed locations. It will also point out the location of doorways, windows, furniture, and other relevant details. The rough sketch should also include exact measurements of the perimeter, a legend, compass direction north, and case information (officer, address of the scene, case number, date, measurement scale, etc.).

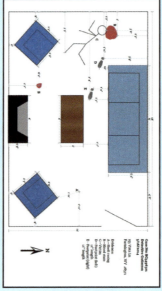

rough sketch   final diagram

The finished sketch (or final diagram) is usually prepared for courtroom presentation and will be oriented to scale. Therefore, all the measurement details will not be visible on the final sketch. The finished sketch will also only include those key items that were directly related to the investigation. It is not uncommon for investigators to utilize a form of CAD (computer-aided design) software. Using CAD software provides 3D capability to move around the crime scene and look at the evidence from different angles. As with the rough sketch, the finished sketch should include a legend, directional heading, case information, and scale measurement.

Notes. The third component to recording a crime scene is detailed notes. Detailed notes should be documented continuously from the point of the lead investigator's initial walkthrough to the point where investigators close the scene. The most important point to remember when taking notes is that the investigator should never provide their personal opinion, assumptions, or theories. The notes should only be what you observe with your five senses, not what you think may have occurred.

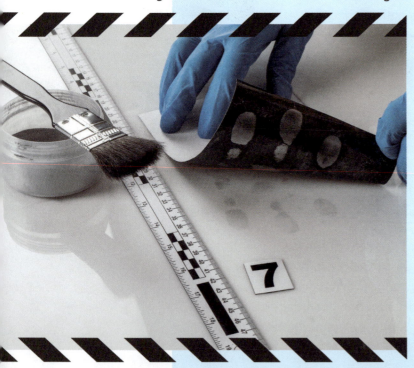

A puddle of brownish-red liquid should not be described as a pool of blood since it has not been verified by a lab. A gun left at a scene could be described as a revolver or semiautomatic handgun, but no other specific details related to brand or caliber should be provided unless verified by the lead investigator or expert on the scene.

The required list of chronological notes, as well as the report format, will vary by department. On average, the notes will consist of:

- An overview or summary of the scene
- Any weather and environmental conditions that may have affected the scene
- Detailed descriptions of key areas or specific scenes directly related to the crime
- How each piece of evidence was processed and collected at the scene by their identification marker
- If the scene requires multiple days to complete, there should be notations about what is pending further investigation.

Once again, it is important to remember that, when the crime scene is considered processed and complete, the investigator will only have the photography, sketch, and notes to refer back to for analysis. Therefore, it is imperative the notes be as detailed as possible to ensure a thorough description of the scene has been documented.

Search Patterns. During the recording of the crime scene, there are different types of search patterns that investigators may utilize in the search for evidence. The most common search patterns are grid, spiral (both inward and outward), parallel, and zone. The grid search is the most common type used by investigators because it ensures small pieces of evidence are not missed.

But the type of search pattern used largely depends on the type of scene. If investigators need to search a large field, then they are likely to use a parallel or grid search pattern. When there is only one investigator assigned to a scene, which is not uncommon, a spiral or zone search may be the best choice.

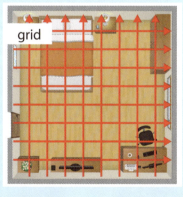
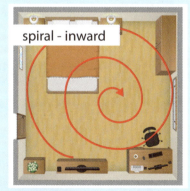
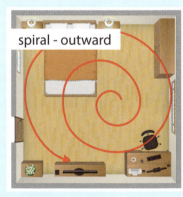
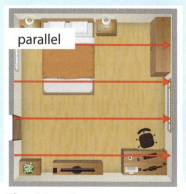
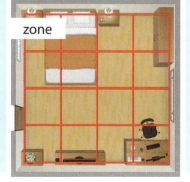

Regardless of the search pattern, each type requires the keen observational skills of the investigators in their search for evidence.

The Crime Scene

Crime Scene Safety. Crime scenes have the potential of subjecting the investigators and officers to multiple health hazards. It is of the utmost importance that personnel investigating the crime scene protect themselves with the appropriate safeguards. Updated vaccinations are just one requirement outlined by OSHA (Occupational Safety and Health Administration). Investigators will also be required to wear protective gloves, eyewear, and footwear. When biological hazards or infectious agents are prevalent, protective suits with respiratory masks may be required. Protective wear not only keeps the investigator safe from noxious substances, but it also aids in preventing cross contamination of evidence.

CONCLUSION

The recording of a crime scene is a tedious process involving three key components: photography, sketches, and notes. Each of the processes has a departmental policy and procedure that must be followed in an organized fashion to ensure scene integrity. A detailed, accurate recording of a crime scene is only possible because an intelligence and order is behind each of the processes described in this lesson. Colossians 1:16 states, "For by him all things were created, in heaven and on earth, visible and invisible … all things were created through him and for him." The one true God created the universe with complex organization. This systematic orderliness confirms the God of the Bible.

Lesson 4
Evidence Collection and Documentation

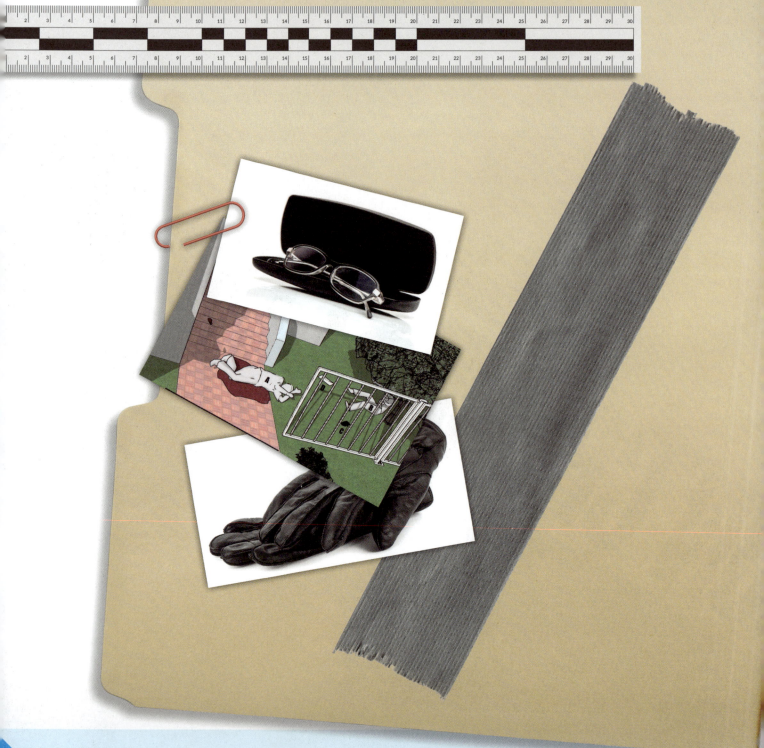

A single witness shall not suffice against a person for any crime or for any wrong in connection with any offense that he has committed. Only on the evidence of two witnesses or of three witnesses shall a charge be established (Deuteronomy 19:15).

Cold Case: Nicole Brown Simpson and Ron Goldman

Recognized as the trial of the century, the O.J. Simpson murder trial was the most televised and watched criminal case in the history of the United States. O.J. Simpson (the "Juice") is a Pro Football Hall of Fame 1985 recipient, actor, broadcaster, and well-known celebrity. Leading up to the beginning of the case, O.J. Simpson and Nicole Brown had been divorced for two years. Their relationship had been plagued with violence and domestic abuse prior to and following the divorce. The case began on the evening of June 12, 1994, at 6:30 p.m. Nicole Brown Simpson had dinner with her family after her daughter's dance recital. Her mother left her prescription eyeglasses at the restaurant table.

- Sometime before 10:30 p.m. — Ron Goldman, a waiter at the restaurant, offers to drop the prescription eyeglasses at Nicole's residence.
- 10:50 p.m. — A neighbor sees Nicole's dog barking and notices the dog has bloody paws.
- 11:01 p.m. — O.J. Simpson is driven from his residence, only a couple miles from Nicole's, to the airport and flies to Chicago.
- 12:10 a.m. — Nicole's dog leads the neighbors to the murdered bodies of Nicole Brown Simpson and Ron Goldman.
- 4:30 a.m. — The police drive to O.J. Simpson's mansion to inform him of the death of his ex-wife Nicole, only to discover that O.J. is not home, and they find "his blood-stained Bronco and a bloody glove that matches one found near Goldman's body."[37]
- 10:45 a.m. — Investigators arrive at Simpson's mansion with a search warrant and discover more evidence.
- 12 p.m. — O.J. Simpson has arrived home from Chicago and is taken away for questioning in the death of Nicole Brown Simpson and Ron Goldman.
- June 17, 1994 — O.J. is charged with the murders of Nicole Brown Simpson and Ron Goldman. After stating he will surrender to police, he flees police and is spotted in the passenger seat of his white Bronco. Police immediately follow the Bronco on a 60-mile chase. To date, this is the most watched and televised police chase in American history.
- June 17, 1994, 9 p.m. — O.J. is arrested and placed in custody.
- January 24, 1995 — The Trial of the Century begins.
- October 3, 1995 — After a lengthy trial, hundreds of pieces of evidence, and testimony, O.J. Simpson is acquitted of the murder of Nicole Brown Simpson and Ron Goldman.

There were over 108 exhibits of DNA evidence alone in this trial. The amount of circumstantial evidence that linked O.J. Simpson to the crime scene was extensive. Below is a list of a few other pieces of evidence found during the investigation:

- 911 call history from Nicole Brown reporting O.J.'s violent behavior.
- O.J. had fresh wounds on his hand the day after the murders.[38]
- O.J.'s blood was identified at the murder scene.
- Hair samples consistent with O.J. were found on Ron Goldman's shirt.
- Inside O.J. Simpson's Bronco and his residence, police identified blood, hair, and fibers from Brown and Goldman.
- O.J. Simpson's glove was found at Nicole's home, and the matching glove was found outside O.J.'s house.
- Bloody shoeprints found at the murder scene matched shoes owned by O.J. Simpson.[39]

As Sherlock Holmes said, "There is nothing more deceptive than an obvious fact."[40] The O.J. Simpson trial will be studied by law schools and trial experts for decades. O.J. Simpson was found liable for both murders in 1997 in a civil trial. This case had a lot of evidence, but the criminal trial for Simpson ended in a verdict of not guilty. Yet there was enough evidence for him to be found guilty in a civil trial that followed. This highlights the difference in criminal and civil law. Civil trials focus on disputes between individuals while criminal trials focus on a person's crimes against the state or federal government. This includes breaking a law established by local, state, or national government. Criminal law requires a higher burden of proof to convict, with the possibility of incarceration, while civil law is based on the preponderance of evidence and results in financial restitution. As seen in this case, even the most thoroughly documented evidence doesn't guarantee a specific outcome in a case. Though Simpson was ordered to pay $33.5 million in damages per the civil trial, the Goldman family has collected less than 1% from him.

This lesson will discuss the difference between physical and circumstantial evidence, both of which were utilized in the O.J. Simpson trial.

Evidence, as it relates to the criminal justice system, is defined as data presented to a court or jury as proof of the facts in issue and which may include the testimony of witnesses, records, documents, or objects.[41] Evidence has a twofold purpose: to establish criminal intent to commit a crime and indication of a criminal act. Evidence can stem from both physical (nonliving origin) and biological (living origin) forms. The search for evidence stems from Locard's Exchange Principle, as an unavoidable cross transfer occurs between two items that come into contact at the crime scene. This cross transfer results in physical evidence linking a suspect or victim with a crime. Crime scene evidence can be classified into two basic categories: direct evidence and circumstantial evidence. Direct evidence requires no inference and directly connects a suspect to a crime scene. Circumstantial evidence requires inference, but sufficient circumstantial evidence is capable of conviction even when there is no direct evidence. Circumstantial evidence provides the majority of the evidence presented in court, though both types of evidence are equally important and neither holds more weight than the other.

EVIDENCE FROM A BIBLICAL WORLDVIEW

Skeptics and nonbelievers often ask for the "evidence" of God's existence or the "evidence" that the history in the Bible is true. But do we need evidence to prove God is real? God's perfect, Holy Word reveals who He is. Genesis 1:1 begins with, "In the beginning, God." The Bible never argues for the existence of God, as it is understood from the very first verse and throughout the entire Bible. First Corinthians 8:6 states, ". . . yet for us there is one God, the Father, from whom are all things and for whom we exist, and one Lord, Jesus Christ, through whom are all things and through whom we exist." There is no one who has an excuse for denying the existence of God, as stated in Romans 1:20, "For his invisible attributes, namely, his eternal power and divine nature, have been clearly perceived, ever since the creation of the world, in the things that have been made. So they are without excuse."

So ultimately, a person must have faith in the existence of God and His truth found in the Scriptures. Hebrews 11:6 tells us, "And without faith it is impossible to please him, for whoever would draw near to God must believe that he exists and that he rewards those who seek him." As Christians, we can boldly and confidently defend our faith with the Bible, God's perfect Word. The confirmation of His existence lies in our relationship with Him, what He reveals to us in the Bible, and His very creation that is present all around us. What is truly wonderful is the additional confirmation from archaeological evidence; the tens of thousands of biblical records and manuscripts supporting the authenticity of the Bible; and the unchanging message, meaning, and context of God's Word.

IDENTIFICATION OF PHYSICAL EVIDENCE

Very few crime scenes do not yield some type of physical evidence. Learning to identify viable evidence is a trained skill. Perfecting this technique often takes years of experience in crime scene work. It is not uncommon for novice investigators to miss key evidence, and this demonstrates the necessity for new personnel to receive hundreds of hours of training under the mentorship of an expert. The phrase "practice makes perfect" applies to investigative crime scene work. Often, equipment plays a role in the ability to identify trace evidence. If an agency has limited funding, the technology they have available to aid in the detection of hidden evidence (which may include alternate light sources or evidence vacuum sweepers) may be limited. As in any profession, an individual should complete their job to the best of their ability with the tools they have available. This provides a living testimony of service to the Lord.

Crime scene evidence is either physical (of nonliving origin), biological (living origin), or testimonial. Physical evidence is composed of tangible items, while biological evidence would include fluids and other items that contain the potential for DNA. The lists below provide an overview of evidence found at crime scenes:

Physical evidence:
- Documents
- Explosives
- Firearms
- Glass fragments
- Fibers
- Impressions (shoes, tires)
- Paint samples
- Powders (drugs, poisons)
- Security footage
- Serial numbers
- Weapons and tools
- Fingerprints
- Impressions (lips)

Biological evidence:
- Bodily fluids (blood, saliva, semen)
- Human hair
- Animal fur

Testimonial evidence:
- Victim and/or bystander eyewitness accounts
- Confessions

The type of evidence will affect the collection, packaging, and analysis required to process it. These processes will be discussed in detail throughout the textbook. Physical evidence is further classified as either direct evidence or circumstantial evidence.

DIRECT EVIDENCE

Direct evidence links a suspect to a crime or scene through personal knowledge or observation. This type of evidence does not require any inference to draw conclusions since the connection between evidence and suspect is clear and is able to prove a fact on its own. Examples of direct evidence may include surveillance video footage or eyewitness testimony.

To distinguish between direct evidence and circumstantial evidence, review the following scenario: An eyewitness observed a woman laying her wallet on the restaurant table. When the woman turned her head, a man with a spider tattoo on his right hand, wearing a black hoodie, walked by her table and took her wallet when she was not looking.

This would be considered direct evidence since the eyewitness saw the crime occur and can describe the suspect's features. Now imagine the same scenario, but in this case, an eyewitness tells police they saw a man with a spider tattoo on his right hand, wearing a black hoodie, walking out of the restaurant with a woman's wallet in his hand. Since the actual theft was not observed by the eyewitness, this would be considered circumstantial evidence.

CIRCUMSTANTIAL EVIDENCE

Circumstantial evidence differs from direct evidence in that it is not gathered from direct observation but from inference. Many people have a misconception that circumstantial evidence is of less value than direct evidence, but this is not the case. Circumstantial evidence comprises the majority of evidence in criminal convictions. In the court of law, circumstantial evidence must prove *mens rea*, or the state of mind of the suspect when they engaged in the illegal act. The Latin root for *mens rea* means guilty mind.[42] When determining *mens rea*, there are questions the criminal justice system needs to consider: Was the suspect acting purposefully and willfully? Was the suspect aware of the harm their actions could cause? The American Law Institute's Model Penal Code outlines four standards for defining *mens rea*: a guilty individual is one who acts purposefully, knowingly, recklessly, or negligently.[43] Additionally, circumstantial evidence must show *modus operandi* (MO), or the method and habits a criminal utilizes to commit their crimes. Recognizing a pattern in criminal activity allows the investigator to link possible evidence and related crimes together, as well as predict the future behavior of the suspect.

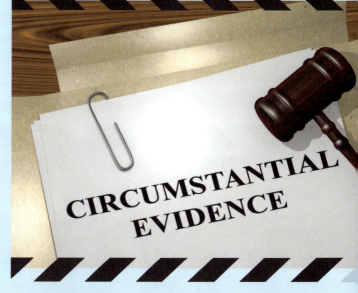

Types of circumstantial evidence are similar to those providing direct evidence, but foundationally, the difference is the context of the evidence, such as, "Was there direct observation?" and "Is there security video footage available?" The following examples are a sampling of what is considered circumstantial evidence and may include types of physical evidence such as computer browser history, shoe impressions, trace evidence, and fingerprints. The more circumstantial evidence at a crime scene, the greater possibility of a connection between the suspect and the evidence, but often this may or may not result in a conviction in the courtroom. This was the case in the O.J. Simpson case study at the start of this lesson.

Evidence Collection and Documentation

CLASS CHARACTERISTICS

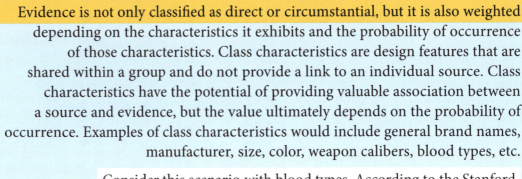

Evidence is not only classified as direct or circumstantial, but it is also weighted depending on the characteristics it exhibits and the probability of occurrence of those characteristics. Class characteristics are design features that are shared within a group and do not provide a link to an individual source. Class characteristics have the potential of providing valuable association between a source and evidence, but the value ultimately depends on the probability of occurrence. Examples of class characteristics would include general brand names, manufacturer, size, color, weapon calibers, blood types, etc.

Consider this scenario with blood types. According to the Stanford School of Medicine, the occurrence of blood types in individuals can be seen in the list below.[44]

- AB negative (0.6 percent)
- B negative (1.5 percent)
- AB positive (3.4 percent)
- A negative (6.3 percent)
- O negative (6.6 percent)
- B positive (8.5 percent)
- A positive (35.7 percent)
- O positive (37.4 percent)

Generally, if a blood sample retrieved from a crime scene is identified as an AB− (0.6% of the population) or B− (1.5% of the population) blood type, it would be considered an important class characteristic due to the low probability of occurrence. This in conjunction with other blood factors would assist in the identification and elimination of possible suspects.

INDIVIDUAL CHARACTERISTICS

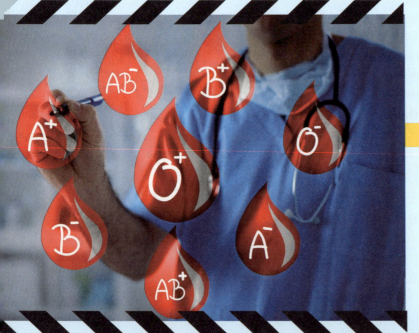

Individual characteristics are unique features that have a high probability of being associated with a standard source. Probability in relation to evidence refers to the fact that the association between source and unique features defies human comprehension or a mathematical prediction. An example of this would be the probability of wear marks on the outsole of a shoeprint pattern. Based on studies conducted on shoe wear outsole patterns, the probability that identical shoes worn by two different individuals will have the same wear marks is one in one octillion. See the chart on the next page.

Number of Characteristics	Probability of Occurrence
1	1 out of 16,000
2	1 out of 127,992,000
3	1 out of 683 billion
4	1 out of 2.7 quadrillion
5	1 out of 8.7 quintillion
6	1 out of 23 sextillion
7	1 out of 53 septillion
8	1 out of 106 octillion
9	1 out of 189 nonillion
10	1 out of 300 decillion

Source: Stone 2006[45]

Other examples of evidence exhibiting individual characteristics include fingerprints with matching minutiae (details), DNA fingerprint identifications, striation marks on tools and bullets, and handwriting characteristics.

DOCUMENTATION OF EVIDENCE

The correct collection, handling, and packaging of evidence is often a tedious process and, if not processed correctly, will result in a failure to admit the evidence into court. Regardless of the size of the evidence, proper procedures must be followed and maintained to ensure the integrity of the evidence. Often, the value of the evidence is apparent at the crime scene, but in many cases, there is latent information that is only retrievable through testing procedures in the forensic lab, such as biological fluids, trace hair or fiber evidence, and latent fingerprints.

The primary goal when collecting and packaging evidence is to preserve its integrity by handling it in such a way that no change or damage is incurred from the removal at the scene to when it arrives at the forensic lab, and ultimately to the court room. Proper protective equipment is necessary to avoid cross contamination of evidence and to assist the investigator in accomplishing evidence integrity. This may require the investigator to use latex gloves, facial masks, hair nets, disposable shoe coverings, and, if necessary, additional biohazard gear. The collection of evidence will be discussed in detail in the respective lessons, but each type of evidence requires specific handling, packaging, and storage. The type of packaging to secure and protect the evidence is determined by the form of the evidence (solid, liquid, or gaseous) and the size of the evidence (microscopic to massive in size).

Once evidence has been secured, the investigator should proceed with the collection of reference samples from the crime scene. Reference samples are those from the victims at the scene of the crime, carpet fibers from known sources, hair or fur samples from known sources, handwriting examples, and other related samples that will aid in the elimination or connection of evidence to the scene. The number of reference samples required for examination will differ based on the source.

Chain of Custody. The chain of custody is critical to ensuring the integrity of the evidence. The chain of custody provides a documented, chronological record of those individuals who have interacted with each piece of evidence from the moment of collection, through analysis, and into the courtroom. Essentially, it is a documented "continuity of possession of evidence."[46] Chain of custody records verify to the court that the evidence being submitted is authentic in nature and has not been tampered with prior to court submission. The document also ensures that every testing analysis completed on the evidence had the proper authorization. A violation in chain of custody will result in the inadmissibility of evidence into the court system. This is just one of the many reasons to maintain a well-documented chain of custody to present to the court. Chain of custody will be discussed in more detail in Lesson 34.

Evidence is one of the pathways to criminal prosecution. This lesson provided an overview of the features associated with crime scene evidence. Whether evidence is physical, biological, or testimonial, each piece will fit together into a puzzle that completes the picture of the crime.

Collect

Preserve

Present

PHYSICAL EVIDENCE

UNIT 3

Lesson 5
Drugs

> Or do you not know that your body is a temple of the Holy Spirit within you, whom you have from God? You are not your own, for you were bought with a price. So glorify God in your body (1 Corinthians 6:19–20).

Case Study: Death of Michael Jackson

The afternoon of June 25, 2009, at 2:26 p.m., Michael Jackson, the "King of Pop," was pronounced dead from cardiac arrest. He was only fifty years old. As Sherlock Holmes said, "To begin at the beginning,"[47] Michael Jackson rose to fame at the young age of 11 when his family group from Gary, Indiana, the Jackson 5, opened for Diana Ross in 1969. Jackson released his first solo album in 1979. His best-selling album in 1982 sold over 66,000,000 albums worldwide. Jackson came to be known as the King of Pop, selling a total of 750,000,000 albums during his career.

It is alleged that Jackson first turned to drugs after receiving second-degree burns to his scalp while filming a commercial for Pepsi® in 1984. The burns caused permanent damage to his scalp and hair growth, which caused him to be self-conscious about his appearance.[48] A few years later, in 1993, Jackson was accused of inappropriate behavior with children at his personal estate called Neverland. Due to the pressures of a legal battle and investigation, in conjunction with media coverage of the event, Jackson began taking a wide variety of antidepressants, antianxiety pills, and other medications. Ultimately, Jackson settled out of court with the accusing family for $22 million. Police reopened the investigation into inappropriate behavior with children in 2003.

Michael Jackson was a drug addict for 15 years leading up to his death. He was also $400 million in debt. Though he attempted rehabilitation, Jackson was never able to curb his addictions. Jackson's drug addiction became so severe, it caused him to have an implant in his abdomen to diminish the effects of opiate drugs.[49] Also, Jackson battled with chronic insomnia for years and relied on drug cocktails to achieve sleep. Jackson's addiction to propofol developed over the years from multiple dental and facial reconstruction surgeries. Leading up to the day of his death, Dr. Murray, Jackson's physician, administered propofol on a regular basis to help him sleep. Propofol is a dangerous anesthetic and, in conjunction with the numerous other drugs Jackson was taking, is believed to have contributed to his death.

The day before Jackson's death, on June 24, he left his last rehearsal for his new *This Is It* tour around midnight. Here is the account:

- 1:30 a.m. — Jackson is administered a 10-mg tablet of Valium®.
- 2:00 a.m. — Jackson is administered Ativan®, an antianxiety drug, through an IV.
- 3:00 a.m. — Jackson is administered another sedative called Versed®.
- Later that morning, Jackson received two more mg of Ativan and two more mg of Versed®.

At dawn, Jackson was still not able to sleep and requested a dose of propofol. Dr. Murray denied his requests until 10:40 a.m., when he administered 25 mg of propofol. At 10:50 a.m., Dr Murray noticed that Jackson was not breathing and administered 0.2 mg of Anexate® (a drug used to counteract sedatives). At 12:22 p.m., one of Jackson's security guards called 911, almost two hours after he was found not breathing. Doctors pronounced Michael Jackson dead at 2:26 p.m.

Facts to consider about this case:
- According to the coroner, the drugs found in Jackson's system during the autopsy included:

    Propofol, a sedative

    Lorazepam (Valium®)

    Midazolam, a sedative

    Diazepam (Valium®)

    Lidocaine, a painkiller

    Ephedrine, a stimulant and decongestant

    Nordiazepam (Valium®)

- Previous employees of Jackson testified that the singer would take 30–40 Xanax® pills every night.
- Dr. Conrad Murray had also been hired (informally) by the *This Is It* tour company (AEG) to have Jackson ready for performance and a lengthy tour.[50]
- Dr. Conrad Murray, Jackson's personal physician, was charged and convicted of voluntary manslaughter in his death. Dr. Murray served two years of a four-year term in prison.
- Numerous drugs were found at the scene of Jackson's death in addition to the 13 drugs found in his system. They included:

    An antidepressant

    A sleep aid

    Medication to treat panic attacks and seizures

    Two types of medications used to treat vitiligo

    Medication used to reverse the effects of an overdose of a different medication used to treat anxiety, seizures, and alcohol withdrawal

    A muscle relaxant

    A corticosteroid

    A medication used to treat an enlarged prostate

    Two antibiotics

    A stimulant

    Aspirin

An excessive number of prescription medications paired with irresponsible behavior regarding dosage amounts is likely what contributed to Jackson's untimely death. This lesson will outline the positive and negative aspects of drugs while examining this topic through the lens of God's Word.

==All drugs carry a risk factor, and there is no level of drug use that can be deemed safe.== What is a drug? A drug is any substance that when administered or ingested produces an effect. Drugs are derived from two basic sources, either natural or synthetic. Drugs affect an individual either physiologically, psychologically, or both.

Over 31.9 million people in the United States over the age of 12 admit to using some kind of illegal drug in the past month. Fifty percent of Americans admit to using an illicit drug at least once in their lifetime.[51] Drug use, both prescription and illegal, along with drug crimes are a serious problem in the United States and around the world. Drug crimes present many challenges for law enforcement due to the lucrative nature of the business and the violent measures offenders engage in within the drug world.

Drugs have the potential to cause physiological (physical) and psychological (mental) dependency, as well as addiction. Many people assume that a physiological dependence and an addiction are synonymous, but that is not the case. A person can be dependent upon a drug without being addicted. People will often be dependent on blood pressure medication or insulin for diabetes but are not addicted to the drugs. Drugs are also organized into schedules (see **Table 7**) based on their potency and medical value. Whether natural or synthetic, legal or illicit, drugs are classified into categories dependent upon their effects on the body.

DRUG USE FROM A BIBLICAL WORLDVIEW

The Bible provides guidelines on how Christians should view intoxication, drunkenness, and intentionally putting things in their bodies that would cause harm. Genesis 1:27 describes the creation of humans as divine. Humans are the only creation by God made in His image. First Corinthians 6:19–20 describes the body as a temple of the Holy Spirit and that it is not our own but bought with a price. First Corinthians 10:13 tells us, "No temptation has overtaken you that is not common to man. God is faithful, and he will not let you be tempted beyond your ability." First Peter 5:8 reminds us to "Be sober-minded; be watchful. Your adversary the devil prowls around like a roaring lion, seeking someone to devour." Intoxication and illicit drug use are discouraged because they lower inhibitions and increase the likelihood of committing sinful activity against the Creator God. Ephesians 5:18 tells us, "And do not get drunk with wine, for that is debauchery, but be filled with the Spirit." A sober, clear mind that is filled with the truth of God's Word is able to withstand "the flaming darts of the evil one" and the dependency that is likely to follow.

Caution should be taken with prescribed medications as well. Yes, prescribed medicines are necessary to treat illness, curb the negative side effects of cancer treatments, help those with disorders, etc., but many individuals become addicted to prescribed medications (especially painkillers) when there is no valid medical explanation. Also, people acquire prescribed medications from friends or family, or by theft, and become addicted. Sadly, these individuals need the truth of God's love for them to fill the voids they are trying to mask through drug use. As followers of Christ, we should strive to keep our minds clear so that we can be alert to fight the spiritual battle, guide those who are lost, be a light for truth in a very dark world, and most importantly, be ready when Christ returns. First Peter 1:13 says, "Therefore, preparing your minds for action, and being sober-minded, set your hope fully on the grace that will be brought to you at the revelation of Jesus Christ."

DEPRESSANTS

Like the word states, depressants depress, or slow down, the central nervous system. The central nervous system (CNS) consists of the brain and spinal cord and controls the functions of the entire body. A few of the functions of the CNS include thought processes, emotions, breathing, and heart rate. Another common term for depressants is barbiturates, or "downers." Examples of depressants include alcohol (which will be discussed in detail in Lesson 12), antianxiety drugs, and methaqualone.

The effects of a depressant on an individual will vary. Factors such as body weight, body size, previous use of depressants, existing health conditions, dosage amount, and the overall strength of the drug can all affect how a person responds to the drug. Dependence and addiction are common in users of depressants. Regular use of depressants can lead to both physical and psychological dependence. When depressants are used in conjunction with alcohol or other drugs, the dependence is far more serious. They do not necessarily cause someone to be depressed, though extended drug use and addiction can lead to depression. Consistent use of depressants will also lead to tolerance for the drug. Tolerance occurs when the body becomes accustomed to taking a drug, and the body adapts, requiring a higher dosage of the drug to achieve the same effects. Withdrawal from addiction is very difficult and often requires other drugs to wean the individual off of the barbiturates under medical supervision. **Table 1** outlines the general effects of depressants based on low and high doses.

Table 1: Effects of Depressants[52]

Low Dose	High Dose
Reduced anxiety	Vomiting
Impaired judgment	Irregular breathing
Elevated mood	Unconsciousness and memory loss
Reduced reaction time	Coma and death

STIMULANTS

Stimulants have the opposite effect of a depressant. Stimulants, or "uppers," speed up the CNS by making a person feel awake, energized, and overly confident. In essence, stimulants speed up brain activity, making people more alert. The chemicals in stimulants can be found in naturally occurring substances and prescription medications, as well as illicit drugs. Examples of stimulants include caffeine, cocaine, crack, methamphetamine, nicotine, amphetamines, and mephedrone. Factors that affect the potency of stimulants include body weight and size, prior use and tolerance, dosage amount, and preexisting conditions. As with any drug use, combining stimulants with other forms of drugs such as alcohol, cannabis, or prescription medications is extremely dangerous. The general effects of stimulants are outlined in **Table 2**.

The majority of stimulants are prescribed by medical doctors, but clandestine labs illegally acquire stimulants and modify or remarket them on the drug market. It is common for those taking stimulants, both legally and illicitly, to develop a dependency on the drug. This dependency is both psychological and physiological. As the human body becomes physiologically accustomed to having regular doses of stimulants, it will develop a tolerance over time. Tolerance fosters increased cravings for the drugs and can lead people to irrational behavior as they try to fill the addictive desires. As a user becomes more addicted to the drug, higher and higher doses are required to achieve the same effect. Stimulants may be taken intravenously, smoked, and sniffed.

> **Clandestine lab:**
> A lab that produces illicit drugs, primarily methamphetamine, which is 80–90% of the production in the United States.

A Focus on Cocaine. Cocaine has been used as a stimulant since the ancient Incas chewed coca leaves. Peruvian and Bolivian natives continue to chew coca leaves today.[53] In 1859, cocaine was extracted from the coca leaves for the first time by a chemist named Albert Niemann. Sigmund Freud was the first public person to advocate for cocaine use and even published a paper in 1884 titled *Über Coca* ("About Coke"). In his paper, he wrote,

A few minutes after taking cocaine, one experiences a sudden exhilaration and feeling of lightness . . . One senses an increase of self-control and feels more vigorous and more capable of work. Long-lasting, intensive mental or physical work can be performed without fatigue.

Freud went on to recommend the drug to his girlfriend, friends, colleagues, and patients. Sadly, those connected to him had adverse side effects, and some even died. Further popularity for the drug came in 1886, when John Pemberton invented Coca-Cola®. You guessed right, one of the ingredients in Coca-Cola® was coca leaves.[54] This new, amazing drink provided energy and euphoria, but around 1903, the coca leaf was eliminated as an ingredient. Coca-Cola® claims there are no coca leaves in their products today.

Cocaine use continued into the early 1900s. After multiple cocaine-related deaths and instances of nasal damage (due to sniffing), the United States banned the drug in 1922. It was not until the 1970s that the drug became popular in the entertainment, college, and white-collar circles. The drug's ability to provide extended periods of energy was enticing to people working long hours or college students looking for an extra boost to finish term papers. What many did not realize is the addictive effect of cocaine. Users can become addicted after just one hit of cocaine, and many become lifelong prisoners to the drug. A study in 2015 found that cocaine is the third most addictive drug after alcohol and heroin.[55] By the end of the 1980s, cocaine had become not only affordable, but also the most dangerous drug on the drug market at that time. Cocaine is most often snorted through the nose and results in a high that lasts only 30 minutes. Crack, concentrated cocaine combined with baking soda (or other substance), is usually heated and smoked. Its name comes from the fact that it crackles when heated. Crack is even more addictive than cocaine and results in a high lasting 2–3 minutes.

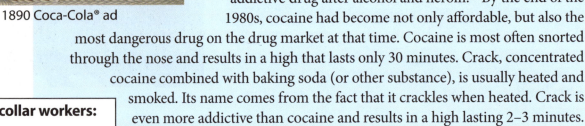

1890 Coca-Cola® ad

White-collar workers: People who work in an office or professional environment.

Table 2: Effects of Stimulants

Low Dose	High Dose
Cheerfulness	Anxiety
Exhilaration	Nausea
Alertness	Tremors and seizures
Reduced appetite	Coma and death

Caffeine, a well-known ingredient in coffee, tea, and many sodas, is also classified as a stimulant. Though these beverages are not the same as more serious stimulant drugs, problems can still arise from substance abuse of any kind, including addiction and various medical issues. We should always be aware of what we are putting into our bodies, as the Bible says our bodies are temples of the Holy Spirit (1 Corinthians 6:19–20). We should also be a good example to others in our conduct, reflecting the image of Jesus Christ.

OPIATES AND OPIOIDS

Opioids are naturally derived from the seed pods and sap of an opium poppy plant or can be synthetically manufactured. Opioid drugs activate receptors in the brain that depress the central nervous system. As the bodily systems slow down, the body

releases dopamine, a pain reliever. Most people who are prescribed opioids are dealing with severe pain. The most common names for opioids are narcotics or painkillers.

Opioid use has the potential to lead to both physiological and psychological dependency, addiction, and tolerance. Examples of prescription opioids include morphine, codeine, Vicodin®, fentanyl, opium, and oxycodone. Illegal opioids, such as heroin (though in some countries it is prescribed), are used to get "high" and are far more potent than prescription opioids.[56] Prescription opioids are the most prescribed medications in the United States. According to the Center for Disease Control (CDC), there are 58 opioid prescriptions for every 100 Americans.[57] An opiate refers to natural opioids such as heroin, morphine, and codeine. All opiates are classified as opioids. Opiates are extremely addicting, and those who use opiates for extended periods of time may experience irreversible damage to vital organs.

A Focus on Heroin. Opium has been used by ancient civilizations dating back to 3400 B.C. The use of opium as treatment for pain came to the United States in the 1700s. By the end of the 1700s, physicians began to document the addictive behaviors of opium use. Doctors began to look for a cure to opium addiction and successfully isolated morphine and codeine in 1805. Morphine, which produced 10 times greater effects than opium, was not the answer to opium addiction as originally hoped by researchers. Attempts were made to find a drug that could be used in place of morphine. In 1874, heroin was first synthesized from morphine and, by 1898, was being manufactured by the Bayer Pharmaceutical Company.[58] It did not take long for researchers to realize that heroin was not the answer for those addicted to morphine, due to its highly addictive nature. By 1924, heroin was deemed an illegal drug in the United States.

The first major trend in heroin use came after World War II and steadily increased

until its peak in the 1960s. Several celebrity deaths in the early 1970s (Janis Joplin, 27 years old; Jim Morrison, 36 years old) due to heroin overdose sparked attention to drug use in the United States, but because it is so addictive,

the number of users only increased. A large percentage of heroin addicts are located in large, inner-city neighborhoods. Heroin addiction continues to surge and is considered the second most addictive drug in the United States. Celebrities succumbing to heroin addiction and death far too young include River Phoenix (1993, 23 years old), Curt Cobain (1994, 27 years old), Chris Farley (1997, 33 years old), Cory Monteith (2013, 31 years old), and Philip Seymour Hoffman (2014, 46 years old). It is estimated there are currently over 467,000 people addicted to heroin in the United States.[59]

Table 3: Effects of Opioids

Low Dose	High Dose
Lethargy	Cold, clammy skin
Drowsiness and disorientation	Blue lips and fingertips
Slurred speech	Sleepiness
Slowed breathing and heart rate	Death by respiratory depression

HALLUCINOGENS

Hallucinogens (or psychedelics) are derived from natural sources, such as trees, fungi, and seeds, and from synthetic chemicals. They are the oldest class of drugs that people have used to alter the perception of the mind. Hallucinogens are considered alkaloids due to their nitrogen content and physiological effects on humans. Synthetic hallucinogens became widely available in the 1960s. Hallucinogens are placed into two categories: classic hallucinogens (LSD) and dissociative drugs (PCP).[60]

> **Alkaloid:**
> Nitrogenous organic compounds from a plant that produce physiological effects on humans.

Common hallucinogens are LSD, peyote, DMT, ketamine, marijuana, Ecstasy (club drugs), and PCP. Scientists believe that hallucinogens interrupt the communication between the brain and spinal cord and cause serious side effects such as changing the perception of time, distorting reality, causing mood swings, and fostering hallucinations. Users of hallucinogens are likely to develop a psychological dependence on the drugs. Side effects are further classified into short-term and long-term categories (see **Table 4**).

Table 4: Effects of Hallucinogens

Short-Term	Long-Term
Increased heart rate	Paranoia
Nausea	Mood changes
Dry mouth	Memory loss
Insomnia	Flashbacks
Psychosis	Suicidal tendencies

A Focus on LSD. LSD (lysergic acid diethylamide) was first isolated in 1938 by Albert Hoffman while he was analyzing fungi. The hallucinogenic effects of LSD were not realized until 1943, when Hoffman accidentally ingested a small quantity.[61] Hoffman began to experiment and document the psychoactive effects of LSD. The drug grew in popularity during the 1960s to the 1970s. When using LSD, perceptions are altered so dramatically, the use of hallucinogens is often referred to as a "trip" to a new world of reality. Users will differentiate their "trips" as good or bad, depending on their overall experience. There are many contributing factors that influence a "trip," such as environment, companions, and the use of alcohol or other drugs. The danger of LSD is that there is no such thing as a "good" trip. Illicit drugs that alter perception violate God's design for human lives. The Bible clearly states in 1 Peter 5:8, "Be sober-minded; be watchful. Your adversary the devil prowls around like a roaring lion, seeking someone to devour."

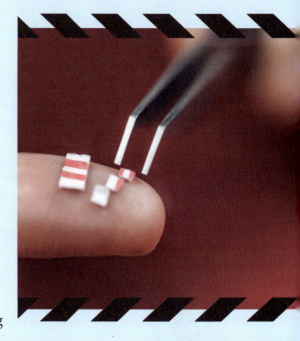

Table 5: Hallucinogens "Trip" Effects

Short-Term	Long-Term
Exhilaration	Frightening hallucinations
Alteration of the senses	Anxiety and panic
Hallucinations	Unpredictable behavior
Rapid breathing with irregular heartbeat	Flashbacks

CANNABINOIDS

Cannabinoids are any group of related compounds that include cannabinol and the active constituents of cannabis. Cannabis is derived naturally from the hemp plant (a cousin of the marijuana plant) *Cannabis sativa*. Various parts of the plant are used to create different potencies in drugs for recreational, medicinal, or synthetic uses. Scientific research has discovered that the cannabis plant produces between 80 and 100 cannabinoids and roughly 300 non-cannabinoid chemicals.[62] The two types of cannabinoids are delta-9-tetrahydrocannabinol (THC) and cannabidiol (CBD).[63] Delta-9-tetrahydrocannabinol (THC) levels are what determine the potency and euphoric (high) effects of cannabis. The higher the THC level, the greater the euphoric effect. In contrast, cannabidiol (CBD) is estimated to have the opposite effect by offering a calming, anti-psychoactive response. CBD is extracted from either the hemp plant or the marijuana plant. Cannabinoids come in many forms, such as butane hash oil, cannabis, medicinal cannabis, and synthetic cannabis. Common examples of cannabinoids include hashish, marijuana (a hallucinogen), pot, weed, CBD, Mojo, and Godfather. Effects of cannabinoids are shown in **Table 6**.

Butane Hash Oil. Since the legalization of cannabis and the reduced cultural stigma in cannabis use, a new method of ingesting cannabis has emerged in the form of butane hash oil. This concentrated THC, when processed with butane oil, results in a product that has 80% THC concentration. This is substantially more potent than the THC of marijuana, which ranges between 10–25%.[64] Butane hash oil is smoked through a bong or similar device.

Cannabis. The most common name associated with cannabis is marijuana. Marijuana is the most widely used and illicit drug in the United States, though it is likely to gain legal status across the country in the future. The entirety of the *Cannabis sativa* plant can be used to make a variety of drug products. Marijuana is the dried leaves of the cannabis plant. When trichomes from the flower buds are extracted and pressed into a concentrate, the result is hashish. The stems and seeds will be added to different products for potency of THC. The highest levels of THC are found in the resin of the cannabis plant and is called sinsemilla. Sinsemilla can only be extracted from the unfertilized flowering tops of the female plant and is difficult to cultivate and therefore more expensive. Cannabis is most often smoked, but it can also be baked and vaporized.

A Focus on Medicinal Cannabis. Historical records show that cannabis has been used to treat illness as early as 2737 B.C. in China. The first physician to publish scientific research on the medicinal properties of cannabis was Dr. William O'Shaughnessy in 1839. At the time of O'Shaughnessy's publication, it was not known that there were individual cannabinoids. This discovery came about a century later as technology improved. In 1942, Roger Adams discovered the first cannabidiol (CBD) and later THC.[65] Since the 1960s, Dr. Raphael Mechoulam has conducted extensive research into the medicinal properties of CBD and has theorized it has the potential to treat epilepsy, glaucoma, schizophrenia, type 2 diabetes, tumors, side effects of chemotherapy, and drug dependency and addiction.[66] According to the World Health Organization (WHO), "In humans, CBD exhibits no effects indicative of any abuse or dependence potential. . . . To date, there is no evidence of public health related problems associated with the use of pure CBD."[67] All fifty United States have legalized some form of CBD, though the federal government still classifies it as marijuana. There are three types of medicinal cannabis: pharmaceutical cannabis derived from both natural and synthetic sources; standardized cannabis, which are plant products legal in some countries; and illegal cannabis, which is dangerous due to harmful impurities and unknown potency.[68] Medicinal cannabis, depending on the legal definition that can vary state by state, is not inhaled, and smoking marijuana does not have medicinal properties. CBD is often administered in tincture form, as drops of oil are placed under the tongue, added to food such as smoothies, etc. There are also CBD gummies and topical ointments.

According to experts, there are several problems with medicinal cannabis and CBD oils. First, medical doctors are not convinced of its medicinal benefits since the research on a variety of subjects is still in process. The only illness that has been adequately tested and demonstrates significant benefits from CBD is epilepsy. Doctors are not even clear on the correct dosage amounts to recommend to people. Secondly, there is also little regulation on the products being produced. This causes a disparity in the quality of the product and the ability of the product to help physical conditions. The danger lies in what elements may be added to the products being purchased. Basically, any person who wants to start a CBD company "could say whatever he wants on the label and sell it to people."[69] With no licensing required to distribute, mislabeling as a supplement and not a medicine, and no regulations, it will be difficult to correctly analyze the medical properties of CBD in treating illnesses. Lastly, using CBD has negative side effects such as nausea, dizziness, drowsiness, slowing of thought processes, memory loss, and irritability. Currently, there is legislation in the United States that will begin to regulate this industry.

Synthetic Cannabis. Synthetic cannabis (K2 or Spice) is a laboratory manufactured version of cannabis with similar effects to the natural option. Because it is synthetic, users may experience different side effects than those of natural cannabis. Studies have surfaced concluding that using synthetic cannabis is far more dangerous than those forms derived from the *Cannabis sativa* because it can cause seizures, dehydration, anxiety, heart attacks, strokes, and psychosis.[70] The synthetic version of cannabis is 30 times more likely to cause harm to the user due to the product being largely unregulated, mass produced, and every dose has a different potency. Synthetic cannabis is sold as herbs, teas, potpourri, and more.

Table 6: Effects of Cannabinoids

Low & High Dose	Combined with Alcohol or Drugs
Exhilaration	Nausea and vomiting
Bloodshot eyes	Anxiety and panic
Increased appetite	Paranoia
Laughter with quiet moods	Impaired memory

Long-term use of cannabinoids has the potential to lead to psychological dependence. Cannabis is often viewed as the gateway drug, which means those who engage in regular marijuana use will often experiment with more serious drugs that lead to physiological addiction. Other repercussions of long-term use are a lower IQ, negative outlook on life, lack of success in achieving personal life goals, mental disorders, and little academic success.

DRUG SCHEDULES

Prior to 1970, drug laws varied by state, and there was no federal regulation of controlled substances. In 1970, President Richard Nixon enacted the Controlled Substances Act (CSA). The CSA brought the various existing laws under one federal statute. Under the Controlled Substances Act, drugs are categorized into five schedules (see **Table 7**).[71]

Table 7

Schedule I Controlled Substances

Substances in this schedule have no currently accepted medical use in the United States, a lack of accepted safety for use under medical supervision, and a high potential for abuse.

Some examples of substances listed in Schedule I are: heroin, lysergic acid diethylamide (LSD), marijuana (cannabis), peyote, methaqualone, and 3,4-methylenedioxymethamphetamine ("Ecstasy").

Schedule II Controlled Substances

Substances in this schedule have a high potential for abuse which may lead to severe psychological or physical dependence.

Examples of Schedule II narcotics include methadone (Dolophine®), meperidine (Demerol®), oxycodone (OxyContin®, Percocet®), and fentanyl (Sublimaze®, Duragesic®). Other Schedule II narcotics include morphine, opium, codeine, and hydrocodone.

Examples of Schedule II stimulants include amphetamine (Dexedrine®, Adderall®), methamphetamine (Desoxyn®), and methylphenidate (Ritalin®).

Other Schedule II substances include: amobarbital, glutethimide, and pentobarbital.

Schedule III Controlled Substances

Substances in this schedule have a potential for abuse less than substances in Schedules I or II and abuse may lead to moderate or low physical dependence or high psychological dependence.

Examples of Schedule III narcotics include products containing not more than 90 milligrams of codeine per dosage unit (Tylenol with Codeine®), and buprenorphine (Suboxone®).

Examples of Schedule III non-narcotics include: benzphetamine (Didrex®), phendimetrazine, ketamine, and anabolic steroids such as Depo®-Testosterone.

Schedule IV Controlled Substances

Substances in this schedule have a low potential for abuse relative to substances in Schedule III.

Examples of Schedule IV substances include alprazolam (Xanax®), diazepam (Valium®), lorazepam (Ativan®), and others.

Schedule V Controlled Substances

Substances in this schedule have a low potential for abuse relative to substances listed in Schedule IV and consist primarily of preparations containing limited quantities of certain narcotics.

Examples of Schedule V substances include cough preparations containing not more than 200 milligrams of codeine per 100 milliliters or per 100 grams (Robitussin AC®, Phenergan with Codeine®), and ezogabine.

As we discussed earlier, the increasing drug use in the United States in the 1960s to 1970s, in addition to several celebrity overdose deaths, called attention to new drug regulations by President Richard Nixon. In 1973, the Drug Enforcement Administration (DEA) was formed to oversee and regulate controlled substances in the United States. The severity of the penalty for drug possession and criminal activity is dependent upon where the drug falls within the five schedules. Trafficking in Schedule I drugs will result in harsher penalties than Schedule IV. A discrepancy occurs with such substances as marijuana. According to the federal government, marijuana is a Schedule I controlled substance. As of January 2020, marijuana has been legalized in 11 states for adults over the age of 21 and for medicinal use in 33 states.[72] If someone is found possessing marijuana in one of these states, federal regulations should take precedence, but this is often a battle the states do not want to engage in.

DRUG COLLECTION AND TESTING

Drug evidence comes in many forms, from powders and liquids, pills and other solid forms, to even biological samples such as blood or urine. As we discussed in Lesson 4, evidence should first be photographed, then packaged in an appropriate container, tagged with chain of custody documentation, and sent to the lab for analysis. Whenever handling and collecting any type of evidence, proper PPE (personal protective equipment) must be utilized for the safety of the investigator and to maintain the integrity of the evidence. Depending on the drug scene, especially if a clandestine lab, this may include facial mask, gloves, and other protective clothing. If the drug is a dry substance, plastic bags are the optimal packaging material. But if you are collecting plant-based material or anything that may contain moisture, such as hashish, marijuana, bedding, or clothing, the evidence must be packaged in paper bags to avoid the growth of mold and other substances that would damage the evidence. Biological materials require their own special packaging in tubules and other types of containers. Any sharp object, such as a syringe or needle, would be packaged carefully in sharps containers. Every single piece of evidence will have its own evidence label and chain of custody. Each agency will have a specific outline of procedures for packaging each form of drug evidence.

Drug testing has three levels: weight, presumptive, and confirmatory. A weight test is simply the weight of the drug evidence. A weight test can be used to determine if there is enough of the drug to continue testing. Presumptive testing quickly determines whether the substance is a drug versus baking soda or a similar powder and possibly another type of drug.

Presumptive testing includes:

- Color tests: reagents react with a mixture of chemicals to determine if a type of drug is present. A few examples are provided below:

Test	Drugs	Color Results
Marquis Color	Heroin, morphine, and most opium Amphetamines	Purple Brown
Cobalt Thiocyanate	Cocaine	Blue
Dillie-Koppanyi	Barbiturates	Violet blue
VanUrk	LSD	Blue purple
Duquenois-Levine	Marijuana	Purple

- Microscopic analysis: analyzes the structure of the material; most useful in plant-based drugs.

- Microcrystalline tests: analyze crystal formation by diluting drugs with solvent.

- Ultraviolet spectroscopy: analyze the absorption rate of UV light.

Drug testing

Confirmatory testing confirms the type of drug, the individual components of the drug, and other trace details. Types of confirmatory testing include:

- Gas chromatography: separates the individual components.

- Mass spectrometry: beams of electrons break apart the individual components, creating a unique spectrum.

- Infrared spectroscopy: infrared light is used to examine the chemical bond between atoms.

The only drug testing performed in the field is a presumptive color test to determine if the evidence is a drug. All confirmatory drug testing is conducted in a forensic laboratory by trained forensic drug chemists. We will take a closer look at the equipment used to perform these tests in Lesson 28.

CONCLUSION

The most important statement in this lesson is from the very first sentence, "All drugs carry a risk factor and there is no level of drug use that can be deemed safe." Drug use and addiction continues to be a serious problem worldwide. In 2018, over 67,000 people died of drug overdose in the United States.[73] This statistic includes illicit and prescription opioids, which constitute the majority of overdose-related deaths. As followers of Christ, we must be of clear mind, alert, ready to defend the Word of God, and ready to serve those in need. But being a Christian does not make you immune to becoming a victim of regular drug use. Many Christians suffer from drug addiction as well. Economic burdens, peer pressure, and the cultural expectations of this physical world influence believers to turn to drugs in order to deal with the pressures instead of focusing on the peace found only in God.

We should remember what Jesus said in John 16:33, "I have said these things to you, that in me you may have peace. In the world you will have tribulation. But take heart; I have overcome the world."

Lesson 6
Toolmarks

Whatever you do, work heartily, as for the Lord and not for men, knowing that from the Lord you will receive the inheritance as your reward. You are serving the Lord Christ (Colossians 3:23–24).

Case Study: "Lady in the Box"

In the state of Ohio in 1974, 23-year-old Janice Hartman disappeared. Janice Hartman graduated high school in 1970 and married her boyfriend, John David Smith III. Four years later, they divorced. To support herself, Janice took a job at a club as a dancer. Janice started partying after work, where drugs and alcohol were prevalent. After an altercation with some men at one of these parties, Janice told her mother she was going to leave town for a while. Janice disappeared. She left behind her car, clothing, and all personal effects. For the next 26 years, no one heard from Janice Hartman. In 1974, police started an investigation, but the case went cold. The police assumed that the "party girl" lifestyle had caught up with Janice.

Twenty years after her disappearance, Janice's brother received a phone call from a woman whose sister was married to John Smith, Janice's former husband. The woman told Janice's brother that John Smith lied to the woman's family about who he was and that John was married to her sister (Betty) for a few short months in 1990 before she disappeared in 1991. John Smith denied any wrongdoing in his first and second wives' disappearances. The cases remained unsolved.

Facts about the case:

- Eyewitness testimony stated that the night Janice disappeared, she was seen leaving the club with her ex-husband, John Smith.
- While John and Janice were married, John had been abusive to her and had a temper.
- 1979 — Five years later, Michael (John's younger brother) and John's grandfather came across a wooden (coffin-sized) box in the barn and opened it. They discovered the decomposed remains of Janice. When John was confronted by his brother and grandfather, John Smith denied any knowledge of Janice's death. John claimed that someone else had killed Janice and that he hid the body because he was afraid he would be blamed for her death. John disposed of the body alongside a highway in the state of Indiana in 1979.
- 1980 — The box was found in Indiana, but since DNA analysis had not been developed, the skeletal remains could not be identified other than it was a female. The remains were buried in a pauper's grave, or an inexpensive grave for unknown remains. Police coined the discovery as the "Lady in the Box."[74]
- 1991 — John Smith's second wife, Betty Smith, also disappeared.
- 1999 — The FBI interviewed John's brother (Michael). After years of guilt, Michael revealed the incident with the box and his brother John. Michael relayed this story to the FBI: After Janice disappeared in 1974, Michael found John in the barn building a wooden box about four feet in length. John told his brother the box was to store Janice's personal items. Michael later observed John rolling up Janice's clothes and placing them in the wooden box. Michael observed John nailing the box shut. Michael dismissed the box until his grandfather came across it in 1979.

- 2000 — DNA testing links the "Lady in the Box" to Janice Hartman through mitochondrial DNA analysis. Mitochondrial DNA can be linked through the female line. The DNA analysis matched Janice's mother's mitochondrial DNA.
- 2000 — John Smith is arrested while living with his third wife, whom he married in 1998.
- 2001 — John Smith is convicted and sentenced to 15 years in prison.
- 2019 — John Smith is indicted for Betty's murder, though her remains have never been found.
- Janice Hartman's remains were found but were not intact. Her legs below the knee were missing, having been removed with a saw after her death. The saw left marks, and the upper leg bones were sent to a forensic anthropologist for analysis, where identifiable saw marks in a "V" shape were found on the leg bones. Toolmark analysis verified that the "V" shapes were smooth on one side and jagged on the other, which fit the description of a serrated knife with 8.1 or 11.3 teeth per inch.[75]
- No murder weapon was ever found.
- Inside a storage locker owned by John Smith, police discovered skull fragments and teeth. These remains did not belong to Janice or Betty and have never been identified. In addition, police found two pictures of women who have never been identified.[76]

Toolmarks leave behind clues to the original tool used in a crime. In this case, the toolmarks left behind in bone were compared to the serrated knife used in the disposal of the body. Tools have the potential of revealing both individual and class characteristics, and it is these identifiers that are the key to the value of toolmark evidence covered in this lesson.

"To a great mind nothing is little." — Sherlock Holmes[77]

Oblique lighting:

A light source positioned at a low angle to create shadows. The shadows allow minute details in the surface to be visible for photography.

A toolmark is defined as the impression (or indentation) left by the contact of a tool (or similar object) onto a surface, leaving behind a pattern of the tool. The pattern varies due to the different ways people hold tools, the angle at which the tool was used, and the amount of wear on the tool. Toolmarks appeared in forensic investigation in the early 1900s. Dr. R. Kockel was the first scientist to correctly match knife striations carved in wood using oblique lighting and to address the geometry behind angle of impact in relation to the tool in the hands of an attacker.[78] In 1969, the Association of Firearm and Tool Mark Examiners (AFTE) was formed.[79]

TOOLMARK COMPARISON FROM A BIBLICAL WORLDVIEW

The earliest mention of tools in the Bible is in Genesis 4:22, "Zillah also bore Tubal-cain; he was the forger of all instruments of bronze and iron." Our early ancestors were highly intelligent and capable of forging iron and bronze into tools and weapons. Adam, God's original, perfect creation before sin, was still living at this time. This is not the image that evolutionary ideas provide about early civilizations. Evolutionists are forced to believe that we descended from a primate ancestor; therefore, "early" humans (imagine the classic grunting caveman) were not capable of manipulating metals into tools. They believe that humans are only improving, but this is not the case. The farther humans get from the original creation of humans, the more of a decline there is in genetic mutations, disease, etc. Amazingly, we can be sure that humans have been making tools for 6,000 years with ingenuity provided by our Creator God.

In every forensic discipline, a scientist has the potential to bring glory to the Lord. Colossians 3:23–24 tells us, "Whatever you do, work heartily, as for the Lord and not for men." Forensic toolmark comparison experts have an important job of identifying characteristics or marks left behind on soft surfaces and relating them back to the type of tool used. The expert analysis has the potential to aid detectives in their search for the weapon or tool used at the crime scene. Excellence in work, even toolmark identification, aids the investigators, victims, and judicial system in the search for answers. Titus 2:7 states, "Show yourself in all respects to be a model of good works, and in your teaching show integrity, dignity." As in any profession, completing your work with integrity and honesty is a living testimony to the one true God who governs your life.

CLASS CHARACTERISTICS VS. INDIVIDUAL CHARACTERISTICS

Remember Locard's Exchange Principle? When two things come into contact with one another, there is an exchange of materials between them. When tools come into contact with a surface, there is an exchange of information in the form of characteristics, markings, or impressions. Markings are often found on windowsills by a screwdriver a burglar used to pry open a window, the back of a hammer that was used to open a car door, or a saw that was used to slice evidential materials. These characteristics left behind on surfaces group the evidence into one of two categories: class characteristics and individual characteristics. While class characteristics are most often identified in impressions, individual characteristics are far rarer in occurrence.

Class characteristics are defined as general characteristics that do not provide any unique, individualized information. Class characteristics cannot be connected to one individual source or tool. Examples of class characteristics include brand, color, size, and shape. When we look at the hammer in **Figure 1**, there are a few class characteristics visible:

Figure 1
Brand: Craftsman®
Model: CMHT 51398
Head weight: 16 oz

> **Tools are manufactured by:**
>
> **Stamping:** The shape of a tool is stamped on a solid piece of metal.
>
> **Forging:** The metal is shaped into a tool under high pressure through hammering.
>
> **Milling and grinding:** Creates the final shape of the tool and refines the edges.

Individual characteristics are far more valuable for an investigation because they provide unique information to one specific tool or piece of evidence. During the manufacturing process of tools, machine marks leave behind striation patterns (imperfections) on the heads of hammers, edges of crow bars, chisels, knives, etc. When the striations are observed under a microscope, they resemble the peaks and valleys (ridges and furrows) seen in friction ridge skin of fingerprints (see **Figure 3**).[80] Since these striations can be easily affected by the use of the tool, unique characteristics develop. Individual characteristics in tools would be damage to the tool like marks, nicks, scratches, breaks, rust, and other identifiers caused by using the tool. Damage and wear to the tool will affect the marks and impressions the tool leaves behind and will be evident in the impression. What is the probability that two identical hammers owned by two different individuals would develop the exact same wear, damage, nicks, and breaks and leave behind the exact same impressions? We can confidently conclude that it is extremely unlikely, or just about 0%. By examining the hammer in **Figure 2**, there are individual characteristics we can identify:

Figure 2
Damage to paint
Number taped to handle with tape. Potential for fingerprints on the tape.
Nicks on the handle

Figure 3

questioned striations | known striations

Once the individual striations have been identified, they are compared side by side with the original source under a comparison microscope. This is the reason why locating the original tool that created the impressions is so important. The final challenge is to create a link between the identified tool's impression and the crime scene toolmark impression.

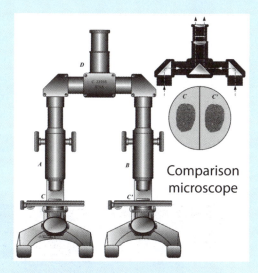

Comparison microscope

FIVE CLASSIFICATIONS OF TOOLS

Tools have a design purpose, or action, when they are being used. Actions may include slicing, gripping, shearing, flat action, or compression. Each of these actions provides a different function.

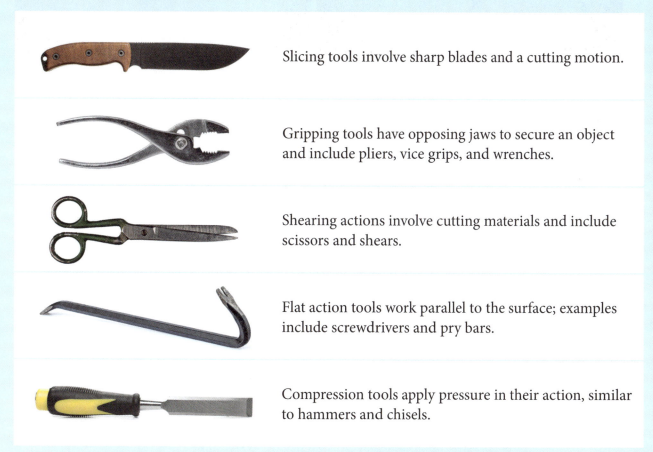

Slicing tools involve sharp blades and a cutting motion.

Gripping tools have opposing jaws to secure an object and include pliers, vice grips, and wrenches.

Shearing actions involve cutting materials and include scissors and shears.

Flat action tools work parallel to the surface; examples include screwdrivers and pry bars.

Compression tools apply pressure in their action, similar to hammers and chisels.

Depending on what tool is used to apply an action, an individualized impression or mark of some form will be transferred onto the surface applied. This transferred mark is the "fingerprint" for that tool. There are two types of toolmarks that result from the transfer between tool action and surface: impressed toolmarks and striated toolmarks.

Impressed toolmarks (or compression marks) are produced when a tool is applied to a surface or another object with enough pressure and force to leave an impression (see **Figure 4**). The impression creates a mirror image of the pattern on the tool to the applied surface. The individual characteristics of the tool (nicks, chips, gauges, rust, etc.) will be transferred onto the impression. The impression can then be photographed or molded for comparison purposes. Striated toolmarks are created by a motion parallel to the surface, where enough pressure is applied to produce a striated mark (see **Figure 4**).

Figure 4
A. Impression toolmark
B. Striation toolmark[81]

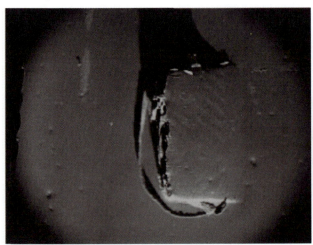

TOOLMARK COMPARISONS

Toolmark comparisons involve a two-fold process. First, a viable toolmark impression must be retrieved from the crime scene. The toolmark impression is often retrieved and preserved at the scene with a casting compound. If possible, the entire structure where the toolmark impression is discovered will be sent to the lab, but it is often not feasible to remove victims' entire windows or doors where these marks are located. The examiner will then use the class characteristics of the impression to determine the type of tool used to create the mark. Second, the questioned tool must be identified, collected, and submitted to the lab for analysis. Once the suspected tool has been received, examiners will create "test" marks to compare with the crime scene impression. Depending on the tool, it may include creating marks in lead (a soft metal) or other soft surface that will not damage the integrity of the evidence. The examiner will apply the same putty compound used on the impression to create a cast of the "test" mark. The two castings, crime scene and "test" mark, will be compared side by side under a comparison microscope with the goal of identifying matching unique, individual characteristics in both casts.

Casting compounds:
Putty-like substances that enable casting on horizontal and vertical surfaces (metal, wood, plastic, and paper). The cast creates an exact, detailed mirror image of the impression.

New technology called ToolScan™ System has been developed that allows for 2D and 3D scanning and comparison of toolmark impressions.[82] After a scan of the marking or impression, a digital silicon casting image is created. This allows for 3D rotation with a texture-free image of the impressions. Use of this new technology is also the best method to ensure the integrity of the evidence. Once the images are scanned, they can be stored in a digital database for future reference and additional examination.

Figure 5: Toolmark comparison under a comparison microscope[83]

CONCLUSION

Toolmarks are a valuable piece of evidence when investigating burglaries, car theft, and other crimes where materials and surfaces have been pried or forced open. Because tools are manufactured, striated marks are impressed into the metal. These special markings become damaged with use and appear as dents, nicks, rust, etc., into the striated pattern. Individual features distinguish each tool to its owner.

No two tools will wear in the exact same pattern, thereby providing a unique, identifiable signature. It is important to remember that individual characteristics in toolmarks are rare. The majority of knowledge learned in investigative work regarding toolmarks lies within class characteristics. Identifying the style of tool, size of tool, and type of tool from an impression has the potential to greatly influence the direction of an investigation toward resolution and provide valuable circumstantial evidence. As a Christian in the field of forensic science, your work ethic, integrity, and attention to detail can provide valuable insight into the field of toolmark identification.

Lesson 7
Weapons

For the word of God is living and active, sharper than any two-edged sword, piercing to the division of soul and of spirit, of joints and of marrow, and discerning the thoughts and intentions of the heart (Hebrews 4:12).

Case Study: Beltway Snipers

On October 2, 2002, a man was killed by sniper fire while walking in a parking lot in Wheaton, Maryland. This was the beginning of a chain of attacks that swept through the Washington, D.C., area for the next 22 days. Five more murders followed in Maryland and Washington, D.C. Between October 4–22, there were an additional four murders and three wounded in Maryland, Virginia, and the D.C. area. All the attacks were the result of sniper fire along a stretch of Interstate 95, coining the name for the attackers — the "Beltway Snipers."[84]

After the October 3 shooting, police investigators quickly linked the events together, and 400 FBI agents were assigned to investigate the case. Agents worked the tip hotline, created digital maps of the crime scenes, aided the Montgomery County Police Department, and created profiles for the suspects. Though there were exhaustive investigative efforts by hundreds of officers, a break in the case did not come until October 17, by none other than the sniper himself. As an attempt to brag to and tease police, one of the snipers called and stated he was responsible for an attack on two women a month earlier in Montgomery, Alabama. During this attack, one woman was murdered and one wounded. This call changed the course of the investigation and led to the capture of John Muhammad (age 41) and Lee Malvo (age 17) four days later.

Below are the investigative steps taken by the FBI according to their website:[85]

- Investigators soon learned that a crime similar to the one described in the call had indeed taken place and that fingerprint and ballistic evidence were available from the case.

- An agent from our office in Mobile gathered that evidence and quickly flew to Washington, D.C., arriving Monday evening, October 21. While ATF handled the ballistic evidence, we took the fingerprint evidence to the FBI Laboratory.

- The following morning, our fingerprint database produced a match — a magazine dropped at the crime scene bore the fingerprints of Lee Boyd Malvo from a previous arrest in Washington State. We now had a suspect.

- The arrest record provided another important lead, mentioning a man named John Allen Muhammad. One of our agents from Tacoma recognized the name from a tip called into that office on the case. A second suspect.

- Our work with ATF agents revealed that Muhammad had a Bushmaster .223 rifle in his possession, a federal violation since he'd been served with a restraining order to stay away from his ex-wife. That enabled us to charge him with federal weapons violations. And with Malvo clearly connected, the FBI and ATF jointly obtained a federal material witness warrant for him. [A material witness warrant allows law enforcement to detain an individual when they have reasonable cause to believe a person has information related to a criminal act or if they believe a person will not be responsive to a subpoena for a scheduled time of testimony.] The legal papers were now in our hands.

- Meanwhile, on October 22, we searched our criminal records database and found that Muhammad had registered a blue Chevy Caprice with the license plate of NDA-21Z in New Jersey.

CASE STUDY

- At 3:19 in the morning on October 24, 2002, to be exact, we closed in on the snipers and their 1990 Chevy Caprice.

John Muhammad (born John Allen Williams) was a decorated Army veteran who was honorably discharged in 1994. After Muhammad's second marriage ended in divorce, he fled to Antigua with the couple's three children. It is believed that Muhammad met Lee Malvo during his time in Antigua.[86] Muhammad returned to the U.S. Soon after, authorities discovered he was back in the country and returned the three children to their biological mother. Lee Malvo and his mother moved to the United States during this time period. It is theorized, mourning the loss of his biological children, Muhammad began to focus his attention on Malvo. While living together in a homeless shelter, Muhammad and Malvo developed a father-son relationship. This led to Muhammad training Malvo on military techniques.

Muhammad and Malvo began their multi-state crime spree in the winter of 2002. Between February of 2002 and October 24, 2002, when they were apprehended, Muhammad and Malvo were responsible for the murder of 17 people and wounding 10.

As Sherlock Holmes said, "It's every man's business to see justice done."[87] Due to a thorough investigation and collection and handling of evidence, the FBI was able to secure a conviction of John Muhammad and Lee Malvo. In September of 2003, Muhammad was convicted of capital murder (the act of murder) and sentenced to death. Malvo, being a minor, received six consecutive life sentences without parole in just one state. On November 10, 2009, John Muhammad was put to death by lethal injection. He chose to not make a last statement and never showed any remorse for his actions. Lee Malvo remains incarcerated at a maximum-security prison. Malvo has expressed regret for his actions.

This case utilized not only ballistic evidence, but also fingerprints. This is common in most case work. Since fingers are used to load and fire weapons, fingerprint pattern evidence often becomes just as important as the ballistic information. The following lesson will highlight the essential features of weapons that produce evidence characteristics.

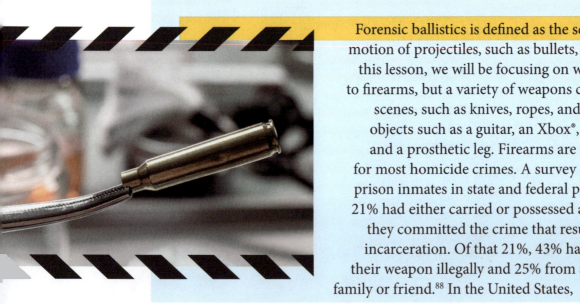

Forensic ballistics is defined as the science or study of the motion of projectiles, such as bullets, shells, or bombs. For this lesson, we will be focusing on weapons as they relate to firearms, but a variety of weapons can be found at crime scenes, such as knives, ropes, and bottles, and stranger objects such as a guitar, an Xbox®, stiletto heeled shoes, and a prosthetic leg. Firearms are the weapon of choice for most homicide crimes. A survey conducted in 2016 of prison inmates in state and federal prisons found that 21% had either carried or possessed a firearm when they committed the crime that resulted in their incarceration. Of that 21%, 43% had retrieved their weapon illegally and 25% from a family or friend.[88] In the United States, the Second Amendment to the Constitution outlines the right to bear arms. Though some states restrict this constitutional right more than others, this freedom gives all Americans the right to legally own firearms for self-defense purposes. Criminals often abuse this right by acquiring firearms illegally. Because weapons can be acquired from a variety of sources (dealers, stores, pawn shops, gun shows, underground markets, etc.) and are used by criminals in a variety of crimes, proper investigation and analysis are imperative to correctly connect the ballistic evidence to a crime scene.

WEAPONS FROM A BIBLICAL WORLDVIEW

When you hear the word "weapon," you may immediately think of a firearm, knife, or explosive, but a weapon can also include hands, fists, feet, cloth, ropes, bags, writing utensils, vehicles, nuclear arsenal, or a remote-controlled drone. A weapon is defined as anything that is designed or used to inflict bodily harm. Humans have been developing weapons for thousands of years. From a biblical worldview, we recognize the necessity for weapons is a result of man's sin. In God's original, perfect creation, there was no death, disease, or suffering. Man's disobedience against God's commands resulted in a sin-cursed world. As a result, the necessity for weapons developed as a defensive mechanism against man's sinful nature and to hunt and obtain food (primarily after the global Flood when God gave man permission to eat meat in Genesis 9:3). Unfortunately, man also uses these inventions to inflict harm on other humans. Weapons are inanimate objects and do not harm anyone on their own; therefore, weapons themselves are not the problem behind criminal acts. The problem is the sinful nature of humans that use the weapon to hurt their fellow man.

Genesis 9:3:
"Every moving thing that lives shall be food for you. And as I gave you the green plants, I give you everything."

Based on biblical and historical records, some of the earliest man-made weapons were likely spear-type projectiles that could be thrown or aimed at a target. An extensive account of the variety and type of weapons used in early civilizations after the global Flood are described in the forty-first book of Job in the Bible. See if you can point out the different weapons used to attack the fire-breathing creature called Leviathan:

Can you draw out Leviathan with a fishhook
or press down his tongue with a cord?

Can you put a rope in his nose
or pierce his jaw with a hook?

Will he make many pleas to you?

Will he speak to you soft words?

Will he make a covenant with you
to take him for your servant forever?

Will you play with him as with a bird,
or will you put him on a leash for your girls?

Will traders bargain over him?

Will they divide him up among the merchants?

Can you fill his skin with harpoons
or his head with fishing spears?

Lay your hands on him;
remember the battle—you will not do it again! . . .

When he raises himself up, the mighty are afraid;
at the crashing they are beside themselves.

Though the sword reaches him, it does not avail,
nor the spear, the dart, or the javelin.

He counts iron as straw,
and bronze as rotten wood.

The arrow cannot make him flee;
for him, sling stones are turned to stubble.

Clubs are counted as stubble;
he laughs at the rattle of javelins.

(Job 41:1–8, 25–29)

Though the Leviathan is believed to be extinct, it was a fearsome creature that was uniquely created by God to withstand an onslaught of weaponry.

HISTORY OF WEAPONS

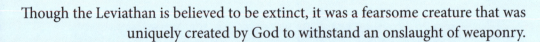

Genesis chapter 4 provides us with the account of the very first murder, but the Bible does not tell us the weapon that was used. Regardless, Cain killed Abel, and though the method and weapon remain a mystery, the Bible is clear that Abel's blood was "crying to me [God] from the ground" (Genesis 4:10). It is therefore plausible to assume that a weapon was used and that it drew a substantial amount of blood. Possible theories for the weapon include a plough spear, a knife, a stone, etc. Though there were no human eyewitnesses mentioned in the Bible, the perfect eyewitness and judge, the Creator God, was watching and passed judgment on Cain.

In Genesis 27:3, we see the first mention of weapons, "Now then, take your weapons, your quiver and your bow, and go out to the field and hunt game for me." Deuteronomy 1:41 and Judges 18:16 talk about the weapons of war. The Bible uses the plural "weapons" to provide insight that different types of weapons had been developed at this point in history, such as swords, spears, javelins, and quivers and bows. But it was not until A.D. 850 that gunpowder would be invented in China.

In 1364, history records the first use of a firearm.[89] These "hand cannons" were the earliest version of the handguns used today. They were developed during the medieval era, were made of solid iron, weighed up to 35 pounds, and were highly inaccurate. Hand cannons were fired by lighting a wick that would in turn ignite the gunpowder and project arrows, lead balls, and other items that would fit inside the barrel.[90]

An important advancement in ballistics came in 1540 with the discovery of rifling. Rifling forces the bullet to spin, which increases distance and accuracy through angular momentum. This is accomplished by engraving helical grooves inside the barrels of handguns, rifles, tank guns, etc. The grooves can either spin right or left. The development of rifling is important to forensic ballistics and will be discussed further in the next section.

In 1835, Samuel Colt produced the first commercial percussion repeating revolver with multiple chambers. This was also the year for the first case involving firearm examination that successfully linked a bullet to the suspect. Henry Goddard successfully matched imperfections on the homemade bullets to the mold in the home of the suspect where the bullets were made. The first semi-automatic handgun was designed by Joseph Laumann in 1892, but it is the Borchardt pistol created in 1893 that set precedence for semi-automatic handguns today. The Borchardt pistol provided the ability to have replaceable magazines in the grip.[91]

Colt revolver

Borchardt pistol

In contemporary firearms, improving accuracy is the primary goal. Scopes, lasers, fiber optic sights, and other technological advances have brought firearms to a new level of proficiency. A variety of extra parts, products, and accessories are available for customization. Gun enthusiasts refer to some current rifles as so-called "Lego rifles" due to the number of interchangeable parts. This culmination of firearms, ammunition, parts, and merchandise contribute to the body of evidence within the field of forensic ballistics.

RIFLING

Rifling marks in a barrel

Lesson 4 introduced the concepts of class characteristics and individual characteristics. In the field of forensic ballistics, these same characteristics can be identified from the evidence (see **Table 1**). Class characteristics help investigators determine the type and caliber of gun used in the crime, but it is the individual characteristics that have the potential to individually link a weapon to the ammunition (evidence) fired from that weapon. When a gun is fired, the rifling (lands and grooves) inside the barrel creates unique markings, or striations, on the bullet (see **Figure 1**). Lands are the raised areas. These markings are so individualized that two bullets from the same gun will have identical markings, whereas two bullets from two different guns (even if they are the same make and model) will not be identical under a comparison microscope. The markings occur because of the tools used to create the lands and grooves inside the barrel during the rifling process. Rifling in firearms occurs through one of these manufacturing processes: cut rifling, broach rifling, button rifling, hammer forging, or ECM (electrolytic cationic machining rifling).[92]

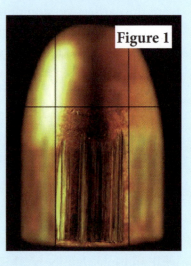
Figure 1

- *Cut rifling*: A time-consuming rifling process that is the oldest method used. Each land and groove is cut individually by a single-bladed cutter.

- *Broach rifling*: A steel rod composed of cutting rings, each slightly larger than the previous ring, with evenly spaced lands and grooves is twisted through the gun barrel.

- *Button rifling*: A button (made of tungsten carbide), with the reverse pattern of lands and grooves, is pushed through the barrel at high pressure. This process is quick and efficient and leaves the barrel with a smooth finish.

- *Hammer forging (polygonal rifling)*: A steel mandrel (with rifling pattern) is inserted into the barrel while the outer surface is machine hammered.

- *ECM (electrolytic cationic machining rifling)*: The inside of the barrel is "wet-etched" with an electric current and salt solution by twisting an electrode to create lands and grooves.[93]

Table 1

Class Characteristics	Individual Characteristics
Type	Striations
Caliber	Imperfections
Width of lands and grooves	Rust/corrosion

COLLECTING AND ANALYZING BALLISTIC EVIDENCE

The first step in analyzing any type of firearm is to determine if it is safe to examine. This includes verifying the firearm is not loaded with live ammunition. Many accidents have occurred because a firearm misfired and injured the investigators. Unlike what is shown on TV, a gun should never be picked up with a pencil or other object inserted into the barrel since it could damage the evidence (markings) inside the barrel. Personnel must also be careful to not damage potential fingerprints on the outside of the gun. Therefore, firearms must be handled with care by wearing gloves and collecting it by handling the trigger guard.

Firearms always need to be unloaded prior to packaging. Each piece of ammunition must be extracted from the firearm, the exact location of that ammunition in the magazine or revolver marked on the evidence collection documentation, and placed into small sliding cardboard "matchboxes." Each round of ammunition should be packaged separately, labeled, and contain a chain of custody documentation. If possible, the investigator should initial the bullet itself. Once the firearm is safe to handle, the technician will log the make, model, serial number, damage, and any unique identifiers. Recovered projectiles, wads from shotguns, empty magazines, and other forms of ballistic evidence will all be collected and packaged carefully so as not to damage any potential evidence.

A crime scene gun should never be picked up with a pencil or other object inserted into the barrel.

Before examination by ballistic experts, guns are often processed for fingerprints by a latent print examiner, especially on the magazine of a semiautomatic weapon. If the ballistic experts handled the gun first, they would potentially damage any partial fingerprints. Super glue fuming (covered in Lesson 18) and other processing methods do not often yield viable prints for comparison due to heat, perspiration, and other environmental factors involved in the handling of firearms that prevent the deposit of fingerprints. Occasionally, a partial print is found that can be linked back to a suspect.

In the lab, the projectiles will be examined and logged according to their caliber. Caliber is the diameter of the bullet or barrel of the gun in 100ths of an inch (e.g., .45 caliber, or .45") or in millimeters (e.g., 9mm) (see **Figure 2**). Caliber does not always determine the make and model of the gun, since it is possible for certain guns to fire projectiles of calibers that are not specific to the weapon, but the caliber does yield clues as to the type of weapon used in the crime.[94]

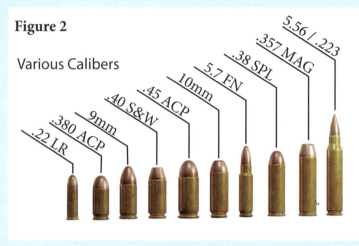

Figure 2

Various Calibers

Projectiles collected at the crime scene will be viewed through a comparison microscope. The comparison microscope was developed in 1923 for the purpose of analyzing ballistic evidence, and it continues to be the most important tool for examiners today.

Comparison microscopes allow scientists to view two projectiles under the same view, magnification, and orientation to look for identical features. Since there is no feasible method to compare lands and grooves inside the barrel to fired ammunition, the ballistics expert will test fire the guns to produce ammunition that can now be compared against those collected at the scene. Two different guns can never produce identical striated markings, or a unique "fingerprint," that is impressed onto each projectile when discharged from a gun. A test-fired bullet in the lab will match the striated markings on the projectile found at the scene if fired from the same gun. This sounds fairly simple, but matching striation patterns between projectile and firearm is not an easy process. Dirt, rust, and debris inside the barrel obscure the impression of the striated patterns. Striations are also not permanent and can be easily damaged over time.

SHOTGUNS

There are different factors that must be considered when examining ballistic evidence from shotguns. Shotguns do not have lands and grooves inside the barrel, but a smooth surface. To be considered a shotgun, the barrel must be at least 18 inches in length and no larger than 2 inches in diameter. Therefore, there are no impressed striations or markings to compare. Shotguns fire shots that are lead balls or pellets inside a case or shell (see **Figure 5**). The size of the recovered shot is sometimes helpful in determining the type of shot fired, gauge of the shotgun, and the maker of the shell. These class characteristics are not sufficient to link one shot to the gun it was fired from.

When the trigger is pulled on a shotgun, the firing pin hits the back of the primer, igniting the powder inside the shell and forcing the projectile forward. Due to the force of the ignition, when the projectile is propelled forward, the shell is forced backward, hitting the breechblock (see **Figure 4**). Newton's Third Law of Motion is at work in this situation — for every action (or force), there is an equal and opposite reaction. Just like the lands and grooves impress unique markings on a bullet from a firearm, the breechblock has the potential to impress unique markings (a fingerprint) on the back of shotgun shells (see **Figure 3**). Other unique markings may be visible on the brass end of the shotgun shell. These markings occur during the firing process and are largely due to imperfections or wear inside the gun itself. Unique markings can be compared similarly to the striated marks on firearm projectiles to establish a verifiable match between the shot and the gun that fired it.

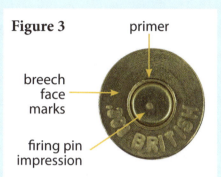

Figure 3

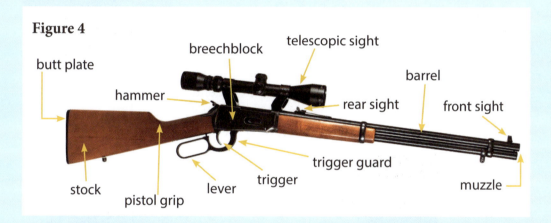

Figure 4

IBIS (INTEGRATED BALLISTICS IDENTIFICATION SYSTEM)

The captured digital images of striated patterns and shell cases are entered into a database called IBIS. IBIS is the database for these images and has the ability to compare digital striation patterns with images of others found at crime scenes and those that are classified as test fires. IBIS is connected to NIBIN (National Integrated Ballistics Information Network), which is the storehouse for IBIS images. NIBIN is the only interstate automated ballistic system in the United States and is operated by the ATF (Bureau of Alcohol, Tobacco, Firearms, and Explosives).[95] Only criminal case–related firearm evidence is entered and stored in the NIBIN system. Since the system was implemented in 1999, NIBIN has resulted in over 110,000 hits, or matches.[96]

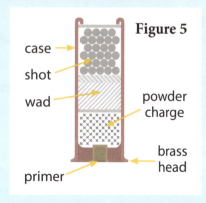

Figure 5

Weapons

SERIAL NUMBER RESTORATION

Every legally manufactured firearm after 1968 is stamped with a unique serial number. The use of serial numbers became law as a way to establish traceability in weapons. The serial number is stamped into the side of the barrel or action (see **Figure 6**). The serial number is registered to the purchaser of the firearm. Though the owner of a firearm may sell the gun in the future (perfectly legal), the serial number will always be linked to the original purchaser of the gun.

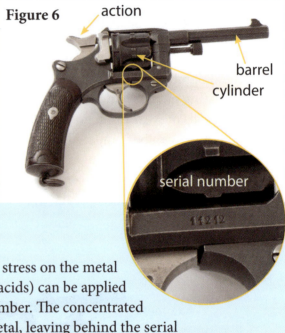

Figure 6

Criminals will often try to mask the identity of the firearm by filing or grinding off the serial number, but grinding does not always remove all traces of the serial number (see **Figure 7**). The stamping of the serial number into the metal is done with such force that the numbers put stress on the metal underneath. Restoration agents (acids) can be applied to the original area of the serial number. The concentrated hydrochloric acid eats away the metal, leaving behind the serial number. This process is referred to as "raising the serial number"[97] (see **Figure 8**).

Figure 7

Serial number removed

Figure 8

Serial number restored

GUNSHOT RESIDUE (GSR)

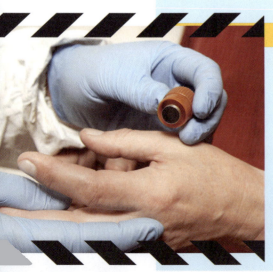

GSR is defined as the residue (burnt and unburnt particles) found on the hands, clothing, and other areas of the body from someone who:

- Has recently discharged a firearm.
- Was in proximity of a firearm when it was discharged.
- Handled a firearm that was recently discharged.
- Handled an object touched by a person who has recently discharged a firearm.

This includes both the suspect and victim involved in a crime. GSR is also found on the entry and exit points of a gunshot, as well as any other materials used as targets. The amount of GSR present becomes less prominent as you move away from the end of the barrel of the firearm. The range where GSR has been detected is up to 20 feet, depending on the weapon.[98] There will be more GSR found on the entry wound than the exit wound simply because the entry wound is the closest to the barrel. GSR also varies by the type of weapon discharged. GSR is extremely transient evidence, meaning it is easily transferable. It can be transferred from the firing hand to non-firing hand easily, and vice versa.

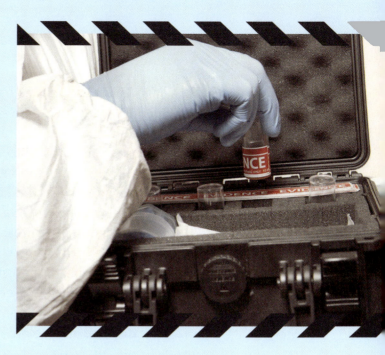

The GSR released upon discharging a weapon is both organic and inorganic in composition and varies according to where the ammunition was manufactured. Organic components originate from the primer and propellant and consist of over 23 compounds. The inorganic particles are primarily composed of elements such as lead, barium, and antimony. For a GSR validation, all three of these inorganic components must be present in a lab test. Having just one of the inorganic elements present could mean the person could have been exposed to barium while working in a firework manufacturing plant.[99]

GSR particles are very small and are, on average, 1–10 µ in range. This means they are not always visible to the naked eye. Therefore, chemical and laboratory testing are often necessary to determine if GSR is present on the surfaces involved in the crime. Before applying any chemicals to the surface, it is important that the evidence undergo preliminary microscopic examination and photography since chemicals can permanently alter the evidence. Physical characteristics that may be identified during the preliminary examination and help in distance determination include a ring around the bullet hole, ripped material in the form of a star shape called a stellate, singed material, and melted fibers.

GSR presumptive test kits are available for forensic personnel and provide a quick, colorimetric test right at the scene. The chemical reagents in the Modified Griess Test kit react with the nitrates and change color if the heavy metals associated with GSR are present. In the lab, investigators will verify the presence of GSR with a Scanning Electron Microscope (SEM) or Atomic Absorption Spectrometry (AAM).

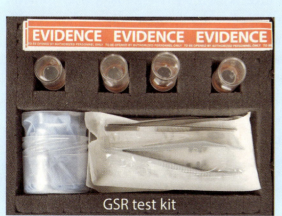
GSR test kit

Inorganic components: Derive from metallic components of the firearm, including the primer used. Examples include barium and antimony.

Organic components: Created by the propellant and forces the bullet out the barrel due to the explosion. Examples include hydrocarbons.

µ: µ represents a micron. A micron is 0.00038 inch.

Stellate: Arranged in a radiating pattern like that of a star.

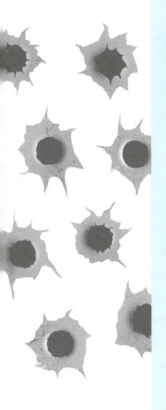

DISTANCE DETERMINATION

Part of an investigation is estimating the distance between the point at which the weapon was fired and the resulting target, and the angle at which a firearm was discharged. This is often accomplished with a series of test fires, under controlled conditions, on similar surfaces to those of the evidence. Distance determination is always used in conjunction with chemical testing and is not sufficient evidence on its own. In rifles and handguns, contact wounds exhibit evidence such as ripping of fabric, singeing and burning of fibers, lead deposits around the bullet hole, and concentrated areas of nitrate deposits. The more distance that occurs between the firearm and the entry point, the greater the dispersion of nitrate particles. The maximum distance to achieve a positive result in nitrate residue is between 5–7 feet.[100] When examining shotgun pellets, a wide dispersion of pellets represents distance from the target. On average, 12-gauge shotgun pellets will disperse at a rate of 1 inch for every yard. As with all ballistic evidence, distance determination evaluations must be conducted with the original weapon, using the exact same type of ammunition, and under the same environmental conditions, since any one of these factors would alter the results.

20 ft – dispersion circumference, 12 cm

40 ft – dispersion circumference, 28 cm

60 ft – dispersion circumference, 47 cm

To determine the location from where the gun was originally discharged, the angle and height from which the gun was fired is calculated with basic trigonometry and geometry. Bullet holes are rarely perfectly round since rarely is a gun fired at a perfect 90° angle to the floor. Bullet holes are often found as an ellipse shape. An angle of entry can be measured on the surface where the bullet entered. Ballistic experts used to use metal rods, the same size as the bullet hole, inserted into the elliptical holes. The problem with this classic method is it damages evidence inside the bullet hole. Current methods involve the use of trigonometry and geometry to determine the angle from which the gun was fired.[101]

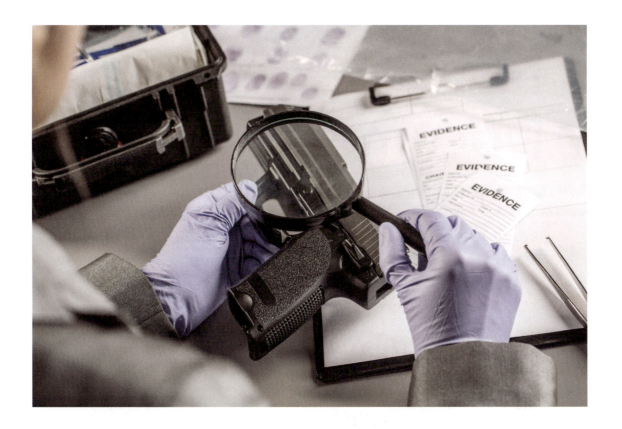

CONCLUSION

The primary goal in the collection of ballistic evidence is the preservation of the unique (fingerprint) markings that appear on bullets during discharge. The development of rifling was the key to the impression of these striations. The class and individual characteristics identified on the weapon are essential to connecting a firearm to a crime scene. During the investigative process, ballistics experts follow detailed safety protocols for the handling of ballistic evidence.

Though the use of weapons is the result of man's sinful nature, the systematic scientific processes behind ballistic investigation points to a Creator God. Mathematical certainties, measuring capabilities, laws of motion, and angles of measurement testify to the orderly design present all throughout nature. These laws of nature in science require a law giver, and this is the all-powerful Lord of the universe.

Lesson 8
Documents

I, Paul, write this greeting with my own hand. This is the sign of genuineness in every letter of mine; it is the way I write (2 Thessalonians 3:17).

Case Study: The Unabomber

Ted Kaczynski is a math prodigy who was accepted to Harvard University on scholarship at the age of sixteen. While in college, he was described by peers as a recluse but extremely brilliant. During his time at Harvard, he participated in a voluntary research study. During this three-year research study, Kaczynski was subjected to over 200 hours of insults and personal attacks as part of the research.[102] It is believed that participating in this research study contributed to the deterioration of his mental health. In 1967, he earned a Ph.D. in mathematics from the University of Michigan. His dissertation, *Boundary Functions*, was praised for its mathematical ingenuity and cited as one of the best dissertations on record at the university.

The same year, at the young age of 25, Kaczynski went on to become the youngest professor of mathematics at the University of California at Berkeley, but his career in teaching lasted only two years.[103] After resigning in 1969, Kaczynski moved to the wilderness of Montana, where he lived a survivalist lifestyle in isolation (no electricity or running water). During this period in the early 1970s, Kaczynski began to formulate his own "anti-government and anti-technology philosophy."[104] In 1978, Kaczynski accepted a factory job in Chicago with his brother, but this failed as well. He then returned to isolation in Montana.

The crimes of the Unabomber began in the year 1978 when a primitive homemade bomb exploded at Northwestern University outside the city of Chicago. Another bomb was sent to Northwestern the following year. Two more bombs were sent between 1979 and 1980 to American Airlines. In 1979, the FBI, ATF, and U.S. Postal Inspection Service formed a task force to investigate the "UNABOM" case (university airline bombs).[105]

Facts about the case:

- Over a span of 17 years, the task force involved over 150 full-time investigators and analysts.
- The 17-year manhunt for the Unabomber was the longest and most expensive manhunt in FBI history.
- Throughout most of the investigation, the task force was uncertain of the suspect's gender, occupation, location, and connection with victims.
- The Unabomber was careful to remove all forensic traces from bomb components by making his own glue from deer hooves, removing all packaging and wrappers from the batteries, and leaving no fingerprints.
- After 1987, the Unabomber did not send any more bombs for six years.
- In 1990, the Unabomber began sending letters to the media about the bombings.
- In 1993, the Unabomber emerged with more lethal bombs.

- In 1995, the Unabomber authored a 35,000-word manifesto entitled *Industrial Society and Its Future*. He stated that if the manifesto was published, the bombing attacks would stop; if not, he would blow up a passenger plane. Reluctant to give in to terrorist threats, Janet Reno (Attorney General) authorized the publication of the manifesto in *The Washington Post* and *The New York Times*.
- Also in 1995, FBI criminal profiler James R. Fitzgerald was assigned to the case. Fitzgerald began to use linguistics, or the ability to identify word usage, phraseology, and other terminology. This aided in determining the age of the suspect, birthplace, and other relevant facts.[106]
- When David Kaczynski, Ted's brother, read the manifesto in 1995, the narrative and linguistic style resembled letters he had received from his brother. David's suspicions led him to contact the FBI.
- By the time the Unabomber was captured in 1996, 16 total bombs had been built, 3 people had been killed, and 23 people had been injured. Each incidence involved a U.S. Postal Service mail bomb or, on rare occasion, was personally delivered.
- James R. Fitzgerald stated about the case, "And it came down to about 600 separate blocks of individual phraseology, sentences, short paragraphs in which we had virtually identically written sentences from Ted Kaczynski and the Unabomber."[107]
- This case was the first time in history that phraseology was used as evidence.

Ted Kaczynski (the Unabomber) was arrested on April 3, 1996, by the FBI at his cabin in Montana. Investigators discovered one completed bomb (most likely for his next victim), bomb components, and 40,000 pages of personal diaries. Though Kaczynski's attorneys recommended he plead insanity, he refused repeatedly by stating he was not insane. In an effort to avoid the death penalty, Kaczynski pled guilty to 13 federal bombing charges. In 1998, Kaczynski was sentenced to life in prison. He committed suicide on June 10, 2023.

It is fascinating to think that the way a person writes and the very paper they write on (or print a manuscript on) could become valuable evidence in a case.

"It is a pity he did not write in pencil. As you have no doubt frequently observed, the impression usually goes through."
— Sherlock Holmes[108]

Documents provide a wealth of information for both criminal and civil cases. Consider a ransom note found at the scene of a kidnapping, a bank robber's note passed to the bank teller, or a forged check to pay for goods at a department store. Questioned documents are any suspicious materials that may contain imprints or markings of writings, symbols, and other characters that are intended for communication. Forensic Document Examiners examine these materials to verify identity, forgery, and possible alterations to the original document. Sometimes markings are visible, such as an identifiable signature on a forged check, but occasionally they are hidden on a blank piece of paper that was underneath the document evidence. Have you ever written a note and then realized the message copied to the paper underneath?

Early in the 20th century, the three fundamental processes of document examination were instituted:

- The identification of individuals through their signature and handwriting samples.
- The determination of whether an individual's signatures and/or handwriting samples are genuine or copied (forged).
- The determination of the origin and history of the document in question.

> **Indented writings:**
>
> Impressions left on papers positioned under another piece of paper that has been written on.

HISTORY OF DOCUMENT EXAMINATION

Ransom notes have been used for coercion as early as the Middle Ages. The first ransom note in the United States was largely forgotten until 2013, when a woman uncovered a bundled stack of letters in a plastic bin in her home.[109] She uncovered 22 ransom letters regarding the kidnapping of four-year-old Charley Ross by two men in a horse and buggy in 1874. The ransom notes were written by a fairly illiterate person. This is a portion of one letter:[110]

> Mr. Ross— be not uneasy you son charly bruster he al writ we got him and no powers on earth can deliver out of our hand. You wil hav two pay us befor you git him from us. an pay us a big cent to. If you put the cops hunting for him you is only defeeting yu own end. we is got him fitt so no living power can gits him from us a live. if any aproch is maid to his hidin place that is the signil for his instant anihilation. if yu regard his lif puts no one to search for him you money can fech him out alive an no other existin powers don't deceve yuself and think the detectives can git him from us for that is one imposebel yu here from us in a few day.

As you will learn in this lesson, a poorly written ransom note still contains valuable clues. In this example, we can quickly determine the writer had little education and was aware of the Rosses' family wealth. This case is a cold case and remains unsolved to this day. Other famous ransom notes throughout history include the Lindbergh kidnapping in 1932, the Peter Weinberger kidnapping in 1956, and the murder of JonBenét Ramsey in 1996.

The first case where handwriting analysis was used to solve a crime was in the kidnapping of Peter Weinberger. On July 4, 1956, one-month-old Peter was left in his carriage by his mother on the patio of the family home. Peter's mother returned a few minutes later to find the baby missing and a ransom note left behind. After two ransom notes and the required seven-day waiting period for FBI involvement in the 1950s, the FBI began the daunting task of comparing the two ransom notes to over two million handwriting exemplars. The FBI successfully matched the ransom note to the probation notes of Angelo LaMarca.[112]

LaMarca following his first-degree murder conviction

The greatest embarrassment to handwriting experts was the "lost" Hitler diaries. Between 1981 and 1983, master forger Konrad Kujau developed a 60-volume set of Hitler diaries. Kujau then went on to pose as an antiques dealer, claimed the diaries were found in a plane crash in East Germany, and sold the set for $3.7 million to a West German magazine called *Stern*. *Stern* sold publication rights to *The London Times*, who requested verification of authenticity. Three handwriting experts in forensic handwriting analysis were assigned to the case, and all three agreed the diaries were written by the same person and were, in fact, real. The diaries were published internationally as skepticism about the authenticity continued to circulate. Ultimately, a West German agency determined the diaries were forgeries by analyzing the paper under UV light. An ingredient in the diary papers was not used in production until 1954. Hitler is believed to have died in 1945. Additional testing verified the ink was no more than a year old, tea had been used to "age" the documents, and Hitler's signature was not verifiable. Interestingly, the initial forensic analysis was correct in saying that all three volumes were written by the same person, who turned out to be the master forger. In fact, Kujau had even forged some of the handwriting exemplars the experts used to verify the three diaries.[113]

Fake Hitler diary (Spanish)

DOCUMENTS FROM A BIBLICAL WORLDVIEW

There is biblical evidence that documents and books were being written as early as Genesis 5:1 when it mentions "the book of the generations of Adam." Many people have a misconception that early civilizations were illiterate and uneducated, but the Bible clearly tells us that humans are created in the image of a perfect God. Adam and Eve would have been highly intelligent and communicating intelligently through both oral and written languages. It is likely that Noah would have stored documents and artifacts safely on the Ark to preserve human history from the global Flood. Deuteronomy 6:9 tells us that the Israelites were instructed to "write them [the commands of the Lord] on the doorposts of your house and on your gates." Joshua 18:9 tells us that a group of Israelite men "wrote in a book a description of [the land]." There is no question that Adam and his direct descendants were reading and writing.

The Creator God Himself also wrote visible messages to His people. The finger of God wrote the Ten Commandments (Deuteronomy 9:10). Have you ever wondered what God's handwriting looked like?

The Bible also provides insight into the uniqueness of handwriting. In 2 Thessalonians 3:17, Paul authenticates his letter by telling the recipients they can trust the contents because they should recognize his handwriting: "I, Paul, write this greeting with my own hand. This is the sign of genuineness in every letter of mine; it is the way I write." Every individual writes with a unique style or overall signature. This is why the foundational philosophy behind handwriting analysis is the *unconscious* handwriting of two different people will never be the same. This is yet another unique gift that God the Creator gave to every single person.

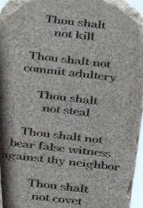

Documents   Lesson 8

HANDWRITING COMPARISONS

Handwriting comparison involves the identification of both class characteristics and individual characteristics. There are three basic steps in handwriting comparisons:

1. Analysis between the evidentiary writing sample and a known writing sample for unique identifiers such as slant, spacing, unusual formation of letters, exaggerations, etc.

2. Comparison of key elements for similarity in the spelling, overall grammar, and phraseology.

3. Evaluation of the totality of similarities between the evidentiary and known writing samples. One positive match in handwriting comparison is insufficient to demonstrate guilt. The examiner must acknowledge several identifiable characteristics.

Analysis. When analyzing handwriting, examiners will inspect the evidentiary writings side by side with exemplars from possible suspects. Exemplars are simply handwriting examples and include collected handwriting samples and requested handwriting samples. Exemplars may include official documents with signatures, checks, passports, wills, or applications. Investigators will request that suspects provide written samples with the same narrative as in the evidence, in addition to signatures. When collecting signatures for comparison against a questioned document, the analyst should request 20–30 repetitions of signatures. Collecting an adequate number of exemplars within the right time frame for comparison is one of the most important facets of analyzing forensic documents. Suspects may not "plead the Fifth" (the right to remain silent) when requested to submit a handwriting sample. In the case *Gilbert v. California*, the Supreme Court upheld the right of law enforcement to take handwriting samples prior to the appointment of counsel, and thus this right lies outside of Fifth Amendment protections.

If the questioned document was written in the past, the investigator will acquire writing samples from the same general time frame. The established principle is the writing sample must be within 2–3 years of the questioned document; any longer reduces the likelihood of credibility. This principle is based on research that shows a person's writing style and signature will change over time. Think about it: Do you write your signature exactly like you did five years ago?

Not only do two people write distinctly different, but one person will never write the exact same information the exact same way twice. There are natural variations that occur in every person's writing style while still exhibiting unique identifiers. Additionally, the officials will provide the suspect with similar pens and paper to the evidentiary document. Most importantly, the suspect must not be provided the original questioned document. Suspects may purposely attempt to disguise their handwriting.

Identifiers play a key role in the analysis of a handwriting sample. They include a variety of characteristics:

Fifth Amendment:

No person shall be held to answer for a capital, or otherwise infamous crime, unless on a presentment or indictment of a grand jury, except in cases arising in the land or naval forces, or in the militia, when in actual service in time of war or public danger; nor shall any person be subject for the same offense to be twice put in jeopardy of life or limb; nor shall be compelled in any criminal case to be a witness against himself, nor be deprived of life, liberty, or property, without due process of law; nor shall private property be taken for public use, without just compensation.

Slant	Right	Left	Middle
	Slant	*Slant*	*Slant*
Letter size	Large	Medium	Small
	letters	*letters*	*letters*
Slope	Up	Down	Straight
	Slope	*Slope*	*Slope*
Spacing	Close	Wide	Normal
	wordspacing	*word spacing*	*word spacing*

	Dots "i"	Does not dot "i"	Stylized "i"
Letter formation "i"	i	ι	i̊
Letter formation "t"	Cross "t"	Does not cross "t"	Stylized "t"
	t	l	t t
Letter formation "r"	Pointed "r"	Flat-topped "r"	Stylized "r"
	r	r	r
Letter formation "e"	Looped "e"	Not looped "e"	Stylized "e"
	e	ι	e

Comparison. In addition to identifiers, examiners will compare the overall spelling, punctuation, age of the questioned document, and phraseology of the evidentiary with known handwriting samples. Are the same spelling errors present in both documents? Do they both contain similar grammatical context? How long ago was the evidentiary material written when compared to the known exemplars? Does the individual use unusual phraseology in their manuscripts? Identifying these features, in union with a number of identifiers, establishes credibility when the two samples are established as a match.

Phraseology. Phraseology is defined as the way in which words are used to express an idea or thought in speech or writing. The use of phraseology in document examination came to the forefront of forensic investigation during the almost 20-year Unabomber investigation. As discussed in the case study at the beginning of the lesson, federal agent and criminal profiler James Fitzgerald joined the FBI manhunt in 1995. The FBI suspected Ted Kaczynski, but they did not have enough evidence to obtain a search warrant. Using the phraseology from Kaczynski's Ph.D. dissertation, letters and documents provided by his brother David, and the Unabomber's manifesto, *Industrial Society and Its Future*, analysts found similar linguistic context used in all documents. One phrase that was a significant match in both the dissertation and the manifesto was the transposition of verbs in the expression, "You can't eat your cake and have it too."[114] The final case against the Unabomber came down to 600 separate pieces of phraseology within sentences and paragraphs in which almost identical narrative and context was used.[115]

1—format-margin
2—baseline slope
3—letter formation
4—letter spacing
5—slant
6—diacritic placement
7—word spacing
8—complete letters
9—format-punctuation
10—pen lifts

Figure 1

Similar to people who have unique fingerprints, typebar typewriters also had specific characteristics that differed from typewriter to typewriter.

TYPESCRIPT COMPARISONS

Typewriters were first patented in the United States in 1868. Rapidly, typewriters revolutionized the way offices conducted correspondence, handled business transactions, drafted wills, etc. The emergence of the home computer in the 1980s resulted in typewriters becoming almost obsolete. Occasionally, criminals use typewriters in an attempt to disguise the original source of ransom notes, threats, and/or extortions on individuals. What they don't realize is that typewriters hold a wealth of class characteristics that can be traced back to each individual machine in the form of individual characteristics. The most common type of typewriter is called a typebar typewriter (see **Figure 1**). Iron bars with molds of the letters strike on an ink ribbon to impress characters onto paper (see **Figure 2**).

Though typewriters were bulk manufactured, similar to tools, the wear and tear on each machine is unique. Different brands of typewriters reveal class characteristics that will also have varying typefaces (see **Figure 3**). Depending on how frequently the typewriter is used and for what purpose, certain letters (or typebars) can exhibit more wear, resulting in misprints, defects, or other marks on paper that are considered individual characteristics.

When a typewriter is used to produce a questioned document, the first task for the examiner is to determine the make and model of the typewriter. Identifying the make and model of the typewriter allows the examiner to procure examples of the typeface. The next step would be to match the typeface in the evidentiary note with a sample from the suspected typewriter. Analysts will examine the ink, spacing, misaligned letters, variation in pressure of typeface, and spurs or marks unique to the machine. Additionally, the typewriter ribbon should be examined.

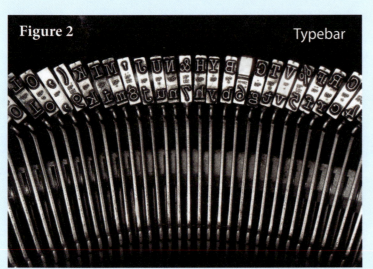

Figure 2 — Typebar

Typewriter ribbons contain text that was transposed onto the paper. Sometimes, characters on the ribbon can be matched to the questioned document. In the case of the Unabomber, analysts successfully matched Kaczynski's typewritten manifesto to the typewriter in his Montana cabin.

Figure 3 — Typefaces

```
pay me 5 mill in cash or else.
PAY ME 5 MILL IN CASH OR ELSE.
```

PAPERS AND INK

Paper is examined for its class characteristics such as weight, weave pattern, fibers, color (both external and internal), watermarks, and thickness. Ultraviolet light will reveal further details that the unaided eye may not be able to see. Thickness is measured using special calipers. Weaves and fibers reveal whether the paper is comprised of wood pulp or other materials. Watermarks contain information regarding manufacturing and production, as well as the type of paper, and are best viewed under a light source. Paper examination would also apply to computer-generated documents where a printer is used to copy the text.

Facsimile papers should be examined for the TTI (Transmit Terminal Identifier) number that identifies the sender's name, fax number, recipient's fax number, date, and time of the transmitted fax. As with all machines, with repeated use, imperfections in printing emerge. These imperfections are the unique "fingerprints" or individual characteristics used in comparison in both the sending and receiving fax machines.

Though the TTI information provides clues to the make and model of the fax machine, this information is programmable by the sender and can be altered by a knowledgeable person.

Indentions are defined as impressions left on papers positioned under another piece of paper that has been written on. If a bank robber wrote a robbery note for a bank teller on a hotel notepad, the remaining papers on the notepad may contain indentions of his robbery note. This can now be linked to the person who reserved the hotel accommodations. A device called an EDD (Electrostatic Detection Device), along with special lighting, is used to visibly observe hidden indentions or erasures. This device has been successful in revealing indented text for up to seven layers of paper thick.

The ink used on questioned documents can be analyzed to determine the first date of commercial availability. If the date on the document predates the manufacturing of the ink, then there is evidence of a forgery. Using gas chromatography/mass spectrometry, the ink can be analyzed for its volatile components, which diminish over a two-year period. Based on the age of the ink, it is possible to estimate an age of preparation. Similar to pen ink, computer-printed documents can be analyzed to determine the commercial availability of the printer ink, but determining an exact age is difficult and unlikely. Xeroxed copies also contain ink samples that are evaluated for age and provide information on their exposure to environmental conditions like fading, water damage, weather, temperature, etc.

When examining ink samples on questioned documents, analysts will first begin with non-destructive tests. These may include ultraviolet and infrared technology, microscopy, and a basic visual examination. Other tests include thin layer chromatography. A microsample of the ink is removed from the document for chemical analysis. Since each brand of ink pen will be composed of several organic dyes, separating out those dyes results in a distinct pattern. The pattern will be different for inks with different dye compositions. Chromatography is the best method to compare the composition of ink samples (see **Figure 4**). The U.S. International Ink Library contains over 9,500 ink compositions for comparison.[116] Though it is possible to determine the commercial availability of an ink sample, it is difficult to identify the exact pen used on the questioned document. But comparisons of the ink used on both a questioned document and a known source could be analyzed to determine if the same pen was used.

Figure 4 Chromatography

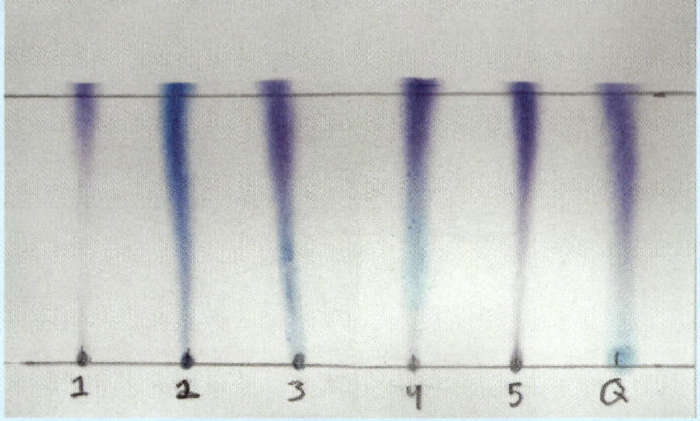

DELETIONS, ERASURES, AND OTHER MODIFICATIONS

Another job of the forensic document examiner is to determine if the original document was altered or modified for fraudulent purposes. Modifications are often visible to the naked eye due to the abrasion and disruptions caused on the original paper. Chemical processing, infrared or UV light, or special lighting are also used to reveal erasure features. Modifications include insertions, additions, and deletions to the original text. The forensic document examiner must ascertain which of the modifications are intentional and those that are fraudulent. Things to look for include:

- Do the staple holes on all the documents align?
- Are there marks that would be consistent across the paper if it were folded?
- If the document was subject to a fire, is there a way to decipher the information?
- If the document was ripped in two pieces, do the fibers align under microscopic examination?

Careful analysis with the appropriate processing techniques have the ability to reveal the hidden clues in questioned documents.

COLLECTION AND EVALUATION OF DOCUMENTS

Similar to other fragile evidence, each piece of document evidence should be photographed, placed into a plastic zip bag, and labeled with the appropriate documentation. If the paper is damp or contains any moisture, the document must be placed in a paper bag to avoid contamination on the document. Once in the lab, the moist document will be hung to dry.

The majority of document processing techniques are nondestructive. As stated earlier in the lesson, a visible examination will yield the majority of identifiable characteristics. If more invasive testing is warranted, a holepunch the size of a period on a typewriter provides a sufficient number of chemical tests. In some cases, the perpetrator purposely obliterates text. Similar to etching agents used in serial number restoration, oxidizing agents can be placed over the ink to produce hidden text. The text must then be examined under a microscope, UV light, or infrared lighting.

Another technique called infrared luminescence is a property within some dyes that causes them to emit infrared light when they are exposed to blue-green light. By using special photography filters in conjunction with blue-green light, analysts have been able to capture full written texts thought to be damaged. Infrared luminescence is also used to detect counterfeit money. United States bills will floresce fibers under infrared luminescence as well as reflect broad bands on the back of monetary notes.

CONCLUSION

Questioned document examination should not be confused with graphology. Graphology is the study of human personality through an individual's writing. Graphologists study handwriting samples and hypothesize a person's personality, mental health, intellect, and a variety of other factors. There is no scientific justification for the accuracy of graphology, and it is currently not admissible in court. The science behind questioned documents is historically supported to be accurate when the correct analysis has been completed with a sufficient number of exemplars and examined by trained personnel.

Forensic document examiners receive an average of two years of formal training in their field. They are also required to have a bachelor's degree in one of the natural sciences. Analysts must have an attention to detail coupled with an interest in the unique styles of written language. Because of the tedious work, they are subject to regular eye exams to ascertain their ability to distinguish details. They must also be excellent communicators and will be required to testify to their expertise and the evidence in court.

One of the largest criminal investigations in history was the assassination of President John F. Kennedy in 1963. Imagine if you were a document examiner assigned to review the JFK assassination records when they were released to the public in 2017... these records contained over five million pages of documentation![117]

Lesson 9
Computer Forensics

All things were made through him, and without him was not any thing made that was made (John 1:3).

Case Study: The Morris Worm

In 1989, the World Wide Web was invented. A year prior, on November 2, 1988, Robert Tappan Morris, a student working on his master's degree at Cornell, released the first "recognized" computer worm by hacking a terminal at Massachusetts Institute of Technology (MIT) from his location at Cornell University in New York. Morris was known for his technological expertise in the Unix® operating system. Morris' father was one of the computer scientists who helped develop the Unix® system, a system still used in iPhones® today. Morris had designed a worm that would slowly spread through computers using the Unix operation system. A computer worm is different from a computer virus since a worm does not need a software hosting platform but is simply a self-replicating computer program. Robert Morris claimed he did not intentionally design an attack on computers but wanted to see how big the internet was in 1988. He thought he had created an experiment with a slow, stealthily moving program. This program would be passed through the internet to determine the size of it. Unfortunately, the program moved through the internet much faster than expected, wreaking havoc online. The first computer attack had been implemented.

Facts about the case:[118]

- Though the Morris Worm has received notoriety for being the first major computer attack, computer viruses had been detected for five years prior to 1988.
- Within the first 24 hours of the released computer worm, 6,000 of the 60,000 computers connected to the internet received a "denial of service" (DoS) attack.
- The worm was able to decipher weak passwords.
- The worm was programmed to reinfect a computer 1 in 7 times, causing machines to malfunction.[119]
- The worm did not destroy files or attempt to retrieve sensitive information, but it did cause damage, slow down processing times, and cause widespread outages.
- It is estimated the Morris Worm resulted in millions of dollars in damages in 1988.
- The Morris Worm infiltrated Berkeley, Harvard, Princeton, Stanford, John Hopkins, NASA, the Lawrence Livermore National Library, and more.
- As a result of this attack, the Department of Defense launched the first computer emergency response team.

A flaw in the program caused it to multiply much faster than anticipated and revealed its presence in computer systems. When Morris realized the worm was out of control, he contacted two friends. One friend sent out an "anonymous" apology across the internet on behalf of Morris. The other friend called *The New York Times*, stating the initials of the person who wrote the program was RTM. It did not take long for *The New York Times* to figure out the culprit was 23-year-old Robert Morris. The FBI launched an investigation into Morris and his friends.

In 1991, Robert Morris received the first conviction in history under the 1986 Computer Fraud and Abuse Act. His sentences were three years in prison, 400 hours of community service, and a $10,000 fine. He never served prison time and was only given parole. Morris went on to earn a Ph.D. and is now a professor at MIT, the very institution where he initiated the attack.

- A special exhibit in the Computer History Museum in Mountain View, California, contains the original floppy disks of the Morris Worm. This case was not only the beginning of thousands of computer hacks, but it also marked the launch of the cybersecurity industry. Next time you leave your tablet, laptop, or phone on, consider this quote from Spafford, "The only truly secure system is one that is powered off, cast in a block of concrete and sealed in a lead-lined room with armed guards and even then I have my doubts."[120]

Every email, text, digital photograph, social media post, etc., leaves behind trace computer signatures — signatures containing unique identifiers that point to the author and user.

"I am somewhat exhausted; I wonder how a battery feels when it pours electricity into a non-conductor?" — Sherlock Holmes[121]

Computer forensics (cybercrime) is a field dedicated to the search, preservation, and analysis of information computer systems with the goal of presenting evidence to the court. In the forensics discipline, this is one of the fastest growing fields of investigation. A survey conducted in 2018 found that almost 33% of adults in the U.S. had experienced a hack of their social media and/or email account, with an over 362.5-million-dollar loss in scams.[122] Computer forensics includes the investigation of computer hard drives, CDs, DVDs, thumb drives, deleted files, encrypted files, email, chats, social media, cache, bookmarks, and more. Analysts use Computer Forensic Tools (CFT) to collect data from computers, copy the information, and locate hidden data.

COMPUTER FORENSICS FROM A BIBLICAL WORLDVIEW

Though there is no direct computer-related terminology in the Bible, God's Word clearly states multiple times that all things were created by Him. "All things" include the raw materials needed to build computer systems, the intelligent minds that develop computer software and hardware, and the complex, orderly mathematical processes necessary for computer operation.

Intro to Forensic Science

And the Bible does mention technology. A variety of tools and technology would have been necessary for humans to achieve the architectural wonders described in the historical record in the Bible. Genesis 4:17 states that Cain built a city, and verse 22 says that Tubal-Cain was a user of bronze and iron. Genesis 6 describes the dimensions of the Ark, and Genesis 11 tells of man's self-glorification through a collective effort to build a tower. The book of Nehemiah describes how Nehemiah rebuilt the great wall in Jerusalem. Jesus Himself was a carpenter and would have used tools and technology in His trade. The Bible was written by the hands of men inspired by the very Word of God. In the Bible lies truth, and just as a computer requires a programmer, creation requires a Creator.

Data structure:

A method of organizing information (data) in the virtual system of a computer. Data structures and algorithms work hand-in-hand to build computer programs.

HISTORY

Computer history includes the development of computer language, hardware, software, and network connections. Each one of these components is necessary for a computer system to connect, collaborate, and process information.

Binary Language. The precursor to the binary code used in computers today originated between the 2nd and 3rd centuries B.C. Pingala, a mathematician from India, developed a binary numeral system. Though he did not use "0" and "1" like the modern system, he used light (*laghu*) and heavy (*guru*). The systematic process he used is very similar to the binary code used today.[123] In the 1700s, binary logic was formalized by German mathematician Gottfried Leibniz. He used 0 and 1 to represent commands. Leibniz also invented a calculating machine called a Stepped Reckoner that could add, subtract, multiply, and divide.[124]

Stepped Reckoner

Algorithms. Algorithms are the step-by-step instructions that define a set of procedures that must be carried out in specific order to obtain a desired result. Algorithms serve as the underpinnings that operate computer programs and are organized by a data structure. Algorithms are derived from algebra, which was first introduced in the 7th century by Brahmagupta, an Indian mathematician. "Algorithm" is a term derived from *Algoritmi de numero Indorum*, the Latin translation of a work by the 9th-century mathematician al-Khwarizmi.

Computers. Charles Babbage invented the Difference Engine in 1823, which performed computations up to eight decimals. In the 1830s, Babbage outlined plans for the Analytical Engine, considered to be the forerunner to the modern computer.[125] Though Babbage worked on the Analytical Engine for the rest of his life, the machine was never completed due to the cost of producing new hardware components. The machine was forgotten until 1937, when Babbage's notebooks were discovered. It is important to note that Charles Babbage was a devoted Christian and attributed his study to the Creator God. It is said of Charles Babbage, "[He] believed that the study of the works of nature with scientific precision, was a necessary and indispensable preparation to the understanding and interpreting their testimony of the wisdom and goodness of their Divine Author."[126]

> **Analog computer:**
> A non-digital computer that analyzes data directly without converting into numerals or codes.

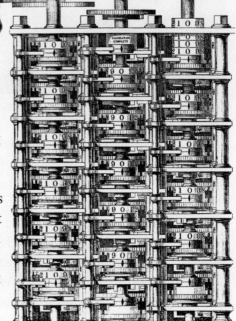
Difference Engine

The Analog Computing Machine is an early version of the modern computer.

With the discovery of Babbage's personal notes, the Analytical Engine No. 2 was built and accurate up to 31 digits. The first computer programmer was Ada Lovelace, who worked closely with Babbage and published the first algorithm to be carried out by the Analytical Engine.

The field of computer forensics began in the mid-1940s, when the age of analog computers (left) was going to be replaced by digital computers. The first microprocessor was invented in the 1960s. The first computer crime to be prosecuted was in 1966, but the emergence of what is considered computer crime today resulted from the invention of the home computer in the 1980s. The Morris Worm in 1988 (described in the case study at the beginning of the lesson) brought to the forefront the need for cybersecurity forces. As a result, by the early 1990s, law enforcement agencies across the country had implemented protocols for the investigation of computer-related crimes.

HARDWARE AND SOFTWARE

Hardware is defined as a device that is physically connected to a computer. Software is the computer programs that perform tasks on the operating system. The primary differences between hardware and software can be reviewed in **Table 1** below.

Table 1	Hardware	Software
Types	Input Storage Processing Control Output	System software Programming software Application software
Function	Delivery system Infrequently changed Dependent on software	Perform tasks Easily changed, updated, modified Dependent on hardware
Examples	Hard drives, monitors, printers, CD ROM, video cards	Microsoft® Word, Keynote®, QuickBooks®, Adobe®, internet browser
Nature	Physical	Logical[127]

COMPUTERS

Every computer consists of three main components: the CPU (Central Processing Unit), RAM (Random Access Memory), and the control bus. The CPU is the brain of the computer and controls the processing of any and all information. How fast information moves through the control bus is determined by the CPU. The four basic operations of the CPU include fetch, decode, execute, and store.[128] RAM is short-term memory. When a Microsoft® Word document is open on a computer, it is a visual representation of what is currently stored in RAM that a user is accessing. But as soon as that file is saved permanently, it moves to long-term storage on a physical disk (hard drive, USB, SD card, etc.). The control bus is the communication pathway between the data, the hardware, and the software. The control bus is located in the system board. To understand a control bus, imagine the traffic lane a school bus travels for student pick-ups and the route it takes to arrive at the school, or the central nervous system in the human body as the nerves detect sensory information and carry it back to the brain. These pathways are similar to the control bus, controlling the movement of information throughout the computer. Computers can also be extended with additional hardware like a Network Interface Card (NIC), which is a circuit board. This allows the computer to connect to a network. NICs work in both wired and wireless formats.

OPERATING SYSTEM

The operating system (OS) is the essential software that serves as the interface, or bridge, between the software and the hardware.[129] A computer cannot function without an operating system. The operating system controls the input and output, file management, memory, commands, resources, and security. The OS uses a series of drivers that allow the application software to talk to the hardware. An example would be pulling up a social media app (which is the application software) on your mobile device (which uses a mobile device operating system) and taking a picture with your camera (which is a piece of hardware).

FORMATTING

Format is the instructions for an operation system to read and write to a drive (physical device you put data on). Formatting is the preparation of the drive to receive the set of instructions (or format). Basically, it is a file system or layout to allow data to be written. During the formatting, a set of instructions on how to read and write data to a system, its restrictions and limitations, is provided to the operation system.

For example, one cabinet in a kitchen is usually designated for dishes. The dishes are organized by type and size of dish (big and little plates, big and little bowls, platters, etc.) while being confined to the size of the cabinet. Or a student is assigned a research paper, and the teacher requires a certain format — Times New Roman type, size 12 font, 1-inch margins, 1,000-word length, etc. The text must fit within this required format. Just as you can organize your dishes or prepare a research paper according to a specific size and shape, your computer has to be able to format data in a specific way in a specific place according to the space limitations provided.

When a hard drive is formatted, the platter (flat circular piece of metal), which is coated with iron oxide or chromium dioxide (magnetic substances), spins. While spinning, a read/write device sends small amounts of electricity through the head of the device, magnetizing the platter. Binary code, in the form of 0's and 1's, records the data on the hard drive.[130]

platter

ERASING DATA

There are four different terms that are associated with erasing data on computer systems. Those are reformatting, wiping (deep formatting), shredding, and erasing. Though they are often used interchangeably, they are distinctly different in their overall function. Each one presents a unique set of challenges to a forensic investigator.

Reformatting. When someone reformats their computer, or essentially attempts to erase current data and replace with a new set of instructions and new data, residual data still remains. Residual data is traces of data that remain on a system. Imagine an old-fashioned chalkboard. When you erase a chalkboard, there are usually visible letters, sentences, or numbers remaining. Often with chalkboards, it requires multiple erasure attempts or a wet wash to remove the data. A drive retains residual data in much the same way. A shadow of data still remains on the system. Multiple formatting attempts will continue to reformat or clean the system. Forensic computer analysts will attempt to retrieve this residual or shadow data for information regarding the criminal case using data recovery software.

Wiping (Deep Formatting). Wiping attempts to permanently delete records and makes recovery almost impossible. During this process, data is overwritten with new data. As with formatting (or wiping a chalkboard), multiple wipes are required to ensure the data is irretrievable.

Shredding. When you feed a piece of paper through a shredder, it slices that paper into hundreds of little strips. A similar device is available for computers. A physical shredder can be used to destroy the hard drive and the data remaining on the device. There are also digital shredders. A digital shredder erases portions of a hard drive, but instead of replacing it with structured data, it replaces it with random data.

Erasing. Erasing means to permanently eliminate any attempt to retrieve data. There are three methods to achieve this goal: using a destructive wiping (deep formatting) program described above, degaussing, or physical destruction. Degaussing is to use a magnetic field to neutralize (erase) the data on a device. It does this by removing the magnetic properties existing in the iron oxide or chromium dioxide. Degaussing results in a permanent erasure or randomization of files.

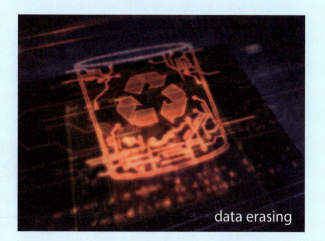

data erasing

THE INTERNET

The birth of the internet began in the 1960s as scientists and military experts, worried about foreign breaches of information, developed a method of communication separate from the telephone. They discovered a way for computers (the size of a small house at the time) to talk to one another by a method called packet switching.[131] By 1970, four computers were now connected to the new ARPAnet (Advanced Research Project Agency Network). Now move forward to the late 1970s, when a computer scientist named Vinton Cerf invented the TCP (transmission control protocol). The TCP/IP is the "handshake" that allows different computers to communicate.[132] Cerf's invention provided the needed mechanism for the worldwide network, which allowed files to be interchanged around the world. The year 1991 was important to the history of the internet. Tim Berners-Lee, a computer programmer, introduced the world to the internet. No longer was it limited to file exchange, but virtual access was now open to everyone. The first search engine was developed in 1992, as well as the ability for companies to create websites. Over 230 nations are now connected to the internet.[133]

Packet switching: A digital network transmission process in which data is broken into bite-sized pieces or blocks of information for fast, efficient transfer through network devices.

The ability to search topics on the internet is a resource that has opened the door to easy knowledge acquisition. When a topic is searched on the internet, the computer begins to record information (artifacts) about that search, such as browser history, bookmarks, IP addresses, storage in the cache, and permission access to cookies. Each of these terms are described below.

- *Browser history*: a record of the website addresses that the computer has recently visited and any data associated with the websites. Browser history retains information about search queries, logins, passwords, social networks, and financial information.

- *Bookmark*: a shortcut to a particular website. Just as a page in a book can be bookmarked by folding the corner of the page down or using a paper bookmark, an electronic bookmark saves a web address to your profile.

- *IP addresses*: fundamental protocol for communication on the internet. It determines how information is packaged, addressed, transferred, and routed by networked devices. It is an address that points to a location on the internet.

- *Cache*: temporary storage that retains information about browser history, frequently visited sites, and search terms in a file cache. The cache stores downloaded images, videos, documents, and files.

- *Cookies*: a piece of data inside the browser that gives feedback about the user to the server. Cookies mark and track information and are software that lives in the browser. For example, a user will search a certain product or be talking about specific merchandise on or near their computer, only to discover later that afternoon that the exact product is now offered to them in the computer ads popping up on their screen.

A computer forensics investigator will conduct a thorough examination of all related activity mentioned above. Web browsers offer the ease of integration between browser service and synchronization of passwords, and users unknowingly save important information, like their interests, personal life, and future plans. The history in the computer browser is stamped by date and time and provides a timeline for investigators. Even when a user attempts to delete internet history and cache data, it is likely the data remains. Often, no data is actually removed from the hard drive and, even when deleted, is retrievable. Though computer history and frequently visited webpages are only circumstantial evidence, it does provide supporting documentation of intent to commit a crime. For example, in 2009, Krenar Lusha of the U.K. was arrested based solely on his internet searches. Investigators monitored key word searches from Lusha on how to make explosives; investigated his downloads, which contained manuals on building explosives; and reviewed his chat session, which revealed he referred to himself as a terrorist. This evidence helped to convict Lusha, and he received seven years in prison.[134]

Email. The ability to email messages and files from computer to computer transformed the world. There is debate over who invented the email delivery system. Some say it is Ray Tomlinson, who in 1971 created a system of communication for the ARPAnet system discussed earlier. Others give credit to Shiva Ayyadurai, who claims to have written a program in high school called EMAIL in the late 1970s. Regardless of the true inventor, since 1971, email has evolved into over 2.6 billion active users and is the most used form of communication for personal and professional use. Email-related crimes include phishing, spam, harassment (threats, doxing, or other abusive language), illegal (pornographic) images, and sensitive information (e.g., banking information, medical records, etc.).[135] Email investigation is challenging since the majority of email is not encrypted. The primary goal in computer forensics is to verify the sender and receiver of the email by means of the email header. The header contains information regarding the pathway in which the email traveled, but this can be easily manipulated by a knowledgeable user.

Encryption: The process of encoding information from plaintext to ciphertext.

Instant Messaging. Instant messaging (chat) crimes are similar to those of emails, except whereas email can be delayed by hours or days (dependent upon when the email is opened), instant messaging is in real-time. Difficulty in investigating instant messaging crimes is due to the different platforms' methods of time stamping, the location of system folders, which vary according to operating system, and the storage fluidity of historical information.[136]

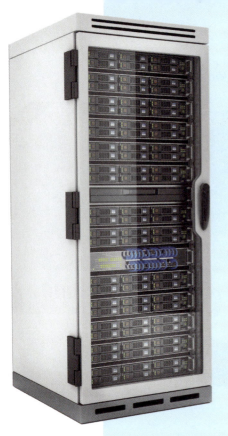

Servers. Information is not only stored in the memory of personal or business computers, but on servers as well. Servers are virtual filing cabinets that store information. Whereas in the past, servers simply sent and received messages, their role has drastically changed. Servers now function as collaborative tools that monitor databases and store documents, contacts, etc. When a terrorist searches, "How do I build a bomb?" on the internet, a series of events occurs. As the terrorist types and hits the search button, the computer will begin to store that information, any websites visited, permission access in the form of cookies, etc. Additionally, that information is sent to the offsite server that hosts the internet service. The Communications Assistance for Law Enforcement Act passed in 1992 allows law enforcement to "conduct electronic surveillance while protecting the privacy information outside the scope of investigation." The law goes on to state that communication companies are required to have "all necessary surveillance capabilities to comply with legal request for information."[137] There are hundreds of varying servers monitoring information, such as web servers, email servers, proxy servers, and identity servers.[138]

Media (CD & DVD) and USB Drives. CDs (compact disc) and DVDs (digital versatile disc) are optical discs that read and write information. DVDs have the capability to store significantly more information than a CD and provide information on both sides of the disc. Recovery of information on DVDs and CDs is often challenging due to the variety of file system formats. Professional data recovery software is available that will not only read all system formats, but is also equipped with CD imaging and the ability to report over 50 data items.[139] A USB (universal serial bus) drive (thumb drive or flash drive) is a small, durable device used for data storage that can only operate when plugged into a USB port. Compromised USB drives contain malware that can infect a computer system. God created humans to be curious, but it is never wise to insert a USB drive from an unknown source into a personal computer.

SECURITY

Computer security protects computer systems from theft, unauthorized access, and security breaches. Computer security is a top concern among businesses due to the number of data breaches that continue to occur on a regular basis. Computer hackers have cost consumers and business owners billions of dollars. The Yahoo!® data breach that occurred between 2013 and 2016 resulted in over three billion compromised personal records and billions of dollars in damages.

There are a variety of protections available to guard information stored on a computer hard drive or in virtual locations such as clouds. But it is important to recognize that computer hackers are on the forefront of technology and are continuing to find ways to bypass the latest updates in computer security. The seven layers of cyber security are laid out similar to an arc, with humans providing the ultimate shield of protection.

THE 7 LAYERS OF CYBERSECURITY

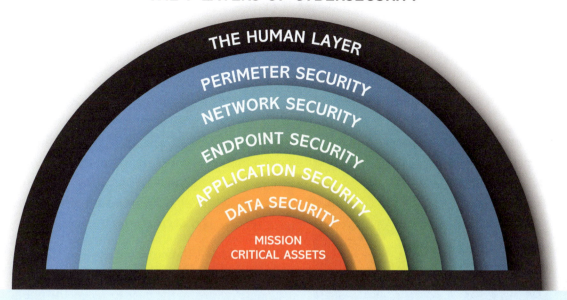

Humans. Humans are the preeminent layer to computer security. Humans ultimately are the number one key to the protection of personal and business information. Human error and failure to follow security protocols are the primary reason for computer crimes. Human cybercrime falls within these categories:

- *Phishing*: an email disguised as professional in which the user is requested to provide passwords, address, telephone number, etc.
- *Ransomware*: hackers access computer files and lock the user out, often demanding ransom to regain access.
- *Webcam managing*: hackers hijack the user's webcam in hopes of watching the user's keystrokes for passwords, conversations, and other data.
- *Screenshot managing*: hackers access the user's screen and take screenshots of passwords, etc.
- *Keylogging*: hackers record the user's keystrokes to decipher passwords, etc.
- *Ad clicking*: hackers display advertisements that may entice the user to click on an ad and open malware.

Perimeter. Authentication methods validate a person's access to the system. When a user logs into their email account, the provider authenticates their permission to access the system. Due to security breaches, many websites and emails have instituted multifactor authentication. Multifactor authentication requires two or more pieces of evidence to receive access to a system. Evidence may include passwords, email codes, text codes, personal information, etc. This verification through authorization validates the authentication. An example of perimeter security is passwords. Passwords are a set of characters, words, numbers, etc., that are used to authenticate user access to a digital system. Passwords ensure the user has permission to view or access information.

Network. A computer network is a group of computers, using similar protocols, that are connected to one another for the purpose of communicating data electronically. A network is capable of instituting a series of security protocols to protect the information of the computers connected to its system. An example of network security is firewalls. Firewalls prevent unauthorized access to specific devices, such as hardware or software, and protect from people trying to get into the computer system. Based upon a set of security rules, a firewall will either allow traffic to access or block information on a computer or network. Another example of network security is a Virtual Private Network (VPN). When an individual uses a VPN to connect to the internet, your request is encrypted and it masks your location.

Endpoint. This is the breaking down of a network into individual systems. An example of endpoint security is Google® allowing the user to access the public tools, such as Google Docs™, Slides™, and Sheets™.

Application. This refers to individual authorization within a single application or service. For example, a college presentation group project has been assigned by a professor, and the group decided to use Google Slides™. Google Slides™ is hosted on the internet. Each user will have to be granted access to use the individual application, Google Slides™ from Google®.

Data. Data is an extension of application security and allows an individual to grant access to files for the purpose of modifying those files. Refer back to the group Google Slide presentation. The creator has full control of the presentation, but the other members of the group need to be granted access to read, write, and update data. Data security permissions allow authorized individuals to change, delete, or copy the individual files.

ANTI-FORENSIC TOOLS

Even with the development of computer security measures to counteract cybercrime, there is a continual and steady increase in breaches of sensitive information. By the year 2024, there is an expected 70% increase in cybercrime, as well as an estimated cost of $5 trillion due to breaches of information.[140] Almost on a daily basis, the FBI website publishes another arrest related to cybercrime. One of the issues facing law enforcement is the use of Anti-Forensic (AF) tools, which have the ability to erase and alter information, create "chaff" that hides information, plant fake evidence, and leave tracer data that prevents computer forensic software from revealing hacker information.

Chaff:
Worthless information designed to lead an investigation awry.

There are four goals for AF tools:

1. Avoid detection.
2. Disrupt the collection of data.
3. Increase the period of time allotted for investigation.
4. Cast doubt on forensic testimony.

The use of AF tools does not completely eliminate the possibility of identifying criminal activity or traceable information, but it does impede investigations and increase the time frame for analysis and resolution.

CYBERCRIME INVESTIGATION

Computer crime investigations fall within both criminal and civil court cases, but the method of investigation varies between the two types. A computer forensic analyst may be utilized for either scenario.

I. Criminal Computer Forensic Investigations

1. Law enforcement obtains a search warrant and secures the computer. The Fourth Amendment to the Constitution provides protection against unreasonable search and seizure. A search warrant is required to seize and search not just the computer, but the files as well. The warrant must specify the exact information (and potential files) the investigators are looking for on the machine. They cannot just randomly search a suspect's computer. Securing the computer by preventing any unauthorized access is the key to evidence integrity and court admissibility. Search and seizure include the correct storage, labeling, and chain of custody as outlined by the law enforcement agency.

2. Identify and copy all files on the system by using Computer Forensic Tools (CFT). This includes deleted, encrypted, protected, and overwritten files. Difficulties occur within this area of computer forensics. Once detectives begin opening computer files, there is no way to verify they did not change anything, and it can be contested in court. Documentation of every single step and every single piece of evidence is essential to maintain integrity.

3. Examine unused or hidden storage space on the computer.

4. Document every step of the investigation and maintain chain of custody.

5. Prepare for courtroom testimony.

Ultimately, a conviction in a criminal investigation will result in incarceration, parole, community service, criminal record, or other form of criminal punishment.

II. Civil Computer Forensic Investigations

1. A private investigator is hired to investigate a dispute or lawsuit claim. Search and seizure do not apply in this situation; instead, the party negotiates a time and place for the investigator to examine the related computer materials. If the private investigator is provided access, then they will follow similar protocols regarding CFT, copying, etc.

2. Interview all involved parties in the investigation.

3. Since the private investigator does not have the rights and privileges of law enforcement, they may need to implement surveillance measures to gain information. Though they are permitted to eavesdrop on conversations, according to privacy laws, they are not permitted to record private conversations through a listening device.[141]

The resolution of a civil court case results in some form of monetary payments, a service, or property.

CONCLUSION

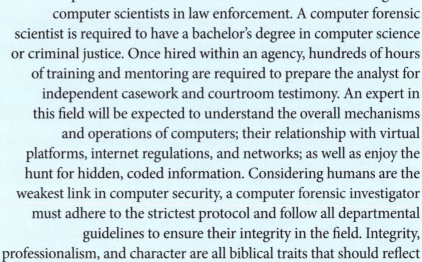

The field of computer forensics is one of the fastest growing divisions in law enforcement. The expected increase in computer-related crime, in addition to the innovative methods of computer hackers, has established the need for knowledgeable computer scientists in law enforcement. A computer forensic scientist is required to have a bachelor's degree in computer science or criminal justice. Once hired within an agency, hundreds of hours of training and mentoring are required to prepare the analyst for independent casework and courtroom testimony. An expert in this field will be expected to understand the overall mechanisms and operations of computers; their relationship with virtual platforms, internet regulations, and networks; as well as enjoy the hunt for hidden, coded information. Considering humans are the weakest link in computer security, a computer forensic investigator must adhere to the strictest protocol and follow all departmental guidelines to ensure their integrity in the field. Integrity, professionalism, and character are all biblical traits that should reflect a follower of Christ. Even within this technical field, a person can give glory to the Creator of knowledge, and the One who is knowledge, Jesus Christ.

BIOLOGICAL EVIDENCE

UNIT 4

Lesson 10
DNA

I charge you in the presence of God, who gives life to all things (1 Timothy 6:13a).

Case Study: DNA Profiling

DNA profiling is the process of determining an individual's characteristics from a DNA sample. This process was developed in 1985. Prior to that, the ability to compare DNA profiles, or "fingerprints," was a goal of the science community. DNA samples were stored in hopes that when technology improved, DNA profiles could be processed. As advancements in DNA processing were established, many cold cases have been resolved over the decades. The case below describes the very first time that DNA profiling was used to solve a series of crimes.

On November 21, 1983, 15-year-old Lynda Mann was walking home from a friend's house. She lived in the small village of Narborough in the English Midlands. Though most people stayed on the well-trafficked pedestrian paths, Lynda is believed to have accessed a secluded path called "Black Pad."[142] She was never seen alive again. Her assaulted, murdered body was found lying in the path the following morning. A semen sample was collected from her body and found to belong to a male with type A blood with an enzyme profile attributed to only 10% of males. There were no suspects, and the case went cold.

Over two years later, on July 31, 1986, 15-year-old Dawn Ashworth also took a shortcut home and never arrived alive. After a two-day search, her body was found near a different path called Ten Pound Lake. Dawn had been assaulted and strangled like Lynda, and the blood type retrieved from the semen sample matched the first suspect.

An important advancement was made in 1985, when Dr. Alec Jeffreys developed the first DNA profiling test.

Facts about the case:

- The prime suspect, 17-year-old Richard Buckland, admitted to the crime of Dawn Ashworth during police questioning but denied involvement in the first crime. Buckland was known to have learning disabilities.
- Alec Jeffreys compared a blood sample from Buckland to the two semen samples. He discovered that Buckland's did not match the DNA profile from either crime but that both crime scene DNA samples matched the same person. The girls had, in fact, been killed by the same man.
- Richard Buckland was the first person in history to be exonerated of murder by the process of DNA profiling.
- Every man in three local villages, over 5,000, were asked to voluntarily provide a blood or saliva sample. Over the next 6 months, no match was found.
- One day at a local bar, a man named Ian Kelly was bragging about impersonating his friend Colin Pitchfork when he provided a DNA sample on his behalf.
- Colin Pitchfork was a local baker, 22 years old, and a married man with two sons. Pitchfork was arrested, and using Jeffreys' DNA profiling, his DNA was found to match the killer's DNA samples.

- Colin Pitchfork confessed to the murders of Lynda and Dawn.

Pitchfork was the first person in history to be convicted of murder through DNA fingerprinting. Pitchfork was sentenced to a minimum of 28 years to life in prison. A miniseries was made about the case in 2014 called *The Code of a Killer*. Due to good behavior, Pitchfork was moved to an "open prison"[143] sometime before 2017. In 2017, Pitchfork was permitted to leave the prison for six hours and visit Bristol City, where he was seen dining on a pork sandwich. Over the next few months, he was permitted to stay overnight in Bristol, always returning to the prison after his outings. Pitchfork also changed his last name to "Thorpe." He was denied parole in 2018.[144] In February of 2020, a petition with over 27,000 signatures requested that Pitchfork be denied parole.

Since Pitchfork, DNA continues to be the gold standard in criminal identification.

"I know, my dear Watson, that you share my love of all that is bizarre and outside the conventions and humdrum routine of daily life." — Sherlock Holmes[145]

DNA (deoxyribonucleic acid) is the instructional code book of life. The Bible states in 1 Timothy 6:13 that God "gives life to all things." Every single living thing, whether human, animal, protozoa, bacteria, etc., contains the building blocks of information that comprise a DNA molecule. Within the DNA instruction manual is genetic and heredity information (genotype), physical characteristic information (phenotype), as well as health-related factors. Since 1984, police authorities have been collecting DNA samples from individuals charged with certain offenses, but as of 2003, every charged offense is required to submit a DNA sample. Today, the United States has one of the world's largest databases of DNA profiles, containing over 5.6 million samples.[146] Due to advancements in DNA analysis, cold cases that have remained unsolved for decades have been solved, giving families closure.

DNA FROM A BIBLICAL WORLDVIEW

The Bible clearly states in Genesis 1:27 that God created humans in His image. All humans are descendants of Adam and Eve and are of one humankind. Does the DNA in the human genome confirm the Bible? Yes! The Human Genome Project (1990–2003) was an extensive research study to map out the human genome. Many of the top scientists in the world were involved in this important research study. After a decade of DNA research, the Human Genome Project began to publish their results. Geneticist Dr. Venter (head of the Celera Genomics Corporation) stated about the Human Genome Project, "They had put together a draft of the entire sequence of the human genome and . . . unanimously declared, there is only one race – the human race."[147] Humans share more than 99% of their DNA. Those who believe in the authority of God's Word already recognized there is one human race because in Acts 17:26a, the Bible states, "And he made from one man every nation of mankind to live on all the face of the earth." The Bible is God's perfect Word and contains no errors; therefore, we can trust the historical account of the divine creation of the one human race (kind).

Human genome: The 23 chromosome pairs found in the cell nuclei that make up the nucleic acid sequences in humans.

What about plants and animals, does their DNA confirm the Bible? Yes! The Bible describes the creation of plants and animals in Genesis 1 as "according to their kind." In fact, God uses the phrase "according to their [or its] kind" ten times in the first chapter of the Bible. The study of DNA has verified that both plants and animals can only reproduce within their created kind (order and/or family level in taxonomy). This means that rose plants can only produce more rose plants, Venus fly traps can only produce more Venus fly traps, and dogs only have more dogs. The Human Genome Project published a quote on their project website in 2015 that stated, "We all know that elephants only give birth to little elephants, giraffes to giraffes, dogs to dogs and so on for every type of living creature."[148] Once again, valid observational science confirmed what the Bible already told us thousands of years ago.

Taxonomic Pyramid

- KINGDOM
- PHYLUM
- CLASS
- ORDER
- FAMILY ← KIND
- GENUS
- SPECIES

HISTORY OF DNA

Robert Hooke (1635–1703). Robert Hooke was the first scientist to publish information about cells. By studying a slice of cork under a lens, Hooke noticed empty spaces joined together by walls. He coined the term "cells" since they looked very much like the cell arrangement (or rooms) where monks resided. Hooke published his research in a book titled *Micrographia: or Some Physiological Descriptions of Miniature Bodies Made by Magnifying Glasses*. This is important to the history of DNA because it was in cells that scientists discovered DNA 200 years later.

Antonie van Leeuwenhoek (1632–1723). After reading Hooke's book *Micrographia*, Leeuwenhoek was inspired to explore the world of microscopes and microscopy. In 1682, he wrote a letter to Robert Hooke about an important observation:

> Thus I came to observe the blood of a cod and of a salmon, which I also found to consist of hardly anything but oval figures, and however closely I tried to observe these, I could not make out what parts these oval particles consisted, for it seemed to me that some of them enclosed in a small space a little round body or globule, and at some distance from this body there was round the globule a clear ring and round the ring again a slowly shadowing contour, forming the circumference of a globule.[149]

Though he did not realize it at the time, Leeuwenhoek had discovered the cell nucleus, the location of chromosomal, nuclear DNA.

Gregor Mendel (1822–1884). The history of DNA begins with the father of genetics, Gregor Mendel. In 1854, Mendel, an Austrian monk who enjoyed studying botany, began to purposefully cross green and yellow pea plants to observe the offspring. He studied and recorded seven characteristics in the pea plant: plant height, pod shape, pod color, seed shape, seed color, flower position, and flower color. He tediously recorded his discoveries and included mathematical ratios and predictions of heritable traits in offspring. He was the first to use the terms "recessive" and "dominant" regarding traits.[150]

Gregor Mendel presented his research to the Brünn Natural History Society in 1865 and published his research in 1866 in a paper titled *Experiments on Plant Hybridization*.[151] Due to the unassuming title and failure of Mendel to make a proclamation that he had discovered a new understanding of heredity, his research went unnoticed. Contributing to the oversight by the scientific community, a few years prior to Mendel publishing his research, Charles Darwin published *The Origin of Species* in 1859. Darwin's evolutionary ideas captured the attention of the scientific elite, and Mendel's research was forgotten. Mendel died in 1884 without ever knowing how important his research would be to the study of DNA, heredity, and genetics.

But Gregor Mendel had made groundbreaking research in the laws of heredity. His paper described "invisible" factors that contributed to the visible traits (green vs. yellow plant, etc.) he observed occurring in the pea plant offspring. Scientists now understand that these "invisible" factors are genes.

> **Genes:**
> A unit of heredity; a segment of DNA or RNA that is passed on from one generation to the next and carries the genetic information.

1900. Sixteen years after Mendel's death, his research is discovered and replicated by three independent scientists around the world. His work is now heralded as the foundation for the Laws of Heredity.

Oswald Avery (1877–1955). Oswald Avery was an immunochemist at the Rockefeller Institute of Medical Research. His focus of research was bacteria and what mechanism in bacteria allowed it to become so lethal. During a process of bacteria purification, Avery discovered a substance that was identified as a nucleic acid. Further analysis revealed that the substance was DNA and that DNA was responsible for heritable traits. He published his research in 1944, but it received little attention.

Erwin Chargaff (1905–2002). Erwin Chargaff was an Austro-Hungarian Jewish biochemist who immigrated to the United States after World War II. After reading Avery's research, Chargaff became so inspired to study DNA that it changed the course of his scientific studies. As a biochemist, he analyzed and isolated the chemical components of DNA. He developed what is now called Chargaff's Rules:

1. In double-stranded DNA, the number of guanine units equals the number of cytosine units (G = C), and the number of adenine units equals the number of thymine units (A = T).
2. DNA composition varies between species.

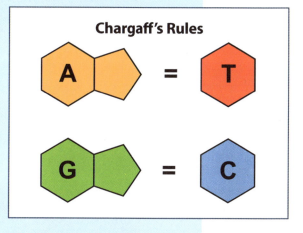

Chargaff was not included when the Nobel Prize (1962) was awarded to the scientists credited for the discovery of DNA.

Rosalind Franklin (1920–1958). Rosalind Franklin not only earned a doctoral degree in physical chemistry but became an expert in x-ray diffraction. She received an appointment at King's College, where she worked closely with Maurice Wilkins and Raymond Gosling, her assistant. Under Franklin's direction, Gosling was able to capture two images. One of the images is considered in science to be the most important x-ray crystallography photograph ever taken and is called Photograph 51. After close examination, Franklin concluded that DNA is a helical structure with the phosphate groups located on the outside. Scientists now recognized that DNA was composed of four nucleotides and phosphates, but the discovery of actual structure is credited to Maurice Wilkins, James Watson, and Francis Crick. Franklin was never awarded the Nobel Prize for her discovery because she passed away from cancer before the prize was awarded in 1962.

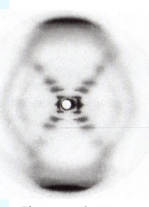

Photograph 51

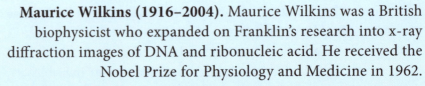

Maurice Wilkins (1916–2004). Maurice Wilkins was a British biophysicist who expanded on Franklin's research into x-ray diffraction images of DNA and ribonucleic acid. He received the Nobel Prize for Physiology and Medicine in 1962.

James Watson (1928–present) and Francis Crick (1916–2004). Francis Crick was a British biophysicist researching at Cambridge University Cavendish Laboratory. After visiting Crick at the university, James Watson, an American geneticist and biophysicist, joined Crick at Cambridge to study the structure of DNA. Using Franklin's photographs and research in addition to other research by Avery, Chargaff, and others, Watson and Crick are credited as the first scientists to solve the mystery surrounding the structure of DNA. They formulated the double helix model and verified that DNA does replicate. They received the Nobel Prize for Physiology and Medicine in 1962.

Sir Alec Jeffreys (1950–present). Alec Jeffreys is a British geneticist who developed a technique to isolate and identify the components of DNA into an individual genetic profile, or "fingerprint," in 1985. This led to the first criminal conviction as a result of DNA fingerprinting (see case study at the beginning of the lesson). Alec Jeffreys was knighted in 1994, an honor because of his extraordinary research in DNA profiling.

The Human Genome Project (1990–2003).[152] The Human Genome Project was initiated in 1988 and officially launched in 1990 by the National Institute of Health and U.S. Department of Energy. The goals of this research initiative were to:

- Map out the human genome.
- Determine the 3.2 billion letters in the human genome.
- Map out the genome of other living organisms.
- Develop new technology to study DNA.

CODIS (Combined DNA Index System). The Combined DNA Index System allows for an electronic search and comparison of DNA profiles. CODIS was launched in 1990 and was ordered under the FBI's authority in 1994. Today, over 270 police agencies around the world utilize CODIS to maintain DNA databases.[153]

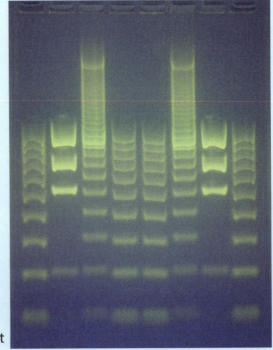

DNA fingerprint

DNA STRUCTURE

The human body is made up of over 30 trillion cells. While not all cells contain nuclear DNA, such as red blood cells or corneated cells, the majority of cells do contain chromosomal, genetic information. DNA is microscopic and cannot be seen with the naked eye or with a compound microscope. DNA can only be observed under a high-power electron microscope. Five thousand strands of DNA laid side by side would be as wide as a single human hair.[154] The three main types of DNA are nuclear DNA, mitochondrial DNA, and y-DNA. The human cell contains one nucleus. In the nucleolus of the nucleus is found the 23 pairs of human chromosomes, or 46 total (23 from the mother and 23 from the father). The first 22 pairs of chromosomes contain genetic information and the markers used in DNA profiling. The 23rd pair of chromosomes determines sex. If the pair is XX, it is a female, and XY is a male. The human karyotype confirms the Bible in Genesis 1, when God describes the creation of humans as male and female (see **Figure 1**).

Corneated cells: Dead cells similar to those found in hair.

Karyotype: A picture or photograph of the chromosomes in an organism, which includes the number, size, and shape.

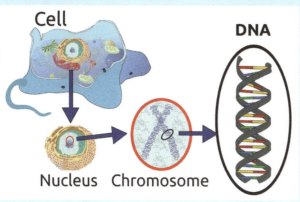

Figure 1

23rd chromosome determines sex. XY is a male; XX is a female.

Chromosomes are made of tightly coiled DNA. The DNA found in the nucleolus of a human cell is classified as nuclear DNA and is the only DNA that can distinguish one individual. DNA is also found in the mitochondria, the powerhouse of the cell. One cell contains over 2,000 mitochondria. Mitochondrial DNA is far more prevalent than nuclear DNA, but it only contains the maternal genome and not the paternal. Mitochondrial DNA is passed through the female line, meaning that a mother will pass her mitochondrial DNA information to all her children (both male and female), but only females pass on the information through the female egg during reproduction (see **Figure 2**).

Figure 2

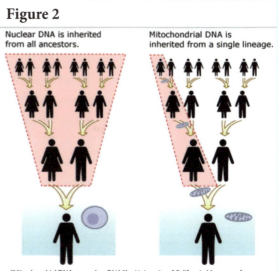

"Mitochondrial DNA vs. nuclear DNA," by University of California Museum of Paleontology (CC BY-SA 3.0, creativecommons.org/licenses/by-sa/3.0/deed.en)

A third type of DNA, y-DNA, only contains one paternal genome and not that of the mother. Y-DNA is passed from father to sons on the Y chromosome. Though mitochondrial and y-DNA may provide valuable genetic information, nuclear DNA is the only type that provides a profile unique to one individual (see **Figure 3**).

Figure 3

Y-line

A DNA molecule in a human cell is a three-meter chain of monomer nucleotides. If all the DNA inside one human could be uncoiled and laid out end-to-end, in astronomical units, it would wrap the solar system twice. A DNA nucleotide is composed of three basic components: one of four nitrogen bases (adenine, thymine, cytosine, and guanine), phosphate group, and a deoxyribose (5-carbon) sugar molecule. Adenine and guanine are categorized as purines, while cytosine and thymine are pyrimidines. A purine is a two-ring organic compound structure that is the most widely occurring nitrogen containing heterocycle in nature. Pyrimidines are organic rings of six atoms — four carbon and two nitrogen — and are involved in the processes of enzyme regulation and protein manufacturing. The DNA molecule is held together by hydrogen bonds between the nitrogen bases and covalent bonds between the phosphate of one nucleotide and the sugar of the next. Genes are segments of the DNA molecule that code for specific heredity information and are responsible for all body functions.

Monomer:
A molecule that can be reacted together with other monomer molecules to form a larger polymer chain.

Heterocycle:
Containing more than one kind of atom joined in a ring.

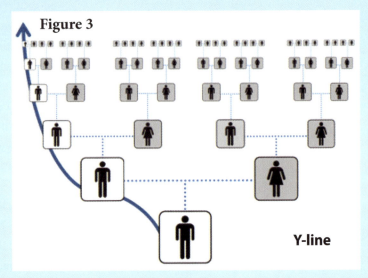

The DNA nitrogen bases strictly follow an organized pattern called complementary base pairing. There are over three billion base pairs in one human genome. In base pairing, a purine will always pair with a pyrimidine and vice versa. This means that adenine (purine) always pairs with thymine (pyrimidine), or A pairs with T, and guanine (purine) always pairs with cytosine (pyrimidine), or G pairs with C. Though complementary base pairing determines the "steps" on a ladder, there is no specific order for the bases to follow. The pattern will vary between individuals. For example, if a DNA strand is found with the bases CCA GGT on the left side of the strand, how would the complementary base pairs be represented on the right side?

Using the information encoded in the genes (similar to ingredients for a recipe), DNA becomes the code book (or recipe) for protein manufacturing in the human body. DNA sequences and forms amino acids, which are the basic unit of proteins. There are twenty amino acids that are considered building blocks to human life. The shape and order of the amino acids result in chains of amino acids that build the proteins. Proteins are responsible for metabolism, DNA replication, providing structure to cells, and many more important functions.

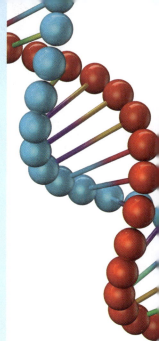

COLLECTION AND PRESERVATION OF DNA

The method of collection, packaging, and transportation of biological evidence is dependent upon whether the evidence is in a wet or dry condition. Biological evidence, with a potential for DNA, includes blood, skin, semen, and saliva. As stated in earlier lessons with other types of evidence, the preferred method for collection is to submit the complete, entire item where evidence is identified. It is often not possible to collect and submit an entire piece of flooring, bed, door frame, etc. Therefore, proper collection protocols must be followed in addition to the proper individual packaging and storage of every piece of evidence.

Wet Biological Evidence

When collecting wet blood and/or other biological fluids, specific protocols must be followed to ensure the evidence does not become contaminated. The key factor is to adhere to the two-hour window. Wet evidence must not be packaged longer than two hours, as mold growth and other factors destroy the evidence.

1. Wet biological evidence that can be transported to the lab should be packaged in a paper bag or envelope to prevent mold growth. The evidence will need to completely air dry before repackaging in the lab.
2. If the wet evidence cannot be transported due to the surface or location, the blood or fluid can be absorbed using a 1" x 1" square of 100% cotton sheeting. It is then packaged for transportation to lab. The cotton squares will need to air dry before repackaging in the lab.

Dry Biological Evidence

Dried blood and biological fluids should be collected and packaged dependent upon the manner in which the sample is found.

1. If the entire sample (such as bed sheets or clothing) can be collected and sent to the lab, the sample should be secured in a paper bag or envelope for transportation.
2. If the sample cannot be transported, the sample should be lifted using fingerprint tape and placed on a backer card or scraped into a paper envelope. If wet, absorb the stain with ½-inch long threads that have been soaked in distilled water. The threads must be air dried before packaging or transported to the lab for drying.

DNA PROFILING AND ANALYSIS

The origins of DNA profiling began with Dr. Alec Jeffreys in 1983. When DNA profiling was first developed, it was a long, tedious process that analyzed repeating sequence lengths hundreds of bases long through a process called gel electrophoresis. To receive an analysis would take between 6–8 weeks when there was not a backlog at the laboratory. But backlogs developed, and investigators would wait between 6–8 months for DNA results and analysis. Additionally, a large sample the size of a dime was required for a DNA fingerprint. Though a 6- to 8-month turnaround time is not uncommon today, the overall process has become more efficient.

Once the biological evidence is received at the laboratory, the technicians will first separate the DNA molecules from other cellular material. Once separated, the DNA will be isolated and extracted. This process can take between two to three hours. After extraction, the DNA must be verified as human and not that of animal or bacteria origin through a process called quantitation. Specific DNA sequences are then copied using polymerase chain reaction (PCR) in a process called amplification. DNA is then cut into sections (or pieces) using restriction enzymes, which are designed to look for specific base pairs as points for separation.

Electrophoresis:

The key difference between gel electrophoresis and capillary electrophoresis is that gel electrophoresis is performed in a vertical or horizontal plane using a polymer gel of standard pore size, whereas capillary electrophoresis is performed in a capillary tube with a polymer liquid or a gel.

Chromosomes Structure

Paternal homologue — Maternal homologue

Three gene pairs at three different loci

In the 1990s, DNA analysis began using STRs (Short Tandem Repeat). Analysts use one loci on select chromosomes and determine the length. The length of the STR provides the markers scientists need to create a DNA fingerprint. Distinct markers with repeating units are found on DNA in the human chromosome. Each person has two sets of the STR markers because they receive one from each parent.[155] The number of times the markers repeat varies between individuals. Specific DNA sequences are then copied using polymerase chain reaction (PCR) in the amplification process. Using PCR and capillary electrophoresis, the repeating markers can be analyzed for unique identity. The benefit of using STR for analysis is it only requires a small DNA sample (see **Figure 4**).

Figure 4

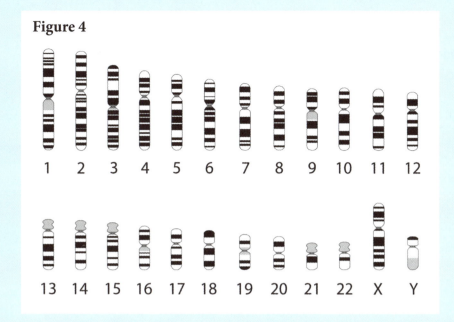

Figure 5

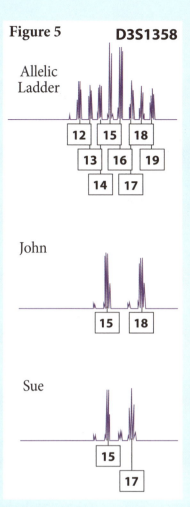

The number of repeats on a specific marker is identified as a two-numbering system (one for each parent). When a DNA profile is entered into CODIS, the two-number system is entered for the specific STR (see **Figure 5**).

In this example, the STR for locus point D3S1358 would be logged into a DNA database as:

John: 15, 18   Sue: 15, 17

Electrophoresis. DNA is a negatively charged substance. When the extracted DNA is injected into the sample wells on an electrophoresis device, an electric current is applied. The positive terminal is attached at the opposite end. The DNA has already been cut into different sized pieces or lengths; therefore, the pieces have a different weight. Since negative charges are attracted to positive charges, the DNA pieces (negative charge) are pulled through the gel or capillary (depending on the type of electrophoresis) to the positively charged opposite end. The different-sized pieces of DNA will stop at different locations, with smaller pieces traveling the farthest and larger pieces traveling the shortest distance. The stopping points for the sections of DNA is what creates the band patterns used for analysis.

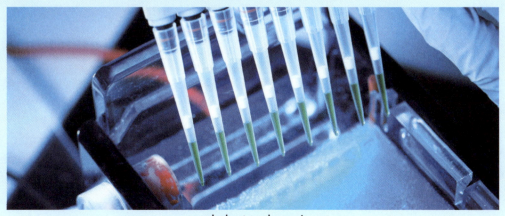

gel electrophoresis

GENETIC GENEALOGY

Genetic genealogy is a relatively new field of forensic work. Genetic genealogists (detectives) are specialists in researching family history and are able to take unknown DNA profiles, search those profiles in a public DNA database, and build a family tree. Based on the family tree, the genealogist is able to provide police agencies with names of potential suspects. The following are the steps to conduct a genetic genealogy investigation:[156]

1. Create a DNA profile from a biological sample.

2. Search the DNA profile in a public database. Individuals wanting to learn more about their family history will submit their DNA profiles to free, public databases. DNA profiles are obtained through voluntary, paid submission of a sample of DNA to companies such as AncestryDNA®, MyHeritage DNA®, etc. The profile is added to a public genealogy database, such as GEDmatch®. The database will search for other people (relatives) with similar DNA profiles. The DNA from the suspect will be 50% similar to their parents, 25% similar to their grandparents, and so on through their family tree.

3. Build the family tree. Genetic genealogists participate in extensive research into birth, marriage, and death records; social media profiles and stalking; newspapers; census data; etc., in an effort to establish family links between the results of the DNA profile search in the database and the unknown sample submitted for analysis.

4. Identify suspect. Once genetic genealogy has identified a possible suspect, police begin an investigation into the facts of the original case, such as eyewitness testimony, the original suspect's physical characteristics, and retrieval of DNA for comparison.

Because of advances in DNA, the creation of DNA heredity databases, and the work of genetic genealogists, hundreds of cold cases have been solved.

THE FUTURE OF DNA

DNA is the code book of life, a code written by the one true Creator God. Every living thing has species-specific DNA. DNA technological advancements are occurring at a rapid pace. As the understanding of DNA advances, the ability to profile, search, and identify samples will become even more of an efficient process.

Rapid DNA. Rapid DNA methods were first developed in 2010. Rapid DNA are DNA profiles created from a buccal (cheek) swab without human intervention. A Rapid DNA machine takes a buccal swab through a completely automated process of extraction, amplification, separation, detection, and allele identification in just 90 minutes.[157] The profile is then searched in CODIS. The Rapid DNA Act of 2017 allowed for the FBI to issue standards and procedures for the use of Rapid DNA machines and analysis.[158] Rapid DNA is permitted for those in custody if the state has a DNA collection law, but if a DNA sample is collected from a crime scene, it must be analyzed in an accredited lab or it may not be submitted to CODIS.[159]

DNA Storage. DNA is capable of volumes of storage. Scientists have stated, "DNA can store more data far more densely than silicon, you could squeeze all of the data in the world inside just a few grams of it."[160] Similar to binary code, which uses 1's and 0's, DNA storage uses the four nucleotide bases: adenine, thymine, cytosine, and guanine. DNA storage research began in the 1980s, but it was not until 2011 that scientists successfully stored five files onto strands of DNA. In 2016, they were able to store one kilobyte of data, Robert Frost's poem *The Road Not Taken*, onto strands of DNA. In 2019, scientists developed the first automated system for "storing and retrieving data in the manufactured genetic material."[161] Benefits of DNA storage are minimal storage space, low maintenance, and the limitless potential. Unfortunately, the process of DNA storage is extremely expensive and has the potential for substitutions, insertions, or deletions in the genetic code. In the forensics community, scientists envision the ability to create DNA codes for inanimate (nonliving) objects. The objects would be coated in DNA for tracing and identification.

SNPs. In 2013, scientists isolated five differences called single nucleotide polymorphisms (SNPs) between identical twins. Prior to that, it was believed that identical twins (monozygotic) were 100% genetically the same. This discovery has aided in paternity cases and related issues regarding identical twins.

Epigenetics. Geneticists are focusing on epigenetics, the study of heritable phenotype changes that do not involve alterations in the DNA sequence. *Epi* means on top of the genes. For example, imagine a DVD. The DVD contains recorded information, pictures, etc., of a film, but the DVD cannot be viewed unless there is a DVD player. Whereas genes in DNA are similar to the information recorded on the DVD, epigenetics is like the DVD player. Epigenetics is the mechanism that will turn off or turn on certain traits in the genetic code that contribute to protein manufacturing. Factors that influence epigenetics include environment, nutrition, emotional factors, exercise, etc. There will be many new discoveries in the field of epigenetics in the coming years.

Lesson 11
Serology

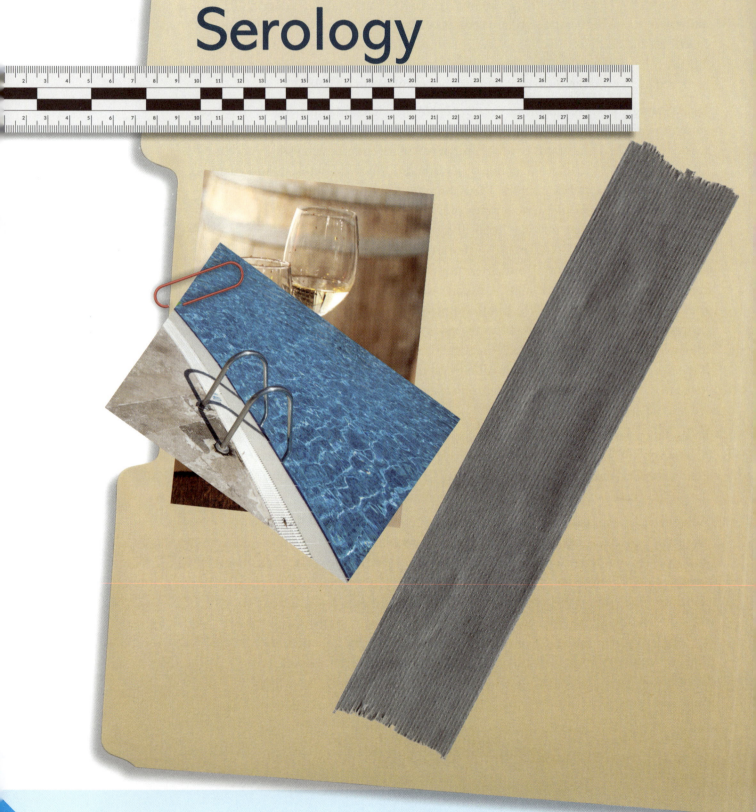

For the life of every creature is its blood: its blood is its life (Leviticus 17:14a).

Case Study: The Peterson Mystery

In 1997, Michael and Kathleen Peterson were married. They were affluent, owned a 14-room dream home and appeared to their children, family, and neighbors as happy. But as Christmas of 2001 approached, the Peterson household was tense. The couple's children were now out of the house, and troubles at work pushed Kathleen to begin taking Valium®. Michael had run for mayor and lost due to lying in public. There were also other stressors.

According to testimony, on December 8, Michael suggested an afternoon of Christmas shopping. The couple had a nice dinner at home, watched a movie, and drank some wine. Kathleen received a call from a coworker at 11 p.m. Testimony states that the couple enjoyed some time by the pool, and then Michael decided to go to bed.

At 2:41 a.m. on December 9, 2001, Michael Peterson called 911.

911: Durham 911. Where's your emergency?

Michael Peterson: Uuuuh, 1810 Cedar Street. Please!

911: What's wrong?

Peterson: My wife had an accident, she's still breathing.

911: What kind of an accident?

Peterson: She fell down the stairs. She's still breathing, please come.

At 2:46 a.m., Michael Peterson called 911 again.

911: Durham 911. Where is your emergency?

Peterson: Where are they?! It's eighteen-ten Cedar. She's not breathing! Please! Please! Would you hurry up!

Detectives arrived at the home to find Kathleen lying dead in a pool of her own blood at the bottom of the stairs. Blood was splattered up the stairwell and over the walls. Michael was cradling his wife's body, and police had to pull him away. He was barefoot with bloody shorts on. A blood expert was called in to review the scene. Based on the presence of blood on the walkway outside the home, blood stains on the front door, blood smears up the staircase and on the walls above, blood on the kitchen sink, and a severe injury on the back of Kathleen's head, the police immediately felt this was not an accident, but a homicide.

Two months after Kathleen's death, the autopsy report stated that she had been killed by blunt force trauma to the back of the head. Michael Peterson was charged with first-degree murder for the death of his wife. Michael continued to proclaim his innocence and stated that Kathleen had an accidental fall down the stairs.[162]

Facts about the case:
- Wine glasses in the kitchen sink did not have Kathleen's fingerprints on them. If the couple had been drinking by the pool, there would have been prints on the glasses.
- Police investigators believe the death was not accidental because there was too much blood everywhere.

- The blood found around the victim was mostly dry. This showed that time had elapsed before Michael called police.
- Red neurons were found in Kathleen's brain. This meant there had been a two-hour period where Kathleen lacked oxygen and had been slowly dying during this time frame.
- Kathleen had seven tears to her scalp.
- Expert witnesses for the defense included Dr. Werner Spitz, forensic pathologist; Dr. Henry Lee, forensic scientist; and Tim Palmbach, DNA expert. The defense experts claimed that Kathleen had tripped on the stairs, fell backwards, and hit her head on the door frame. She then tried to stand, slipping on her own blood, and fell a second time, causing the additional injuries.
- It was discovered that Michael Peterson had an email exchange with a man with whom he wanted to have sex.
- A month before Peterson's trial, it was discovered that another woman, Elizabeth Ratliff, had died after being with Michael Peterson by "falling down the stairs." This occurred in 1985. The body was exhumed for examination. There were seven cuts in the bone of the scalp. The death of Elizabeth was deemed a homicide.

Michael Peterson was found guilty and went to prison for eight years until new evidence was presented. There were issues with the forensic evidence used in the criminal trial. Though methods used to search for bloodstains on Michael's clothes and DNA analysis were requested, they were never conducted nor was the evidence stored properly.[163] The forensic science discrepancies allowed the defense to request an Alford plea for manslaughter in 2017. This is a plea that states the defendant does not admit to guilt but acknowledges the state has enough evidence to convict, or the defendant does not want to endure a new trial. He was sentenced to serve time but was awarded his time served awaiting trial and released from prison. He now lives in a house with no staircase.[164]

There is a lot of uncertainty surrounding this case. Remember, forensic science is a historical science, meaning the original events are unobservable. Therefore, investigators are tasked with evaluating the evidence left behind and drawing conclusions. Often, not all the answers are there, which leads to frustration in the overall justice so often expected by the victims in these cases. But with each unanswered question, forensic science techniques improve and get one step closer in the search for resolution. The study of blood and the information it holds has advanced significantly in the last century. This lesson will discuss the importance of blood evidence while pointing to the most significant blood shed in history — the blood poured out by the Savior Jesus Christ as payment for man's sin.

"My name is Sherlock Holmes. It is my business to know what other people do not know." — Sherlock Holmes[165]

Forensic serology is the scientific study of blood serum and bodily fluids such as semen, saliva, breast milk, and other fluids. Serology focuses on the proteins in blood that are manufactured by the immune system and the antibodies produced in the blood. The Bible tells us the life is found in the blood (Leviticus 17:14). In just 60 seconds, blood will circulate throughout the 60,000 miles of track in the human body, traveling from the heart to the extremities and back again. That is twice the circumference of the earth. Every second, two million blood cells are produced in human bone marrow. Red blood cells are replaced every few months and white blood cells every few days. Blood is essential to life; it is responsible for oxygen transport, defense against pathogens, and protection against hemorrhages. The importance of blood to human life should not be overshadowed by the significance of Christ's blood, shed on the Cross as payment for the sins of mankind.

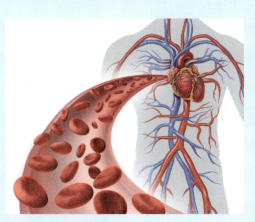

Leviticus 17:14:

"For the life of every creature is its blood: its blood is its life. Therefore I have said to the people of Israel, You shall not eat the blood of any creature, for the life of every creature is its blood. . . ."

Hemorrhage:

A heavy loss of blood.

FORENSIC SEROLOGY FROM A BIBLICAL WORLDVIEW

The Bible refers to blood 447 times in the New King James Version. Why does God talk so much about blood in the Bible? Blood is obviously important to God; blood is essential to human earthly life, but more importantly, to eternal life. To truly understand the importance of blood, life must be equated to blood. After the first sin, God shed the blood of at least one animal, not only to cover Adam and Eve, but also because a blood sacrifice was necessary for the forgiveness of sins. The Bible states in Hebrews 9:22, ". . . without the shedding of blood there is no forgiveness of sins." To protect their lives during the Exodus Passover event, the Hebrews were required to shed the blood of lambs and cover their doorposts. Most importantly, the shedding of Christ's (the Lamb of God) blood on the Cross was necessary for the payment of all human sin. Christ's blood is a protective covering of life over the death humans deserve due to their sinful nature. Only through repentance and forgiveness of sin can humans spend eternity with Christ. Ephesians 2:13 says, "But now in Christ Jesus you who once were far off have been brought near by the blood of Christ." Blood becomes a fascinating topic to study through the lens of life and the truth of God's Holy Word.

Serology

Lesson 11

HISTORY

Blood has been recognized as important to life for the last 6,000 years of human history. The first murder victim in the Bible involved the loss of blood. God tells Cain regarding the murder of his brother Abel (Genesis 4:11), "And now you are cursed from the ground, which has opened its mouth to receive your brother's blood from your hand." Though it would be thousands of years before scientists would understand the properties of blood, blood types, and the importance of DNA, blood was still recognized as the essence of life. As with most pioneers in early scientific study, Christian scientists (such as Harvey and Leeuwenhoek) were at the forefront of discoveries in the field of serology. The following dates are the key discoveries in the understanding of blood and its properties.

1492 — Pope Innocent VII of Rome received the first recorded blood transfusion from three different individuals. Unfortunately, the science of blood typing had not been developed and the pope died.

1628 — William Harvey discovered how blood circulates through the human body. He documented the ability of the heart to pump blood through the arteries and back to the heart via the veins.

1674–1719 — Antonie van Leeuwenhoek researched red blood cells (RBCs) and accurately measured them to be 0.003 inches. He also identified the connections between arteries and veins as capillaries. In 1700, he drew the very first sketch of a human red blood cell.[166] Leeuwenhoek spent his entire life fascinated by the microscopic world that God had created. He stated,

> It is to be hoped then, that the enquirers into Nature's works, by searching deeper and deeper into her hidden mysteries, will more and more place the discoveries of the truth before eyes of all, for as to produce aversion to the errors of former times, which all those who love the truth ought diligently to aim at. For we cannot in any better manner glorify the Lord and Creator of the Universe than that, in all things, how small forever they appear to our naked eyes, which yet have received the gift of life and power of increase, we contemplate the display of his Omniscience and Perfections with the utmost admiration.[167]

1826 — Lord Joseph Baron Lister and Dr. Thomas Hodgkin published research on the morphology of RBCs as concave discs and their stacking pattern as an identifier of disease. Lister also made advancements in the study of white blood cells (WBCs) and their importance in immunity.[168]

1895 — Dr. Eduard Piotrowski publishes the first study on blood spatter analysis titled *Concerning the Origin, Shape, Direction and Distribution of the Bloodstains Following Head Wounds Caused by Blows*.

Morphology: The form and structure of an organism.

1900 — Karl Landsteiner discovered that blood contained three different groups: A, B, and O. He was awarded the Nobel Prize for Medicine in 1930. And in 1902, two of Landsteiner's students discovered the fourth blood group, AB.

1937 — The first blood bank in the United States is opened in Chicago.

1939 — The blood group systems of RH (Rhesus + and −) are discovered by Philip Levine and R.E. Stetson, but the name of RH was not given until 1940 by Landsteiner. The name "Rhesus" was assigned because it was first discovered on a rhesus macaque primate.[169]

1940 — Edwin Cohn developed cryopreservation of blood, which allows samples to be stored for long periods of time.

1955 — Dr. Paul Kirk testified to the effectiveness of blood spatter analysis in determining suspect position in the famous case *State of Ohio v. Samuel Sheppard*. This case set the precedence for blood spatter testimony.

1983 — The International Association of Bloodstain Pattern Analysis (IABPA) was founded.

Properties of Blood. Blood is a connective tissue that consists of plasma, blood cells, and platelets. Blood is part of the circulatory system; it carries the essential oxygen and nutrients to and waste materials away from all body tissues. Formed elements (or corpuscles) of the blood contain three types of blood cells, red blood cells (99.9% RBC or erythrocytes), white blood cells (>0.1% WBC or leukocytes), and platelets (<0.1% thrombocytes). The primary purpose of red blood cells is oxygen transport throughout the body. White blood cells fight off infections. Platelets are responsible for blood clotting. Formed elements comprise 45% of blood. The remaining 55% of blood composition is plasma, which is 91.5% water and 8.5% solids. Plasma provides the medium that suspends the formed elements and aids in the transportation of nutrients. Dissolved within the plasma are proteins, electrolytes, carbohydrates, minerals, and fats.[170]

Mature RBCs do not contain a nucleus; therefore, there is no DNA information in these types of cells. DNA is found in WBCs. Considering that RBCs are 99.9% of the formed elements compared to the WBCs (<0.1%), it is not as easy to identify complete DNA profiles from a blood sample. Profiles will often be determined by the quantity and viability of the sample (see **Figure 1**).

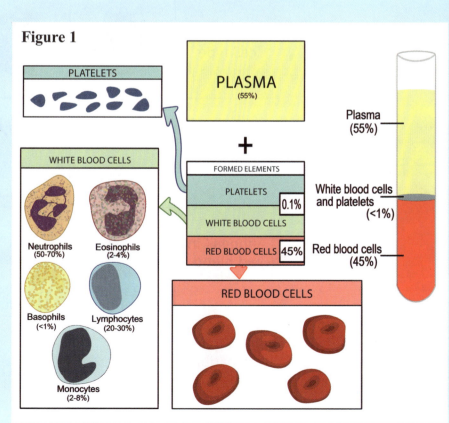

Figure 1

BLOOD TYPING

On the surface of red blood cells are found antigens. Antigens are chemical protein structures designed to function as an immune response and will attack foreign substances with antibodies. Scientists have discovered four principal blood antigens: A, B, O, and Rh systems.[171] The presence or absence of antigens determines a person's blood type. The infusion of the wrong blood type into a person's system will result in a defensive response from the leukocytes in the immune system and will often lead to death. In summary:

- Group A blood has A antigens on the surface with B antibody in the plasma.
- Group B blood has B antigens on the surface with A antibody in the plasma.
- Group AB blood has both A and B antigens on the surface and neither A nor B antibody in the plasma.
- Group O blood has neither A nor B antigens on the surface and both A and B antibody in the plasma.
- Rh factor (D antigen): The presence of the D antigen results in a Rh+, whereas the absence of the D antigen results in Rh−.

BLOOD TYPES AND CROSS-REACTIONS

Group	A	B	AB	O
Red blood cell type	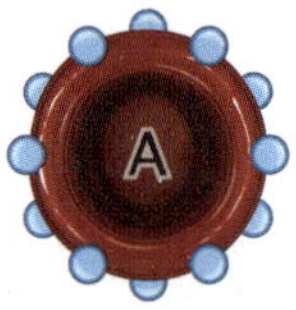 (A)	 (B)	 (AB)	 (O)
Antibodies in plasma	 Anti-B	 Anti-A	None	 Anti-A and Anti-B
Antigens in red blood cell	A antigen	B antigen	 A and B antigens	None
Blood types compatible in an emergency	A, O	B, O	A, B, AB, O (AB⁺ is the universal receipent)	O (O is the universal donor)

Lesson 11

Intro to Forensic Science

For every antigen in blood, there is an identifiable antibody (immunoglobulin). Antibodies are found in the blood serum. Antibodies will only react with their corresponding antigen. Antiserums (anti-A, anti-B, etc.) have been developed to react with the antigens in blood to identify blood type. For example, if anti-A serum is added to a blood sample containing A antigens, the antibodies in the serum and the antigens will combine and clump together in a process called agglutination (see **Figure 3**). Similar to a lock and key, the structure of the antibodies will lock with its corresponding antigen. If there is no match, they will not join together or agglutinate (see **Figure 4**).

Figure 3

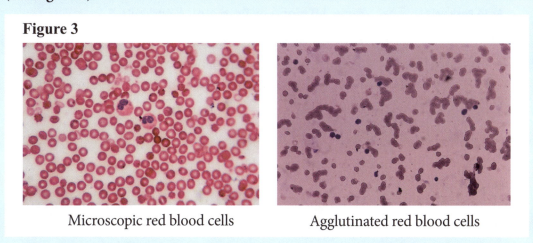

Microscopic red blood cells   Agglutinated red blood cells

Figure 4

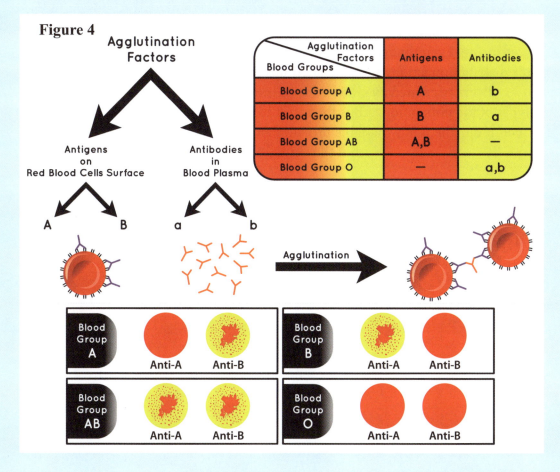

Serology

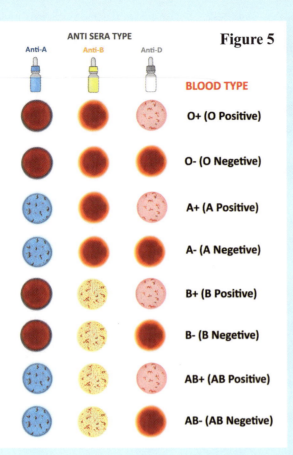

Figure 5

Blood Typing. As stated at the beginning of the lesson, serology is the study of blood serum and the antigen and antibody reactions. When determining blood type, serologists will use the serums anti-A, anti-B, and anti-D. A serologist will apply the antiserums to a blood sample and look for signs of agglutination (or granulation) to determine blood type.

- Type A blood is agglutinated by anti-A serum.
- Type B blood by anti-B serum.
- Type AB blood by both anti-A and anti-B.
- Type O blood by neither serum.
- The presence of agglutination from anti-D serum is positive for Rh, and no agglutination is negative for Rh (see **Figure 5**).

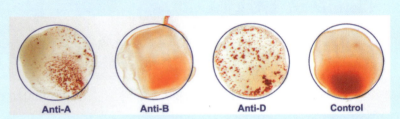

Heredity. Blood type is genetic and is passed down from the parents to their offspring. Even though blood type is the result of genetic properties, there is a wide distribution among the people groups (ethnicities) in the world. The genetic diversity created by God in the cells of humans is represented in the blood types of the population. AB is the rarest blood type, with type O being the most common. The following table provides an estimated breakdown of blood types within the United States by percentage of ethnic groups.

Summary of ABO and Rh Blood Types within the United States

Blood Type	African-Americans	Asian-Americans	Caucasian-Americans	Latino/Latina-Americans
A^+	24	27	33	29
A^-	2	0.5	7	2
B^+	18	25	9	9
B^-	1	0.4	2	1
AB^+	4	7	3	2
AB^-	0.3	0.1	1	0.2
O^+	47	39	37	53
O^-	4	1	8	4

BLOOD TESTING AND ANALYSIS

The first questions for the forensic investigator when arriving on a scene with potential biological fluids are "Is the fluid biological?" and "Is it of human origin?" Similar to other evidential procedures, they will begin their investigation with presumptive tests and then conduct confirmatory tests either on site or in the lab. The five steps in the search for blood evidence include:

1. Visual examination of the crime scene.
2. Photograph and record the evidence.
3. Collection and preservation of the evidence.
4. Presumptive testing.
5. Confirmatory testing.

Presumptive Testing. When searching for blood evidence, investigators will often conduct a visual examination of the crime scene. Sometimes, blood evidence is not visible to the naked eye. It is not uncommon for people involved in blood-related crimes to clean up the evidence. Also, blood spatter can leave behind extremely small quantities or droplets that are very difficult to see with a visual exam. Presumptive testing establishes the possibility that biological fluids such as blood, saliva, or semen are present.

Luminol reaction

A luminol test is one of the presumptive tests that investigators will use to identify the location of possible blood. Through a chemical reaction and oxidization, luminol reacts with the hemoglobin in blood to emit a blue light, or luminescence, under a UV light that only lasts about one minute in fresh blood and several minutes in aged blood. Photography is necessary to capture the results of the luminol reaction. The problem with luminol is that it has the potential to destroy other types of evidence as well as reacting with chemicals other than blood. Follow-up presumptive testing is necessary to verify the location of blood evidence.

A Kastle-Meyer test (phenolphthalein test) is the first step to determine if a sample is blood. Phenolphthalein reacts with a heme molecule present in blood. Phenolphthalein also reacts with the peroxidase property of the hemoglobin in blood, which catalyzes phenolphthalin through a process of oxidization into phenolphthalein. To test a sample:

1. Retrieve the sample to be tested with a cotton swab or filter paper.
2. Apply one drop of the phenolphthalein reagent and wait a couple seconds.
3. Apply one drop of hydrogen peroxide.

Testing:

The Kastle-Meyer test was first developed in 1903.

A positive reaction for blood will result in a pink color within five seconds. It is important that the test be monitored and positive results recorded promptly. Due to oxidization from the air, a phenolphthalein test will turn pink in about 30 seconds, even if the sample is not blood. Positive results are not limited to human blood or any particular species, and since this test is only preliminary, false positives are possible. There are also substances that will register a false positive to phenolphthalein, like nickel and copper salts, without the addition of the hydrogen peroxide.[172] This is why following procedure and applying chemicals in the correct order is necessary for test integrity.

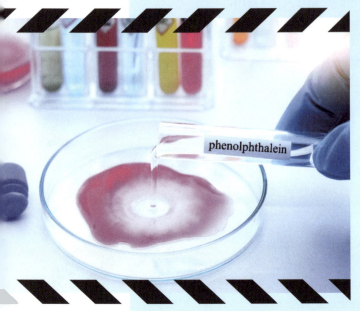

Alternate Light Source (ALS). Alternate light sources use visible, UV, or infrared light to cause biological material to glow (fluoresce) or darken. An ALS device is equipped with the ability to change the wavelength of light to react with different types of fluids. Blood will be absorbed by ALS (or darkened).

Confirmatory Testing. Confirmatory tests provide conclusive results while identifying the biological material. This type of testing is time consuming and expensive, but necessary for confirming the substance and for courtroom testimony. It is important to note that DNA is not a confirmatory test for blood. DNA only provides the DNA, not evidence of the origin of the blood.

The Takayama test was discovered in 1912. This test will confirm that a sample is blood but does not confirm the species of origin. The Takayama test also works best with fresh blood samples. To perform this test in a lab:

1. Apply a drop of the Takayama reagent to the suspected stain on a microscope slide and apply a coverslip.
2. Heat the slide over a low flame.
3. A positive test will result in dark pink crystals of pyridine hemochromogen.

The Rapid Stain Identification (RSID™) Test of Human Blood is effective in isolating human blood from ferret blood, primate blood, semen, saliva, urine, and human breast milk. The RSID™ of Human Blood is capable of detecting the presence of blood in a sample as small as 1 µL (microliter). This test detects the presence of glycophorin A found in the membranes of red blood cells. To perform this test:

1. Mix the sample with a buffer specifically designed for the human blood test.
2. Apply the sample to a paper wick attached to the RSID™ device. Through a process of diffusion, antibodies will react with the sample and form a colored line. If the sample is not human, no line will appear.

3. The device will store the date of the test and an image of the results that can be downloaded to a computer.

The benefit of this test is that it can be completed in just ten minutes.

RSID™ is the preferred test, but a backup test called ABAcard® HemaTrace® can be used to detect the hemoglobin in blood. Antibodies in the test strip react with the hemoglobin in the blood sample. A pink dye band in the window of the device is a positive result. The result only provides a positive result to blood and not to the individual whom the blood is from.

Individualization Testing. Once a sample has been confirmed as human blood, individual testing may be necessary to determine the origin. One test used to distinguish origin is Ouchterlony double immunodiffusion. In this test, antigens and antibodies present in the blood sample are diffused into a gel. Depending on the geometric pattern created by the antigens, similarities between origins can be determined. Identity is determined when the two antigens are immunologically identical. Additional individualized testing will include DNA analysis (Lesson 10) and blood typing.

Viscosity: Having a thick or sticky texture that does not flow easily.

COLLECTION AND PRESERVATION OF BIOLOGICAL FLUIDS

When collecting and preserving biological fluids, such as blood, semen, saliva, and urine, the same procedures that were discussed in Lesson 10: DNA under the "Wet and Dry Biological Evidence" headings will need to be followed. Please refer to this section on the proper methods for collection and preservation of biological fluids.

BLOOD SPATTER ANALYSIS

Due to the viscosity of blood, when it is dispelled during a criminal act, it leaves behind patterns, stains, and shapes that investigators use as clues to determine the location of suspects and victims. The science of blood spatter analysis has gained credibility since the famous case involving Dr. Sam Sheppard and the testimony by Dr. Paul Kirk. An overview of the science of blood spatter patterns and how to interpret the clues will be discussed in detail in Lesson 25: Residues and Patterns.

OTHER BIOLOGICAL FLUIDS

Saliva. Saliva is a mixture of extracellular fluid secreted by the salivary glands in the mouth. Saliva is 99.5% water and also contains white blood cells (DNA), proteins, and digestive enzymes. Saliva is often found at crime scenes, especially those involving a sexual assault.

Areas to search for saliva include cups, mugs, cans, bottles, partially eaten food, bathroom items, and other areas where bite marks, lip prints, or licked items are visible.[173] Once the potential for saliva on evidence has been identified, the investigator will proceed through the presumptive testing, collection, preservation, and confirmatory testing.

Presumptive Testing: The Phadebas® Forensic Press test is used to detect alpha-amylase enzymes in saliva. A positive result applies to any organism that produces alpha-enzymes and is therefore only preliminary. Other biological fluids also produce the alpha-amylase enzyme. If the alpha-amylase enzyme is present in the sample, it will react with a rich blue color on filter paper. To determine if the sample is saliva, confirmatory testing will be performed.[174]

Confirmatory Testing: RSID™ Test of Human Saliva works similarly to the test for saliva described above. Instead of the alpha-amylase enzyme, this test detects the alpha-amylase molecule from human saliva. A suspected saliva sample will be applied to the wick and through a process of diffusion, the device will provide a positive or negative result. There have been cases when primates, bacteria, and fungi have registered positive results, so caution must be taken and repeated testing performed for verification.

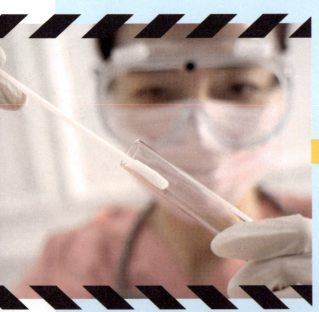

Using Raman spectroscopy, a new portable device developed by Dr. Lednev allows investigators to scan possible samples of saliva with a 92% accuracy rate. This device not only verifies the sample is human saliva but is capable of correctly identifying the gender.[175] The device uses lasers and scattered light readings to create a unique fingerprint without damaging the genetic information in the saliva sample.

Semen. Seminal fluid is a mixture of secretions from four male urogenital glands. One sample of a seminal fluid secretion is approximately 3.5 mL and will contain between 10–50 million sperm cells. Identifying the presence of seminal fluid and subsequently sperm is extremely important because sperm contain high quantities of DNA. Sperm are located by staining the cells and microscopy.[176]

Presumptive Testing: Presumptive testing helps to identify the possibility of a seminal fluid sample and does not guarantee a positive result. The following are presumptive tests used when detecting semen.

The Acid Phosphatase Test (Walker Test) detects the presence of an enzyme called acid phosphatase (AP) produced by the male prostate gland. A positive result for semen will turn the sample a dark purple color in less than one minute. Other biological secretions can produce the same results; therefore, this test is only presumptive.

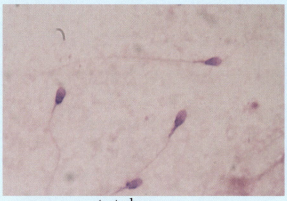
tested semen

Alternate Light Sources (ALS) cause semen to fluoresce due to proteins found in the fluid. This aids in the detection of a semen sample for collection and further testing.

Confirmatory Testing: Once a possible semen sample has been identified and collected, confirmatory testing is required for verification. Christmas Tree Stain is used to highlight anatomical features of the individual sperm. Picroindigocarmine stain turns the neck and tail of the sperm green and blue. Nuclear Fast Red stain turns the head of the sperm red and the tip of the head pink. The ability to quickly identify the anatomical features of a sperm is important because sperm degrade quickly, with the tails breaking down first. To perform this test:

1. Prepare the slide by fixing the cells by heating.
2. Cover the cell debris with red stain and allow to sit for 10 minutes.
3. Wash the stain away with deionized water.
4. Cover the stain with green stain and allow it to sit for 15 seconds.
5. Wash the stain with ethanol.
6. Place over a heat source to dry.
7. Examine the slide under a microscope.

RSID™ Test of Human Semen works similarly to the test for blood and saliva described above. A semen sample will be applied to the wick and through a process of diffusion, the device will provide a positive or negative result in the form of a red line.

CONCLUSION

The study of biological fluids is a complex and tedious process, but when an investigator follows the appropriate protocols, there is potential to uncover important information about the victim and the suspect. Information may include DNA profiles, blood type, genetic disease, species origin, and other identifiers. Blood was the focus of this lesson because it is so important to physical life and spiritual life. An adult human can lose up to 14% of their total blood volume before experiencing major side effects, 20% before experiencing hemorrhagic shock, and up to 50% before death. God has designed the human body with amazing resiliency against injury sustaining blood loss. But nothing compares to the blood loss of Jesus Christ. Every single drop of His blood shed on the Cross was for the redemption of billions of people — billions of people who deserve eternal suffering in hell. Be thankful that the Lord loved you enough to cover your sins in His blood, and now you have the opportunity for eternal life in heaven with Him. The choice is yours.

Lesson 12
Toxicology

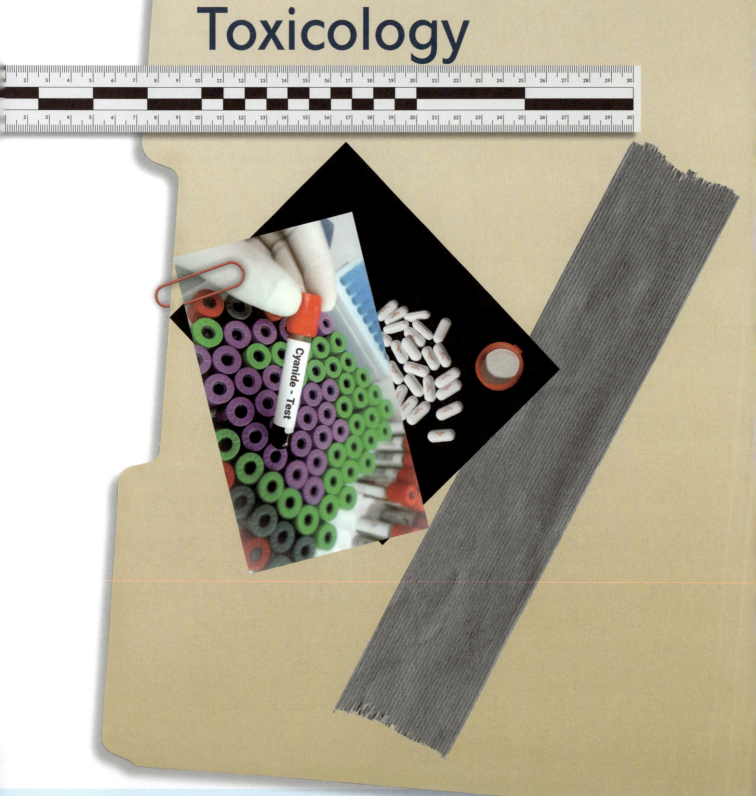

Be sober-minded; be watchful. Your adversary the devil prowls around like a roaring lion, seeking someone to devour (1 Peter 5:8).

Case Study: Toxicology

The following case is one of the most famous unsolved toxicology crimes in history. Prior to 1982, over-the-counter medication did not have tamper-resistant packaging. There were no plastic or foil factory seals on medication bottles. During this period in history, a series of seven poisoning deaths began on September 29, 1982, in Chicago.[177] The first victim was 12-year-old Mary Kellerman, who died after taking an Extra Strength Tylenol® gelatin capsule early in the morning. The same day in a nearby Chicago suburb, Adam Janus died after taking Tylenol® medication. Adam's brother and sister-in-law returned home from the hospital after his sudden death, developed headaches, took the same Tylenol® medication, and both died. In the next few days, three more healthy people mysteriously died. As police began to investigate this series of deaths, it was not until October 1982 that authorities identified the common variable, the ingestion of an Extra Strength Tylenol® gelatin capsule.[178] Toxicological analysis revealed the capsules had been laced with potassium cyanide.[179] Immediately, all Tylenol® was pulled from the shelves across the United States, and the public was warned to not ingest any products containing acetaminophen. This recall involved over 31 million bottles of Tylenol® medication.

The first question for investigators was did the bottles of Tylenol® medication come from the same factory? The answer was no. The bottles originated from different factories but were all located within the Chicago suburbs. This showed that the bottles were not tampered with at the factory level but within the individual stores, likely by the same person. Investigators hypothesized that the suspect had taken the bottles off the shelves in the stores, laced the medication with cyanide, and returned the packages to the shelves unnoticed. The next question was were only the Tylenol® capsules contaminated or did it apply to all forms of medication? Analysts determined it was limited to capsules only. It was believed this was the easiest form of medication to tamper with, since a capsule can be taken apart, emptied of the original contents, and refilled with potassium cyanide.

Facts about the case:

- This case has never been solved and remains open. All documents related to the investigation remained sealed.
- As of 2009, there was a reward of $100,000 for information leading to an arrest and conviction. It is unknown if the reward is still active.
- More than 140 FBI and police investigators worked on this case.
- More tainted bottles were discovered in October in the Chicago area, but they had not been purchased before the recall. Over 75 pills were found to be laced with cyanide.[180]
- Standards on medication tamper-proof packaging were implemented in Tylenol® products but not universally adopted by all medication manufacturers until 1989.
- Tampering with medication became a federal crime under the "Tylenol Bill."
- A medication alternative was developed, the solid caplet shape. This offered the public an option that made medication easier to swallow and without a refillable capsule.

- During the investigation, a man named James William Lewis mailed letters of confession with ransom demands to Johnson & Johnson, the manufacturers of Tylenol®. Lewis claimed if he received $1 million, the poisonings would end. It was finally determined that Lewis lived in New York and could not have been involved in the Chicago poisonings. Due to his false claims and demands for ransom, he was charged with extortion and sentenced to twenty years in prison. Lewis was released from prison in 1995.[181] He still claims he is innocent of the crimes.
- Tylenol® (Johnson & Johnson) is still praised for its immediate response and recall even though it would result in the loss of millions of dollars to the company.

Investigators still hope they will one day solve this case, but as witnesses and original analysts have retired or died, it is unlikely. One still from video surveillance shows one of the victims, Paula Prince, a mother of four, purchasing the Tylenol® capsules on the day she died. A bearded man watching her in the background is believed to be a possible suspect, but this person has never been identified. With the advances in DNA technology, a smudge found on one of the laced Tylenol® bottles is believed to contain a possible fingerprint and/or DNA, but this has not been confirmed. In 2009, court-ordered DNA and fingerprint samples were collected from Lewis, and in 2011 from Ted Kaczynski (Unabomber), but neither were found to have a connection to the crime.[182]

This case is an example of how the negative aspects of a crime initiate a positive move toward consumer safety in an industry. Due to the toxic chemicals in drugs and alcohol, moves toward safer measures are important to protect children and others who are vulnerable from accidentally accessing these substances. And while the analysis of drugs also falls under the field of toxicology, this lesson will focus on the number one drug — alcohol.

As Sherlock Holmes said, "Now is the dramatic moment of fate, Watson, when you hear a step upon the stair which is walking into your life, and you know not whether for good or ill."[183]

Toxicology is a field that analyzes how chemical substances, similar to drugs and alcohol, affect living organisms. This field overlaps with many other disciplines, such as biology, chemistry, pharmacology, and medicine. For forensic scientists, toxicology is primarily focused on the presence and concentration of toxins in biological specimens.

A toxicology report is helpful in providing insight into the drugs that may have affected the physical and/or mental state of a person under the influence of drug and alcohol toxins. Questions that need to be answered by a forensic toxicologist are: Was the person within the legal limit of substance use? Was the dosage appropriate for the individual? Did the influence of toxins impair the person physically and/or mentally? To answer these questions, a forensic toxicologist must be knowledgeable about a wide range of chemical substances and their effects on living organisms. Though toxicology includes a wide range of drugs and toxins, this lesson will focus primarily on the number one drug in the United States — alcohol.

TOXICOLOGY FROM A BIBLICAL WORLDVIEW

The most popular verse associated with drinking alcohol in the Bible is Ephesians 5:18, "And do not get drunk with wine, for that is debauchery, but be filled with the Spirit." The Bible is clear: do not get drunk because it is a gateway to morally objectional behavior. The Bible directly forbids a Christian to be drunk at any time. Drunkenness is described in Galatians 5:19–21 as a selfish desire and sinful: "Now the works of the flesh are evident . . . drunkenness, orgies, and things like these. I warn you, as I warned you before, that those who do such things will not inherit the kingdom of God." And 1 Peter 4:3 describes drunkenness as Gentile (or pagan) behavior. Though the Bible is clear regarding drunkenness, what about a casual drink or one drink? The Bible provides direction when answering this question. There are positive aspects of alcohol use in the Bible that highlight medicinal and celebration purposes. In 1 Timothy 5:23, Paul tells Timothy, "No longer drink only water, but use a little wine for the sake of your stomach and your frequent ailments." Psalm 104:14–15 credits the Creator God as the maker of wine, for it "gladden[s] the heart of man." Interestingly, a small glass of red wine has been shown to help people who have heart conditions.[184] And the very first miracle of Jesus involved Him turning water into wine at a wedding celebration (John 2:3–11).

Though the Bible does not directly state that alcohol is inherently wrong, there are clues and warnings to drinking it, and what is revealed in Scripture is that the negative aspects far outweigh the positive. Alcohol consumption diminishes inhibitions and has been directly linked to shattered families, disorderly behavior, irrational decision making, sexual assaults, vehicular manslaughter, domestic disturbances, and many other criminal acts. Proverbs 23:31–32 compares alcohol consumption to that of a biting serpent, "Do not look at wine when it is red, when it sparkles in the cup and goes down smoothly. In the end it bites like a serpent and stings like an adder." The Bible warns of this behavior in Proverbs 20:1, and Romans 13:13 says, "Let us walk properly as in the daytime, not in orgies and drunkenness, not in sexual immorality and sensuality, not in quarreling and jealousy." The Bible also warns Christians that their consumption of alcohol should not cause another believer to stumble in their walk with Christ. Romans 14:21 tells Christians, "It is good not to eat meat or drink wine or do anything that causes your brother to stumble." Most importantly, drunkenness inhibits the message of the gospel. As a Christian, it is necessary and expected by God to abstain from behaviors or substances that could inhibit the ability of believers to be the light of Christ. This is modeled by the Apostle Paul in 1 Corinthians 9. Paul states in verse 4, "Do we not have the right to eat and drink?" And then he says in verse 12, ". . . but we endure anything rather than put an obstacle in the way of the gospel of Christ." Think about it — if you were a sinner who observed a person you knew to be a Christian in a drunken stupor, what is the first thought that would come to your mind? Most likely it would not be, "How can I become a follower of Jesus?"

WHAT IS TOXICOLOGY?

As stated earlier, toxicology is basically the study of a chemical's effect on living organisms. This field would include studying the effects of those chemicals on biological bodily systems, diagnosis, and proposing treatments. This is why the field is a multidisciplinary approach and includes pharmacists, medical doctors, chemists, biologists, and forensic scientists. Since every person will respond differently to drugs and alcohol due to their personal health, metabolism, and other environmental factors, a toxicologist must consider a number of variables, including exposure time and dosage amount. For a forensic toxicologist, the role primarily involves laboratory testing on bodily fluids, tissue samples, and organs collected from suspects and victims, and is limited to those cases falling under criminal law. Laboratory analysis determines the levels of illicit drugs, prescription drugs, and alcohol in a system, as well as environmental and workplace exposures to toxins.

One of the major branches of forensic toxicology deals with measuring alcohol levels in the body. Alcohol is one of the most dangerous drugs in the United States, with both short-term and lifelong problems. As of 2018, over 86% of adults (18 years and over) had drunk alcohol at least once in their lifetime, over 70% in the last year, and over 55% in the last month.[185] Not only is drinking alcohol an important issue in the adult population, but statistics also show that underage drinking continues to be a serious problem in the United States and that teens use more alcohol than cigarettes or marijuana.

- By age 15, approximately 30% of teens have had at least one alcoholic drink.
- By age 18, approximately 58% of teens have had at least one alcoholic drink.
- Youth ages 12–20 years drink 11% of all alcohol consumed in the United States.
- 4.3 million youth report binge drinking (four or more drinks within a few hours) at least once in the last month.[186]

Alcohol is the number one drug related to violent crime. Since one of the side effects of alcohol consumption is reduced inhibitions, there is an increased likelihood for aggressive behavior.[187] A few statistics include:

- 37% of sexual assaults are committed by intoxicated individuals.
- 50% of all traffic accidents involve alcohol.
- 50% of all homicides involve alcohol intoxication.
- Over 40% of incarcerated criminals were under the influence of alcohol when committing the crime related to their offense.[188]
- Over 65% of domestic disturbances and abuse involve alcohol.

Due to the serious and widespread use of alcohol and its direct connection to violent crime, this lesson will focus primarily on alcohol and how it relates to forensic toxicology.

ALCOHOL

Alcohol is a family of organic compounds that includes methanol, ethanol, and isopropanol. When alcohol is discussed in this lesson, it will be referring to ethanol or ethyl alcohol, which is the primary ingredient in alcoholic beverages. Chemical properties of ethanol include a colorless, volatile, soluble-in-water liquid that is often used as a solvent. Physical properties of ethanol include its ability to depress the central nervous system (CNS). In Lesson 5, you learned that a depressant slows down metabolic systems, including thought processes and reaction times. The depression of the CNS is directly proportional to the concentration of the alcohol in the blood. The proportion of concentration of alcohol is determined by the BAC (Blood Alcohol Content) level. This will be discussed in more detail below.

Metabolism. Understanding how alcohol is metabolized in the body is important to determining the effects on the organs of the body. After alcohol is swallowed and travels down the esophagus, the stomach begins the absorption process. Twenty percent of alcohol is absorbed by the stomach. The small intestine takes up the remaining 80% of the absorption. Finally, alcohol enters the bloodstream. Once it enters the blood, it is distributed in the water-containing components of the body, thereby affecting those organs with high concentrations of water. Two of the organs most affected by alcohol are the liver and the brain. As the blood circulates alcohol through the body, it will pass through the liver and be metabolized. The liver will metabolize 95% of alcohol in the body, while only 5% is eliminated.

Elimination. The remaining 5% of alcohol not metabolized by the liver is eliminated by the kidneys in the form of urine, breath, sweat, breast milk, and saliva. On average, the body will eliminate 0.5 oz (15 mL) of alcohol from the body per hour. The rate of elimination can be affected by a number of factors:

- *Food:* Stomach contents can delay the absorption of alcohol by up to three times more than an empty stomach, but this rate varies based on the type of foods consumed. Foods high in protein and fats will delay the absorption rate at a higher rate than carbohydrates and other types of food.

- *Gender:* Females are generally smaller in their body mass than males. Therefore, females will have a higher BAC when consuming the exact same quantities of alcohol as males.

- *Body weight:* Taller or larger individuals will be able to consume more alcohol than smaller people because they have more volume for the alcohol to circulate throughout the body. Alcohol is also water soluble and will not be absorbed by fat but is absorbed by muscle. A person who is lean and muscular can consume more alcohol than a person of the same size with sufficient fat supplies.

Blood Alcohol Content (BAC). BAC is the amount of alcohol in the bloodstream measured by a percentage and is equivalent to grams of ethanol per 100 mL of blood in the body. The BAC of a person is largely affected by the amount of water in their body, the amount of alcohol consumed, and the metabolism rate. The higher the BAC percentage, the greater the health risk to the individual (see **Table 1**).

Table 1

BAC	Effect on the Body
0.02–0.04%	Feelings of relaxation with impaired memory and judgment
0.08%	Loss of coordination and impaired driving
0.3%	Loss of consciousness, coma, and repressed breathing
0.4–0.5%	Death

What Is Considered a Drink? What is considered a drink is the same regardless of the person's size or gender. What is different is the effect of the drink on a person, which will vary depending on the factors discussed above. In the United States, one drink contains about 14 grams of pure alcohol. This is equivalent to:

- 12 oz of beer containing 5% alcohol
- 5 oz of wine containing 12% alcohol
- 1.5 oz of 80-proof liquor[189]

12 oz.   5 oz.   1½ oz.

The liver can process one standard alcoholic drink per hour. If a person starts to feel the effects of alcohol in the brain, they have consumed more than one alcoholic drink in an hour. Of course, body weight, stomach contents, tolerance, and other factors can affect the metabolism rate.

BIOLOGICAL EFFECTS OF ALCOHOL

Due to its toxic properties, alcohol will have negative biological effects on every system in the human body. For this section, the focus will be on the two primary organs that are negatively affected by alcohol, the liver and the brain.

The Liver. As stated earlier, the liver will metabolize 95% of the alcohol in the blood. Since the liver receives the blood directly from the small intestine (organ of alcohol absorption), it is highly sensitive to excessive drinking. Alcohol is basically a poison that the body must process, and the liver is the first line of defense. During the metabolism of alcohol in the liver, byproducts are created that are toxic to the liver. It is these byproducts that are responsible for the swelling and damage to the liver. There is no question that people who are heavy drinkers are at risk of permanent liver damage, and alcohol is the leading cause of liver failure in the United States. But God created the liver with an amazing feature. Unlike other organs, a healthy liver can regenerate half of itself in one year.[190] An alcoholic with minor to moderate liver damage has the potential to heal the damaged organ over a period of time, assuming they abstain from drinking alcohol. Often, liver damage in heavy drinkers becomes so severe that only liver replacement will save their lives.

The Brain. The human brain is a marvel to scientists. God designed the brain with billions of nerve cells. The nerve cells (neurons) transmit electrical messages to one another through a process called neurotransmission. Scientists have discovered that alcohol directly interferes with the messages relayed through neurotransmission. Not only does alcohol inhibit neurotransmission, but with repeated and increased drinking, the brain will develop a tolerance to the effects of alcohol. The brain can also be permanently damaged due to alcohol use in the form of memory loss, difficulty learning new concepts, slurred speech, and blurred vision.[191] As tolerance develops, people will need to drink more and more alcohol to achieve the same desired feelings. Effects on the brain include loss of coordination, memory loss, and potential death due to the suppression of the activity in the brainstem (see **Figure 1**).

Figure 1 [192]

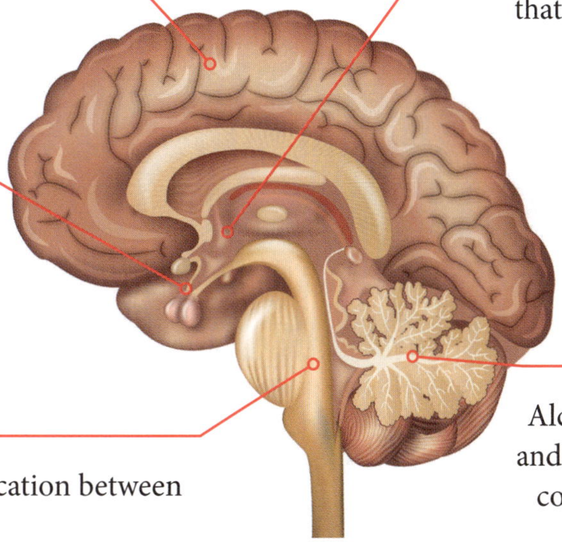

Bad Decisions
Alcohol damages the frontal lobes of your brain, increases the possibility of depression and impacts your emotional state, impulses, and ability to plan or develop ideas.

Learning and Memory
Alcohol will wreck the ability to remember or learn, permanently damages the hippocampus, and destroys memories.

Delayed Responses
Alcohol slows down the communication between the brain and spinal cord.

Impair the Body
Alcohol can damage the part of the brain (hypothalamus) that controls the temperature, blood pressure, and even the rate of your heart.

Slowed Senses
Alcohol will affect the senses and awareness. It destroys the coordination and awareness of potential danger.

Underage drinking is very dangerous to the brain because it is still developing until age 25. Drinking alcohol will slow the overall function of the brain and lead to long-term cognitive impairment. Alcohol affects the nerve cells in the brain and interrupts the communication between the nerve cells and other cells in the body by slowing everything down. Alcohol also inhibits the ability to make wise decisions. Alcohol causes people to be more outgoing and participate in activities they would not normally take part in. Teens find it difficult to control urges when intoxicated, and binge drinking also leads to blackouts and memory loss. Forty percent of youth who start drinking before the age of 15 will develop alcohol disorders lasting their lifetime.[193]

BLOOD ALCOHOL TESTING AND ANALYSIS

Presumptive Testing

Field Sobriety Tests. A standard sobriety test during a routine traffic stop where the individual driving is suspected of intoxication consists of three individual tests: the horizontal gaze nystagmus (HGN), the walk and turn, and the one-leg stand. Sobriety tests are accurate in over 90% of diagnosing alcohol-impaired people.[194] For field sobriety tests to uphold in court, it is generally accepted that the officers strictly follow the 1981 federal procedures outlined by the National Highway Traffic Safety Administration (NHTSA).

- Horizontal gaze nystagmus (HGN) is the "involuntary jerking of the eye" when the eyeballs move from side to side. When intoxicated, the eyes jerk at various angles and with higher frequency. The eyes will also have difficulty following a moving object. The HGN test also provides the positive identification of drug use, some medications, and inhalants.

- The walk and turn test involves the person taking nine steps, heel-to-toe, along a straight line. After taking nine steps, they are then required to turn around and repeat the process back to the officer. A few of the indicators that the person is intoxicated are loss of balance, using the arms to balance, does not follow instructions, and does not take the correct number of steps.

- The one-leg stand test involves the person lifting one leg six inches off the ground and counting by ones (one-one thousand, two-one thousand, and so on) until told to stop by the officer. The process lasts about 30 seconds. Indicators of intoxication include swaying, loss of balance, hopping, and putting the foot down.[195]

- In 1874, Francis E. Anstie discovered there was alcohol in the breath of people who had been drinking.[196] In 1927, the first breathalyzer device was invented by William McNally. Interestingly, this device was used by women to test their husband's breath when he came home at night. The first mobile breath analyzer was called the "drunkometer" and was capable of detecting alcohol in a person's breath but not the BAC. It was not until 1954 that the first breathalyzer was developed that could measure the level of alcohol content. As a person exhales into the breathalyzer device, an electric current measures the amount of ethanol present and sends the information to a microprocessor. A breathalyzer test is not as accurate as a blood test in measuring alcohol content, but it is recognized in court as a valid measure of BAC. Though a person has the right to refuse to take a breathalyzer, they will be subject to a minimum of a 12-month license suspension or possible revoking of all driving privileges.

CONFIRMATORY TESTING

Blood Alcohol Test. If a person is suspected of drunk driving and/or tests positive to a breathalyzer, a blood alcohol test may be ordered. A medical technician extracts a blood sample directly from a vein, and the blood sample is analyzed for BAC. This method of analysis is more accurate than the breathalyzer but is only required in rare cases where confirmatory testing is warranted. Since BAC diminishes over time, in the time it takes between when a person is pulled over for suspected drunk driving and transporting them to a medical facility for a blood test, the percentage of alcohol in the system is likely to decrease and may not reflect the actual BAC at the time of initial contact.

Gas Chromatography. Head space gas chromatography is used in conjunction with a blood sample to separate the components of alcohol from other volatile materials in the blood. The blood sample is placed into a sampling reservoir. The sample is then heated to a predetermined temperature and the vapor analyzed. By comparing the peaks on the graph to known alcohol concentration standards (see **Figure 2**), an accurate determination of BAC can be calculated.

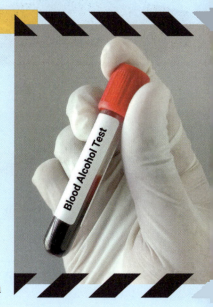

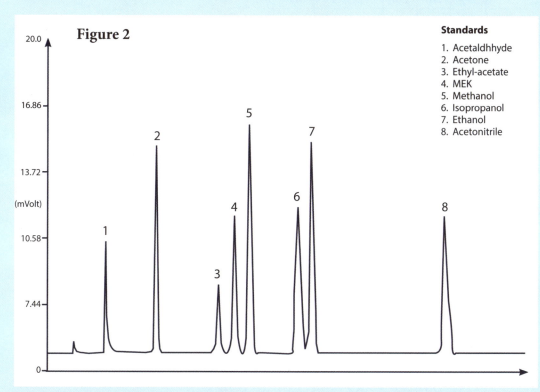

Figure 2

Standards
1. Acetaldhhyde
2. Acetone
3. Ethyl-acetate
4. MEK
5. Methanol
6. Isopropanol
7. Ethanol
8. Acetonitrile

BLOOD ALCOHOL LAWS

In 2000, a federal law to measure drunk driving was enacted that requires all fifty United States to require a limit of 0.08 percent blood alcohol concentration. Basically, this law states that any noncommercial (ordinary individual) driver over the limit of 0.08 percent BAC can be charged as intoxicated. For commercial truckers and bus drivers, the limit is 0.04 percent. Many countries have also adopted this policy, but Sweden has the lowest BAC level at only 0.02 percent. **Figure 3** identifies gender, body weight, and number of drinks within these limits.

Laws were put in place to protect the lives of drivers. The more an individual has consumed, the more likely they are to be impaired behind the wheel of a car and are at an increased risk of injuring themselves and others. Every day in the United States, 29 people die due to alcohol intoxicated drivers, or one death every 50 minutes.[197]

Figure 3[198]

Men									
Approximate Blood Alcohol Percentage									
Drinks	Body Weight in Pounds								
	100	120	140	160	180	200	220	240	
0	.00	.00	.00	.00	.00	.00	.00	.00	Only Safe Driving Limit
1	.04	.03	.03	.02	.02	.02	.02	.02	Impairment Begins
2	.08	.06	.05	.05	.04	.04	.03	.03	Driving Skills Affected - Possible Criminal Penalties
3	.11	.09	.08	.07	.06	.06	.05	.05	
4	.15	.12	.11	.09	.08	.08	.07	.06	
5	.19	.16	.13	.12	.11	.09	.09	.08	
6	.23	.19	.16	.14	.13	.11	.10	.09	
7	.26	.22	.19	.16	.15	.13	.12	.11	Legally Intoxicated
8	.30	.25	.21	.19	.17	.15	.14	.13	
9	.34	.28	.24	.21	.19	.17	.15	.14	Criminal Penalties
10	.38	.31	.27	.23	.21	.19	.17	.16	

Your body can get rid of one drink per hour. One drink is 1.5 oz. of 80 proof liquor, 12 oz. of beer, or 5 oz. of table wine.

Women										
Approximate Blood Alcohol Percentage										
Drinks	Body Weight in Pounds									
	90	100	120	140	160	180	200	220	240	
0	.00	.00	.00	.00	.00	.00	.00	.00	.00	Only Safe Driving Limit
1	.05	.05	.04	.03	.03	.03	.02	.02	.02	Impairment Begins
2	.10	.09	.08	.07	.06	.05	.05	.04	.04	Driving Skills Affected - Possible Criminal Penalties
3	.15	.14	.11	.10	.09	.08	.07	.06	.06	
4	.20	.18	.15	.13	.11	.10	.09	.08	.08	
5	.25	.23	.19	.16	.14	.13	.11	.10	.09	
6	.30	.27	.23	.19	.17	.15	.14	.12	.11	
7	.35	.32	.27	.23	.20	.18	.16	.14	.13	Legally Intoxicated
8	.40	.36	.30	.26	.23	.20	.18	.17	.15	
9	.45	.41	.34	.29	.26	.23	.20	.19	.17	Criminal Penalties
10	.51	.45	.38	.32	.28	.25	.23	.21	.19	

Your body can get rid of one drink per hour. One drink is 1.5 oz. of 80 proof liquor, 12 oz. of beer, or 5 oz. of table wine.

COLLECTION AND PRESERVATION OF BLOOD

Blood Samples from the Living. As stated earlier, the collection of a blood sample occurs at a licensed medical facility by trained personnel. Unlike other times when the skin is disinfected by an alcohol swab prior to blood being drawn from the vein, when retrieving a blood sample for BAC analysis, a nonalcoholic swab must be used to avoid any conflict between results and equipment used in the testing. Once the blood is extracted within an airtight tube, the blood will require a preservative (to inhibit growth of microorganisms) and an anticoagulant (to avoid clotting). To ensure the levels of alcohol concentration remain stabilized in a blood sample, it must be refrigerated. Additionally, a blood sample cannot be stored for a long period of time since alcohol levels have been shown to decrease while in storage.

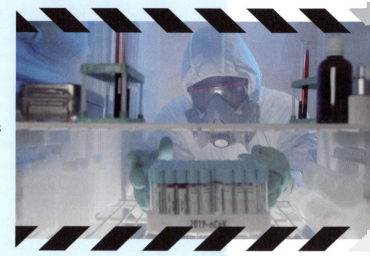

Blood Samples from the Deceased. When a person dies, the blood concentrations can vary in different parts of the body as bacteria begins the decomposition process. During this period, ethyl alcohol is released in the body. This makes it necessary to extract a blood sample from various parts of the body. Similar to living specimens, the blood must be stored in an airtight container with an anticoagulant and preservative and then refrigerated.

WHAT IS ALCOHOLISM?

Alcoholism is classified as a disorder caused by the physical and mental dependency of the human body on alcoholic beverages. The dependency is simply caused from a person drinking too much alcohol, causing a chemical change to occur in the brain. As alcohol consumption increases, dependency increases, thereby increasing the likelihood of physical and mental disorders. Once a person becomes an alcoholic, the physical need for alcohol will override logical decision making, healthy personal relationships, employment, and many other factors. The need for alcohol becomes the primary focus of their daily life.

Alcohol abuse is different from alcoholism. Alcohol abuse occurs when someone drinks a sufficient amount of alcohol, causing behavioral problems, but the person is not physically dependent on alcohol. The reliance on alcohol is more psychological than physiological in those dealing with alcohol abuse. Any use of alcohol by underaged youth is considered alcohol abuse. **Table 2** outlines the key differences between alcohol abuse and alcoholism.

Table 2

Alcohol Abuse	Alcoholism
Failing to complete responsibilities	Compulsion to drink, even when alone
Drinking when dangerous, such as driving a car	Abuse of alcohol consumption regardless of consequences
Drinking even when having problems made worse by drinking behaviors	Failure to acknowledge addiction
Psychological dependence	Physical dependence
Psychological withdrawal symptoms	Physiological withdrawal symptoms

The only treatment for those suffering with alcoholism or alcohol abuse is complete detoxification, rehabilitation, and biblical counseling. Alcohol-related addictions are largely attributed to emotional problems, low self-esteem, and previous family-related alcohol drinking patterns.[199] Sadly, these individuals do not recognize their value and self-worth to the Almighty Creator God. They do not realize that they are image bearers of God and that their bodies are temples of the Holy Ghost upon salvation through Christ. Their comfort is found in a substance that will never be fulfilling.

Alcohol is a depressant to the central nervous system, and the first step in healing is to remove this factor from the brain and body systems so that recovery can take place. Detoxification can last between 4–7 days after the last drink but is largely affected by how much and how long the person has been an alcoholic. General detox side effects include anxiety, irritability, sweating, and nausea. After the last drink is consumed, severe detox side effects may include:

- After 6 hours: possible seizures
- 12–24 hours: hallucinations
- 24–48 hours: headaches and upset stomach
- 48–72 hours: delirium exhibited by increased heart rate, seizures, and fever

Fetal Alcohol Syndrome Disorders (FASDs) are conditions that occur in people whose mother consumed alcohol during pregnancy. Alcohol passes through the umbilical cord in the transfer of blood from mother to child. The severity of the disorder varies based on toxicity. The signs of FASDs can be physically visible as well as behavioral and cognitive. Fetal Alcohol Syndrome (FAS) is the most severe case of the FASDs. These children can be born with physical deformities, learning impairments, behavioral issues, brain damage, growth problems, and other complications. FAS children will experience similar detox side effects to those of an alcoholic adult and will require treatment. Another FASD is Alcohol-Related Birth Defects (ARBD), where children are born with heart, kidney, hearing, or bone issues. FASDs last for the entirety of a person's lifetime, and there is no cure. There are treatments available that can help reduce some of the symptoms. The only way to avoid FASDs is for mothers to abstain from the consumption of alcohol during pregnancy.

CONCLUSION

Contrary to popular television and social media, which portray alcohol as necessary to have a good time, alcohol is an extremely dangerous, addictive drug. Alcohol is the most used and abused drug in the United States. Alcohol is a depressant to the central nervous system with dangerous side effects to every part of the body, with the brain and liver affected the most. Regular alcohol consumption has been linked to liver disease, stroke, memory loss, sleep deprivation, and shorter life expectancy. These health risks are the same for college students who only binge drink on the weekends. Additionally, alcohol use has also been found to be a gateway to other, more dangerous drugs and negative behaviors. The best way to avoid becoming a slave to alcoholism and/or alcohol abuse is to abstain from taking the very first drink. First Corinthians 6:19 says, "Or do you not know that your body is a temple of the Holy Spirit within you, whom you have from God? You are not your own."

Lesson 13
Anthropology

For these things took place that the Scripture might be fulfilled: "Not one of his bones will be broken" (John 19:36).

Case Study: The Killer Clown

In the earlier part of 1978, neighbors living around a home on 8213 Summerdale Avenue in a suburb of Chicago notified police of a putrid smell coming from the home. The home belonged to John Wayne Gacy. Later that year in the month of December, John Wayne Gacy was brought into a Chicago police precinct for questioning. He was under suspicion for the disappearance of a 15-year-old boy named Robert Priest, who went missing from a pharmacy after telling his mom he was meeting a man about a contract job. The pharmacist identified Gacy as the man talking to boys about some work. The police questioned Gacy and searched his house but found nothing. The police were forced to let him go, but he was placed under surveillance. Gacy was so bold that he cooked dinner for the stakeout team one night. While the officers were enjoying a fish dinner in Gacy's home, one of them smelled a familiar stench coming from the floorboards of the house . . . human decomposition. A second search warrant was granted, and this time police made a gruesome discovery — multiple bodies decaying under the floorboards of the house, as well as in a river near the house. As police questioned Gacy, he began confessing to a number of gruesome murders. Two forensic anthropologists, Charles Warren and Clyde Snow, were called in to help identify the bodies. After sorting through all the recovered bones, the anthropologists determined they had identified skeletal remains of 33 male victims. Dr. Snow created a chart for each skull with 35 points of reference to be used in identifying each victim.

John Wayne Gacy was born in Chicago in 1942. He married in 1964 and moved to Iowa to manage his father-in-law's Kentucky Fried Chicken® restaurant. Gacy and his wife had two children and appeared to be happily married. But in 1968, he was accused of sexually assaulting a male employee, and his wife divorced him and won custody of the children. Gacy never saw his children again. In the early 1970s, Gacy moved back to his hometown of Chicago, started a construction company, remarried, and by all public appearances seemed "normal." In 1975, Gacy joined the Jolly Joker clown club, which was an organization that performed for the community and at children's hospitals. His stage name was Pogo the Clown. Gacy went through a second divorce in 1976. In 1978, the year his crimes were discovered, he became the captain of his democratic precinct and escorted Rosalynn Carter, President Jimmy Carter's wife, around Chicago during a visit.[200] Gacy was so dangerous because, by all public appearances, he was an upstanding member of the community, but in reality, he was a serial killer hiding in plain sight. Dr. Jeffrey Walsh, a criminal justice professor at Illinois State University, explained,

[Serial killers] tend to blend into society relatively efficiently . . . that's another thing people are disturbed by. Because of how horrible their acts often are, we sometimes think they look different than us or that we would recognize them. The fact is, many of them have regular lives and blend in, so they don't meet the stereotypical views of what a monster would be like.[201]

Facts about the case:

- Growing up, Gacy was repeatedly abused by an alcoholic father.[202]
- When Gacy was 20 years old, he worked at a morgue. He later confessed to psychiatrists that he slept in coffins and was fascinated with the deceased.
- After his arrest, Gacy confessed that his first murder was in 1972. His murdering spree lasted until 1978.
- The majority of Gacy's victims were prostitutes or runaways. The victims would be brutalized and assaulted before being murdered.
- 29 bodies were uncovered under the floorboards of his home and four in the river behind the house.
- 9 victims were never identified. A facial reconstruction expert created profiles of the 9 victims, and the pictures were distributed, but no one has ever identified these individuals. They remain unknown to this day.
- For his final meal, Gacy requested KFC® chicken, fried shrimp, French fries, and fresh strawberries.
- After repeated appeals, psychiatric evaluations, and claims of split personalities, Gacy was executed by lethal injection on May 10, 1994.
- After his execution, his brain was analyzed for abnormalities by Dr. Helen Morrison. No abnormalities were identified.
- To this day, John Wayne Gacy is considered one of the most dangerous and sinister serial killers in history.

This case utilized skulls to identify the victims and bring closure to their families. Bones hold a wealth of information about a person, their age range, health, biological sex, and much more.

"I am not the law, but I represent justice so far as my feeble powers go." — Sherlock Holmes[203]

There is a famous line from a song released by The Four Freshmen in 1950 called "Dry Bones" that goes like this: "Them bones, them dry bones." The song goes on to teach the skeletal structure of bone configuration in the human body. The word anthropology is derived from the Greek word *anthropos*, which means "man," and *-ology*, meaning "to study." Basically, anthropology is the study of man. There are three basic types of anthropology: cultural, physical, and linguistic. While cultural anthropology deals with people groups and their customs, cultures, and how they interact with the land, and linguistic anthropology focuses on languages, physical anthropology focuses on the study of identifying skeletal remains. Forensic anthropology is the study of skeletal remains to identify deceased individuals for civil and criminal investigation. "Them dry bones" leave behind a wealth of clues into a person's gender, age, overall health, past injuries, and ethnicity.

ANTHROPOLOGY FROM A BIBLICAL WORLDVIEW

Bones are mentioned over 80 times in the Bible. Often when someone thinks of bones, they think of death, but in reality, the bones of a living human are very much alive. Bones contain living cells, blood vessels, nerves, and pain receptors. Ecclesiastes 11:5 talks about the bones in the life of a baby in the womb of its mother: "As you do not know the way the spirit comes to the bones in the womb of a woman with child, so you do not know the work of God who makes everything." What a testimony to the value of human life in the womb! Some verses use analogies between dry, rotting bones and the association with envy or restlessness (Proverbs 14:30; Psalm 38:3); other verses talk directly about physical bones (Job 10:11–12; Psalm 109:24). Also, the Old Testament prophesied that Jesus would not have any of His bones broken during His suffering and death on the Cross (Psalm 34:20), but He would experience something even more painful, as all of his bones would be pulled out of their joints (Psalm 22:14).

When we look at physical anthropology through the lens of the Bible, there are important references to skeletal structure. In Genesis 1:27, the Bible states, "So God created man in his own image, in the image of God he created him; male and female he created them." When examining the skeletal structure between the male and female sexes, there are identifiable differences that cannot be altered. This lesson will discuss those later in detail, but in the skull and pelvis, there are clear differences between the two sexes that reflect God's purpose and design.

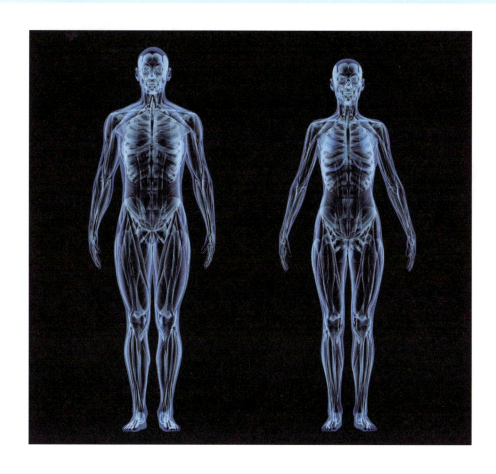

Genesis 2:21–22:

"So the Lord God caused a deep sleep to fall upon the man, and while he slept took one of his ribs and closed up its place with flesh. And the rib that the Lord God had taken from the man he made into a woman and brought her to the man."

There are also skeletal differences in the overall size between males and females. When God created the first female, the Bible reveals that God caused Adam to fall asleep then took one of Adam's ribs and made woman (Genesis 2:21–22). Some Christians believe that males have one less rib than females because of this biblical account, but that is not accurate. Males and females have the same number of ribs — 24, or two sets of twelve. But women's ribs are on average 10% smaller than men's ribs because their overall structure is more petite than that of a male. And God created ribs with an amazing ability: they can regenerate in just two to three months.

God created living bones to grow, repair, and change as we grow. Bones are also as strong as steel and designed with an exquisite composite structure that provides optimum strength. The complexity of the bone testifies to a Master Designer and not to evolutionary chance. It is only when we study human anatomy through the lens of the Bible that we can appreciate the handiwork of God, and when bones are mentioned so often in the Bible, it must be important to human life and to God.

HISTORY

God created bones approximately 6,000 years ago, but the use of bones in criminal investigation is far more recent. In 1894, Thomas Dwight gave a famous lecture at Harvard University about the identification of skeletal remains for forensic analysis. Though investigators were not utilizing these techniques yet, Dwight is recognized as the father of forensic anthropology. It was not until the early 1930s that a more prominent role for forensic anthropologists arose during a historic period called the gangland murders. During the 1920s, the rise of mafia-controlled gangs caused havoc in major cities across the United States. By 1926, there were more than 12,000 murders taking place per year.[204] The gangland murders forced the FBI to turn to anthropologists to aid in the identification of the skeletal remains from murdered victims and gang members.

An important development in a searchable anthropological database occurred after World War II and the Korean War.[205] It became necessary to have an organization dedicated to identifying the skeletal remains of fallen soldiers from war. An organization called JPAC (Joint POW/MIA Accounting Command) was assigned the task of identifying soldiers and returning their bodies to the families. As they began to study and identify skeletal remains, JPAC started a database of bone type, gender, and ethnicity. Today, JPAC is one of the largest human identification laboratories in the world.

In 1962, Wilton Krogman published *The Human Skeleton in Forensic Medicine*, which is now recognized as the "bible" of forensic anthropology. And in 1980, Dr. William Bass started the "Body Farm" at the University of Tennessee in Knoxville, which researches human decomposition in various types of settings. Today, forensic anthropologists are regularly used for crime scenes involving skeletal remains, as well as for archaeological sites where human remains are uncovered in crypts, tombs, and burial sites.

ANATOMY OF BONE

There are 206 bones in the adult human body, and they comprise about 20% of the total body weight. Though bones reach a point where growth stops and they no longer increase in length, bones continually form, repair, and respond to changes in the human body throughout a lifetime. To do this, bones contain two types of cells: osteoblasts (bone makers) and osteoclasts (bone breakers). Osteoblasts are responsible for making bone matrix in which the cells (osteocytes) are buried. To maintain an exchange of gases and nutrients between cells, a special projection called a process connects with other cells inside the bone in a microscopic canal. Osteoclasts (bone breakers) remove bone by secreting a special acid that dissolves bone. While humans are still growing, osteoblasts make bone faster than osteoclasts can dissolve it. Once a person stops growing, these two types of cells work together to create and replace bone without causing further growth.

osteoclasts degrade, causing osteoporosis

There are two types of bone in the human body: compact bone and spongy bone. The two types of bone are what provide the lightweight yet strong design found in bones. Dr. David Menton, an expert in human anatomy, describes the two types of bone below:[206]

- *Compact bone:* The strong tubular shaft of long bones, such as our thigh bone (femur), is made of compact bone. Compact bone itself appears to be completely solid but is actually permeated with many blood vessels running lengthwise within hollow tunnels called Volkmann's canals. Surrounding each of these canals are concentric rings, or layers, of bone that form osteons. This architecture helps give compact bone its great strength.

- *Spongy bone:* Spongy bone occurs mostly inside each end of long bones. Spongy bone receives its name from its appearance, not because it can be squeezed like a sponge. The surface area of spongy bone is vastly greater than that of compact bone, so it is mostly in this type of bone that calcium and phosphorus are stored and removed to maintain mineral balance in our body fluids. Each of the little beams of spongy bone is oriented precisely to impart the greatest strength for the load placed on the bone. Amazingly, when the load placed on bone changes, such as during pregnancy, the spongy bone can change its shape to best accommodate the new load.

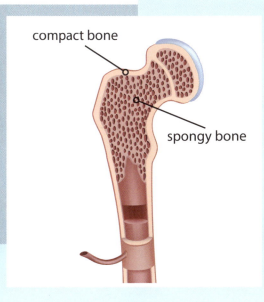

Function of Bones. Bones are responsible for mechanical and biological functions in the human body. Bones have three basic mechanical functions: to protect vital organs, to provide support and structure, and to allow muscle movement. The biological functions of the bones include maintaining the mineral levels in the blood and corresponding tissue fluids. The blood relies on the bones to regulate the levels of calcium and phosphorus for muscle contraction, as well as the formation of DNA and RNA.[207] Bones are also responsible for the production of red blood cells, white blood cells, and platelets in the bone marrow.

Types of Bones. Bones are classified into five types:[208]

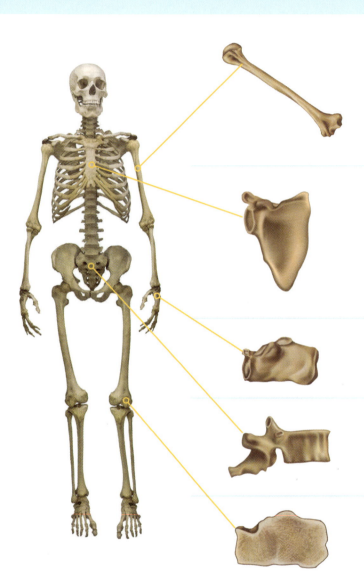

Long bones: The long bones are longer than they are wide. Examples of long bones include the femur, tibia, fibula, humerus, radial, and ulna. Long bones are very useful in determining the height of a deceased person. In the anthropological database are the long bones with their association to a person's gender and ethnicity.

Flat bones: Flat bones are curved in form and protect vital organs. Examples of flat bones include the scapula (shoulder blade), sternum (breastbone), cranium (skull), ilium (hip bone), pelvis, and ribs. As with long bones, flat bones such as the pelvis provide valuable clues into the gender of deceased individuals and are the most reliable of all bones.

Short bones: The short bones are equal in length and width. Examples of short bones include those in the hands and feet, like the carpals and tarsals.

Irregular bones: Irregular bones have a variety of shapes and are neither flat nor long. Examples of irregular bones include the vertebrae, sacrum, and mandible (lower jaw).

Sesamoid bones: Sesamoid bones are short or irregular bones found within tendons. Examples of sesamoid bones include the patella (kneecap) and pisiform (carpal).

EVALUATING BIOLOGICAL SEX FROM BONES

In Genesis 1:27, the Bible tells us, "So God created man in his own image, in the image of God he created him; male and female he created them." This statement is sufficient confirmation that though both males and females are made in the image of God, they are distinctly different as well. God specifically designed males and females for unique roles and to exhibit different features, and this purpose can be seen in their skeletal structures.

The Skull. There are several skeletal differences between males and females in the human skull: cranial mass, superciliary arch, shape of the eye, zygomatic cheek bone, zygomatic process, and mandible. Each reflects the overall design and structure of the two sexes, females with softer curvature and males with more pronounced features. See **Table 1** for more details.

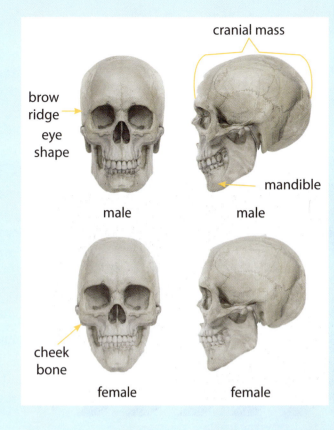

Table 1	Male	Female
Cranial Mass	Thick, dense cranium bone, causing it to be blocky and larger in size	Rounder and tapered
Brow Ridge	Prominent and thick with large features	Thinner, softer, and slenderer
Eye Shape	Square with blunt upper margin	Round with sharp edges in the upper margin
Cheek Bone	Prominent	Softer, less prominent
Mandible	Square in shape	Round in shape

The Pelvis. The pelvis is the most reliable bone in the body to determine sex. God designed females distinctly different from males for one unique purpose: childbirth. Compared to adult males, the typical adult female pelvis has a rounder, flatter inlet from the top and a larger, rounder outlet below. Both features facilitate childbirth (see **Figure 1**). The pubic arch is the angle formed where the hip bones meet in the front. In males, the pubic angle is sharper and more V-shaped. The wider pubic angle of the average adult female pelvis, closer to 90°, facilitates childbirth. The fan-shaped ilium bone makes up the largest section of the hip bone. The ilium bears the upper body weight and supports the spine. The fan-shaped ilium is higher in males but wider in adult females, a wise design considering that females carry extra weight during pregnancy. These anatomical features show forethought and ingenuity from the Creator God.

Figure 1

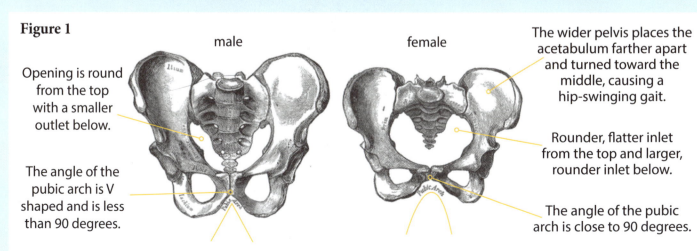

EVALUATING AGE FROM BONES

During fetal development in the womb, bones remain mostly cartilage. The flexibility and bendable nature of cartilage allows the baby to develop within the confined safety of the womb. Whereas an adult has 206 bones, a newborn baby will have 300 bones. As humans grow, cartilage turns into bone (ossification) and bones fuse together. Cartilage grows from within the bone, and this allows for the bone to grow in length at the same time. God created the long bones with a cartilaginous epiphyseal plate, or growth plate. As a person grows, the growth plate will be replaced with bone. Once the cartilage has turned to bone along the epiphyseal plate, growth in length is no longer possible. The absence or presence of a growth plate helps in determining the age of a person.

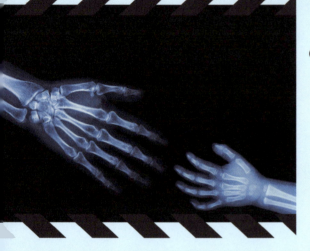

Another method for estimating age is bone fusion. This x-ray shows the noticeable gaps between the bones of the child's hand compared to the same bones that have been fused in the adult's hand. Bone fusion is an ongoing process that continues throughout a person's life, with some bones (sutures in the skull) not fusing until well into their 60s. Sutures are fibrous joints that connect the bones in the skull (see **Figure 2**).

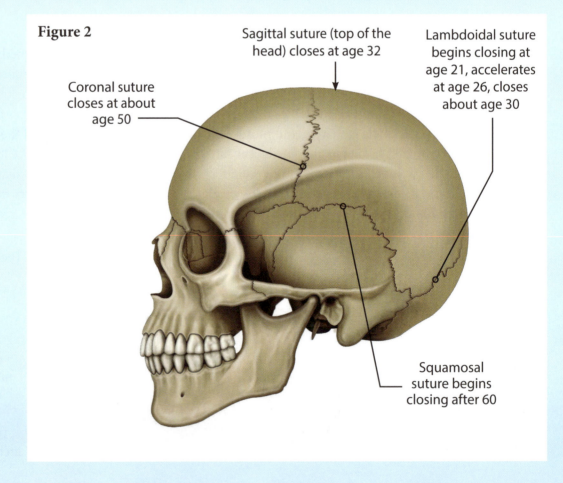

Figure 2

Sagittal suture (top of the head) closes at age 32

Lambdoidal suture begins closing at age 21, accelerates at age 26, closes about age 30

Coronal suture closes at about age 50

Squamosal suture begins closing after 60

EVALUATING ETHNICITY FROM BONES

The overall skeletal structure of humans is similar within the created sexes, but there are identifiable features that differentiate between ethnic groups (or people groups), primarily when examining the skull. First, it is important to answer the question, where did ethnicities (or people groups) come from? Most people use the term "race" to distinguish between the different people groups, but this is an inaccurate term. The Bible states in Acts 17:26a, "And he made from **one** man every nation of mankind to live on all the face of the earth" (emphasis added). There is only one race, the human race.

The human race began in the Garden of Eden approximately 6,000 years ago. God created humans in His image, and they are the only creation for which Jesus sacrificed Himself on the Cross. Adam and Eve willfully chose to disobey God's commands and were expelled from the Garden of Eden. In just 1,500 years, the human population became so vile the Bible tells us in Genesis 6:5 that their thoughts were "only evil continually." A righteous God had to pass judgment with a global Flood to destroy all life that breathed air in their lungs. Only Noah and his family were spared the global catastrophe. When the waters receded and Noah and his family were able to exit the Ark, God told them to multiply and fill the earth. Once again, humans disobeyed God's commands. They did not disperse and instead settled as one people in the land of Shinar. It was here they decided to build a tower to heaven to glorify themselves, not the one true God. Once again, a righteous God must pass judgment for disobedience, and this resulted in the confusion of languages.

The human race was separated into people groups when God confused the languages at the Tower of Babel. As the people groups moved across the face of the earth, they reproduced within their isolated groups, causing certain genetic features to become more pronounced. These genetic features are visible on the skull and can provide insight into the possible ethnicity of an unidentified skull. The three main ethnic categories where these features are classified are European, Asian, and African. Of course, these are general classifications, and there can be exceptions.

Babel:
The modern-day location of the city of Babel in Shinar is south of Baghdad, Iraq.

European

Asian

African

Anthropology

COLLECTION AND PRESERVATION OF BONES

When skeletal remains are located, a series of steps are required to safely collect the evidence and transport them to the lab for examination.[209]

1. **Mapping the scene.** Map out the scene to determine the location of all the bones. Occasionally, ground penetrating radar (GPR) or cadaver dogs may be necessary to ascertain the areas to be excavated.

2. **Surface examination.** Examine the ground for other types of evidence, such as clothing, weapons, bullets, etc. Collect this evidence before extracting the bones.

3. **Soil evaluation.** Topsoil must be carefully removed or sifted for evidence.

4. **Collection.** Depending on whether the body is found buried or aboveground will affect the method of retrieval. Buried skeletal remains tend to be intact. All clothing, jewelry, bones, and any other evidence must be carefully packaged in paper packaging or boxes to prevent contamination. Skeletal remains found aboveground often result in a larger crime scene since animals will ravage the remains and scatter the bones across large areas. The weather and insect activity will also affect the decomposition rates. After one year, the likelihood of locating a complete skeleton is minimal.

5. **Examination.** In the lab, forensic anthropologists will clean the bones and lay them out in the correct anatomical position to determine how much of the skeleton is present. They will also collect samples for DNA analysis.

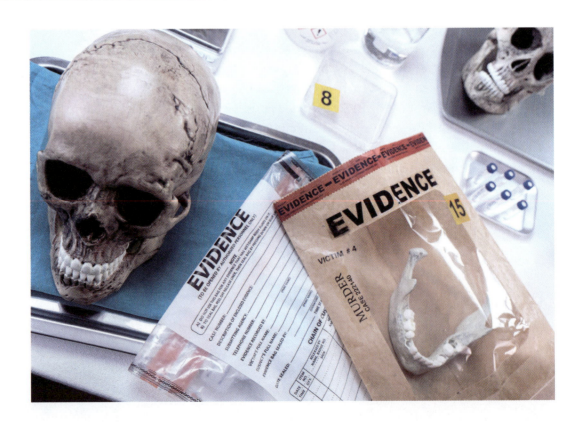

CONCLUSION

Bones serve important biological functions by giving the body support, protecting vital organs, producing blood cells, and storing vital minerals. The living skeleton was designed by God to reflect His glory and design. Once a person is deceased, bones offer insight into the life of that person. Forensic anthropologists analyze bones to determine the health of the individual, any prior fractures and injuries, ethnicity, age, and gender. Forensic anthropology is yet another systemic method of analysis that is only possible because an orderly God created an orderly universe.

Lesson 14
Entomology

All winged insects that go on all fours are detestable to you. Yet among the winged insects that go on all fours you may eat those that have jointed legs above their feet, with which to hop on the ground. Of them you may eat. . . . But all other winged insects that have four feet are detestable to you (Leviticus 11:20–23).

Case Study: Shoo Fly, Don't Bother Me

The murdered body of a man was found on the side of the road. The local investigator was called to the scene. The investigator initially thought the man was robbed and then killed, but upon close examination, the personal effects were still on the man's body, ruling out a robbery. The body had ten wounds, which appeared to be caused by a sickle. The violence of the injuries convinced the investigator the murder was instigated by hatred or jealousy. The investigator proceeded to question the wife of the victim about possible enemies of the deceased. She claimed he had no enemies, but one man had asked to borrow some money.

Since this was a large rice farming community, a sickle was a piece of equipment owned by all farmers in the area. The investigator asked the farmers to bring their sickles for examination. The investigator warned that if anyone refused to participate or tried to conceal their sickle, they would be charged with the crime. According to the investigator's notes, between 70 and 80 sickles were brought for examination and laid on the ground. The investigator noticed that flies gathered on only one sickle. This is the actual historical account of what happened next:

> At the time the weather was hot. The flies flew about and gathered on one sickle. The inquest official pointed to the sickle and said, "Whose is this?" One man abruptly acknowledged it. He was the same man who had set the debt time limit. Then he was interrogated, but still would not confess. The inquest official indicated the sickle and had the man look at it himself. "The sickles of the others in the crowd had no flies. Now, you have killed a man. There are traces of blood on the sickle, so the flies gather. How can this be concealed?" The bystanders were speechless, sighing with admiration. The murderer knocked his head on the ground and confessed.[210]

Facts about the case:

- This is the very first recorded case in history involving forensic entomology.
- This case occurred around A.D. 1235 in China during the Song Dynasty (960–1276).
- The Song Dynasty was one of the first governments to issue an imperial decree requiring investigations into every human death.[211]
- The investigator was a lawyer and death investigator who recorded detailed notes of his investigation. His notes have been translated into English and can be purchased as a book titled *The Washing Away of Wrongs* by Sung Tz'u (A.D. 1247), translated by Brian E. McKnight.
- *The Washing Away of Wrongs* by Sung Tz'u is the first forensic textbook known in history. Tz'u wrote over 53 chapters on his forensic investigations into death scenes.

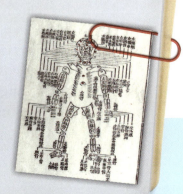

This case is fascinating because Tz'u was able to solve many murder cases without fingerprints or DNA. His intuitive investigations and keen insight into death scenes laid the foundation for forensic investigation. Though he did not understand the complex life cycle of necro-insects nor how this relates to determining time of death, Tz'u will always be known as the first forensic entomologist.

This lesson will provide an overview of forensic entomology and how crime scene insects reveal the timeline of a crime.

"Crime is common. Logic is rare. Therefore, it is upon the logic rather than upon the crime that you should dwell." — Sherlock Holmes[212]

Entomology is the study of insects. In the field of forensic entomology, scientists focus on insects (and other arthropods) that are drawn to decomposing remains and study their life cycles to help in determining time of death. Forensic entomology falls into three distinct fields: urban, stored product, and medicolegal.[213] Urban entomologists will study insects at an individual's place of business or home. This is the person who sprays a home for ants or other pests. Stored product entomologists investigate insects contaminating the food industry. The FDA (Food and Drug Administration) permits insect parts to be present in a variety of foods, but anything beyond the permissible amounts would be subject to investigation.[214] Medicolegal entomology is the investigation into the order of succession of insects on a body, the location of insects on the body, and determining elapsed time of death (postmortem interval, or PMI). This lesson will focus on forensic investigation using medicolegal entomology.

ENTOMOLOGY FROM A BIBLICAL WORLDVIEW

The Bible is not clear on what day of creation week God created insects, but there are clues given to us in Genesis chapter one. The Bible states that flying creatures were created on day five of the creation week (Genesis 1:20–23). The Bible also tells us that God ordered all plants and animals in His creation to reproduce according to their kind. Since insects reproduce according to their kind in their adult form and most adult insects are flying, it is likely they were created on day five of the creation week as an important part of the ecosystem.

Although God created insects for a variety of purposes, their important role in human decomposition would not have occurred until after Adam's sin entered creation. Prior to that, an insect's role likely would have been exclusively related to plants and poop. Genesis chapter one is clear that God's creation was very good, meaning there was no death, no sin, and no suffering. Genesis also outlines God's mandate to all living things to eat of "every plant yielding seed that is on the face of all the earth, and every tree with seed in its fruit" (Genesis 1:29). Insects would have likely been plant eaters with the rest of the animals and Adam and Eve. Once Adam's sin and death entered the world, the insects became an important part of the decomposition process, as well as a food source to birds, reptiles, and other created things, including humans.

The Bible also tells us that some insects were designed as food for humans. Leviticus 11:20–23 says, "All winged insects that go on all fours are detestable to you. Yet among the winged insects that go on all fours you may eat those that have jointed legs above their feet, with which to hop on the ground. Of them you may eat: the locust of any kind, the bald locust of any kind, the cricket of any kind, and the grasshopper of any kind. But all other winged insects that have four feet are detestable to you." John the Baptist lived off locusts and honey: "Now John wore a garment of camel's hair and a leather belt around his waist, and his food was locusts and wild honey" (Matthew 3:4).

> **Spontaneous generation:**
> A debunked scientific theory stating that organisms could arise from nonliving things.

HISTORY

As described in the case study at the beginning of the lesson, in A.D. 1235, investigator Sung Tz'u solved the first recorded case using forensic entomology. A couple hundred years later, insects were used to disprove spontaneous generation in 1668 when Francesco Redi observed maggots becoming flies while exposing them to meat in both enclosed containers and ones open to the environment. Additional information about insect evidence on decaying bodies was documented in the late 1800s by Hermann Reinhard, a German entomologist. Reinhard worked closely with Eduard von Hofmann by completing detailed observations about insects attracted to the remains of exhumed bodies.[215] Because of their research, they are heralded as the fathers of forensic entomology. In 1855, Bergeret d'Arbois was the first scientist to use insect succession (the arrival of different insects to decaying biological material) to determine postmortem interval, known as PMI.[216] Postmortem interval is the time since a person's death.

In 1894, Jean Pierre Mégnin published a book on the applied aspects of forensic entomology. Mégnin was one of the first scientists to publish work on insect life cycles in relation to cadavers. This is an excerpt from his investigation into the discovery of a mummified infant covered in mites:

Entomology   Lesson 14

Mégnin calculated that on the whole body, 2.4 million acari (mites) were present dead or alive. He also calculated that after 15 days, the first generation with 10 females and five males had developed; after 30 days, 100 females and 50 males; after 45 days, 1000 females and 500 males. Finally, after 90 days, 1 million females and 500,000 males were present.[217]

Based on his calculations of the insect activity, Mégnin estimated the infant had been dead a minimum of 5–8 months. This case demonstrated the beginnings of insect life cycles and generations to determine time of death.

By the 1920s, several research articles had been published, providing specific details about the common insect species attracted to corpses. After World Wars I and II, advancements in postmortem interval were further perfected, as well as insect life cycles in a variety of environmental conditions. One of the primary scientific research centers in the world today is at the University of Tennessee's Forensic Anthropology Center Body Farm. These scientists study decaying remains in various conditions to learn about insect activity, life cycles, environmental factors, and anthropological effects in determining postmortem intervals.

CRIME SCENE CREATURES

Flies. Many different types of insects are attracted to decaying remains, but flies are the first insects to arrive on the scene. Within ten minutes of death, flies will begin their life cycle process in the open, exposed wounds and crevices on the deceased animal or human. On average, flies will be attracted to decaying matter up to three months after death. The maggots (larvae) of the life cycle process are the primary scavenger in feeding on the decaying material. There are four types of flies that are considered crime scene creatures in forensic entomology:

 Blow flies (*Calliphoridae*) are larger than the typical housefly and have a green shimmer in their exoskeleton. These are typically the first of the four flies to be attracted to decaying remains.

 Flesh flies (*Sarcophagidae*) love to feed on flesh, hence their name. Whereas most of the fly species lay eggs on decaying materials, the flesh fly deposits maggots directly onto carrion (decaying flesh).

 House flies (*Musca domestica*) are the most common type of domestic fly. One female is capable of laying 500 eggs in her lifetime. They are capable of carrying dangerous pathogens and disease on their bodies, as well as aiding in the decomposition process.

 **Skipper flies** (*Piophila casei*) are "fat loving" and are drawn to decaying fatty tissues and flesh. They get their name from their tendency to skip or jump when startled in the larva form.[218] Skipper flies are one of the most valuable specimens on human remains due to their consistent life cycle process.

Beetles. Whereas flies arrive early in the decaying process, beetles tend to arrive later and feed on the fly maggots. There are over 30,000 species of beetles, and they are the most common type of insect.[219] Of the 30,000 species, only certain types of beetles are attracted to decaying material. From approximately three months until over three years after death, different necro-species of beetles will be frequent visitors to the scene. Depending on the location and temperature, there could be over ten different species of beetles on a decomposing body. A few of the more popular necro-beetles are discussed below.

 Dermestid beetles (*Dermestidae*) are one of the most common beetles collected from carrion specimens. Dermestid beetles arrive between 3–6 months and 1–3 years after the soft tissues have been consumed by other insects.

 Carrion beetles (*Silphidae*) are attracted to decaying animals and humans and have signature orange markings. There are approximately thirty species of carrion beetle, and each one is drawn to different decaying plant, animal, and human remains. Their primary role is to "transform rotting corpses into the much less offensive form of their own bodies"[220] by breaking them down into usable components that can be absorbed by the soil.

 Scarab beetles (*Scarabaeidae*) are identifiable by their unique, club-shaped antennae. This species of beetle is primarily involved in the decomposition of manure and plant materials, but approximately 14 different species have been found on decaying human bodies.

Moths. Moths are one of the last insects to arrive, and the larvae help in the breakdown of hair and fur on mammalian species.[221] This moth is the traditional "clothes" moth that feeds on the natural fibers in clothing.[222] Moths have been very helpful in determining if a body has been moved from one location to another. When the moth larvae pupate, they leave the body to prepare the cocoon. When a body is moved, the DNA of the moth in the cocoon can be tested to connect the body to its original location.

The following chart provides a summary of the information on insect succession and corpse decomposition.

Entomology

Crime Scene Creature Succession Chart

Order of Succession	Insect Fauna	Features in the Corpse Decay	Age of Corpse
1	Blow flies	Fresh	0–3 months
2	Blow flies and flesh flies	Putrid/odorous	0–3 months
3	Dermestid beetles	Rancid	3–6 months
4	Flies (various species)	Rancid	3–6 months
5	Flies and beetles (various species)	Ammonia fermentation	4–8 months
6	Dermestid beetles	Dry (dehydrated)	1–3 years
7	Carrion beetles	Dry (dehydrated)	Over 3 years
8	Moths	Dry (dehydrated)	Over 3 years

LIFE CYCLE OF INSECTS

Once the insects have been identified and collected from a corpse, the next step in the investigation is to determine the age of the insects, as well as the postmortem interval (PMI) of the body. Depending on the insect, they will go through one of two life cycles: complete metamorphosis or incomplete metamorphosis. The word metamorphosis means change. Complete metamorphosis involves four stages, which are egg, larva, pupa, and adult. Within the larva stage, insects will go through instars, or larva stages of growth. In complete metamorphosis, the larvae do not resemble the adult insect since the insect undergoes a complete change while pupating. Incomplete metamorphosis has three stages, which are identified as egg, nymph, and adult. The nymph will often resemble the adult insect since these insects will not pupate or make a complete change. Depending on the insect, each stage of metamorphosis follows a specific time frame under certain temperatures and environmental conditions. The circled areas in the image highlight the instar stages in both types of metamorphosis.

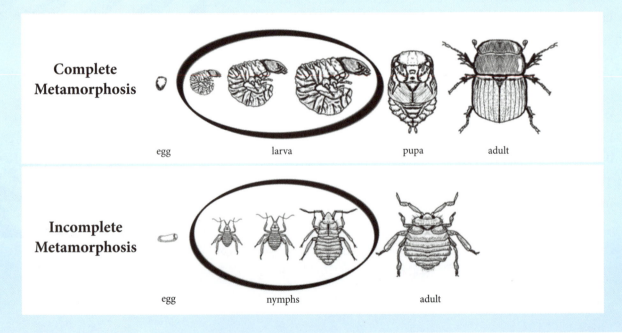

The blow fly is the first insect to arrive on a scene of a decaying corpse. A blow fly's life cycle has been thoroughly researched by scientists when it undergoes complete metamorphosis. During this process, a blow fly will have six stages: egg, first instar, second instar, third instar, pupa, and adult. At each stage, the length of the insect can be used to determine age. Based on the size of the larvae, while considering the temperature and location, an accurate PMI can be established.

The established timeline for a blow fly in each of these stages is applicable when the temperature is 70 degrees. At 70 degrees, the complete blow fly life cycle is approximately two weeks. Anything above or below that temperature will affect the length of the timeline. If the temperature is above 70 degrees, the two-week time frame will be sped up. Imagine a warm day in Miami, Florida, with a temperature of 98°. The two-week time frames may be reduced to just 4–5 days. In the winter months, the life cycle time frame can be slowed down dramatically. Extremely cold temperatures will increase the two-week period to 4–6 weeks or longer depending on frost and snow. If a body is frozen, insect activity and decomposition may not occur until warmer temperatures arrive in the spring. By calculating the Accumulated Degree Hour (ADH), the amount of thermal energy the insect received in the day can be determined. ADH is defined as the heat units calculated by multiplying the environmental temperature by the number of hours in a day. This information assists in age or time since colonization of the insect population.

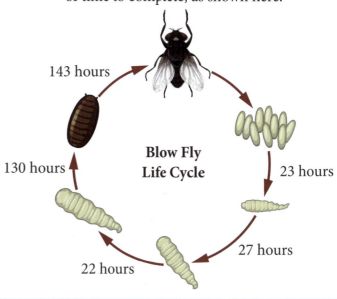

The blow fly life cycle has six parts: the egg, three larval stages, the pupa, and the adult. At 70°F, each stage takes a known amount of time to complete, as shown here.

COLLECTION AND PRESERVATION

Insect evidence should be collected in a certain order to ensure that all life cycle stages present are identified and collected. First, adult flies and beetles should be collected from the natural openings on the body (mouth, ears, eyes, etc.) as well as from any possible wound sites. Adult insects should be placed in a kill jar containing 80% ethyl alcohol and then stored in glass vials containing 80% ethyl alcohol. Second, the eggs, larvae, and pupae need to be collected and stored in the same manner. To collect living specimens for rearing, capture 50–75 larvae of varying sizes, wrap with aluminum foil and ground meat, and place in a ventilated container for transportation to the lab. Pupae do not require ground meat, but they do require oxygen; therefore, a ventilated container is required to preserve these specimens. As with all evidence reviewed throughout the textbook, every vial and/or bag of evidence should be labeled and documented with the required information of the assigning agency. Labels should include the geographical location, location on the body, date and hour collected, case number, and investigator name.

Formula for ADH:

Temperature x 24 hours/day = heat units

THE NECROBIOME

The necrobiome is a microbial community eagerly anticipating the death of plants, animals, and humans. Just as insects aid in the breakdown of decaying material into usable forms of energy, the necrobiome plays an important role as well. This is an excerpt from the article *A Ticking Clock to Determine Cause of Death*:[223]

It [the necrobiome] breaks down their bodies with such systematic, clocklike efficiency that forensic scientists believe it can help them determine the time of death more precisely, especially when other forms of forensic evidence are not available.

The timetable of necro-communities appears to be fairly uniform, no matter what species are involved. So, this method has the potential to be useful anywhere.

After seven to ten days, evidence of insect activity (one of the main traditional ways to measure time of death) begins to rapidly lose its value, but the necro-microbial clock provides a time frame far beyond that of insects.

The necrobiome can be useful to identify more recent deaths, too. Insects attract very different necrobiomes to a decaying organism, depending on the stage of decay. Scientists have discovered a marked shift in the bacterial community within just 24 hours of death.

Simply by classifying the type of bacteria or fungi present and the abundance of certain species, investigators can uncover valuable clues as to time of death. The study of the necrobiome is still in its infancy, and researchers expect us to find even more hidden clues that will help future forensic investigations.

This is just one surprising way humans can benefit by recognizing the complex, organized, systematic community that came from an all-powerful Creator God, who created everything for its purpose (Proverbs 16:4).

CONCLUSION

When God created insects, the world was very good with no death or disease. Once Adam chose to disobey God, sin and death entered the world. Insects became an important part of the decomposition cycle in animals and humans. The ability to study and record the exact timing involved in an insect's life cycle points to the Creator God, who put logical, mathematical processes in motion to reflect His glory. Without necro-insects, decaying plants, animals, and humans would spread disease and be harmful to the environment, but a decomposition process was put in motion by a God with great forethought. It's a process that not only provides insight into the time of death, but that also naturally breaks down substances into the soil while providing nutrition to the insect population. As one biological clock stops, others begin.

Lesson 15
Death Scenes

For as in Adam all die, so also in Christ shall all be made alive (1 Corinthians 15:22).

Case Study: Jonestown

On November 18, 1978, Reverend Jim Jones of the People's Temple (a cult) instructed his members to commit "revolutionary suicide."[224] Nine-hundred eighteen people lost their lives to coerced suicide — murder. The death scene held the record for the single largest loss of American life due to a non-natural disaster until the terrorist attacks on September 11, 2001.[225] Jim Jones rose to fame in the late 1960s. His congregation called him "Father" and his wife "Mother." His church (cult) promoted inclusivity for all people, regardless of ethnicity. Hundreds flocked to his charismatic teaching because he was a showman and able to be whatever the people needed him to be, such as a healer, their god, a politician, and professed savior. Through a narcissistic need for power and propagation of fear, Jones had the unique ability to brainwash his cult members into following him anywhere.

By the early 1970s, defectors of the People's Temple began to reveal the truth about Jones' staged (fake) healings, false teachings, socialist/Marxist ideology, sexual abuse, beatings, whippings, and other coercion tactics. As the authorities and the media began to investigate, Jones became fearful of being exposed and purchased land in Guyana, South America, for a new refuge. The People's Temple began flying its members down to the new compound located in the middle of the jungle. Jones told his people they were going to the "Promised Land" for a socialist utopia.

Facts about the case:

- In 1956, Jim Jones started the first multi-ethnic church in Indiana when he was only 25 years old.

- In 1965, Jones prophesied an impending nuclear war and convinced his congregants to move to California. One-hundred forty church members followed him to Redwood Valley. During this time, he began to preach socialist/Marxist ideology and is recorded saying, "Socialism is God."[226] He separated husbands and wives, and parents from children in communal living. Jones believed that families were the "sickest relationships of all."[227]

- During this time, Jones became addicted to drugs. His trademark sunglasses were to hide the drug use, but he told his church members that he wore glasses because the spirit was so strong in him that looking in his eyes would be too bright of an experience for them.

- Jones continued to propagate his agenda of fear by telling his followers that the government was coming for their children, they would take all the poor people away, and blacks would be put in concentration camps. He fostered paranoia to the point that everyone began to live and be consumed by the church.

- The People's Temple moved to San Francisco, and Jones was able to gain political power. He became so powerful that he was invited to the inauguration of President Jimmy Carter.

- In 1973, Jones decided to build an agricultural settlement in English-speaking, socialist Guyana called the "Promised Land." The settlement contained a clinic, pharmacy, kitchen to feed hundreds, schools for the children, and everything a community needs for survival.

- The "Promised Land" called Jonestown in Guyana was built in an isolated area in the jungle, 160 miles from the closest city. There were only two ways into Jonestown: flying over the jungle or a 19-hour boat trip. This kept the residents of Jonestown separated from society, and it was virtually impossible to escape.

- In Jonestown, beatings continued. A pit was dug where people could be thrown for periods of time. All mail coming in and going out was censored. Food and sleep were scarce. Every day began at 5 a.m., and Jones would wake up the residents almost every night over the loudspeaker with "White Night" drills, ranting and raving about how they needed to work harder.[228]

- Over 900 people were living in Guyana by 1977. Relatives in the United States became concerned about their safety and formed a group called the Concerned Relatives. The Concerned Relatives began writing their congressmen for help. Congressman Leo Ryan from California's 11th congressional district decided he would take a delegation to Jonestown to investigate.
- On November 14, 1978, Ryan, 17 Concerned Relatives, NBC staff, and a few members of Ryan's staff landed in Georgetown, the capital of Guyana.
- After heated negotiations with Jones, on November 17, 1978, Ryan and 16 others boarded a small plane and landed on an airstrip a few miles from Jonestown.
- The People's Temple congregation had been rehearsed in what to say and how to act for the delegation. In a desperate attempt to escape, Vernon Gosney (Temple member) slipped NBC correspondent Don Harris a note stating, "Vernon Gosney and Monica Bagby: please help us get out of Jonestown."[229] Ryan spoke to Gosney, who warned him of the terrible danger he was in, but Ryan believed that as a member of the United States Congress, he had a hedge of protection.
- On November 18, 1978, Ryan and a few others stayed the night in Jonestown. By 3 p.m. that day, 14 more Temple members expressed wishes to defect. Ryan decided he would stay another night and be sure there were not others wanting to leave the compound when an attempted assassination on his life failed. Ryan, realizing the danger, left on the truck with the defectors, his staff, and media.
- Ryan's delegation arrived at the airfield at 4:45 p.m., but the planes did not arrive until 5:10 p.m. A Jones loyalist, Larry Layton, open fired on one plane as it taxed off the runway. Several were wounded, including Vernon Gosney. Other Temple members arrived at the runway. They shot and killed Congressman Ryan, three journalists, and a defecting Temple member, and wounded nine others.
- Once Jones received word that Congressman Ryan was dead, he summoned everyone to the pavilion. He told them that the U.S. government would be arriving to kill them all. His entire last statement to the people of Jonestown was recorded. He told them, "If we can't live in peace, then let's die in peace."[230]
- Large vats of Flavor Aid® (generic Kool-Aid®) laced with cyanide were prepared. Children were killed first by injection while the parents watched. Jones then instructed those remaining to drink the Flavor Aid® cyanide. Some members resisted and were injected by needle.
- Jim Jones, after watching the slow and horrifying death by cyanide of hundreds of his people, was the only member to die of a single gunshot wound to the head.
- Nine-hundred eighteen people lost their lives in Jonestown, and over 300 bodies were never identified, almost all of them children. They are buried in Evergreen Cemetery in Oakland, California.

The Jonestown massacre was a challenging case for U.S. officials to investigate. Not only did it occur in a foreign country, but there were multiple crime scenes, weapons, and victims. Amazingly, God, knowing the depravity of sinful humans, created biological processes in decomposition that provide clues to when, how, and in what position a person died. These fascinating details will be discussed in the following lesson.

"Education never ends, Watson. It is a series of lessons, with the greatest for the last." — Sherlock Holmes[231]

==Any death scene, with one human life or multiple, are all traumatic to investigate.== The loss of one human life is tragic, but when there are many individuals, the question asked most often is "Why?" Why did people drink the cyanide? Why do people follow the direction of cult leaders? Why do individuals carry out mass murder on innocent civilians? Why does a loving God allow these deaths? These are difficult questions to answer from a secular perspective, but Christians recognize the depravity of sin and the need for a Savior. Death occurs because humans willfully chose to disrupt a perfect creation and disobey a righteous God.

Because death scenes contain sensitive evidence, they require an expert to analyze the scene, point out essential evidence, and identify trends or similarities to other crimes. Looking for patterns in death scenes can often link to the trail of a serial killer. Death investigators are responsible for conducting the investigation of a human corpse, outlining the circumstances surrounding the death, and providing the medical examiner with details about the scene. These responsibilities are targeted toward determining the cause, mechanism, and manner of death. If possible, the medical examiner should view the body at the crime scene prior to removing it from the scene. Actions by the death investigator (i.e., medical examiner or pathologist) include:

- Investigation of a death scene by documenting a general description of the location of the body, clothing on the body or near the body, and trauma to the body.

- Examination of the body for trace evidence. This would include looking for fibers, hairs, blood spatter, or fingerprints.

- Determining an ID on the deceased based on identification found on the body (such as a driver's license) or through fingerprint, DNA, and/or dental records. Sometimes, this includes a positive ID by someone who knows the deceased.

- Obtaining medical records for the deceased. It is important to determine if the deceased had any preexisting health conditions, fractures, or other injuries that may be discovered during the autopsy.

DEATH FROM A BIBLICAL WORLDVIEW

Death was never part of God's original plan for His creation. At the end of the creation week, everything was very good (Genesis 1:31). Something that is very good in the eyes of a perfect God does not include death or suffering. Many people ask how a God of love can allow so much pain, suffering, and death. The answer is that Adam and Eve willfully chose to disobey God's command, bringing sin and death into the world. This was not God's choice, but man's. Romans 5:12 tells us, "Therefore, just as sin came into the world through one man, and death through sin, and so death spread to all men because all sinned." The Greek word used here for men, *anthropoid*, means men and women. And the consequence of sin is death (Romans 6:23).

Death is hard to reconcile with for both Christians and nonbelievers. The loss of a family member or close friend is heartbreaking. This loss is handled very differently depending on whether someone is a follower of Christ or a follower of the world. Those who willfully reject Christ view death as a final act. They believe there is no hope of seeing their loved ones again. Bill Nye the Science Guy, a well-known evolutionist and atheist, stated, "It looks like to me this life is all you get. This is it. There's nothing afterwards."[232] This is the common ideology in the secular culture. But Christians recognize that eternity awaits them after death. According to God's perfect Word, eternity will be spent one of two ways: in heaven with our Creator God or separated from God in the eternal torment of hell (Matthew 25:46). Whereas nonbelievers experience hopelessness in death, Christians cherish the hope of seeing those who are fellow believers restored one day in heaven.

God is sovereign and therefore knew that man would sin against His commandments, but in His mercy, God sent His only Son, Jesus Christ, to earth to die for the sins of humanity. When Christ arose from the dead, He conquered death and provided a way for us to spend eternity with Him. First Corinthians 15:55–57 says, "O death, where is your victory? O death, where is your sting? The sting of death is sin. . . . But thanks be to God, who gives us the victory through our Lord Jesus Christ."

Romans 6:23:
"For the wages of sin is death, but the free gift of God is eternal life in Christ Jesus our Lord."

Matthew 25:46:
"And these will go away into eternal punishment, but the righteous into eternal life."

STAGES OF DECOMPOSITION

Decomposition of the human body begins within four minutes of death.[233] The rate of decomposition is affected by several factors but primarily by the environment in which the body is located. There are four overarching stages of decomposition: autolysis, bloat, active decay, and skeletonization.[234]

Autolysis. Autolysis begins immediately after death and is a form of cellular self-digestion. When the circulation of oxygen stops, excess carbon dioxide causes cell membranes to rupture. Enzymes that are released from the membranes begin to eat the cells from the inside out. During this stage, *pallor mortis* is the first indicator of decomposition.

- *Pallor mortis* begins between 15–20 minutes of death and results in an extremely pale color in the skin.

- *Rigor mortis* is the stiffening (Latin meaning of *rigor*) of the joints and muscles due to a loss of adenosine triphosphate (ATP). ATP is the substance that allows energy to flow to the muscles for them to function. Without ATP, muscles become stiff and inflexible.[235] The stiffening of muscles begins between 30 minutes to one hour after death. *Rigor mortis* peaks at 12 hours before diminishing. This time frame can be affected by the environmental conditions, drugs in the system, and other factors. Occurring almost simultaneously with *rigor mortis* is *livor mortis*.

- *Livor mortis* (or lividity) is the pooling of blood from gravity to the lowest point as the heart stops the circulation of blood through the body. This results in a purplish-blue color on these portions of the body. The location of *livor mortis* provides clues as to whether a body has been moved from one location to another. If a person died on their back and *livor mortis* forms in this region, and then the body is discovered on its stomach, investigators would know that the body had been moved due to the purplish-blue color on the back of the individual.

- *Algor mortis* is the gradual cooling of the body after death until it reaches the ambient temperature.

Bloat. Bloating is the result of the cellular digestion occurring during autolysis. The gases created from autolysis cause the body to double in size. During this stage, the body will also begin to emit putrid odors called putrefaction. Bloating begins 4–10 days after death. Insect activity is often prevalent in the orifices of the body.

Active Decay. During active decay, all the fluids in the body seep into the surrounding ground surface where the body is lying. The odor is very strong, and insects continue to break down the body tissues and begin to pupate in the surrounding soil. Skin beetles may become active on the decomposing body. This process, also called butyric fermentation, occurs 10–25 days after death.

Skeletonization. Skeletonization begins 25–50 days after death and can last for years. Since the process is influenced by several environmental factors, there is no exact time frame for skeletonization. After several weeks, the nails will become dislodged from the body. When the process is complete, only dry skin, hair, and bones will remain. Common insects to the scene are beetles, mites, and the clothes moth. Additionally, plants and fungi begin to inhabit the body.

skeletonization

FACTORS AFFECTING DECOMPOSITION

As stated above, the process of decomposition can be expedited or impeded by a variety of factors. Depending on whether the body is located inside a climate-controlled setting or open to weather and temperature changes can greatly determine the speed of decomposition. The factors below are the primary mechanisms that will influence the rate of decomposition:

- **Temperature and Humidity.** Lower temperatures will slow down the microbes and insect activity, while low humidity dries the corpse and aids in the mummification of the remains. Higher temperatures and high humidity will speed up the rates of decomposition.

- **Accessibility.** Is the body buried beneath the ground versus above the soil? How acidic is the soil? Is the body in the shade or directly in the sunlight? Is the body wrapped? Each of the factors will affect the decomposition timeline. Buried bodies will decay slower than bodies exposed to direct sunlight, warm temperatures, and the elements. It is not uncommon to find bodies tightly wrapped in blankets, tarps, or other types of coverings. When a body is wrapped, it will decompose at a slower rate. Clothing can also have the same effect. Bodies found in heavier clothing will decompose slower than those found in thinner, lighter clothing. The more exposed the body is to the environment, the faster the rate of decomposition.

- **Cause of Death.** Large, gaping wounds lead to faster decomposition, and the scent will attract predators and scavengers to the remains.

- **Percent of Body Fat.** The more fat on the body, the faster the rate of decomposition. Leaner, thinner bodies will decompose slower.

- **Drugs.** As discussed in Lessons 5 and 14, when there are amphetamines in the system, the accelerated nature of this type of drug will cause insects to speed up their rate of decomposition. In contrast, depressants will slow down insect activity and life cycles.

THE AUTOPSY

Once a body has been cleared from the crime scene, it will be transported to the medical examiner (pathologist) for an autopsy. During the autopsy, the pathologist will be looking for the cause of death, injuries, toxicological influences, and the identification of the deceased.

The autopsy will begin with a thorough external exam and then include a detailed internal exam. The wound sites will be analyzed to determine the type of weapon used. The autopsy is completed in six stages:

1. *Y-incision:* The Y-incision is a y-shaped incision that opens the breastplate of the body to reveal the major organs. The incision is from shoulder to shoulder to the lower sternum and then straight down to the pubis.

2. *Removal of organs:* The organs are removed from the body, sometimes as one unit and occasionally one at a time, and subsequently weighed. During this stage, blood samples will be taken to analyze for toxins and DNA signatures.

3. *Stomach contents:* Stomach contents are examined to determine if the person had eaten recently and what the contents include. Since the process of digestion is a determined time frame, observing the stage of digestion in the stomach contents provides clues to the time of death.

4. *Sample collection:* Additional liquid samples are extracted from the ocular fluid, gall bladder, liver, and urine. Since toxin distribution is not always consistent in body organs and tissues, these additional samples are examined for drugs and poisons.

5. *Head and brain:* The head is first examined for external injuries. An incision is then made on the scalp to open the head and remove the brain for a thorough examination.

6. *Conclusion:* Once this systematic process is complete, the organs are returned to the body and it is sewn up for burial.

Once the autopsy and the toxicology analysis are completed, the pathologist will review the results and prepare a report for the investigators. One of the key conclusions needed by the officers is the cause of death. Was it natural or murder? A stabbing or a heart attack? Understanding the mechanism and the manner of death will lead the investigators toward their next course of action. The mechanism of death is how a person dies. Was the death caused from asphyxiation by strangulation, hemorrhaging due to blood loss, or a drug overdose?

Manner of death falls into five categories:

1. *Natural:* Natural death is the largest category and includes death by old age, heart attack, cancer, strokes, and other natural causes.

2. *Accidental:* Accidental deaths are caused by unplanned events, such as a car crash, house fire, or head trauma.

3. *Suicide:* Suicide is a death inflicted by an individual's own choice. This can occur by a self-inflicted gunshot, drug overdose, hanging, drowning, or other form of suicide.

4. *Homicide:* A homicide is the deliberate killing of one human by another. Homicide falls into three categories: murder, manslaughter, and justifiable homicide.

5. *Undetermined:* An undetermined death is a death that has an unknown cause or cannot be determined by the medical examiner.

Asphyxiation: Suffocation; unconsciousness or death caused by a lack of oxygen.

COLLECTION AND TRANSPORTATION OF BODIES

In preparing a body for transportation to the medical examiner, the investigator should first place paper bags over the hands and feet to ensure preservation of key evidence. As reviewed in previous lessons, all biological evidence (DNA, bodily fluids, blood, etc.) is packaged in paper bags to inhibit the growth of bacteria. Second, the body should be wrapped in a sterile, white sheet for transportation. Wrapping the body ensures any hairs or fibers that become dislodged from the body during transportation are collected for analysis. Any personal effects found with the body must remain with the person and be transported to the morgue. Personal items will often aid in determining the identity of the deceased.

CONCLUSION

Contrary to the ideology of the mainstream culture, earthly death is not final. Hebrews 9:27 is a reminder of the punishment of sin: "And just as it is appointed for man to die once, and after that comes judgment." Every human body will die an earthly death, but the soul will live for eternity. As Christians, there is hope in the death of loved ones, the hope of seeing believers again in heaven with the Lord. Those who do not believe in the truth of God's Word often feel hopelessness, finality, and separation upon the death of those closest to them.

Regardless of one's belief about death, everyone wants answers surrounding a deceased loved one. Did they die naturally or due to suspicious circumstances? The team of police investigators, medical investigator, and pathologist work together to bring resolution to families. Utilizing analysis of the crime scene and evidence visible on the body, the team will successfully ID a deceased individual while determining cause and manner of death.

TRANSITORY EVIDENCE

UNIT 5

Lesson 16
Human Fingerprints

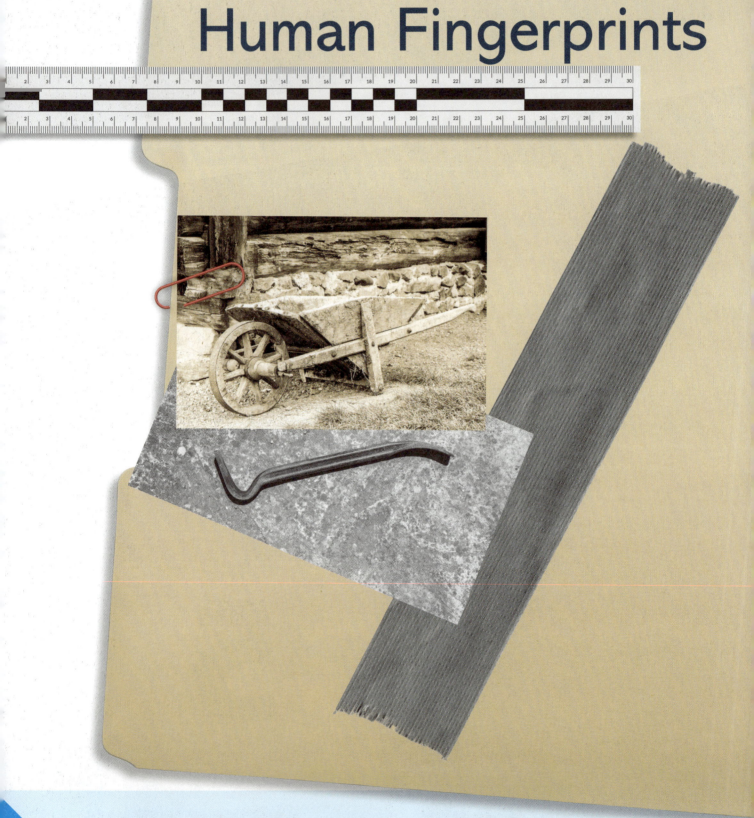

I praise you, for I am fearfully and wonderfully made. Wonderful are your works; my soul knows it very well (Psalm 139:14).

Case Study: The Patent Fingerprints

Prior to 1900, fingerprints had never been used to convict a criminal in court in the United States. This changed in 1910, when the very first criminal case to use fingerprints as evidence resulted in a conviction using said evidence. Around 2:00 a.m. on September 19, 1910,[236] Thomas Jennings rolled a wheelbarrow under a window at 1839 West One Hundred and Fourth Street. Standing on the wheelbarrow and using a crowbar, Jennings pried open the window and entered the home of Clarence Hiller and his family in South Chicago. Jennings entered the bedroom of Hiller's daughters. The two daughters were alerted to the intruder and began screaming, which woke up Clarence. Clarence confronted the intruder, Thomas Jennings, and during the scuffle, both men fell down the staircase. Hiller's daughter Clarice told police she heard gunshots before Jennings fled through the front door. Hiller collapsed lifeless from two gunshot wounds at the foot of the stairs.[237] Sherlock Holmes so famously said, "To a great mind nothing is little."[238] In a case, the smallest detail is important. Neighbors notified the police, who apprehended Jennings a few blocks from the Hiller home. Jennings gave the police a false name of William Jones. During the crime scene examination, Captain William F. Evans observed "fingermarks," an early term for fingerprints, on the front porch rail. The porch rail had been freshly painted. Clear, visible fingerprints were impressed into the wet paint. Impressed fingerprints in a soft surface that result in a three-dimensional impression are called plastic prints. Investigators cut the wood away from the rail and delivered it to the police station. Black powder was sprinkled over the impressed prints to make them more visible for examination. It was quickly discovered that William Jones was really Thomas Jennings, a convict and recent parolee.

Facts about the case:

- When police apprehended Jennings, his coat was covered in blood, and he was carrying a loaded revolver.
- Captain Evans was a fingerprint operator in the Bertillon identification system (also known as anthropometry). This case occurred during the period between Bertillon identification (identification based on body measurements) and the change to fingerprint identification.
- Captain Evans had a son named Emmett, who was also a police investigator. In 1904, Evans sent his son to the World's Fair in St. Louis to learn about the new technique of fingerprinting. He told his son, "I don't think it is any good but look and see."[239] Emmett returned with positive remarks for the new system of identification, and Chicago began collecting fingerprints from criminals in 1905.
- Captain Evans compared the fingerprints to those on file for the suspect and found 33 points of minutiae to be a perfect match.[240]

- Other than the three fingerprints (index, middle, and ring fingers of the left hand) left behind on the front porch rail, all other evidence linking Jennings to the case was circumstantial.
- Captain Evans was one of the first fingerprint examiners in the United States.

During the trial, Jennings' defense attorney, W.G. Anderson, questioned the veracity of fingerprint identification. In forensic science, it is difficult to enter new evidence into the courtroom proceeding if it does not have precedence in the system. In an attempt to disprove the uniqueness of fingerprints, the defense team acquired random fingerprints from the public to show that two people could have the same fingerprint patterns, only to discover that it backfired. It was quickly discovered in the courtroom that their sample did not have matching fingerprints.

Jennings was convicted of the murder of Hiller and sentenced to be hanged. He appealed the conviction on the basis that fingerprints were not infallible. But in 1911, in *People v. Jennings*, the Illinois Supreme Court made a ruling that stands as the landmark case for the use of fingerprints as a form of unique identification. The court upheld the conviction due to "Standard authorities on scientific subjects discuss the use of fingerprints as a system of identification, concluding that experience has shown it to be reliable."[241] Thomas Jennings was hung for his crimes in 1912.

The unique characteristics that make up the friction ridge skin on every individual (and some animals) point to the ingenuity of the Creator God. Job 37:7 tells us, "He seals up the hand of every man, that all men whom he made may know it."

Fingerprint patterns are the primary tool used for criminal identification. Fingerprints are the patterns created by the friction ridge skin located on the entire surface of the hands and feet. Due to the design of friction ridge skin, an uneven surface is created that provides a nonslip surface and firmer grip. Fingerprints develop in the mother's womb between 10 and 16 weeks of fetal development and remain with an individual until the dermal and epidermal skin fully decomposes after death. The value in fingerprint identification lies in three qualities: individuality, identifiable characteristics, and unchanging structure. The beauty, design, and complexity behind the structure of friction ridge skin testifies to a Master Artist and Creator God who loved every single person so much He gave them 20 unique friction ridge skin patterns (ten on the fingers and ten on the toes) unlike anyone else who will ever live on the face of the earth . . . past, present, or future.

FINGERPRINTS FROM A BIBLICAL WORLDVIEW

When studying friction ridge skin, the book of Psalms most closely manifests the unique design reflected in fingerprint patterns. Psalm 139:13–14 says, "For you formed my inward parts. . . . I am fearfully and wonderfully made." Job 10:8 describes the hands of God as having "fashioned and made me." Genesis 1 clearly describes the creation of humans as supreme to all other created things because they are formed in the image of God. God designed fingerprints to develop early in the womb. This is a testament to the value of a human life. At ten weeks of fetal development, humans have unique fingerprint patterns that remain with them for their entire lifetime. There is no question this person is fully human and entitled to the life God has planned for them. Also, at the moment of fertilization, a human has six feet of DNA that contains all the genetic instructions to form their fingerprints, as well as the information needed to fully develop. At the moment of fertilization, that tiny single-celled person is fully human. The abortion of a child in the womb at any point in a pregnancy is nothing short of the murder of a human life.

Fingerprints not only provide identifiable features, but the surface of friction skin is extremely sensory and can relay information directly to your brain. Imagine if you were blindfolded and someone placed a feather in your hand. Would your sense of touch allow you to distinguish the object? Absolutely! The intricate design of the hands (and feet) provides humans with the ability to pick up a heavy gallon of milk and an air-filled marshmallow at the same time while discerning the difference.

Also, the Creator God recognized the benefit of providing humans with a nonslip surface on their hands and feet. Therefore, the hands can grasp a cup without dropping it, and the feet walk barefoot without slipping. The uneven surface created by friction skin provides grip. Think about it — what is on the bottom of sneakers? Ridges and an uneven surface. Shoe manufacturers simply copied God's brilliant design when they developed nonslip footwear. And what is even more amazing is that God could simply have created friction skin to aid in gripping, but He went one step further and gave humans a special identity through their friction skin patterns in the form of over 10,000 unique details. In the estimated 108 billion humans that have lived in the last 6,000 years, there are not two people who even had one identical fingerprint, much less even ten points of minutiae that are identical. And imagine what the fingerprints of Jesus, who was born as a perfect human, must look like. Those who are believers know they will be able to look at the fingerprints on the nailed-scarred hands of the Savior when they get to heaven.

HISTORY OF FINGERPRINTS

The history of fingerprints dates back over 4,000 years. There is evidence on early stone artifacts, clay seals, pottery, and documents that demonstrates early civilizations recognized that fingerprints held value in someone's identity. Though there is no evidence to suggest these civilizations recognized every person has a unique set of prints, it does demonstrate recognition of a personal mark of identification.

Other historical documents have identified fingerprints as having patterns and include descriptions of spirals and loops, as well as descriptions of the thickness of the skin. In a petroglyph from the early 1700s, the Mi'kmaq peoples carved the ridge detail from a person's hand into slate.[242] There is clear recognition of patterns on the tips of the fingers and a whorl on the thumb, as well as ridge detail (lines) on the palmar area.

Chinese fortune tellers used fingerprint patterns and the number of whorls for their predictions. Though this is a form of witchcraft and holds no validity, it does demonstrate an awareness of friction ridge skin patterns.

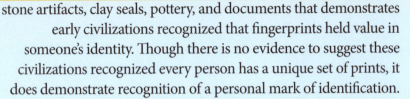
Purkinje

But it was not until 1788 that Dr. Johann Mayer published the first information about the uniqueness of friction ridge skin. Mayer stated, "Although the arrangement of skin ridges is never duplicated in two persons, nevertheless the similarities are closer among some individuals. In others the differences are marked, yet despite their peculiarities of arrangement all have a certain likeness."[243] The first person to organize the patterns into a form of classification system was J.E. Purkinje in 1823. Purkinje was also one of the first to publish observations on primate friction ridge patterns as well as the fingerprint-like pattern on the prehensile tail of spider monkeys. Animal fingerprints will be discussed in Lesson 17.

In 1879, an important advancement was made in identification by Alphonse Bertillon. Bertillon was a French criminologist who recognized everyone has unique body measurements. He devised the first system of classification based on a series of nine core body measurements. This system came to be known as anthropometry and was so successful that it spread to North America and was used in the United States as a means of filing criminals according to measurement. In 1903, the system was found to have fallibility and was discontinued. This occurred during the West case, the importance of which in relation to the science of fingerprints will be discussed later in the lesson.

Though various publications continued to surface over the next few decades, it was not until 1880 that the first article was published suggesting that fingerprints left at a crime scene could be used for identification. Dr. Henry Faulds is given credit for first publishing this practice, but it is Sir William Herschel, in response to Faulds' article, who stated he had been practicing this method for over twenty years in India. Therefore, Herschel is credited as the first European to implement the methodology of fingerprint identification.

First fingerprints taken by Herschel, 1859

Now that fingerprints were recognized for their value in identification, it became necessary to develop a way to organize fingerprint files aside from someone's name. During this period, scientists also began toying with the idea of creating a superior human race. This initiative was called eugenics. Eugenics is defined as the study of how to force reproduction within a human population to increase the occurrence of heritable characteristics regarded as desirable. The scientist who coined the term eugenics and is considered the father of the eugenics movement, Sir Francis Galton, collected one of the largest repositories of fingerprint files for this period in history. As part of his eugenics research, he spent ten years studying over 8,000 ten-print fingerprint cards and classified each print according to pattern type and ethnicity for the sole purpose of determining what pattern type was special to a particular "race" of people. He published a book titled *Finger Prints* in 1892 that included an important conclusion:

> It may emphatically be said that there is no peculiar pattern which characterizes persons of any of the above races (English, Welsh, Hebrew, Black). There is no particular pattern that is special to any one of them, which when met with enables us to assert, or even to suspect, the nationality of the person.[244]

Human Fingerprints

Once again, observational science confirms the truth of God's Word. The Bible states in Genesis 1 that God created Adam and Eve. Therefore, everyone in the human population is descended from them. In Acts 17:26a, the Bible emphasizes this again by saying, "And he made from one man every nation of mankind to live on all the face of the earth." Galton's own research confirmed that there is no particular fingerprint pattern that can be attributed to one particular people group but that patterns are randomly distributed across the whole of humankind, one human race made in the image of God.

It is important to note that the eugenics movement influenced the Nazi agenda and the extermination of millions of humans they considered less desirable, including those of Jewish descent, the disabled, and other minority groups. But the eugenics movement did not end with the defeat of the Nazi agenda. Eugenics still occurs today. Some countries like Iceland pride themselves on eliminating Down Syndrome,[245] but this is nothing short of eugenics. These countries have made it legal for parents to participate in selective abortions for the sole purpose of eliminating those babies that society deems less desirable.

In his book *Finger Prints*, Galton, who is also considered the father of fingerprint classification, developed the first system of organized fingerprint classification based on pattern type. In his book, he described the three types of fingerprint patterns still used today: arch, loop, and whorl. Expanding on Galton's research, Sir Edward Henry, a British official in India, developed a systematic method to classify fingerprints by assigning numerical values to fingers with the presence of the whorl pattern. The Henry system was so successful that it was brought to the United States in 1903, though it was used secondarily to the Bertillon method of anthropometry, which remained the primary means of identification until the historic West case.

Galton

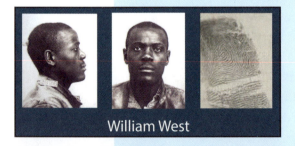

William West

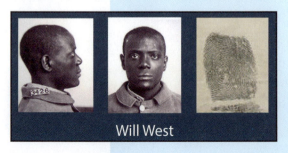

Will West

In May of 1903, a man was arrested and taken to Leavenworth Penitentiary in Kansas for processing. The clerk recognized the arrestee named Will West. When searching his anthropometry measurements, they found they were very close to another prisoner's — William West — measurements. Upon closer examination, they discovered these two men were identical twins who were unaware they had a twin brother. This case brought to light a discrepancy, or fallibility, in the method of anthropometry. When the fingerprints of Will and William West were analyzed, the technicians discovered they were uniquely different. Identical twins do not have the same fingerprints. The West case forever changed the use of fingerprints, and fingerprints remain the primary means of identification today.

ANATOMY OF FRICTION SKIN

Skin is the largest organ on the human body and covers an average of 22 feet on an adult. The ridged skin found on the hands and feet is distinctly different than the skin found on most of the body. Not only are the palms of the hands and bottoms of the feet two of three places on the body where there is no hair, but this is the location of unique pattern formation. Ridges develop in the womb and create identifiable characteristics. These ridges aid in gripping, and the creases in the ridges allow the skin to flex and bend. Friction skin is composed of two distinct layers: the epidermis and dermal layers. The epidermis is the thinner, outer layer of skin. This layer serves as a barrier against contagions and contains the sensory receptors. Damage to the epidermis in the form of cuts, burns, warts, etc., will undergo cellular repair, and often, no damage is visible in the friction skin patterns after healing.

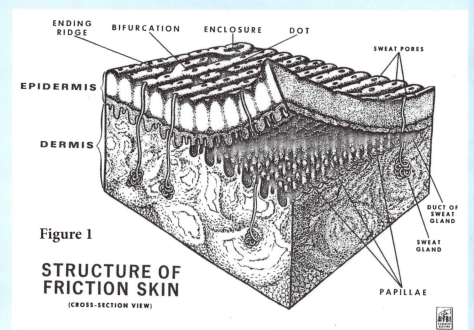

Figure 1

STRUCTURE OF FRICTION SKIN
(CROSS-SECTION VIEW)

The dermal layer is the connective tissue that nourishes the epidermis. **Figure 1** shows that the fingerprint ridges and furrows are anchored deep within the dermal layer. A deep wound into the dermal layer will result in a permanent scar on the surface of the friction ridge skin. Permanent scars have the potential to become an identifiable feature as unique as minutiae characteristics. Sweat ducts from the dermal layer make their way to the surface of friction skin, secreting perspiration in the form of water (99%), fatty acids, amino acids, sugars, and other chemicals through the eccrine sweat glands. These eccrine sweat glands are the only appendage of friction ridge skin.

THE INDIVIDUALITY OF FINGERPRINTS

Analysis of fingerprints for over a century has confirmed the randomness of minutiae in friction ridge skin as a unique form of identification. In theory, it is a 100% certainty that no two people will have identical fingerprint patterns. God's design is truly amazing to study when you consider that all ten fingers will vary from those of the ten toes on one person. The 20 unique pattern arrangements on each finger (though some people may have more or less than twenty) will be unlike anyone else who will ever be conceived. All fingerprint patterns can be grouped into three basic categories: loops, whorls, and arches. Loops are the most common fingerprint in humans, consisting of 65% of all patterns, whorls are the second most frequent at 30%, and arches are the rarest at 5%.

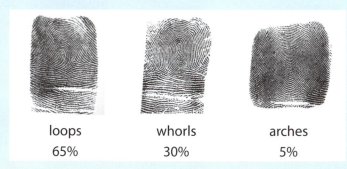

loops 65%   whorls 30%   arches 5%

Human Fingerprints

Considering there are an estimated 108 billion people who have been conceived in human history and there are only three general fingerprint patterns, what makes a person's fingerprints unique? Friction skin is made of thousands of little characteristics. The unique, comparable characteristics are called minutiae.

IDENTIFIABLE CHARACTERISTICS

The word minutiae basically means "details," and fingerprint patterns are made of thousands of details. It is estimated there are over 10,000 minutiae characteristics covering the entire surface of the hands and feet. Common examples of minutiae are listed below (though deltas and cores are not technically minutiae but common locations in a print).

Figure 1

- *Ridge ending*: the location where a ridge abruptly ends and does not continue.
- *Bifurcation*: the location where a single ridge splits into two separate ridges.
- *Island*: the location of a single spot of friction skin.
- *Crossover*: the location where two ridges cross and form an "X."
- *Delta*: the location where two ridges diverge and a point of reference or friction skin is visible at the center of the divergence. The term comes from the geographical term for a river delta.
- *Core*: the location of the center of the pattern area.

What makes minutiae characteristics so useful is the location of each point in relation to each other. The orientation of minutiae and how they make up the patterns of fingerprints are what is unique to everyone. The minutiae can be compared, counted, and analyzed against other known prints. Biometric software on phones, tablets, and computers are searching minutiae characteristics, not overall pattern type. When two points of minutiae on two different prints occur in the same location, it is considered one matching point. The examiner now begins the process of establishing additional concurring points (see **Figure 2**).

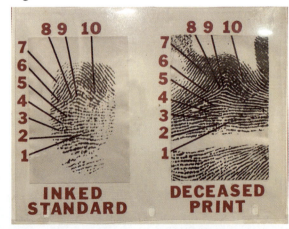

Figure 2

With over 10,000 characteristics on the surfaces of the hands and feet, it only takes between seven and ten minutiae on average to confirm a unique match. There is no official number of minutiae required for an identification, and each comparison is evaluated on its own merit. The greater the number of matching points, the greater the confidence level. If there is even one characteristic that does not match or cannot be explained, the examiner should begin leaning toward an inconclusive opinion. It is fascinating to think that ten minutiae only make up a surface area of about 1 cm² of one fingerprint, and this is enough information to confirm someone's identity. God created every single human with identifiable precision in friction ridge skin, made up of tiny details that form recognizable patterns unlike anyone else in His creation.

Biometrics: A system of body measurements and calculations related to human characteristics for identification. (This topic is discussed further in Lesson 18.)

Unchanging Structure. The structure of friction skin remains unaltered during an individual's lifetime. There may be a wearing down of the ridges due to a person's profession or permanent scarring from injuries, but the identity found in the structure of the patterns is unchanging. The patterns that develop in the mother's womb between 10–16 weeks remain with a person until they decompose beyond the dermal layer of the skin. There have been cases when a body's epidermis is gone due to decomposition, but their identity has been verified by using the dermal layer of skin.[246]

FINGERPRINT CLASSIFICATION

Fingerprints are classified into three pattern groups: arch, loop, and whorl. These three basic patterns are further subdivided into eight total patterns, described in the following sections.

The Arch. Arches are characterized by not having a delta or core. The ridges in an arch enter one side and flow out the other side.

 Plain arch: The ridges of a plain arch flow, or tend to flow, from the left side of the print to the right side of the print and create a gentle hill within the pattern area. A plain arch has no upthrust in the core of the fingerprint as seen in the tented arch.

 Tented arch: The tented arch has a distinct upthrust in the shape of a camping tent or tepee in the core of the print. A tented arch may also be classified as such when it resembles a loop but lacks one of the three requirements to be classified as a loop.

The Loop. The type of loop is determined by the flow of ridges in relation to the ulna and radial bones of the arm. A loop must meet three essential points: sufficient recurve, presence of a delta, and a ridge count of at least one. A ridge count is the number of ridges between the core and the delta.

Ulnar loop: Of the total eight pattern types, ulnar loops are the most common. In an ulnar loop, the ridges flow or tend to flow toward the pinky finger or ulna bone of the arm. The flow of ridges resembles a slide, as the ridges start at the base (delta) and flow upward over the core and then slope down off to the other side of the print.

Radial loop: Radial loops are less common and are characterized by ridges that flow or tend to flow toward the thumb or radius of the arm.

The Whorl. Whorls are characterized by the presence of two deltas and a core. There are four types of whorls:

plain whorl — central pocket loop whorl — double loop whorl — accidental whorl

When looking at all eight subclassifications of fingerprints and their frequency by pattern types, the following percentages reflect their commonality or rarity.

Loops		Arches	
Ulnar	Radial	Tented	Plain
60%	4%	1%	4%

Whorls			
Plain	Central pocket loop	Double loop	Accidental
21%	4%	4%	1%

HENRY CLASSIFICATION

Henry

Sir Edward Henry is given credit for the fingerprint classification system used in the United States. The system is based on the presence of whorls in fingers or thumbs. A point value is only given if a whorl is present. If no whorl is present, no value is given for that finger or thumb. The fingerprint classification is written in fraction form. To avoid a value of "0" when no whorls are present, an arbitrary "1" is always added to both the numerator and denominator. Therefore, an individual who has no whorls present on any of their fingers or thumbs has a primary classification of $1/1$. Someone who has whorls on all ten of their fingers, after applying the Henry system, will have a classification of $32/32$. Therefore, all primary fingerprint classifications fall within the range of $1/1$ to $32/32$.

A complete fingerprint classification includes the components below in the format of a large fraction.

	Key	Major	Primary	Secondary	Sub-Secondary	Final
Numerator	The ridge count of the first loop. If there are no loops, there is no key.	The ridge count or whorl tracing of the right thumb. If a small letter group, this will take precedence.	The value of fingers 2, 4, 6, 8, 10 + 1.	The capital letter representation of the right index print pattern (A, T, U, R, W).	The ridge count codes (I, O) or whorl tracings (I, M, O) in fingers 2–4 of the right hand. If a finger has a print in the small letter group, this will take precedence.	The ridge count of the pinky finger in the right hand. If there is no loop in the right pinky, the left-hand pinky is used and placed in the denominator. If there is no loop in either pinky finger, there is no final.
Denominator	If there is no value for the key, this is left blank.	The ridge count or whorl tracing of the left thumb. If a small letter group, this will take precedence.	The value of fingers 1, 3, 5, 7, 9 + 1.	The capital letter representation of the left index print pattern (A, T, U, R, W).	The ridge count codes (I, O) or whorl tracings (I, M, O) in fingers 2–4 of the left hand. If a finger has a print in the small letter group, this will take precedence.	The ridge count of the left-hand pinky finger when there is no loop in the right pinky. If there is a loop in the right hand, this is left blank. If there is no loop in either pinky finger, there is no final.

Step 1: Identify the pattern of each finger with a letter under the finger: whorls (capital W in all fingers), arch (lowercase a in all fingers except the index finger where a capital A is used), tented arch (lowercase t in all fingers except the index finger where a capital T is used), radial loop (lowercase r in all fingers except the index finger where a capital R is used). The only exception is for ulnar loops, which are the most common type of fingerprint. A diagonal line slanting in the direction of the loop is used to signify an ulnar loop — "\" in the right hand and "/" in the left hand. Notice that the diagonal line follows the flow of ridges toward the ulna bone in that hand. See the fingerprint card to the right.

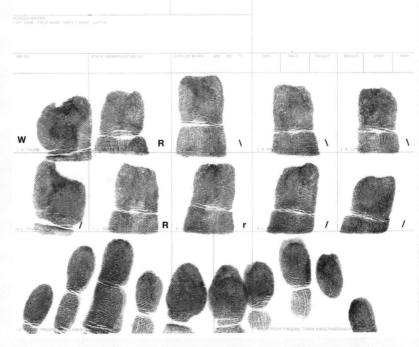

Human Fingerprints

Lesson 16

Step 2: Once the patterns have been identified, identify the ridge counts in the loops and the type of tracing in the whorls.

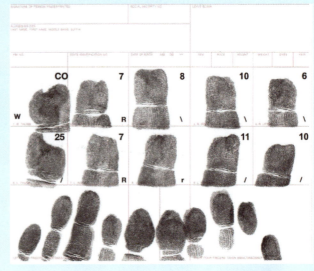

- *Ridge counts in ulnar and radial loops:* Count the number of ridges that cross an imaginary straight line from the delta to the core of the fingerprint. This value is written in the top right corner of the fingerprint block.

- *Whorl tracings:* Trace from the center of the left delta to the center of the right delta. Assign a value of I (inner) for a tracing that flows inside the right delta, M (meet) for a tracing that aligns with the core of the right delta, or an O (outer) for a tracing that flows outside the right delta. The tracing is written in the upper right corner of the fingerprint block along with the type of whorl (plain "P," central pocket "C," double loop "D," accidental "X").

Inner tracing (I) Meet (M) Outer (O)

Step 3: Record the Key. The key is the ridge count of the first finger with a loop pattern. The first finger to have a loop is the right index finger, and when counting the number of ridges from the delta to the core, the count is 7. The key is placed in the numerator. If there are no loops in the ten fingers on the fingerprint card, there is no key.

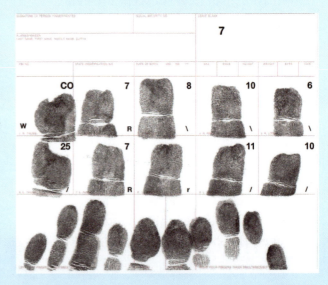

Step 4: Record the Major. The major is either the whorl tracings or ridge count code in the thumbs. If a whorl tracing, only use the capital letter for the trace type, I (inner), M (meet), or O (outer).

For ridge counts, the coding for the thumbs is:

	Coding	Grouping Sizes		
		Small	Medium	Large
Right hand	When the left thumb is 16 ridge counts or less	1–11	12–16	17 and over
Right hand	When the left thumb is 17 ridge counts or over	1–17	18–22	23 and over
Left hand		1–11	12–16	17 and over

The right thumb's information is placed in the numerator and the left thumb's in the denominator.

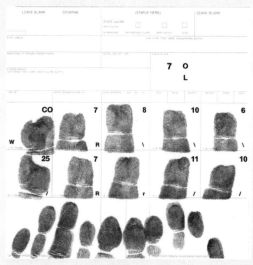

Step 5: Record the Primary. Calculating the primary is the most important step in the classification process. A point value is given only if a whorl is present in the assigned finger block. The chart below provides the point value given to each finger. The whorl can be any one of the four types of whorl patterns.

Finger 1	Finger 2	Finger 3	Finger 4	Finger 5
Right thumb	Right index	Right middle	Right ring	Right pinky
16 points	16 points	8 points	8 points	4 points
Finger 6	Finger 7	Finger 8	Finger 9	Finger 10
Left thumb	Left index	Left middle	Left ring	Left pinky
4 points	2 points	2 points	1 point	1 point

Human Fingerprints

To formulate the primary or numerical portion of a classification, the whorl value assigned to each finger is added to create a numerator and denominator.

The numerator is the sum of the values of fingers 2, 4, 6, 8, and 10, if a whorl is present, plus arbitrary 1.

Numerator: sum of fingers
2, 4, 6, 8, 10 +1

The denominator is the sum of the values of fingers 1, 3, 5, 7, and 9, plus arbitrary 1, only if a whorl is present.

Denominator: sum of fingers
1, 3, 5, 7, 9 +1

Observe the fingerprint card below. Using the Henry system of classification, the primary is calculated as $1/17$.

Numerator: no whorls in fingers
2, 4, 6, 8, 10 + 1 = 1

Denominator: 16 points for finger 1, no whorls in
3, 5, 7, 9 + 1 = 17

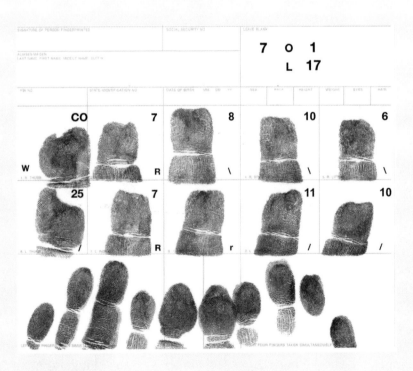

Step 6: Record the Secondary. Following the primary is the secondary, which is simply the pattern type in the index fingers. This is represented by a capital letter:

Whorl	Plain arch	Tented arch	Ulnar loop	Radial loop
W	**A**	**T**	**U**	**R**

Observe the fingerprint card below. Using the Henry system of classification, the secondary is R/R.

The secondary is written directly next to the primary.

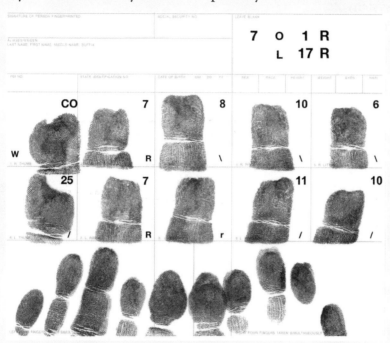

Step 7: Record the Sub-secondary. The secondary is followed by the sub-secondary, which is the pattern types in the index, middle, and ring fingers of both hands, unless there is a member of the "small letter group" such as a radial loop, tented arch, or plain arch in the middle fingers (fingers 3 and 8), ring fingers (fingers 4 and 9), pinky fingers (fingers 5 and 10), or thumbs (fingers 1 and 6) of either hand. Due to the rarity of these pattern types outside of the index fingers, they are given priority in the classification. Small letters are brought up to the classification in their exact position adjacent to the index finger (secondary) in both the numerator and the denominator. If there are multiple small letters, a dash is used in between the letters to indicate an absence. If a small letter is in the thumb, that letter is placed to the left of the index (secondary).

If there are no small letters present in the middle fingers, ring fingers, pinky fingers, or thumbs, then the following process is followed for loops and whorls.

Ulnar loops: In the example below, there is a ridge count of 17. The number of ridges present in each finger determines the code of I or O.

Code	Index	Middle	Ring
I	9 or less ridges	10 or less ridges	13 or less ridges
O	10 or more ridges	11 or more ridges	14 or more ridges

The ridge count is written in the upper right corner of the fingerprint box. The right-hand codes are written in the numerator and left hand in the denominator.

Observe the fingerprint card to the right. Using the Henry system of classification, the sub-secondary is R/Rr.

This is because the radial loop in the middle finger is considered in the small letter group. Since it is in the middle finger of the left hand, it is placed in the denominator directly next to the index finger.

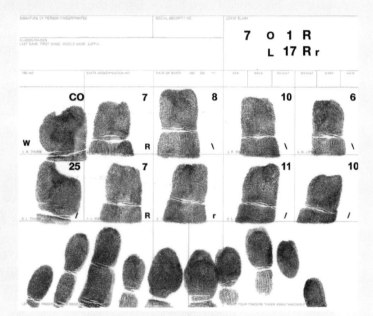

Step 8: Record the Final. The final is the ridge count of the pinky in the right hand. If the pinky of the right hand does not have a ridge count (such as when an arch or whorl is present), then use the ridge count in the left pinky finger and write in the denominator. If no ridge count is present in either pinky, leave this section blank. Observe the fingerprint card below. Using the Henry system of classification, the final is 6.

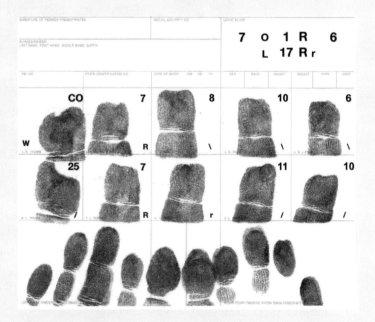

CONCLUSION

Fingerprints are fascinating to study because every single one is different. There is always something new to discover in the field of dactyloscopy (classification of fingerprints). God's ingenuity and creative design is reflected in the arches, loops, and whorls through the functionality of friction ridge skin. The rippled surface aids in gripping and provides a nonslip surface on the hands and feet. There is no question that fingerprints are just one example of how the human body is fearfully and wonderfully made.

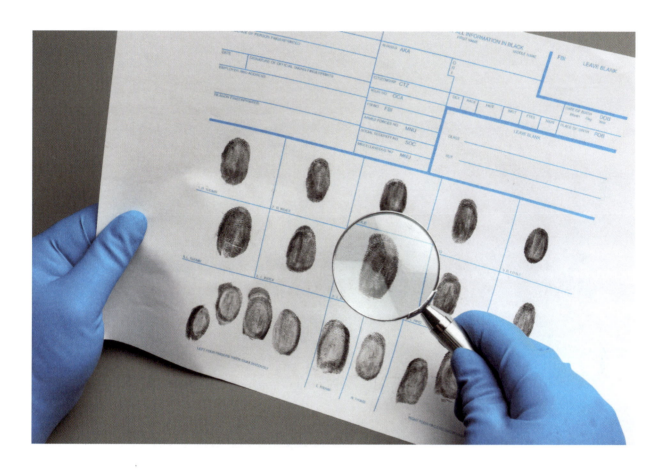

Lesson 17
Animal Fingerprints

For his invisible attributes, namely, his eternal power and divine nature, have been clearly perceived, ever since the creation of the world, in the things that have been made. So they are without excuse (Romans 1:20).

Case Study: The Monkey Caper

In the year 1975, history was made in fingerprint science when the first police raid on zoo primate houses occurred in Europe. The British investigators went to retrieve fingerprints from six chimpanzees and two orangutans. The primate houses were located at the London Zoo and at Twycross Zoo in Leicestershire.[247] It is well known among fingerprint experts that primates have friction ridge skin, the three types of fingerprint patterns, and unique identity. More research is needed in examining primate fingerprints, but scientists have theorized that all ten of a primate's digits have different fingerprint patterns and are unlike any other primate that has lived in the past, is living in the present, or will be born in the future. It is also common knowledge that primates are often not suspects in a crime. So why would British police want to fingerprint primates?

In 1975, British police were baffled by a series of unsolved crimes. When the police found smudged or smeared prints at a crime scene, they jokingly referred to them as "monkey prints." After repeated unsuccessful attempts to identify a suspect by matching human fingerprints to those found at the crime scenes, police thought they would determine if a primate, or monkey, was responsible. The operation was led by Steve Haylock from the Hertfordshire Police Department. The juvenile chimps and orangutans happily allowed the Hertfordshire police officers to take their digit prints.[248] The officers dusted the digits with fingerprint powder and pressed them into sticky fingerprint tape. The officers then attempted to match the primate prints to latent prints found at the crime scenes. Not to anyone's surprise, the primates were found not guilty. The police did confirm previous research on the unique qualities of primate digit prints. All eight of the primates had different digit prints.

Twenty years later, another animal would come under suspicion, but this time it was not a primate. In 1996, the first major study on koala digit prints was published. Scientists determined that koala friction ridge skin is almost indistinguishable from those of humans. Under the microscope, their morphology is identical. They are so similar that if a human and koala were both at a crime scene and left their fingerprints behind, fingerprint experts may have trouble discerning the difference between the two.[249] But police investigators are not too concerned with similarities between human and koala prints. As with primates, it is unlikely a koala will be participating in criminal activity anytime soon. But as Sherlock Holmes said, "Life is infinitely stranger than anything which the mind of man could invent."[250]

It is not surprising God created some animals with friction ridge skin. These animals need to climb, and grab and hold their food, all activities that benefit from having a nonslip surface on their hands and feet. And God values His creation so much, He created these animals with unique fingerprint identification as well.

Human fingerprint patterns are a viable form of identification for three distinct reasons: they provide unique identity, they are distinguished by minutiae characteristics, and they do not change during a person's lifetime. God created human friction ridge skin on day six of the creation week approximately 6,000 years ago. But humans are not the only creation from day six that possess friction ridge skin and fingerprints. God created some animals that share this anatomical feature with humans. Primates, marsupials, and some carnivores have been analyzed and verified to have friction skin and fingerprint patterns. Though evolutionists like to use this similarity in design as evidence of common descent, there are distinct differences between human and animal friction ridge skin. Additionally, a similarity in design (or homology) would still be expected if one Designer created all things. God's Word is the only reliable source of truth, and the historical record provided in Genesis can be trusted from the very first verse. God clearly states that He created all things according to their kinds — plants according to their kind, primates according to their kind, marsupials according to their kind, and humans in the image of God.

ANIMAL FINGERPRINTS FROM A BIBLICAL WORLDVIEW

The observable fact that animals have friction ridge skin and fingerprints is somewhat of a mystery to secular scientists. For Christians, this would be expected based on what is seen in creation. Romans 1:20 states that creation is evidence of the Creator. When observing creation, there is clear design, beauty, complexity, pattern, and organized information all throughout living things. Patterns are not just visible in human and animal friction skin but are also evident in sand dunes, clouds, water, flower blossoms, fish, zebras, tigers, birds, and much more. And even more amazing is the fact that each one has unique identity as well. There are not two sand dunes that have the same pattern, or two flower blossoms, or two zebras, tigers, fish, etc. When describing these patterns in nature, John Upchurch (2016) stated, "... all these similarities aren't infinite, unrelated, random patterns. Instead, He placed complex but discernible patterns all over that show similarity and diversity. In turn, these point back to the attributes of their three-in-one Maker. It's sort of like He stamped His fingerprint over and over on creation so that we couldn't miss it."[251]

Not only are these fingerprint patterns all throughout nature a reflection of God's design, but there is also evidence of forethought in the structure of friction ridge skin. When you consider the function of friction ridge skin, it makes sense why God designed certain animals with these features. The uneven surface of friction skin provides traction and aids in a firmer grip. The animals that have friction ridge skin are primarily climbing, arboreal-dwelling creatures. Would having a nonslip surface on their hands and feet benefit these animals who live in trees? Absolutely, and it simply confirms a God who loves His creation. Psalm 104:24 states, "O Lord, how manifold are your works! In wisdom have you made them all; the earth is full of your creatures."

Romans 1:20:

"For his invisible attributes, namely, his eternal power and divine nature, have been clearly perceived, ever since the creation of the world, in the things that have been made. So they are without excuse."

PRIMATE FINGERPRINTS

Primates have friction skin on their hands and feet along with unique digit prints. All ten of their digit prints are different and reflect the same three patterns seen in humans — arches, loops, and whorls (see **Figure 1**). Other similarities to humans include the fetal development of the ridges and ridges lined with sweat pores.

Figure 1

human palm print

gorilla palm print

Though there are similarities, it is the distinct differences in friction skin structure and overall pattern distribution that separate humans from primates. Noticeable differences in human and primate fingerprints include pattern distribution and morphology. Chrisman (1996) stated, "Primate friction skin is notably different. It is characterized not only by contoured ridges on hands and feet, but also features sweat pores placed at semiregular intervals on the top of ridges."[252]

Pattern Distribution. One of the major differences between humans and primates is in the frequency of loop and whorl patterns present on both the hands and feet. In human fingerprints, the most common pattern type is the loop with a 65% frequency and whorls with 30%. Primates have a high frequency of whorl patterns on their digits, ranging between 50–65%. Primate loop frequency ranges between 30–40%, depending on the species.[253] Primates also have noticeably more whorls on their palmar surface. In both the hypothenar and interdigital areas of the palms (see **Figure 2**), primates have a high prevalence of whorl patterns (see **Figure 3**). Some research has concluded that there is a less than 1% chance of a whorl visible in these areas of the palm.[254]

Figure 2
Sections of the palm in both humans and primates

Figure 3
Palmar whorls in primates

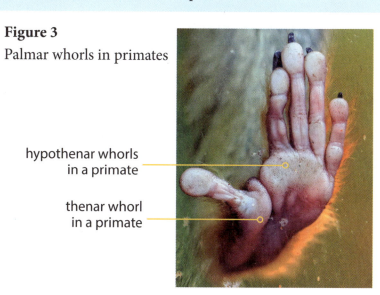

hypothenar whorls in a primate

thenar whorl in a primate

Animal Fingerprints

MORPHOLOGY: STRUCTURE AND DESIGN

The overall structure of primate hands differs from that of humans. God created primates with longer, curved fingers and a short thumb, allowing them to survive in their arboreal habitats. Scientists have recognized the ingenuity of this design as well:

> Each hand features four fingers in addition to the opposable thumb, but the human fingers are shorter and flatter. The primate's longer, curved fingers assist with the animal's ability to swing through the trees. The longer human thumb would be hindrance for primates, getting in the way of the hook-like grasp they need for swinging from the trees.[255]

Dermatoglyphics: The scientific study of skin patterns.

In addition to the overall shape of the hands, the structure of primate friction skin differs from human friction skin in their thinner, less dense ridges. Scientists use a density of ridge analysis to compare the ridge density of humans and animals. Basically, they evaluate the number of ridges to cross a straight, one-centimeter line on a fingerprint. This is called the ridge breadth. One of the most comprehensive studies conducted on primate fingerprint patterns (with a focus on chimpanzees) was conducted in 1938 by Harold Cummins and Shirley Spragg. Cummins was a pioneer in primate dermatoglyphics. After examining multiple chimpanzee specimens, Cummins and Spragg concluded that there was a distinctive average of 10+ ridges per centimeter increase over that of humans.[256] On average, primates have 22 ridges per centimeter while humans have 11 ridges per centimeter.[257] To summarize, primates' ridges are less dense (thick); therefore, they have approximately double the ridges within the same surface area when compared to humans.

Other variations in structure include primate whorls having curved ridges that are not seen in human ridges[258] and "distinct tented arch patterns on fingertips that are clearly different from human patterns"[259] (see **Figure 4**). Some species of primates also have ridged skin on their knuckle pads, a feature not visible on humans. Another prominent difference between humans and primates is in the number of minutiae characteristics. Scientists refer to this as minutiae complexity. After careful study of primate minutiae, scientists have concluded that primate ridges are more linear with less division. This results in less minutiae variation in the friction skin patterns of both the hands and feet when compared to human diversity in minutiae.[260] There are still sufficient minutiae to determine individual identity in every primate.

Human and Primate Friction Skin: Similarities and Differences

Similarities	Differences
Raised friction skin with three basic patterns: arch, loop, and whorl.	Pattern distribution Humans: 65% loops, 30% whorls Primates: 65% whorls, 30% loops
Frequency of 5% arch patterns.	Primates have curved ridges.
Sweat pores line ridges.	Primates have tall tented arches.
Friction ridge skin on the hands and feet.	Primates have a low occurrence of minutiae complexity on both the hands and feet.
	Primates have a high prevalence of hypothenar and interdigital whorls.
	Some primate species have friction ridge skin on knuckle pads of three middle digits.[261]
	Ridge breadth Humans: average of 11 ridges/centimeter Primates: average of 22 ridges/centimeter
	Ridge density Humans: higher Primates: lower

Figure 4: Primate hypothenar whorl

God not only equipped primates with friction skin on their hands and feet, but He provided some monkeys with friction skin on the underside of their prehensile tail. Scientists have printed spider monkey tails and discovered that every tail print is different.[262] Spider monkeys rely on their tails to secure themselves to branches while feeding and to move through the trees. Would a spider monkey benefit from having a nonslip surface running the entire length of its prehensile tail? As the anatomist Dr. David Menton often said, "The Lord God thinks of everything."

MARSUPIAL FINGERPRINTS

Like humans and primates, marsupial fingerprints are unique to each individual animal. This amazing trait points toward our intelligent Creator God, who made everything for a purpose (Proverbs 16:4). Think about it — would a koala or sugar glider benefit from having a nonslip surface? Do they climb and grip food? Yes, and God not only equipped them with this feature, but He loves His creation so much that He also gave them unique identity as well. In the marsupial family of animals, arboreal and climbing marsupials such as koalas, tree kangaroos, and sugar gliders (**Figure 6**) have friction skin and unique fingerprint patterns. This is different from the terrestrial (land-dwelling) marsupials, which do not have friction ridge skin.

Figure 6

sugar glider   tree kangaroo

Koalas. The existence of friction ridge skin on the surface of koalas' hands and feet is a mystery to evolutionary scientists. Koalas have the three types of fingerprint patterns, the patterns are composed of minutiae, and all ten of their digits are unique. Scientists have discovered that the morphology of koala friction skin is almost identical to humans. In fact, when they studied koala friction skin microscopically, they discovered that koala and human friction skin are so similar that if a koala and human were to leave their fingerprints behind at a crime scene, investigators would have a difficult time telling them apart (see **Figure 7**).[263]

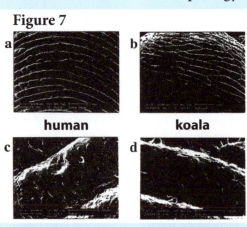

Human and koala ridge breadth is almost identical as well. Studies have calculated the density of ridges for koalas to be on average 12 ridges per centimeter compared to the 11 ridges visible in humans.[264] This scientific fact poses serious problems for evolutionists. This similarity between human and koala friction ridge skin does not coincide with the evolutionary tree of life or fit in their timeline. On the evolutionary tree of life, there are branches that divide to represent animal evolutionary development.

Figure 8

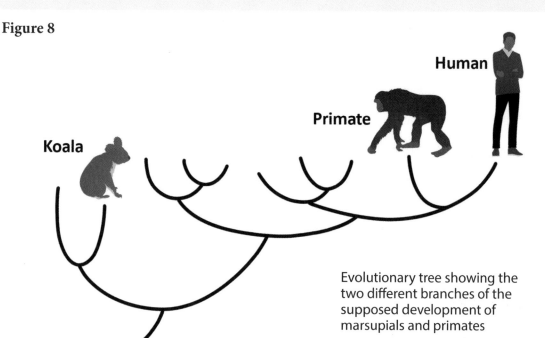

Evolutionary tree showing the two different branches of the supposed development of marsupials and primates

The earliest marsupials and primates are on different branches of the evolutionary tree (see **Figure 8**). Humans, which evolutionists claim are linked with an early primate ancestor, are positioned on the same branch as primates, whereas the marsupial is on a distinctly different branch. Considering human and koala fingerprints are almost identical yet distinctly different from primates, this fact cannot be answered by evolutionary ideas. According to evolution, the koala and early primate ancestor are separated on the evolutionary tree by 70 million years. This separation in the timeline would also be evident in the development of friction ridge skin. Why would marsupials, which are not closely related to primates, have similar fingerprints to humans? Secular scientists have to admit they are mystified:

Figure 9

Koala fingerprint

> Koala fingerprints are somewhat of a scientific mystery. Apes such as gorillas and chimpanzees are, evolutionarily speaking, a lot closer to humans than koalas. Koalas are not exactly anywhere near those particular evolutionary branches.[265]

For Christians who believe in biblical authority, the answer is simple. God designed creatures with the features they need to survive in their environment. Friction skin aids in a firmer grip. But the Bible also describes God's love for His creation, and this is reflected in the unique identity given to every animal and human with friction skin.

Though the structure of koala fingerprints is very similar to humans, there are differences in the type of fingerprint patterns, surface area of friction ridge skin, and minutiae detail. The primary pattern type on koalas is the arch (see **Figure 9**), whereas in humans there is only a 5% occurrence.

Additionally, koalas do not have friction skin on the entire surface of their palms or lower sections of their digits nor the level of minutiae complexity seen in humans.

Human and Koala Friction Skin: Similarities and Differences

Similarities	Differences
Raised friction skin with three basic patterns: arch, loop, and whorl.	Koala: arch is the dominant pattern.
Ridge breadth: average of 11 ridges/centimeter.	Koalas have friction ridge skin on portions of the hands and feet, not the entire surface.
Minutiae characteristics.	Koalas have a low occurrence of minutiae complexity on both the hands and feet.
Morphology.	

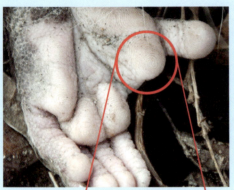

opossum friction ridge skin

Other arboreal marsupials, like tree kangaroos, have friction skin and fingerprint patterns. Scientists studying tree kangaroos have verified, "And like fingerprints, their pattern is unique to each animal."[266] God equipped rock wallabies to climb by giving them a nonslip surface along with unique patterns: "They have reduced claws and they have highly developed transverse ridges at the ends of their toes, much like a human fingerprint."[267]

Much like the climbing rock wallaby, opossums also have friction ridge skin and unique fingerprints. The opossum is the only marsupial native to the United States. Scientists studying opossums have confirmed that their digits have patterns very much like a human fingerprint.[268]

Interestingly, kangaroos, which are terrestrial (land-dwelling) marsupials, do not have friction skin or fingerprints. They do have a textured skin surface, similar to a dog's nose, but there is no unique fingerprint pattern detail (see **Figure 10**).

This applies to the land-dwelling wallabies. Wallabies are in the same created kind as kangaroos. Once again, there is a textured surface on the hands and feet, but no fingerprint patterns (see **Figure 10**).

Figure 10

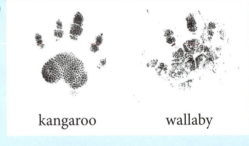

kangaroo   wallaby

Only a God with infinite wisdom would distinguish skin texture between land-dwelling and tree-dwelling marsupials. He designed tree-dwelling marsupials with a friction, nonslip surface to provide them with exactly what they need to survive in their arboreal environment. God knew they would be climbing and grasping food, which would require a friction surface.

Currently, there is only one carnivore known to have friction skin with unique patterns. The fisher weasel (right) has been discovered by forest rangers to have raised friction patterns. The rangers have been able to identify the weasels by their print patterns.[269]

When we examine this from a biblical worldview, we can see that friction skin and unique fingerprint patterns align with the truth in God's Word. Proverbs 16:4 tells us that God created everything for a purpose, and this is evident in the unique features God designed on animals to survive in their environments. Romans 1:20 reminds us that creation is evidence of our Creator. Friction ridge skin, a nonslip surface, provides a unique feature that humans, primates, and marsupials benefit from to survive in their environments. The love and care of our Creator is simply evident on the surface of your little finger.

CONCLUSION

Though there are several identifiable differences between primate and human fingerprints, secular scientists continue to claim this shared feature is evidence of common ancestry through evolutionary processes. These same secular scientists admit there is a "well designed" functionality to ridged skin in primates: "Fingerpads intuitively seem to be well designed mechanically to improve their grip."[270] The functional design in conjunction with unique identity in the structure of this type of skin reflects an intelligent designer, the Creator God, not the result of random processes in evolution over millions of years. The primary conclusion visible throughout secular literature regarding primate friction skin is an evolutionary adaptation to climbing:

> An increased friction rate between fingertips and a gripped surface would benefit human ancestors as well. These hominins, which lived primarily in trees, would use these unique grooves to help them grasp branches. This idea is supported by the evidence of fingerprints in some of *Homo sapiens* closest living relatives — chimps and gorillas. In fact, it is likely that fingerprints are an attribute evolutionarily acquired by animals with an arboreal lifestyle.[271]

Ultimately, the issue is worldview. Do you believe the world's ideology of molecules-to-man evolution or God's created kinds as described in the book of Genesis? Observing shared features with other created kinds — such as skeletal structure, internal organs, or finger and toe prints — simply points toward one all-powerful Designer and Creator. It seems logical that God would use a similar design, or homology, in different creatures: "After all, he did make us to live in the same world, eat the same food, and breathe the same air."[272]

Proverbs 16:4:

"The Lord has made everything for its purpose, even the wicked for the day of trouble."

Lesson 18
Fingerprint Processing

Before I formed you in the womb I knew you, and before you were born I consecrated you (Jeremiah 1:5a).

Case Study: Miami Spa Murder

Fingerprints have been lifted from a variety of surfaces, but they had never successfully been lifted off human skin until 1978. On July 23, 1978, three homicide victims (one male and two females) were found in the World of Health Spas in North Miami Beach, Florida. All three had been shot to death. Officers immediately reached out to the Public Safety Department's Crime Scene Section at the Metro Dade (now Miami Dade) Police Department. The spa provided the perfect controlled environment to process the body for fingerprints. One police technician who had success in processing fingerprints on human skin in the past was assigned the task of examining the body of one of the female homicide victims. As the technician dusted the body of Patricia Lynn Beck with black magnetic powder, three latent prints were revealed two inches above the left ankle on the outside of the leg. One of the prints was found to be viable and contained sufficient ridge detail to make a comparison against possible suspects. The fingerprints were first photographed. The technician then lifted the prints off the skin using standard fingerprint lifting tape. The tape was then placed on a white backer card.

The evidence was submitted to the Latent Unit of the Identification Section in the Metro Dade Police Department. A latent print technician compared the lifted prints to those of the spa owner, Stephen William Beattie. After a lengthy examination, the technician successfully matched the left middle finger to that of Beattie. The other two fingers did not contain sufficient ridge detail for comparison. This was the first time in history that a fingerprint lifted from human skin was successfully matched to the fingerprints of a suspect.[273] Since this was the first case of its kind, the state attorney's office requested verification from the FBI Identification Division, who confirmed the ident. An ident is when an unknown print is successfully matched to a known print.

The suspect was arrested and went on trial January 2, 1979. Stephen William Beattie pled not guilty. Numerous witnesses were presented to the court, in addition to multiple fingerprint experts verifying the positive identification.[274] The jury returned a guilty verdict, and Beattie received the death sentence. He committed suicide on August 9, 1981, while in prison.

Processing fingerprints is an artistic skill that improves with experience. The team of fingerprint experts working on the Miami spa murder case were not novice investigators. The author's father, Richard Hall, was one member of the experienced team working on this case. Experience and technological advances are two key factors in retrieving viable fingerprints.

"You have brought detection as near an exact science as it ever will be brought in this world." — Dr. Watson to Sherlock Holmes[275]

As a well-renowned fingerprint expert once said, "It has frequently been stated, and often found to be true, that the best evidence against an accused is finding his fingerprints at the crime scene."[276] Over 25% of crime scenes yield fingerprint evidence, which are found on almost any solid surface. Why are fingerprints so prevalent? The single file line of sweat pores on the peaks of friction ridge skin secrete perspiration continually. This is one of the involuntarily controlled anatomical features in God's design. No one can look at their hands and stop themselves from sweating. The fingerprint left behind from the perspiration in friction ridge skin sweat pores is identical to the fingerprint of the individual who left it.

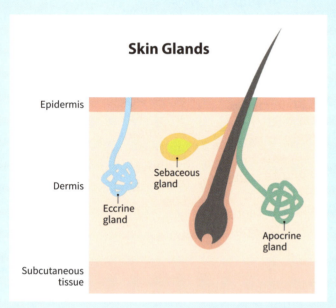

There are three types of glands in the human body: eccrine, apocrine, and sebaceous glands. Eccrine glands are largely concentrated on the hands and feet. Eccrine glands secrete sweat that is composed of 98% water. The remaining 2% consists of fatty acids, amino acids (250 nanograms [ng] per fingerprint), and other minerals.[277] When a surface is touched, the secretion leaves behind a reproduction of the fingerprint formed by friction ridge skin.

The viability of the prints left behind at a scene is dependent on several factors. An investigator must consider the health of the friction ridge skin of the person leaving the print. A person's age and occupation play a key role in the "wear and tear" on friction ridge skin. Older individuals are more likely to have creases and damage to the friction ridge skin versus youth, who will have firm, undamaged skin. Welders (contact with hot surfaces), carpenters (sanding), health care professionals (frequent washing of hands), and even teachers (handling large volumes of paper) may have worn ridges on their fingers because of their occupation. If the friction ridge skin is worn, the minutiae detail left behind may be difficult to detect. Also, the conditions at the crime scene have a direct impact on the secretions left behind. The composition of the surface, the pressure applied, temperature, and weather conditions will all contribute to the quality of the prints.

> **John 1:3:**
> "All things were made through him, and without him was not any thing made that was made."

FINGERPRINT PROCESSING FROM A BIBLICAL WORLDVIEW

God created all things (John 1:3). This includes things that are unseen with the naked eye, like atoms, molecules, and the laws that govern the chemical reactions in the field of chemistry. Colossians 1:16a says, "For by him all things were created, in heaven and on earth, visible and invisible." Atoms are the fundamental building blocks of all things. Atoms comprise the 90 naturally occurring elements on the periodic table. Copper, lead, gold, silver, and iron are some of the first elements utilized by humans for their unique properties. The Bible gives clues in Genesis 4:22a when God states, "Zillah also bore Tubal-cain; he was the forger of all instruments of bronze and iron." Bronze is an alloy made mostly of copper.

Over the next 5,500 years, humans would begin to identify, record, and discover other elements. An element is composed of atoms with the same atomic number and cannot be broken down further. The last naturally occurring element, Rhenium, was discovered in 1925 by Walter Noddack, Ida Tacke, and Otto Berg.[278] Other elements have been synthesized in labs, resulting in the 118 elements represented on the periodic table.

Over the years, several scientists attempted to organize the elements into a logical format. Finally, in 1869, a Russian chemist named Dmitri Mendeleev had a dream of how the 63 known elements should be presented. The following morning, he began to write down his ideas and develop the periodic table. Mendeleev structured the elements by increasing atomic mass and grouped them by similar properties. He left holes where he predicted more elements would be discovered.

Mendeleev Periodic Table, 1869[279]

This resulted in a periodic table of elements. The table has changed since 1869 as more elements have been discovered, but it is important to recognize that the table is organized in the actual physical nature and structure of each element. The elements perfectly align by increasing atomic mass. This is not a forced system created by humans, but a systematic, sequenced design with order and complexity. The organized structure of the periodic table testifies to an Architect and Designer. The periodic table of elements is one more example of the all-powerful, all-knowing God of the universe who created everything with order and consistency.

Figure 1

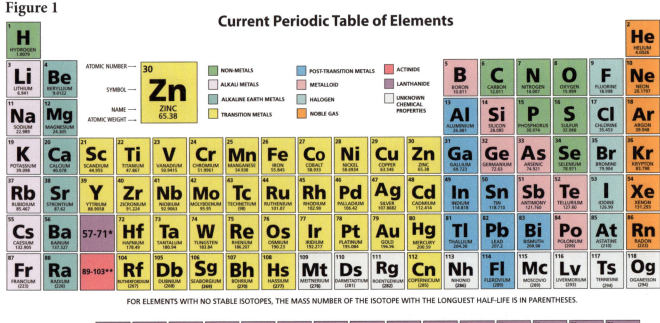

How is this related to fingerprint processing? Being able to understand the chemical properties of elements allows scientists to make predictions about how certain chemicals will react with others. Foundational methods in fingerprint processing were possible due to the sweat pore design of friction ridge skin; the anatomical and involuntary perspiration secretions; and the ability of different chemical reactions to react with the amino acids, fatty acids, and other biological components present in perspiration. This would not be possible if random evolutionary processes were the mechanism. The ability to predict, test, and synthesize results are processes put in place by the Creator God. God is a God of order, not chaos. In 1 Thessalonians 5:21, God challenges us to "test everything." The very ability to use a systematic, sequenced, structured method of experimentation to produce the advanced fingerprint processing techniques available today are only possible because the Creator God established the orderly laws of the universe.

TYPES OF FINGERPRINTS

Crime scene fingerprints have been grouped into three categories: patent, latent, and plastic. Each one requires a different technique of processing, collection, and preservation to ensure the integrity of the evidence and to preserve the important minutiae details.

Patent. A patent print is a print that is clearly visible to the unaided eye. Often these types of prints are found in blood, paint, dust, grease, tape, or moist soil. The first tool investigators will use in the search for patent prints is a visible examination with a light source, like a simple flashlight. Patent prints are photographed before any type of lifting technique is administered.

Latent. The word *latent* means concealed or hidden. Latent prints are not visible to the unaided eye and require some form of physical or chemical processing to reveal their hidden design. Fingerprint dusting powders or fuming chemicals are a few of the techniques used on surfaces containing latent prints.

Plastic. Plastic prints are left behind in soft surfaces and create a three-dimensional impression of the fingerprint. A pliable surface will record the friction ridge details as the fingers are pressed into the surface. Examples where plastic prints are discovered are soap, putty, clay, wax, and wet paint (see Lesson 16 case study). Once a plastic print has been identified and photographed, a silicone mold can be made of the print to preserve the minutiae details.

TYPES OF SURFACES

One factor that affects the type of fingerprint left behind is the type of surface where contact is made. All surfaces fall within two broad categories, porous and nonporous. A third category, semiporous surfaces, exhibits properties of both porous and nonporous surfaces. The type and texture of the surface will determine the form of processing needed to protect and preserve the fingerprint.

Porous Surfaces. A porous surface is defined as something made from an absorbent material. Fingerprints deposited onto porous surfaces will absorb into the substrate where the print is left. This makes the fingerprints more durable and have a high probability of delivering usable prints. Examples of porous surfaces are cardboard, paper, and untreated wood. When processing porous surfaces, there is a sequential order (or protocol) in processing techniques that must be followed. Each subsequent processing technique will destroy the properties necessary for success in the previous techniques. The technician can never reverse or go back to previous testing once progressing sequentially down the list. See **Table 1** for a list of each technique by type of surface.

Nonporous Surfaces. Anything nonporous is nonabsorbent. Therefore, these prints are considered fragile and must be handled with care. Since they do not absorb into the surface, they can survive on the surface for a long time, and if undamaged, the probability of retrieving usable prints is high. These types of surfaces are often smooth or rough. Examples of a nonporous surface are glass, glazed ceramics, plastic, metals, vinyl leather, and varnished wood. Fingerprint powders and cyanoacrylate ester (super glue) fuming are the two techniques that are most often used to process prints on smooth nonporous surfaces. On rough nonporous surfaces, technicians will use a form of casting material or gel lifter. It is important to follow the sequential order of techniques when processing fingerprint secretions on nonporous surfaces.

Semiporous Surfaces. Semiporous surfaces absorb and resist absorption at the same time. Glossy cardboard, waxed surfaces, types of varnished wood, high gloss wall paint, glossy magazine covers, and cellophane are all examples of semiporous surfaces. Processing of semiporous surfaces will require a combination of the methods used on porous and nonporous surfaces. Based on the level of porosity, the technician will use their experience and knowledge to determine the best techniques to enhance the fingerprint minutiae.

Handprint on dirty glass

Table 1: Sequential Order of Processing by Surface Type[280]

Porous	Nonporous	Semiporous
Visual examination	Visual examination	Visual examination
Photography	Photography	Photography
DFO (1,8-Diazafluoren-9-one)	Super glue (cyanoacrylate ester)	Technique is determined by the level of porosity of the surface. Often, a combination of methods.
Ninhydrin	Fluorescent dye stain	
Physical developer (silver nitrate)	Fingerprint powders	

PROCESSING TECHNIQUES

A variety of resources are available in the search for fingerprints. The location of the evidence ultimately determines the type of processing technique the technician will use. Questions to consider when selecting a processing technique include:

- Is the surface porous or nonporous?
- If the surface is semiporous, what combination of methods should be used?
- Is the evidence wet or sticky?
- Is fuming or powdering going to best illuminate the friction ridge detail?

Crime scene investigators will use their training and expertise to answer these questions directly at the crime scene. The list below is not all inclusive, but it does describe the most common tools, techniques, and processing methods used in forensic science.

- *Alternate light source (ALS):* ALS is a device that emits wavelengths of light and works in conjunction with a variety of light filters. An ALS allows an investigator to quickly search windows, railings, doorknobs, and other frequently touched areas for friction ridge detail by accessing the naturally reacting UV capabilities inside fingerprints and biological fluids. When illuminated with an ALS, fingerprints will glow. Depending on the color of the surface, the technician can select varying filters to illuminate invisible prints on contrasting backgrounds.

- *Cyanoacrylate ester (super glue) fuming:* Super glue was discovered by accident in 1942 while scientists were trying to create clear plastic gun sights. The unusual substance caused fingers to stick together and created a white film on surfaces. The process of using super glue fuming for the development of latent fingerprints was not used until the 1970s. This technique is used on nonporous surfaces. This process relies upon the deposition of polymerized cyanoacrylate ester on the fingertip secretions.[281] The evidence is placed in a fuming chamber with a small amount of super glue. The application of heat speeds up the time needed for deposition. Fuming results in white, crystallized, durable prints. Due to the white color of the fingerprints, technicians will often further process the evidence with contrasting-colored powders. This process is very effective on handguns, knives, and other types of weapons.

footprint found with UV light

- *1,8-Diazafluoren-9-one (DFO):* DFO is one of the more recent processing techniques. It was first used on fingerprints in 1990. DFO reacts with the amino acids present in fingerprint secretions and is often used in conjunction with ninhydrin. There are approximately 14 different amino acids present in every fingerprint.[282] After treatment with DFO, fingerprints will glow when exposed to blue-green light at 470 nanometers (nm) and will result in emission at 570 nm.[283] DFO is effective on porous surfaces and results in reddish-pink prints. DFO is applied by spraying, dipping, or brushing. The evidence is then allowed to dry before heating in a low-humidity oven to facilitate development of latent prints.

Fingerprint Processing

- *Dusting powders:* Dusting powders are applied to surfaces using a type of brush or sifter. This the oldest method used in the search for latent prints and dates to the 1800s when investigators were expected to make their own fingerprint powder. Now manufacturers provide a plethora of colors and types of powders. Once the friction ridge detail is visible, prints are lifted with clear fingerprint lifting tape and secured to a contrasting-colored backer card. Powdered prints are often bagged in plastic evidence bags for protection. Currently, there are four general categories for fingerprint powders.

  - Conventional carbon-based: Black powder is the most widely used powder for a variety of surfaces. Since a colorant can be added to the base to make the powder, a wide assortment of colors is available to use on contrasting backgrounds. There is white powder for black backgrounds and red powder for yellow backgrounds. Carbon-based powders are effective on fresh fingerprints on both porous and nonporous surfaces. Conventional powders are inexpensive and cover a large area with just a little powder, but they are very messy. These types of powders are applied with a natural hair or synthetic hair brush.

  - Magnetic: Magnetic powder is made of a colorant and iron shavings. Each iron shaving is wrapped in colorant. A magnetic wand attracts the iron filings, and as the filings are rubbed over a surface, the colorant adheres to the residue. Magnetic powders are easy to use and clean up due to their magnetic properties. Using a magnetic wand, extra iron filings can easily be picked up and returned to the original storage container. The downside of magnetic powders is they are ineffective when attempting to brush a surface upside down, such as a ceiling.

  - Fluorescent: Fluorescent powder consists of a light-stimulating color and a base (conventional and magnetic). The colorant reacts with UV light and is used alongside an ALS. The variety of colored powders and the purple/blue wavelengths in the ALS have illuminated fingerprints on surfaces that would have otherwise been invisible using conventional powders. A minimal amount of powder with a feather duster is the best method to apply fluorescent powder.

  - Nano-powder: The latest development in fingerprint powders applies nanotechnology. SupraNano™ particles are added to conventional, magnetic, and fluorescent powders. Tiny silica balls hold the colorant and result in a 30% improved latent print definition over that of other powders.[284] The nanotechnology in the powder can quickly analyze the fingerprint residue for demographic information of the depositor, such as drug intoxication, explosive chemical signatures, and ethnicity.

- *Iodine fuming:* Next to powders, iodine fuming is one of the oldest methods used to search for latent prints. Unlike ninhydrin that involves a chemical reaction, iodine causes a physical reaction to take place in the fatty acids present in fingerprint residues. Evidence is placed inside a fuming chamber with a sample of solid iodine crystals, and heat is applied. As the fatty acids absorb the iodine, they turn an orange/brownish color. The reaction will fade over time, so iodine fumed prints need to be photographed and processed further to preserve the information. This type of fuming is considered nondestructive, meaning it will not impede other forms of chemical processing. This is the reason that iodine fuming is often tried before other techniques.

- *Ninhydrin:* Ninhydrin is the most widely used chemical to detect latent prints on porous surfaces. Ninhydrin chemically reacts with the amino acids present in fingerprint residue. When the amino acids react, it results in a purple color called Ruhemann's purple. Ruhemann's purple is named after Siegfried Ruhemann, the scientist who accidentally mixed the compound in 1910 and discovered its reaction to amino acids.[285] Ninhydrin can be sprayed, dipped, or brushed onto the evidence. Once the evidence is dry, it is processed in a dark, humid location for 1–2 days at room temperature. Or it can be placed in a heat/humidity chamber (80% relative humidity) for approximately 30 minutes.

- *Physical developer (silver nitrate):* Physical developer is a solution of iron salts that reduces silver nitrate to metallic silver. Physical developer is effective on dry and wet porous surfaces, including sticky surfaces like duct tape, but is most often utilized with wet, porous evidence. Like the effect of photographic physical developer on film, porous evidence reacts to the chemical in a similar redox reaction. A redox reaction is when electrons are shared, resulting in a change in oxidation in the reactant. The fingerprints result in a dark gray or black color due to the absorption of metallic silver on the fatty acids in the perspiration residue.[286] Evidence is dipped in physical developer and then rinsed with water. The evidence is then allowed to air dry, or a dryer can be used to speed up the drying time. The prints should be photographed immediately after the evidence has dried because the developed print is sensitive to light, just like film removed from a camera.

PRESERVATION AND COLLECTION

There are many processing and preservation methods that can be used at a crime scene, and each crime scene will yield a unique set of situations. A common method used in the search for latent fingerprints includes the investigators starting with an observational overview of the crime scene by scanning the surfaces with the ALS. As potential friction ridge detail is illuminated, the technicians will dust the areas with fingerprint powder. Magnetic powder is the preferred powder and is available in a variety of colors. Investigators should always wear gloves to avoid cross contamination of their own friction ridge skin. The Crime Scene Unit (CSU) will often request copies of the fingerprint cards of police officers who were present at the scene for elimination prints. Elimination prints are fingerprints of anyone who was at the crime scene, including the residents, property owners, medical personnel, and officers.

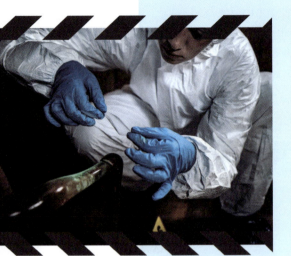

After dusting the fingerprints, personnel will attempt to lift the prints with clear fingerprint lifting tape and apply them to a white backing card. Depending on the agency, lifted prints are packaged together (since they are protected behind the tape) or packaged separately in either paper or plastic, depending on the type of print collected. If the evidence contains any moisture, it should be allowed to air dry and then placed in paper packaging to provide breathable storage and reduce the chance of fungal contamination.

The surface where fingerprint evidence is located will determine whether the evidence is collected and brought to the lab for processing or processed and packaged directly at the scene. If the surface is large, like a door frame, window, or unmovable object, the technicians will process directly at the scene. For high-profile cases, the evidence may be physically removed and transported to the lab to ensure the sequential order of processing is completed in a controlled environment.

As with all evidence, proper packaging, labeling, and securing of evidence is a priority to establish the integrity of the evidence for the judicial proceedings. Chain of custody procedures must be followed as the evidence transfers from the scene to the lab for processing, back to the experts, to the evidence storage facility, and finally to court. One break in the chain of custody will invalidate the evidence and jeopardize the meticulous work of the forensic investigators.

ANALYSIS OF FINGERPRINTS

As fingerprint evidence arrives at the latent print unit, experts will begin an analysis of its value. They will attempt to classify the prints into one of the three types: arch, loop, and whorl. These are considered class characteristics. If the class characteristics are not a match between the latent and known prints, they can quickly be eliminated. If the class characteristics are a match, the technician will begin to search for individual characteristics, or minutiae. A sufficient number of minutiae characteristics are necessary to make an identification. There is no standard number of required minutiae to establish an identification, but historically, the minimum is between 7–10 matching characteristics. Many times, there is not sufficient ridge detail for comparison, and the latent is labeled as having no value for comparison. If there are no known prints or possible suspects to compare the evidence prints against, the responsibility falls on the detectives to investigate and procure these prints for comparison or request an AFIS search to help develop a suspect.

Once known comparison prints are available, the latent print expert evaluates the evidence print and the suspect print side by side, and they will begin the process of comparing minutiae characteristics. The minutiae must be in the same order, location, and spatial relationship in both prints. If there are no unexplained differences, the prints are considered to have originated from the same person.

Once the first examiner has confirmed an ident, the latent print and known print will be assigned to a second examiner for verification. The second examiner will complete all the steps conducted by the initial examiner. If both examiners arrive at the same conclusion, the veracity of the ident is likely to be upheld in court.

When an ident is verified and the case scheduled for court, an attorney may request a comparison chart be prepared. The side-by-side comparison chart outlines the matching characteristics point by point to show the same orientation, order, and placement between the crime scene print and the known print (see **Figure 2**).

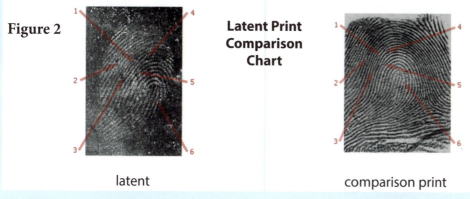

Figure 2

Latent Print Comparison Chart

latent　　　　　　　　　　　　comparison print

It is not uncommon to find differences between the two prints that can be scientifically explained. Differences between known and latent prints include varying pressure, surface type, contaminants, and type of fingerprint development. When a difference falls within these categories, it does not preclude an identification.

If no known fingerprints are available and no viable suspects are identified, another tool for the examiner is to submit the latent prints into AFIS (Automated Fingerprint Identification System) for a biometric search against a database of known prints. This system will be discussed in the next section.

A positive identification is not only the responsibility of the initial examiner and second examiner, but the supervisor also verifies the ident. Depending on the case, each one may be required to testify to the veracity of the evidence in court. A positive identification is taken very seriously since one wrong ident can ruin a fingerprint expert's career and the wrongly identified individual's livelihood.

BIOMETRICS

Biometrics is defined as a system of body measurements and calculations related to human characteristics for identification. Over the last fifty years, biometric technology has advanced at an accelerated rate. The most common uses for biometric technology are fingerprint identification and facial recognition, though there are many other forms of biometric platforms. The Department of Homeland Security (DHS) in the U.S. uses a system called IDENT that currently holds more than 260 million unique identities and processes more than 350,000 biometric transactions per day.[287] A ten-print rap sheet request to the FBI's Criminal History Record Information (CHRI) can search millions of prints in just 20 seconds.[288] The biometric platforms described below provide an overview of the trending forensic biometric identification systems.

Live Scan. Over five decades of research has been dedicated to developing an automated method to search for the minutiae characteristics that provide unique identity in individuals.[289] Live Scan is an inkless electronic device that collects fingerprints and palm prints for storage in known databases. Live Scan is used for criminal and civil ten-print cards. Live Scan will capture the fingerprint and palm print images for search in the AFIS system (more on this below). The AFIS system can complete a criminal background search against the national database in approximately 20 seconds and a civil fingerprint search in 3–5 days.

AFIS (Automated Fingerprint Identification System). After WWII, the space race was launched. The primary goals were to be the first to reach space and eventually the moon. This mission employed hundreds of scientists and engineers for decades. When the space race ended in the 1970s, these same scientists and engineers, whose mission was now complete, recognized they would soon be out of work and were looking for a new venture. According to Alex Tichy, one of the aerospace engineers involved in the Apollo Program, a group of scientists were sitting around a table, discussing their next venture in 1973. The scientists began to brainstorm a computer system that could read and search fingerprint patterns. This group launched the AFIS project in 1974. The group sold the first AFIS system to the Minnesota Law Enforcement Agency in 1977.[290]

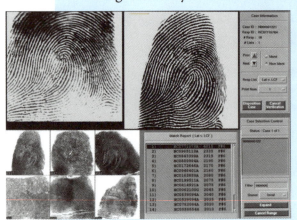

In 1980, AFIS was available worldwide and was recognized as the first tool to biometrically match latent fingerprints to known fingerprints stored in databases. There were several challenges leading up to the successful implementation of AFIS. The system had to be read and capture the ridge detail on traditional ten-print inked fingerprint cards. It then had to be able to record and store the information. Finally, it needed to compare the minutiae on latent prints to those from fingerprint cards in the system.[291] But the tenacity of the scientists had resulted in a successful platform that searched friction ridge detail.

By 1999, over 500 AFIS systems were in operation around the world, with hundreds more functioning today. As technology advances, with the ability to store iris scans and facial recognition software, AFIS is quickly becoming ABIS (Automated Biometric Identification System). "With the new generation of ABIS software, fingerprint examiners can process multiple complex biometric transactions with high accuracy and link face recognition to fingerprint or iris scanning."[292]

Though it appears that computers can effectively search these characteristics in a fraction of time, the human factor behind the information is the most important aspect. A human must fingerprint a criminal on the Live Scan during arrest, a human must search and collect the latent prints, a human must input the data into AFIS, a human must set up the parameters for searching, and a human must verify the results. The training to be an effective AFIS operator who not only uploads images but is also qualified to compare patterns and make identifications takes between 12–18 months and is not a simple task.

NGI. The Next Generation Identification (NGI) system is the upgraded FBI version of the IAFIS (Integrated Automated Fingerprint Identification System). The FBI started using the NGI in 2013, and it is recognized as containing the most extensive criminal history collection in the world. NGI contains over 154 million criminal, civil, and military fingerprint ten-print cards.

Next Generation Identification system

CONCLUSION

The probability that two individuals will have identical characteristics is 1 in 64 trillion.[293] The search for these unique characteristics is one of the first pieces of evidence uncovered at a crime scene. Fingerprint processing techniques will continue to evolve as new methods are discovered. Twenty years ago, it was impossible to successfully retrieve a fingerprint from fabric, but recent developments in the last decade have made this a reality.[294] The scientists on the project describe the process:

> We take these fabrics, place them in a vacuum chamber, then heat up gold to evaporate it and spread a fine film over the fabric. We then heat up zinc, which attaches to the gold where there are no fingerprint residues. This helps reveal the fingerprint — where contact has been made we see the original fabric, where there was no contact we're left with the grey colour of the metal film.[295]

Once again, understanding the chemical properties of fundamental elements in nature, in this case gold and zinc, has led to significant advances in the field of fingerprint processing. Additionally, most elements on the periodic table are some form of metal. Due to the properties of metals, these surfaces provide challenges in the search for fingerprints on knives and firearms. But new technology called Time-of-Flight Secondary Ion Mass Spectroscopy (ToF-SIMS) has been found to develop high resolution fingerprint images from metal surfaces where traditional methods have failed.[296] Scientists discovered when using ToF-SIMS that "The technique is capable of revealing fingerprints in so much detail, defined ridge definition and the position and shape of the sweat pores are clearly visible."[297] The future of latent fingerprint development is limitless, and it will be exciting to see what techniques are discovered in the coming years.

Lesson 19
Trace Evidence Part I: Hair vs. Fur

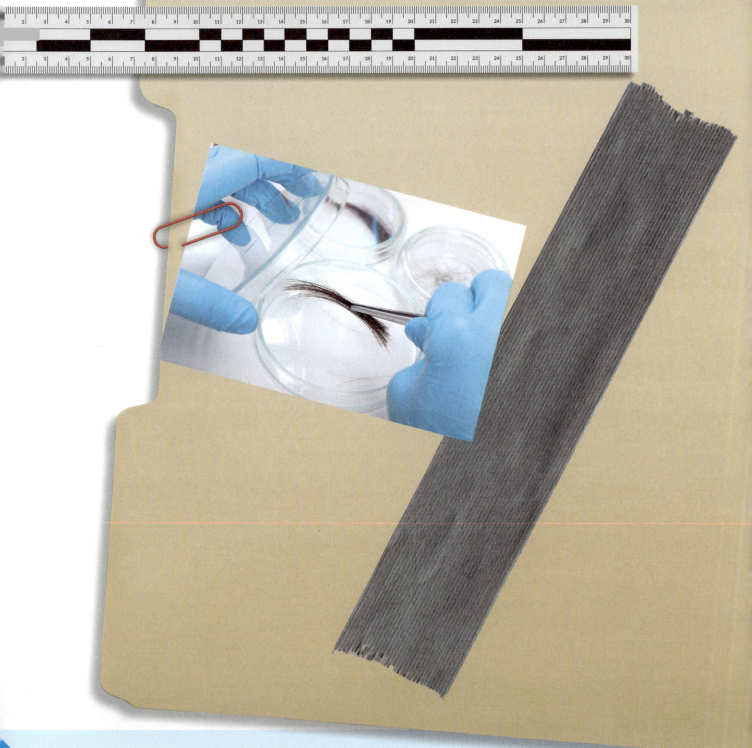

Why, even the hairs of your head are all numbered. Fear not; you are of more value than many sparrows (Luke 12:7).

Case Study: Thwarted by a Single Hair

In March of 1998, Christopher Faviell and Charles Martinez boasted about a murder and coverup to their close friends. The friends relayed this information to the police. The first goal of the Ruidoso Police Department was to find the body of the woman they believed to be deceased. The police were able to piece together the driving route to the possible location of the body. The murdered body of Elizabeth (Liz) Langhorst-Ballard was found in a desert in Tularosa, New Mexico. The woman had been strangled to death, wrapped in plastic, and buried in a shallow grave. Coyotes had discovered the body first and had pulled half of it out of the shallow grave and carried it across the desert. This was helpful to investigators because the decaying body released a scent. A cadaver dog on his last mission before retiring was able to locate the remains of Ballard.

When the Ruidoso police arrived at the location of the murder on Evergreen Street to begin the investigation into her death, they found a crime scene cleaned, vacuumed, and thoroughly wiped of evidence related to her murder. The car used to transport the body from the apartment to the desert had also been cleansed of all trace evidence. Investigators examined Ballard's body and found hair, with the root, lodged in the fibers of her sock. A microscopic examination quickly determined it was not a human hair and resembled the fur of the suspects' pet dog. Since animal fur microscopy is considered a class characteristic, the fur sample was sent to a lab in California that specialized in forensic animal DNA. A DNA match would provide the individual identification needed for conviction.

Facts about the case:

- One of the defendants, Charles Martinez, was known as "Eva." Charles and Christopher Faviell were involved in a 13-year relationship and lived on Evergreen Street. They met Ballard at a bar in 1997.
- Faviell decided he no longer wanted to live that lifestyle. Martinez moved out and Ballard moved in, but the relationship between Faviell and Ballard was tumultuous from the beginning. Their relationship only lasted a few months.
- During their brief relationship, Liz Ballard had filed assault and battery charges against Christopher Faviell.
- By January 1998, Faviell and Martinez reunited. On February 14, 1998, Christopher and "Eva" (Charles Martinez) had a wedding ceremony. Charles, now "Eva" 100% of the time, despised Ballard for separating him from Chris those few short months.
- Christopher left several threatening telephone messages on Liz Ballard's answering machine the week before her murder. Christopher and "Eva" told close friends that "Liz is going down" and "I'm going to kill her."[298] These same friends notified police when Faviell and "Eva" started bragging about getting rid of Liz in early March 1998.
- Police questioned Christopher and "Eva" and searched their home. Among the evidence they collected were fur samples from the pet dog, a pit bull mix named Hercules.

- After an exhaustive search based on the geographic descriptions relayed by Christopher and "Eva," on April 7, 1998, police discovered the remains of Liz Ballard.
- Investigators were able to collect hairs from one of her socks. This trace evidence was sent to the lab for examination. Examiners were able to identify the hairs as canine and match them to fur samples taken from Hercules, but it was not conclusive enough for a conviction.
- Ruidoso police contacted Dr. Joy Halverson. Dr. Halverson created the very first canine DNA database and had previously aided police in evaluating dog DNA, which resulted in a conviction. Dr. Halverson successfully matched the dog fur from Liz's sock to the sample collected from Hercules.[299]

It was discovered that Liz appeared uninvited at the Evergreen home the night of her murder. After a night of drinking, she claimed to want peace with the two men and went to their home around 2:30 a.m. Martinez was angry over Ballard's previous attachment to Christopher, and this led to the attack and subsequent murder of Liz. The two men, Christopher Faviell and Charles "Eva" Martinez, both pled guilty. Faviell accepted a plea bargain for second-degree murder, as well as aiding and abetting Liz's murder. He only served four and a half years in prison. Charles "Eva" Martinez was convicted of first-degree murder, but he battled the conviction and was granted a plea of second-degree murder in 2007. He was released in 2016.

"The case left its mark nationally as the first time DNA was extracted from a dog root hair."[300]

Though forensic scientists still cannot match an animal hair to one specific animal (such as "Fido" or "Fluffy"), microscopy does allow for a quick identification of animal kind origin. Any type of evidence that requires magnification to study its details is called trace evidence. The next few lessons will discuss different types of trace evidence and the unique characteristics hidden to the naked eye.

"You see, but you do not observe." — Sherlock Holmes[301]

Trace evidence is evidence resulting from two objects or people coming into direct contact with one another. This is based on Dr. Edmond Locard's Exchange Principle: When two objects come into contact with one another, there is an exchange of material between them. When a suspect and victim interact through physical contact, an exchange of trace materials is inevitable. The exchange of trace evidence can be linked to the scene, the individuals involved, and mechanisms of transport. Trace evidence can also be created through movement of environmental factors such as wind, sand, or weather such as rain or snow. Trace evidence is often plentiful, easily transferable, and microscopic. An expert in this field will require training to effectively evaluate and identify the relevant characteristics in trace evidence as well as relate it back to a specific source, event, or time. Trace evidence will often yield class characteristics, but it is far more difficult to produce individual characteristics. The next four lessons will focus on trace evidence as it relates to minute characteristics in human hair, animal fur, textile fibers, glass, paints, soil, wood, and pollen.

HAIR

Hair is composed of keratin, which makes it durable. There are three fundamental reasons why hair is valuable trace evidence:

1. It resists decomposition.
2. It retains its structural features for a long period of time.
3. It contains chemical markers for health and drug use.

Hairs are one of the most common biological pieces of evidence found at crime scenes. On average, one human scalp contains between 80,000 and 100,000 hairs,[302] and humans shed an average of 100 hairs per day.[303] A quick microscopic examination can determine if the hair is of human or animal origin, as well as whether the hair fell out naturally or was pulled out in a violent altercation. Human hairs provide clues to ethnicity, area of the body, length and color of the hair, overall health, chemical treatments, and method of removal from the source.[304] However, it is extremely difficult to link one human hair to one individual. When the skin, tissue, and/or root of the hair are present, it increases the likelihood of a match through DNA typing. There have been a few cases where an ample number of hair samples were available and trace analysts were able to create a DNA profile without the hair follicle. A mitochondrial DNA analysis is possible without the hair follicle,[305] but remember, mitochondrial DNA can only verify female ancestry.

Animal fur (hair) samples will often yield the kind, or taxonomic family, species, and breed of the source animal. Unique features in the scales and medulla of animal kinds differentiate them from each other. Genesis 1 describes the creation of animals "according to their kind," and this is exactly what is observed in the microscopic world of animal fur examination.

HAIR ANALYSIS FROM A BIBLICAL WORLDVIEW

A microscopic examination of human hair against animal fur confirms the creation account found in Genesis 1 in the Bible. God describes the creation of animals according to their kinds on days five and six of the creation week. Humans were fashioned in the image of God (Genesis 1:27). This description is used again in Genesis 7 when the Bible describes the animals sent to Noah's Ark, according to their kinds. What is a kind? Dr. Georgia Purdom, a molecular geneticist, explains that the original kind "represents the basic reproductive boundary of an organism. That is, the offspring of an organism is always the same *kind* as its parents, even though it may display considerable variation."[306] A biblical kind is usually equivalent to the family level in Linnean taxonomy.

Based on these descriptions in the Bible, there should be observable differences in the created kinds. And though obvious differences exist on the macro level, they are also visible on the micro level in something as simple as a single strand of fur. Each animal kind (or family level in biological taxonomy) exhibits unique traits that distinguish them from every other animal family. This confirms the Bible and refutes evolutionary ideas that all life evolved from one common source. An analyst can observe a hair sample and quickly determine whether it is of human or animal origin, as well as which animal family it is from. Both the scale and medulla patterns provide clues into the source of hair or fur sample. The medulla of a cat will resemble a chain of small pearls, while a dog's looks like small blocks stacked together and a horse's has a mosaic pattern. Primates' fur samples are clearly different from that of a human. Human hair is set apart from the animal kingdom. This lesson will outline the created differences between human and animal hair in both form and function. These are a few examples of the amazing artwork of God visible in the fur of animals.

dog

primate

domestic cat

camel

HISTORY OF HAIR EVIDENCE

The history of hair examination can be traced back to 12th-century China. In the book *The Washing Away of Wrongs* written by investigator Sung Tz'u, Tz'u describes his observations of hair analysis: "The difference of a hair is the difference of a thousand li." (A li is equivalent to a mile in the Chinese language).[307] During his criminal investigations, he recognized there were unique properties that differentiated hair samples.

Investigators first recognized the value of trace hair evidence in the late 1800s. The first book to mention the use of hair in forensic investigation was *The Principles and Practice of Medical Jurisprudence* by Taylor and Stevenson in 1883. John Glaister, a pioneer in mammalian fur microscopy, published a photomicrograph collection titled *Hairs of Mammalia from the Medico-legal Aspect* in 1931. Glaister spent many years photographing the microscopic medulla patterns in animal families, and his publication provided a reference upon which to build forensic hair analysis. The next major publication in this field came in 1977, when John Hicks published *Microscopy of Hairs: A Practical Guide and Manual*. This manual has become the "bible" of forensic hair examiners and is a required reading for experts in the field.

It was not until 1980 that scientists successfully analyzed the concentration of cocaine in a hair sample.[308] This breakthrough allowed for the routine practice of drug analysis from hair samples.

HAIR ANATOMY AND GROWTH

Hair Anatomy. Hair is made of a protein called keratin, which is also the same substance comprising nails and the primary protein in skin. Hair keratin is an outgrowth of skin found in mammals. Hairs are anchored to the skin by the hair follicle. The hair follicle resembles a bulb that contains living cells. The cells are nourished by blood vessels that contain hormones. The variation in hormonal levels throughout someone's life directly affects hair growth, texture, and health. Living cells result in cell division that occurs in the hair follicle and are responsible for the growth of the hair shaft.

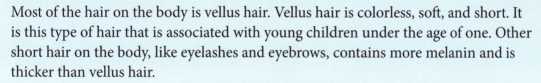

Humans have hair on their entire bodies, except for three specific areas: on the palms of the hands and bottoms of the feet (friction ridge skin) and the lips. Remember, the design of friction skin present on the hands and feet aids in a firmer grip and would be hindered if hair were present. The Lord God thinks of everything! Though not friction skin, the creases in lip patterns also provide unique identity. Imagine what it would be like to eat ice cream if God had created humans with hair on their lips. Human hair characteristics vary depending on their origin, such as the head, pubic region, chest, arms, legs, eyelashes, etc.

Most of the hair on the body is vellus hair. Vellus hair is colorless, soft, and short. It is this type of hair that is associated with young children under the age of one. Other short hair on the body, like eyelashes and eyebrows, contains more melanin and is thicker than vellus hair.

Head hair has two overarching anatomical features: the hair shaft and the hair follicle. The hair follicle is the living part of the hair where cell division is occurring. It is the part of the hair that is needed for nuclear DNA analysis. Since it is living, there is a slight feeling of pain when hair is forcibly removed from the scalp. In contrast, the hair shaft is the nonliving portion of the hair. When the hair is cut at the salon, there is no pain because the cells in this section of the hair are dead.

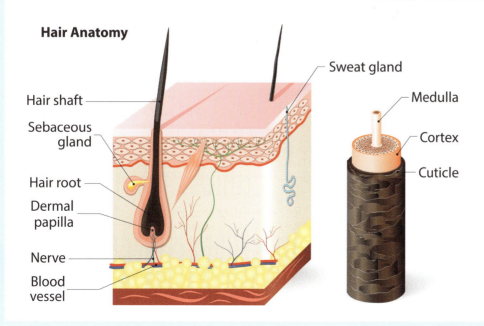

The hair shaft has three basic parts: medulla, cortex, and cuticle.

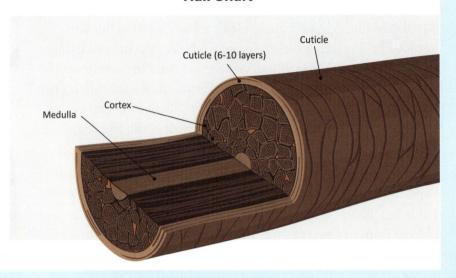

Hair Shaft

✔ *Medulla:* The medulla is the core, or central canal, of the hair. The medulla runs the entire length of the hair shaft. The medulla contains sugars and amino acids. In humans, the medulla is present in one of three patterns: continuous, fragmented, or absent. The medulla pattern can vary by hair in one individual. Therefore, multiple hair samples from varying areas on the head are collected for analysis.

continuous

fragmented

absent

✔ *Cortex*: The cortex surrounds the medulla and is made of keratin. This is the thickest layer of the hair shaft, and it contains the melanin that determines the hair color. The color of hair is created by the pigment cells that contain melanin in the hair follicle. As a person ages, the pigment cells die and no longer produce melanin. This results in a gray hair color. The cortex also contains elongated cells that run parallel to the length of the hair. The cortex is useful in examining the overall health of the individual.

✔ *Cuticle*: The cuticle protects the hair with overlapping scales made of keratin. These flattened cells on the cuticle always point away from the root of the hair. There are three types of cuticle patterns:

Coronal: The coronal scale pattern resembles stacked children's play cups and is found in rodents, bats, and other animal species.

Spinous: The spinous pattern resembles the top of an asparagus in appearance. This pattern is found in cats, seals, and other animal species.

Imbricate: The imbricate pattern resembles a brick wall with no repeating pattern. This is the primary pattern found in humans.

Hair Growth. Hair grows on average half an inch per month. The maximum growth length of hair is dependent on a person's genetics. For most people, the maximum hair length is around 40 inches in an adult, around 24 inches in children, and 6 inches in infants under the age of one. There is a genetic variation where some people have grown their hair much longer due to elongated periods in the anagen stage (see below). The Guinness World Records holder for hair length is Xie Quiping, who has a recorded hair length of 21.7 feet.

Hair growth occurs in three cycles: anagen, catagen, and telogen. Most hairs recovered at crime scenes are in the telogen phase.

Phase	Biological Factors	% of Hair Follicles	Length in Phase
Anagen	Growth phase above and around the dermal papilla of the follicle.	80–90	Approximately 1,000 days
Catagen	Transitional phase where the hair follicle withers and prepares to dislodge.	2	10–14 days
Telogen	Resting phase that includes: 1. No hair growth. 2. The old hair detaches. 3. The new hair enters the growth phase (anagen).	10–18	100 days

Trace Evidence Part I: Hair vs. Fur

ETHNICITY AND HAIR

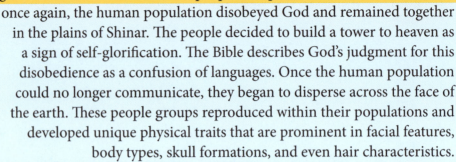

After the global Flood, God commanded people to reproduce and fill the earth. But once again, the human population disobeyed God and remained together in the plains of Shinar. The people decided to build a tower to heaven as a sign of self-glorification. The Bible describes God's judgment for this disobedience as a confusion of languages. Once the human population could no longer communicate, they began to disperse across the face of the earth. These people groups reproduced within their populations and developed unique physical traits that are prominent in facial features, body types, skull formations, and even hair characteristics.

The FBI has categorized hair types into three major ethnic groups: European, African, and Asian. Within these three groups, observed variation is visible in the pigment granules, overall hair type, and cross sections.[309] These characteristics help the hair analyst determine probable ethnic origin of the evidence collected at the scene.

Ethnic Group	Pigment Granules	Hair Type	Cross Section
European	Fine to medium in size / Distributed evenly	Straight or wavy	Round or oval
African	Large / Clumped into groups	Curly or kinky	Oval
Asian	Medium size / Grouped in patches	Straight	Circular

HUMAN HAIR AND ANIMAL FUR

Humans are the only creation made in the image of God and set apart from the animal kingdom. Distinct, observable differences can be seen in human hair when compared against animal fur. According to the FBI, "Each species of animal possesses hair with characteristic length, color, shape, root appearance, and internal microscopic features that distinguish one animal from another."[310] This is another example of how observational science always confirms the Bible. A few of these differences occur in the way hair/fur grows, the diameter, medulla patterns, and textures.

Animals' medulla patterns help to differentiate between animal kinds. Some animals have beautiful patterns in their medulla, and others generally have continuous or fragmented patterns. The primary difference between animals and humans is the width of the medulla. This is measured by the medullary index, which is the diameter of the medulla divided by the diameter of the hair, both measured in microns. In humans, the medullary index is less than one-third, whereas in animals it generally is greater than one-half.

| human | dog | deer | rabbit | rat |

Evolutionists claim that the presence of hair/fur on all mammals confirms common ancestry, but a simple examination refutes this ideology. There are clear observational differences between humans and animals. The chart below outlines several of the key distinctions between human hair and animal fur.

Differences Between Human Hair and Animal Fur

	Human Hair	Animal Fur
Growth	Grows continuously, independently, and replaces in a mosaic pattern unrelated to a season.	Growth stops and is synchronized by season.
Overall Diameter	Thinner	Wider
Medulla (Medullary index)	Thinner < ⅓	Wider > ½
Melanin Distribution	Consistent color and dense near the follicle	Abrupt color change or "banding" with density near the medulla
Root Shape	Club shaped	Varies by animal kind
Scale Pattern	Imbricate	Varies by animal kind, but mostly spinous or coronal
Texture	Soft and potential to grow long	Coarse and generally short in length
Temperature Regulation	No ability to regulate temperature	Regulates temperature

Animal fur is classified into three types outside of the tail and equine mane hairs. Tail and equine mane hairs are often considered "hair" since their appearance and growth are similar to human hair. Within the three types of animal fur, God provided an array of variation, form, and function.

Trace Evidence Part I: Hair vs. Fur

- Guard hairs are the protective outer hairs.
- Fur hairs are the inner coat and provide insulation.
- Tactile hairs (whiskers) are located on the head and provide sensory functions.[311]

The most common animal samples recovered from crime scenes include domestic pets, such as cats and dogs, cattle, deer, and rabbits. Animal fur can be matched to the species and breed of the animal kind, but they cannot be linked to one individual animal without DNA. According to the FBI, "Animal hairs do not possess enough individual characteristics to differentiate individual animals from other similar animals."[312]

Ligature:
Something used to tie or bind.

COLLECTION

In the search for trace hair evidence, the investigator will begin with a focused search of suspect and victim clothing, ligatures, weapons, bodies, clothing, jewelry, and other items found in the crime scene. Because trace evidence is often plentiful and easily transferred, investigators will prioritize using a holistic approach while considering the location of the evidence in proximity to the crime. There are several tools available to search for and collect trace evidence. These include forceps to collect and bag the evidence, clear tape to pick up hairs, as well as combs, clippers, specialized vacuums, swabs, alternate light sources, and more. Evidence vacuum sweepers are one of the favorite methods of collecting trace evidence. Investigators simply vacuum one area then replace the filter and evidence collection bag. They can efficiently vacuum multiple rooms at a scene with no cross contamination. The entire filter and collection bag are then submitted to the trace unit at the lab for analysis.

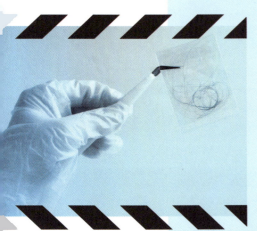

The investigators will collect control samples and, if possible, suspect hair samples. Samples will include those that are associated with the crime scene, victims, and any animals within the proximity. Hairs will reveal different characteristics, depending on the area of the body and section of the scalp. In humans, this variation requires that 50 hairs, both pulled and combed, be collected for analysis. They will also collect from different areas of the head by selecting ten hairs each from five sections, as well as similar samples from other parts of the body if warranted.

Holistic:
Looking at the whole rather than its parts.

EXAMINATION

Examination begins under a microscope. A simple compound microscopic examination will reveal the shape and bodily origin of the hair, its color, ethnic origin, and other visual features. Hair samples are evaluated in a two-step process, first for their origin and second for comparison against suspect hairs. Scientists use a comparison microscope (see **Figure 1**), which allows them to look at both the suspect and known reference samples simultaneously. This process can take hours, days, weeks, and sometimes months as one single hair is compared individually.

Figure 1

questioned hair

known hair

Comparison Microscope

Establishing a statistical certainty between suspect and known hair samples is challenging. Though it appears that hair analysis is consistent and reliable, there are several factors that hinder both class and individualistic identification. Some reasons for this include:

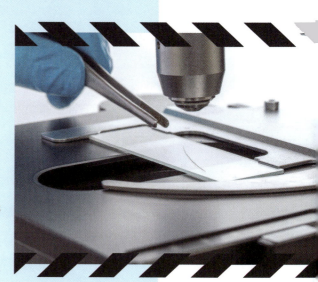

- ✔ The necessity of the hair follicle and root tissue to establish a nuclear DNA profile. When DNA is sufficient for typing, a complete DNA profile is only successful in 60–70% of the cases.
- ✔ Chemical treatments and peroxides in hair dyes break down the DNA and alter the cuticle.
- ✔ The frequent use of cleaning agents, such as shampoos and conditioners, can reduce the likelihood of DNA typing.
- ✔ The age of the sample has a direct impact on the ability to extract viable DNA for profiling. The older the sample, the less likely technicians will be able to construct a DNA profile.

CONCLUSION

Though the examination of trace evidence can be a long, tedious process, it has the potential to provide connections between people and places, people and people, and as seen in the case study, people and animals. Small microscopic traces of information are easily transferred when two things come into contact with one another, and this is unavoidable. The unique characteristics of human hair and animal fur, within their created kinds, confirm the truth of God's Word from the very first chapter in Genesis. And every person is so valuable to God that at every moment in their life, He knows the exact number of hairs on their head. Considering that number varies between 80,000 to 100,000 daily, this is one more example of God's amazing devotion and attention to His creation.

Lesson 20
Trace Evidence Part II: Fibers

She seeks wool and flax, and works with willing hands (Proverbs 31:13).

Case Study: Wayne Williams

On July 28, 1979, the bodies of two young males were discovered on the side of a road in Atlanta. One had died of a gunshot wound and the other of asphyxiation. This began a string of 30 murders over a 22-month period. Since most of the victims were children, the killings were coined the Atlanta Child Murders. Investigators were able to link the crimes due to rare yellow-green nylon fibers present on many of the victims. By the spring of 1980, the FBI was called in to help solve the case and to develop a criminal profile. The MO (*modus operandi*) for the murderer was to dump the bodies in wooded areas. As the cases became more public and the murderer was in fear of capture, the killer changed the pattern and started disposing of the victims in the Chattahoochee River in the spring of 1981. Though tragic for the victims and their families, this turned out to be very helpful for police investigators. There are only 14 bridges that cross the Chattahoochee River, and the FBI narrowed their watch to these specific areas. In May of 1981, officers heard a loud splash at 3 a.m. They observed a car fleeing the scene. The officers immediately pursued and pulled over 22-year-old Wayne Williams. Since officers did not know the reason for the splash and had no probable cause, they had to let Williams go. But two days later, a body was discovered downstream from the location of the splash, and Williams was brought in for questioning. Williams failed three polygraph examinations and had no reliable alibis. He was arrested for the murders.

Authorities obtained search warrants for Williams' residence and car. During a search of Williams' home, police discovered that his carpet was Luxaire English Olive carpet, a rare yellow-green nylon carpet made by a Georgia carpet company. This evidence in conjunction with head hair, dog fur from his German shepherd, yellow blanket fibers from Williams' bed, and eyewitness testimony linked Williams to the crimes. The probability that more than one person could have the same dog fur and carpet fibers on multiple pieces of evidence became the focus of the prosecution.

Williams was convicted of two counts of murder in 1982 and sentenced to life in prison. In this example, trace evidence was the primary focus of the prosecutor's case, and only careful evidence collection and examination by the crime scene professionals made it possible.[313]

Facts about the case:

- After Williams was arrested for the two murders, the killings immediately stopped.[314]
- Rare green nylon carpet fibers were found on 19 of the bodies.
- Statisticians estimated that only one in 8,000 Atlanta homes had Luxaire English Olive carpet installed.
- Red fibers were found on a victim's shoe that matched the carpet fibers from inside Williams' car.

- Fibers from the yellow bedspread collected from Williams' home were found on eight teenage and four adult victims.[315]
- An FBI expert testified that the presence of fibers and dog fur on nine of the murdered youths originated from Williams' home or car.[316]
- During the court proceedings, Williams became very angry and yelled at the prosecutors, "You want the real Wayne Williams? You got him right here."[317]
- Williams was never tried for the other 28 murders for which he was believed to be responsible. Those murder investigations have been closed.
- Williams is currently serving his sentence.
- He was denied parole in November of 2019 and will not be eligible again until November 2027.
- Wayne Williams maintains his innocence to this day.

Fibers are another form of trace evidence and require magnification for analysis. Though a certain color may be visible macroscopically, the individual construction of the fibers hold a wealth of information.

"I might not have gone but for you, and so have missed the finest study I have ever come across: a study in scarlet, eh? Why shouldn't we use a little art jargon. There's the scarlet thread of murder running through the colorless skein of life, and our duty is to unravel it, and isolate it, and expose every inch of it." — Sherlock Holmes[318]

Textiles are a yearly $70-billion industry and one of the most lucrative economies in the global market.[319] The United States produced more than 35,000 pounds of textiles in 2018.[320] India is the leader in cotton manufacturing and produced over 6,420 thousand metric tons in 2019.[321] Due to the quantity of fabric production worldwide, forensic fiber evidence is an integral part of investigation. A single fiber is defined as the smallest unit of a textile material. Fiber evidence has a length that is many times greater than its diameter. There are two fundamental types of fibers: natural and synthetic (man-made). Natural fibers include those of both animal- and plant-based origins. Both types of fibers can be spun together into a yarn, which is then woven into fabric. The value of the fiber to an investigation is dependent upon the type and color of fiber, the number of fibers, the location of the fibers, and the number of fibers that complete the triangle between the crime scene, victim, and the suspect. The greater the number of fibers, the greater the significance of the evidence.

In fiber investigation, experts will attempt to differentiate between primary and indirect transfer of evidence. Primary transfer is the direct exchange of materials between the crime scene and the victim, whereas indirect transfer is an exchange of already present fibers from the scene on the perpetrator transferred to the victim. Not all fibers will be exchanged or transferred between the crime scene, victim, and perpetrator due to tight weaves and a fabric's ability to "hold" fibers.[322] Even still, a single fiber has the potential to link an individual to a specific location or person due to Locard's Exchange Principle.

FIBERS FROM A BIBLICAL WORLDVIEW

In God's original creation, humans were not intended to wear clothing. When He created Adam and Eve, the historical record in Genesis 2:25 states, "And the man and his wife were both naked and were not ashamed." The perfect, sinless world would not have caused Adam and Eve to feel any shame or drive them to hide anything from God. So, why do people wear clothes today? When Adam and Eve chose to disobey God's commands, sin entered the world, and everything changed. The Bible says, "Then the eyes of both [Adam and Eve] were opened, and they knew that they were naked. And they sewed fig leaves together and made themselves loincloths" (Genesis 3:7). Sin affected Adam and Eve's perception of their nakedness. Nakedness in itself is not sin, but they now felt shame in their disobedience against a holy God and in their exposure. In fact, the wearing of clothes confirms the truth found in the Bible:

> Even today, nakedness is bonded with shame, as people the world over wear clothes. In fact, this doctrine of clothing that comes out of a literal rendering of Genesis reveals that, by wearing clothes, cultures and religions all over the world are confirming the Bible's account is true.[323]

Another point to think about is if evolution were true and humans are simply evolved animals and thereby animals themselves, why don't animals wear clothes? Answers to these challenging questions only make sense when viewed through the lens of the Bible. To adequately clothe Adam and Eve, God performed the first sacrifice, or shedding of blood, as payment for sin. Genesis 3:21 says, "And the Lord God made for Adam and for his wife garments of skins and clothed them."

The Creator God knew mankind would sin against Him, and yet He provided a wide variety of plants and animals to provide the necessary fibers for clothing. When fibers are examined in the Bible, there are direct references to wool, flax (linen), and fabrics. Clearly, Adam and Eve and their descendants would have relied on animal skins and natural fibers for coverings. Since these civilizations were quite advanced in metallurgy, weaponry, and architecture, they would have been skillful in the weaving of fibers into fabric, though there were certain laws to follow. Deuteronomy 22:11 forbid the Israelites from wearing garments containing wool and linen woven together. They were to wear clothing of one type of weave. Wool from goats and sheep would have been their primary source for clothing. Interestingly, historians have not discovered any evidence that the Israelites used cotton, the most popular fiber for clothing today.[324]

TYPES OF FIBERS: NATURAL VS. SYNTHETIC

Deuteronomy 22:11:
"You shall not wear cloth of wool and linen mixed together."

The first step in the investigation of fiber evidence is for the analyst to determine if the fiber is natural, synthetic, inorganic, or a mix. Proper identification of the fiber is necessary so that subsequent analysis and testing is properly administered. In the production of fabric, the use of natural and synthetic fibers is approximately a ratio of 50/50.

Natural fibers are those that stem from an organic (living), natural source. Natural fibers are further divided into two subcategories, dependent on whether they originate from cellulose (plants) or protein (animals). Animal (protein) fibers are the most common natural fiber encountered at crime scenes. Wool is the primary protein fiber used in textile production. Other animal fibers include camel, alpaca, and mohair. Silk is also classified as a natural protein fiber and is the only natural fiber to have a filament structure.[325] Due to its construction, there are no hair/fur characteristics. The most common plant (cellulose) fiber used to make fabrics is cotton. The United States produces 4,000 metric tons of cotton a year, with over 25 million tons produced worldwide.[326] Cotton grows on shrub plants. Other common plant-based fibers include flax, jute, and hemp. Natural fibers can also be classified into a subcategory of vegetable fibers. Within this category, analysts would be classifying the types of fibers as stem, leaf, or seed.

The first synthetic fibers were derived from raw cellulose materials like cotton or wood. The cellulose is extracted, chemically treated, and forced through production jets. These fibers are referred to as regenerated fibers. True synthetic fibers are made from the manufacturing of raw materials that are not derived from natural fibers. Nylon and polyester are the two most common synthetic fibers produced, followed by acrylics, rayons, and acetates.[327] Rayon was the very first manufactured regenerated fiber and was invented in France in the late 1800s by a scientist named Hilaire de Chardonnet. Rayon was followed by acetate in the 1920s.[328] History records an interesting story about the naming of rayon. When rayon was discovered, manufacturers were trying to decide what to name this new fiber. They created a naming committee, who decided to have a contest and offered a $1,000 prize. Over 10,000 name suggestions were received, but none were approved by the committee. During a meeting, one of the committee members said, "Let's just see if we can send a ray of light [on this problem]," and used the word *rayon*, which is a French word meaning "ray of light."[329] Rayon became the official name of this new fiber.

In 1933, an important discovery was made by Wallace Carothers. He invented the first truly synthetic fiber from glass filaments and called it nylon. Since this time, scientists have invented dozes of synthetic varieties. In 1954, under the Textile Products Identification Act, the Federal Trade Commission established generic names for manufactured fibers with approved trademarks.

FIBER COMPOSITION

All fibers are made of polymer chains. The word polymer comes from the Greek word *poly*, meaning "many," and *meros*, which means "part." Polymers are large molecules that connect like chain links. These chains are made of repeating groups of atoms that are bonded together. A good example of a polymer chain is to imagine a pile of paperclips. The individual paperclips can be seen in the pile. Now imagine someone picks up one of the paperclips and finds they are all linked together. This is similar to a polymer chain, with each paperclip representing the basic structure or monomer (repeating unit) of the polymer.

Polymers are present in both natural and synthetic fibers. When synthetic fibers were designed, scientists copied similar patterns existing in natural polymers like DNA. DNA has complex repeating units composed of amino acids. Animal hairs and cellulose-based fibers are also composed of polymer chains. This molecular structure is part of God's design throughout nature. Once again, God's creation is the template upon which man models to create new substances like manufactured fibers.

The design of polymers gives them both strength and flexibility. Polymers are arranged into crystal networks that provide their strength. Fibers have strength in their lengthwise direction and are their weakest at right angles to the fiber's direction. The parallel orientation of the polymer chains along the axis of the fiber is one of the properties that gives them their strength.[330] Amorphous or "jumbled" sections give fibers their unique flexibility.

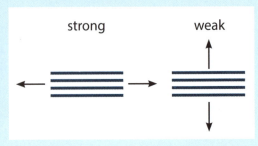

THREE PROPERTIES OF FIBERS

Fibers have three basic properties in their structure: orientation, crystallinity, and amorphousness. Orientation refers to the parallel alignment of the polymer chains along the long axis of the fiber. Orientation, along with crystallinity, provide fibers with their strength. Crystallinity is the order of the molecular chains in the fiber molecule. Crystallinity can be compared to scaffolding in a building, providing a framework for support and strength. The denser the crystalline structure, the more likely that the fiber will be inflexible and water repellant. For example, polyester is 65–85% crystalline and only 15–35% amorphous.

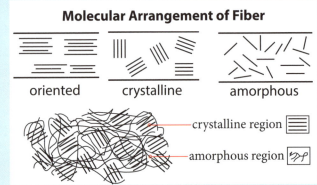

The amorphousness characteristic in a fiber is the regions of air space in between the crystalline scaffolding where no polymer chains are present. When a fiber has a higher percentage of amorphous regions, the fiber will tend to be more absorbent.[331] Wool is extremely absorbent. It is 70–75% amorphous and only 25–30% crystalline.

COLLECTION

As discussed in Lesson 19 in the collection of hair and fur trace evidence, fiber evidence is secured with the same types of tools — forceps, tape, vacuums, and other specialized tools. The process of collecting fiber evidence can be tedious, with each piece of evidence requiring separate packaging and labeling. This explains why vacuums with changeable filters are used so that collection is expedient at the crime scene and the fibers can be analyzed in detail at the lab. Review the information in the Lesson 19 "Collection" section for a reminder about proper collection of trace evidence. Most importantly, significance increases when the number of collected fibers on the victim's clothing matches that of the suspect's clothing, residence, car, etc. The more fiber evidence, the greater the percentage of certainty the two are connected.

EXAMINATION AND ANALYSIS

According to the FBI, when a fiber examiner matches fiber evidence to a known piece of clothing, fundamentally, either the fiber did or did not originate from the known source.

> In order to say that the fiber originated from the item of clothing, the clothing either had to be the only fabric of its type ever produced or still remaining on earth, or the transfer of fibers was directly observed. Since neither of these situations is likely to occur or be known, fiber examiners will conclude that the fibers could have originated from the clothing or that the fibers are consistent with originating from the clothing. The only way to say that a fiber did not originate from a particular item of clothing is to know the actual history of the garment or to have actually observed the fiber transfer from another garment.[332]

The problem with fiber evidence is that it is not individualized like a fingerprint and thereby is not sufficient evidence on its own to convict a suspect. It is theoretically only circumstantial and must be supported with corroborating evidence. The discovery of a less used natural or synthetic fiber increases the significance of the discovery. Examiners will also look at the dyes used to achieve a variety of colors in textiles. Other unique identifiers include fading, discoloration, and staining, which have the potential to increase the value of the fibers to the scene.

Though there are many examination tools available to study fiber evidence, the four primary methods discussed in this lesson are microscopic examination, chemical analysis, burn test, and solubility.

Microscopic Examination. Examination of natural animal fibers resembles that of human hair analysis. As discussed in detail in Lesson 19, microscopic analysis will reveal the species origin, color, diameter, medulla characteristics, and scale patterns. Examiners should also be able to distinguish between the two types of animal hair, the animal's fur and their guard hairs.

A microscopic exam of cellulose fibers will reveal the diameter, length, crimp, and color. The diameter of natural fibers is measured in micrometers, while synthetic fibers are measured in deniers, or linear density, based on weight per unit length.[333] Length is the second most important property of fibers. Natural fibers (excluding silk) have a staple length of 2–46 cm. Silk and synthetic fibers are called filaments and can be of unlimited length due to the manufacturing process used to create them. The crimp of fibers is described as the waves, bends, and twists that occur along their length. Color application used to dye fibers and fabrics occurs in one of three methods:

1. Fibers are colored prior to being spun into yarns.
2. Yarns are dyed prior to being woven into fabrics.
3. Dyes are added to the surface of the fabric.

The application and absorption of the color into the fibers will determine the visible characteristics, method of comparison, and resulting analysis.

When studying synthetic fibers, a compound microscope uses light to reflect off the surface of the fiber and reveal the striation patterns and cross-sectional design. A unique feature and identifying quality of synthetic fibers is their cross-sectional shape. Under the microscope, synthetic fibers can be classified by their cross-sectional design, dye composition, and birefringence qualities.

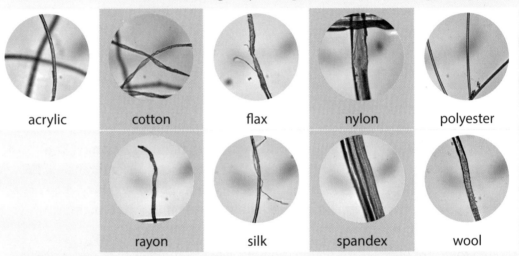

acrylic | cotton | flax | nylon | polyester
rayon | silk | spandex | wool

Analysts will also measure the length and diameter of the fiber, as well as examine the luster and damage, and attempt to identify any visible debris. Another unique feature in fibers is the addition of delustering particles (titanium dioxide) to reduce shine. The observant properties of these delustering particles can assist in fiber identification. Other microscopic analysis includes a phase contrast microscope to observe the structure of each fiber and a scanning electron microscope, which uses electrons to create an image of the fiber structure and patterns.

Once a suspect fiber and known fiber have been observed to be a potential match, they will be compared under a comparison microscope. When fibers are compared side by side, they should be viewed using the same magnification, lighting, and mounting on a microscope slide. Controlling these outside variables will help reduce the risk of missing or misidentifying a potential match.

Another property of manufactured fibers is their ability to exhibit double refraction, or birefringence. Synthetic fibers are polymers that are aligned in the direction of the length of the fiber. The crystalline structure formed by the polymers is what gives fibers their double refraction property. The fiber is placed in a fluid with similar refractive index and then placed under a polarizing microscope. The analyst will observe the disappearance of the Becke lines, and the index of refraction can be measured for the fiber. Becke lines will be discussed further in Lesson 21, as this is an important test in forensic glass analysis.

Luster:
A quality that causes material to reflect light and give them a sheen.

Chemical Analysis. The next significant step after microscopic characteristics is to perform an analysis of the chemical composition. Not only must there be similarity on the microscopic level, but the chemical make-up of each fiber must be identical. Chemical analysis will not only identify the generic classification, but the sub-classifications as well. Several generic manufactured fibers, like nylon and polyester, have multiple subclasses that exhibit unique chemical properties.

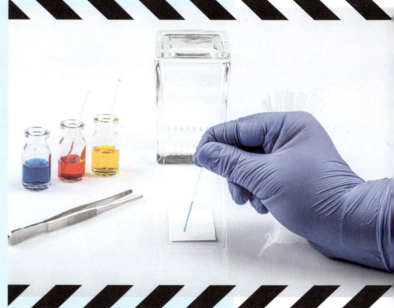

The chemical interaction between dyes and fabric is one of the most important pieces of information when analyzing fibers. Natural dyes have been used for thousands of years. The modern dye industry began over 150 years ago with the first manufactured, synthetic dye, mauve.[334] There are now thousands of dyes used in the clothing industry. The way a dye is attracted to a piece of cloth is called the cloth's affinity. Natural fibers have a higher affinity for dyes than those found in synthetic fibers. Remember the crystalline and amorphous structure of fibers discussed earlier in the lesson; this affects the water-soluble compounds found in dyes. Dyes have an electrical charge, meaning that natural fibers are easier to dye because of their molecular properties, which attract positive and negative charges. Hydrophobic synthetic fibers are far more difficult to dye. The only exception is nylon, which has many water-soluble compounds.

Hydrophobic: Water-repelling.

Another technique available to analysts is the extraction of the dyes for chromatography analysis. Once extracted, the dye is placed on a thin layer chromatography plate. The spectrum of the colors used in the dyes will be separated out into their individual components and can be observed for similarities under a comparison microscope.

The Burn Test. Different types of fibers exhibit unique properties when subjected to a flame. The way the fabric reacts to the presence of heat is an identifier to its origin. Fibers also give off a noticeable odor when burned. Cotton smells like burning paper, wool like burning hair, and nylon like celery.[335] See **Table 1** for more information on the odors attributed to natural and synthetic fibers. The presence or lack of ash will also provide insight into the classification of the fiber evidence. Natural fibers will often burn into some form of ash, while synthetic fibers will result in hard plastic black beads and will curl away from the flame.

Trace Evidence Part II: Fibers

Solubility Test. Solubility tests are very helpful in distinguishing synthetic regenerated fibers from truly manufactured. A microscopic exam can quickly separate natural from synthetic, but when examining synthetic fibers, a solubility test aids in the identification of hard-to-classify manufactured fibers. In a forensic lab, a variety of expensive solvents are available for testing, but fibers can also be analyzed with acetone, acetic acid, and hydrochloric acid. To review how common fibers react to the solubility testing, see below.

Table 1	NATURAL FIBERS		
Types	**Identification**	**Characteristics**	**Properties**
Cotton Flax Silk Alpaca Wool *Source:* Natural Fibers	Microscopic Exam Colors and Dyes Morphology (Structure) Birefringence: Polarizing Infrared Spectrophotometry Burn Test Solubility	Longest history of fiber use Produced from natural sources	Diameter Determine lengthwise striations Delustering particles Medulla and scale patterns Does not dissolve in sulfuric acid
Cotton *Source:* Cellulose (Plant)		Most common textile *Design:* flat, twist *Color:* creamy white/dirty gray	*Diameter:* 16-20 micrometers *Length:* ⅛ to 2½" *In flame:* burns, does not curl away from flame *Odor:* burning paper *Ash:* fluffy, gray Afterglow with smoldering Luster
Flax		First fiber used for textiles *AKA:* Linen *Color:* Light blonde to gray, blonde	*Diameter:* 40-80 micrometers *Length:* 8-24" *In flame:* burns, does not curl away from flame *Odor:* burning paper *Ash:* crystalline High heat resistance Afterglow with smoldering Bright luster Dissolves in high density acids

Types	Identification	Characteristics	Properties
Silk *Source*: Protein		Only natural filament fiber Composed of 2 filaments *Color*: translucent, white, yellow, brown, gray	*Diameter*: 12-30 micrometers *Length*: up to 656 yards *In flame*: burns slowly, and curls away from flame *Odor*: burning feathers *Ash*: crushable, black Self-extinguishing Bright luster Dissolves in sodium hydroxide *Exception*: will dissolve in sulfuric acid
Alpaca		Silky with tenacity Fleece sheared biannually *Color*: Over 22 colors Hypoallergenic	*Diameter*: < 30 microns *Length*: 9-10" *In flame*: Flame resistant, burns slowly Curls away from flame *Odor*: burning hair *Ash*: crushable, black Water resistant Dissolves in sodium hydroxide
Wool		Wool is most plentiful and resilient Weak fiber *One sheep*: 5500 miles of wool fiber/yr *Color*: off white to brown Hypoallergenic	*Diameter*: 14-45 micrometers *Length*: 1.5-15" Burns slowly, curls away from flame *Odor*: burning hair *Ash*: crushable, black Self-extinguishing Dissolves in sodium hydroxide
SYNTHETIC FIBERS			
Acetate Acrylic Nylon Polyester Rayon Spandex *Source*: Synthetic Fibers	Microscopic Exam Color Morphology (structure) Birefringence: Polarizing Microscope Infrared Spectrophotometry Burn Test Solubility	Discovery of polymers in late 1800s launched production Produced from synthetic chemicals	Diameter Determine lengthwise striations Delustering particles Cross sectional shape of fibers

Trace Evidence Part II: Fibers

Types	Identification	Characteristics	Properties
Acrylic		Latin *acryl*, meaning bitter Manufactured in 1950 *Color*: ivory or white	*Diameter*: 15-25 micrometers *Length*: varies *In flame*: yellow flame Melts and shrinks from flame *Odor*: chemical *Appearance*: brittle tan/black bead Continues to burn and melt *Microscopic*: dog-bone/kidney bean shape Resistant to acidic breakdown
Nylon		First manufactured fiber in 1933 80% used in carpet Stronger than steel wire *Color*: ivory	*Diameter*: 14-24 micrometers Length: varies *In flame*: burns with melting Melts and shrinks from flame *Odor*: celery *Appearance*: hard gray/tan bead Self-extinguishing *Microscopic*: round w/ smooth surface Slowly dissolves in acetic acid and hydrochloric acid
Polyester		Manufactured in 1951 2nd to cotton, with 40% in apparel *Color*: white, ivory, or transparent	*Diameter*: 12-25 micrometers *Length*: varies *In flame*: burns Melts and shrinks from flame *Odor*: sweet *Appearance*: hard black bead Self-extinguishing *Microscopic*: no features Dissolves slowing in sulfuric acid

Types	Identification	Characteristics	Properties
Spandex		Anagram of "expands" Manufactured in 1950s 80% of clothing contains spandex Stretches up to 5x its length *Color*: white	*Diameter*: 12-25 micrometers *Length*: varies *In flame*: burns Melts with no shrinking *Odor*: chemical *Ash*: soft black Continues to burn and melt *Microscopic*: groups of fibers fused together Resistant to acidic breakdown
Rayon *Source*: Cellulose Synthetic		Silky with tenacity Fleece sheared biannually *Color*: Over 22 colors Hypoallergenic	*Diameter*: 12-25 micrometers Length: 1-21" *In flame*: burns, does not curl away from flame *Odor*: burning paper *Ash*: fluffy, gray ash Afterglow with smoldering *Microscopic*: striations & serrations Dissolves in hydrochloric acid

CONCLUSION

Though fiber identification is not as conclusive as fingerprints, a positive match between suspect clothing, carpet, or similar fiber and the victim is valuable circumstantial evidence. The FBI reiterates the importance of fiber evidence:

> Another important consideration is coincidence. When fibers that match the clothing fibers of the suspect are found on the clothing of a victim, two conclusions may be drawn: The fibers originated from the suspect, or the fibers originated from another fabric source that not only was composed of fibers of the exact type and color but was also in a position to contribute those fibers through primary or secondary contact. The likelihood of encountering identical fibers from the environment of a homicide victim (i.e., from his or her residence or friends) is extremely remote.[336]

Whether natural or synthetic, every fiber can be tested for unique characteristics that testify to their origin, manufacture, and location, and ultimately link a victim to the suspect.

Lesson 21
Trace Evidence Part III: Glass and Paint

Again Jesus spoke to them, saying, "I am the light of the world. Whoever follows me will not walk in darkness, but will have the light of life" (John 8:12).

Case Study: Green River Killer

"I didn't have no morals or conscience to stop me."[337]

Two boys were riding their bikes home across Green River on Meeker Bridge near Kent, Washington, on July 15, 1982, when they saw bright white tennis shoes in the water below. They parked their bikes and climbed down to the river to investigate. As one of the boys started to pull on what looked like a bag, the other boy cried, "Stop!" The boys suddenly realized it was the dead body of a young female. The victim was identified as 16-year-old Wendy Lee Cofferd. One month later, the bodies of four more women were pulled out of Green River. The women ranged from late teens to early thirties in age. Some of the bodies were found weighted down by rocks. All of them had been killed by strangulation.

By October 1982, the police realized they had numerous missing females. The FBI provided a criminal profile: white male, mid-30s, likely lives with mother, and a loner. A development occurred ten months after the discovery of the first victim in April 1983. Marie Malva is last seen by her boyfriend getting into a red pickup truck. The boyfriend tries to follow the truck but is unsuccessful. When Marie never returns home, her father goes to the boyfriend's house, looking for her. The boyfriend and father now go on a search for the truck and find it. The truck belonged to a man named Gary Ridgway. The father notified police, and they sent an officer to the house. The officer knew Ridgway from high school, and Ridgway convinced the officer he was not involved; unfortunately, his next victim was still alive inside the house. No further investigation was conducted on Ridgway. By February 1984, there were over 21 dead females, with many still missing.

Police were baffled and did not have any suspects. In February 1985, the killings stopped for a time. The police theorized that the killer either was dead or in prison. Though the killings appeared over, many decomposing bodies continued to be found throughout the year. By June 1986, a total of 36 bodies had been recovered, and several females were still missing.

There was a break in the case when police received a description of a truck that had been seen near or around the victims, as well as a composite sketch of the suspect driver. A friend of one of the victims was able to identify Ridgway from a lineup. Police discovered he had been arrested for solicitation in 1982, two months before the first victim was found. In 1984, Ridgway was put under surveillance, a search warrant was issued for his house, and his wife was brought in for questioning.[338] At this point in history, DNA analysis did not exist as an option, but police collected biological samples from Ridgway. No physical evidence was found; Ridgway passed a polygraph test and was released. The case was closed, and in 1990, the police task force assigned to identify the serial killer was disbanded. The murder spree ended, and the case went inactive for over a decade.

By November 2001, technology had improved, and the preserved suspect DNA evidence collected from the victim was tested against saliva samples taken from Ridgway in 1987. There was an identical match, and Ridgway was arrested. Police made a deal with Ridgway; if he told them where the missing victims' bodies were located, they would not seek the death penalty. The police wanted closure for the families with missing loved ones. Ridgway was clearly a sociopath, and with joy and excitement, Ridgway took them on what he called "field trips" to the locations of the disposed bodies of his murdered victims.

Unique to this case was the presence of minute traces of spray paint on six of the victims. Ridgway was known to work at a truck factory in the paint shop. Spray paint is unique in that when it goes through the air, it forms tiny balls that dry where they land. These balls can only be seen with a microscope.[339] Police had collected thousands of paint samples that had been associated with Ridgway, in addition to paint samples collected from the time of the murders. Skip Palenik, a forensic investigator, was able to match the spray paint found on these victims to the paint used in the auto body shop where Ridgway worked.[340]

Facts about the case:

- As a child, Ridgway had a reputation for abusing animals.
- Ridgway joined the U.S. Navy and married Claudia Barrows in August of 1970 before he was deployed to the Philippines. They were divorced by January 1972. He married a second time in 1973, and they had a son named Matthew. His second wife divorced him in 1981. Bitter toward his ex-wife's rejection of him, Ridgway claimed that the killings resumed after his second divorce as a way of releasing his anger.
- Nightmares tormented Ridgway during this time, and he contemplated burning his house down.
- Ridgway met Judith Mawson in early 1985, and he claims that she filled the void in his life. They married in 1988. When Ridgway was questioned in 1987 and then later arrested in 2001, Judith claims to have had no knowledge or suspicion that he was the Green River Killer.
- Ridgway admitted to having a fascination with his victims.
- From prison, serial killer Ted Bundy assisted in the creation of a psychological profile of Ridgway.
- As far as police know, only one woman was able to escape from the Green River Killer.

Ridgway pled guilty to the murder of 48 women in 2003 and a 49th victim in 2001, though he estimates there are over 90 victims. Gary Ridgway received 49 consecutive life sentences with no chance of parole. He is serving his life sentence in solitary confinement. To this day, Gary Ridgway is considered the second most prolific serial killer in the United States.

"It may be that you are not yourself luminous, but that you are a conductor of light. Some people without possessing genius have a remarkable power of stimulating it." — Sherlock Holmes[341]

As outlined in the last two lessons, the key to trace evidence is the exchange of information during direct contact. This lesson will continue the study of trace evidence by taking an in-depth look at glass and paint. Glass and paint are two of the most common pieces of evidence found at the scene of car accidents, in addition to shootings, burglaries, arson, and vandalism. Fragments of broken glass can easily become lodged in victims' clothing, hair, and personal belongings. Headlight glass left behind from a hit-and-run will provide clues to the make and model of the car. Broken glass ranges in size from tiny shards to large pieces that are easily identifiable. During the impact of two cars, a transfer of paint is not only exchanged between cars, but onto the victims as well. When a burglar uses a hammer to gain entry through a window of a house, paint and broken glass can become lodged in their hair and clothing. The identifiable properties present in both glass and paint evidence provide not only class characteristics but have the potential to be discriminating to one specific source.

GLASS ANALYSIS FROM A BIBLICAL WORLDVIEW

Historical records describe the first evidence of glass production in Egyptian glass beads dated at 2500 B.C. The first civilization to discover the process of making glass remains a mystery, but the Bible provides information. Genesis describes the creation of Adam and Eve as made in the image of God and therefore extremely intelligent. Since Adam lived to be 930 years old (Genesis 5:5), it is likely the methods to produce glass materials would have been explored during his lifetime. It would not be surprising for archaeologists to discover glass production much earlier than 2500 B.C.

Ancient Egyptian bead

Genesis 5:5:

"Thus all the days that Adam lived were 930 years, and he died."

The Bible refers to glass when describing heaven. The book of Revelation describes glass has having the appearance of crystal and pure gold:

- *Before the throne of God:* "and before the throne there was as it were a sea of glass, like crystal" (Revelation 4:6).

- *The Holy City:* "The wall was built of jasper, while the city was pure gold, like clear glass" (Revelation 21:18).

- *Streets of gold:* "And the twelve gates were twelve pearls, each of the gates made of a single pearl, and the street of the city was pure gold, like transparent glass" (Revelation 21:21).

Imagine heavenly gold so pure it appears as transparent glass. Heaven will be a place unlike anything sinful humans living on earth can imagine. But for those who have accepted Christ as their Savior, they will enter a home of many mansions, prepared for them by a loving God for His children.

HISTORY OF GLASS

stained glass window by Tiffany

The technique of making modern glass originates in Alexandria in ancient Rome.[342] The art of glass blowing is believed to have originated in Syria in the first century B.C. Crystal was first developed in the 15th century in Venice, Italy, and quickly became a product of high demand in world trade. From 1878–1933, Louis Comfort Tiffany was the primary manufacturer of a unique type of glass called Favrile. The glass Tiffany created was opalescent — when more than one color is used in making the glass. This decorative glass is still desired today, and an original piece from this period is quite valuable. As the science of glass production continues to develop, it is important to remember the Creator God spoke into existence the elements on the periodic table that are necessary to produce a product like glass.

PROPERTIES OF GLASS

Glass is defined as the inorganic product of fusion, which has cooled to a rigid condition without crystallizing.[343] Unlike most crystalline solids, glass has no definite arrangement and instead reflects a network of atoms lacking long-range symmetry.[344] Glass includes amorphous materials such as lime, sodium oxide, and silica. Amorphous refers to any noncrystalline solid in which the atoms and molecules are not organized in a definite lattice pattern. Therefore, glass is technically a liquid, though it appears as a solid due to its high viscosity. Viscosity is resistance of a fluid (liquid or gas) to a change in shape, or movement of neighboring portions relative to one another.

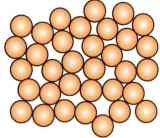

crystalline   amorphous

Glass has a high melting point of over 2,500 degrees Fahrenheit. The process of creating glass includes the heating of silica sand, soda, lime, and other substances into a molten state. Rapid cooling is applied to ensure that there is no crystallization in the new piece of glass. A unique feature of broken glass is in the irregular shape of the fragments. This characteristic separates it from items that can appear similar, like table salt, which has a regular, crystalline structure.

258 ▶ Lesson 21   Intro to Forensic Science

COMPOSITION OF GLASS

Due to the frequency of broken glass at crime scenes, it is important that investigators are knowledgeable in the composition of different types of glass. Identifying the ingredients in glass aids the examiner in differentiating the manufacturer of the glass and how much of the glass was produced in a certain time frame. Glass is made of metal oxides, which are chemical compounds containing a metal and one or more oxygen atoms. The primary metal oxides present in glass are aluminum, sodium, magnesium, and calcium. By substituting varying percentages of these oxides, different types of glass are formed. There are three major categories for the ingredients found in glass:

- *Formers*: aid in creating the glassy, noncrystalline structure present in glass through strong chemical bonds.
- *Fluxes*: softeners that increase the melting capability while lowering chemical resistance.
- *Modifiers*: provide stability to the glass by providing chemical and corrosion resistance. Common modifiers include calcium, aluminum, and zinc.

Glass modifiers are the mechanism for the diversity seen in the types of glass manufactured. Glass can be "precisely tuned and augmented" to meet the demand of various scientific and industrial applications.[345] Soda lime glass (70% silica, 15% sodium oxide, 9% calcium oxide, and other compounds)[346] is the most common type of glass collected at crime scenes, though there are several other types of glass an examiner should be familiar with. For example, by observing the melting properties in glass windows at the scene of an arson, it is possible to estimate the temperature of the fire and the accelerants used to start the fire.

Trace Evidence Part III: Glass and Paint

Types of Glass: Characteristics and Examples

Type of Glass	Characteristics	Examples
Commercial soda lime glass	Chemically stable Hard Inexpensive Green-yellow tint due to an iron impurity	Light bulbs Windowpanes Bottles
Float glass	Special coating Weather resistant	Mirrors Tough panels Sensors
Borosilicate glass	Heat resistant Withstands sudden changes in temperature Instead of sodium oxide, contains boron and aluminum	Car headlights Lab glassware Pyrex®
Laminated glass	Sandwiched between tempered glass	Car windshields
Tempered glass	Also called safety glass Four times stronger than window glass When impacted, shatters into tiny pieces (dices) with no jagged edges	Side and rear windows of cars Shower doors Windows less than 1 foot from the ground
Photochromic glass	Adjusts the light level in the environment Darkening and fading is due to the photolysis of tiny silver crystals suspended in the glass	Eyeglasses
Tinted glass	Absorbs heat Reduces glare by adding gray, green, or blue pigments to increase the density, thereby reducing the transmission of light	Automobile windows Commercial building windows Residential home windows
Leaded glass (crystal)	High refractive index Sparkles Contains lead oxide	Fine dining glassware Collectible figurines

CHARACTERISTICS OF GLASS FRAGMENTS

In the exchange of glass evidence, the closer the something is to the breaking glass, the more fragment evidence will be present. The farther away an item or person is from the breaking glass, the less evidence that will be recovered. Additionally, the number of fragments is directly related to type of impact and force applied to the glass. Different types of glass will exhibit varying shatter patterns. The location of glass fragments is also affected by the surface on which they land. Silky-type clothing or a slippery surface will cause the glass to slide off, whereas rough fabrics, carpet, and wet clothing will cause glass to adhere to the surface.

Locating broken fragments of glass provides clues to the projectile used in the crime, the velocity of the projectile, sequence of impacts, and possible injuries. If the glass fragments are of correct size, they can be matched back to the original source. The goal is to eliminate extraneous sources and identify the direct glass involved. Like pieces of a puzzle, broken glass fragments can be fit together to reveal a picture of the impact. When trying to determine the direction of force on a glass fragment, the spine must be analyzed for stress marks. The stress marks created by the impact are perpendicular to the force applied and run parallel to the other edge of the glass. This foundational principle in glass analysis is called the 4R Rule:

> **R**idges on **R**adial cracks are at **R**ight angles to the **R**everse side of impact.

Upon impact, radial cracks form on the edge of the broken glass. By viewing these stress marks under magnification, an examiner can determine the direction of impact, such as the outside versus inside of a glass bottle or windowpane, etc. Unfortunately, glass fragments are usually too small to piece back together, and alternative testing is required to determine the physical properties of the glass.

GLASS FRACTURES

Glass bends upon impact and will ultimately fracture after enough force is applied. For glass to break, it must be exposed to one or all three types of stress force:

- *Comprehensive force*: the force that presses the glass.
- *Tensile force*: the force that stretches the glass.
- *Shear force*: the force that separates the glass by causing it to move in two different directions.

The fracture patterns will reveal the direction of impact and order of impact when there is more than one point of impact. When glass is impacted, the opposite side will stretch and crack first. Two types of cracks will form on glass: radial cracks and concentric cracks.

Radial cracks form on the opposite side of impact. One of the most important characteristics of radial cracks is that they terminate when meeting an existing line fracture. This allows analysts to number the order of radial cracks by determining where each crack ends.

Crack B terminates at A; therefore, A came first.

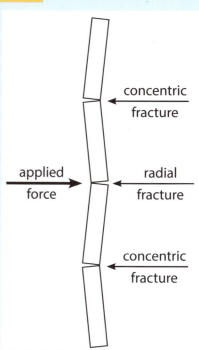

Trace Evidence Part III: Glass and Paint

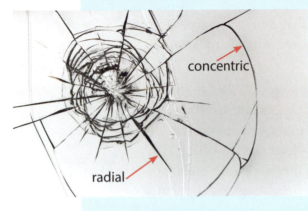

Concentric cracks are circles around the point of impact that originate on the surface where the force was applied. Concentric cracks occur after radial cracks and are located on the same side as the force.

When a projectile is fired at glass, the impact creates a crater. The crater is wider on the exit side versus the entrance. The higher the velocity of the projectile, the cleaner the entrance and exit cracks. A low velocity impact will result in a highly irregular-shaped hole and surrounding crack patterns. This provides clues to the investigator on the direction of the force of impact.

Radial cracks, concentric cracks, and craters are valuable forms of evidence. Crack patterns form a unique pattern or "fingerprint" to that individual piece of glass. Craters determine the orientation and location of the weapon firing the projectile. There will never be two impact fracture glass patterns that are identical.

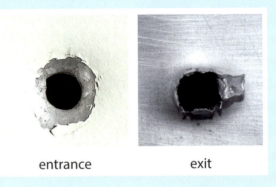

entrance   exit

PRESERVATION AND COLLECTION

Glass evidence should be handled with care at the crime scene. The investigator should follow all safety protocol when collecting and securing sharp-edged glass. A puncture in the safety gloves would require immediate attention to avoid contamination. Every piece of glass evidence is packaged in plastic or glass containers for transportation to the lab. If shards of glass exist in clothing, bedding, carpet, etc., the entire item should be secured for analysis.

In the lab, glass evidence can be collected after shaking garments recovered from the scene. Any fragments must be individually separated by similarity for examination. Individually bagged evidence will be evaluated separately. As the evidence is found to be relevant to the investigation, glass will be grouped by type for examination.

EXAMINATION OF GLASS

The size and shape of the glass fragments will determine the type of testing. The list below is not all inclusive, but it provides an overview of the testing techniques available in the examination of glass analysis. Each of these methods is nondestructive, meaning the glass sample remains undamaged. These should be used before other forms of analysis that consume the evidence and prohibit any further testing.

Microscopy. The first step in identifying the class characteristics of glass is under the magnification of a microscope. A physical match is the most conclusive proof of the original source, considering no two fractures will ever be identical.

Physical Characteristics. The next step would be to identify the physical characteristics of glass. The primary characteristics include:

- *Color:* Glass can be produced in any color and is examined by placing the glass on a white background in natural light.

- *Fluorescence:* Fluorescence is visible on glass surfaces when the surface that contains the fluorescent capability has been preserved. Certain surfaces of glass are exposed to chemicals that allow the glass to have fluorescent characteristics. Sometimes fluorescence spectroscopy can be used on trace evidence.

- *Thickness:* The thickness of glass reflects its origin. Thickness is measured with a micrometer. Glass is usually not consistent in thickness (think of a curved glass bottle), and several areas are measured and recorded. Since car windows are often the source of glass analysis, analysts must be familiar with the thickness of both tempered glass (3.0 mm thick) used on side windows and laminated glass (3.3–3.6 mm thick) used in windshields.

- *Curvature:* The curvature of the glass can be measured using an interferometer. The interferometer confirms if the glass is from a windshield, glass container, or other curved glass surface.

- *Density:* Density is examined using the sink or float method. Denser glass will sink versus less dense glass, which will float. This method is called density gradient column method. The challenge to this test is the size of the sample. The sample must be between 2–3 mm in diameter to use this method. This method also requires the use of toxic liquids in the density gradient column. Additional analysis includes displacement and flotation methods. When using the displacement method, the mass of the glass and the amount of water displaced is used to calculate density. The FBI has collected over 1,400 densities for glass samples and created a searchable database.

- *Refractive index:* Light exists as a dual wave, and when the wave travels through a medium, it will bend. The bending of light is called refraction. The density of a glass specimen will affect the amount of light passing through the object and the direction of the bending of light. The refractive index is the most common property analyzed in forensic glass analysis because any material that allows light to pass through has refractive index. The refractive index provides a measurable number that can be compared against other samples and helps to eliminate evidence from crime scenes. The refractive index of common glass found at crime scenes includes:

    Automobile glass: 1.47–1.49

    Bottles: 1.51–1.52

    Window glass: 1.51–1.52

    Eyeglasses: 1.52–1.53

Trace Evidence Part III: Glass and Paint

- *Oil immersion:* When the refractive index of the glass is different than the refractive index of a known oil, a halo will appear around the edge of the glass. This halo effect is called a Becke line. This method was named after Friedrich Johann Karl Becke (1855–1931), who developed the method. The halo is a result of the refracted light focusing on the edges of the glass. The location of the Becke line, whether inside or outside the perimeter of the glass, determines the refractive index. When the refractive index of both the glass and the liquid is the same, the glass will seem to disappear, and no Becke line is present.

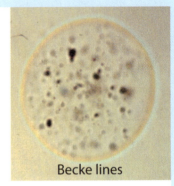

Becke lines

- *Chemical analysis:* Determining the elemental composition of glass is the final testing used after all other methods have been exhausted. An instrument called the XRF is used to focus a beam of X-rays onto a piece of glass evidence. The device then measures the energy emitting from the X-rays off the glass. Different elements will respond differently to the X-ray emission. This method can be expensive. Another test called flameless atomic absorption spectrophotometry requires the glass sample to be dissolved in acid for analysis, thereby destroying the evidence.

Glass is a common piece of evidence at crime scenes, but it is not without problems. First, is not always feasible to evaluate every piece of glass for comparison. Secondly, fragments may be too small for testing, or pieces can be destroyed, overlooked, or damaged at the crime scene.

PAINT

Paint is one of the most common pieces of evidence found at crime scenes due to the thousands of painted objects. Paint is easily transferable between two objects and recognizable (largely due to color) in the form of scrapes, gashes, and other forms of contact. This is especially true in hit-and-run and burglary cases.

The earliest mention of paint in the Bible is in 2 Kings 9:30, "When Jehu came to Jezreel, Jezebel heard of it. And she painted her eyes and adorned her head and looked out of the window." This describes Jezebel using some form of early eye shadow. And in Ezekiel 13:12 is the first reference to painting a wall: "And when the wall falls, will it not be said to you, 'Where is the coating with which you smeared it?'" The Bible confirms that the art of painting has been around for thousands of years.

PAINT COMPOSITION

Paint is a liquid consisting of a pigment that is suspended in a binder. A pigment is a group of compounds that are used to color other materials. The binder is a resin dissolved in solvent that allows the pigment to adhere to a surface. As the paint dries, the solvent evaporates and leaves behind the hard binder and pigments. To achieve the variety present in paint colors, manufacturers use a mix of organic (red, yellow, white) and inorganic compounds in different percentages. Paint can provide both class and individual characteristics. A class characteristic would be the type of paint, such as artist's paint, house paint, automobile paint, and other types. An individual characteristic is recognized as the unique, matching layer sequence of two different paint samples. Even when a positive individual match is confirmed, it is difficult to discriminate to just one source.

PAINT ANALYSIS

The PDQ (Paint Data Query) database contains over 45,000 paint samples from automobile manufacturers dating back to the 1930s.[347] Most vehicles have four layers of paint: the electrocoat primer, primer surface, basecoat, and clear coat. Each layer has a different mixture of substances in polymers, pigments, fillers, and other substances.[348] Since there are unique qualities in each layer of paint, different testing is used to analyze and differentiate the components.

- *Electrocoat primer:* electrically bonded to the steel frame of the vehicle to prevent corrosion. The electrocoat ranges from black to gray in color.
- *Primer surface:* bright color that smooths out the surface of the car. This layer is light gray for light-colored cars and red oxide for dark-colored cars.
- *Basecoat:* the paint coat that reflects the actual color you see with your eyes.
- *Clear coat:* clear, glossy coat that protects and extends the life of the basecoat.

Trace Evidence Part III: Glass and Paint

PRESERVATION AND COLLECTION

After photographing each piece of evidence, forceps should be used to collect paint samples. As with glass, the evidence should be secured in small plastic or glass containers. Placing in a paper envelope or plastic bag would risk bending or breaking the paint sample. If the paint is impressed into a piece of evidence, the entire item should be secured for analysis at the lab. If there is paint evidence on a car bumper or similar surface, a straightedge razor is used to scrape a ¼-inch piece of paint that is then placed in the proper container.

As with all other types of evidence, it is important to collect reference samples of comparable ¼-inch squares for comparison against the crime scene samples. This includes vehicles, tools, furniture, and anything else that reflects a transfer paint evidence.

EXAMINATION OF PAINT

When examining paint, the color is the primary distinguishing characteristic of paint chips recovered from crime scenes. The color layers of the paint fragments provide a unique sequence that can be compared against a known sample. The more layers of matching paint, the higher percentage of an identical match. A stereo microscope is used to determine the layering of paint by examining a cross section for sequence, color, thickness, and texture of the paint fragment.[349]

paint layers

Since most recovered paint samples are incomplete and do not contain all the necessary layers for a match, the paint fragments must be sent to the lab for chemical analysis. Chemical analysis is destructive to the paint sample and should only be considered when there are a sufficient number of samples to test.

- *Pyrolysis gas chromatography*: Chromatography is a method of chemical analysis that separates mixtures into their components. In this method, paint chips are heated at high temperatures for several seconds to the point of reaching an oxygen-free, gaseous state. The gas is processed through the gas chromatograph to produce a pyrogram of the polymers present in the sample.

- *Infrared spectrophotometry*: Binders present in the paint sample absorb infrared radiation and produce a unique spectrum. As a thin beam of light is shone through the sample, the light that is not absorbed is detected and measured.[350]

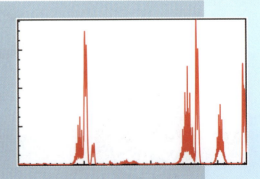

- *Emission spectroscopy*: Some of the elements in paint are common across manufacturers, while others have signatures that are useful in forensic analysis. The elements in paint will produce a colored barcode spectrum for each individual sample.[351]

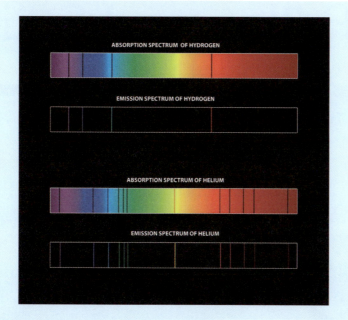

CONCLUSION

Glass fragments and paint chips are two more examples of the numerous pieces of trace evidence waiting to be uncovered at crime scenes. Though glass and paint primarily reveal class characteristic information, there is potential for both to yield individualized links between the suspect and the crime scene. The examination of trace evidence continues in the next lesson in the field of forensic botany with an in-depth look at soil and pollen.

Lesson 22
Trace Evidence Part IV: Pollen and Soil

As for what was sown on good soil, this is the one who hears the word and understands it. He indeed bears fruit and yields, in one case a hundredfold, in another sixty, and in another thirty (Matthew 13:23).

Case Study: A Trip Down the Danube

A man disappeared near Vienna, Austria, in 1959. A search for the man ended in vain. Those close to the missing man identified a friend and business partner as having motive for killing the missing man.[352] Police arrested and charged the business partner with the murder. The problem for police was that there was no body, no confession, no murder weapon, and only motive. During the search of the defendant's house, police discovered boots that were caked with muddy soles. The mud was collected and sent to a palynologist, one who studies pollen, Wilhelm Klaus from the Department of Paleobotany at the University of Vienna. Klaus' analysis of the mud identified trace pollen from modern spruce, willow, alder, and hickory, estimated to be thousands of years old.

The secular dating of the hickory pollen was 20 million years, but through a biblical lens, it is clear the pollen could not be older than 4,500 years, which marks the end of the global Flood around 2500 B.C. Klaus deduced the hickory pollen was present due to erosion of sediment. The sediment exhibited traits that have been associated with the post-Flood Miocene period. Interestingly, there was only one small area 20 kilometers north of Vienna along the Danube River that exhibited Miocene eroded soil, as well as spruce, willow, and alder.

Facts about the case:

- Once police presented the defendant with the analysis from the palynologist, he confessed to the murder.
- The defendant led the police to the location of the body, and it was in the exact geographic area that Professor Klaus had identified from the pollen analysis.
- Forensic palynology expert analysis is not recognized in the United States court system as conclusive evidence.
- Today, a request for pollen analysis can take between 8 months to 2 years due to a shortage of forensic palynologists.

Soil and pollen transfer from the crime scene to a suspect and/or victim's car or home often occurs unknowingly. These tiny pieces of trace evidence have the potential to point to the geographic location and movement of those involved in the crime scene triangle. Pollen is so durable, it can remain in an individual's clothing after repeated washings.

"Give me problems, give me work, give me the most abstruse cryptogram or the most intricate analysis, and I am in my own proper atmosphere. I can dispense then with artificial stimulants. But I abhor the dull routine of existence. I crave for mental exaltation. That is why I have chosen my own particular profession, or rather created it, for I am the only one in the world." — Sherlock Holmes[353]

Trace evidence is often microscopic evidence, and this is clear in the two examples covered in this lesson: soil and pollen. Under magnification, both soil and pollen manifest characteristics that can lead to identification and geographic location. These two types of evidence are often found together and provide clues to whether evidence was moved from one location to another or if a suspect was present at the scene of the crime and carried away soil on the bottom of their shoes or pollen granules on the legs of their pants. Often, criminals are unaware they have carried away microscopic signatures that can track their movement from one location to the next.

SOIL

Soil is not often equated to a fingerprint or something that possesses unique characteristics. But God designed the minerals in soil with distinctive characteristics relative to geographic regions. Once again, in the study of soil, Sherlock Holmes was a pioneer in soil analysis, long before real crime labs. In Sir Arthur Conan Doyle's book *A Study in Scarlet* (1888), Dr. Watson says of Sherlock Holmes, "Knowledge of Geology: Practical, but limited. Tells at a glance different soil from each other. After walks has shown me splashes upon his trousers, and told me by their colour and consistence in what part of London he had received them." This narrative makes Sherlock Holmes the world's first forensic edaphologist, or an expert in soils.[354] It was not until 1904 that the first case was solved using soil scrapings from under a suspect's fingernails.[355]

Doyle

Soil is the result of weathered rock and decaying organic matter called humus. Weathering is the process by which rocks are broken down into soil and is the result of weather, water, and interaction between living things. There are three types of weathering: biological (tree roots and lichen), chemical (water acids and gases), and physical (wind, rain, and thermal expansion).

When undisturbed, weathering breaks down bedrock and forms small particles in a layer called the C horizon. As organisms die and decay, they form a nutritionally rich top layer called the A horizon. The process of weathering then breaks down the A horizon carrying the nutrients downward and creates the B horizon. To summarize, the C horizon forms first, followed by the A horizon, and over time the B horizon. The combination of weathering and bedrock results in the formation of identifiable soil layers with recognizable characteristics. This is called soil geomorphology.

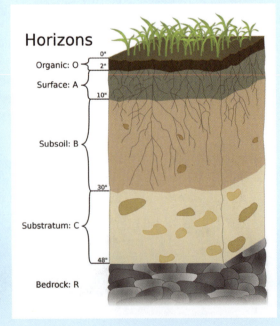

Horizons
- Organic: O — 0"–2"
- Surface: A — 10"
- Subsoil: B — 30"
- Substratum: C — 48"
- Bedrock: R

SOIL FROM A BIBLICAL WORLDVIEW

God created dry land on day three of the creation week. "And God said, 'Let the waters under the heavens be gathered together into one place, and let the dry land appear.' And it was so. God called the dry land Earth, and the waters that were gathered together he called Seas. And God saw that it was good" (Genesis 1:9–10). Though soil is the result of weathered rock, it is likely that God created soil instantaneously to support the vegetation also created on day three. God ordered the vegetation to reproduce according to their kind; therefore, pollen would also have been created on day three. Angiosperms, or flowering plants, are the largest

group of plants, and pollen is necessary for their reproduction. The Bible states in Genesis 1:12, "The earth brought forth vegetation, plants yielding seed according to their own kinds, and trees bearing fruit in which is their seed, each according to its kind. And God saw that it was good." For plants to begin reproducing according to their kind, they would have had to be producing pollen.

The parable of the sower is the only parable to begin with the command to "Listen." In Matthew 13, Mark 4, and Luke 8, Jesus uses four conditions of soil to describe the hearts of people when they hear the Word of God. In Matthew 13:3–8, the Bible says, "A sower went out to sow. And as he sowed, some seeds fell along the path, and the birds came and devoured them. Other seeds fell on rocky ground, where they did not have much soil, and immediately they sprang up, since they had no depth of soil, but when the sun rose they were scorched. And since they had no root, they withered away. Other seeds fell among thorns, and the thorns grew up and choked them. Other seeds fell on good soil and produced grain, some a hundredfold, some sixty, some thirty." How do these types of soil relate to the human heart?

First, it is important to recognize that in this parable (recorded in three gospels), there is only one sower, one type of seed, one plot of ground, and one type of soil but in four different conditions. The only variable that is changing in this parable is the condition or location of the soil where the seeds are sown, and this directly affects the viability of the seed. This parable is relaying an important truth, and that is everyone—all humans who are equally made in the image of God—has a potential to produce a bountiful harvest when they choose a life with Christ. The sower (Jesus Christ) provides one message (the seed), salvation through Christ alone. The problem occurs in the heart of people. How receptive are they to the message? Are they willing to let Jesus work in their lives and cultivate their lives to reflect a follower of Christ? Are they willing to stand on the authority of God's Word and produce visible fruit?

Trace Evidence Part IV: Pollen and Soil

Jesus describes four results when the seed is sown on these soils:

- *On the path:* For a farmer, the path is walked on repeatedly, causing the ground to become compacted, hard, and impermeable. This type of soil represents the hardened hearts of man. When the "seeds" are scattered on the path, they are an easy target for the influences of Satan, and their hard hearts reject the gospel message, leaving them lost in their sins.

- *On the rocky ground:* In farming, this ground is shallow. Plants have little roots to anchor to the soil and receive proper nourishment, therefore, are easily withered by the sun. These are people who accept Christ but fail to cultivate and grow their faith. Ultimately, they abandon the faith when they experience trials and tribulations as a result of their new life in Christ.

- *In the thorns:* When considering a plot of land, the thorn-infested soil is on the edges where a plow cannot reach. Since these seeds did not fall within the area that is cultivated and cared for, even if they sprout, they will be quickly overtaken by weeds. Sadly, these people sit on the edges, occasionally attend church, and are resistant to committing to the body of Christ. They are not diligent to cultivate a relationship with Christ by seeking him through prayer and studying his Word. Though they may produce one small fruit, they are easily overtaken by worldly pleasures and fall away from Christ.

- *On good soil:* The good soil is a well-plowed, cultivated area that has been broken up into a porous, nutritionally rich soil ready for seed. This soil has been essentially changed and turned over by the plow. Individuals with good soil, or hearts ready for the Word, experience seeds of truth and are fundamentally changed by the power of Christ in their lives. Now that they are firmly rooted in Christ, they recognize that cultivation is a lifelong process as God continually brings to light the faults and sins within their newly softened heart. Sometimes this may be a painful process as people work through sins in their lives, such as relationship problems, addictions, inappropriate behaviors, etc. But they recognize this is part of God's love for them and that a changed heart is a changed mind, resulting in a changed life. Fruit is bountiful and observable in their lives.

In every church, ministry, and school, all four conditions of soil (or people) are present. Each person will hear the seeds of truth and willfully affect how/if those seeds will be cultivated in their life. Since Jesus, the ultimate sower, has commanded us to go out and spread the gospel, we can imitate him and be sowers in our areas of influence (Matthew 28:19–20; 2 Corinthians 9:10).

SOIL COMPOSITION

Soil is composed largely of minerals, followed by air, water, and 4% organic material. Minerals include hematite, limonite, calcite, dolomite, and gypsum, to name a few.[356] The composition of the minerals in varying percentages is what gives soil its color. Soil also provides important minerals to plant growth, as well as the human diet. These include calcium, phosphorus, iron, magnesium, copper, and zinc.

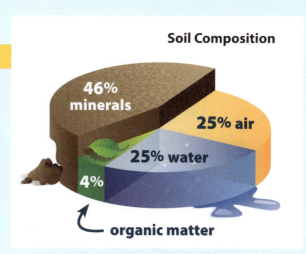

UNIQUE PROPERTIES IN SOIL

Soil is classified by its texture, color, structure, porosity, permeability, and depth. In the field, soil scientists will simply use their hands to determine the texture. By picking up a handful of soil and rubbing it between their hands, the softness, hardness, compactness, or porosity of soil can be determined. A Munsell color chart is used to distinguish the color. Munsell color charts have been used for over 55 years to classify soil. The chart leaves a hole in every color so that the chart can be placed directly over the soil for correct color identification.

The structure of soil is defined as whether it is single grain or in another granular form. Examples of granular structure can be seen in the chart below. The structure of the grains in the sediment is the unique "fingerprint" in soil analysis. Sediment is defined as the solid particles that are weathered from a parent material and transported. Structure is the single grain particle or other granular form visible microscopically.

Soil Structure

granular

platy

wedge

prismatic

columnar

blocky (angular)

(subangular)

Trace Evidence Part IV: Pollen and Soil

TYPES OF SOIL

Soil is often identified by its gross appearance, meaning the visible structure varies by the type of soil. Since soil changes color and consistency when wet, soil is always evaluated when dry. Types of soil include:

Sand is light, warm, dry, acidic, low in nutrients, and has quick water drainage. Sand is present in a large range of environments and geographic regions.

Clay is dense with high nutrients, moist, drains slowly, and tends to crack in the summer. Clay is only formed through chemical weathering.

Silt is light, moisture retentive, carried by moving water, nutritious, well drained, and tends to compact.

Peat is high in organic matter and retains moisture.

Chalk is light or heavy and contains high alkaline with calcium carbonate or lime composition.

Loam is a mixture of sand, silt, and clay, is fertile, and has good drainage.

SOIL COLLECTION

Soil collection at crime scenes will vary by location. The primary concern is to collect a representative sample from the scene for comparison and elimination purposes. This requires that soil be collected at various points within a 100-yard radius of all locations related to the crime. In large scenes, it is not uncommon to assign an individual investigator to every collection point to ensure there is no cross contamination of soil. Since soil analysis is often microscopic, only 1–2 tablespoons are collected from each point. And as with all forensic evidence, each sample would be individually packaged in plastic containers and labeled with the exact location.

Soil collection will also vary depending on the type of evidence where it is located. When compacted soil evidence is collected from the bottom of a shoe or tire, the investigator should not scrape the soil out for collection, but instead wrap the entire artifact in paper and place in a bag for transportation to the lab. Any loose, visible soil on clothing, furniture, bedding, etc., should be carefully collected and placed in small paper packaging. If a clump of soil is discovered under the bumper of a car or attached to a suspect tool, the entire clump should be packaged intact. Loose soil in cars, garages, or homes can be collected with specialized trace evidence vacuums. As discussed in previous lessons, a new bag would need to be used for each new location.

SOIL EXAMINATION

The first step in soil analysis is to complete a visual exam. The soil must be completely dry before analysis is conducted, which may include drying the soil in a chamber. A visual exam includes identifying the color, consistency, and matrix characteristics. Color indicates the chemical composition in the soil. White or gray indicates the presence of lime; gray or black the presence of organic material; and red, brown, or yellow is the presence of iron. Consistency is the texture of the soil: Is it wet or dry, clumpy, or dusty? The matrix characteristics are the presence or absence of roots, sticks, seeds, insects, and decomposing leaves. Examining the matrix characteristics requires varying sifting screens to filter out the larger particles.

Once a visual exam is complete, a microscopic analysis brings into view the soil structure. Based on the type of soil, the granule geometric structure will be analyzed for identification and can be compared side by side under a comparison microscope. Another important method of analysis is to study the density of the soil samples. The density gradient method is one method where the soil sample is added to a solution with varying levels of density. As the soil sinks through the density column, it will suspend at the point of equal density between the soil and solution.[357] The soil will create bands in the cylinder (resembling an electrophoresis DNA banding) that reveal a unique signature for fingerprint of the soil sample. Soil density ranges between 1.5 g/mL to 2.7 g/mL.[358] Soil found on the forest floor has been recorded to have a density less than or equal to water at 1.0 g/mL, while the soils with the highest density of 4.0 g/mL are composed of dense minerals.

Trace Evidence Part IV: Pollen and Soil

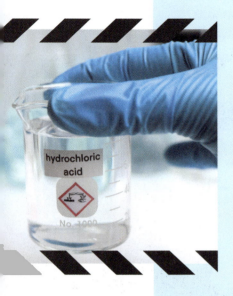

The pH of soil is another indicator used in soil identification. In this test, the soil is mixed with a small amount of water. The pH of the supernatant (liquid part that remains after the soil has settled) is measured with a pH indicator. A reading between 0 and 6 is an acid, 7 is a base, and any measurement between 8 to 14 is a base.

Occasionally, soil testing requires the addition of hydrochloric acid (HCl). When soil contains reactive metals like lead, tin, iron, magnesium, or zinc, and HCl is added to the soil, a reaction occurs in the form of hydrogen gas. If carbonates or bicarbonates are part of the soil composition and HCl is added, there will be a release of carbon dioxide (CO_2).

The presence of lead is an indicator of the geographic location of a soil sample. To test for the presence of lead, water is mixed with the soil. Once the soil settles, potassium chromate solution is added to the supernatant. If lead chromate is present in the soil, the supernatant will turn a milky yellow color.

PALYNOLOGY

Forensic palynology is the study, identification, and analysis of pollen and spores to investigate criminal and civil cases. Forensic palynology has been in use for over 50 years, but in the United States, this field of science does not meet the Daubert standard. The Daubert standard was established by the Supreme Court in 1993 in the case *Daubert v. Merrell Dow Pharmaceuticals Inc.*[359] Basically, the standard is used by a trial judge to determine whether the expert witness scientific testimony is valid and applies to the facts of the case. Methodology considered by the judge includes:

- Has the technique been tested?
- Has the technique been published and scrutinized in peer review?
- What are the standards and error rate of the technique?
- Is the technique widely accepted in the scientific (forensic) community?

To date, forensic palynology has not met this standard in the United States, but in New Zealand and Great Britain, the technique has been utilized in criminal court since the 1970s. The first recorded case that used forensic palynology to solve a murder occurred over fifty years ago in Austria (review this case under the case study at the beginning of the lesson). More recently, palynology was used in the discovery of Ötzi the Iceman to track his movement before his death over 3,400 years ago.

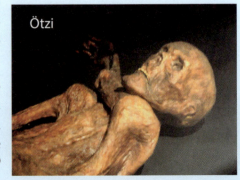

Ötzi

In 1991, a freeze-dried body of a male was discovered in the Ötztal Valley Alps between Austria and Italy. The body was in a trench about 10,500 feet above sea level. Due to the location of the body, he was named Ötzi.[360]

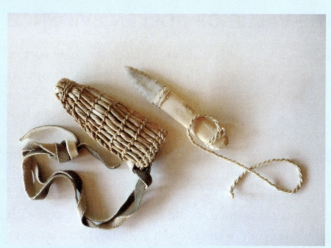
Reconstruction of Ötzi's knife and scabbard

Replica of Ötzi's copper axe

The man still had his traveling items on him, including a copper axe, bow and arrows, dagger, dried grass fibers, and many other artifacts. The artifacts date the body at over 3,400 years old. Estimates believe he is older than the Egyptian pyramids (mummies) and Stonehenge.

Examinations of the body determined the man had over 50 charcoal tattoos believed to be some form of acupuncture therapy. Genetic DNA testing has revealed that Ötzi has 19 living relatives.[361] What is most interesting is the evidence of wounds that occurred within 24 hours of his death. Wounds on his hands show defense-style injuries, suggesting he had been in an altercation not long before his death. Initial exams concluded that he had died of hypothermia, but computer imaging in 2001 discovered an arrowhead lodged in his left shoulder. This evidence was missed in the initial exam. The arrowhead had clipped his subclavian artery, which would have caused death within minutes. Scientists now theorize that Ötzi was, in fact, murdered, resulting in the oldest and longest cold case that will never be solved.

What does this have to do with pollen? Ötzi's stomach contents were still intact. It was determined that he had had three meals in the last 33 hours of life. In the contents, over 30 types of pollen were identified, in addition to grains and meat from an ibex and red deer.

During digestion, food moves from the stomach (2 hours) to the small intestine (4–5 hours), large intestine (9–12 hours), and finally to the rectum (14–55 hours). Based on where the pollen was in the digestion tract, the timing involved in digestion, and knowing the geographic location of the pollen, scientists have been able to trace his movements. It is truly amazing to see how God's unique design in pollen assisted scientists over 3,400 years later to trace the movement of Ötzi.

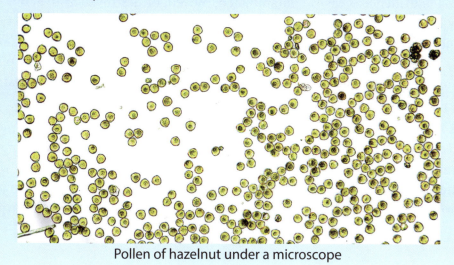
Pollen of hazelnut under a microscope

Trace Evidence Part IV: Pollen and Soil

THE VALUE OF POLLEN EVIDENCE

Pollen is defined as a fine, powdery yellow substance that is discharged from the male part of a flower or cone. Pollen is produced in the microsporangium in the anther of an angiosperm flower, the male cone of a coniferous plant, or in the male cone of other seed plants. Pollen contains microscopic forensic characteristics. God created pollen grains with a protective coating made of sporopollenin that protects the gametophytes during the process of their movement and fertilization. There are some pollens that can survive between one and four years in water and even up to a year in liquid nitrogen. Once again, God's providence and forethought is seen in the durability of pollen. He knew He would eventually send a global Flood to destroy the earth and that the plants He created would need to be equipped with the ability to reproduce after the Flood waters receded. Today, there are over 380,000 different species of plants, each with their own unique pollen type.

Pollen is so small that criminals are not aware that microscopic evidence travels with them from the scene to their car, home, work, etc. The smallest pollen grain is from the forget-me-not flower and is only 0.006 mm in diameter.

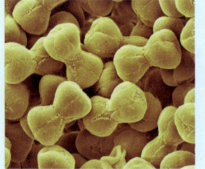
Forget-me-not pollen

The largest pollen grain is from the Cucurbitaceae and is visible with the naked eye at 200 microns. Each geographic region has its own unique pollen print generated from the plants that grow in the surrounding area. "Think of it," says Andrew Laurence, head palynologist of U.S. Customs and Border Protection, "as a fingerprint for a region." And it's a relatively indestructible fingerprint. Even if you put clothes through a washing machine, a pollen print remains.[362] The complex morphology, or structure, of the pollen granules allows them to be traced back to the parent plant and the source environment.[363]

Other benefits of pollen evidence include many types of dispersal mechanisms (birds, insects, wind, water, etc.) and the durability of pollen. Pollen is resistant to biological, chemical, and mechanical attacks.

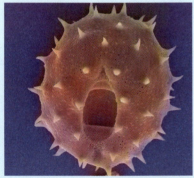
Cucurbitaceae pollen

PRESERVATION AND COLLECTION OF POLLEN

If a scene is believed to contain important palynology evidence, it must be collected quickly. Pollen evidence is easily contaminated, moved, or destroyed at an active crime scene.[364] As with soil collection, the investigator must collect both standard and reference samples. Standard samples are collected with the pinch method. Simply pinch dirt samples throughout the crime scene in an area of 50 to 100 meters square. Typically, 10–20 pinches of dirt are adequate. Each sample should be sealed in a separate container.[365]

To collect loose pollen evidence, a clean paintbrush or cosmetic brush is used to brush samples into a sterile plastic bag, container, or paper envelope. A new brush must be used for every collection site. If the investigator is collecting soil to analyze for possible pollen grains, and the soil is damp, the soil must first be dried in an oven on low heat. The addition of alcohol to the wet soil is another method to preserve the pollen and to kill any microbes that may compromise the pollen. Another method is to use transparent cellophane tape to collect pollen samples. The tape is then placed in Ziploc® plastic bags.

Due the properties of hair and fur, pollen is often lodged within the individual strands. The same characteristics occur in woven fabrics and bags; pollen can become lodged within the fibers. If hair, animal fur, or fibers contain pollen samples, the substance must be washed with detergents and warm water to dislodge the pollen. The wash water is stored and frozen to prevent microbe contamination.[366]

Pollen can also become lodged inside packing materials and taped boxes. A special portable vacuum is the best tool to extract pollen from these surfaces. The pollen becomes lodged in the lint trap of the vacuum and can be collected quickly over a large area. As in the case of Ötzi the Iceman, pollen granules on food in the digestive tract can also provide clues to time of death, location of the death, and the movement of the individual.

Many other items have the potential to contain pollen evidence, such as honey, tea, coffee, paper money, tobacco, air filters, and so much more. The search for pollen can be challenging, but a single grain can hold the key to an important link between suspect, victim, and crime scene.

Trace Evidence Part IV: Pollen and Soil

EXAMINATION OF POLLEN

Pollen has the potential to not only point to a geographic area, but it can pinpoint the exact season of the year as well. This requires palynologists to be familiar with the pollen cycles of various plants. Another point of examination is the health of the pollen grain. Scientists examine the cytoplasm (or intine) of the pollen grain and measure the degradation of the intine. Since cytoplasm degrades rapidly after dispersal, a fairly accurate timeline can be created.[367]

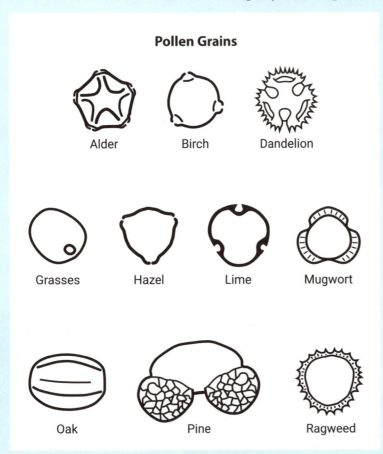

Examining pollen is a slow, tedious process, as each grain is reviewed under a microscope. Pollen washed from clothing, hair, fur, and fibers must first be extracted from the wash water before examination can begin. If the pollen is collected on cellophane tape, the tape can be stuck to a microscope slide and stained for analysis. Often, the exact species is difficult to identify with just the pollen sample, and very few forensic scientists are specialized in this field. Therefore, a request for pollen analysis will take between eight months to a year and half.

The most effective application of forensic palynology is in the illegal drug market. To link specific drug dealers with individual shipments of drugs, pollen has been used to make the connection between geographic locations and the travel of drugs during shipping. By examining the pollen on marijuana seized during a drug raid in New York City, scientists were able to identify that the drugs had pollen traces to multiple geographic regions in New Zealand, as well as Asia. Identical evidence on other drug raids allowed police to identify multiple drugs that all linked back to one large shipment from Asia.[368]

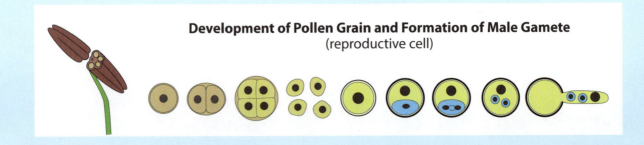

Development of Pollen Grain and Formation of Male Gamete
(reproductive cell)

CONCLUSION

Forensic soil and pollen analysis are interconnected. Both contain unique properties that provide a connection to a geographical location, a season, and the parent material, whether geological or botanical. Each contains unique, identifiable shapes and patterns, pointing back to the source. Soil often contains pollen; therefore, collection of soil has the potential to yield evidence in both areas. These pieces of trace evidence have helped solve crimes and will only become more valuable as technology improves.

Recent developments have allowed researchers to DNA barcode pollen. Pollen contains the male gamete information from the source plant. DNA is extracted and then put into high-throughput DNA sequencing, where multiple pieces of DNA are sequenced at the same time. This advancement is important because pollen evidence contains several species, and this allows to differentiate each one at one time.[369]

High-throughput DNA sequencing: Allows for thousands to millions of samples to be run at once. This method drastically reduces the time required in traditional DNA sequencing methods; also known as Next-Generation.

ligularia flower

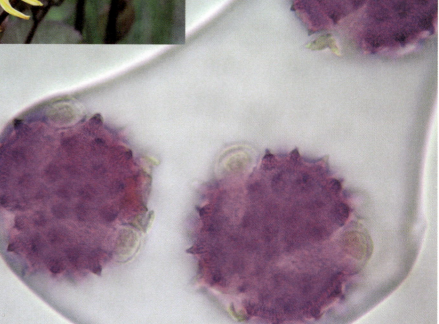

ligularia pollen

Lesson 23
Impressions

Ponder the path of your feet; then all your ways will be sure (Proverbs 4:26).

Case Study: The Bloody Print

The mid-1800s in Europe was a period of great poverty. It was not uncommon for several people from different families to be living in communal apartments, renting by the room. This was the case in Glasgow, Scotland, in a unit labeled No. 17 at Sandyford Place. On July 4, 1862, the body of 38-year-old Jess McPherson was found in her home, half naked and lying in her own blood. In the pool of blood were three small footprints. Historical facts state that Jess McPherson was described as a big, brawny woman who had worked in maid service since the age of ten. Jess McPherson was best friends with a woman named Jessie M'Lachlan. Jessie M'Lachlan was married to a sailor, and the couple were very poor. Jess and Jessie were as close as sisters. Jess gave Jessie money on a regular basis, as well as paid off her debts at the local markets. On the evening of July 4, 1862, Jessie M'Lachlan went to visit her good friend Jess McPherson, leaving her son at home with a maid. Early in the morning of July 5, 1862, Jessie's son was heard crying. The wash maid went to check on him, only to discover that Jessie was not home. The maid put the little boy back to bed and glanced out the window around 5:30 a.m. Jessie did not return home till 3 ½ hours later, approximately 9:00 a.m., in clothing her wash maid had never seen before. She carried a large bundle under her cloak.

Within one hour of returning home, Jessie left and went to an ironmonger, where she purchased a locking iron box. She placed the large bundle in the box, locked it, and took the key. She told the shop owner she would return for the box, but she never got the chance. Around 11:30 a.m., Jessie visited the accountants where she was four pounds behind on her rent and paid the bill. A little after noon, Jessie visited Lundie's Pawn shop, gave a name of Mary M'Donald, and pawned several pieces of silver, all which had an "F" stamped on them.

Mr. John Fleming returned home (the same apartment as Jess) on Monday, July 7, 1862, after being away all weekend. John Fleming had a son named John, who answered the door and told his father that Jess had been missing all weekend. Mr. James Fleming, the elderly father of John and grandfather to younger John, had been home all weekend and did not seem concerned. Mr. John Fleming was immediately alerted since reliable Jess had not been seen since early Friday. Her bedroom door was locked from the inside. When the men were able to open the bedroom door of Jess McPherson, they found her bloody body face down, the furniture was in disarray, and there were splotches of blood all over the space. The police investigators counted over 40 wounds on her face and hands. Next to the window were three bloody footprints of a bare left foot (friction ridge skin). Investigators began to identify blood drops in the kitchen, in the lobby of the apartment, and in old Mr. James Fleming's chest of drawers. The floors had been recently cleaned, as well as the face, neck, and chest of the victim. Mr. James Fleming was arrested on Wednesday, July 9. But was he the guilty party?

Meanwhile, Jessie's sailor husband returned home. She told him about the iron locked box, and how inside were some clothes from her late friend Jess. Jessie asked her husband to conceal the contents at his sister's house, but the box had been shipped to the Glasgow Police. The contents of the box led investigators to Jessie M'Lachlan, and both she and her husband were arrested for the murder of Jess. It was quickly discovered that the husband had been at sea and was innocent.

Facts about the case:[370]

- A Miss M'Intyre was walking home around 11:15 p.m. near the home of Jess McPherson. She reported hearing a wailing noise and moaning that frightened her.
- A jeweler named Mr. Steward, who lived next door to Jess McPherson, reported to be awoken around midnight.
- Three sisters walking home from a wedding celebration around 3:30 a.m. the night of the murder reported seeing a light on in the home of Jess. This was highly unusual considering the time of night in Glasgow.
- The milk boy, who was accustomed to being greeted at the door every morning between 7:30 a.m. and 8:45 a.m. by Jess McPherson, reported that an elderly man who also lived in No. 17, a Mr. Fleming, answered the door the morning of July 5, 1862, and told the boy they did not want any milk.
- A young girl, Miss Sarah Adams, who had performed work for Jessie M'Lachlan in the past, was called to her home to deliver a trunk to Hamilton Station with strict instructions to not open the trunk.
- P.C. Campbell, a patrol officer, was performing his nightly checks in Sandyford Place. The No. 16 unit was locked, but he noticed that No. 17's door was open, and two women were having a conversation.
- The investigator examining the body measured the length of the three bloody footprints against those of the deceased, but they were significantly smaller. The footprints were not Jess'. It was stated they were from a female.
- A cleaver (knife) found in the kitchen drawer is believed to be the murder weapon and is on display at the museum at the police headquarters in Glasgow. The slight penetration of the wounds pointed to a woman killer.
- The size of the bloody footprints did not match those of James Fleming, but when they replicated the stepping of blood onto a wood floor with Jessie M'Lachlan, it was a perfect match. The original bloody footprints were cut away from the house and sent to the police department for analysis. In the Glasgow Police Department Museum, there is a piece of wood with one of the three bloody footprints on display.
- Jessie relayed three different accounts of her whereabouts the night of the murder.
- The only defense given for the suspect, Jessie M'Lachlan, was that she was nowhere near the scene at the time of the murder and that it must have been committed by another person, Mr. James Fleming.
- The jury returned with a unanimous guilty verdict in just 15 minutes. Jessie M'Lachlan was sentenced to be hung on October 11, 1862. Jessie screamed in the courtroom, "I am innocent."
- The Queen of England pardoned the hanging and sentenced Jessie to life in prison.
- Several months after her conviction, she "confessed" to her lawyer in a fourth version of the crime.

- In 1877, after 15 years in prison, her sentence was lifted, and she was set free. She immigrated to the United States. After her husband died, she remarried and died in 1899.
- The true account of the murder of Jess McPherson remains a mystery, but this is the first documented case where footprints were used in the conviction of a suspect.

During this period in criminal investigation history, there were no crime labs or trained investigators. There was no protocol for securing the scene, protecting evidence, and preventing contamination. Examples like this case are an important reminder of why procedures are so important and why the appropriate preservation of evidence is key to solving a case.

" 'I must thank you,' said Sherlock Holmes, 'for calling my attention to a case which certainly presents some features of interest.' "[371]

Though criminals will attempt to cover their tracks, they are often unaware they have left clues to their identity in the dirt below their feet. This lesson continues the study of impression evidence. According to the National Institute of Standards and Technology, pattern and impression evidence includes any markings produced when one object comes into direct physical contact with another object, such as fingerprints, shoeprints, tool marks, bite marks, blood stains, fabrics, ballistics, and tire treads. This classification also includes pattern analysis. Pattern analysis includes evaluating handwriting, typewriting, printers, copiers, and writing instruments.[372] Everyone leaves impressions everywhere they go; it is unavoidable. This is why impression evidence, whether 2D or 3D, is so prevalent. For example, a bloody shoeprint is a two-dimensional piece of evidence, while tire tracks in mud are three dimensional.[373] On a hard surface, like concrete, a latent (or hidden) shoe pattern is referred to as a latent impression. The unique characteristics in every shoe and tire impression have the potential to provide a link to one individual source. This lesson will focus on shoes and tires as impression evidence.

SHOEPRINT IMPRESSIONS

The importance of shoes in forensic science is unquestionable. Nearly everyone wears shoes, and shoes leave behind traces of evidence. The United States shoe market is a multi-billion-dollar industry and the largest footwear market in the world.[374] In 2019, retail shoe sales exceeded 1.9 trillion dollars in the U.S. The number of shoes added to the market every year are in addition to the shoes sold in previous years. There are literally millions of shoes. Depending on the manufacturer, brand, size, and other factors, the patterns on the soles of shoes vary and exhibit distinctive markers.

Examples of Shoe Tread Patterns

piecewise lines	lines & circles	lines & ellipses	only circles arc

lines, circles, & ellipses	only ellipses	circles & ellipses	only texture

When a questioned shoeprint is located at a crime scene, investigators will attempt to collect and preserve the print for analysis. A variety of methods are available, depending on the surface where the shoeprint is located. These will be explained later in the lesson. Once viable questioned shoeprints are collected, they are first compared to a suspect shoe. If the impression design is different from the suspect sole design, the design is searched through a database to identify class characteristics. The United Kingdom has the most comprehensive footwear pattern inventory, and the FBI has a database with over 14,000 searchable shoe prints.[375]

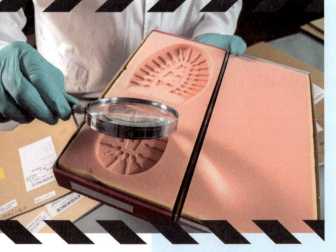

Impression evidence expresses both class and individual characteristics. Though class information helps to eliminate other variables, the examiner will only continue to search for individual characteristics if the class characteristics match between a questioned shoe and suspect shoe.[376] See **Table 1** for examples of both class and individual characteristics in shoe impressions and prints.

Table 1

Type	Definition	Characteristics	Examples
Class	General or generic characteristics Not unique to any one object or person A feature that is shared by two or more items of footwear or tires[377]	Shape (right/left) Brand Size* Outsole design (pattern) General wear Mold defects Dimension	Adidas® sneakers Size 10 hiking boots Worn dress shoes
Individual	Narrowed down to one single, individual source A feature on a footwear outsole or tire tread resulting from random events	Wear (holes) Indentations Cuts Scratches Gouges	Worn heel (pattern or hole) Cuts running through the outsole

*When considering shoe size, there is no strict relationship between the manufacturer-labeled shoe size and the measured dimensions of the outsole. A size 10 men's work boot will measure larger than a size 10 men's athletic shoe.

THE VALUE OF INDIVIDUAL CHARACTERISTICS

The value of even one identifying characteristic is sufficient to proceed with further investigation. William J. Bodziak (2000) stated, "Positive identifications may be made with as few as one random identifying characteristic, but only if that characteristic is confirmable; has sufficient definition, clarity, and features; is in the same location and orientation on the shoe outsole; and in the opinion of an experienced examiner, would not occur again on another shoe."[378] With the thousands of shoe designs, mold variations, and sizes, manufacturers have stated the "estimated frequency of any particular shoe design in a specific size is much less than 1% of the total shoe population."[379] The statistical probability of unique marks developing on the outsoles of two different shoes from the same brand and manufacturer was developed by R.S. Stone in 2006 (see **Table 2**).[380] Based on his analysis, there is a 1 in one octillion chance that two different people wearing the same shoe will have the exact same wear on their shoes. The more identifying characteristics, the higher the probability they are unique factors.

Table 2

Number of Characteristics	Probability of Occurence
1	1 out of 16
2	1 out of 127,992,000
3	1 out of 683 billion
4	1 out of 2.7 quadrillion
5	1 out of 8.7 quadrillion
6	1 out of 6 sextillion
7	1 out of 53 septillion
8	1 out of 106 octillion
9	1 out of 189 nonillion
10	1 out of 300 decillion

The following excerpt from Forensic Science Simplified discusses the value of probability in the shoeprints recovered in the famous trial of the century, the O.J. Simpson case:

> One of the most famous cases involving shoeprints was the 1995 O.J. Simpson murder trial. The bloody shoeprints found on the walkway in front of Nicole Brown Simpson's condominium received worldwide media attention. Upon forensic examination, they were identified as imprints from the sole of a size-12 designer Bruno Magli shoe.

Information from the manufacturer indicated that only 299 pairs of this size-12 shoe were sold in the U.S. Two of these pairs were sold at a Bloomingdale's store in New York where Simpson was known to have shopped. However, Simpson denied ever owning a pair of these shoes. It wasn't until the 1996 wrongful death civil trial that pictures surfaced of Simpson at a Buffalo Bills football game, wearing a pair of black Bruno Magli® shoes of the same style that left the bloody shoeprints. This was key evidence in the civil trial that led to the judgment against Simpson.[381]

FOOT IMPRESSIONS FROM A BIBLICAL WORLDVIEW

God created humans with an identifiable stride, sometimes referred to as a gait. Humans walk in a heel-toe rhythm, have distinctive arch characteristics, a short stride, and feet that slightly point outward while walking. The directional angle of human feet is due to the design of the human pelvis.

In 1978, in Laetoli, Tanzania, a 27.5-meter trail of fossilized tracks was discovered by Dr. Mary Leakey and her team. The tracks were discovered under rocks dated at 3.6 million years on an evolutionary time scale using potassium-argon dating. The research team recognized the human-like appearance of the fossilized footprints. Visible in the tracks is an ordinary heel-toe strike (with a deep impression at the heel), arch pattern, short stride, and slightly pointed out feet that are all unique characteristics of the human gait.

human footprints in Laetoli[392]

But there was a major problem for the evolutionary scientists. The evolutionary timeline does not allow for humans to be walking on the earth at that time. Evolutionary estimates place the first hominid around 1.9 million years ago. Leakey concluded these were related to the same species as the upright walking, bipedal primate ancestor called *Australopithecus afarensis*. This assumption was based upon a single jawbone fossil of *afarensis*, found in the Laetoli area in the same layer as the fossil footprints and another *A. afarensis* fossil (the famous Lucy) discovered 1,000 miles away from the Laetoli tracks. Think about it: How would this forensic anthropology analysis hold up in a court of law if it was a criminal case? The problem is *Australopithecus afarensis* is nothing more than a knuckle-dragging ape. On occasion, when apes are walking upright, their stride is distinctly different from humans. God designed the pelvis of the primate in such a way that human bipedal motion is impossible for them. Additional fossils of *Australopithecus afarensis* were discovered later and confirm that *afarensis* was an extinct primate. In Dr. Mary Leakey's book, R.H. Tuttle outlined his analysis of the Laetoli footprints:

> Strictly on the basis of the morphology of the G prints [prints found at a site labelled 'G'], their makers could be classified as *Homo* sp. because they are so similar to those of *Homo sapiens*, but their early date would probably deter many paleoanthropologists from accepting this assignment. I suspect that if the prints were undated, or if they had been given younger dates, most experts would probably accept them as having been made by *Homo [sapiens]* . . .
>
> If the prints were produced by a small species of *Australopithecus* (southern ape) then we must conclude that it had virtually human feet which . . . were used in a manner indistinguishable from those of slowly walking humans. . . . The feet that produced the G trails are in no discernible features transitional between the feet of apes . . . and those of *Homo sapiens*. They are like small barefoot *Homo sapiens*.[382]

Potassium-argon dating: Determining the age of something "based on the assumption that the amount of radioactive argon in a . . . sample all came from the decay of radioactive potassium."[393] Radiometric dating is "founded on unprovable assumptions such as 1) there has been no contamination and 2) the decay rate has remained constant."[394]

cast of Laetoli footprints

The Laetoli footprints look human because they are human. The Bible describes the creation of animals on day six about 6,000 years ago. God also created Adam and Eve on the same day. Genesis 1:26–27 says, "Then God said, 'Let us make man in our image, after our likeness.' . . . So God created man in his own image, in the image of God he created him; male and female he created them." The Bible is the only source of truth and should be the foundation upon which scientific evidence is studied. What would happen in the future if a fossil were discovered that had the clear anatomy of a bipedal primate? Can the Bible still be trusted? Consider this statement from Dr. Elizabeth Mitchell,

> Even *if* a truly bipedal apelike animal with an arched foot and human-like stride had walked across Laetoli, that would not mean that humans evolved from bipedal apelike animals. A bipedal ape, if it existed, would just be an animal. But human beings are not animals. Human beings have a spiritual nature, and it is sinful human beings—descended not from apelike animals but from Adam—that Jesus Christ died to redeem.[383]

The Laetoli footprints are the earliest human footprints discovered, but they are not 3.6 million years old. Based on a biblical timeline, they could not be older than 4500 B.C., the point in history when the global Flood waters receded. The Laetoli tracks were made by fully human, image bearers of the Creator God.

PRESERVATION AND COLLECTION

There are three types of shoeprint impressions, categorized as visible (or patent), plastic, and latent prints. Visible prints are a direct transfer from the shoe to a surface and can be seen with the naked eye. An example would be a shoeprint in blood or a muddy tire track. Plastic prints are impressed into a soft surface like sand or snow. A latent print is not observable to the naked eye and requires a form of processing to make it visible. There are different methods available in the search for latent shoe prints. These include, but are not limited to, alternate light sources, oblique lighting, magnetic powders, dust lifters, chemicals, etc.

When collecting three-dimensional impression evidence, the most common method is casting. A special plaster is prepared and poured into the impression. A cast is the result of filling a three-dimensional impression with an appropriate material.

Types of casting material include dental stone, sulfur, or other materials specifically used to accurately recover three-dimensional impressions.[384] Some casting materials are also successful for lifting two-dimensional impressions. A plaster cast is movable about thirty minutes after pouring. It is then cured for 24–48 hours before cleaning any dirt and debris. Care must be taken to avoid destroying the detail marks. Maintaining the integrity of the print is a priority. Other methods of impression collection include:

dental stone cast

- *Electrostatic dust lifter*: an instrument that utilizes an electrostatic charge as a means of transferring dry origin impressions from a substrate to a Mylar® film.
- Gel lifter, tape, electrostatic lift, etc.

This image represents the original shoe print in mud, followed by the cast, and then the comparison against the suspect shoe.

SHOEPRINT EXAMINATION

The outsole of the shoe is the part that leaves the impression. This is the area that is examined for unique identifiers such as wear (holes), nicks, cuts/scratches, and gouges. These individual characteristics on the questioned shoe are then compared to a suspect shoe side by side. All variations in manufacturing must be considered during this process. Some manufacturers leave the exact same outsole pattern regardless of size, and others expand the pattern as the size increases or create the soles oversized to only cut them down to fit the upper part of the shoe. The pressure applied while leaving the impression can also affect the resulting image. When a match is confirmed by two or more examiners, a comparison chart may be required for courtroom testimony. The chart will point to the matching characteristics. The position of each characteristic must be represented in the known shoe, questioned print, and test print if applicable. This provides a clear presentation to the jury by showing the shoes are undeniably from the same source.

If a series of shoeprints are discovered, the investigator can take up to four measurements:

1. *Stride length:* the distance between two successive steps of the same foot.
2. *Step length:* the distance between the left and right foot.
3. *Stride width:* the transverse distance between the left and right foot impressions measured perpendicular to the direction of travel.
4. *Foot angle:* angular measurement of the midline of the foot in relation to the direction of travel.

The distance in the stride can be correlated to someone's height (though this is very limited due to the fact that the stride will be different if the person was walking slowly or briskly, or jogging or running). By using these four measurements, the suspect profile can be created.

TIRE AND TREAD PATTERNS

The first rubber tire with tread created for vehicles was developed by Harvey Firestone in 1900. His name should sound familiar since Firestone® is still a leading manufacturer of tires today.

Firestone

Tire impressions are made from the tread design on an individual tire. The tread design affects the performance of the tire. Tires have certain dimensional features that distinguish the branding. In contrast, tire tracks result from two or more tires. Tires are classified as original equipment tires or replacement tires. Original equipment tires are the tires that are sold as brand new on new vehicles. Replacement tires are what is purchased when the original tires become worn and damaged.

Tire Impression. Today's tires are made of radial ply construction. Radial construction of tires provides flexibility, stability, strength, and shock absorption. The structure of a tire consists of:

- *Bead:* The bead is made of a metal structure and ensures the fit on the rim and provides the air pressure seal.
- *Carcass:* The carcass wraps around the bead and includes layers of rayon and nylon in a rubber compound.
- *Side wall:* The side wall is made of rubber and protects the carcass.
- *Belt:* The belt surrounds the carcass and is made of layers of steel wires.
- *Tread:* The tread is in direct contact with the ground and is represented in many different designs based on the terrain and needs of the tire.[385]

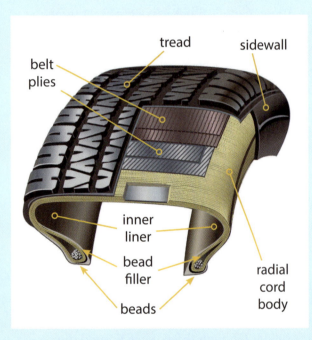

Tire tread is designed with raised tread called ribs and grooves called slots. There are two types of grooves on tires, those that circumvent the tire and those that run sideways, or transverse, to the tire. Pitch lengths are included on each tire to reduce sound, which is also known as noise treatment. Different tires will have a different pitch sequence to allow for a preference in sound reduction. Every tire is labeled with DOT (Department of Transportation) identification number, which includes the manufacturer, plant code identifier, and date of manufacture.

Tires are also designed with a wear bar called a Tread Wear Indicator. When a tire is new, the wear bar is 1/16" raised above the base of the grooves. The DOT has a national standard that requires all tires to have at least six wear bars. As the tires become used, the wear bars become worn in size and signify when the tires need to be replaced.

Tire tracks provide valuable information about what occurred at the crime scene. Investigators may learn how many cars were present at the scene and the direction of travel. Also, when a car is out of alignment, specific wear patterns will be visible in the patterns they leave behind. Tire tread can be recovered from mud, pavement, clothing, and any other surface that comes into contact with tires.

Tire marks are classified according to the direction of the tires during motion. Rotating tires are further divided into the following categories:[386]

- *Prints*: two-dimensional marks left behind on the road surface after traveling through a wet substance.

- *Impressions*: three-dimensional indention made in a soft surface like mud, sand, dirt, etc.

- *Scuff marks*: while the car is turning, these marks are left behind by sliding wheels.

Sliding tires leave different markings because of the car tires not being rotated. Sliding marks are further subdivided into:[387]

- *Skid marks*: the result of locking brakes as the vehicle continues to move in a straight direction. Front tire skid marks are darker on the edges while rear tire skid marks are lighter on the edges.
- *Yaw marks*: the result of turning tires while the car is still moving in a forward direction.
- *Skip marks*: the result of braking over a bump or hole. Skip marks are typically one to two feet long when traveling at normal speed.
- *Gap marks*: the result of a release on the brakes and then pressure reapplied on the brakes, causing a gap in the skid mark.[388]

yaw marks

Impressions

COLLECTION AND PRESERVATION OF TIRE TREAD

As seen in the collection of every type of evidence, all evidence must be photographed before any attempt is made at collection. Tire tread patterns should be photographed from multiple angles. The dark portions in the skid marks should be outlined with chalk and then photographed again. Written documentation would include the direction of travel, measurements, and number of impressions. Like shoe impressions, a poured casting material is used to preserve the tread pattern. Depending on the length of tire impression or tire track, this could be a significant amount of casting material. Sometimes only certain portions of the pattern may be cast for analysis. Other collection methods include photography, powders, and chemical enhancement.

When a suspect vehicle is identified, all the tires should be collected for analysis. The investigator should also collect elimination tire prints from any police, emergency, and victim vehicles at the scene. As tire impressions are examined, these will need to be eliminated from involvement in the case. Remember, tire track evidence is the impression left behind by two or more tires. Tire track evidence at the scene is examined for:[389]

- *Track width*: measurement from the center of one wheel (front) to the center of the opposite wheel (front).
- *Wheelbase dimensions*: measurement from the center of the front wheel to the center of the rear wheel directly behind it.
- *Turning diameter*: diameter of a circle that a car makes when the steering wheel is fully turned. This measurement applies to front wheels only.

When examining tread patterns at the crime scene, it is important to note whether the vehicle traveled in a straight path and made any turns. Often, the rear tires will only be visible if turns were made.

EXAMINATION OF TIRE TREAD

Once the tire patterns have been reduced to only the suspect vehicle, the questioned tire impression is examined against the known suspect vehicle. The known vehicle may not be recovered until after the initial examination of the tread evidence, and the make and model of the tire is determined. The investigators will compile a list of suspect vehicles.

The first step in examination is to print a full circumference test impression from all seized tires.[390] This is easily done by applying a thin coat of a silicone-based product to the tire and driving it over paper. The impression can then be developed with magnetic powder, and the analyst will take the test impression and compare it to the impression evidence.

Tire Track – Known Standard: Sections A–C

Tire Track – Known Standard: Sections D–F

Impression examinations are conducted by a well-trained impression examiner at a public or private crime lab. They will use a variety of tools to document the details of the tires. These will include calipers, lighting, 3D printing, and magnification. During the examination, the examiner will document:[391]

- Manufacturer
- Size of the tire
- Wear characteristics
- Individual characteristics (cuts, gouges)
- Arrangement of the tires on the suspect vehicle (driver front, driver rear, etc.)
- Arrangement of the tires on the vehicle at the crime scene
- Number of grooves
- Tread design

CONCLUSION

Impression evidence is extremely valuable to forensic investigators. Shoeprints can provide the number of people present at the scene, the direction of travel, and sometimes which shoeprint came first at the scene. Tire impressions point toward the size and type of vehicle involved in the crime, and tread patterns help determine the type of tire. Impression evidence requires that the class characteristics exhibit brand or design before proceeding to identify individual markers. New technology in tire tread examination has utilized the chemical analysis of the rubber left behind in the skid marks to test it against the rubber of the suspect tire. This provides just one more link in the connection between the suspect and the crime scene.

Lesson 24
Arson and Explosive Investigation

He drove out the man, and at the east of the garden of Eden he placed the cherubim and a flaming sword that turned every way to guard the way to the tree of life (Genesis 3:24).

Case Study: Death by Fire

On December 23, 1991, in Corsicana, Texas, Diane Barbee was alerted that her neighbor's house was on fire. Diane saw Cameron Todd Willingham, the owner of the home, outside the burning house, screaming, "My babies, oh, my babies! My babies are burning!"[395] Diane yelled at Willingham, "Go back in! Go try to get the babies!" Neighbors tried to gain entry to the bedrooms in the house, but they were reportedly engulfed in flames. A firefighter also attempted to gain access to the children's bedrooms and emerged from the fire with a tiny little girl (Amber) in his arms. As the firefighter fell to the ground, Amber's arms were limp; she died when she arrived at the hospital. The twins (Karmon and Kameron) were still in the house and pronounced dead. Their mother, Stacy, was out Christmas shopping when the fire started.

Investigators questioned Todd, who was unharmed except for minor burns on his shoulder. The fact that he had no injuries and did not try to save the children was found to be inconsistent with his statement. The night after the tragic house fire, Todd Willingham went out for a night of partying. The town also held a fundraiser to raise money for the burial of the three children, since Todd and Stacy claimed they could not afford it. At the fundraiser, Todd was overheard bragging about how the money would begin rolling in since people felt sorry for him. He also insisted on buying a new set of darts with the funeral donation money.

The fire investigation of the house revealed there was no evidence of wire shorting that could be responsible for starting a house fire. When the police found charcoal lighter fluid on the threshold of the door, they began to view the scene as arson.[396] After an interview with Todd, it became clear he was the prime suspect. He was arrested, and his bail was set at one million dollars. He was offered a plea deal that if he confessed, he would avoid the death penalty. Though his attorney urged him to take the deal, Willingham refused. The trial lasted only three days, and the jury deliberated for just one hour, returning a guilty verdict. Willingham was sentenced to death.[397]

Facts about the case:

- Stacy had called police on a few occasions for domestic abuse issues. The neighbors even told police they were afraid Todd would kill Stacy.
- Todd stayed home with the three girls while Stacy worked as a waitress. The couple had financial issues.
- Todd had multiple extramarital affairs.
- Todd was never observed trying to rescue any of his children. Willingham emerged from the burning house barefoot but claimed to have crawled around on his daughter's bedroom floor, looking for her as she screamed "Daddy," before fleeing from the house. His feet showed no burn marks, though the hallway to the bedroom was badly burned.
- Investigators cited 20 indicators of arson.
- The first witness at the trial was a jailhouse informant named Johnny Webb, who claimed that Willingham confessed to him in prison, but he later recanted this story.

- Twelve years later and only weeks before Willingham's execution, an appeal was made to have the arson evidence reexamined. The science of arson investigation had advanced over the years.
- A well-known chemist and respected arson analyst, Dr. Gerald Hurst, was asked to review the evidence. After evaluating the evidence, Dr. Hurst stated, "Todd Willingham's case falls into that category where there is not one iota of evidence that the fire was arson. Not one iota."[398] This was just four days before execution.
- Appeals failed, and Willingham was executed on February 17, 2004. At the execution, he made a last statement that he was wrongly convicted and that he was innocent. His ex-wife Stacy attended the execution.
- The original arson investigators still insist that the fire was the direct result of arson.

The interpretation of arson evidence is considered by many in the field as very subjective. This means that the analysis of point of origin, motive, etc., may vary among investigators. It is very challenging to investigate a scene where the majority of the evidence has been burned, sometimes with only ashes remaining. Arson investigation requires years of training and field work.

"... and meanwhile take my assurance that the clouds are lifting and that I have every hope that the light of truth is breaking through." — Sherlock Holmes[399]

Arson is the willful or malicious intent to burn property. Arson crimes often involve buildings, vehicles, boats, and forests. Arson is a criminal act that not only includes those that started the fire, but also anyone who aided, counseled, or supplied materials in the arson. There are four classifications for arson: aggravated arson, simple arson, attempted arson, and setting negligent fires. The primary difference between aggravated and simple arson involves the danger to human life. Aggravated arson, a more serious crime, results in a direct danger to life, while simple arson does not. Human life has an inherent value. Whenever there is a direct threat to a human life, as seen in a burglary versus a robbery, it results in a more serious crime and possible sentence. Attempted arson is the intent to set a fire or preparation to commit arson. Negligent fire is simply causing a fire to burn and letting it get out of control (e.g., a campfire left unattended).

In many circumstances, arson is difficult to prove because the evidence is destroyed in the process. The two most common causes of arson are revenge and insurance fraud. Within a five-year span, over 261,000 people set purposeful fires for insurance claims, resulting in over $1.5 billion in fraud.[400] When a fire incident occurs, the first responder is the fire department. The fire investigators will determine if the police need to be contacted. In cases involving arson, both the fire and police departments will work together to build a case for arson.

FIRE FROM A BIBLICAL WORLDVIEW

Humans have been using fire for around 6,000 years. The first mention of fire in the Bible is in Genesis 3:24, "He drove out the man, and at the east of the garden of Eden he placed the cherubim and a flaming sword that turned every way to guard the way to the tree of life." Adam and Eve willfully chose to disobey God. As a result, they were cast out of the Garden of Eden. God placed an angel with a flaming sword at the entrance to prevent any human from gaining access to the Tree of Life, the tree that produced the fruit granting eternal life. Many ask the question, "Where is the Garden of Eden located on the earth today?" The answer is nowhere. Using God's perfect Word as the starting point, the Bible provides a clear answer. The global Flood of Noah forever altered the face of the earth. As the fountains of the great deep broke open (Genesis 7:11) and the Flood covered the earth in water, a major catastrophic geologic activity took place. This changed the entire face of the earth, and the original location of the Garden of Eden was forever lost.

The Bible is also clear that man was smelting very early on in human civilization. Since humans are made in the image of God, it is not surprising they had advanced technology from the very beginning. Genesis 4:22 describes Cain's descendant Tubal-cain as "the forger of all instruments of bronze and iron." Based on this passage, it is clear he was using fire to melt down these elements to form tools, weapons, and other items needed for an advanced society. Tubal-cain was in the eighth generation from Adam.

Did Adam and Eve use fire in the Garden of Eden to heat food? The Bible does not state that they did. The only information provided is that God instructed them to eat of "every plant yielding seed that is on the face of all the earth, and every tree with seed in its fruit. You shall have them for food" (Genesis 1:29).

The all-powerful God created the essential ingredients for fire during the creation week, and though it may not have been needed in the Garden of Eden, it was likely the need to cook food and produce heat that would have resulted in the use of fire shortly after the expulsion from the Garden.

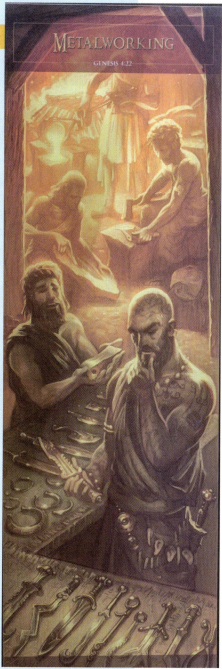

Tubal-cain

Arson and Explosive Investigation

RECIPE FOR FIRE

Fire is essentially a process of transformation that occurs when oxygen combines with a substance to produce both heat and light. This chemical reaction is called oxidation. But oxidation does not always result in fire. For example, rust is the result of oxidized iron, and when methane and oxygen combine, they will burn but not produce a visible flame.[401] Fire results when enough heat is applied to a fuel source and when sufficient oxygen is present. Therefore, the recipe for fire includes a fuel source, heat, and oxygen: Fire = fuel + oxygen + heat.

The Fire Triangle

Fuel: a solid, liquid, or gas combustible material

Heat: energy required to increase the temperature of the fuel to the flash point

Oxygen: minimum 16%

When heat is applied to fuel, the atoms in the fuel become excited and begin to move around until they reach the point when they have enough energy to break the chemical bonds that hold them together. This is the flash point. The flash point is the lowest temperature to which something can be heated for the substance to give off vapors that will burn when exposed to a flame. For a substance to reach its flash point, sufficient energy must be applied. The chemical change in the amount of energy applied to the substance influences the amount of energy given off. In this reaction, the energy given off is always more than the energy required for the flash point. The exothermic chemical reaction results in the release of volatile gases. The gases mix with the oxygen in the air and produce heat. Where there is a supply of fuel and oxygen, the liberation of heat and light (flame) will continue. The liberation of heat and light by the rapid combination of oxygen with a substance is called combustion.

There are other factors besides temperature that influence the rate of oxidation. Fuels exist in three basic states of matter, which are solids, liquids, and gases. In a solid, particles are tightly compacted together with definite volume. An example of a solid fuel is wood. In liquids, the particles are attracted to one another, but they have no definite volume. Gasoline is an example of liquid fuel. Particles in a gas are not attracted to each other and have no definite volume. Hydrogen gas is an example of a highly flammable gas.

The state of a physical fuel will affect the rate of oxidation. Fuel will only ignite by flame in its gaseous state due to the requirement of freely colliding molecules. As a fuel is heated, kinetic energy is produced, causing the molecules to move around. As the molecules collide, heat energy is released. Consider a log sitting in a campfire. How is this solid fuel transformed into a gaseous form for oxidation? Burning a log requires sufficient heat energy to break down the molecules in the solid fuel into a gaseous form, which will then ignite into flame. The process of converting a solid fuel into a gas is pyrolysis.

Glowing combustion:

Glowing combustion is an example of a fuel burning without a flame. Examples would be the smoldering embers of a campfire or a burning cigarette butt on the ground. In these examples, the carbonaceous residue continues to combust after the flames have diminished.

Another factor that affects combustion is the flammable range of a fuel. A mixture of gaseous fuel and air cannot ignite unless its composition lies within a range of gas in air concentration known as the flammable range.[402] If the fuel/air mix is below the range or high above the range, combustion will not occur. See **Table 1** for the flash range of common fuels.

Table 1	Common Flash Points and Flammable Ranges	
	Flash Point °F	**Flammable Range** % of fuel to mixture
Gasoline	40	1.3–6.0
Kerosene	110	0.7–5.0
Acetone	−4	2.6–13.0
Ethyl alcohol	55	3.3–19.0

Spontaneous combustion:

Spontaneous combustion is the result of a substance self-heating by an exothermic reaction in a poorly ventilated area. This process is often a slow buildup of temperature until it surpasses the flash point.

Why does fire always burn upwards? This is an interesting characteristic of fire. As heat energy is released, it heats up the temperature of the air around the flame, thereby reducing its density. Since the density of hot air is less than that of cold air, the hot air will rise while the cold air begins to sink. The sinking cold air fuels and accelerates the fire and the continued rise of hot air.[403] Also, fires will burn from areas of high temperatures to areas of low temperatures. This occurs through a process called heat transfer. There are three fundamental forms of heat transfer: conduction, convection, and radiation.

- *Conduction:* heat transfer occurs between the contact of solid objects.
- *Convection:* heat transfer by the molecular movement through a liquid.
- *Radiation:* heat transfer by electromagnetic waves. As the temperature increases, the electromagnetic waves carry with them the energy from the source.

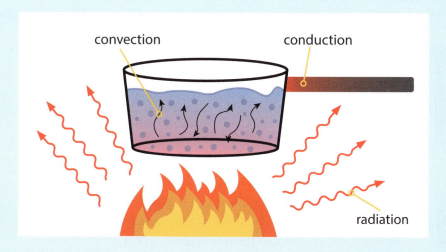

FIRE INVESTIGATION

Responding to the Scene of a Fire. When arriving at the scene of an arson, it is important to immediately assess the needs of the victims and to begin videotaping the scene. Video will capture the people at the scene, any vehicles leaving the scene, and the fire itself, as well as the effort to extinguish the fire. Photography is also key to accurately recording all the details. Remember, the three fundamental components of investigation include photography, sketches, and notes. Notes at the scene of an arson will document:[404]

- *Victim(s)*: name, age, and gender.
- *Witness(es)*: name, age, gender, contact information, and their observations.
- *Vehicles*: make/model, license, or VIN of all vehicles at the scene, around the scene, or leaving the scene.
- *Flame*: record all characteristics of the flames, such as color, intensity, height, etc.
- *Smoke*: record the color of the smoke. The color of the smoke can indicate the spark or accelerant that started the fire.
- *Surroundings*: record information about the surrounding houses, property, etc., that may be in proximity to the fire.
- *Alarms and sprinklers*: document if alarms and/or sprinklers were activated because of the fire.

Point of Origin (PoO). As soon as the fire has been extinguished, the investigation of the scene should begin. Evidence is in a fragile state, and any remaining accelerant will disappear within a couple days. The prompt and immediate need for an investigation often overrides the requirement of a search warrant. The investigator will begin the search for the point of origin (PoO). The PoO is the location or point where the fire started. PoO methodology has been developed to help investigators pinpoint the origination of the fire. The PoO holds clues to the ignition used to start the fire (candle, match, etc.), accelerants (gasoline or kerosene), and other pieces of evidence. Below is a list of characteristics that can direct the investigator to the point of origin.

- *"V" patterns:* Fire burns up and will form a V-shaped pattern. A narrow V-shape signifies a hot fire, likely the result of an accelerant. A wide V-shape is indicative of a slow-burning fire, and a U-shaped burn indicates a puddle of accelerant. The point of the V provides clues to the where the fire started.

- *Char patterns:* A char pattern results from a fast-moving, hot fire that leaves behind sharp lines between the burned and unburned areas. A visible char pattern on the inside of a bedroom door versus the outside would indicate the fire originated inside the room.

- *Heat shadows:* A heat shadow is the result of large, dense furniture shielding part of a wall or floor.

- *Glass:* Glass melts, cracks, and sometimes shatters under high heat and pressure. Observing the condition of glass can provide clues to PoO. For example, light bulbs melt toward the heat source while abnormal cracking patterns reflect an extremely hot fire.

- *Chimney effect:* The chimney effect occurs when an upward-burning gas forms a fireball and bursts through the ceiling. This is because heated gases have less density than the cooler air surrounding them and therefore rise toward the ceiling. As the heated gases rise and build up, they will explode and burn a hole through the ceiling. Often, a hole in the ceiling points to the PoO beneath it.

- *Blistering concrete:* When concrete is heated, the water trapped inside begins to expand. The pressure will build to the point the concrete becomes compromised and begins to blister. The areas of blistering focus on or near the point of origin.

Trained canines called ACDs (Accelerant Detection Canines) are often used to search for the point of origin. Dogs have a high sensitivity to odor detection. Canines have been trained to detect explosives, narcotics, electronic components, cancer, and other amazing things. The chart below describes the exquisite capabilities God gave canines to identify the unique scents of accelerants, which far surpass man-made chemical detectors.

K-9	Parts per trillion*
Human	Parts per billion
Sensor equipment	Parts per million

*1 part per 1 trillion parts

PRESERVATION AND COLLECTION

==Evidence at arson scenes is extremely fragile.== The collection of ashes, residues, and other debris begins as soon as it is safe to enter the scene. The focus will be on the point of origin. Solid and liquid evidence is stored in airtight containers like paint cans or glass jars. Each container should be clearly labeled with location. Reference samples will also be collected for comparison in the lab.

In the lab, technicians will extract the vapors that collect inside the cans to perform gas chromatography. Gas chromatography will separate the vapors into their individual components. The results are then searched in a national database of ignitable liquids. Ignitable Liquids Database and Reference Collection was created as a storehouse for the compositions of ignitable liquids. The database is maintained and updated by the University of Central Florida and the National Center for Forensic Science.[405]

CHALLENGES IN ARSON INVESTIGATION

==Arson investigation is riddled with challenges.== The primary hindrance is the destruction of physical evidence in the fire. Arson investigators must coordinate with the fire department and are dependent on the fire department to notify them of a potential arson case. Determining whether the fire is accidental or intentional is not always clear. Was the fire started by natural, accidental, or malicious causes? Finding truthful witnesses is not always possible, especially in cases of insurance fraud.

EXPLOSIVES

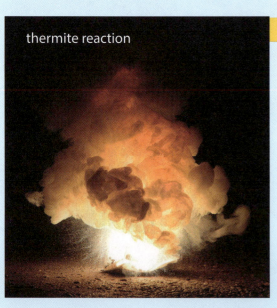

thermite reaction

==The same components necessary for an arson are required for an== explosion. The primary difference between arson and explosions is the rapid rate of reaction observable in explosive materials. Since there is a rapid buildup of gas pressure, the results are a physical expulsion of that pressure up to 7,000 miles per hour. Explosives contain one of three explosive materials in solid, liquid, or powder form and an incendiary device.

For an explosion to occur, there must be a fuel, an oxidizer, and a spark to generate heat. An oxidizer feeds the reaction with the necessary oxygen to sustain it. This is because the reaction is so fast that there is no time for the reaction to extract oxygen from the air.[406] Oxidizing agents are chemicals that supply oxygen to the reaction. Black powder is an example of an oxidizing agent. Other chemicals, like nitroglycerin, have the oxygen and fuel combined in one molecule. An explosion is essentially an exothermic (release of heat) oxidation reaction.

TYPES OF EXPLOSIVES

Explosives are classified according to their reaction speed.

Low Explosives. Low explosives burn at a slow rate of 1,000 meters per second. Low explosives, like black powder, are often used as the propellant for a high explosive and in ammunition.[407] When confined to a small container, low explosives have the potential to produce large explosions resulting in death. The two most common low explosives are black powder and smokeless powder. Black powder is a nitrate-formulated powder that simply burns when not packaged in small containers. Smokeless powder, also nitrate based, is the safest low explosive.

High Explosives. High explosives react instantaneously, faster than the speed of sound, and have a loud detonation. High explosives have a velocity exceeding 1,000 meters per second. High explosives differ from low explosives in that they do not have to be confined to a small container to have a significant damaging effect. High explosives are categorized by primary and secondary explosives. Primary explosives are very sensitive to shock, heat, and friction and are often used as a primer to detonate larger explosives. Secondary explosives are not affected by shock, heat, and friction, and thereby rely on the primary explosive to initiate detonation. Examples of high explosives are TNT, C-4 (RDX), and dynamite.

Dynamite was developed by Alfred Nobel in 1867, the namesake of the Nobel Peace Prize. Nobel was searching for a way to stabilize nitroglycerin. He found that by adding pulp to the nitroglycerin, it stabilized the material while still maintaining its explosive qualities. Today, the use of dynamite has been replaced by ammonium nitrate–based explosives. Ammonium nitrate is high in oxygen and, when combined with a fuel source, produces a cost-effective, stable form of explosive.

Homemade Explosives. Domestic and terrorist explosives often include one of three common homemade bombs: pipe bombs, IEDs, and Molotov cocktails. Pipe bombs are a section of a pipe containing low explosives. The pipe is capped, and a fuse is inserted into a form of explosive powder. When the pipe bomb is ignited and successfully explodes, large fragments of steel pipe are jettisoned with rapid speed. The potential for life threatening injuries is very high. An IED (Improvised Explosive Device) is made of five components: explosive material, a switch, a main charge, a power supply, and a container. These components usually survive the explosion.[408] IEDs are delivered via vehicles (e.g., terrorists), physically thrown by the assailant, delivered in a package (e.g., Unabomber), or hidden in backpacks (e.g., Boston Marathon bombings).[409] The Molotov cocktail was named after the Soviet foreign minister in World War II named Vyacheslav Molotov. The term Molotov cocktail was coined by the Finns as an insult. A Molotov cocktail is a glass bottle with motor oil, a flammable material, and a wick or cloth soaked in kerosene or gasoline. The wick is usually set on fire and the bottle thrown prior to explosion. This device is normally used by amateurs to start fires.

Liquid Explosives. There are hundreds of solid explosives but approximately a dozen frequently used liquid explosives. Liquid explosives are simple to construct, and the chemicals are easy to purchase. Nitroglycerin is a common liquid explosive that is sensitive to shock. If shaken, nitroglycerin begins to break down into water, oxygen, and carbon dioxide and releases a significant jolt of energy. In 2006, authorities in the United States and Great Britain were alerted to a terrorist plot against the airline industry. The intel described the use of what appeared to be ordinary liquids smuggled onto airlines and combined in flight to make an explosive device. This resulted in a ban on liquids, such as bottles of water, any other beverages, and shampoos. This ban is still in effect today.

Military-grade Explosives. Within the United States, the use of military-grade explosives in terrorist activity is not as common as in other parts of the world. In these countries, obtaining military-grade explosives is not difficult, and therefore, they are key components in homemade terrorist bombs. TNT and RDX (C-4) are the two most common military-grade explosives encountered outside the United States.

EXPLOSION INVESTIGATION AND ANALYSIS

Explosives investigation uses many of the same practices employed in arson investigation. As in all investigations, the use of photography and videography are required to accurately record all the details. A detailed analysis of the blast site begins with the point of origin (PoO), or crater.

Once the point of origin has been identified, a bomb specialist is brought in to verify that the device and location are safe for investigation. Specialists use robots to verify that the device has detonated. K-9s trained in detecting explosive residues or an IMS (ion mobility spectrometer) will be used to detect the location of chemical residues. If an explosive device is concealed inside a box, bag, or other medium, a portable X-ray machine is used to reveal the components before being secured and removed from the scene.

From the PoO, the investigation will expand outward to all buildings, vehicles, and areas affected by the blast. The investigator will likely find components from the explosive device, such as wiring, timers, fuel or powder residue, and circuit boards. Evidence collection could reach into the hundreds, depending on the size of the blast site.

If terrorists are believed to be involved in the explosion, the FBI's Terrorist Explosive Device Analytical Center (TEDAC) and Homeland Security are contacted to examine the evidence.

Crater from an explosion in Ukraine

The examination of evidence begins with a microscopic analysis of small fragments and soils in search of any unconsumed explosive materials. Analysis of large fragments will begin with a search for fingerprints or DNA. Collected residues will be analyzed using gas chromatography or infrared spectroscopy. The goal is to determine the type of explosion, the explosive materials used, and the origin of the materials constructing the device. Results can be searched in national registers that contain information about terrorist groups and serial bombers.

There are limitations in explosion investigation. One is weather, since rain can wash away key residue evidence. Additionally, the blast may destroy the evidence beyond identification. Criminals may be careful to leave behind no trace evidence when constructing their bombs, as occurred with Ted Kaczynski, the Unabomber.

Incidents of explosions in the United States have been on a 28% decline since 2013, in addition to the number of people injured and killed. The state with the most explosion incidents is California. The most bomb threats are brought against educational institutions.[410]

CONCLUSION

It is interesting to note that 90% of arsonists go unpunished due to insufficient evidence. Many of these are committed by juveniles experimenting with fire. Circumstantial evidence is often misinterpreted or overlooked due to the lack of training in this field. Many investigators lack the scientific understanding of the chemistry behind combustion and the factors affecting its spread, patterns, and characteristics of origin. Continual training and education are essential for arson investigators as technology improves.

All forensic disciplines have their own organizations dedicated to the research, education, and support of professionals in their respective fields. The International Association of Arson Investigators (IAAI) is an international association of more than 10,000 fire investigation professionals. This group of arson experts is committed to suppressing the crime of arson through professional fire investigation.[411]

Lesson 25
Residues and Patterns

This is he who came by water and blood—Jesus Christ; not by the water only but by the water and the blood. And the Spirit is the one who testifies, because the Spirit is the truth (1 John 5:6).

Case Study: Murder of Marilyn Sheppard

On the night of July 4, 1954, Dr. Sam Sheppard had fallen asleep on the couch when he was awakened by a cry of "Sam" from his wife upstairs. When he entered their bedroom, he claimed to have seen a "bushy-haired man" attacking his wife. Sheppard was hit on the head and fell to the floor unconscious. When he regained consciousness, he checked the pulse of his wife and found her to be dead. Their son, Sam Sheppard Jr., was unharmed and asleep in the home. Sheppard heard noises in the lower level of the house, found the back door open, and saw someone running toward the lake. He attacked the man. During the altercation, Sheppard claimed he was rendered unconscious a second time. When he regained consciousness again, he was shirtless, and his watch was missing. Sheppard called a family friend before calling the police.[412]

Dr. Sam Sheppard was a well-known neurosurgeon and the son of a prominent doctor, but investigators did not believe his story. Dr. Sheppard had a history of marital affairs, and there were rumors of friction in the marriage. To the police, it appeared as a simple domestic murder case. The police did not investigate the "bushy-haired man" or any other suspect. Dr. Sheppard was arrested, tried, and convicted of second-degree murder on December 21, 1954. The trial drew lots of attention and not only had a very biased judge ruling over the proceedings but is also recognized "as a mockery of justice" by the federal courts and studied by law students.[413] He was sentenced to life in prison. Maintaining his innocence, Sheppard began the appeal process. F. Lee Bailey took over as Sheppard's chief counsel on July 30, 1961. On July 16, 1964, Sheppard was released on the grounds that during the original trial, there were multiple violations of his constitutional rights. But it was not over. In May of 1965, his conviction was reinstated by a federal appeals court, and Sheppard went through a second trial.

Blood spatter analysis had never been introduced in court as evidence. During the second trial, blood spatter analysis and testimony by Dr. Paul Kirk was entered as evidence. Dr. Kirk pointed to the blood spatter patterns as evidence. He testified that Dr. Sheppard could not possibly be guilty. This was the first case where blood spatter analysis was key to the exoneration of a suspect. Based on this new testimony and other credible facts from the case, Sheppard was found not guilty. Sheppard returned to his surgical practice, but after killing two patients and having a pattern of alcoholism, he was forced to quit practicing medicine. He tried professional wrestling and used the stage name "Killer Sheppard."[414] Since his second trial, Sheppard had become addicted to barbiturates and was an alcoholic. Sheppard died of liver failure in 1970 at the age of 46. He never admitted guilt to friends, family, or even his lawyers and claimed his innocence until his death.

But there's another piece to this mystery — a man named Richard Eberling. But who is he? Richard Eberling owned a window cleaning company at the time of the murders, and the Sheppards were one of his clients. Eberling was arrested for grand larceny in 1959. When police later searched his home, they found nothing of the Sheppards except a cocktail ring belonging to Marilyn Sheppard.[415] The ring is claimed to have been stolen three years after the murder from the home of a Sheppard family member. Eberling consented to a lie detector test regarding Marilyn's murder, and the results were found to be inconclusive. It did become clear that Eberling found Marilyn attractive and appealing. Eberling was never addressed as a possible suspect in either the first or second trial. Eberling was later convicted of murdering Ethel Durkin in 1989. Kathie Collins, a nurse for Durkin, told police that Eberling confessed to her that he killed Marilyn Sheppard. Eberling denied making this claim. His murder conviction renewed interest in his possible involvement in Marilyn's death.

The question remains to this day: Who really killed Marilyn Sheppard? According to a statement by Eberling, "The Sheppard answer is in front of the entire world. Nobody bothered to look."[416]

Though there are extensive facts surrounding this case, these are a few of the highlights.

Facts about the case regarding the Sheppards:

- At the time of the murder, Marilyn was four months pregnant with a baby boy. The baby was Sam Sheppard's, dispelling the theory that Marilyn was having an affair and Sam killed her in anger.
- No fingerprints were found in the house besides those of the family.
- Prosecutors claimed there were no signs of forced entry into the home. Years later, it was revealed that the Scientific Investigation Unit never told the prosecution they had found evidence of forced entry outside the cellar door, enough to warrant a toolmark casting.[417]
- There were visible signs of a robbery (or staged robbery), such as open drawers and broken items.
- Sheppard claimed to be wearing a t-shirt on the night of the murder. A t-shirt was found a few yards from the Sheppards' property line that was Sam's size. No blood was found on the shirt. There was also no blood found on Sam's pants, belt, socks, or shoes, other than one stain on the knee area of his pants. This was believed to have occurred as he was checking his wife's pulse.
- Marilyn died from 35 blows to the head, and blood spatter covered the room. The act was clearly passion driven and not an arbitrary robber.
- Marilyn had described her husband to a family friend as a "Jekyll and a Hyde."[418]
- The coroner testified in court, "In this bloodstain I could make out the impression of a surgical instrument."[419] No surgical instrument matching the description was ever found.
- Sheppard's bloody watch was found inside a green bag on the bluff above Lake Erie. The watch had stopped at 4:15 a.m.
- Dr. Kirk's blood analysis testimony stated the killer was left-handed; Sheppard was right-handed.

- F. Lee Bailey was Sam Sheppard's second attorney. Bailey would go on to become a famous attorney and would be one of the people on the defense team representing O.J. Simpson in 1995.
- The Sam Sheppard case inspired a popular TV series and movie.

Facts about the case regarding Eberling:

- Richard Eberling had type A blood; no type A blood was identified in the blood evidence.
- When Eberling was arrested for larceny in 1959, he did not have "bushy hair," but he was known to wear toupees.
- During his 1959 arrest, Eberling told police he had cut himself while installing a screen at the Sheppards' home two days before the murder in 1954. He had a scar on his left wrist.
- When Eberling was testifying for the defense in Sheppard's second trial, Sheppard never identified him as the man with the "bushy hair" or the suspect who attacked him the night of Marilyn's death.
- Eberling identified the cellar door on a detailed sketch he drew of the Sheppard home in 1992 during the reinvestigation, a detail not visible on the police sketch in 1954.
- In 1998, a DNA profile developed from a bloodstain near the closet in the bedroom showed that Eberling's profile fit within a rare blood DNA profile.
- On July 25, 1998, Eberling died in prison.
- In August of 1998, an inmate at the same prison with Eberling told police that Eberling had confessed to Marilyn's murder before he died.

Several books have been published on the murder of Marilyn Sheppard, some pointing to Dr. Sheppard and some pointing to Eberling as the killer. Blood spatter analysis has come a long way in validity since the 1960s. This lesson will cover the techniques used in interpreting blood patterns and the value found in a single drop of blood.

"The most common place crime is often the most mysterious, because it presents no new or specific features from which deductions may be drawn." — Sherlock Holmes[420]

Blood spatter analysis is the field of forensic examination that deals with the physical properties of blood and the shapes, locations, and distribution patterns of bloodstains. The goal of blood spatter analysis is to provide a knowledgeable, expert interpretation of the physical events that produced the blood evidence. The first major case that involved blood spatter analysis was the Sam Sheppard case in 1955 discussed above.

Remember from Lesson 11 that the components of blood are 45% formed elements and 55% plasma. The formed elements comprise red blood cells, white blood cells, and platelets. Ninety-one percent of plasma is water. As the Bible says in Leviticus 17:11, life is in the blood. A human would have to lose 40% of their blood volume, either externally or internally, to produce death. A cut vein or artery will result in a loss of half a liter of blood per minute. Investigators understand that dead people do not bleed. The heart must still be circulating blood for bleeding to occur. When a living person is struck with an object, the initial injury does not cause the blood spatter. There must be an open, bleeding wound that is then struck a second, third, or more times to leave a blood spatter pattern.

Blood exhibits a high level of surface tension (0.058 N/m), and this characteristic causes blood to form the spherical shapes visible in blood spatter patterns. Surface tension is the result of the intermolecular forces at work between the liquid and the surface. The liquid molecules adhere together and give the appearance of an elastic membrane in the droplet. Blood is also very viscous. Viscosity is the blood's resistance to flow. The phrase "blood is thicker than water" describes the viscosity. Blood will flow more slowly than water due to its cellular components. The surface tension and viscous nature of blood contribute to the unique shape of the patterns left behind.

BLOOD SPATTER FROM A BIBLICAL WORLDVIEW

Blood spatter analysis requires an understanding of mathematical calculations in the field of geometry and a fundamental understanding of physics. The reliability of mathematical laws used in this discipline demonstrates that there must be a law giver. Someone set into motion the mathematical principles measurable throughout creation. Though blood spatter analysis is often the result of man's sin against another human, God put principles in place that allow investigators to solve these crimes using the scientific method and mathematical predictability. Dr. Dana Sneed relates how math confirms the biblical Creator God:

Leviticus 17:11:

"For the life of the flesh is in the blood, and I have given it for you on the altar to make atonement for your souls, for it is the blood that makes atonement by the life."

Math is predictable because our God, who upholds the universe (Hebrews 1:3), is consistent—he does not change (Malachi 3:6). In fact, we see the foundation of math in Genesis 1, when God counted the days of creation and marked the beginning of time. The concept of infinity or even irrational numbers (that have decimal places that continue on into infinity) remind us that God is beyond measure (Psalm 147:5); infinity can only exist because God is infinite. Math, like operational science, depends on the uniformity of universal laws and the certainty of absolute truths, which depend on the God of truth (Isaiah 65:16).[421]

HISTORY OF BLOOD SPATTER

The history of blood spatter analysis is young compared to other forensic disciplines. The first detailed study of blood spatter analysis was published in 1895 by Dr. Eduard Piotrowski and was titled *Concerning the Origin, Shape, Direction and Distribution of the Bloodstains Following Head Wounds Caused by Blows*. His research laid the groundwork for future pioneers such as Dr. Victor Balthazard (1939), who was the first to use physical interpretation of stains to determine point of origin, and Dr. Paul Kirk (1902–1970), who was the first to use bloodstain pattern analysis in court during the Sam Sheppard case in 1955 (see the case study at the beginning of this lesson). In 1983, the International Association of Bloodstain Pattern Analysts (IABPA) was formed to standardize this branch of forensic science. The science of blood spatter stains continues to develop into a very accurate and predictable form of analysis.

Balthazard

A DROP OF BLOOD

A single drop of blood has three characteristics: the parent drop, spines, and satellite spatter. The parent drop is the drop of blood from which the satellite spatter originates. The spines are pointed edges on the parent drop that radiate out like a sun. Spines help pinpoint direction. The satellites are small drops of blood that broke free from the parent drop when the blood hit the surface.

If the parent drop falls at an angle less than 90 degrees, it will have a tail. The tail always points toward the direction of travel. The type of surface the droplet falls upon will affect its characteristics. A smooth, hard surface will leave no distortion of the blood around the edges. Examples of a smooth, hard surface are glass, tile, finished hardwood floors, etc. Textured surfaces, like linoleum flooring, will result in a bloodstain with visible spines and satellite droplets.

The elongated shape of these droplets can be measured to determine the following characteristics:

- The direction from which the blood originated
- Angle from which the blood originated
- The time of the attack
- Location and position of the victim
- Movement of the bleeding suspect or victim
- Number of blows to the victim
- The type of injuries
- The location of the attacker

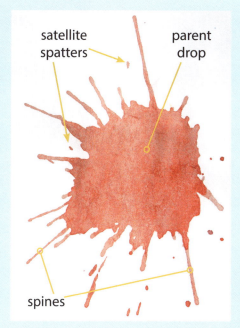

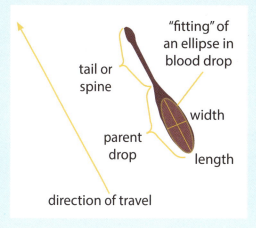

Residues and Patterns

CATEGORIES OF BLOODSTAINS

Bloodstains are categorized into three broad categories: passive, transfer, and projected.

- **Passive.** Passive drops of blood are pulled down by gravity alone. The distance between the source and the surface affects the size of the blood droplet. The greater the height, the larger the spatter.
    - There are four types of passive patterns, which are identified as drops, drips, pools, and clots.

- **Transfer.** Transfer bloodstains are the result of a bloody surface coming into contact with a clean surface, thereby leaving bloody residue. This direct transfer can occur from a bleeding body being dragged across a floor or when an assailant rubs bloody hands on a door frame. Transfers have the potential to leave identifiable, individualized characteristics like fingerprints, palm prints, and shoe prints. Types of transfer bloodstains include:

    - *Swipe or smear*: This is when wet blood is transferred to a surface that did not originally have blood on it.
    - *Wipe or smudge*: Occurs when a clean, non-blood-bearing object moves through a wet bloodstain and alters the appearance of the original stain.
    - *Contact bleeding*: A simple person-to-person transfer of blood.

- **Projected.** Projected bloodstains are the result of a force or action that causes exposed blood to be expelled. The amount of spatter and the spatter area is directly affected by the force applied. This force is greater than the force of gravity. Analyzing the cast-off patterns is crucial to determine the direction and location of the force.
    - *Back spatter*: The result of blood spatter on the perpetrator from the attack on the victim.

TYPES OF SPATTER

Learning to distinguish between the various types of blood spatter is key to an investigator's analysis. Each type of spatter holds distinguishing characteristics that will help in the interpretation of events at the crime scene.

Impact Spatter. This is when a blood source is impacted by a blow that causes a random dispersion of smaller drops of blood. The surface texture and velocity greatly impact the appearance of the blood drops. Velocity is defined as an object's speed and direction of motion.

impact spatter

- Low velocity: 0–5 ft/sec, with stains 3 mm or greater in diameter. These reflect dripping blood due to gravity.
- Medium velocity: 5–25 ft/sec, with stains 1–3 mm in diameter. These reflect a blunt force trauma or cast-off pattern.
- High velocity: 100+ ft/sec, with stains less than 1 mm and resembling a fine mist.

There are four phases of impact that every blood drop will progress through:

1. Contact and collapse is the flattening of the blood droplet upon impact.
2. Displacement is the spreading out of the blood droplet.
3. Dispersion is the separation of spatter or small droplets from the main droplet.
4. Retraction is the adhesion of blood particles that do not completely separate and are drawn back into the parent droplet.

Gunshot Spatter. This is the forward blood spatter emitted from the exit wound and back spatter from the entrance wound. If the bullet becomes lodged in the body, only back spatter is visible.

gunshot spatter

If the gunman is near the victim, the gunman will likely have back spatter visible on their clothing, hands, and other parts of their body. Occasionally, blood spatter will spray into the muzzle of the firing gun. This is called drawback effect.

Cast-off Spatter. This is caused by the blood released from a bloody projectile. For example, a blood-covered fist, knife, baseball bat, gun, or other object flings blood onto the walls and surfaces as it is in motion. The pattern may resemble an arc shape. The amount and range of spatter is dependent on the object inflicting the blows, the amount of bleeding incurred from the injury, and the direction of the object at impact. Cast-off provides clues to the minimum number of blows inflicted on the victim. The investigator will count the number of forward/backward spatter patterns. Other factors that can be gleaned from cast-off patterns are the height of the attacker, angle of impact, and direction of the weapon.

cast-off spatter

Arterial Spray Spatter. This pattern occurs when a main artery or the heart is ruptured. As the blood builds up, the pressure of the pumping blood will spurt blood outward from the injuries. The area with the biggest spurt is the location of the first burst artery. Since this blood is highly oxygenated, it can be distinguished by its bright red color.

arterial spray spatter

Expired Blood. These patterns are caused by a bleeding mouth or nose from an internal injury. Often in expired blood, oxygen bubbles expressed in the blood spatter provide another characteristic for comparison by providing insight into the type of injuries present in the victim.

expired spatter

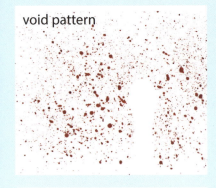
void pattern

pool pattern

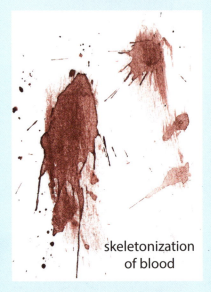
skeletonization of blood

trail pattern

Void Pattern. This is a space where there is no visible blood spatter. The void is created when an object or person blocks projecting blood spatter from reaching a surface. The blood adheres to the blocking material instead. Analyzing void patterns can alert the investigator to the height, size, and shape of the object or person causing the void.

Flow Patterns. These are the result of the flow of blood downward due to the force of gravity. There are two types of flow patterns, active and passive. Active flow is blood emitting from an open wound, while passive flow is blood patterns due to arterial spurt. Flow patterns provide clues to the movement of the victim and/or perpetrator.

Pool Patterns. These are the collection of blood in a pool on an undisturbed, nonporous surface. If blood collects on a porous surface, it will either be absorbed or, if there is sufficient blood, will diffuse to the surface beneath.

Splash Patterns. These are visible when a pool of blood splashes outward and resemble the shape of an exclamation point.

Skeletonization of Blood Patterns. These occur when the edges of a bloodstain begin to dry. Under normal conditions, this occurs within 50 seconds of deposit. The drying of the edges is referred to as skeletonization. Once the edges have skeletonized, any disturbance to the stain, whether wiping or smearing, will leave the perimeter of the original stain intact. Depending on how much blood is deposited, the center of the stain may dry and flake away if disturbed. This characteristic provides clues to the timing and movement of anyone involved in the act.

Trail Patterns. These patterns are caused by a series of drops that form by the dripping of blood from an object, weapon, or injury. The size of the drop helps in determining the distance from the ground and possible height. This will be discussed in the next section. Additionally, the shape of the drops allows investigators to determine the speed and direction of the person who was injured. Sometimes, by following the blood trail, the drops will lead directly to the weapon. There is also the potential for DNA evidence.

BLOOD SPATTER CALCULATIONS

Analyzing blood spatter requires measurements, accuracy, and calculations. Three areas that impact this analysis are the impact angle, the area of convergence, and the point of origin.

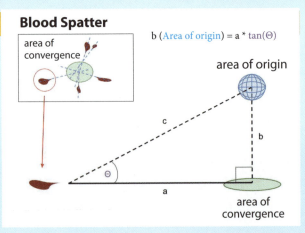
Blood Spatter
b (Area of origin) $= a * \tan(\Theta)$

Impact Angles. Bloodstains have a unique shape, a teardrop with a pointed tail. As discussed earlier, the pointed end of a bloodstain always points toward the direction of travel. To determine the direction and angle of impact, only the circular portion of the stain is measured for the length and width. If the length and width are the same, the blood droplet fell perpendicular to the surface and is a 90-degree stain.

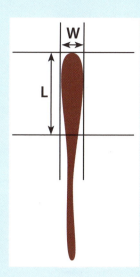

As the angle decreases, the more elongated the stain. The angle of impact is defined as an acute angle formed between the blood drip and the surface. Using trigonometry, the impact angle is calculated. The formula to measure the impact angle is:

$$\sin A = \frac{\text{width of bloodstain}}{\text{length of bloodstain}}$$

Area of Convergence on a Two-dimensional Plane. The area of convergence is the point at which the drops of blood in an impact pattern originated. To determine this point, lines are drawn from the long axis of several individual bloodstains through their tails to determine the area of convergence.

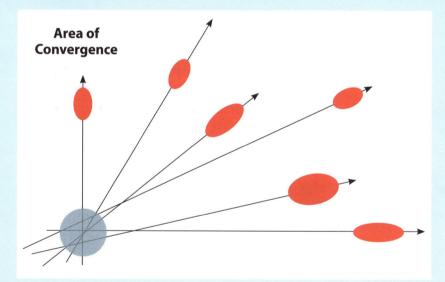

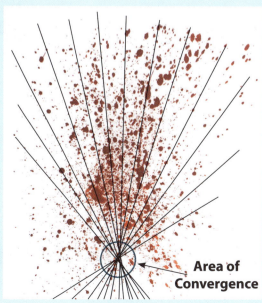

Residues and Patterns   Lesson 25 ◂ 317

Area of Origin in a Three-dimensional Space. The area of convergence in a three-dimensional space is the area in which the victim or suspect was present when the blood spatter stain was produced. Investigators use strings or lasers at the point of each bloodstain from the long axis of the stain to the approximate point of origin. They will then use the angle of impact measurement to pinpoint the exact location of the attacker. Any interruption or discrepancy in any of the patterns is a clue in the timeline of events.

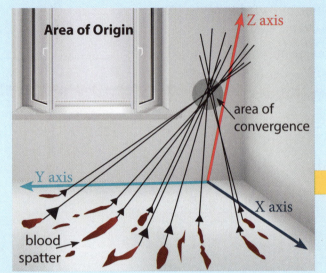

DOCUMENTING BLOODSTAINS

As with all evidence, the first step is to photograph each pattern and drop of blood from a distance to observe the overall pattern and then up close to identify spines, tails, or spatter. They should also be photographed with and without a scale measurement. The perimeter rule method is to use a rectangular ruler with scale measurements around each pattern and stain. In addition, the location of each bloodstain is recorded with the size.

Of all the search patterns, the grid method is the best search methodology to locate and identify all blood spatter evidence. In this method, a grid of known dimensions is placed over the pattern for scale and to accurately record the pattern.

CONCLUSION

Bloodstains reveal clues to the direction and angle of the weapon, and the location of the assailant and victim. Based on the patterns, investigators can determine movement through the scene, the number of blows, and other important characteristics. Blood spatter reveals the person was alive when the attack began, and the length of time blood is on a surface allows for an estimated time of attack and possible time of death. Forensic bloodstain experts are expected to be knowledgeable in the different patterns, shapes, and angles of blood spatter.

It is unfortunate that this type of expertise is needed in forensic work, but man has rebelled against their Creator God. In His wisdom, God put into motion mathematical laws that allow crime scene experts to resolve these mysteries.

FORENSIC TOOLS

UNIT 6

Lesson 26
Microscopes

Whatever your hand finds to do, do it with your might (Ecclesiastes 9:10a).

Case Study: The Power of a Lens

In August of 1889, a road repairman reported a foul smell to the police. Police discovered the decomposing body of a male wrapped in a cloth. Rope found with the body verified death by strangulation. A court bailiff from Montmartre, France, 300 miles away, had been reported missing on July 26, 1889. During this period in crime scene investigation, police rarely collected bodies for examination. This was a rare case when the decomposing body was collected and examined for evidence. The police suspected the body belonged to the missing Parisian court bailiff Toussaint-Augustin Gouffé, but his family failed to identify the body as Gouffé. The body was buried in a pauper's grave.[422]

Not long after the burial, the chief of the Paris Investigative Unit, Goron, had the body exhumed for examination by a famed criminologist. Dr. Alexandre Lacassagne spent an entire week performing an in-depth review of the deceased. His process set a precedent for future medical examiners that is still used today. Dr. Lacassagne was able to verify the body as Gouffé after comparing a hair taken from the comb of the missing person's apartment to that of the victim. Dr. Lacassagne examined the two hairs under a microscope and successfully identified an exact match. This is one of the earliest cases where microscopy was used to solve a case.

Facts about the case:

- Prior to Gouffé's disappearance, he had been sighted associating with two known con artists, Gabrielle Bompard and her partner, Michel Eyraud.
- History records that Bompard met Gouffé at a cafe and lured him to her apartment while Eyraud hid behind a curtain. While Gabrielle distracted Gouffé, Eyraud wrapped a rope around the neck of Gouffé and strangled him.
- The murderers hid the body in a trunk and shipped it by railway to Lyon. They picked up the trunk, rented a truck, and began to transport the body. But the smell of putrefaction became too powerful, and the couple left the trunk on the side of the road.
- Bompard and Eyraud fled to the United States.
- After authorities found the body of Gouffé, they began to piece together the story. One of the first wanted posters was created for the murderous couple and distributed across Europe.
- The thorough autopsy by Lacassagne set a precedent for medical examiners. He used anthropometry to correctly estimate the height of the deceased, he matched a hair sample to one from a comb in Gouffé's apartment, and he also identified a fracture in the right ankle that had not healed correctly and matched it back to an injury Gouffé had as a child.[423]
- Gabrielle Bompard fell in love with an American adventurer who convinced her to return to France and confess. She did so in January 1890 and was imprisoned. Eyraud eluded police until June of 1890, when he was apprehended in Havana, Cuba.

- Eyraud was found guilty in December of 1890 and sentenced to death by guillotine. He was executed on February 3, 1891. The attorney of Bompard convinced the court that Eyraud had hypnotized her into committing the heinous act.
- A lament was composed for Miss Gabrielle Bompard about her misfortunes. Below is the poster to advertise the song.
- She was sentenced to twenty years of hard labor in a women's prison. She was released in 1905 for good behavior and died in 1920.

"The game is afoot." — Sherlock Holmes[424]

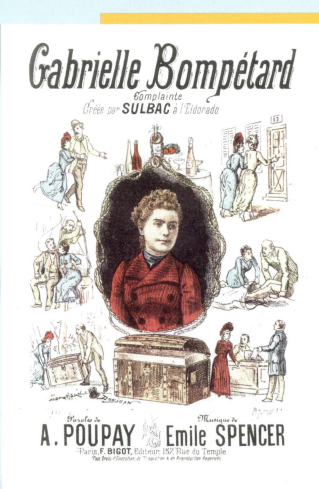

Microscopy reveals the unseen world of God's creation. Microscopes rely on light to illuminate hidden details. Light is energy in the form of waves. Light waves emanate from the source of the light at a rapid speed of 300,000 km/second (186,000 miles). When light passes through different materials, it will bend, diffract, and/or be reduced in speed. The components of a microscope utilize these properties of light to magnify images that would be impossible to see with the naked eye.

Microscopes were only invented a little over 400 years ago, which is fairly recent in the timeline of history. Prior to that, the world had little knowledge of the vast number of tiny protozoa in water; the structure of viruses; the cells that comprise plants, animals, and humans; or the characteristics in fur, hair, and fibers. The innovation of microscopes continues to be an integral tool in every scientific discipline from geology to microbiology, but it is without question one of the most important pieces of equipment in the field of forensic science.

MICROSCOPY FROM A BIBLICAL WORLDVIEW

The father of microscopy, Antonie van Leeuwenhoek, was a Christian scientist who lived in the mid-1600s. Leeuwenhoek devoted his life to studying God's creation through the tiny lenses he personally ground from small pieces of glass. One of the most fascinating aspects of Leeuwenhoek's microscopes is though they were made from only one lens (see **Figure 1**), they were far superior in clarity to the compound microscopes of his day. He did not invent the microscope, but he is considered the father of microscopy due to his years of research in the field. He was a pioneer in protozoology and bacteriology, in addition to the study of human cells and tissues. It is estimated he made over 247 microscopes and 419 lenses.[425]

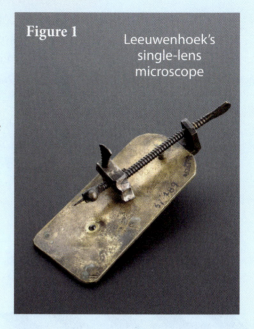

Figure 1 — Leeuwenhoek's single-lens microscope

Leeuwenhoek believed the beauty and detail magnified through a tiny lens glorified the Creator God more than the visible world around him. All throughout his writings, it is evident he gave God the glory for everything he observed. One of his favorite things to study was protozoa, which he called animalcules. He recorded detailed notes about protozoa like Vorticella, Volvox, and rotifers. He wrote in his journal:

> From all these observations, we discern most plainly the incomprehensible perfection, the exact order, and the inscrutable providential care with which the most wise Creator and LORD of the Universe had formed the bodies of these animalcules, which are so minute as to escape our sight, to the end that different species of them may be preserved in existence. And this most wonderful disposition of nature with regard to these animalcules for the preservation of their species; which at the same time strikes us with astonishment, must surely convince all of the absurdity of those old opinions, that living creatures can be produced from corruption of putrefaction (Schierbeek 1959, p. 171).[426]

Protozoology: The study of protozoa.

Bacteriology: The study of bacteria.

It is important to recognize that many of the pioneer scientists in history believed in the biblical God, and their scientific study was for the sole purpose of understanding the mysteries in creation. Psalm 104:24 is a good reminder of the wondrous works of the Lord, both microscopic and macroscopic: "O LORD, how manifold are your works! In wisdom have you made them all; the earth is full of your creatures." Leeuwenhoek devoted his life to the study of God's creation. He truly was a testament to Ecclesiastes 9:10a, "Whatever your hand finds to do, do it with your might."

TYPES OF FORENSIC MICROSCOPES

In this lesson on microscopes, there are sections written by Dr. David Menton from his microscope manual called *Scope It Out!* Dr. Menton's experience in microscopy included 34 years of teaching histology (microscopic anatomy) to medical students at Washington University School of Medicine in St. Louis and serving as the histology consultant for several editions of *Stedman's Medical Dictionary*. Over a period of 40 years, he used several types of light and electron microscopes in biomedical research at Mayo Clinic, Brown University, Washington University School of Medicine, and Woods Hole Marine Biology laboratory. Due to his extensive experience, Dr. Menton's explanations are clear and concise and some of the best information on microscopes for students. He gave permission for these sections to be included in this textbook.

Compound Light Microscope
(By Dr. David Menton)

This type of microscope uses visible light to produce an image, similar to the function of human eyes. The wavelength of visible light limits how much a light microscope can usefully magnify things. For all practical purposes, a light microscope cannot magnify an object more than about 1,000 times its original size (and in typical use no more than 500 times).

The compound microscope gets its name from the fact that more than one lens is used in its optical path. While a simple lens, like a magnifying glass, uses only one lens between the eye and the object of study, a compound microscope uses two lenses, an eyepiece lens (or ocular) and an objective lens, mounted on each end of a tube. Each "lens" itself may consist of two or more lens elements cemented or grouped together to correct for optical distortions. The comparatively high magnifying power of the compound microscope arises from the fact that the eyepiece lens magnifies the already magnified image from the objective lens. Thus, the combination of a 10x eyepiece and a 40x objective gives a magnification of 10 x 40, or 400-times magnification.[427]

There are two main limitations to the compound microscope:

1. The object of study must be small enough or thin enough to allow light to be transmitted through it, and
2. it provides only a two-dimensional image.

As a result, to look at the cells, fibers, or hairs, we must use a very thin section. One of the greatest challenges of using a compound microscope is to understand the three-dimensional structure of an organ while examining a thin slice from it in essentially two dimensions.[428]

One of the things that can cause confusion for the beginning microscopist is the effect that microscopes have on the orientation of the image. Microscopes make your specimen look upside down and backward from its real orientation. A forensic analyst must keep this in mind when examining evidence under the microscope.

Microscopists must also be familiar with depth of focus. Depth of focus basically means how much of the thickness of a specimen is in acceptable focus. Most prepared slides of biological organs and tissues consist of thin sections about 5–10 microns thick. As thin as this is, it is still too thick to be entirely in focus with the higher power objectives. The higher the magnification we use, the shallower the depth of focus. A good microscopist compensates for this by constantly focusing up and down with the fine focus during the study of a specimen.

Another feature on a compound light microscope is the ability to measure the size of the specimen. The most common tool is a stage micrometer. This is a special glass slide with fine lines etched on it. These lines are usually 0.01 mm (10 microns) apart. Some microscope eyepieces are fitted with an ocular micrometer, which makes measuring easier. When looking through such an eyepiece, a scale is visible which has 10 divisions superimposed on the field of view. A stage micrometer is used to measure the size of the divisions in the ocular micrometer (which will be different for each objective). Thus, knowing the size of the divisions in the ocular micrometer for each objective, one can easily and accurately measure any object in the field. The most precise measurements of size and area of structures under the microscope are currently achieved with the use of special digital cameras and computer software.

The following list summarizes the key facts about compound light microscopes:

- Light is passed through an object from beneath.
- The image is viewed upside down and backward.
- There are multiple objectives for magnification: 4x, 10x, 40x, 100x.
- They are available in either monocular (one eye piece) or binocular (two eye pieces).
- The higher the magnification, the greater likelihood for depth of focus issues.
- The size of specimens is measured with a stage micrometer.

Parts of the Compound Microscope

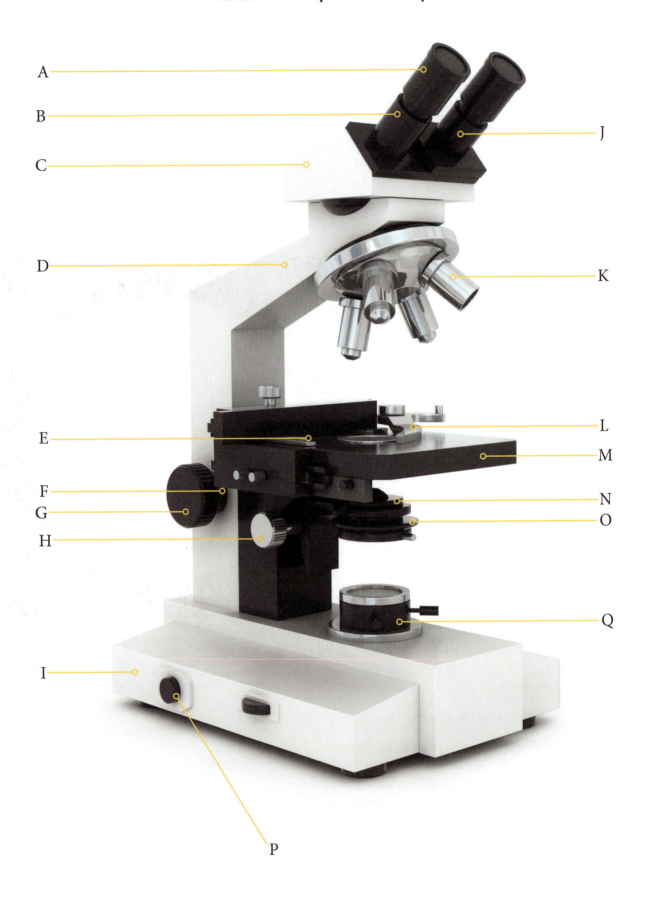

Microscope Parts Identification Key

A. *Eyepiece* (ocular) – 10x magnification, wide field.
B. *Focusing ring for left eye* – independently adjusts for left and right eye focus.
C. *Binocular head* – relieves eyestrain by permitting use of both eyes.
D. *Microscope arm* – part of the microscope frame.
E. *Slide clip control tabs* – these open the clips that grip a glass slide.
F. *Coarse focus knob* – allows coarse focus of the objective lenses.
G. *Fine focus knob* – allows fine focus of the objective lenses.
H. *Condenser focus knob* – focuses light from the condenser on to specimen.
I. *Microscope base* – the lowest portion of the microscope frame.
J. *Body tube* – tube runs from base of eyepiece to the base of the objective.
K. *Objective lens* – one of four objective lenses.
L. *Stage clip* – holds microscope slide securely on stage.
M. *Mechanical stage* – precisely and mechanically moves slide on stage.
N. *Condenser* – a substage lens that concentrates light on slide specimen.
O. *Condenser diaphragm* – adjusts to make light just fill the objective lens.
P. *On/off switch for substage illuminator* – turns light on and off.
Q. *Substage illuminator* – the light source for the microscope.

Stereo Microscope
(By Dr. David Menton)

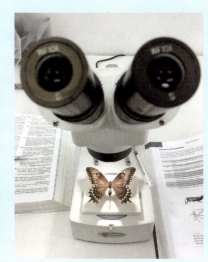

The stereo microscope is sometimes referred to as a dissecting microscope because it may be used to assist in the dissection of small specimens. It is also useful when examining items that are too thick to be seen through the compound microscope. The key feature of a stereo microscope is that it shows its object of study in three dimensions (stereo). A stereo microscope resembles a pair of binoculars in that it has two eyepieces and two objective lenses. Although some compound microscopes have two eyepieces for the comfort of the viewer, they use only one objective lens. While such a microscope may have several objectives of different magnifications, only one objective can be used at a time, and thus it is not possible to see a stereo image. Stereo microscopes are best suited for getting a 3D view of objects such as insects, plant parts, bullets, shell casings, minerals, etc.[429]

The main limitation of the stereo microscope is magnification. Stereo microscopes typically magnify things in a range of only 10 to 40 times. If a stereo microscope were designed for much greater magnification than 40x, its depth of field (or depth of focus) would become very shallow as it is in the compound microscope.[430] Another disadvantage of a stereoscope is the inability to examine what is inside a sample or piece of evidence.

Most modern stereo microscopes provide an illumination source under the specimen whose light passes up through the specimen (diascopic illumination) as well as an illumination source above the specimen whose light illuminates the specimen surface (episcopic illumination). These light sources may be used together, for example, to transilluminate a plant leaf, showing structures within the leaf while illuminating the cells and other details on the leaf's surface.

The following list summarizes the key facts about stereoscopes:

- This is the most frequently used microscope in forensics.
- Light is passed either through an object from beneath or from above. Light from above is used for opaque specimens, while the light from beneath allows for the viewing of microscope slides or other translucent pieces of evidence.
- Image is right side up with correct orientation from right to left.
- Good for opaque forms of evidence, soil, entomology, and large pieces of evidence.
- Does not allow for viewing inside an item.
- Magnification ranges from 2x to 125x.

Comparison Microscope

The first comparison microscope was invented in 1920 by an American Army colonel named Calvin Goddard, who was working for the Bureau of Forensic Ballistics. He was trying to find a way to examine ballistic evidence side by side, and he was successful. A comparison microscope allows for two pieces of evidence to be viewed side by side simultaneously. In essence, a comparison microscope is two compound light microscopes connected by an optical bridge. The optical bridge is made of a series of lenses and a mirror that brings the two images being compared into one single eyepiece.[431] Many comparison microscopes are equipped with multiple magnifications ranging from 6x to 144x, as well as multiple illumination options, video, and camera capabilities.

Utilizing digital technology, the images viewed on the comparison microscope are transferred to a larger screen for comparison. More sophisticated comparison microscopes are equipped with the ability to superimpose both images on top of one another for comparison of minute details. This type of microscope is primarily used in ballistics, but it also has uses in dactyloscopy, impressions, trace analysis, paleontology, and archaeology.

The following list summarizes the key facts about comparison microscopes:

- The scope is two compound microscopes joined by an optical bridge.
- Essential to conduct side-by-side comparisons between two pieces of evidence, hair and fibers or ballistics.
- Offers multiple magnification and light options, as well as photo and video capability.

Polarizing Microscope

A polarizing microscope is used to detect birefringence in materials such as pharmaceutical and drug samples, botanical evidence, as well as minerals. Birefringence is the refraction of light in an anisotropic (e.g., soils) material in two different directions to form two rays of light. To measure birefringent properties, two filters (analyzer and polarizer) are required to filter out one-directional linear polarized light. The two filters are oriented at 90° to one another to create a dark background and only reveal the birefringent properties of the sample. Filter one is called the polarizer. This is positioned between the microscope light source and the sample. Filter two is called the analyzer. This filter is located between the sample and the microscope eyepiece.[432]

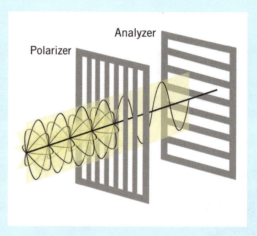

The following list summarizes the key facts about polarizing microscopes:

- Microscope built with a compound light microscope and a polarizer and analyzer filters.
- Polarization impacts the incoming light waves to reveal special properties (birefringence) in the evidence.
- Useful in soils, minerals, and artificial fibers.

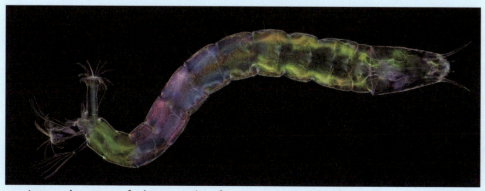

internal organs of a larva via birefringence and polarized light microscopy

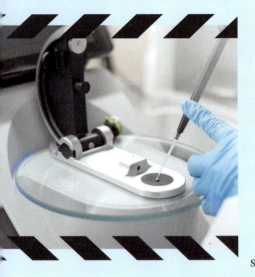

Microspectrophotometer

Microspectrophotometers are used to measure the spectra in trace samples, like a single textile fiber or paint fragment. The spectra are the molecular and/or structural composition of a sample and are unique "fingerprints" that can be used for comparison. These microscopes can measure samples smaller than the thickness of a human hair. According to a manufacturer of microspectrophotometers, they can measure the "transmittance, absorbance, reflectance, polarization, fluorescence, and photoluminescence microspectra of sample areas smaller than a micron."[433] One of the most important benefits of using this microscope is the nondestructive nature of analysis. The microscopist can measure the spectra of these small samples without ever physically touching the sample.

The following list summarizes the key facts about microspectrophotometers:

- Beam of light is directed at the object, and its spectrum information is collected.
- Spectrums are unique to chemicals, fibers, etc.
- Unique spectral fingerprints can be used like fingerprints.
- The analysis is nondestructive to the sample.

Electron Microscope (EM)

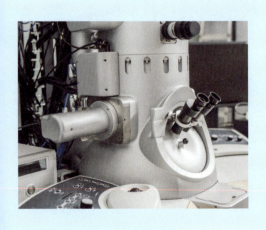

In 1897, J.J. Thompson discovered the electron, but it was not until 1933 that the first electron microscope was contracted by Ernst Ruska. Ruska was awarded the Nobel Prize in 1986 for his work in electron microscopy. Electron microscopes (EMs) use beams of electrons for illumination instead of photons of light. Electrons have a much shorter wavelength than light. Electrons travel in waves and can magnify an image. While high-end light microscopes are improving and have been able to magnify biological cells up to 20,000x, the electron microscope is capable of one million times magnification. This is why electron microscopes average several hundred thousand dollars.[434] The U.S. Department of Veteran Affairs (2021) describes the basic steps involved in the use of EMs:[435]

- A stream of high voltage electrons is formed by the Electron Source and accelerated in a vacuum toward the specimen using a positive electrical potential.
- This stream is confined and focused using metal apertures and magnetic lenses into a thin, focused, monochromatic beam.
- This beam is focused onto the sample using a magnetic lens.
- Interactions occur inside the irradiated sample, affecting the electron beam.
- These interactions and effects are detected and transformed into an image.

Applications for EMs in forensic science include gunshot residue analysis, forensic geology, paint samples and fibers, bulb filaments, document examination, and many more. The following list summarizes the key facts about EMs:

- A beam of electrons instead of photons of light are aimed at the object.
- Extremely high magnification between 10x to 100,000x.
- Useful in analyzing gunshot residue.
- Very expensive.

Transmission Electron Microscope

MICROSCOPIC UNITS OF DIMENSION

(By Dr. David Menton)

Fractions of an inch may suffice for measuring most of the small pieces of evidence encountered at crime scenes, but when using the microscope, such units of dimension are useless. In these cases, the metric system is used. The metric system is based on a unit of length called the meter (a little over 39 inches long). One meter is divided into 1,000 millimeters (mm). One millimeter is approximately the thickness of a dime and thus still too large a unit of measurement for the microscopic world. One millimeter may in turn be divided into a thousand micrometers, which are often

6 microns

referred to as microns (μ). When considering sizes under the light microscope, scientists use microns as the unit of measurement. A red blood cell, for example, is about 6 microns in diameter. Because God created similar red blood cells nearly everywhere in humans and mammals, they serve as a handy "measuring stick" for estimating the size of other nearby cells and structures.

MAGNIFICATION VS. RESOLUTION

(By Dr. David Menton)

It is important to understand the difference between magnification and resolution when using the microscope. Magnification is the process of enlarging something to the point it becomes visible. When viewing a slide or piece of evidence under a compound microscope, it is good practice to always begin with the lowest objective magnification.

The term resolution refers to how small an object can be visibly seen. Technically, it means how close two dots can be to one another and still be seen as two dots rather than one. The resolution of the normal unaided eye is about .2 millimeters (or 200 microns). This is about how long a hair grows every day. The best possible resolution of a compound microscope is about .2 microns, or about a thousand times better than the resolution of the human eye. Thus, the microscope opens a whole new world to examine forensic evidence.

Keep in mind that magnification without resolution is useless. For example, one could magnify a small photograph to the size of a billboard and still not see any more detail (resolution) than could be seen in the original small photograph. We call magnification with no increase in resolution empty magnification. Empty magnification may be useful when viewing an image from a long distance away, like a highway billboard, but it is not very useful when looking through a microscope.

MICROSCOPE LENS AND OBJECTIVE

(By Dr. David Menton)

Figure 1

Both the eyepiece lenses and the objective lenses of most microscopes have useful information stamped on the side of the lens barrel.

Eyepiece Lens Information. The eyepiece always shows the magnification of the lens (**Figure 1**). While eyepiece magnification is usually 10x (the best and most common size) it may be 5x, 15x, or even 20x. Eyepieces more powerful than 10x are likely to produce some degree of empty magnification, though they may be useful for someone with impaired vision. There may be other information on the eyepiece as well, such as the name of the manufacturer and special characteristics of the eyepiece. One might see the letters "WF," indicating the eyepiece shows a wide field of view (the disk of the illuminated specimen you see when looking through the microscope is extra wide). Some special eyepieces may show the letters "HEP," meaning a high eye point, which allows the user to wear eyeglasses while looking through the eyepiece.

Objective Lens Information. There is information stamped on the side of all objective lenses that tells us how much the lens magnifies. Usually there is also information related to the resolution of the lens. The four traditional objective lenses on microscopes have a magnification of 4x, 10x, 40x, and 100x. Combined with 10x eyepieces, these four lenses give a total magnification of 40x, 100x, 400x, and 1,000x respectively (4 x 10 = 40, etc.).

The objective lens of a traditional microscope also provides all the information to determine the numerical aperture, or NA, which allows a scientist to calculate the resolution of each objective lens by using the following formula:

$$r = .61\lambda/NA$$

Where r = resolution in microns, .61 is a constant, and λ = the wavelength of light (.52 microns as an average wavelength for the full spectrum of visible light). For example, the 10x objective on a microscope shows an NA of .25. To calculate the resolution of this lens, use the resolution formula: r = .61 x .52 / .25 = 1.3 microns.

Would it be possible to resolve a single red blood cell with this low power lens? Yes! The red blood cell is about 6 microns in diameter, and this lens can resolve things as small as 1.3 microns.

PREPARING MICROSCOPE SLIDES

(By Dr. David Menton)

Microscope slides are thin, rectangular plates of glass that typically measure one inch by three inches (25x75 mm) and are 1.0 to 1.2 mm thick. A microscope slide may be either a *blank slide* with no specimen on it or a *prepared slide* with a specimen mounted under a *coverslip*. Blank slides are used to make prepared slides. Special blank slides, called *concavity slides*, have a shallow well (concavity) in the slide that can be used to examine living freshwater invertebrates.

Coverslips are rectangular or circular plates of very thin glass (or plastic) measuring 0.13 to 0.17 mm in thickness. To obtain full resolution, a coverslip must always be used to cover a specimen. It is important for good resolution that there is no air between the coverslip and the slide. For this reason, the space under the coverslip must be filled in with some medium that has a refractive index as close as possible to that of glass. For a temporary mount that will be used only a few hours, similar to a hair or fiber sample, the medium may be water or glycerin. Glycerin lasts much longer than water, but it never hardens, so the slide must be stored flat. For a permanent mount . . . the mounting medium is a special mounting cement. This requires dehydration of the specimen, as permanent mounting cements do not mix with water. If your specimen is essentially dry (like an insect wing . . .), clear fingernail polish may be used to make a permanent mount.

CONCLUSION

Every student should have a microscope in their home. A person is never too young to become proficient in microscopy, and a quality microscope will last a lifetime. The lens of a microscope reveals an unseen world full of beauty and wonder. The microscopic world is a testament to its Creator God. But to become accomplished in microscopy requires practice. Scientists develop their microscopy technique through training and trial and error. Considering that the microscope is an essential tool for forensic science, learning to use it correctly and efficiently is imperative.

Lesson 27
Crime Labs

All Scripture is breathed out by God and profitable for teaching, for reproof, for correction, and for training in righteousness, that the man of God may be complete, equipped for every good work (2 Timothy 3:16–17).

Case Study: St. Valentine's Day Massacre

The 18th Amendment to the Constitution banned the manufacture, transportation, and sale of intoxicating liquors. The 18th Amendment was ratified on January 16, 1920. This legislation sparked a rise of illegal production and sale of alcoholic products. One group that rose to power on the back of the illegal alcohol trade in the 1920s was the mafia. Between 1920 and 1930, neighborhood gangs organized into a sophisticated criminal network of twenty Italian American crime "families" that operated throughout the United States.[436] These families participated in gang warfare with each other, fighting for control in bootlegging, gambling, and prostitution.

During this period, Chicago's North Side family was ruled by the famous Al "Scarface" Capone. Capone's long-time enemy was rival Irish gangster George "Bugs" Moran. On February 14, 1929, a bloody massacre of seven men occurred in the Lincoln Park garage on the North Side of Chicago. The assailants used 70 rounds of ammunition during this execution-style assault. History records reveal that Bugs Moran was only minutes behind his men and barely missed being a victim himself. Out of the four men who murdered the victims, two were dressed as policemen. Though this crime remains unsolved to this day, it is believed that Capone ordered the hit on Moran's men.[437] After this attack, Capone ruled Chicago and was labeled by the authorities as Public Enemy No. 1. A focused investigation on Capone ultimately resulted in his arrest and imprisonment for 11 years due to federal tax evasion. He served his time in Atlanta, Georgia, and at the famous California prison called Alcatraz.

What does this case have to do with crime labs? As a result of the St. Valentine's Day Massacre, Chicago recognized the necessity for a crime lab. One of the most prominent forensic scientists at the time, Major Calvin H. Goddard (Lesson 7), was called in to examine the ballistic evidence from the massacre. Goddard was responsible for the refinement of the comparison microscope to examine ballistic evidence side by side. Goddard was asked to determine if the assailants were really police officers or gangsters. He tested the guns used by Chicago police at the time next to the ballistic evidence from the two Thompson submachine guns found at the crime scene. He determined that Chicago police officers were not responsible for the murders. Due to his success in the ballistic analysis of the St. Valentine's Day Massacre, he was asked to develop and head the very first crime lab in the United States. The Chicago Crime Lab was born at Northwestern University in 1929, becoming the second forensic laboratory in the United States.

Facts about the case:

- Leading up to the massacre, Moran and Capone had been gangster rivals for ten years, and both had survived several attempted murders on each other.
- Five of the seven men murdered were known Moran gang members, one was an associate, and one was an innocent man. One of the victims (and Moran's best killer), Frank Gusenberg, was still alive when police arrived, but he refused to break the code of silence and reveal any information about the assault.[438]
- A raid on the home of one of Capone's hit men in 1929 uncovered two machine guns that Goddard matched back to the massacre scene.[439]

- At the peak of Capone's organization, his net worth was estimated at $100 million.
- On February 15, 1936, one day after the 7th anniversary of the St. Valentine's Day Massacre, one of the believed hitmen, Jack McGurn, was gunned down at a bowling alley in Chicago. It is believed that Moran ordered the hit, though he was not charged in the crime.
- Capone was released in 1939 from Alcatraz and died as a recluse in Florida in 1947.
- Moran was imprisoned in 1946 on robbery charges. He died in 1957 of lung cancer at Leavenworth Federal Prison.
- The St. Valentine's Day Massacre remains one of the most famous technically unsolved cases in history.

This case reflects the necessity of proper investigation and the protocols established within crime labs. But even today, with state-of-the-art technology and surveillance, a crime lab can only process the evidence collected by the human investigator involved in the case. The lab is only as effective in solving the case as the officer is in the proper collection and handling of evidence.

"You know my method. It is founded upon the observation of trifles." — Sherlock Holmes[440]

==Crime labs (or forensic laboratories) are responsible for analyzing evidence collected== from criminal or civil cases. Crime labs employ specialists in the fields of biology, chemistry, physical science, and digital forensics. Crime labs also specialize in criminal behavior, profiling, and pathology. Most crime labs are considered public facilities and are interconnected with law enforcement, the medical examiner, and coroner at all levels of government (local, state, regional, and federal). There are also private labs that operate separately from the public sector. England and Wales are two of the few countries in the world that operate only with private crime labs.[441] Crime labs are very expensive to operate, and therefore not every jurisdiction has their own lab. They are often only found at the higher levels of government and/or in large cities where there is enough crime to warrant a forensic laboratory.

All crime labs have an evidence intake unit that assigns identification numbers for the evidence submitted for examination. The unique identifying number provides a tracking system for chain of custody as the evidence moves through the analysis process. Typical crime labs perform a variety of services: fingerprint and DNA analysis, ballistics, document examination, toxicology, explosives, computer forensics, and trace evidence. While the evidence is being examined at the crime lab, it is stored in a secure location. The department and examiner the evidence is assigned to will determine the storage area for the evidence so that only that one specific examiner has access.

CRIME LABS FROM A BIBLICAL WORLDVIEW

Crime labs rely on preexisting information to process evidence. Where was the evidence found? What is its composition? How could the environment have affected the crime scene? Using observational science, labs process evidence from a past event that is unobservable in its original form. The analysis of that evidence is then interpreted in light of the events of the crime. The evidence from the past is referred to as historical science. (This topic was discussed in more detail in Lesson 2.) What is important to realize is that any valid scientific test relies on direct observation using preexisting information. Nothing only produces more nothing. There have been many labs trying to play "god." Though they make claims of creating life in a test tube, these proclamations are false. Man has never been able to create life from nothing. Often, these claims are nothing more than a reorientation or alteration of existing cells to form one created kind into similar organism within the same kind. The fervor to create life from nothing continues for proponents of evolution. When Darwin reduced the value of human life to nothing more than pond scum, the pursuit of attempting to recreate this

"pond scum" has never ceased. Evolutionary scientists are eager to create life in a lab since it would be the breakthrough required to support the idea of life from nothing. The field of synthetic biology is dedicated to synthesizing life from chemicals. Synthetic biology is defined in this way:

> Synthetic biologists seek to assemble components that are not natural (therefore synthetic) to generate chemical systems that support Darwinian evolution (therefore biological). By carrying out the assembly in a synthetic way, these scientists hope to understand non-synthetic biology, that is, 'natural' biology.[442]

What has been observable in the study of biological life? The law of biogenesis states that life always comes from other life. Additionally, the cell theory states that all cells come from preexisting cells. When scientists claim to be creating new life, in reality, they are "taking preexisting cells, modifying them, and developing new life forms using premade components."[443] The Bible is clear that these premade components were designed by the Creator God. Even when scientists modify the cells, they are primarily restricted to new life within the barriers of the kind or taxonomic family. Dr. Georgia Purdom, a molecular geneticist, wrote about synthetic biology in an imaginary dialogue between a secular scientist and God:

> A scientist tells God that they no longer need Him because of all the things "science" can now do. God challenges him to a man-making contest, to which the scientist agrees. God says He wants the scientist to do just like He did when He created Adam starting with dirt. The scientist agrees and picks up some dirt, to which God replies, "No, no, no. You go get your own dirt!" To today's scientists who think they are showing in the lab that life can come from non-life all I have to say is, "Get your own dirt!"[444]

The question remains, will proponents of evolution ever discover the bridge between life and non-life by synthesizing chemicals in a lab? The answer is a confident "no." The information to create life was designed by an all-powerful, all-knowing Creator God who spoke into existence all living things on days three, five, and six of the creation week (Genesis 1). God created life fully formed to fulfill His mandate to reproduce after their kind, and this is exactly what has been observed in nature for the last 6,000 years.

HISTORY OF CRIME LABS

==The very first police crime lab was launched by Edmond Locard in the country== of France in 1910. The United States was not far behind France in recognizing the need for labs dedicated to fighting crime. The first crime lab in the United States was in the city of Los Angeles in the year 1923 and was created by August Vollmer. This was prior to the start of the FBI crime lab in 1932, which is now the most comprehensive forensic laboratory in the world. Since crime labs exist at all levels of government, there are many different types of services provided at each level. The number of crime labs grew exponentially after legislation in the 1960s required police to scientifically analyze evidence.[445] Coinciding with legislation changes, crime rates in the United States began to steadily increase, putting pressure on the criminal justice system for more laboratory services. The development of a DNA profiling test in the 1980s further identified the importance of crime labs in processing evidence.

As the number of crime labs grew at all levels of government, the necessity to distinguish their individual roles became necessary. The following section provides an overview of each type of lab and the specialty services they offer.

TYPES OF CRIME LABS

City Labs. City crime labs service one local police department and district attorney. The very first city crime laboratory, and the first crime laboratory in the United States, was the Los Angeles Police Department in 1923. Today, the LAPD is one of the most comprehensive city crime labs in the United States, encompassing eight specialized units: the Questioned Documents Unit, the Field Investigation Unit, the Firearm Analysis Unit, the Narcotics Analysis Unit, the Serology/DNA Unit, the Toxicology Unit, the Trace Analysis Unit, and the Quality Assurance Unit.[446] Though the LAPD is equipped to address all facets of forensic science, most city labs only offer select services. Because operating crime labs is very expensive, they are only found in larger, urban cities. As in all levels of government, the city lab will work independently of the county lab unless they cannot provide the services requested by the police department or prosecutor.

County Labs. County labs serve all the cities within that county's law enforcement that do not have their own working lab. Whereas city labs serve their local municipalities, county labs serve the county sheriff's department. County labs are typically full-service labs.

Regional Labs. Regional labs support a specified region of the state that includes multiple counties. Regional labs serve as a conduit of information between local, county, and state labs.

State Labs. One of the first state crime labs in forensic history was in North Carolina. The North Carolina State Bureau of Investigation began in 1938. Today, all states have their own publicly operated crime lab. State labs exist to serve any agency in their respective state that does not have access to their own lab. Typically, there is only one state lab in the state and not a system of labs. In larger states with higher populations, they will have access to multiple labs, each lab providing specific services that vary from the other labs in the state. For example, New York has four state crime labs:

- *Forensic Investigation Center*: Provides a full range of forensic science services, including the state's DNA Databank.

- *Mid-Hudson Satellite Crime Laboratory*: Specializes in controlled substances examinations.

- *Southern Tier Satellite Crime Laboratory*: Specializes in controlled substances examinations.

- *Western Satellite Crime Laboratory*: Specializes in controlled substances analysis.

Federal Labs. The leading federal forensic laboratory in the world is the FBI Forensic Laboratory in Quantico, Virginia. J. Edgar Hoover became the director of the Bureau of Investigation (the FBI) in 1924 and remained in that position until his death on May 2, 1972. He had a vision for a federal crime lab that would use science to fight crime. The St. Valentine's Day Massacre on February 14, 1929, had sparked the creation of the Scientific Crime Detection Laboratory at Northwestern University in Chicago. This facility became the training center for Hoover's special agents. One of those agents, Charles Appel, proposed the creation of a separate division with the Bureau that would oversee criminal research and analysis.[447]

Hoover

His proposal was sent to Hoover, and Hoover immediately approved the creation of the Bureau Criminal Laboratory. The new lab was assigned room 802 in the Southern Railway Building in Washington, D.C. Calvin Goddard was called in to assist in the development of the new Bureau lab. The lab was equipped with only an "ultraviolet light machine, a microscope, a moulage kit (trauma kit), a wiretapping kit, photographic supplies, chemicals, a drawing board, and other office equipment."[448] The lab processed 963 examinations during its first year of operation and now evaluates well over one million pieces of evidence a year. Due to its success, the FBI Crime Lab serves as a model for crime labs around the world.

FBI Lab firearms collection, 1933

Research & Specialty Labs. Research labs are often located on university campuses. These labs focus on developing new, innovative forensic techniques and methods of evidence processing. Specialty lab services include forensic entomology, odontology, wildlife forensics, genealogy, microbiology, and facial reconstruction.

FBI Laboratory in Quantico, Virginia

FBI's mobile forensics laboratory

PROBLEMS WITH CRIME LABS

One of the primary issues facing crime labs in the United States and around the world is accreditation. Currently, the United States has a voluntary process for accreditation, which is monitored by the American Society of Crime Lab Directors.[449] Accreditation is a tedious process. The lab must demonstrate that it meets both the analytical processes as well as employs the professional personnel to operate a forensic lab.

Another issue facing labs is the appearance of bias. Since crime labs often work exclusively with a specific jurisdiction and the prosecutors and detectives receive the labs' services for free, accusations for the tampering of evidence are common. Criminal defense attorneys do not have access to the free services provided by public crime labs. If a defendant cannot afford a private attorney and a public defender is assigned, there is limited funding provided for forensic testing. This "imbalance" in the criminal justice system gives the appearance of bias toward the prosecution in criminal cases.

Lesson 28
Mobile Forensics

Now may the God of peace . . . equip you with everything good that you may do his will, working in us that which is pleasing in his sight, through Jesus Christ, to whom be glory forever and ever. Amen (Hebrews 13:20–21).

Case Study: London Bombings (7/7 Attacks)

On the morning of July 7, 2005, at 8:50 a.m., a series of coordinated suicide bombers attacked the transit system of the city of London, England. The initial terrorist attack occurred on three of the main train lines, resulting in the death of 39 people. Then, an hour after the first attack, another bomb detonated on the upper deck of a bus in Tavistock Square, killing 13. The four attacks caused injuries to over 700 people.[450] The London bombings are considered the single worst terrorist attack on British soil and the first suicide attacks in modern Western Europe.[451]

This criminal act was important to the development of mobile forensics. Forensic historians signify this event as a turning point in the use of cell phone evidence. Several victims used their cell phones to take digital photographs and record what occurred immediately following the attack, individuals in the vicinity, and other important details about the aftermath. These photos were used to piece together the clues left behind by the bombings and helped to identify the four suicide bombers. The value of digital evidence was brought to the forefront in forensic investigations.

Facts about the case:

- The bombs were constructed from ordinary, easy-to-obtain materials and carried in backpacks.
- Witnesses described the suicide bombers as "ordinary British citizens."[452]
- Prior to the bombings, the four men traveled together to a central transit interchange where they said their goodbyes to one another. Witnesses observed their separation onto four different transportation systems and claimed that "four men fitting their descriptions are seen hugging. They appeared happy, even euphoric."[453]
- Investigators reviewed over 6,000 hours of security footage to construct a timeline of events.
- All four bombers were identified as radicalized al-Qaeda, and all four were killed in the bombings. The four bombers were:

    Mohammad Sidique Khan: age 30, married, father of one child, employed as a primary school learning mentor

    Shehzad Tanweer: age 22, employed in a fish and chip restaurant

    Germaine Lindsay: age 19, married, pregnant wife and one young son

    Hasib Hussain: age 18, lived with his brother and sister-in-law

- Pieces of evidence included a credit card found at the scene with the name Khan, a driver's license belonging to Hussain, and video footage of the four men arriving in vehicles to the train station.
- Another four men attempted to copy the July 7 bombings on July 21, but their devices failed to detonate.
- The late Queen of England visited victims of the bombings in the Royal London Hospital.

CASE STUDY

- The response of the London emergency departments is heralded as one of the most effective and efficient responses to a terrorist attack. Emergency authorities had a plan in place, and everyone knew their roles and responsibilities. They were able to save many lives.

In the last decade, cell phone evidence, specifically tagged call detail records (CDR), has demonstrated its value in criminal case work. Be aware, cell phone data is currently not protected by the 4th Amendment to the Constitution (which prohibits unreasonable search and seizure). This means your entire cell phone record is subject to review if subpoenaed by the court.

"My business is that of every other good citizen — to uphold the law." — Sherlock Holmes[454]

Mobile forensics is a branch of computer forensics that focuses on the recovery and investigation of information found on digital devices such as computers, cell phones, tablets, and digital cameras. Mobile evidence is very sensitive and can easily be altered and/or deleted. To ensure there is an immediate lockdown of transmissions from mobile devices at crime scenes, mobile forensics investigations have specific protocol that must be followed to ensure the data is safely seized and secured. Once secured, mobile evidence will be sent to the lab for analysis. A variety of mobile extraction and analysis tools are available in hardware and software formats. Following proper procedure both at the scene and in the lab is essential to ensure the evidence is admissible in the court of law.

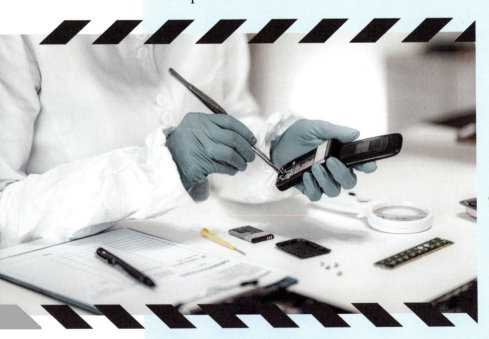

Of all the types of mobile devices, cell phones are the primary piece of evidence found at crime scenes. It is not surprising that cell phones have become an important connection between people, society, and the world. Today, 95% of American adults own cell phones.[455] These small computers have the capability of 64 GB (gigabytes) of memory and storing volumes of data daily. According to the Info Institute, at a minimum, one cell phone can contain:[456]

- Incoming, outgoing, and missed call history
- Phonebook and contact lists
- SMS text, application-based, and multimedia messaging content
- Pictures, videos, audio files, and sometimes voicemail messages
- Internet browsing history, content, cookies, search history, analytics information
- To-do lists, notes, calendar entries, and ringtones
- Documents, spreadsheets, presentation files, and other user-created data
- Passwords, passcodes, biometric data, swipe codes, and user account credentials
- Historical geolocation data, cell phone tower–related location data, and Wi-Fi connection information
- User dictionary content
- Data from various installed apps
- System files, usage logs, and error messages
- Deleted data from all the above

A PICTURE IS WORTH A THOUSAND WORDS

In the field of mobile forensics, digital pictures provide a wealth of information about the lifestyle, friends, family, and social connections of people involved in criminal investigations. Interestingly, digital pictures are now accepted by many 911 call centers as evidence. Individuals in emergency situations are directly sending pictures and videos to call centers to document a variety of crimes. The images and digital videos from both victims and witnesses are immediately forwarded to emergency responders and police personnel en route to the 911 call. This also allows medical staff to prepare for possible injuries. One example of this technology is an app that allows for instant crime reporting and "GPS tagged distress messages."[457] Mobile forensics is now labeled as technology that travels to the scene of the crime.

FROM CELL PHONE TO SMART PHONE

Cell phones have been around since 1973. The first cell phone was called DynaTAC 8000X and cost $3,995 (equivalent to $10,000 today). The phone had a 30-minute use time and required 10 hours to recharge.[458]

By 1990, there were an estimated 11 million cell phone users. In 1992, the very first text message was sent from a developer to the director of Vodafone™, and it simply stated, "Merry Christmas."[459] It was not until 1992 that IBM invented the very first smart phone. The smart phone was released in 1994 and sold for $1,100. IBM® called it the Simple Personal Computer (SPC). The SPC had a touch screen, the ability to send and receive emails, a calendar, and an address book.[460] The phone only lasted for one hour before requiring a charge.

In 2001, there was breakthrough in cell phone technology. The very first wireless internet 3G network became available for cell phones. This significant development allowed for video conferencing. The downside was the high cost for data to operate this fancy phone. This prevented the average consumer from investing in the expensive phone.

DynaTac 8000X

Smart phone technology was forever changed with the introduction of the iPhone® by Steve Jobs and Macworld™ in 2007. People were thrilled to learn that the new iPhone® had 8 hours of battery life and up to 8 GB of memory.

the SPC (Simple Personal Computer)

original iPhone®, iPhone® 3G, and iPhone® 4

By 2009, smart phones were equipped with Google Maps™. By 2019, over 21 smart phones had been developed with thousands of apps. As of 2021, there are an estimated 2.5 billion people who own a smart phone. Today, the two primary operating systems on smart phones are Google Android™ and Apple iOS®.

Four significant societal changes are attributed to smart phones:

1. *The phrase "Ask Google®"*: Humans now expect instant access to a world of information in only seconds. If they do not know an answer to just about any question, they say, "Ask Google®."

2. *Telecommunication:* Mobile devices forever have changed the makeup of a workforce. Employers have people that work from home and work remotely in other states or countries. This has also influenced the field of education with numerous online schooling opportunities at all levels.

3. *Advertising:* Voice identifying key words and phrases from mobile searches, as well as personal conversations, have allowed for advertisers to promote directly to the mobile user. For example, a simple search for hiking boots on a smart phone results in two weeks of hiking boot ads from multiple vendors on a user's personal device.

4. *Social networking:* The platforms for social media connections are evolving daily. Since smart phones are almost always in the user's hand, it is not surprising that over 80% of social media interaction occurs on a cell phone.

MOBILE FORENSICS FROM A BIBLICAL WORLDVIEW

Mobile devices are the lifeline to social media in the culture today. Individuals are tied to their phones for the sole purpose of checking their status, likes, and views on social media posts. The term "private life" has little meaning for those under the age of thirty, since the posts are filled with overly personal details about family, daily living, and friendships. This technology-driven generation has placed their identity in their popularity on social media. Further, most posts are not reflective of a person's true-life experiences but exaggerated dreams of their desired reality. The most distressing fact about social media is that posts are self-focused and not God-focused.

So how should Christians approach the use of mobile technology and social media? Is it the next mission field? Being a Christian on the social media mission field is plagued with challenges. All throughout history, cultures have attempted to attack anything Christian by using different methods. Today, the attack is viral. Using mobile technology, there is forceful, direct shaming on Christianity, and it is on the rise. The Bible warns of this type of behavior toward Christians in 2 Timothy 3:1–5,

> But understand this, that in the last days there will come times of difficulty. For people will be lovers of self, lovers of money, proud, arrogant, abusive, disobedient to their parents, ungrateful, unholy, heartless, unappeasable, slanderous, without self-control, brutal, not loving good, treacherous, reckless, swollen with conceit, lovers of pleasure rather than lovers of God, having the appearance of godliness, but denying its power. Avoid such people.

Mobile Forensics

Considering what is posted on social media today, these characteristics should seem very familiar. Think about the number of social media posts that could have been written to reach the millions of people who need to hear the message of salvation through Jesus Christ. Just as the secular world is attempting to spread false ideologies, Christians should be sharing the truth about sin, salvation, and Christ through social media.

There are other digital resources available for Christians. One tool that can be used to share Scripture via social media is the digital Bible. Use of the Bible app on mobile devices continues to increase in the number of downloads. YouVersion®, one of the most popular Bible apps, has reported that users "spent more than 235 billion minutes using the app and have highlighted 636 million Bible verses."[461] Though digital Bibles can never replace the tangible experience of physically holding God's Word, digital apps provide a searchable database for biblical references. But caution should be exercised when using digital Bibles. Digital Bibles make it easier for the user to pick and choose their Scripture of choice to fit their viewpoint while disregarding the unwanted verses. Often this results in the Scripture being used out of context. Sadly, this frequently occurs with physical Bibles as well.

One other area of caution for Christians is the convenience of online church attendance. Though online church can reach many with the message of Christ, it also creates a disconnection between Christians and the experience of worshipping together. In recent years, online church has exploded, with many ministries streaming entire services online. Church members and church shoppers can now easily watch a variety of services via their mobile device, in their pajamas, while drinking coffee on their couch. But is virtual church equivalent to the in-person experience? Will Christians have the same level of support from their online church versus in-person church family in time of need? The Bible states in Hebrews 10:24–25, "And let us consider how to stir up one another to love and good works, not neglecting to meet together, as is the habit of some, but encouraging one another, and all the more as you see the Day drawing near."

COLLECTION & PRESERVATION OF MOBILE DEVICES

Proper collection, preservation, and security are imperative in mobile forensic investigations. Any breach of protocol can result in the expulsion of the evidence in a court of law. The following steps are the generally accepted procedures followed by most computer forensic investigators.

computer forensic investigation process model

Acquisition > Identification > Evaluation > Admission as Evidence

Step 1: Device Seizure

The immediate seizure of all devices at a crime scene ensures protection of the device from Wi-Fi, telecommunication, and GPS signals. While at the scene, the investigator will secure written consent from related individuals to extract data from all the mobile devices collected as evidence. The challenge is keeping the battery charged to prevent shutdown and loss of information such as a login or PIN.[462] An unexpected shutdown also has the potential to alter files. Special packaging is used to charge the devices and secure data.

Faraday bag

- *Electromagnetic isolation Faraday bags* darken collected devices from radio signals. Faraday bags prevent remote wiping of all information. These also provide charging capability until the phone arrives at the lab.

- *Jammers* block communication between mobile phones, thereby preserving the information on the cell device.

- *Airplane mode* is used to protect the information on the mobile phone and prevent the transmission of radio waves. This is considered risky because the crime scene investigator must touch and interact with the cell phone. If the device is password protected, another method will be used to protect the phone.[463]

- *Cloning the device's SIM card* ensures the data on the mobile device is secure for analysis. The clone will be analyzed so that the original piece of evidence has not been tampered with.

Step 2: Data Acquisition

This step involves the delicate retrieval of information from the mobile device. The investigator will first make a copy of the SIM card. The copy will be used for examination so that the original source is undamaged and intact. This phase will require the owner's PIN, passwords, or biometric (fingerprint) to unlock the mobile device and retrieve the data that may be mobile itself. The use of biometrics may not be protected by the U.S. Constitution. Defendants have attempted to plead the 5th Amendment when asked to provide a PIN or biometrics, but these requests have been denied by the courts. It is good practice for the investigating agency to refer to the prosecutor's office regarding this issue.[464] At this phase, there are many challenges facing a computer forensics expert. Where is the data located — on the device hardware, in the cloud, on a website, in one of a hundred apps?

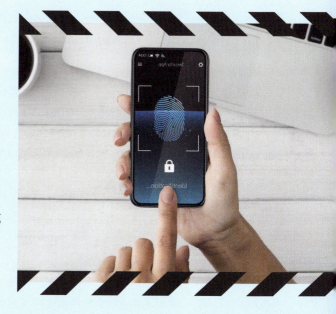

Mobile Forensics

Step 3: Data Analysis

Mobile forensic tools assist investigators in retrieving, analyzing, and preserving information found on mobile devices. These tools are needed to extract deleted content, unlock password-protected files, and bypass encryption barriers. There are several reliable tools on the market for computer crime investigators.[465] A few examples are:

- UFED Ultimate can bypass encrypted devices and export data from almost all mobile devices.
- iOS Forensic Toolkit extracts data from all iOS® devices such as iPhone®, iPad®, Apple Watch®, and Apple TV®. Data extraction includes emails, location history, usernames, and more.
- AccessData Forensic Toolkit FTK® has a specialized filter that provides a fast searching, stable extraction hardware.
- Autopsy® is an Android™ support platform with the capability to extract a wide variety of mobile data.
- Oxygen Forensic® Detective is the leader in cloud extraction, as well as fitness trackers, media cards, and drone history.

PROBLEMS WITH MOBILE FORENSICS

In addition to the challenges in evolving technologies, apps, and other issues surrounding the analysis of mobile evidence, there are several other problems facing investigators.

- *The use of public Wi-Fi.* Wi-Fi uses wireless radio frequency signals to connect to the internet and send messages between devices. Public Wi-Fi is unsecured, meaning anything sent over public Wi-Fi can be intercepted. Using public Wi-Fi opens all the information on a user's computer to anyone else on the public Wi-Fi. Since many people use public Wi-Fi for the convenience, large volumes of information are being exchanged every second. This makes isolating certain information quite a challenge.[466]
- *Prepaid "burner" phones.* Prepaid phones are designed with a disabled data port that cannot be enabled for data extracting. Retrieving data requires an examiner with a high level of expertise and training.
- *Varied operating systems.* With the numerous kinds of phones, each designed with their own operating system, settings, menus, etc., training for forensic computer examiners is extensive and continually requires updating. When describing the number of different operating systems developed by manufacturers, it has turned "the world of mobile phones into a huge diverse zoo . . . sometimes you cannot even trust the manufacturer's name marked on the phone."[467]
- *Encryption.* Due to the rise of identity theft, phone manufacturers have created password and encryption mechanisms that are making it almost impossible for computer forensic investigators to extract data on locked mobile devices. Law enforcement relies on varying software extraction tools to bypass encryption and access the systems without damaging the content. In many cases, the cell phone providers are not willing to assist police in providing access to a user's password information.
- *Cloud storage.* The ease of data sharing from one platform to another presents many problems in trying to retrieve evidence from one device. Tracing evidence from mobile devices to cloud-based storage and then to multiple computers can derail an investigation.

CONCLUSION

Technology is upgrading at a rapid pace. As mobile phones continue to evolve, software developers find it challenging to create new, up-to-date data extraction tools. The unfortunate reality is that computer technology is outpacing the developers. Fortunately, smart phones do contain valuable identifiers. Every time a cell phone is used, a signal is emitted that pinpoints where the user is located via latitude and longitude coordinates. The use of GPS locators and cell phone towers allows investigators to track and locate the position of every device. Retrieving exact locations from cell providers does require a court order and can delay an investigation. But GPS technology has allowed police to track the movement of criminals with accuracy. Another advantage of GPS is the specialized GPS location distress message that can be sent to designated emergency contacts from a mobile device.[468]

There is no debate — a computer forensic team must be equipped with an arsenal of hardware and software tools to extract data from the variety of mobile devices hitting the market. As of 2020, new cell phones are designed with an FBE, or file-based encryption. The FBE encrypts files with a key that is linked to the screen lock passcode of the user.[469] This has significantly increased the time required to retrieve data for analysis. For this reason, many police departments are now providing focused training while instituting expanded digital forensic departments to address the growing increase in computer crimes.

Mobile Forensics

Lesson 29
Facial Reconstruction

So God created man in his own image, in the image of God he created him; male and female he created them (Genesis 1:27).

Case Study: Oklahoma City Bombing

A powerful bomb exploded the morning of April 19, 1995, at 9:02 a.m., destroying a third of the Alfred P. Murrah Federal Building in downtown Oklahoma City. This event occurred just two years after the World Trade Center bombing in 1993. The media, authorities, and society in general assumed this was related to Middle Eastern terrorists. The FBI began an in-depth investigation only to discover a horrible truth — this was not international terrorism but the worst act of "homegrown terrorism in the nation's history."[470]

The truth began to unfold on April 20, 1995, when the rear axle of a Ryder® truck was discovered in the rubble. The axle revealed the VIN (vehicle identification number), which linked to a body shop in Junction City, Kansas. The body shop provided information about the man who had rented the truck. An FBI forensic artist was called in to make a facial sketch of the suspect based on the eyewitness accounts of the employees at the body shop.[471]

The FBI began to canvas the town with the sketch of the suspect. The sketch was identified as Timothy McVeigh by employees at a local hotel. A bulletin was issued for his arrest. Two accomplices were identified: Terry Nichols, who helped McVeigh build the bomb, and Michael Fortier had knowledge of the bomb.

Investigators were astonished to find out that McVeigh was already in police custody. He had been arrested just 90 minutes after the bombing for driving a car with no license plates and having a concealed weapon.[472] Though the suspect responsible for the bombing was apprehended quickly, the actual investigation to convict McVeigh was one of the most extensive in history.

Facts about the case:

- Twenty-seven-year-old Timothy McVeigh was an ex-army officer who had expressed anger about the government involvement in the David Koresh and Waco compound incident, as well as vocalized and written extremist ideology.
- The homemade bomb was made of agricultural fertilizer, diesel fuel, and other chemicals.
- McVeigh parked the rented Ryder® truck in front of the Alfred P. Murrah Federal Building, got out of the car, locked the door, and proceeded to his getaway car before igniting the bomb.
- A daycare was located on the 2nd floor of the federal building. The death toll included 19 children and 149 adults, with several hundred more injured. McVeigh expressed no remorse and called the children killed in the bombing "collateral damage."[473]

- By the end of the investigation, the FBI had conducted 28,000 interviews, followed over 43,000 investigative leads, collected three and a half tons of evidence, and reviewed nearly a billion pieces of information.[474]

On June 2, 1997, Timothy McVeigh was convicted of 15 counts of murder and conspiracy. On August 14, 1997, he was unanimously sentenced to death by lethal injection. In December 2000, McVeigh requested that all appeals for his case cease and that a date for his execution be scheduled.[475] McVeigh was executed in June of 2001. It was the first federal execution since 1963.

The other accomplices were also tried in court and sentenced. Terry Nichols was found guilty on one count of conspiracy and eight counts of involuntary manslaughter and received life in prison. When tried at the state level, Oklahoma charged him with 160 counts of first-degree murder, one count of first-degree manslaughter for the death of an unborn child, and one count of aiding in the placement of a bomb near a public building.[476] Nichols is currently serving his 160 consecutive life sentences. Because of his cooperation with authorities, Michael Fortier was sentenced to only 12 years in prison. He was also fined $200,000 for failing to warn authorities about the bombing.

"The more outré and grotesque an incident is the more carefully it deserves to be examined." — Sherlock Holmes[477]

Facial reconstruction is the process of recreating the face of a deceased individual from their skull or recreating a face that is unrecognizable due to some type of trauma. When a skull is uncovered and the person's identity is unknown, a forensic artist will be called in to create a reconstruction. Molding and shaping the face from only a skull requires knowledge of human anatomy and an idea of gender, ethnicity, age, weight, lifestyle, and health of the person. For gender, age, and ethnicity, examiners will study the skeletal features discussed in Lesson 13. When determining how much tissue and fat needs to be added to a skeleton, artists use standard measurements for facial tissue depths based on years of research into humans of different ages, genders, and ethnicities. The artist then applies clay to recreate the deceased's facial features.

A factor that artists must consider is how a person's physical features are directly impacted by life circumstances. The historical period in which they lived, the available nutrition, housing conditions, etc., will cause variances in someone's appearance. Whether or not a person was malnourished or abused will be reflected in their facial appearance, for example, sunken cheeks, broken nose, or disfigured chin. Obese individuals will require extra fat sculpted on the face, while a thinner person will require less. Other questions to research include: Did the person have an unusually large nose or protruding chin? Were their eyes close together or far apart? Did they have a widow's peak? Have they had any plastic surgery? These are all details that must be factored in when reconstructing a face.

When specific characteristics are unknown, the forensic artists will begin with a set of known, researched standards in facial characteristics provided by a forensic anthropologist. They will consult detectives for any clues to the age, gender, and ethnicity of the individual. The detectives will search the missing person's report for their area. The anthropologist will examine the skull for structural variances that will affect appearance, such as a misaligned nose, missing teeth, and other features that would influence the reconstruction. It is also important to know the history, condition, and location where the remains were found.

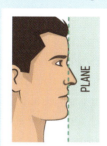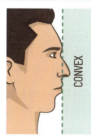

Facial Features

FACIAL RECONSTRUCTION FROM A BIBLICAL WORLDVIEW

<mark>Many interpretative facial reconstructions have been made for ape-like fossils</mark> over the last two hundred years. This is largely because evolutionists begin with the starting point that man evolved from an ape-like ancestor, and therefore, they find ways to make the evidence fit their narrative. As the late Dr. David Menton, an expert human anatomist, stated, "No paleoanthropologists (those who study the fossil evidence for man's origin) would dare to seriously raise the question, '*Did* man evolve from apes?' The only permissible question is, 'From *which* apes did man evolve?' "[478] Evolutionists refer to supposed ape-human ancestors as *hominids*, while living apes are classified as *hominoids*.

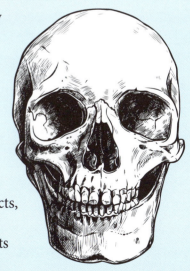

Since there are no observable, living specimens to study, they base their research on fossil evidence. But this is a problem since fossil evidence is so scarce. The fossil record contains 95% marine invertebrates, 4.7% plants and algae, 0.2% insects, and only 0.1% vertebrates. Of the 0.1% vertebrates, only a tiny fraction of those are primates. Because of the rarity of these fossils, very few evolutionary specialists have ever studied an authentic primate fossil firsthand. Most research is based on the study of casts of the original specimen. There have been cases where published research is solely based on the study of photos and measurements.[479]

Lack of evidence along with the desire for fame (the first to discover a supposed transitional species) has led to faulty facial reconstructions. In 1912, Charles Dawson (not Darwin) claimed to have discovered a hominid skull in a gravel pit near the town of Piltdown. This skull had a large, human-like cranium with an ape-like jawbone. Britain claimed that the Piltdown man was "the first Englishman."[480] The truth surrounding the hoax was not discovered until 1953, when geologist Kenneth Oakley, anatomist Wilfrid Le Gros Clark, and anthropologist Joseph Weiner identified the cranium originating from a modern human and the jawbone belonging to a primate.[481] They verified the bones had been stained to look old, and the teeth had been filed down to appear human-like. It was also discovered that Dawson was responsible for over 30 additional fraudulent fossil finds. The fraud of Piltdown man was an embarrassment to the evolutionary community.

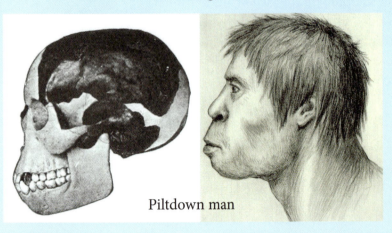

Piltdown man

Another famous example is the Nebraska man, or *Hesperopithecus*, where an entire reconstruction was based on a single tooth. From this single tooth, scientists claimed they knew exactly what the tooth-bearer looked like, their mate, environment, etc., and it was heralded as fact. This "evidence" for human evolution was used in the Scopes Trial in 1925 to discredit biblical creation. In 1927, it was discovered that this famous tooth was nothing more than the tooth from an extinct wild pig.

An artist who has used human anatomy in his sculpting for more than twenty years stated,

Nebraska man

The art of forensic reconstruction, while scientific in process, still requires imagination and interpretation and is therefore very subjective. The process of building up layers of clay at precise thicknesses to represent muscle groups is very accurate and can even be used to identify human remains. But this process is not perfect and falls short when it comes to determining the actual appearance of an extinct specimen.

Artists have displayed their interpretation of hominids and so-called ape men for many years, in books, magazines, movies and museums, using scientific processes where possible, and filling in the missing information with creativity, imagination, and their best guesses based on popular opinion or the opinion of the individual who hired them. As a result, whether intentional or not, the final look of the model or drawing is shaped by the biases of the artist and the scientists who direct the process. In other words, people's starting points influence their view of the evidence, and consequently, their biases show through in their artwork, whether it is forensic or interpretive.[482]

As discussed earlier in this textbook, worldview determines a scientist's starting point. What anatomical features are clear indicators of humans versus apes? When observing a skull from the side, there are several factors that distinguish the two, but the three easiest to observe are the slope of the face, nasal bone, and size of the skull. With this simple understanding, any fossil skull discovered, or any fossil displayed in a museum as an ape-human hominid, can quickly be identified as distinctly created ape or human.

Slope of the face

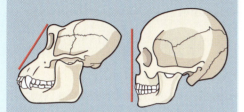

Primates have a sloped profile, while God created humans with a vertical profile.

Size of the skull

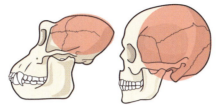

Though there is variety in the human population, the cranium of a human is large due to a larger brain, while the primate has a small cranium.

Nasal bone

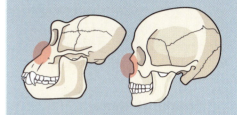

Humans have a distinct protruding nasal bone, while primates do not have a visible nasal bone. In God's perfect wisdom, He distinctly created humans with the exact bone needed to wear glasses.

Evolutionists' search for a transitional species is not over, and they continue to make assumptions with the limited fossil evidence available. It is clear that humans are created distinctly different from primates. Though there may be similarities in design, the observable differences point to the ingenuity and forethought of the Creator God. The Bible provides a clear separation of man and animals in Genesis 1. Humans are the only creation made in the image of God (Genesis 1:27), and animals are created to reproduce after their kind (Genesis 1:24). Humans are the only creation promised eternal salvation through the blood of Jesus Christ.

FACIAL RECONSTRUCTION

There are two types of facial reconstruction, three dimensional and two dimensional. Both types rely on the same information to reconstruct a face.

3D Facial Reconstruction. A forensic artist will begin by making a mold and casting of the original skull. A common casting material used is called alginate. Alginate is a salt of alginic acid, which is also used in making dental impressions.[483] Tools required for a 3D facial reconstruction include:

- Clay shaper tools
- Rulers
- Flexible ruler
- Leather
- Artificial eyes
- Oil-based clay
- Level
- Micrometer
- Sandpaper
- Dremel tool

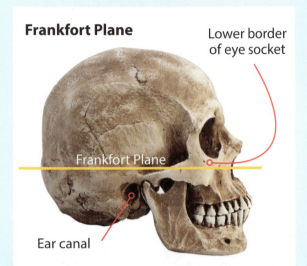

Frankfort Plane

Lower border of eye socket

Ear canal

The skull cast is placed on a special stand in the Frankfort plane position. The Frankfort plane position is the normal position for the human skull, which runs from the orbital rim to central ear hole. The mandible is attached with putty. The skull is leveled to be parallel to the ground using the Frankfort plane.

Sixteen osteometric markers are attached at the designated landmarks for gender and ethnicity, which serve as tissue depth markers. As discussed earlier, the landmarks are based upon over a century of research on facial tissue depths in males and females from different ethnicities. The chart below lists the sixteen markers and their depth in millimeters.[484]

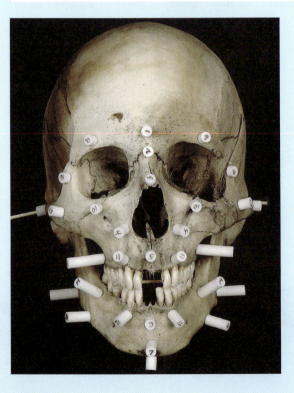

Landmark	Depth (mm)
Glabella	5.5
Gnathion	8.5
Gonion	10
Labrale inferius	13
Mentolabial sulcus	11
Menton	7
Mid-nasal	4
Mid-philtrum	11.5
Mid-ramus	17.5
Nasion	6.5
Pogonion	11.5
Prosthion	11.5
Rhinion	3
Subnasale	13
Vertex	5
Zygion	6

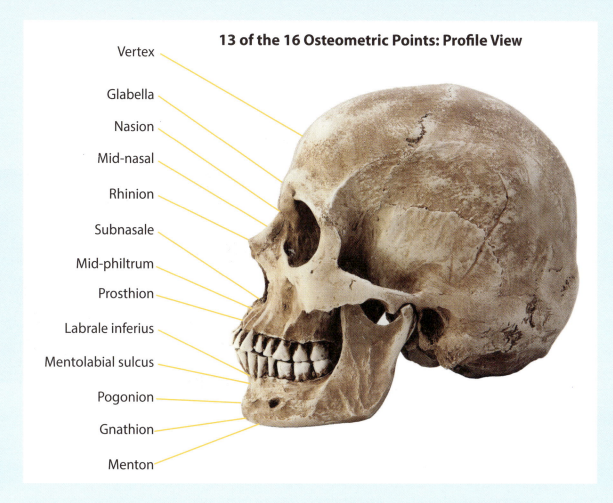

13 of the 16 Osteometric Points: Profile View

- Vertex
- Glabella
- Nasion
- Mid-nasal
- Rhinion
- Subnasale
- Mid-philtrum
- Prosthion
- Labrale inferius
- Mentolabial sulcus
- Pogonion
- Gnathion
- Menton

Using the Manchester technique, clay is then used to fill and form the muscles of the face according to known measurements. The Manchester method was developed by Richard Neave. This method uses the anatomical and anthropometrical measurements to create tissue depth markers as guides.[485] Artificial eyes are inserted to bring life to the reconstruction. Based on researched nasal bones, scientists can estimate the size and shape of the nose. Anthropologists will provide guidance to the artist in the contouring of several major muscles that, if not formed correctly, will affect the reconstruction. The major muscles include:

- *Orbicularis oris* – controls movement of the mouth and lips.
- *Zygomaticus* – controls facial expression.
- *Masseter* – aids in chewing and connects the mandible and the cheekbone.
- *Temporalis* – fan-shaped muscle running from the temporal line to mandible.
- *Parotid glands* – the largest salivary glands; located in the upper part of the cheek in front of the ears.
- *Buccal fat pad* – a mass of fat in the cheek.
- *Chin fat pad* – the small mass of fat in the center of the chin under the lip.

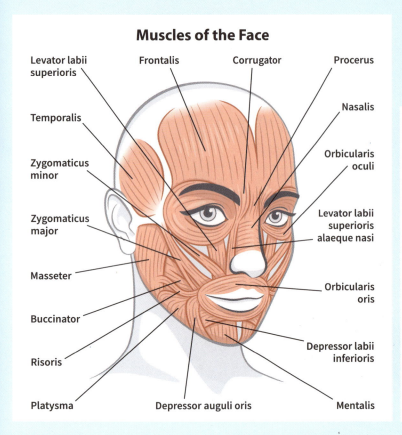

Muscles of the Face

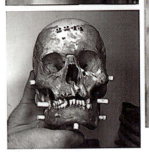
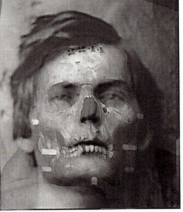

The artist will then flesh the face by covering all markers and muscles. Fleshing also includes texturing to make the face more lifelike. Artists usually use different types of fabric to impress a design onto the surface to give the appearance of skin. The final step is to add a wig that represents the hair of the individual to the best of their knowledge. In skeletons that are thousands of years old, artists will use period hairstyles on the reconstruction.

2D Facial Reconstruction. The primary purpose of 2D facial reconstructions is to provide a comparison image for those who may be able to identify the deceased or to the media. Two-dimensional reconstruction uses the same information needed for a 3D model. According to an expert forensic artist, this is the step-by-step method to accurately create a 2D image:[486]

Step 1 — The process begins by gluing on the proper tissue markers in the proper designated locations. Place the skull on a stand in the Frankfort Horizontal position. Photograph the skull in profile and frontal views, at a 1:1 scale, with a ruler, positioned aside of the skull. The photos then enlarged to life-size dimension. Tape the frontal and profile photo in the Frankfort Horizontal position parallel to one another on two separate flat wood boards.

Step 2 — Upon completion of the above process, tape transparent natural vellum sheets over the printed photographs. Sketching begins, where the artist follows the contours of the skull, along with using the tissue markers as guidelines. Measurements for the mouth, nose, and eyes, is the same for the Two-dimensional process as it is with the Three-dimensional process. Hair type and style determined by samples found on the scene by investigators, or by estimation determined by the victim's race, gender, and/or ethnic background.

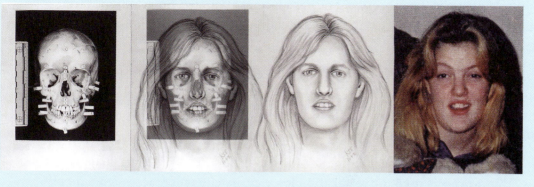

An example of a 2D facial reconstruction conducted by forensic artist Karen T. Taylor, and the subsequent identification, April Dawn Lacy.

FACIAL RECONSTRUCTION SOFTWARE

Another tool available for investigators is facial composite software. This method does not require a forensic artist to operate. Based on the shape of the skull and/or eyewitness descriptions, computer software programs can create a 2D sketch. One of the more popular law enforcement software programs used for facial reconstruction is FACES ID.[487] FACES has over 4,400 facial features in the database, including those of different ethnicities. The software allows for scars, tattoos, piercings, moles, and other unique features, such as headwear, to be added to the composite. The image is given a biometric ID, which is sharable between police agencies and the media, as well as being easily uploaded to websites. This method is cost effective and accessible on any computer.

FACIAL RECOGNITION SOFTWARE

Before ending this lesson on facial reconstruction, it is important to review facial recognition and how it is used in computer forensics. There are two general types of facial recognition: authentication, which is facial recognition via phones and devices, and identification via security footage.[488] Facial recognition software relies on biometrics. The word biometrics comes from the root *bios*, meaning life, and *metric*, meaning measurement. Three basic steps occur in all facial recognition software:[489]

1. *Detection:* Detection is the process of finding a face in an image. Smart phone facial recognition software uses this technology. Detection only focuses on finding a face, not the identity of the user.

2. *Analysis:* Analysis is the step that maps a user's face by measuring the distance between facial characteristics like the eyes, the shape of the chin, and the distance between the nose and mouth. And like biometric fingerprint identification, the software converts those measurements into a string of points called a faceprint.

3. *Recognition:* Recognition is the attempt to confirm the identity of the face mapped during analysis. This process is used for verification for security clearance, access on a mobile device, or identification on any facial recognition software.

Facial recognition software is still developing, and misidentifications are common. The recognition software is limited to its data. To create the data pool, photographs of people are added into the database to train a biometric algorithm how to differentiate a face from another object, like a car. An algorithm is a set of instructions that, given some set of initial conditions, can be performed in a prescribed sequence to achieve a certain goal and that has a recognizable set of end conditions. The more photos in the system, the better the results in "training" the software for more correct idents. People with darker skin shades are more prone to misidentifications simply because there are not as many files in the system. Also, there have been issues with individuals who are attempting to alter their gender. According to the Digital Civil Society Lab at Stanford, when discussing the accuracy of facial recognition software, "Labels are typically binary: male, female. There is no way for that type of system to look at non-binary or even somebody who has transitioned."[490] Even a computer recognizes that God created humans either male or female.

CONCLUSION

Facial reconstruction is one of the unique areas in forensic science for those with artistic abilities. Working closely with anthropologists, a forensic artist has the potential to bring to life skeletal remains. Facial reconstruction artists have been successful in directing police toward possible suspects as well as missing people. Though traditional 2D and 3D facial reconstruction is valuable, the development of facial reconstruction software will continue to be of primary importance in the forensic community. The ability to identify suspects via traffic cameras, department store cameras, and other mediums via facial software requires a fraction of the time than does the traditional method of investigation. The following excerpt demonstrates the value of facial recognition in forensic investigation. In 2019, the NYC Police Department searched their system "10,000 times, looking at 2,500 potential suspects including possible matches in 68 murders, 66 rapes, 277 felony assaults and hundreds of robberies. It's also been used in over 40,000 cases of human trafficking in North America . . . helping rescue 15,000 children over the last five years, and is being used by US Customs in airports and at border crossings."[491]

FORENSIC SPECIALTIES

UNIT 7

Lesson 30
Forensic Odontology

Now when they heard these things they were enraged, and they ground their teeth at him (Acts 7:54).

Case Study: Busted by a Bite

Young, charismatic, smart, articulate, and attractive are characteristics of one of the most prolific serial killers in U.S. history. Theodore Robert Cowell was born on November 24, 1946, to a single mother. The identity of his father is unknown. To hide the shame of birthing a child out of wedlock, Theodore's mother took him to be raised by her parents. Growing up, Theodore believed his birth mother to be his sister. In 1951, Theodore's mother married Johnny Bundy. Theodore eventually discovered the truth about his parentage, though it is not clear as to when this happened. However, he adopted his stepfather's name and now went by the name Ted Bundy. In elementary school, Ted was very shy and was often a target of bullying. His home life was happy, and he had four half-siblings for company. While in high school, Ted Bundy excelled academically and appeared to be a normal teenager. But Ted had a darker side and was caught peering into people's windows and acquired a juvenile record for stealing. Historically, Ted desired to be rich and did not mind stealing items that he wanted or felt he needed to appear part of the upper class. After a series of turns in his life, he graduated college with a degree in psychology in 1972. While at college, he fell in love with a pretty brunette from California. She was wealthy, cultured, beautiful, and had everything he desired in himself. When she ended the relationship with Ted, he was devastated. Many of his future victims would resemble his college girlfriend.

At some point after the breakup, Ted began a killing spree. Best estimates date the first murder to July 1974, when 18-year-old Lynda Ann Healey went missing. There are debates over whether she is the first victim or if there were others. From this point until his capture, Bundy assaulted and killed multiple women between 1974 and 1978. The exact number is unknown; Bundy confessed to 36 in custody, but the number is estimated to be well over 100.

Facts about the case:

- He would lure women to his car by pretending to be injured and asking for help. He was also known for impersonating a police officer and firefighter.
- He profiled women who were brunette and in their late teens or early twenties. The only exception to this was his last victim, 12-year-old Kimberly Leach.
- He had removed the passenger seat from his 1968 Volkswagen Beetle so that when he incapacitated the victims, he could lay them on the floor of the car out of sight.
- Bundy represented himself in one trial in 1977.
- Bundy escaped custody twice in 1977. Once was through the window of the courthouse where he was being tried for murder, and the second was through a hole he created in the ceiling of his prison cell.
- After his second escape, he continued his killing spree, leaving a bite mark on one of his victims. This is ultimately the bite that led to his conviction.
- He was finally captured in February 1978 when he was pulled over for a traffic violation. A dental impression was taken of Bundy's teeth and was matched to the bite mark left on the victim.

- One of his last requests before execution was for his ashes to be scattered in the Cascade Mountains in Washington State. This is the location of at least four of his murders.
- Bundy is recorded as having said, "I don't feel guilty for anything, I feel sorry for people who feel guilt."[492]

He was sentenced to death in 1979 for the murder of two college students and sentenced to death again for the assault and murder of a 12-year-old girl. He was able to delay his execution for ten years by giving police confessions to more killings. But he could no longer escape his punishment, and Bundy was executed in the state of Florida's electric chair (nicknamed Old Sparky) in 1989.[493] It is said he was sobbing uncontrollably in the hours before his execution.[494]

Forensic odontology is a field in forensics that does not stand on its own. This means that additional evidence is needed in conjunction with the dental evidence to secure a conviction. What is often more valuable is the DNA information found in teeth.

"But it is better to learn wisdom late than never to learn it at all." — Sherlock Holmes[495]

Forensic odontology is defined as a branch of dentistry that deals with the proper handling and examination of dental evidence and the proper evaluation and presentation of dental findings. More specifically, it is the recognition of the unique oral features present in an individual's teeth. Teeth leave identifiable marks like tools do. As seen in fingerprints and lip prints, God created each person with a unique teeth arrangement (or dentition); no two are the same. Bite marks reflect this unique design.

Bite marks are left on a variety of surfaces at crime scenes. Pencils, candy, cheese, apples, other foods, and human skin are a few examples of areas to search for impressions. The impressions left behind are compared to a person's dental records. The greatest resource to forensic odontologists is that most people have dental records, with many being digital today, and this is a reliable source of comparison when an impression is recovered from a crime scene. Also, teeth age in a systematic, measurable manner, providing clues to the age of the person when they were living. Since the 1990s and advancements in DNA analysis, teeth have the potential to yield nuclear and mitochondrial DNA through the pulp or crushed tooth. Bite mark impressions can also yield DNA in saliva samples.

ODONTOLOGY FROM A BIBLICAL WORLDVIEW

God created different types of teeth in a specific arrangement in the mouths of humans and animals. Each type of tooth and its placement within the mouth serves a very specific purpose. God designed teeth for mastication, or chewing. Food would not be as easy to consume if it were not for teeth. The Lord God considered every detail when He created all living things. Think about it . . . eating is pleasurable. The act of eating and chewing a delicious meal is enjoyable. Most people do not consider that the act of eating and chewing brings glory to the Creator of the food. First Corinthians 10:31 states, "So, whether you eat or drink, or whatever you do, do all to the glory of God." Food should be enjoyed and appreciated as a gift from God.

Prior to the entrance of sin into the world because of man's disobedience, God commanded all living things, including Adam and Eve, to eat the plants. Genesis 1:29 tells us, "And God said, 'Behold, I have given you every plant yielding seed that is on the face of all the earth, and every tree with seed in its fruit. You shall have them for food.' " All living things were vegetarian before sin.

This is one of the many points in the Bible that evolutionists scoff at. Evolutionists look at the world through a secular lens and see an animal population filled with scavengers and carnivorous activity. They claim that these creatures could never have survived on a vegetarian diet, and they look at their sharp teeth and make certain assumptions. In their minds, teeth obviously evolved for tearing and eating other animals. Similarly, secular paleontologists observe the large, pointy teeth on dinosaurs in the fossil record and conclude these animals evolved as carnivores. Observe the teeth on a *T. rex*; they look pretty scary!

But wouldn't a *T. rex* need those types of teeth if it were eating a large, juicy watermelon or other large fruit?

Scientists have observed many carnivores eating a vegetarian diet. There have been two lions known to be vegetarian. One was Little Tyke, who grew up on a farm and refused to eat meat throughout her life. Though multiple attempts were made to trick her into eating meat, she refused. Her owners (the Westbeaus) were extremely worried that she would not survive if she did not eat meat since that is what all the experts were telling them. But one day, a visitor to the farm said to them: "Don't you read your Bible? Read Genesis 1:30, and you will get your answer."

Forensic Odontology

The record states, "At his first opportunity Georges [Westbeaus] read in astonishment, *'And to every beast of the earth, and to every fowl of the air, and to everything that creepeth upon the earth, wherein there is life, I have given every green herb for meat: and it was so.'*"[496] At that point, after four years of trying to force Little Tyke to eat meat, the Westbeaus finally stopped worrying. Her meals consisted of various grains, chosen for their protein, calcium, fats, and green vegetables. She lived a long, healthy life on a diet of fruits and vegetables. She also developed close bonds with a variety of animals on the farm. Her closest bond was with a lamb named Becky. This relationship was highlighted on the Art Baker show, which ran from 1950–1959. During this episode, Art Baker picked up the Bible and read Isaiah 65:25 (KJV), "The wolf and the lamb shall feed together, and the lion shall eat straw like the bullock." This episode was one of the most popular in the show's history.[497]

Another example is the bonnethead shark (a relative of the hammerhead shark), which has been observed eating seagrass for several years. The scientists studying this behavior assumed the shark was eating the seagrass to feed on the crabs, shrimp, and fish living in the seagrass. They decided to test a theory about the shark's eating habits and captured some bonnethead sharks. The scientists fed the sharks a diet of only seagrass. They were shocked to learn that the sharks were just fine; they even digested the seagrass and were able to extract nutrients from it. One of the scientists working on the project stated in an interview with Fox news:

> We have always thought of sharks as strict carnivores, but the bonnethead is throwing a wrench into that idea by digesting a fair amount of the seagrass that they consume.
>
> Given that bonnetheads have a digestive system that resembles that of closely-related species that we know to be strict carnivores, we need to re-think what it means to have a "carnivorous gut."[498]

There are many more examples where animals thought to be exclusively carnivorous are found to be vegetarian or omnivorous under certain conditions. Though this behavior may be surprising again and again to evolutionists, it is not surprising to those who stand on the authority of God's Word. Science always confirms the Bible 100%. There are also animals with sharp teeth that have never been carnivores, like the panda bear. Pandas need sharp teeth to feed on bamboo, a strictly vegetarian diet.

The pre-sin world was perfect — no death, disease, or bloodshed. But sin changed everything. After sin, animals would eat other animals, and man would likely further disobey God's commands and eat the meat from animals. It was not until after the Flood of Noah that God would give permission for mankind to eat meat. Genesis 9:2–3 says about the animals, "Into your hand they are delivered. Every moving thing that lives shall be food for you. And as I gave you the green plants, I give you everything." The Creator God, in His perfect wisdom, designed all living things with exactly the teeth they needed to survive in a pre-sin and post-sin world.

HISTORY OF DENTAL IDENTIFICATION

The first record of dental work was on a skeleton discovered in a rock shelter in Italy. The skeleton of a 25-year-old male was dated to be 14,000 years old in the secular timeline. Of course, it could not have been older than 4,500 years, the point of the global Flood. A paleoanthropologist observed a partially infected tooth (likely a cavity) on the skeleton that had been cleaned out with a flint tool. This marks the earliest example of dentistry.[499] There have also been teeth discovered with beeswax used for fillings, but these are dated later.

The first dental identification was by Roman Empress Julia Agrippina in A.D. 49. Julia ordered the death of her rival, Lollia Paulina. Lollia was instructed to commit suicide, and then the soldiers were to bring back her head for identification. By the time the soldiers arrived in Rome with Lollia's head, it was decaying and distorted. Julia remembered that Lollia had unique teeth. She examined the head's teeth and verified it was, in fact, Lollia.

Bridge: A permanent fixture that replaces missing teeth by attaching to adjacent teeth.

Paul Revere made the first identification from teeth in the United States. In 1775, he matched the teeth from a body in a Revolutionary War mass grave to a man for whom he made a silver bridge. Revere recognized his work and was able to match the bridge to the deceased man. This ident makes Revere the very first forensic odontologist in the United States. The year 1849 was a significant advancement for forensic odontology when dental evidence became admissible in court. In 1897, Dr. Oscar Amoedo published an in-depth book on forensic odontology and is now considered the father of forensic odontology.

Revere

Agrippina

Records indicate that dental evidence was used to verify the body of Adolf Hitler in May 1945. Charred teeth fragments were matched to Hitler's dental records and radiographs.[500] The story remains that Hitler committed suicide, and then his remains were burned inside his bunker. The face of the body believed to be Hitler was burnt beyond recognition. The details of Hitler's autopsy report were not released until 1968, 23 years after his death. Below is the verbatim report from the autopsy performed on Hitler, taken from the book written by Lev Bezymenski, a Soviet journalist. Bezymenski stated in his book, "The most important anatomical finding for identification of the person are the teeth, with much bridgework, artificial teeth, crowns, and fillings." Hitler's autopsy report reads,

The tongue is charred. its tip is firmly locked between the teeth of the upper and lower jaws. In the upper jaw there are nine teeth connected by a bridge of yellow metal (gold). The bridge is anchored by pins on the second left and the second right incisor. This bridge consists of 4 upper incisors (21 k). 2 canine teeth (31 - 13). the first left bicuspid (14). and the first and second right bicuspids (41 51). as indicated in the sketch. The-first left incisor (b) consists of a white platelet. whith cracks and a black spot in the porcelain (enamel) at the bottom. This platelet is inset into the visible side of the metal (gold) tooth. The second incisor. the canine tooth. and the left bicuspid, as well as the first and second incisors and the first bicuspid on the right. are the usual porcelain (enamel) dental plates. their posterior parts fastened to the bridge. The right canine tooth is fully capped by yellow metal (gold).[501]

Dr. Blaschke, Hitler's dentist from 1934–1945, was interrogated by the United States after his capture in May of 1945. He verified the findings from the Russian autopsy on Hitler's teeth and said they should be "considered reliable."[502]

Dental evidence was also used to identify the victims of the World Trade Center terrorist attack in New York City on September 11, 2001. Over 40 dentists worked to identify the victims as they were recovered from the rubble. According to Oral Health (2001), during the World Trade Center recovery operation, dentists were assigned to one of four teams:[503]

- *Go Team* — Go Team members were dispatched to the scene to safeguard and retrieve dental evidence.
- *Antemortem Team* — This team worked with the dental records of presumed victims, transposing and entering information from radiographs and charts into the computer program.
- *Postmortem Team* — This team received and radiographed remaining dental structures, as well as charted and developed X-rays. One person called out the remaining dental structures, one retracted and cleaned while double-checking the first's assessment, and the third transcribed information and served as an additional pair of eyes.
- *Comparison Team* — These dentists used a view box to compare the radiographs of unknown victims to known people. The number of radiographs to compare had been narrowed down by the identification software programs.

Debate still surrounds the viability and reliability of forensic odontology. There is little argument that identifying deceased individuals by their teeth is one of the most accurate and inexpensive methods available. But the debate largely surrounds the reliability of bite mark analysis. Since the year 2000, 24 men have been released from prison after being wrongly convicted of crimes based on bite mark comparisons on human skin.[504] Though forensic odontology is still a recognized division of investigative sciences, careful examination and multi-expert authentication of findings are necessary to bring this field to a standard beyond a reasonable doubt.

ANATOMY OF TEETH

Teeth have a visible portion, called the crown, and a root that is embedded into a socket in the jawbone. There are four major tissues found in teeth: tooth enamel, dentin, cementum, and pulp. Tooth enamel covers and protects the crown. Enamel is the hardest substance in the human body. Under the enamel is a layer of dentin. Dentin comprises three layers and gives teeth their color while making up much of the tooth composition. Cementum is a calcified substance that surrounds the root and connects the periodontal ligament that holds the tooth in the jaw.

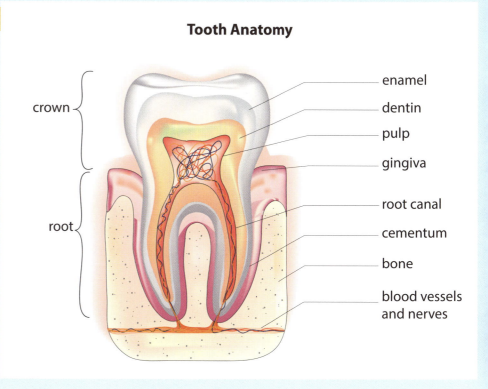

Tooth Anatomy

THE ORAL CAVITY

Quadrants of the Oral Cavity

upper right — quadrant 1
upper left — quadrant 2
lower right — quadrant 4
lower left — quadrant 3

The oral cavity includes the lips, tongue, teeth, and roof and floor of the mouth. There are two arches that are visible inside the oral cavity, the maxillary arch (right and left upper quadrants) and mandibular arch (right and left lower quadrants). Dentists divide the oral cavity into four equal quadrants containing the same number and types of teeth: incisors, canines, premolars, and molars. Each type of tooth was designed by God for a purpose and placed in the exact position to fulfill that purpose.

- *Incisors*: 8 total teeth (four in each arch, two in each quadrant). Incisors are designed for biting and cutting and have a single root.
- *Canines (cuspids)*: 4 total teeth (two in each arch, one in each quadrant). Canines are designed for piercing and tearing and have a single root.
- *Premolars*: 8 total teeth (four in each arch, two in each quadrant). Premolars are designed for crushing and slicing and are only visible in permanent teeth.
- *Molars*: 12 total teeth (six in each arch, three in each quadrant). Molars are designed for chewing, grinding, and crushing food and have multiple roots.

Teeth erupt (grow in) through different stages in life. The first baby tooth often appears around six months, with all baby teeth present by age three. Permanent teeth erupt according to the schedule below.

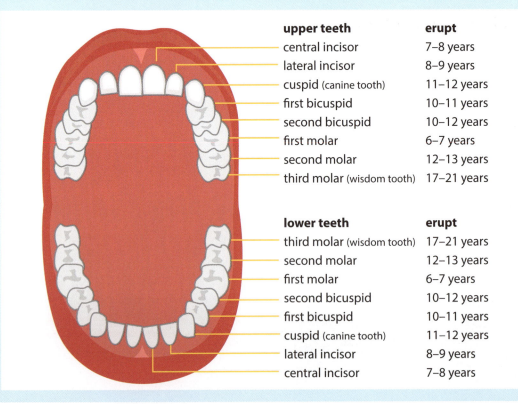

upper teeth	erupt
central incisor	7–8 years
lateral incisor	8–9 years
cuspid (canine tooth)	11–12 years
first bicuspid	10–11 years
second bicuspid	10–12 years
first molar	6–7 years
second molar	12–13 years
third molar (wisdom tooth)	17–21 years

lower teeth	erupt
third molar (wisdom tooth)	17–21 years
second molar	12–13 years
first molar	6–7 years
second bicuspid	10–12 years
first bicuspid	10–11 years
cuspid (canine tooth)	11–12 years
lateral incisor	8–9 years
central incisor	7–8 years

FORENSIC ODONTOLOGY PRACTICES

Forensic odontology relies on dentists who have pursued expertise and certification in forensic analysis in the following areas:

- Identifying unknown remains.
- Identification of remains resulting from mass disasters.
- Age estimates from remains.
- Identification of oro-facial irregularities due to abuse, trauma, lifestyle, or diet in teeth.
- Determining gender and ethnicity from teeth.
- Comparing bite marks on evidence to known dental records with details about bridges, crowns, fillings, false teeth, or orthodontics.

A bite mark is defined as "the physical end product of a complex set of events that occur when human or animal teeth are applied to the skin or foodstuff."[505] Bite marks are unique to each person since the position of the jaw and how the teeth are aligned in the jaw can be differentiated between individuals. Tongue pressure will also leave an identifying mark along with any tooth scraping. When someone bites another human, three movement factors must be considered during the initial evaluation:[506]

1. *Maxilla*: The lack of movement in the maxilla. The maxilla remains stationary as it holds and stretches the skin.
2. *Mandible*: The movement of the jaw and mandible applies the greatest biting force.
3. *Victim*: The reaction of the victim to the biting.

The examiner will begin by pinpointing the class characteristics: Is the bite from a human? Is there a unique pattern or feature to the teeth? Animal bite marks look very different from human bite marks and can quickly be identified during examination.[507] Human bites are very circular in shape, while animal bites are oval. This would be considered a class characteristic. Another class characteristic is the overall shape of the teeth. Central and lateral incisors are uniform in width and leave rectangular marks, while canines are cone shaped and leave rounded marks.

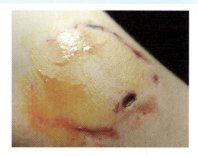

dog bite mark

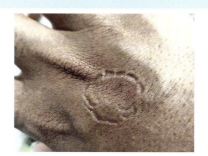

human bite mark

Individual characteristics are what link a bite mark to one individual. Individual characteristics can vary between each tooth. Examples of individual markers include rotation of the teeth, separation between teeth, erosion, abrasions, and restorations (crowns, bridges, etc.).

Any visible bruising must be photographed immediately. Bruising usually appears around four hours after a bite has occurred and will fade after 36 hours. If a bite mark is identified on a deceased person, it is cut away from the skin and preserved in formalin. A silicone cast is then made of the indentation. The bite mark will be swabbed for saliva and sent to the lab for DNA analysis.

Forensic experts label bite marks according to their type:[508]

- Abrasion – an undamaging scrape on the skin.
- Artifact – a piece of the body, such as the tip of a nose, removed as a result of biting.
- Avulsion – a bite resulting in the removal of skin.
- Contusion – a bruise from ruptured blood vessels.
- Hemorrhage – a bleeding spot.
- Incision – a neat puncture or torn skin.
- Laceration – a puncture on the skin.

A tooth impression is classified into one of four categories according to the severity:

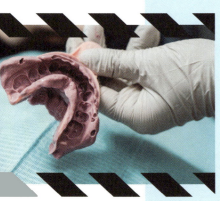

- Clear impression – a bite with significant pressure.
- Obvious impression – a bite with medium pressure.
- Noticeable impression – a bite that exhibits violent pressure.
- Lacerated – the skin is violently ripped from the body.

When examining bite marks, examiners place them into one of four classes:[509]

- Class I – limited class characteristics and lacks individual characteristics; examples include a bruise or abrasion.
- Class II – a single arch bite (either upper or lower) or a partial bite. It may have class or individual characteristics.
- Class III – exhibits both class and individual characteristics due to the applied pressure and penetration of the bite into the tissue. Class III's are used for comparison. Often found on the buttocks, shoulders, upper arms, and chest.
- Class IV – a removal of skin (avulsion or laceration). Class and individual characteristics are not visible. Often found on the ear or finger.

PHOTOGRAPHING BITE MARKS

Once a bite mark is identified on human skin, there are several approaches. As in all forensic evidence discussed in this book, the first step is to photograph the bite mark. There are different lighting techniques that can be utilized to retrieve the best photographic evidence. The bite mark will appear different in all four of the below methods, and each should be considered in order to bring to light any hidden details that could be used for comparison.

- *Conventional camera:* A conventional camera is used to capture the tooth indention with and without scale.

- *Infrared (IR) photography:* IR is best used when there is injured tissue because of the bite mark. Biting human flesh results in a subdermal hemorrhage. The release of blood in the dermal layer of the skin can be captured using IR.

- *Ultraviolet (UV) photography:* UV photography is unique in its ability to capture details on the surface of damaged skin. When the skin is bitten, hemoglobin and melanin are released to heal the injury, and they migrate toward the surface of the skin. UV has the potential to reveal details not visible to the naked eye.

- *Alternate light sources (ALS):* ALS uses fluorescence to illuminate injuries that are not visible to the naked eye. In a darkened environment, the ALS can differentiate between healthy and injured skin, even when it appears completely healed to the naked eye.

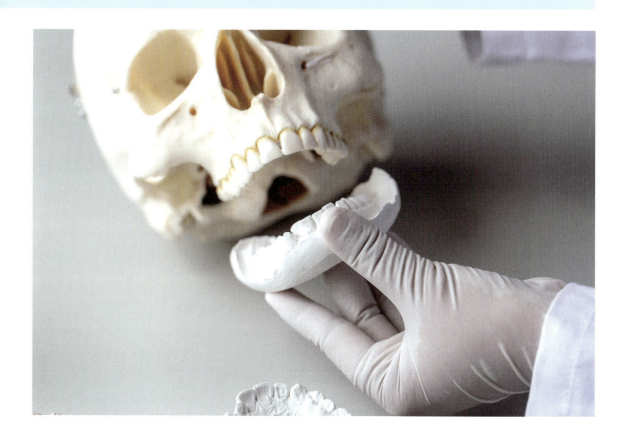

Forensic Odontology

COMPARING BITE MARKS

The investigator will consult with detectives for names of possible suspects and retrieve a court order for the dental records. Once the dental records are obtained, the investigator will proceed with a comparison technique. A dentist will perform an overall examination of the suspect's teeth, outlining any visible identifiers like facial asymmetry, saliva, size of tongue, and condition of the teeth. Any food items in the teeth are collected, photographed, and examined. Two dental casts will be made of each arch for comparison. Comparisons will vary based upon the expertise of the examiners and the technology available.

1. *Direct comparison*: A direct comparison can be made between the suspect's dental cast to the photographs or tooth indentations on the skin.

2. *Overlays:* A life-sized photograph with transparent overlay is created, showing that the bite mark matches the individual's teeth. Using a transparency, a bite mark can be sketched from the photographic evidence and then placed over the dental records for comparison. Bite marks can also be directly overlaid on a suspect's dental cast.

3. *3D dental imaging:* The latest method to compare bite marks to dental records is with computer software 3D imaging. A suspect's dental arch can be scanned using an intraoral scanner. A laser emitted from the scanner detects and records the geometry of the teeth using triangulation from multiple locations. Orthodontists use this technology when developing a plan for braces or Invisalign®. This same technology is used in toolmark analysis. The investigator can also scan the suspect's cast. The result is a 3D image of the person's dentition. A variety of digital overlays are available for comparison. The challenge with this method lies in the need for the suspect's actual oral cavity to complete the scan. If the suspect is unknown or not willing to participate in the scan, another method will be utilized.

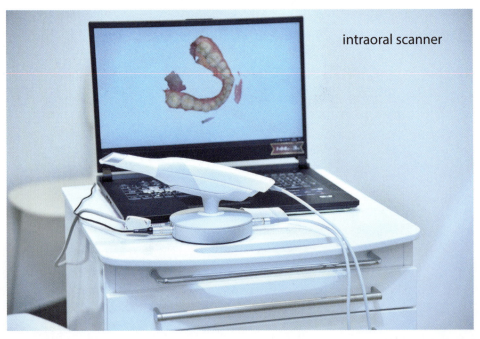

intraoral scanner

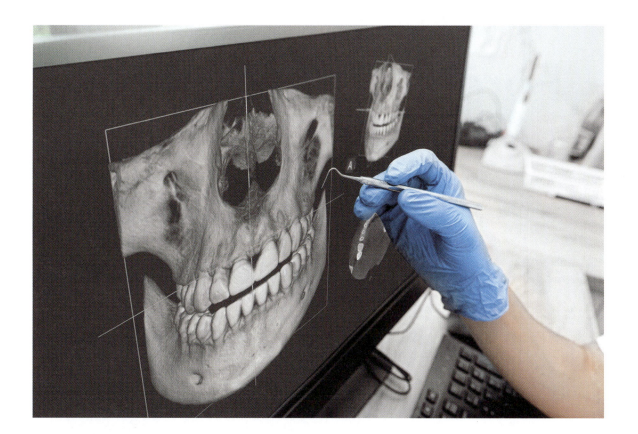

4. *Dental imaging software:* DentalPrint© is one of the most widely used software tools. The software provides exquisite detail, measurements, and the ability to mark and compare the dental records.

CONCLUSION

Human teeth were designed by God to withstand the test of time. Death results in an instant stop to tooth decay, and when someone dies, it is the hair, bones, and teeth that remain for years after death. Teeth remain the longest — in some cases, for thousands of years. The durability and unique nature of teeth point to a Creator God who designed them with forethought in their function and placement within the oral cavity.

Lesson 31
Forensic Psychiatry

Do not be conformed to this world, but be transformed by the renewal of your mind, that by testing you may discern what is the will of God, what is good and acceptable and perfect (Romans 12:2).

Case Study: The Devil Told Me To

On June 20, 2001, 911 received a phone call from a woman named Andrea, who asked police to come to her home. When police arrived, they found Andrea's five small children dead. The children had been murdered by drowning in a bathtub.

Andrea Pia Kennedy graduated as valedictorian of her high school senior class. She was smart and driven and graduated college with a nursing degree. In 1993, she met Rusty Yates, a project manager for NASA. They dated for three years before marrying. Rusty was a follower of a radical preacher named Michael Peter Woroniecki. Woroniecki corresponded with the Yates couple by mail and condemned them for living a hypocritical, middle-class Christian lifestyle. He told them their children were doomed to hell. He also preached that couples should have as many children as possible. The couple sold their moderate home and moved into a mobile home park to live the "simple Christian life." Later, they decided to simplify further and bought a 350-square-foot bus to live in with the four children.

Immediately following the first child, there were mental health problems in the mother. Andrea began to experience severe depression and psychosis. She suffered from visions of Satan, and she claimed he was telling her that she was evil and sinful. She was also having violent tendencies. She received treatment but then suffered a relapse after the birth of the fourth child. In 1999, she was admitted to a facility and treated for postpartum depression and psychosis. Her treatment in and out of mental facilities continued. She became pregnant with a fifth child against the recommendations of the doctors. A doctor took Yates off her antipsychotic medication just months before June 20, 2001.

On the morning of June 20, 2001, Rusty left for work, leaving Andrea with a one-hour window alone in the house with the children. At 9:48 a.m., 911 received a phone call from an unemotional Andrea Yates.[510] Below is a portion of the 911 call transcript:[511]

911: What's your name?

Yates: Andrea Yates.

911: What's the problem?

Yates: Um, I just need them to come.

911: Is your husband there?

Yates: No.

911: Well, what's the problem?

Yates: I need them to come.

911: I need to know why we're coming, ma'am. Is he there standing next to you?

Yates: Pardon me.

911: Are you having a disturbance? Are you ill? Or what?

Yates: Yes, I'm ill.

911: Do you need an ambulance?

Yates: No, I need a police officer. Yeah, send an ambulance.

911: What kind of medical problem do you have, ma'am?

Yates: I just need a police officer.

911: Okay, well why do you need the police, ma'am?

Yates: I just need them to be here.

911: For what?

Yates: I just need them to come.

Andrea did not give police any specific details on why she needed the police at her home. She then called her husband, Rusty, and said something was wrong with all five children. When the first police officer arrived at the home, he found Andrea in wet clothes. He asked her why she needed the police, and she responded, "I just killed my kids."[512]

First, Paul, 3½ years old

Second, Luke, 2 years old

Third, John, 5½ years old

Fourth, Mary, 6 months old

Fifth, Noah, 7 years old

During the confession, police asked Andrea, "After you drew the bath water, what was your intent? What were you about to do?" Andrea answered, "Drown the children."

Facts about the case:

- In the days after the murder, Rusty, Andrea's husband, publicly expressed sympathy for his wife because she was depressed and suffering from mental illness.
- After analyzing Andrea Yates, the defense psychiatrist stated, "She was the sickest person I have ever seen in my life."[513] Yates had been diagnosed with postpartum psychosis.
- To be criminally responsible for the five murders, she had to be found mentally sane.
- The trial began eight months after the five murders, but the prosecution only tried her for three of the murders in case it went in Yates' favor. The withheld two murder cases could then be tried later.
- She tried to kill "the devil" inside her twice in 1999 by trying to commit suicide. She confessed to killing the children to save them from Satan.
- The doctor had advised Rusty to not leave Andrea unattended due to her depression. When Rusty left for work the morning of June 20, 2001, he had scheduled his mother to arrive in just one hour of his departure. Andrea knew she only had the one hour alone with the children to commit the murders.

Andrea Yates was found guilty of all three murders (that she was tried for) on March 12, 2002, and sentenced to life in prison. In 2005, the convictions were overturned due to the false witness of the prosecutor's psychiatrist. Andrea was tried again in 2006. This time, she was found not guilty by reason of insanity.[514] She was sent to Kerrville State Hospital, a mental health facility. Rusty Yates divorced Andrea in 2011.

A forensic psychiatrist is often called into a case where a mental health evaluation is needed to determine fitness for trial. In the Andrea Yates case, the forensic psychiatrist gave false testimony in her first trial, resulting in an overturned conviction and new trial. This case is a reminder of the importance of job integrity in every discipline of forensic science. As a forensic psychiatrist, honesty, trustworthiness, and an unbiased approach would be expected characteristics to display. This lesson will dive into the roles and responsibilities of a forensic psychiatrist, as well as their close relationship with the judicial system.

"I should prefer that you do not mention my name at all in connection with this case, as I choose to be only associated with those crimes which present some difficulty in their solution."
— Sherlock Holmes[515]

The National Institute of Mental Health estimates that one in five people live with mental illness. This is over 46 million people in the United States alone.[516] One in 25 Americans will suffer from a serious mental illness, such as schizophrenia, bipolar disorder, or major depression.[517] The CDC describes mental health as the "emotional, psychological, and social well-being . . . and affects how people think, feel, and act. It also helps determine how to handle stress, relate to others, and make healthy choices."[518] Mental illness impairs how people think, feel, and react to stressors in their life. Sometimes mental illness is temporary, while in other circumstances, it is a lifelong problem.

Interestingly, there is a weak correlation between mental illness and violent acts. The National Academy of Sciences, Engineering, and Medicine estimates that less than 2% of people with severe mental illness will commit a violent criminal act.[519] Therefore, mental illness is not always a factor in a person choosing to commit crime, but with a significant percentage of people experiencing some degree of mental illness, forensic psychiatry plays a key role in understanding criminal behavior.

According to the American Academy of Psychiatry, forensic psychiatry is defined as a "subspecialty of psychiatry in which scientific and clinical expertise is applied to legal issues in legal contexts embracing civil, criminal, correctional or legislative matters."[520] Fundamentally, forensic psychiatry examines the interaction between criminal behavior and mental disorder. Forensic psychiatrists require years of higher education, including medical school and extensive training. Psychiatry is considered a soft science. The soft sciences include psychology, sociology, and political science. Hard sciences are the natural sciences like biology, physics, astronomy, etc. Though a soft science, psychiatry is often more difficult than the tangible hard sciences due to the inability of the specialist to use the scientific method: experimentation, verification, and repeatability. Forensic psychiatrists work closely with the judicial system, city planners, school districts, correctional institutions, and the military.[521] The role of a forensic psychiatrist, or sometimes called a criminal profiler, is to determine why people commit crimes, what type of people commit crimes, and how to prevent people from committing crimes.

Jeremiah 17:9:

"The heart is deceitful above all things, and desperately sick; who can understand it?"

FORENSIC PSYCHIATRY FROM A BIBLICAL WORLDVIEW

Mental illness is defined as a condition that causes serious disorder in a person's behavior or thinking. As a result of sin, both Christians and non-Christians can be victims of mental illness. When psychiatric consultations are necessary for Christians, it is often beneficial to seek out biblical counseling. Biblical counseling applies God's truth to life's struggles, but it is important to note that it is not licensed to provide a professional diagnosis or prescribe medications.

Forensic psychiatry is a challenging field. The study of the mind can be arbitrary, erratic, and unreliable. This field is entirely intangible since there is nothing concrete to observe. Since the earth is marred by sin, the hearts of people are inherently wicked (Jeremiah 17:9). Behavior and thought processes are very subjective. Expertise takes years of counseling and practice to become discerning about the confessions of the guilty as well as professions of innocence.

There is no dispute that most crimes are related to some lapse of mental judgement or temporary insanity. According to a veteran forensic psychiatrist of 40 years, Dr. Louis Schlesinger, many crimes are caused by jealousy and/or committed by someone who knew the victim intimately. History tells multiple accounts of the acts of a jealous rage. Proverbs 6:34 states, "For jealousy makes a man furious, and he will not spare when he takes revenge." In fact, between 50–60% of murders in the United States model the historical account of Abel's murder by his brother Cain in the Bible.

Here is Dr. Schlesinger's explanation:

> If you look at Cain Abel murder case in detail, you'll learn about 50 to 60% of everything you need to know about murder. Cain killed his brother, Abel. There's a close relationship between offender and victim. He killed him because of jealousy. God liked Abel's offering better than he liked Cain's offering. It was a direct violent assault. He rose up and slew him. And most importantly, when the killer is confronted with wrongdoing, he lies. God asked Cain, "Where is your brother, Abel?" And he lied to God. He said, "I know not. I'm not my brother's keeper." That's the prototype of the vast majority of murders.[522]

Jealousy, anger, rage, and envy are all works of the flesh (Galatians 5:19–21). And an unsaved individual is far more susceptible to acting out the works of the flesh than someone who has accepted the free gift of salvation through Christ. Having an authentic relationship with Jesus Christ, in addition to a daily prayer life and Bible study, helps the sinner to avoid the temptation of anger, rage, stages of depression, feelings of incompleteness, and most importantly, violent criminal acts.

When it comes to mental illness, there is no reason to assume that just because a person is a Christian, they do not battle depression, anxiety, jealousy, etc. Sin not only brought physical death into the world, but also mental disease as well. But the body of Christ offers the mentally ill something the world cannot . . . hope, peace, and restoration by following the ultimate Healer, Jesus Christ.[523] While understanding these factors, fundamentally everyone suffers from mental illness. If sin is something that causes a disorder in a person's thinking (the definition of mental illness), then essentially every single person born is plagued by some form of mental illness because of Adam and Eve's sin against God in the Garden of Eden.

DUTIES AND RESPONSIBILITIES

It would be challenging to list all the duties and responsibilities of a forensic psychiatrist. As a profiler becomes experienced, in addition to a recognized expert, the list can become quite lengthy. Below are the generally accepted duties and responsibilities of a forensic psychiatrist.

Duties

- Provide recommendations regarding an individual's competence to stand trial.
- Assess the safety risk for the individual and recommend a level of security.
- The preliminary screening of prisoners.
- Examine the mental state of prisoners for an insanity defense.
- Assess claims of psychiatric malpractice.
- Oversee treatment for the mental disorders.
- Provide expert witness testimony for either prosecution or defense.
- Provide therapy for clients.

Responsibilities

- Exhibit no bias toward the client.
- Protect the rights of the clients (primarily prisoners).
- Provide a professional and honest testimony in the court of law.

CLINICAL EVALUATION AND PSYCHOLOGICAL TESTING

A forensic psychiatrist's clinical evaluation begins with a review of the person's history prior to the interview. Reviewing any past evaluations and diagnoses of mental health is key to understanding the present, especially if there are prescription medications and treatment involved. Once prior history analysis is complete, it is time for the face-to-face interview.

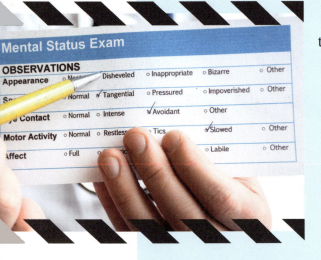

During the self-report interview, the psychiatrist begins to assess the overall mental health of the individual. A self-report instrument relies on the answers of the person interviewed, whether true or false, by using open-ended questions to extract the person's story. If closed-ended questions (yes or no) are used, the person will likely not reveal important information that is needed for an accurate analysis. For example, a closed-ended question could be: Did you cook dinner last night? An open-ended question would be: What did you prepare for dinner last night?

During the interview phase, the psychiatrist will also attempt to determine if the actions of the person stem from situational, medicinal, or behavioral factors.[524] Also, they will investigate if the interviewee is compulsive, obsessive, delusional, or distressed from current treatment. Keen observation is imperative during the clinical interview. Documenting (whether written or video recorded) the person's body language, demeanor, and anxiety are all essential factors in the overall analysis.

In addition to self-report instruments, profilers may use a personality test. The Minnesota Multiphasic Personality Inventory (MMPI-2™) is a psychological testing instrument used by many psychiatrists. This is a reliable test that has been validated through stringent testing measures. The MMPI-2™ includes a Lie Scale to determine if the person is misleading the examiner, lying to find favor, or is severely ill.[525] The issue with this test is its self-report nature. If the person is a habitual liar, it will be challenging to discern the correct facts.

For a full spectrum of a person's mental capacity, a full battery of tests is necessary. A full battery will examine the cognitive and emotional state and personality of an individual while reviewing any prior records. The chart outlines common forensic psychiatry practices and the tests used for evaluation.

Cognitive/Mental Plea	Possible Questions	Assessment Tool
Competency to Stand Trial	Does the person have a basic understanding of the criminal process? Does the person understand the charges, trial process, and the importance of information for their defense?	MacArthur Competence Assessment Tool–Criminal Adjudication (MacCAT-CA™)
Insanity Defense	Did the person understand the difference between right and wrong at the moment of the offense? Is the person suffering from mental illness or mental defect?	McNaughton Standard
Death Penalty Case	Does the individual have a mental defect prior to age 18? Do they have a persistent history of mental illness?	Wechsler Adult Intelligence Scale (WAIS®-R)
Malingering (Act of intentionally feigning or exaggerating physical or psychological symptoms for personal gain.)	Is the person fabricating their psychological symptoms to avoid trial or the death penalty? Is the person faking their inability to remember what happened at the crime?	Structured Interview of Reported Symptoms (SIRS) Test of Memory Malingering
Mental Status	How is the general appearance and behavior of the person? Is the person exhibiting unusual hallucinations, beliefs, moods, or recall?	Montreal Cognitive Assessment (MoCA)
Personality Test	Is the person purposely misleading the examiner? Or lying to find favor with law enforcement? Is the person severely ill and therefore a habitual liar?	Multiphasic Personality Inventory (MMPI-2™)

Forensic Psychiatry

Jack the Ripper:

Thomas Bond's profile of this famous unknown murderer was as follows:

- Probably middle-aged
- Probably not in regular employment
- Physically strong
- Quiet and inoffensive in appearance; neatly and respectably dressed
- Probably lacked anatomical knowledge
- Probably solitary or a loner
- Probably eccentric or odd in behaviour[533]

Each testing instrument is designed with scalar (numbered) measurement to provide a range in severity of factors in the interviewee, such as anxiety levels, depression, hysteria, and psychotic conditions and schizophrenia.[526] Based on the prior history, clinical interview, testing tools, and scalar total, a treatment schedule is developed and recommended. The final analysis will also be used by the forensic psychiatrist to make recommendations to the court, law enforcement, and related agencies.

CRIMINAL PSYCHOLOGY

Criminal psychology and forensic psychiatry are often used interchangeably. Though each field engages in similar duties, there are distinctions. A criminal psychologist is responsible for profiling a suspect, while a forensic psychiatrist would perform the assessment. A criminal psychologist would engage in substantive research about a known suspect, while experimental research falls under a forensic psychiatrist.[527] Therefore, a criminal psychologist focuses on the thoughts, behavior, and actions of criminals. Areas where a criminal psychologist would specialize are profiling, consulting, assessing, researching, and testifying.

Profiling. Criminal psychologists do not interview suspects. They base their profiles on case files, information provided to them by the police, and extensive research. Profiling is not an exact science and is not always recognized as a valid technique used in investigation. The first criminal profiler in history is believed to be Thomas Bond. Bond was the medical examiner who examined the victims of Jack the Ripper (August–November 1888). He released a profile of the psychological make-up of the murderer, though he was never caught. Jack the Ripper is still unidentified and is considered a cold case.[528] The most famous profiler in the modern era is John Douglas. Douglas was a criminal profiler for the FBI and was influential in profiling some of the worst criminals in the United States. As part of his research, he also interviewed Jeffrey Dahmer, Son of Sam, Ted Bundy, the Green River killer, BTK, and Charles Manson. He described criminal profiling as extremely stressful, and it caused him to collapse and have post-traumatic stress disorder when he was only 38 years old.[529] Douglas has published multiple books about his experiences and is now a retired special agent. When asked in an interview why he was so successful, he answered:

> These guys, they'll lie to you. They lie to me. They won't lie to you if they realize that you have studied their crime inside and out, and you're not being antagonistic to them, you're a good listener. You're not shocked or offended. I used this statement for years and years: to understand the artist, you must look at the artwork, right? To understand the criminal—how can you understand the criminal if you haven't looked at the crime?[530]

Profiling falls within four general approaches, which are geographical, investigative, typological, and clinical.[531]

1. *Geographical* would be focused on patterns and links between the location of crimes and the places where suspects live and work.
2. The *investigative* approach predicts suspect characteristics and behaviors.
3. *Typological* approach categorizes the crime scene based on the characteristics present at the scene.
4. The *clinical* approach uses information from psychiatrists to develop a mental health profile.

Consulting. Consulting involves working with police officers and those in the judicial system, as well as any health care workers.

Assessing. Though testing is often conducted by the forensic psychiatrist, it is possible the criminal psychologist will be expected to perform this duty.

Researching. It is often necessary to conduct research outside the scope of casework. Research topics may include eyewitness testimony, evidence collection procedures, confessions, and other legal topics.

Testifying. This is expert testimony on the expert's opinion regarding mental health of the suspect and any other involvement in the case. To be deemed an expert witness by the judicial system, the forensic psychologist will go through a series of rigorous questions surrounding their expertise. These are a few of the questions they will be asked by the prosecution and/or defense:[532]

- What is your occupation/profession?
- What is your educational background?
- What degrees, certificates, or licenses do you have?
- What is your field of expertise/specialty?
- Within the [mental health/social work/social sciences/other discipline] field, is this a recognized professional area of expertise?
- Are there published articles recognizing this field of expertise/specialty? Has this field of expertise/specialty been recognized by any licensing or accreditation body or any governmental agency?
- Is there controversy within the profession about the efficacy or reliability of this field of expertise/specialty? If so, can you articulate why these [opinions/statements/criticisms] should not undermine the value of your opinion?
- What facts or evidence did you rely on?
- Is this the type of evidence relied on in the ordinary course by professionals in your field?
- Is there any other evidence or information relied on in the ordinary course by professionals in your field as part of making such a determination that you did not use?

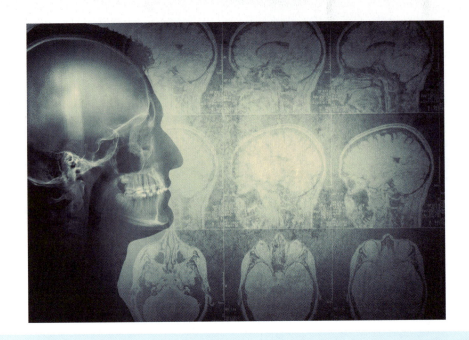

HOW TO BECOME A FORENSIC PSYCHIATRIST

The field of forensic psychiatry is over-glamorized in fictional television series and movies. This division of forensic science will involve tedious research and report writing. Very rarely does a forensic psychiatrist receive a high-profile case that results in fame and fortune. At the same time, the field offers a rewarding career. Psychiatrists will work closely with law enforcement and the judicial system with a goal of resolving criminal activity and bringing resolution for victims and their families. To become a forensic psychiatrist, the following is required:

- Medical school
- Residency in psychiatry
- Fellowship in forensic psychiatry
- State medical license and certification by the medical board
- Continuing medical education to maintain license and board certification
- DEA registration to prescribe controlled substances

The average salary for a forensic psychiatrist is over $200,000 annually. Due to the education required to be a practitioner in this field, this salary far exceeds those in other forensic disciplines except for a pathologist.

CONCLUSION

A forensic psychiatrist diagnosis and treatment is never finite or set in stone. Mental illness can change over time. Therefore, regularly scheduled evaluations are necessary for the benefit of the client. Although there is no single cause that determines a person will experience mental illness, there have been recognized factors that contribute to mental illness, such as childhood physical and/or sexual abuse, domestic violence, chronic medical conditions, chemical imbalances, drug use, personality disorders, and depression.

THE JUDICIAL SYSTEM

UNIT 8

Lesson 32
The Judicial System

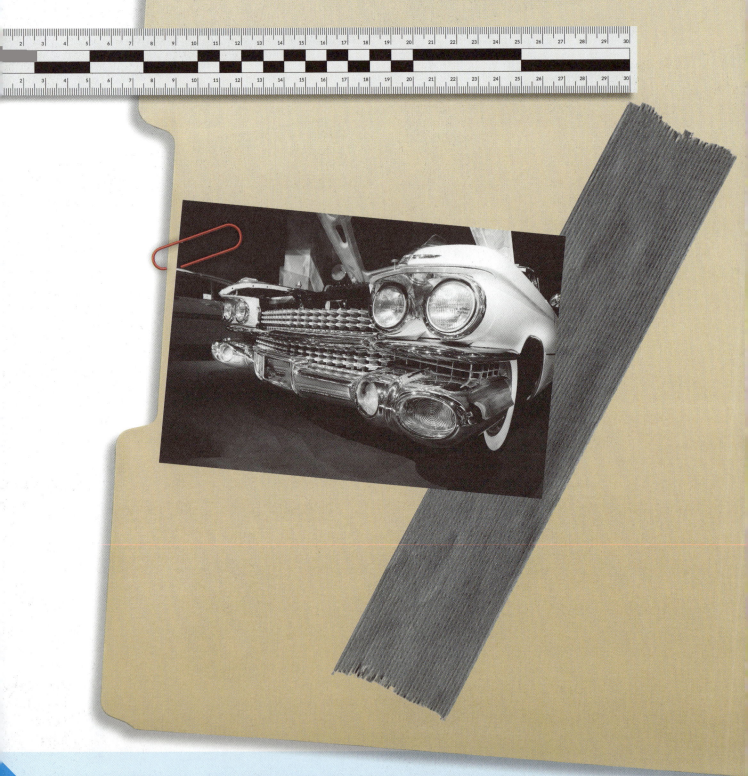

Let every person be subject to the governing authorities. For there is no authority except from God, and those that exist have been instituted by God. Therefore whoever resists the authorities resists what God has appointed, and those who resist will incur judgment (Romans 13:1–2).

Case Study: The Genesis of Miranda Rights

On March 3, 1963, in Phoenix, Arizona, Lois Ann Jameson was walking home after finishing her shift at a local movie theater. She boarded the public bus as usual, exited the bus at her stop, and began to walk down the street toward her home. She noticed a car approaching and within seconds had been forced into the backseat of Ernest Arturo Miranda's vehicle.

He drove the car twenty minutes out of Phoenix to the desert, where he assaulted Lois. He then drove her back to the city and dropped her off on the street. The last thing Miranda said to her was "pray for me."[534] Lois immediately ran home and alerted her family to the kidnapping and assault. The police were notified, and Lois provided a description of the car and the assailant. One week later, Lois' brother spotted a car with similar characteristics driving through their neighborhood. He was able to write down part of the license plate number, which was enough to trace the car back to Ernest Miranda.

On March 13, 1963, Miranda (age 23) was arrested. Miranda already had a police record for burglary, armed robbery, and other offenses. His criminal record had started in the 8th grade. He had dropped out of high school in the 9th grade. He was a drifter and had committed crimes of theft across the United States. He was placed in a lineup, but Lois was unable to positively identify him.

The police then questioned Miranda for two hours without informing him of his 5th Amendment rights. He eventually confessed to the crimes of kidnapping and assault. His confession was used during his trial. His defense team moved to suppress his confession on the grounds that he was not informed of his 5th Amendment right against self-incrimination.[535] But the jury found him guilty of the crimes, and he was sentenced to 20-30 years in prison for each charge.

The case was appealed to the Arizona Supreme Court, and the verdict was affirmed. The court based this affirmation on the fact that at no time during the questioning did Miranda request a lawyer. If he had requested a lawyer and then been denied that right by police, there would have been grounds for a 5th Amendment violation.

The case made it all the way to the United States Supreme Court in 1966. As the Supreme Court was reviewing Miranda's written, signed confession, the members read this statement, "This confession was made with full knowledge of my legal rights, understanding any statement I make may be used against me."[536] Though the police made him include this statement in his confession, the records clearly showed that Miranda was never informed of his right to counsel or that he had the right to not incriminate himself.

In a 5-4 ruling, the Supreme Court reversed the trial court decision and found his confession to be inadmissible under the 5th Amendment. They ruled that all suspects be advised of their 5th Amendment rights prior to questioning while in police custody. The now famous Miranda warning states:

1. You have the right to remain silent.
2. Anything you say can and will be used against you in a court of law.
3. You have the right to an attorney.
4. If you cannot afford an attorney, one will be appointed for you.

The Supreme Court remanded the case for retrial. During the second trial, the unlawful confession could not be used as evidence, but while in jail, Miranda had confessed to his ex-wife. She testified for the prosecution. Miranda was convicted a second time and was sentenced to 20-30 years in prison. He was paroled in 1973. By this time, Miranda was now famous, and it made it difficult for him to find a job. To make ends meet, he would sell autographed Miranda Cards in Phoenix. He was fatally stabbed in a bar fight on January 31, 1976. The killer fled the scene after being read his Miranda warning and was never found.

Ernest Arturo Miranda died without ever realizing his true fame and that his name would be used in almost every popular police thematic television show and movie to this day.

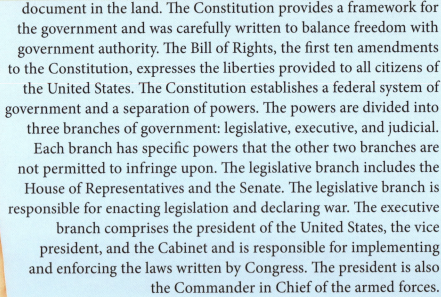

"You have a grand gift for silence, Watson. It makes you quite invaluable as a companion." — Sherlock Holmes[537]

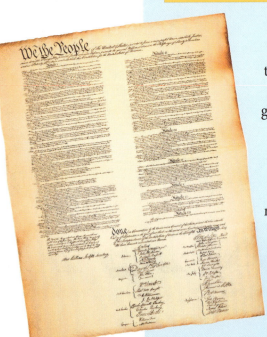

In 1789, the United States Constitution was ratified by the states as the governing document in the land. The Constitution provides a framework for the government and was carefully written to balance freedom with government authority. The Bill of Rights, the first ten amendments to the Constitution, expresses the liberties provided to all citizens of the United States. The Constitution establishes a federal system of government and a separation of powers. The powers are divided into three branches of government: legislative, executive, and judicial. Each branch has specific powers that the other two branches are not permitted to infringe upon. The legislative branch includes the House of Representatives and the Senate. The legislative branch is responsible for enacting legislation and declaring war. The executive branch comprises the president of the United States, the vice president, and the Cabinet and is responsible for implementing and enforcing the laws written by Congress. The president is also the Commander in Chief of the armed forces.

This lesson will focus on the judicial branch, which is outlined in Article III of the Constitution. The judicial branch, at its highest level, is made up of Supreme Court justices, who are appointed by the president of the United States and confirmed by the Senate. There are also lower federal court justices. The Supreme Court is the highest court in the United States. There is a system of courts that branch out from the Supreme Court through the federal system, the individual states, and down to the county systems of government.

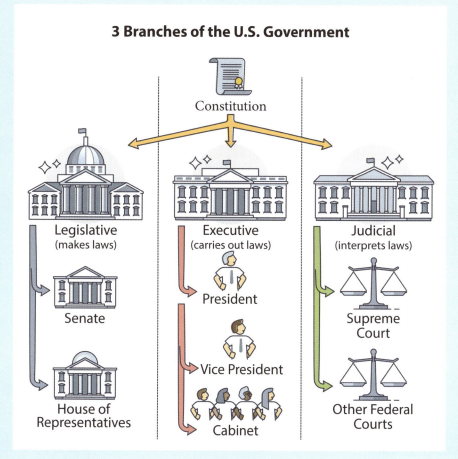

TWO TYPES OF LAW

There are two general types of law in the court systems, civil and criminal. This lesson will focus on criminal law, but a discussion of the two types is important to understand the similarities and differences. The primary difference between the two lies in the purpose. Criminal law exists because of man's sin. Criminal law defines criminal offenses; regulates the apprehension, charging, and trial of suspected persons; and defines penalties and types of treatment for convicted offenders. The sanctions imposed by criminal law help to deter the evil, inherent behavior that every human is born with. Criminal law also provides a sense of justice and retribution for the victims. Another purpose of criminal law is to incarcerate the guilty and punish them through 24-hour monitoring and/or possible death. Though rehabilitation — another important goal for those incarcerated — is preferred, it is difficult to achieve with the limited resources available.

Civil law is generally defined as any law that is not criminal law. Civil law is tasked with providing compensation, often monetary, for people injured by someone else. Civil law is also designed to deter undesirable human behavior. The chart below summarizes the key differences between criminal and civil law.[538]

	Criminal Law	Civil Law
Purpose	Deter the sinful nature of humans Retribution for victims Incarcerate the guilty Rehabilitation	Deter the sinful nature of humans Compensation
Restitution	Fines, imprisonment, counseling, monitoring, capital punishment	Damages
Injured Party	Government (prosecution) government vs. citizen	Plaintiff citizen vs. citizen
Standard of Proof	Beyond reasonable doubt	Preponderance of evidence
Burden of Proof	Government (prosecution)	Plaintiff
Adjudication	Jury	Judge
Attorney Rights	Defendant has a right to an attorney	Plaintiff provides their own attorney; no right to an attorney

Rehabilitation: The ability to successfully reintegrate offenders into the larger society after imprisonment and to equip them with the ability to refrain from criminal activity.

Restitution: A gain-based recovery where one party provides compensation for loss, damage, or injury.

Adjudication: The process of passing judgment, judicial sentence, or decision in a court.

JUSTICE AND CAPITAL PUNISHMENT FROM A BIBLICAL WORLDVIEW

One of the attributes of God is justice. Deuteronomy 32:4 says, "The Rock, his work is perfect, for all his ways are justice. A God of faithfulness and without iniquity, just and upright is he." God has given humans the law, and when they break those laws, He punishes justly. Criminal acts are sins that violate not only God's law, but also the laws established by governing authorities. Capital punishment is one of those punishments for sin that is highly debated. Is it biblical to take the life of a person who has killed another? God says in Genesis 9:6, "Whoever sheds the blood of man, by man shall his blood be shed, for God made man in his own image." The following excerpt from an article titled *Is Capital Punishment for Today?* provides just one version of a possible biblical framework for this topic:

The command of Genesis 9:6 for capital punishment occurs after the worldwide Flood. This command affirms again that the pre-Flood society was reprobate, as mentioned in Genesis 6. "Then the Lord saw," in the words of Moses the lawgiver, "that the wickedness of man was great on the earth, and that every intent of the thoughts of his heart was only evil continually" (Genesis 6:5). In particular, society was given over to violence and murder, "And the land became corrupted before God, and the earth was filled with violence" (Genesis 6:11, 6:13). What began as brother murdering brother (Genesis 4:8) had become endemic—"all flesh had corrupted its way upon the earth" (Genesis 6:12). Clearly, the post-Flood world needed a divine decree to restrain violence.

As the post-Flood world begins, God blesses and commands Noah and his sons. Most of the commands echo God's commands to Adam to multiply and fill the earth. As one of the few survivors of the Flood, Noah became another Adam, but with differences. God's commands to Adam came in the context of a sinless world; the commands came to Noah in the context of a sinful world.

God turns to the lifeblood of man. God prefaces the command of Genesis 9:6 by stating that He will "seek" those who take the lifeblood of man (Genesis 9:5). God will personally seek out and avenge those who commit murder. God emphasizes His determination to "seek" by repeating it (Genesis 41:32), with the addition that He will hold even animals responsible: "From every beast He will indeed seek [and avenge] him" for taking the life of a man. Then God repeats it a third time for even greater emphasis that He will seek out and avenge murder "from all mankind and from every individual man [responsible]."

Then God gives a command to Noah not given to Adam: a prohibition against murder. The Lord orders Noah, "The one who sheds the blood of man, by man his blood will be shed" (Genesis 9:6). The meaning is straightforward: a murderer must be put to death. Moreover, the command charges mankind with the task of executing the murderer—by man the murderer is to be put to death. The reason given for the command is likewise straightforward: "because in the image of God, He made man" (Genesis 9:6). Man may kill and eat animals (Genesis 9:3), but man, because he is made in God's image, may not be unlawfully killed [murdered].[539]

Murder is the most heinous act that one human can inflict on another, and this includes the murder of the unborn through the process of abortion. Every human life is precious and sacred, and each one is an image bearer of the Creator God.

THE SUPREME COURT

According to the Constitution, "The judicial Power of the United States, shall be vested in one supreme Court."[540] There is only one federal Supreme Court. Currently, the Supreme Court of the United States has nine appointed justices. Since there is not a set number of justices outlined in the Constitution, this number has fluctuated throughout history. Congress has been given the power to determine the number of sitting Supreme Court justices as well as the power to shape the federal justice system. Throughout history, there have been six, seven, eight, and ten Supreme Court justices.

U.S. Supreme Court justices

Supreme Court justices serve a lifetime appointment. A lifetime appointment is believed to prevent sitting justices from being influenced or swayed by the governing political party. Therefore, a justice will remain in office until he or she resigns, dies, or is impeached for misconduct.

The Supreme Court is the only federal court required under the Constitution. Most of the cases heard by the Supreme Court are appellate in nature and are not trials. Once the court rules on a case, there is no higher court to appeal to. Their primary duty is interpreting the rule of law and ascertaining if the law was violated. Of the 7,500 requests the Supreme Court receives on a yearly basis, they only grant certiorari to less than 80.[541] Grant certiorari (grant cert for short) means to grant review of the case. A minimum of four justices must vote in favor of the grant cert for the case to be presented before the Supreme Court.

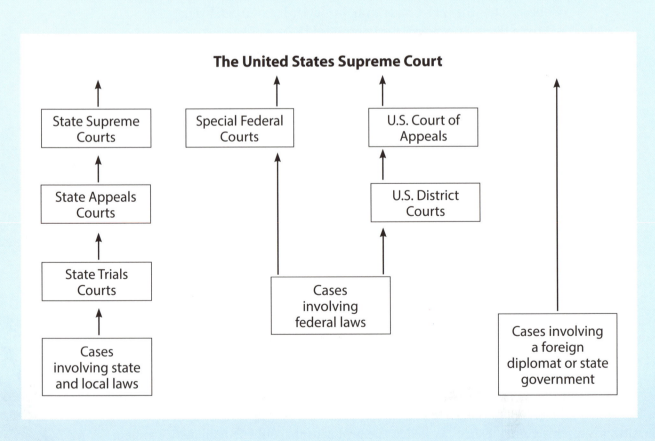

FEDERAL COURTS

Congress has the power to establish inferior (lower) courts to try federal cases. The federal courts oversee any cases involving federal laws, legal battles between states, and cases involving foreign governments. Criminal cases outside of those listed above are handled at the state level. According to the Pew Research Center, of all the 80,000 cases at the federal level in 2018, only 2% even went to trial, while 90% were plea bargained and 8% were dismissed.[542] Of the 2% that do go to trial in the federal courts, less than 1% are found not guilty.

There are two levels of federal courts below the Supreme Court, the U.S. District Courts and the U.S. Circuit Court of Appeals. There are 94 judicial districts in the United States, with at least one in every state. For example, the state of California has four judicial districts, while the state of Kansas only has one. The district court (or trial court) is the first pathway into the federal system.

The federal court system has a Judicial Conference, which comprises 27 members. Members include the Chief Justice of the United States and 26 judges from different regions of the U.S. The conference oversees the administration of the courts, writes court policies, modifies rules of procedure, and monitors the general operation of the judicial branch.

STATE COURTS

All the power not residing with the government is given to the states. Each of the 50 states has their own state constitution, government structure, and judicial system. Because of this freedom, the structure of the governments will vary between the states. State courts are also known as district, superior, county, and circuit courts. Many states have trial courts that are presided over by one judge. These courts hear both civil and criminal cases. Every state has a state supreme court that is primarily a court of appeals. The state judicial branches also have court administrative agencies in place that monitor budgets, recommend rules of procedure, review disciplinary violations, and oversee the general court processes.

In many states, judges are either elected by popular vote or commissioned through nomination by the governor. Since there is no formal training to be a judge, candidates are selected from reputable lawyers with years of experience and who meet the qualifications outlined by the state. Similar to the statistics for the likelihood of a federal trial, in 2017, of all the thousands of criminal cases in the states, less than 3% resulted in a trial.[543] Most cases are settled through plea bargains.

APPELLATE COURTS

When a case results in a trial, the defendant has the right to appeal the decision to a higher court. Depending on the crime, this will be to either a state appellate court or a federal court of appeals. Appellate courts exist to review the verdicts in trial courts and do not conduct trials. Appellate courts look for errors that may have been made during a trial by reviewing legal briefs by the prosecutor and defense attorneys and the official court records. The litigant who is appealing the case must show that a legal error occurred during the trial that affected the decision made by the jury or judge. Attorneys may be permitted to present oral arguments before an appellate court, but no witnesses may testify, and no new evidence may be presented.

Appellate courts can reverse, affirm, or remand a lower court decision.[544] If the appellate court finds there was a clear error and reverses the lower court's decision, the litigant can only be tried on a new set of facts or evidence. If the lower court's decision is affirmed in the appellate court, the litigant may file a petition called a writ of certiorari, which is an official request for the U.S. Supreme Court to review the case. When the appellate court remands the lower court decision, the case is returned to the lower court for some type of action. This many include a new trial.

Federal appellate courts are divided into two levels, the intermediate and the highest. In the intermediate bracket, there are currently 13 United States Courts of Appeals. Appeals from the Circuit Court of Appeals can only be made to the Supreme Court.[545] Appeals are only heard for cases where a guilty verdict was issued. There are no appeals for verdicts of not guilty.

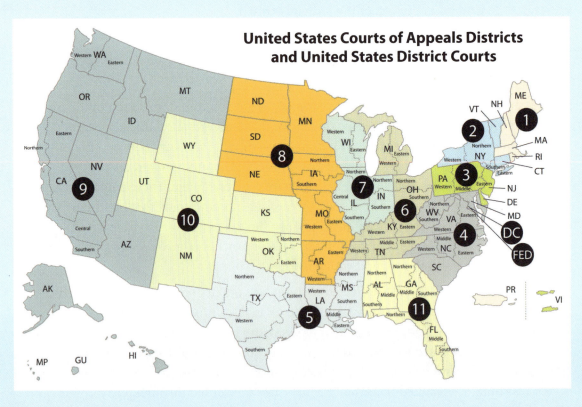

United States Courts of Appeals Districts and United States District Courts

THE JUDICIAL PROCESS

The Constitution grants every person accused of a crime the right to a fair trial. Article III describes a fair trial as a competent judge, a jury of peers, and a trial in the state where the crime occurred. Additional protections for those accused of a crime are outlined in the Amendments of the Constitution. These include:

Amendment	Protection
4th	A guarantee that no person shall be deprived of life, liberty, or property without the due process of law.
4th	Protection against unreasonable search and seizure.
5th	Protection against being tried for the same crime twice ("double jeopardy").
5th	The right to avoid self-incrimination.
6th	The right to a speedy trial by an impartial jury.
6th	The right to cross-examine witnesses and to call witnesses to support their case.
6th	The right to legal representation.
8th	Protection from excessive bail, excessive fines, and cruel and unusual punishments.[546]

The judicial process begins with a crime and subsequent arrest. Once arrested, the accused is brought before a judge, at which time they are formally charged with the crime. It is at this hearing that the accused is asked to enter a plea of guilty or not guilty. The accused is permitted to consult with an attorney. If they cannot afford legal counsel, the state will provide a public defender to assist in the defense of their case. As stated earlier in the lesson, less than 3% of cases go to trial, most cases result in a plea bargain or settlement, and very few are resolved in a trial.

Miranda Rights. A person being read their Miranda rights originates from the Supreme Court case in 1966, *Miranda v. Arizona*. The court ruled that if the police question a person in custody, they must read them their Fifth Amendment rights against self-incrimination. Police must also tell the person that they have a right to an attorney. (See the case study at the beginning of this lesson for the Miranda Warning.)

Contrary to popular television, where the Miranda warning is read with every arrest directly at the scene, *a police officer is only required to read the Miranda warning before custodial interrogation begins.* If a person confesses while in custody and they were not provided with their Miranda rights, the confession and any evidence that stems from the confession is inadmissible in court.

THE ROLE OF THE PROSECUTOR

The American Bar Association (ABA) describes a prosecutor as "an administrator of justice, zealous advocate, and an officer of the court . . . who uses sound discretion and independent judgement to . . . seek justice within the bounds of the law, not merely to convict."[547] The prosecutor is a lawyer who works for a government entity. In the federal court system, the president of the United States appoints United States attorneys for this role. Within the individual states, they are either appointed by the governor or elected by voters with titles of state attorneys or district attorneys. Though it often appears that the prosecutor represents the victim in popular television, this is not their primary obligation. Their job is to find, serve, and represent justice in each case.[548] The prosecutor has multiple responsibilities in every criminal investigation. Those include:

- *Filing criminal charges with the courts.* The prosecutor asks the important question, "Is there probable cause?" Probable cause is the legal standard found in the 4th Amendment that requires police to have adequate justification to arrest a person, conduct a search, or seize property.

- *Investigating crimes.* Prosecutors work closely with the police officers called to the crime scene, the detectives involved in the investigation, witnesses to the crime, the victim, and the family of the victims to investigate the criminal act and serve justice to the best of their ability.

- *Designing sting operations.* A sting operation is when undercover law enforcement creates an opportunity for a possible suspect to commit a crime. Sometimes this includes trained law enforcement posing as members of a group or infiltrating an organization to gain access to suspected criminals. A sting operation can be at a physical location or virtual. With the rise of computer crimes across the United States, creating sting operations via the internet has become common practice.

- *Requesting search warrants.* A search warrant is requested by the prosecutor and granted by a competent authority or judge. If probable cause is met, the search warrant gives police the right to search the location specified in the warrant.

- *Ordering physical surveillance.* Physical surveillance is the undercover observation of a suspect on a 24-hour basis. The surveillance involves using cameras, audio equipment, and direct observation. Either the police or a hired private investigator will conduct the surveillance. Once again, there must be probable cause to invade a person's privacy in this manner.

- *Requesting fingerprints from witnesses and suspects.* If fingerprints are part of the evidence in a case, the prosecutor may request elimination prints from the witnesses and family. Elimination prints do exactly what they are called, eliminate those closest to the crime as possible suspects. As detectives build a list of possible suspects, prosecutors may request for police to fingerprint those individuals for comparison against fingerprints retrieved from the scene.

- *Interviewing witnesses and suspects.* Prosecutors are not required to interview witnesses or suspects to file criminal charges. This is a practice that occurs after criminal charges are filed and is considered part of the investigation.

- *Negotiating plea bargains.* It is normal practice for prosecutors to negotiate with the defense attorney. A plea bargain is a lesser charge for the defendant. Why is this so common? One reason is prison overcrowding. Jails are full of people waiting for an appearance before a judge or those serving sentences. Holding people in jail (a sentence of less than a year) or prison (a sentence of over a year) is also expensive. Depending on the severity of the offense, a better option may be a lesser offense with shorter incarceration. Another reason for plea bargains is the strength of the case. If the prosecutor feels there is not sufficient evidence to support the full extent of criminal charges, a lesser charge may be an option to ensure the defendant receives some form of punishment for their crime. A third reason for a plea bargain is to protect the witness. In cases where young children or sensitive testimony are involved, the prosecutor may elect a plea deal to protect the identity of the witnesses involved in the case. According to a U.S. state attorney for the Sixth Circuit, "The most important aspect for the prosecutor is to consider the rights and concerns of the victim before offering or accepting a plea bargain."[549]

THE ROLE OF THE DEFENSE ATTORNEYS

The ABA describes the function of a defense as "Any attorney – including privately retained, assigned by the court, acting *pro bono* or serving indigent defendants in a legal aid or public defender's office – who acts as an attorney on behalf of a client being investigated or prosecuted for alleged criminal conduct, or a client seeking legal advice regarding a potential, ongoing or past criminal matter or subpoena, including as a witness."[550] The primary role of the defense attorney is to represent the defendant throughout the court process and to provide a vigorous legal defense. Though their responsibilities are multifaceted, the primary expectations of defense counsel include:[551]

- *Developing a solid case.* Developing a case includes investigation, gathering evidence, studying every detail surrounding the case, and interviewing the defendant. All conversations between attorney and client are confidential; therefore, the information gleaned from the defendant, including any confession, remains in the confidence of the defense attorney.

- *Plea bargaining.* In the interest of the client, plea bargaining with the prosecution is an option to reduce the sentence of the defendant.

- *Legal representation.* A defense attorney provides vigorous representation in trial by showing the possibility of reasonable doubt in the evidence presented by the prosecution. The defense team does not have the burden of proving their client's innocence; the burden of proof lies in the hands of the prosecution.

Defense attorneys may also request to interview the witnesses for the prosecution. This would allow the defense team to ascertain the reliability and veracity of the witnesses, to learn additional details not disclosed in the prosecution's reports, and to discover new leads on evidence or other witnesses.

The Judicial System

FORENSIC EVIDENCE IN THE LEGAL SYSTEM

Forensic science is the use of science in the judicial system. The legal system values forensic evidence. Without forensic evidence, the criminal justice system must rely on eyewitness testimony, which is often plagued with inaccuracies. When forensic evidence is validated by scientific techniques, it does not leave much room for injustice. Forensic science techniques have been utilized to both convict and exonerate people throughout history. The forensic scientist plays an important role in the conviction, incarceration, and overall punishment of offenders.

Technically, evidence is defined as anything presented in court for the purpose of proving or disproving a testimony, document, photograph, video, artifact, etc. Trial evidence includes one or all of the following:

1. Sworn testimony of the witness and/or witnesses called by both the prosecution and defense.
2. All exhibits (evidence) submitted to the court during trial.
3. Anything else that all layers have agreed to or stipulated prior to and during the trial.

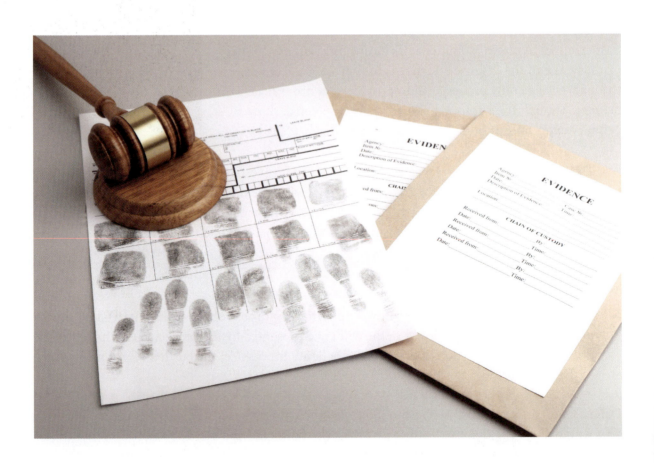

Evidence does not include the oral arguments, rebuttals, questions, or statements presented by the opposing attorneys during the trial.

The gatekeeper for all the evidence submitted in court is the trial judge. In the cases *Daubert v. Merrell Dow Pharmaceuticals, Inc.* (1993), *General Electric Co. v. Joiner* (1997), and *Kumho Tire Co. v. Carmichael* (1999), the federal court clarified this standard. The decision recommended the following considerations for judges when admitting evidence in trial:[552]

- What is the underlying (scientific) principle and was it tested?
- Is the methodology regulated by standards?
- Has peer review or publishing been subject to the concept or technique?
- What is the established or expected level of error?
- Is the principle acknowledged in general?
- Has the specialist found possible theories adequately?

Additional standards have been enacted since 1999. These include that the evidence was analyzed from a forensic specialist in their respective field and a certified lab.

THE FUTURE: ELECTRONIC COURTROOM

The latest advancements in the courtroom are in the use of technology. The new electronic courtroom, or e-courtroom, uses interactive screen displays, webcast testimony, comparison screens, and personal jury screens.[553] Though some attorneys are hesitant to implement technology into trials, polls show that between 72–100% of jurors prefer the incorporation of technology if the attorneys knew how to operate the digital platforms and were knowledgeable in how to retrieve the digital evidence.

CONCLUSION

God provides mankind with laws and commandments in the Bible so that they recognize what constitutes sin in the eyes of a righteous, holy God. The laws of God are not restricting and stifling but give freedom and liberation from sin. Paul describes the law of God in Romans 7:12, "So the law is holy, and the commandment is holy and righteous and good." God's commands are always the ultimate authority, and He calls on Christians to respect the authority placed over them (Romans 13:1–2). Christians must use biblical discernment when considering man's law and how to apply these in accordance with the Scriptures. And though man's judicial system is not perfect, consider the alternative: the absence of man's law, resulting in anarchy, sin, and depravity.

> **Romans 13:1–2:**
> "Let every person be subject to the governing authorities. For there is no authority except from God, and those that exist have been instituted by God. Therefore whoever resists the authorities resists what God has appointed, and those who resist will incur judgment."

Lesson 33
Chain of Custody

He has told you, O man, what is good; and what does the L<small>ORD</small> require of you but to do justice, and to love kindness, and to walk humbly with your God? (Micah 6:8).

Case Study: Fruit of the Poisonous Tree Doctrine

What happens when police enter a home or business without a search warrant and illegally seize evidence? What if that evidence clearly shows proof of guilt? Should the prosecution still be permitted to use it? These are all important questions about the 4th Amendment that courts have wrestled with over the years. The 4th Amendment to the Constitution states, "The right of the people to be secure in their persons, houses, papers, and effects, against unreasonable searches and seizures, shall not be violated, and no warrants shall issue, but upon probable cause, supported by oath or affirmation, and particularly describing the place to be searched, and the persons or things to be seized."[554] This issue was ultimately resolved by *Silverthorne Lumber Co. v. United States* on January 26, 1920.

Fred Silverthorne and his son owned Silverthorne Lumber Co. Due to a series of tips, the federal authorities became alerted to the fact that Silverthorne was not paying his federal taxes. Federal agents detained the father and son for a few hours on February 25, 1919, while they searched their business. Federal agents arrived at their offices without a warrant and proceeded with an illegal search and seizure of their personal files.[555] The agents found the files they were looking for, proof that Silverthorne was not paying his taxes. Once the agents had the files, they released Silverthorne. Silverthorne then petitioned the courts for the return of the illegally seized files.

The district attorney assigned to the case objected to the request. Upon examination of the files, more evidence for additional crimes had been discovered, but the district court ordered the return of the files to Silverthorne. The government made photocopies of all the files before returning them to Silverthorne, but these were impounded by the district court. The district attorney used information he had gleaned from the illegally seized photocopied documents to issue a subpoena to have the original documents returned for examination. Silverthorne refused and was arrested for contempt of court.[556] Even though the district court recognized that the files were illegally seized, they ordered Silverthorne to comply with the subpoenas for the original files. Silverthorne filed a writ of error, stating that the charge should be reversed and the case be reviewed for errors.

The case was appealed and found its way to the Supreme Court. The United States Supreme Court reversed the decision of the lower courts. Fred Silverthorne was released from prison and all charges against him were dropped.

The doctrine of the exclusionary rule, evidence is inadmissible if illegally obtained, was the result of this case and came to be known as the "fruit of the poisonous tree"

doctrine. This phrase was based on verbiage used by Justice Frankfurter on a similar case in 1939, *Nardone v. United States*. The fruit of the poisonous tree doctrine is similar in thought to the biblical account of Adam's sin. When Adam and Eve disobeyed God and ate of the forbidden tree in the Garden of Eden, they brought sin and death to all humans. One man sinned; therefore, death came through sin, and death came to all people because all have sinned (Romans 5:12). Fundamentally, if the tree is tainted, so is the fruit.

"No man burdens his mind with small matters unless he has some very good reason for doing so." — Sherlock Holmes[557]

Chain of custody is defined as the movement, location, and ownership of physical evidence from the time it is obtained at the crime scene until the time it is presented in court.[558] This is also referred to as the continuity of possession. Maintaining an accurate, documented record of chain of custody is the most critical part of evidence. When evidence is submitted to the court, there must be assurance that it is the original evidence that was seized at the crime scene, examined by investigators, and analyzed in the lab. Maintaining chain of custody is an ethical responsibility of all those involved in the handling of the evidence.

The chain of custody provides the names of every single person who had contact with the evidence. This includes officers, investigators, transport personnel, lab technicians, etc. The chain of custody provides a detailed list of all the names of the people who handled the evidence. This is valuable in case any one of them should be needed to testify in court on behalf of the evidence. There is no limit on the number of people who can be included on the chain of custody, but if possible, it should always be kept to a minimum. The more people with hands on the evidence, the greater the likelihood of error or contamination. Liability falls on every single person on the chain of custody, and it is up to the prosecution to verify its integrity. Therefore, the defense team will often look for holes in the chain of custody. By identifying discrepancies in the chain of custody, they hope to cast doubt on the validity of the evidence or have it deemed inadmissible. Remember the fruit of the poisonous tree doctrine? If at any time there is a breach in the chain of custody, all information and analysis received after that point is subject to inadmissibility.

One of the most famous examples of a mishandling of the chain of custody was in the O.J. Simpson trial. The defense team was able to show that the blood samples collected at the crime scene had been passed through multiple officers for varying lengths of time without being recorded on the chain of custody. One blood sample was stored in the trunk of a detective's car overnight. This failure on the part of the police allowed the defense to cast doubt on the integrity of the evidence and the police department's procedures. It also allowed the defense to plant the idea that police wanted to frame Simpson for the murders of Nicole Brown Simpson and Ron Goldman.

WHY IS CHAIN OF CUSTODY IMPORTANT?

There are several reasons why chain of custody is so crucial, but most importantly, chain of custody gives the evidence integrity during the trial. The goal is to ensure that guilty parties are not set free on a technicality, such as evidence being deemed inadmissible due to a break in chain of custody. The sequential record of individuals who handled the evidence is important to ensure that conscientious care was used when handling the evidence. It also ensures that evidence was not planted to give the appearance of a person's guilt. The detailed documentation provides transparency. Transparency makes it clear who has handled the evidence and that no unauthorized, latent examination or tampering was conducted on the evidence. This procedure also helps to deter officers or lab technicians from tainting and misplacing the evidence. Chain of custody is also used in other areas outside of crime scene work:

- Drug testing of athletes
- Chemical testing of foods
- Research on animals
- Clinical trials of new drugs and vaccines
- Proof of authenticity for artwork, antiques, jewelry, coins, etc.
- Package tracking through shipping companies
- Lethal injection procedures

ACCOUNTABILITY FROM A BIBLICAL WORLDVIEW

The players in the criminal justice system (police, attorneys, judges, etc.) are accountable to one another in the pursuit of justice. Just as they may each be called to testify to their actions in a court of law, so will Christians be called to testify to their actions on earth. God is a God of justice, and Christians should strive to always maintain their accountability and integrity.

What is accountability according to God's perfect Word? Accountability is an individual being able to explain their actions with honesty and integrity. Romans 14:12 says, "So then each of us will give an account of himself to God." On the day of judgment, every person will stand before the righteous Judge, Jesus Christ, and be held accountable for their actions. They will give a testimony of what they did for Christ and will answer for their sins. Only through a personal relationship with Christ will a person be spared from eternal suffering in hell. Second Corinthians 5:10 tells us, "For we must all appear before the judgement seat of Christ, so that each one may receive what is due for what he has done in the body, whether good or evil."

The culture today is self-absorbed and focused on self-fulfillment. They do not want to be held accountable to anyone, especially a God who demands justice. But even when humans deny accountability to God, they are still held accountable to and for something, and often this limits their freedom rather than giving them true freedom. True freedom is not the right to do whatever one chooses. Freedom is the ability to do what is right according to the laws and standards of truth found only in God's Word. True freedom is discussed further in this excerpt from an article titled *Accountability* on Bible.org:

> Many see freedom as the right to abandon accountability to God and men in order to do what they please in the promotion of self-gratification. But that is not freedom. It is slavery, or at least leads to slavery. Speaking of false teachers who either twist Scripture to their own self-centered objectives or deny its authority altogether, Peter writes, "…promising them freedom while they themselves are slaves of corruption; for by what a man is overcome, by this he is enslaved" (2 Pet. 2:19). Beliefs or one's world view always has consequences. It is like a train which is free to do what it was created to do as long as it is on its track.
>
> Accountability is one of the means God uses to bring about solid growth and maturity with the freedom to be what God has created us for.[559]

CHAIN OF CUSTODY DOCUMENTATION

Proper chain of custody requires many details. The below list is not all inclusive, but it does highlight some of the information on a chain of custody document:[560]

- Detailed information about the evidence collection, including addresses, lab analysis required, and other relevant facts.
- Some form of unique identifier or identification number.
- Authorization to analyze the evidence.
- Sequential order of people who handled the evidence including their name, date, and signature.
- Any periods of guardianship of the evidence.
- Environmental conditions of handling and storing the evidence.
- The method of delivery between every individual.

Evidence is sealed by the crime scene technician at the location of the crime. When evidence is received by an examiner in the lab, they will open the evidence for examination on a non-sealed edge, examine the items, place everything back into the original bag, seal with new evidence tape, and sign across the new seal and sign the evidence log. Sometimes, depending on the evidence, the evidence bag may simply be resealed and signed. The evidence log is a checkout list, like a library checkout system, where the clerk at the lab or police department records every person who has "checked out" the evidence for examination. The chain of custody should reflect the same order of names, dates, and times as the evidence log.

CHAIN OF CUSTODY

Received from: _____
Received by: _____
Date: _____ Time: _____ am/pm

Received from: _____
Received by: _____
Date: _____ Time: _____ am/pm

Received from: _____
Received by: _____
Date: _____ Time: _____ am/pm

Received from: _____
Received by: _____
Date: _____ Time: _____ am/pm

WHAT IS CUSTODY?

Custody is when "a sample . . . is in actual physical possession of the authorized custodian in a secured place without access to unauthorized personnel or any opportunity for tampering."[561] The key is authorized person. No one should have access to evidence who has not been authorized to do so. Unauthorized handling of evidence is grounds to have the evidence ruled inadmissible in court. Below is an example of a chain of custody:

Crime scene investigator Smith collects a single hair from a crime scene. Smith packages the hair, seals the hair, fills out the relevant information on the evidence label, signs the seal, and begins the chain of custody and attaches it to the evidence. When Smith returns to headquarters, he delivers the evidence to the trace analyst expert, Officer Jones. Jones signs the chain of custody, examines the evidence under the microscope, records all relevant information, reseals the evidence, and turns it in to a clerk at the evidence collection unit named Julie. Julie accepts the evidence, signs the chain of custody, creates an evidence log, and then stores the evidence in a secure location until it is needed for court. If an attorney then requests to review the evidence, Julie will add his or her name to the evidence log, and the attorney would fill out the chain of custody information.

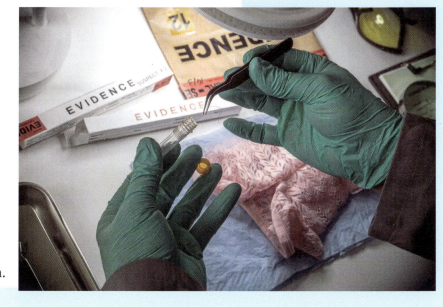

TESTIMONY FOR CHAIN OF CUSTODY

Those involved in a case may be called to testify to the integrity of the evidence and chain of custody. The defense will challenge these individuals to their handling of the evidence. It is very important that the chain of custody be clear, concise, well documented, and complete. This leaves little room for the defense team to make accusations of tainted evidence or the inappropriate handling of evidence. Testimony includes three types:

1. Testimony that the evidence in the evidence bag is what is identified on the chain of custody.

2. Testimony to the continuous possession of evidence in the exact sequence on the chain of custody from the crime scene to the court room.

3. Testimony from each person who handled the evidence that the evidence remained in the same condition through an unbroken chain of custody.

EXCEPTIONS TO CHAIN OF CUSTODY

There are exceptions to the chain of custody requirement. Sometimes, depending on where the chain is broken, the court will permit the evidence in court. If the owner of the property identifies their own evidence, then proving the integrity of chain of custody may not be necessary.[562] Also, if the evidence is inscribed with the crime scene officer's initials, chain of custody discrepancies may be overlooked or deemed unnecessary. Chain of custody integrity may be waived for items with a serial number, like a handgun. One other area where chain of custody is not as important is in unique, one-of-a-kind evidence. Imagine a ransom note written in rainbow-colored markers. This would be unique enough to distinguish itself from tampering, etc. Fundamentally, the value of the evidence is the primary determining factor in chain of custody violations, and the trial judge will decide on its admissibility.

CONCLUSION

Integrity in the chain of custody should be maintained at all times to ensure legal acceptance in court. A break in the chain of custody often results in a motion to suppress evidence. The loss of evidence in a criminal trial can be detrimental to the prosecution, defense, and, most importantly, the victim. Forensic personnel have a great responsibility to follow rules of procedure so that justice is served in each and every case, and chain of custody is just one piece in the puzzle of civil and criminal cases.

Lesson 34
Courtroom Testimony

Does our law judge a man without first giving him a hearing and learning what he does? (John 7:51).

Case Study: Courtroom Testimony – Too Funny to Be True

Lawyers will often ask nonsensical questions during a trial. In addition, the witnesses are often literal in their answers. The courtroom can become a circus at times. Below are excerpts from actual court room testimony.

Testimony of Abbie Hoffman:[563] Hoffman was charged with conspiring to use interstate commerce to incite a riot under the Civil Rights Act of 1968. He was also one of the proponents of the flower power movement in the 1960s and 1970s.

Mr. Weinglass: Where do you reside?

Witness: I live in Woodstock Nation.

Mr. Weinglass: Will you tell the Court and jury where it is?

Witness: Yes. It is a nation of alienated young people. We carry it around with us as a state of mind in the same way as the Sioux Indians carried the Sioux nation around with them. . . . It is a nation dedicated to—

The Court: Just where it is, that is all.

Witness: It is in my mind and in the minds of my brothers and sisters. It does not consist of property or material but, rather, of ideas and certain values. We believe in a society—

The Court: No, we want the place of residence, if he has one, place of doing business, if you have a business. Nothing about philosophy or India, sir. Just where you live if you have a place to live. Now you said Woodstock. In what state is Woodstock?

Witness: It is in the state of mind, in the mind of myself and my brothers and sisters. It is a conspiracy. Presently, the nation is held captive, in the penitentiaries of the institutions of a decaying system.

Mr. Weinglass: Can you tell the Court and jury your present age?

Witness: My age is 33. I am a child of the 60s.

Mr. Weinglass: When were you born?

Witness: Psychologically, 1960.

Mr. Weinglass: What is the actual date of your birth?

Witness: November 30, 1936.

Below are a series of questions by an attorney (Q) and answers of a witness (A) on the witness stand. These were recorded by court reporters during trials.

Q. Now, Mrs. Johnson, how was your first marriage terminated?
A. By death.
Q. And by whose death was it terminated?

Q. Mrs. Thomas, do you believe that you are emotionally unstable?
A. I should be.
Q. How many times have you committed suicide?
A. Four times.

Q. Doctor, how many autopsies have you performed on dead people?
A. All my autopsies have been performed on dead people.

Q. Were you acquainted with the deceased?
A. Yes, sir.
Q. Before or after he died?

Q. What happened then?
A. He told me, he says, "I have to kill you because you can identify me."
Q. Did he kill you?
A. No.

Q. What is your relationship with the plaintiff?
A. She is my daughter.
Q. Was she your daughter on date of the incident?

Q. What can you tell us about the truthfulness and veracity of this defendant?
A. Oh, she will tell the truth. She said she'd kill that idiot — and she did!

Q. Do you have any suggestions as to what prevented this from being a murder trial instead of an attempted murder trial?
A. The victim lived.[564]

Q: How fast was the car coming toward you?
A: I am not a thermometer, so I can't tell you the speed limit.

And finally . . .

Q: Are you a witness, victim, or defendant?
A: I'm the guy who did it.[565]

Appearance, demeanor, and articulation are all key factors when a person provides testimony in the court of law. How professional an individual is dressed will be reflected in the acceptance of their testimony by the jury and judge. This applies to the attorneys as well. Each character in the court room setting directly influences the outcome with these basic, controllable factors.

" 'Well, and there is the end of our little drama,' I remarked, after we had sat some time . . . in silence. 'I fear that it may be the last investigation in which I shall have the chance of studying your methods.' " — Dr. Watson to Sherlock Holmes[566]

Fundamentally, there are two types of evidence, eyewitness testimony and physical evidence. The impact of a truthful eyewitness courtroom testimony in a criminal trial is undisputed and is often the determining factor in convictions. Courtroom testimony is oral evidence given under oath by a witness. The oral evidence is sworn to be truthful, factual, and accurate to the best of the witness' ability. Oral evidence includes courtroom testimony, answers to questions by attorneys, and depositions. Depositions are sworn out-of-court testimony given prior to trial but are still provided under oath with a court reporter.

Since very few cases go to trial, forensic experts and police officers may not be comfortable in court. As with any type of skill, training is required to be successful and includes how to testify under pressure in the courtroom. Every person testifying in court should keep in mind that every word they speak is being recorded. If the case should ever be appealed to a higher court, their testimony transcript will be reviewed and is the only evidence the appellate court will be privy to.

A CHRISTIAN'S TESTIMONY

The Greek root for testimony is *martyria*, or witness. The Greek verb *martyreo* means to bear witness or to testify. This is where the word martyr originates. A martyr is a person who bears witness of the truth and suffers death in the cause of Christ. The New Testament in the Bible speaks on martyrs as witnesses for Christ. The first martyr for Christ mentioned in the Bible was Stephen. Acts 22:19–20 records his death: "And I said, 'Lord, they themselves know that in one synagogue after another I imprisoned and beat those who believed in you. And when the blood of Stephen your witness was being shed, I myself was standing by and approving and watching over the garments of those who killed him.'" The book of Revelation describes martyrs for Christ, as in Revelation 17:6, "And I saw the woman, drunk with the blood of the saints, the blood of the *martyrs* of Jesus. When I saw her, I marveled greatly" (emphasis added). It is very clear that God expects Christians to be a living testimony to the truth of His existence, the truth of His Word, and the truth of salvation only through Christ, even when their testimony results in their persecution and death.

A Christian's testimony is powerful and personal. A testimony is observable in lifestyle, words, and actions. A testimony must also be shared and made public. Luke 8:39 says, " 'Return to your home, and declare how much God has done for you.' And he went away, proclaiming throughout the whole city how much Jesus had done for him." It is impossible to reveal personal experiences with Christ if a person is not telling others. Christians are to testify to things they have seen and things that they know. Luke 24:48 tells us, "You are witnesses of these things" (see also Acts 1:8, 22; Romans 1:9; and others). The Great Commission in Matthew 28:16–20 commands Christians to share their testimonies with the entire world. A testimony should also be truthful (Ephesians 4:25). "Lying lips are an abomination to the Lord" (Proverbs 12:22a). A truthful testimony not only applies to our relationship with Christ, but also to testimony about accounts in our personal relationships and within the judicial system.

The Bible also provides guidelines for the judicial system. God loves justice (Isaiah 61:8), and He demands order (1 Corinthians 14:40) and punishment for crimes (Colossians 3:25). The Bible explains that testimony should only be taken as credible when given by two or three witnesses, never just one. Matthew 18:16 says, "But if he does not listen, take one or two others along with you, that every charge may be established by the evidence of two or three witnesses." Additionally, Hebrews 10:28 says, "Anyone who has set aside the law of Moses dies without mercy on the evidence of two or three witnesses." God recognizes that humans are sinful and flawed. Their eyewitness account is not always accurate, but when two or three people testify to the same incident, there is credibility in the accusation. This is the reason that attorneys will call more than one witness if possible. Christians are fortunate that on the day of judgment (2 Corinthians 5:10), they will not need two to three witnesses to testify to their relationship with Christ; the only perfect eyewitness, Jesus Christ (Revelation 1:5), will testify on their behalf (1 Timothy 2:5–7) to their salvation and right to enter heaven (John 14:6).

John 14:6:

"Jesus said to him, 'I am the way, and the truth, and the life. No one comes to the Father except through me.'"

TYPES OF TESTIMONY

There are three types of witnesses in courtroom testimony: the eyewitness (lay witness), character witness, and the expert witness. The eyewitness is the person who saw the event or crime for which the trial is for. The eyewitness may have experienced one or all the following factors to be considered an eyewitness to the crime: seeing, hearing, smelling, touching, etc. Can a vision-impaired person be an eyewitness? Absolutely — hearing voices and sounds or touching someone's face or clothes are all factors considered eyewitness testimony.

Problems with Eyewitness Testimony. At the turn of the 20th century, a book titled *On the Witness Stand* was written by Hugo Munsterberg. Munsterberg was a pioneer in criminal psychology. His book began to identify the unreliability of eyewitness testimony.[567] Multiple research studies since the 1960s have shown that eyewitness identification and recollection is unreliable. Humans are sinful, flawed, and imperfect, and their memory changes over time. For example, five observers to a hit-and-run accident will each give a different account to the color of the car, make and model of the car, the driver of the car, etc. The fallibility of eyewitness identification was not really brought to light until scientists had the ability to create profiles from DNA evidence. In 1989, the first DNA exoneration occurred. As of 2021, there have been 375 DNA exonerations. Of these 375 exonerations, 69% involved eyewitness identification.[568] Of the 375 wrongly convicted individuals, law enforcement has been able to imprison 165 of the actual assailants. To reduce the number of misidentifications by eyewitnesses, police have been recommended new procedures that have proven effective, especially when using a lineup.[569]

1. Only one suspect should be in each lineup, even if there are multiple suspects.
2. The lineup should be double-blind, meaning neither the eyewitness nor the officer should know who the suspect is.
3. The "fillers," other people in the lineup, should be of the same age, ethnicity, gender, height, etc.
4. Standard instructions should be given to the witness with no hint of bias by law enforcement.

Since human eyewitness testimony has been shown to be fallible, there are some that would claim the Bible cannot be trusted since it was written by humans. To address this point, one can only go to the Word of God, which is divinely self-authenticating. The Bible states:

- Jesus Christ is truth (John 14:6).
- Jesus Christ is the only source of truth (John 17:17).
- Jesus Christ cannot lie (Titus 1:2).
- All Scripture is God-breathed (2 Timothy 3:16).
- God's Word is the judge of truth (John 12:48).
- And truth only exists in Him (Colossians 2:3).
- Any other standard for truth is "empty" (Colossians 2:8).

The Bible is the only book to claim that it is the ultimate authority. When people try to discredit the authenticity of God's Word, they are simply suppressing the truth in unrighteousness (Romans 1:18–21).

The character witness is a person who testifies on behalf of the defendant's morality, character, work ethic, reputation, and any other personal information the attorney feels would be beneficial for their client. There are times when a character witness is inadmissible. If the witness' character is questionable, they may have been involved in the crime, or if their testimony would impeach or confirm the truthfulness of a witness, then it is unlikely a person will be called as a character witness.

The expert witness is defined as a person who is specialized in a field, often technical, who presents their expert opinion without having been a witness to the crime. The expert witness is an exception to normal court proceedings. An eyewitness or character witness is not permitted to provide their opinion, unless directed, when under oath. An expert witness is deemed credible by the court and will be required to testify to their credentials and expertise in the field.

THE COURTHOUSE

The courthouse is the heart of the judicial system. A witness should become familiar with the layout of the courthouse where they will be testifying. It is good practice to either arrive early on the day of the trial or visit the courthouse on a day before the scheduled testimony. Being proactive to learn the layout of the courthouse will reduce stress on the day of the trial. The first step when arriving on the day of the trial is to locate the witness room, or the area where the witnesses are expected to wait until called to testify. Depending on the courthouse, this could be anything from a plush waiting room to a wooden bench outside the courtroom. When in the witness room, the witness should not discuss the case with any of the other witnesses waiting to testify. Some of them may be eyewitnesses, character witnesses, or expert witnesses, and it is unethical for them to discuss the case or share information.

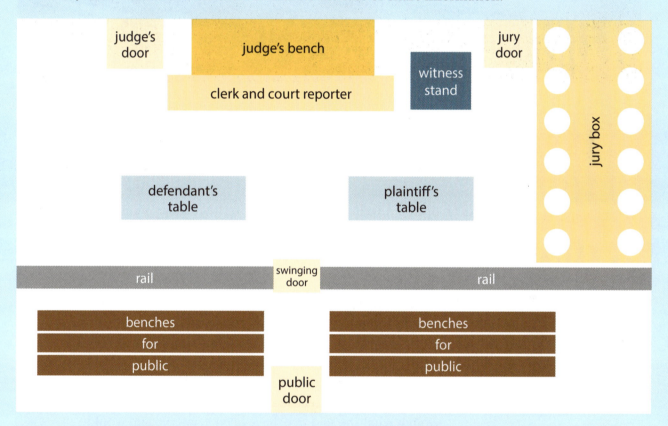

When a witness is called to the stand, they will enter the courtroom from the direction of the witness room. As they walk into the courtroom, this is the first time the jury will see this individual. First impressions are very important at this stage. The witness is sworn in before being seated. It is good practice to fully extend the right hand straight over the Bible (if one is provided) with the palm clearly open and keep the left elbow at a perfect 90 degrees. This gives the appearance of confidence and professionalism. The witness will be asked to swear to the following statement: Do you swear or affirm that the evidence you are about to give will be the truth, the whole truth, and nothing but the truth?

Once the witness is sworn in, they are seated in the witness box. The next section will discuss techniques that should be utilized by each type of witness.

COURTROOM TESTIMONY

Telling the truth is not always enough for a witness in the courtroom. Their demeanor, appearance, and behavior all contribute to their credibility as a witness. Ron Smith, a well-known scientist in the forensic community who has testified in over 500 trials, has conducted numerous seminars and training classes for forensic and police personnel on courtroom testimony. Here is an example he provides on why simply telling the truth is not always enough:

> The best example I can personally recall of this phenomenon was during an armed robbery trial when an eyewitness to the crime was asked under cross-examination, "It was very dark. How is it possible that you can be so sure that the armed man you saw was my client?" The witness dropped her eyes and head and said, "Because I got a good look at him." Even though what she said may have been very true and would have appeared favorably . . . it certainly was not convincing to the jury at all. Just the fact that the witness looked down and away from anyone when she replied, gave the impression that she was not sure. The truth must be presented in a convincing manner for it to be unequivocally believed. This is the responsibility of the witness. Learning how to do this properly is a very important part of becoming a good witness.[570]

There are researched, effective techniques for people who are called to testify. These techniques will vary depending on the type of witness.

EYEWITNESS TESTIMONY

1. Dress professionally. A witness is expected to be clean, groomed, and dressed appropriately. When a person dresses appropriately, they are visually acknowledging the importance of their appearance in court.

2. Behave respectfully. A witness should only speak when directed to do so and should not speak out of turn. This also includes not speaking over the judge or counsel.

3. Tell the truth. A witness should state the facts and not give an opinion. Answer only what you are directed to answer and do not provide additional facts or unrelated information. It is acceptable to pause before answers or ask counsel to rephrase the question. A witness may also restate testimony if there is a reason for the mistake.

4. Be calm. This is one of the most challenging areas for a witness. The attorneys will purposely push witnesses with questions to make them lose their cool. It is important that a witness retain their composure to uphold the integrity of their testimony.

5. Practice good etiquette. A witness' testimony does not end in the courtroom. Media coverage surrounding the case, how a witness behaves, and the information shared outside the courtroom can all have a direct impact on the case. The witness should hold their comments until the case is resolved.[571]

CHARACTER WITNESS TESTIMONY

For a character witness to be successful, they will be expected to adhere to all the testifying techniques that an eyewitness incorporates, but with one addition. They will need to control their emotions. Controlling emotional outbursts is the number one reaction that discredits character witnesses. Since character witnesses know the defendant on a personal level, there are deep feelings, connections, and emotions that are difficult to suppress. In preparation for court, it is common practice for the character witness to participate in practice sessions or online training courses on proper testimony practices.

EXPERT TESTIMONY: THE POLICE OFFICER

1. Remember position and involvement in the case. If an officer is called to testify, it is likely the defendant is claiming innocence. The defense attorney will strive to discredit the officer.

2. Assume the jury is skeptical. There are many people biased toward the police. An officer needs to consider this skepticism when testifying.

3. Study the case prior to trial. It is important that the officer appear knowledgeable and factual about the case, as well as unbiased toward the defendant.

4. Be professional. An officer should know their specific duties, responsibilities, and expectations as outlined in the police handbook. Above all, they should remain calm and collected during testimony.

5. Be concise and to the point. An officer should listen to each question carefully, think before speaking, be accurate, and be brief. Brevity leaves little room for error and reduces the opportunity for the defense to find inconsistencies.

6. Engage with the jury. When an officer answers direct questions, they should always speak to the jury and connect with their eyes. This gives veracity to the testimony and makes it clear the information is truthful. Speak on simple terms so that they can understand.[572]

EXPERT TESTIMONY: THE FORENSICS EXPERT

Areas Requesting Expert Testimony.[573] It is not just during the trial that an expert witness may be called to testify. During the trial process, testimony may be requested in each of these areas:

- *Preliminary hearing (probable cause hearing):* The defense counsel is permitted to cross-examine witnesses against the defendant. During this hearing there is no jury present and testimony is given to the judge. An expert witness is expected to be knowledgeable and well prepared for this hearing.

- *Grand jury:* A grand jury is 12 to 23 jurors chosen from the community. A grand jury will hear the evidence presented by the state and indict an individual if they feel there is enough probable cause. The evidence may include expert witnesses called by the prosecution. Though there is no cross-examination by the defense counsel, the grand jury is permitted to question the expert witness.

- *Motions:* There are two motions the defense counsel files that will require expert testimony: 1) The motion to suppress evidence and 2) The motion to suppress a confession. These hearings are in front of a judge only, but they typically require lengthy testimony from an expert witness. Due to the critical nature of these motions for the defense, the expert testimony can be grueling.

- *Trial:* The expert witness testifies to their observations and analysis for direct evidence or expert opinion.

- *Sentencing hearing:* Expert testimony at a sentencing hearing will vary depending on the state where the trial is held. In severe cases involving capital punishment, expert testimony may be required in front of the jury.

Juries are disengaged with an expert witness if they do not make eye contact, belittle the jury's intelligence by talking down to them, are disrespectful to the courtroom players, use improper speech, have poor posture, and are not prepared. For these reasons, forensic experts need training in public speaking. Agencies will often role-play courtroom testimony to ensure the witness is confident and poised in their testimonial delivery prior to trial.

Techniques for the expert witness include:

1. Request clarification, but not too much. It is perfectly acceptable to ask the prosecution or defense counsel to restate the question, but if this becomes a frequent occurrence, the witness will lose credibility with the jury.

2. Exercise moderate use of the hands. It is okay to use the hands for simple descriptions or measurements, but the hands should not be flailing around as to distract the jury. As much as possible, the hands of the witness should be folded in the lap in a relaxed manner.

3. Lean slightly toward the jury. The posture of the expert witness speaks volumes. A witness should lean slightly toward the jury to give the impression they are engaging them in the conversation. This also allows for easy eye contact with the attorneys and the jury.

4. Organize the case file. An expert witness should have a well-organized, bound file for their results and analysis. A witness should always ask permission to refer to their notes. This demonstrates respect for the courtroom proceedings.

5. Stop talking when it's time. The greatest error committed by expert witnesses is providing too much information. If a witness misspeaks, it is expected they correct themselves by explaining the reason for the correction.

6. Acknowledge limitations. An expert witness should always acknowledge when they do not know something or are not trained in a certain area. This reflects integrity in their testimony and gives them credibility.

7. Be concise and clear. Using technical terminology or phraseology is not recommended. It is far better to use terms the jury can understand. Also, be clear in the delivery of the information by enunciating when appropriate with a good voice volume for the jury. The witness should be enjoyable, not painful, to listen to.

8. Have familiarity with the evidence. A witness needs to be familiar with the evidence they worked on. The appearance of the evidence in court may be different than when originally submitted due to storing and securing of the evidence.

9. Know when to approach the jury. There are times when the witness will be called to show an evidence display to the jury. They may only do so with permission of the judge. The witness must ask permission before leaving the jury stand.

CONCLUSION

Each type of witness plays a key role in the search for justice in the criminal justice system. Eyewitness testimony is valued by juror members and considered reliable. The witness should prepare for the trial, dress appropriately, and remain calm throughout the trial process. Witnessing a crime can be a traumatic event for people. For this reason, it is important that an eyewitness be interviewed swiftly while the facts are still clear in their minds. The longer the time between the crime and the interview, the more skewed the descriptions and details. Witness testimony degrades when there is a long period of time, when children are involved, when the event is extremely stressful, and when attempting to identify an individual's ethnicity than that of the witness. The expert witness is held to a higher standard than the eyewitness. The term "expert" implies expectation by the jury. The expert should be prepared to offer a knowledgeable, professional opinion regarding the evidence examined with integrity and with truth.

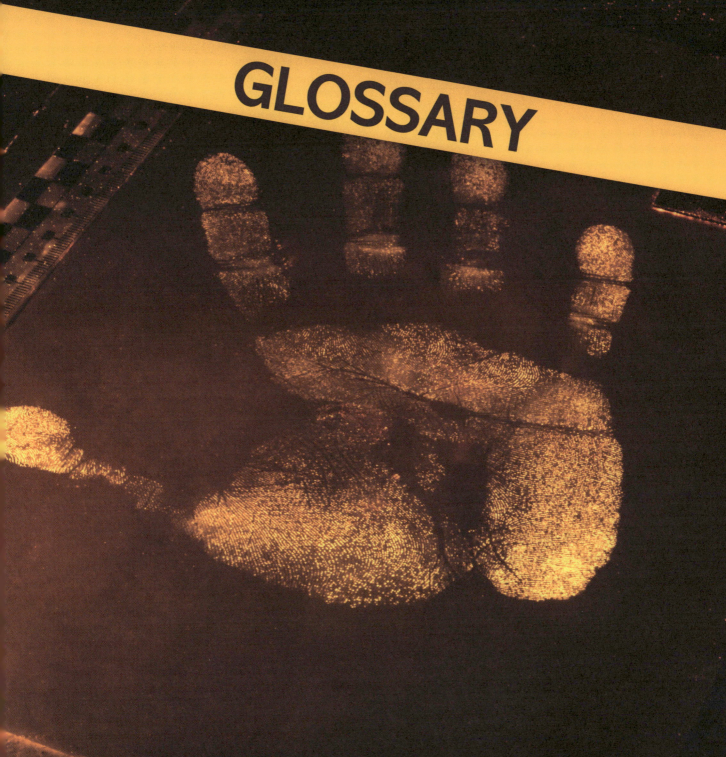

GLOSSARY

1,8-Diazafluoren-9-one (DFO) – reacts with the amino acids present in fingerprint oils and is often used in conjunction with ninhydrin. DFO is effective on porous surfaces and results in reddish-pink prints. DFO is applied by spraying, dipping, or brushing. The evidence is then allowed to dry before heating in a low-humidity oven to facilitate development of latent prints.

4R Rule – the foundational principle in glass analysis that reads: Ridges on Radial cracks are at Right angles to the Reverse side of impact.

ABAcard® HemaTrace® – used to detect the hemoglobin in blood. Antibodies in the test strip react with the hemoglobin in the blood sample. A pink dye band in the window of the device is a positive result. The result only provides a positive result to blood and not the origin of the blood.

Accelerant Detection Canines (ACDs) – trained dogs often used to search for the point of origin.

Accidental whorl – a subdivision of the whorl fingerprint pattern; a combination of two different pattern types, with exception of the plain arch, containing two or more deltas or a pattern that does not meet any of the other conditions.

Accumulated Degree Hour (ADH) – the heat units calculated by multiplying the environmental temperature by the number of hours in a day. The formula for ADH is: temperature x 24 hours/day = heat units.

Acid Phosphatase Test – also called the Walker Test; detects the presence of an enzyme called acid phosphatase (AP) produced by the male prostate gland. A positive result for semen will turn the sample a dark purple color in less than one minute.

Acquit – to find not guilty in a criminal offense.

Active decay – also called butyric fermentation; a stage of decomposition where all the fluids in the body seep into the surrounding ground surface where the body is lying. The odor is very strong, and insects continue to break down the body tissues and begin to pupate in the surrounding soil. Active decay occurs 10–25 days after death.

Adenosine triphosphate (ATP) – the substance that allows energy to flow to the muscles for them to function.

Alford plea – plea that states the defendant does not admit to guilt but acknowledges the state has enough evidence to convict, or the defendant does not want to endure a new trial.

Alginate – a salt of alginic acid, which is also used in making dental impressions.[574]

Alternate light source (ALS) – use visible, UV, or infrared light to cause biological material to glow (fluoresce) or darken. An ALS device is equipped with the ability to change the wavelength of light to react with different types of fluids.

Amino acid – the basic unit of proteins.

Amorphousness – the regions of air space in a fiber in between the crystalline scaffolding where no polymer chains are present.

Amplification – the process of copying specific DNA sequences using polymerase chain reaction (PCR).

Anthropology – the study of man. The three types of anthropology are cultural, physical, and linguistic.

Anthropometry – also known as the Bertillon identification system; one of the first systems of classification based on body measurements.

Anticoagulant – drugs that prevent blood coagulation (clotting).

Anti-Forensic (AF) tools – have the ability to erase and alter information, create "chaff" that hides information, plant fake evidence, and leave tracer data that prevents computer forensic software from revealing hacker information.

Apocrine glands – sweat glands found primarily in areas where there is hair: on the scalp, armpit, and genital regions of humans. These glands secrete a fatty sweat on a continual basis.

Arch – a fingerprint classification characterized by not having a delta or core. The ridges in an arch enter one side and flow out the other side.

Area of convergence (three-dimensional space) – the area in which the victim or suspect was present when the blood spatter stain was produced.

Area of convergence (two-dimensional plane) – the point at which the drops of blood in an impact pattern originated.

Arson – the willful or malicious intent to burn property. There are four classifications for arson: aggravated arson, simple arson, attempted arson, and setting negligent fires.

Asphyxiation – suffocation; unconsciousness or death caused by a lack of oxygen.

Autolysis – a stage of decomposition that begins immediately after death and is a form of cellular self-digestion.

Autopsy – a thorough examination of a corpse through the dissection process. Also, a mobile forensic tool that is an Android support platform with the capability to extract a wide variety of mobile data.

Becke line – a halo effect around the edge of a piece of glass that results when the refractive index of a glass is different than the refractive index of a known oil.

Beyond a reasonable doubt – the legal standard of proof required by the prosecution in criminal cases. This means a juror should be 98–99% sure of the defendant's guilt based on the case presented by the prosecution.

Binder – a resin dissolved in solvent that allows the pigment to adhere to a surface.

Biometrics – a system of body measurements and calculations related to human characteristics for identification.

Birefringence – double refraction; the refraction of light in an anisotropic (e.g., soils) material in two different directions to form two rays of light.

Bite mark – "the physical end product of a complex set of events that occur when human or animal teeth are applied to the skin or foodstuff."[575]

Bloat – a stage of decomposition; the result of the cellular digestion occurring during autolysis. The gases created from autolysis cause the body to double in size.

Blood spatter analysis – the field of forensic examination that deals with the physical properties of blood and the shapes, locations, and distribution patterns of bloodstains.

Bridge – a permanent fixture that replaces missing teeth by attaching to adjacent teeth.

Burden of proof – the obligation of the accusing party to prove their claims in criminal cases beyond a reasonable doubt.

Caliber – the diameter of the bullet or barrel of a gun in 100ths of an inch or in millimeters.

Capillary electrophoresis – performed in a capillary tube with a polymer liquid or a gel.

Carrion – decaying flesh.

Cast – the result of filling a three-dimensional impression with an appropriate material. Types of casting material include dental stone, sulfur, and others.

Casting compounds – putty-like substances that enable casting on horizontal and vertical surfaces (metal, wood, plastic, and paper). The cast creates an exact, detailed mirror image of the impression.

Cementum – a calcified substance that surrounds the root of a tooth and connects the periodontal ligament that holds the tooth in the jaw.

Central pocket loop whorl – a subdivision of the whorl fingerprint pattern; contains two deltas and at least one ridge, making a complete circuit. When an imaginary line is drawn between the two deltas, no recurring ridges must touch the line.

Chaff – worthless information designed to lead an investigation awry.

Chain of custody – also called continuity of possession; the movement, location, and ownership of physical evidence from the time it is obtained at the crime scene until the time it is presented in court.[576] It provides a documented, chronological record of those individuals who have interacted with each piece of evidence from the moment of collection, through analysis, and into the courtroom.

Character witness – a person who testifies on behalf of the defendant's morality, character, work ethic, reputation, and any other personal information the attorney feels would be beneficial for their client.

Chromatography – a method of chemical analysis that separates mixtures into their components.

Civil law – generally, any law that is not criminal law. Civil law is tasked with providing compensation, often monetary, for people injured by someone else.

Civil trial – a trial that handles disputes between parties regarding responsibilities owed amongst the parties involved.

Cold case – an unsolved criminal investigation that remains open, pending the discovery of new evidence. Simply, it has never been solved.

Combined DNA Index System (CODIS) – allows for an electronic search and comparison of DNA profiles.

Combustion – the liberation of heat and light by the rapid combination of oxygen with a substance.

Complete metamorphosis – a process of insect development that involves four stages, which are egg, larva, pupa, and adult. In complete metamorphosis, the larvae do not resemble the adult insect since the insect undergoes a complete change while pupating.

Computer forensics – also called cybercrime; a field dedicated to the search, preservation, and analysis of information computer systems with the goal of presenting evidence to the court.

Confirmative test – a specific test to confirm the identify of a substance.

Controlled Substances Act (CSA) – brought the various existing drug laws under one federal statute; under this act, drugs are categorized into five schedules.

Conventional carbon-based powder – effective on both porous and nonporous surfaces. They are inexpensive and cover a large area with just a little powder, but they are very messy. These types of powders are applied with a natural or synthetic hairbrush.

Crater – a hole left behind from a projectile. Craters determine the orientation and location of the weapon firing the projectile.

Crime lab – also called a forensic laboratory; responsible for analyzing evidence collected from criminal or civil cases.

Criminal law – defines criminal offenses; regulates the apprehension, charging, and trial of suspected persons; and defines penalties and types of treatment for convicted offenders. It also provides a sense of justice and retribution for the victims. Another purpose of criminal law is to incarcerate the guilty and punish them through 24-hour monitoring and/or possible death.

Criminal psychology – the study of the thoughts and behavior of criminals.

Criminal trial – a trial that involves a crime against the state, the breaking of a law, whether to an individual, group of individuals, business, etc.

Criminology – the scientific study of crime and criminal behavior.

Crown – the visible portion of a tooth.

Cryopreservation – a method of biological preservation where cells, tissues, or organs are frozen for a period of time.

Cryptanalyst – an expert in code breaking and cyphers.

Crystallinity – the order of the molecular chains in a fiber molecule.

CSI effect – the influence of the exaggerated portrayal of criminal investigation/forensic science on television and how it directly influences public perception and their courtroom expectations.

Cultural anthropology – the study of people groups and their customs, cultures, and how they interact with the land.

Cyanoacrylate ester (super glue) fuming – This technique is used on nonporous surfaces. This process relies upon the deposition of polymerized cyanoacrylate ester on the fingertip secretions. The evidence is placed in a fuming chamber with a small amount of super glue. The application of heat speeds up the time needed for deposition. Fuming results in white, crystallized, durable prints.

Dactyloscopy – the study of fingerprints.

Data – an extension of application security and allows an individual to grant access to files for the purpose of modifying those files.

Data structure – a method of organizing information (data) in the virtual system of a computer. Data structures and algorithms work hand-in-hand to build computer programs.

Daubert standard – used by a trial judge to determine whether the expert witness scientific testimony is valid and applies to the facts of the case; established by the Supreme Court in 1993.

Defense attorney – "any attorney – including privately retained, assigned by the court, acting *pro bono* or serving indigent defendants in a legal aid or public defender's office – who acts as an attorney on behalf of a client being investigated or prosecuted for alleged criminal conduct, or a client seeking legal advice regarding a potential, ongoing, or past criminal matter or subpoena, including as a witness."[577]

Degaussing – to use a magnetic field to neutralize (erase) the data on a device.

Dentin – the part of a tooth under the enamel. It comprises three layers and gives teeth their color while making up much of the tooth composition.

Dentition – the unique arrangement of teeth in an individual.

Depositions – sworn out-of-court testimony given prior to trial but are still provided under oath with a court reporter.

Depth of focus – how much of the thickness of a specimen is in acceptable focus.

Dermal papilla – finger-like projections in the dermis that are the main source of blood for the hair follicle and provide strength of connection between the epidermis and dermis layers of skin.

Dermatoglyphics – the scientific study of skin patterns.

DNA profiling – the process of determining an individual's characteristics from a DNA sample.

Doctrine of the exclusionary rule – known as the fruit of the poisonous tree doctrine; evidence is inadmissible if illegally obtained.

Double loop whorl – a subdivision of the whorl fingerprint pattern consisting of two separate loop formations with two distinct sets of shoulders and two deltas.

Drug Enforcement Administration (DEA) – federal organization formed in 1973 that oversees and regulates controlled substances in the United States.

Dusting powders – applied to surfaces using a type of brush or sifter. This is the oldest method used in the search for latent prints.

Eccrine glands – glands in the body that are largely concentrated on the hands and feet. Eccrine glands secrete sweat that is composed of 98% water. The remaining 2% consists of fatty acids, amino acids, and other minerals.

Edaphologist – a person who is an expert in soils.

Electrostatic dust lifter – an instrument that utilizes an electrostatic charge as a means of transferring dry origin impressions from a substrate to a film.

Emission spectroscopy – the elements in paint will produce a colored barcode spectrum for each individual sample.

Enamel – the part of a tooth that covers and protects the crown. Enamel is the hardest substance in the human body.

Encryption – the process of encoding information from plaintext to cyphertext.

Entomology – the study of insects.

Epigenetics – the study of heritable phenotype changes that do not involve alterations in the DNA sequence.

Erupt – the term used for teeth growing in.

Eugenics – the study of how to force reproduction within a human population to increase the occurrence of heritable characteristics regarded as desirable.

Expert witness – a person who is specialized in a field, often technical, who presents their expert opinion without having been a witness to the crime.

FACES ID – one of the more popular law enforcement software programs used for facial reconstruction. FACES has over 4,400 facial features in the database, including those of different ethnicities.

Facial reconstruction – the process of recreating the face of a deceased individual from their skull or recreating a face that is unrecognizable due to some type of trauma. There are two types of facial reconstruction, three dimensional and two dimensional.

Fiber – the smallest unit of a textile material.

Filament – silk and synthetic fibers.

Flammable range – a range of gas in air concentration.

Flash point – the lowest temperature to which something can be heated for the substance to give off vapors that will burn when exposed to a flame.

Fluorescent powder – consists of a light-stimulating color and a base (conventional and magnetic). The colorant reacts with UV light and is used alongside an ALS.

Forensic anthropology – the study of skeletal remains to identify deceased individuals for civil and criminal investigation.

Forensic ballistics – the science or study of the motion of projectiles, such as bullets, shells, or bombs.

Forensic odontology – a branch of dentistry that deals with the proper handling and examination of dental evidence and the proper evaluation and presentation of dental findings. More specifically, it is the recognition of the unique oral features present in an individual's teeth.

Forensic palynology – the study, identification, and analysis of pollen and spores to investigate criminal and civil cases.

Forensic psychiatry – a "subspecialty of psychiatry in which scientific and clinical expertise is applied to legal issues in legal contexts embracing civil, criminal, correctional or legislative matters."[578]

Forensic science – the acquisition of knowledge gained from the evidence, analysis, and investigator interpretations, with the goal of presenting this knowledge before individuals in the judicial system (the forum).

Formalin – a clear aqueous solution of formaldehyde and methanol used especially as a preservative.

Frankfort plane position – the normal position for the human skull, which runs from the orbital rim to central ear hole.

Gamete – a reproductive cell containing the haploid (23) number of chromosomes; for example, the male (sperm) or female (egg).

Gel electrophoresis – performed in a vertical or horizontal plane using a polymer gel of standard pore size.

Genetic genealogy – a field of genealogy that combines genealogical DNA tests and genealogy history to discover how humans are related.

Glowing combustion – an example of a fuel burning without a flame. Examples would be the smoldering embers of a campfire or a burning cigarette butt on the ground. In these examples, the carbonaceous residue continues to combust after the flames have diminished.

Grand larceny – theft involving excessive value of property often resulting in a felony.

Graphology – the study of human personality through an individual's writing.

Hair follicle – anchors hairs to the skin; resembles a bulb that contains living cells. The hair follicle is the living part of the hair where cell division is occurring.

Hair shaft – the nonliving portion of the hair.

Heat transfer – the process of fire burning from areas of high temperatures to areas of low temperatures. There are three fundamental forms of heat transfer: conduction, convection, and radiation.

Henry classification system – a system of classifying fingerprints based on the presence of whorls in fingers or thumbs.

High-throughput DNA sequencing – allows for thousands to millions of samples to be run at once. This method drastically reduces the time required in traditional DNA sequencing methods; also known as Next-Generation.

Homology – similarity in design.

Human Genome Project – an extensive research study to map out the human genome.

Humus – decaying organic matter.

Ident – when an unknown print is successfully matched to a known print.

Ignitable Liquids Database and Reference Collection – created as a storehouse for the compositions of ignitable liquids.

Improvised Explosive Device (IED) – a homemade explosive made of explosive material, a switch, a main charge, a power supply, and a container.

Incomplete metamorphosis – a process of insect development that has three stages, which are identified as egg, nymph, and adult. The nymph will often resemble the adult insect since these insects will not pupate or make a complete change.

Indict – a formal accusation that a person has committed a crime.

Infrared spectrophotometry – a thin beam of light is shone through a paint sample, and the light that is not absorbed is detected and measured.

Insect succession – the arrival of different insects to decaying biological material.

Instars – larva stages of growth.

Integrated Ballistics Identification System (IBIS) – the database for captured digital images of striated patterns and shell casings; has the ability to compare digital striation patterns with images of others found at crime scenes and those that are classified as test fires.

Interferometer – an investigative tool that merges two or more sources of light to create an inference pattern.

International Association of Arson Investigators (IAAI) – an international association of more than 10,000 fire investigation professionals.

Iodine fuming – iodine causes a physical reaction to take place in the fatty acids present in fingertip residues. Evidence is placed inside a fuming chamber with a sample of solid iodine crystals, and heat is applied. As the fatty acids absorb the iodine, they turn an orange/brownish color. This type of fuming is considered nondestructive, meaning it will not impede other forms of chemical processing. Iodine fuming is one of the oldest methods in the search for latent prints.

Joint POW/MIA Accounting Command (JPAC) – an organization created after World War II and the Korean War that was assigned the task of identifying soldiers and returning their bodies to the families. As they began to study and identify skeletal remains, JPAC started a database of bone type, gender, and ethnicity. Today, JPAC is one of the largest human identification laboratories in the world.

Jurisprudence – the legal theory behind laws; the science of law with a focus on the historical context and philosophies that shape laws.

Kastle-Meyer test – also called a phenolphthalein test; the first step to determine if a sample is blood. Phenolphthalein reacts with a heme molecule present in blood. Phenolphthalein also reacts with the peroxidase property of the hemoglobin in blood, which catalyzes phenolphthalin through a process of oxidization into phenolphthalein. A positive reaction for blood will result in a pink color within five sections.

Keratin – a protein comprising hair and nails and the primary protein in skin.

Kind – represents the basic reproductive boundary of an organism. That is, the offspring of an organism is always the same kind as its parents, even though it may display considerable variation.[579] A biblical kind of usually equivalent to the family level in Linnean taxonomy.

Latent – concealed or hidden; prints (fingerprints or shoeprints) that are not visible to the unaided eye and require some form of physical or chemical processing to make them visible.

Lifting agent – a black fingerprint powder, magnetic powder, gel lifter, or other medium.

Ligature – something used to tie or bind.

Linguistic anthropology – the study of languages.

Linguistics – the ability to identify word usage, phraseology, and other terminology.

Locard's Exchange Principle – the foundation for forensic science that states that when two items come into contact with one another, there is an exchange of material between them.

Loop – a fingerprint classification; a loop must meet three essential points: sufficient recurve, presence of a delta, and a ridge count of at least one.

Luminol test – through a chemical reaction and oxidization, luminol reacts with the hemoglobin in blood to emit a blue light, or luminescence, under a UV light that only lasts about one minute in fresh blood and several minutes in aged blood.

Magnetic powder – made of a colorant and iron shavings. Each iron shaving is wrapped in colorant. A magnetic wand attracts the iron filings, and as the filings are rubbed over a surface, the colorant adheres to the residue.

Manchester method – in facial reconstruction, this technique uses the anatomical and anthropometrical measurements to create tissue depth markers as guides.[580]

Mandible – the lower jawbone.

Mandibular arch – the right and left lower quadrants of the mouth.

Material witness warrant – allows law enforcement to detain an individual when they have reasonable cause to believe a person has information related to a criminal act or if they believe a person will not be responsive to a subpoena for a scheduled time of testimony.

Matrix characteristics – the presence or absence of roots, sticks, seeds, insects, and decomposing leaves in soil.

Maxilla – the upper, fixed bone of the jaw.

Maxillary arch – the right and left upper quadrants of the mouth.

Medicolegal entomology – the investigation into the order of succession of insects on a body, the location of insects on the body, and determining elapsed time of death (postmortem interval, or PMI).

Medullary index – the diameter the medulla divided by the diameter of the hair.

Mens rea – the state of mind of the suspect when they engaged in the illegal act.

Mental illness – a condition that causes serious disorder in a person's behavior or thinking.

Metal oxides – chemical compounds containing a metal and one or more oxygen atoms.

Micron (μ) – a metric measurement that is one-thousandth of a millimeter; also called a micrometer.

Minutiae – basically means "details"; the unique, comparable characteristics in friction ridge skin (fingerprints).

Miranda warning – a rule (warning) issued by law enforcement to an individual in custody. The Miranda warning states: 1. You have the right to remain silent. 2. Anything you say can and will be used against you in a court of law. 3. You have the right to an attorney. 4. If you cannot afford an attorney, one will be appointed for you.

Mitochondrial DNA – contains the maternal genome and is passed through the female line, meaning that a mother will pass her mitochondrial DNA information to all her children (both male and female), but only females pass on the information through the female egg during reproduction.

Mobile forensics – a branch of computer forensics that focuses on the recovery and investigation of information found on digital devices such as computers, cell phones, tablets, and digital cameras. Mobile forensics is now labeled as technology that travels to the scene of the crime.

Modus operandi **(MO)** – the method and habits a criminal utilizes to commit their crimes.

Molotov cocktail – a homemade explosive; a glass bottle with motor oil, a flammable material, and a wick or cloth soaked in kerosene or gasoline.

Monomer – a molecule that can be reacted together with other monomer molecules to form a larger polymer chain; the repeating unit of a polymer.

Morphology – the form and structure of an organism.

Nano-powder – SupraNano™ particles are added to conventional, magnetic, and fluorescent powders. Tiny silica balls hold the colorant and result in a 30% improved latent print definition over that of other powders. The nanotechnology in the powder can quickly analyze the fingerprint residue for demographic information of the depositor, such as drug intoxication, explosive chemical signatures, and ethnicity.

National Integrated Ballistics Information Network (NIBIN) – the storehouse for Integrated Ballistics Identification System (IBIS) images.

Naturalism – a secular belief in origins without the need for a Creator God.

Necrobiome – a microbial community eagerly anticipating the death of plants, animals, and humans.

Neurotransmission – a process where nerve cells (neurons) transmit electrical messages to one another.

Ninhydrin – the most widely used chemical to detect latent prints. It chemically reacts with the amino acids present in fingerprint oils. When the amino acids react, it results in a purple color called Ruhemann's purple. Ninhydrin is sprayed, dipped, or brushed onto the evidence. Once the evidence is dry, it is processed in a dark, humid location for 1–2 days at room temperature.

Nitroglycerin – a common liquid explosive that is sensitive to shock.

Nuclear DNA – the DNA found in the nucleolus of a human cell.

Nucleolus – the largest structure inside the nucleus, responsible for the synthesis of ribosomes.

Nucleotide – the basic building block of nucleic acids found in DNA and RNA. One nucleotide consists of a sugar molecule attached to a phosphate group, one of the four nitrogen bases (adenine, thymine, cytosine, guanine).

Oblique lighting – a light source positioned at a low angle to create shadows. The shadows allow minute details in the surface to be visible for photography.

Ocular micrometer – a glass disk eyepiece with a built-in ruled scale used to measure the size of microscopic images.

Orientation – refers to the parallel alignment of the polymer chains along the long axis of a fiber.

Original equipment tires – the tires that are sold as brand new on new vehicles.

Osteometry – a branch of anthropometry concerned with the size of different parts of the skeleton.

Ouchterlony double immunodiffusion – in this test, antigens and antibodies present in the blood samples are diffused into a gel. Depending on the geometric pattern created by the antigens, similarities between origins can be determined. Identity is determined when the two antigens are immunologically identical.

Oxidation – a chemical reaction that occurs when oxygen combines with a substance to produce both heat and light.

Oxidizing agents – chemicals that supply oxygen to a reaction.

Packet switching – a digital network transmission process in which data is broken into bite-sized pieces or blocks of information for fast, efficient transfer through network devices.

Paint Data Query (PDQ) – a database that contains over 45,000 paint samples from automobile manufacturers dating back to the 1930s.

Parent drop – the drop of blood from which the satellite spatter originates.

Passive bloodstains – drops of blood pulled down by gravity alone. There are four types of passive patterns, which are identified as drops, drips, pools, and clots.

Patent – prints (fingerprints or shoeprints) that are clearly visible to the unaided eye.

Pathology – a branch of forensic science that involves the examination of human remains and death scenes for diagnostic purposes related to a case. A pathologist will determine the cause and manner of death.

Periodontal ligament – the soft tissue between the teeth and the bone that holds teeth in place.

Phadebas® Forensic Press test – used to detect alpha-amylase enzymes in saliva.

Photomicrograph – a magnified digital image captured through a microscope.

Phraseology – the way in which words are used to express an idea or thought in speech or writing.

Physical anthropology – The study of human biological and physiological characteristics and their development in the identification of skeletal remains.

Physical developer (silver nitrate) – a solution of iron salts that reduces silver nitrate to metallic silver. Physical developer is effective on dry and wet porous surfaces, including sticky surfaces like duct tape. Like the effect of photographic physical developer on film, porous evidence reacts to the chemical in a similar redox reaction. Evidence is dipped in physical developer and then rinsed with water. The evidence is then allowed to air dry, or a dryer can be used to speed up the drying time.

Physical surveillance – the undercover observation of a suspect on a 24-hour basis.

Pigment – a group of compounds that are used to color other materials.

Pipe bomb – a homemade explosive; a section of a pipe containing low explosives.

Plain arch – a subdivision of the arch fingerprint pattern; the ridges of a plain arch flow, or tend to flow, from the left side of the print to the right side of the print and create a gentle hill within the pattern area. A plain arch has no upthrust in the core of the fingerprint as seen in the tented arch.

Plain whorl – a subdivision of the whorl fingerprint pattern; contains two deltas and at least one ridge, making a complete circuit. When an imaginary line is drawn between the two deltas, at least one recurring ridge must touch the line.

Plastic prints – prints (fingerprints or shoeprints) left behind in soft surfaces and create a three-dimensional impression of the print.

Polymer – from the Greek word *poly*, meaning "many," and *meros*, which means "part." Polymers are large molecules that connect like chain links.

Poroscopy – the study of pore patterns on friction ridge skin.

Postmortem interval (PMI) – the time since a person's death.

Potassium-argon dating – determining the age of something "based on the assumption that the amount of radioactive argon in a . . . sample all came from the decay of radioactive potassium."[581]

Prehensile – the ability to grasp or hold objects; some monkeys have prehensile tails.

Preliminary hearing – also called a probable cause hearing; a hearing that takes place after a defendant has entered a plea of not guilty. The prosecution must show that enough evidence exists to officially charge the defendant with the crime. A defendant can choose to waive the preliminary hearing.

Presumptive test – a screening test. A negative test is not tested further, while a positive result is followed by confirmatory tests. The presumptive test helps to reduce the number of confirmatory tests needed.

Probability – in relation to evidence, refers to the fact that the association between source and unique features defies human comprehension or a mathematical prediction.

Probable cause – the legal standard found in the 4th Amendment that requires police to have adequate justification to arrest a person, conduct a search, or seize property.

Projected bloodstains – the result of a force or action that causes exposed blood to be expelled.

Prosecutor – "an administrator of justice, zealous advocate, and an officer of the court . . . who uses sound discretion and independent judgement to . . . seek justice within the bounds of the law, not merely to convict."[582]

Proteins – responsible for metabolism, DNA replication, providing structure to cells, and many more important functions.

Pulp – innermost layer of a tooth containing nerves and blood vessels.

Putrefaction – when a body emits putrid odors; begins during the bloat stage of decomposition.

Pyrolysis – the process of converting a solid fuel into a gas.

Pyrolysis gas chromatography – paint chips are heated at high temperatures for several seconds to the point of reaching an oxygen-free, gaseous state. The gas is processed through the gas chromatograph to produce a pyrogram of the polymers present in the sample.

Quantitation – the process of verifying extracted DNA as human and not that of animal or bacteria origin.

Radial loop – a subdivision of the loop fingerprint pattern; less common and are characterized by ridges that flow or tend to flow toward the thumb or radius of the arm.

Rapid DNA – DNA profiles created from a buccal (cheek) swab without human intervention.

Rapid Stain Identification (RSID™) Test of Human Blood – effective in isolating human blood from ferret blood, primate blood, semen, saliva, urine, and human breast milk. The RSID™ of Human Blood is capable of detecting the presence of blood in a sample as small as 1 μL (microliter). This test detects the presence of glycophorin A found in the membranes of red blood cells.

Rapid Stain Identification (RSID™) Test of Human Saliva – detects the alpha-amylase molecule from human saliva. A suspected saliva sample will be applied to the wick and through a process of diffusion, the device will provide a positive or negative result.

Rapid Stain Identification (RSID™) Test of Human Semen – a semen sample is applied to the wick and through a process of diffusion, the device will provide a positive or negative result in the form of a red line.

Redox reaction – when electrons are shared, resulting in a change in oxidation in the reactant.

Replacement tires – what is purchased when tires become worn and damaged.

Residual data – traces of data that remain on a computer system.

Ridge breadth – the number of ridges that cross a straight, one-centimeter line on a fingerprint.

Ridge count – the number of ridges between the core and the delta.

Root – the portion of a tooth that is embedded into a socket in the jawbone.

Satellite spatter – small drops of blood that break free from the parent drop when blood hits a surface.

Scuff marks – a category of rotating tires; while the car is turning, these marks are left behind by sliding wheels.

Search and seizure – when probable cause exists, police officers have the right to conduct a search of a person and/or their belongings, arrest, and/or seize items. These circumstances are not protected by the 4th Amendment to the Constitution.

Sebaceous glands – exocrine glands that secrete oil (sebum) into the hair follicle to lubricate the hair and skin of animals and humans.

Sentencing hearing – the hearing occurring after the verdict where the court orders the guilty party's penalty.

Serology – the scientific study of blood serum and bodily fluids such as semen, saliva, breast milk, and other fluids.

Sharps container – specially designed plastic tubes used for collecting syringes.

Skeletonization – a stage of decomposition where the body decays down to the bone; begins 25–50 days after death and can last for years. After several weeks, the nails and teeth will become dislodged from the body. When the process is complete, only dry skin, hair, and bones will remain. This term also refers to the drying of the edges of a bloodstain.

Soil geomorphology – the formation of identifiable soil layers with recognizable characteristics caused by the combination of weathering and bedrock.

Spectra – the molecular and/or structural composition of a sample and are unique "fingerprints" that can be used for comparison.

Spectrophotometry – a branch of spectroscopy that measures the amount of light a substance absorbs.

Spectroscopy – an analytical method for identifying a substance by its selective absorption of different wavelengths of light.

Spines – pointed edges on the parent drop of blood that radiate out like a sun.

Spontaneous combustion – the result of a substance self-heating by an exothermic reaction in a poorly ventilated area. This process is often a slow buildup of temperature until it surpasses the flash point.

Spontaneous generation – a debunked scientific theory stating that organisms could arise from nonliving things.

Stage micrometer – a special glass slide with fine lines etched on it; used to measure the size of specimens.

Stellate – arranged in a radiating pattern like that of a star.

Sting operation – when undercover law enforcement creates an opportunity for a possible suspect to commit a crime.

Stored product entomology – the investigation of insects contaminating the food industry.

Subpoena – an order issued by the court requiring a person to appear in court on a designated date to provide testimony.

Supernatant – liquid part that remains after soil has settled.

Synthetic biology – an evolutionary field of science dedicated to synthesizing life from chemicals.

Tail – a spine that results if the parent drop of blood falls at an angle less than 90 degrees. The tail always points toward the direction of travel.

Takayama test – a blood test that will confirm a sample is blood but does not confirm the species of origin; works best with fresh blood samples.

Tented arch – a subdivision of the arch fingerprint pattern that has a distinct upthrust in the shape of a camping tent or tepee in the core of the print. A tented arch may also be classified as such when it resembled a loop but lacks one of the three requirements to be classified as a loop.

Tire impressions – a category of rotating tires; indention made in a soft surface like mud, sand, dirt, etc.

Tire prints – a category of rotating tires; left behind on the road surface after traveling through a wet substance.

Toxicology – a field that analyzes how chemical substances, similar to drugs and alcohol, affect living organisms.

Trace evidence – evidence resulting from two objects or people coming into direct contact with one another.

Transfer bloodstains – the result of a bloody surface coming into contact with a clean surface, thereby leaving bloody residue.

Transmission control protocol (TCP) – also known as the IP; the "handshake" that allows different computers to communicate.[583]

Ulnar loop – a subdivision of the loop fingerprint pattern; the most common print type. In an ulnar loop, the ridges flow or tend to flow toward the pinky finger or ulna bone of the arm. The flow of ridges resembles a slide, as the ridges start at the base (delta) and flow upward over the core and then slope down off to the other side of the print.

Uniformitarianism – the secular belief that rock layers were laid down slowly over millions of years.

Urban entomology – the study of insects at an individual's place of business or home.

Vellus hair – most of the hair on the human body is vellus hair. Vellus hair is colorless, soft, and short.

Viscosity – resistance of a fluid (liquid or gas) to a change in shape, or movement of neighboring portions relative to one another; having a thick or sticky texture that does not flow easily.

Weathering – the process by which rocks are broken down into soil and is the result of weather, water, and interaction between living things. There are three types of weathering: biological (tree roots and lichen), chemical (water acids and gases), and physical (wind, rain, and thermal expansion).

White-collar workers – people who work in an office or professional environment.

Whorl – a fingerprint classification characterized by the presence of two deltas and a core.

Y-DNA – only contains one paternal genome and is passed from father to sons on the Y chromosome.

ENDNOTES

1. "Roman Army," Know the Romans, 2020, https://www.knowtheromans.co.uk/Categories/RomanArmy/.
2. Henry Bettenson, *Documents of the Christian Church* (London: Oxford Press, 1943).
3. Arthur Conan Doyle, "The Adventure of the Blanched Soldier," *The Strand Magazine*, November 1926.
4. "What Is Forensic Science?" American Academy of Forensic Sciences, https://www.aafs.org/careers-forensic-science/what-forensic-science.
5. *Merriam-Webster.com*, 2020, https://www.merriam-webster.com/medical/forensic%20science.
6. *Online Etymology Dictionary*, 2020, https://www.etymonline.com/search?q=knowledge.
7. Don Stewart, "Does God Know Everything?" Blue Letter Bible, 2020, https://www.blueletterbible.org/faq/don_stewart/don_stewart_359.cfm.
8. *Webster'sDictionary1828.com*, 2020, http://webstersdictionary1828.com/Dictionary/science.
9. *Webster's1913.com*, 2020, https://www.websters1913.com/words/Science.
10. *Merriam-Webster.com*, 2020, https://www.merriam-webster.com/dictionary/science.
11. Jeffrey G. Barnes, "History," in *The Fingerprint Sourcebook* (Washington, D.C.: National Institute of Justice, 2010).
12. Sung Tz'u, *The Washing Away of Wrongs*, trans. Brian E. McKnight (University of Michigan Center for Chinese Studies, 1247).
13. James O'Brien, "Sherlock Holmes: Pioneer in Forensic Science," *Encyclopedia Britannica* (March 31, 2014), https://www.britannica.com/topic/Sherlock-Holmes-Pioneer-in-Forensic-Science-1976713.
14. "Edmond Locard," The Forensics Library, http://aboutforensics.co.uk/edmond-locard/.
15. "Types of Forensic Science: Discipline Sections Within the American Academy of Forensic Science," American Academy of Forensic Sciences, 2015, https://aafs.org/AAFS/Resources/Students/Choose-Career.aspx.
16. "Laboratory Services," Federal Bureau of Investigation, 2020, https://www.fbi.gov/services/laboratory.
17. Arthur Conan Doyle, *The Adventures of Sherlock Holmes* (Hertfordshire: Wordsworth Editions Limited, 1992).
18. Jennifer Rivera, "Can Forensic Science Trace the World's Origins?" Answers in Genesis, 2017, https://answersingenesis.org/what-is-science/can-forensic-science-trace-worlds-origins/.
19. See Roger Patterson, "What is Science?" in *Evolution Exposed: Biology* (Petersburg, KY: Answers in Genesis, 2006), https://answersingenesis.org/what-is-science/what-is-science/; and Josh Rosenau, " 'Historical Science' vs. 'Experimental Science,' " National Center for Science Education, October 25, 2019, https://ncse.com/creationism/analysis/historical-science-vs-experimental-science.
20. "What Do Forensic Scientists Do?" American Academy of Forensic Science.
21. Ibid.
22. Shaun Doyle, "CSI and Evolution," Creation Ministries International, November 29, 2012, http://creation.com/csi-evolution.
23. Thomas Young, "Forensic Science and the Scientific Method," Heartland Forensic Pathology, LLC, http://www.heartlandforensic.com/writing/forensic-science-and-the-scientific-method.
24. M. Teresa Scott and Antonio L. Manzanero, "Analysis of the Judicial File: Assessing the Validity of Testimony," *Papeles del Psicólogo* 36, no. 2 (2015): 139–144, http://www.papelesdelpsicologo.es/english/2569.pdf.
25. Bill Nye and Ken Ham, "Bill Nye Debates Ken Ham," Answers in Genesis, February 4, 2014, https://answersingenesis.org/countering-the-culture/bill-nye-debates-ken-ham/.
26. Ken Ham and Bodie Hodge, *A Flood of Evidence: 40 Reasons Noah and the Ark Still Matter* (Green Forest, AR: Master Books, 2016).
27. Jason Lisle, "Is the Present the Key to the Past?" Answers in Genesis, April 4, 2008, https://answersingenesis.org/who-is-god/is-the-present-the-key-to-the-past/.
28. Linda Geddes, "The troubling flaws in forensic science," BBC, May 13, 2015, https://www.bbc.com/future/article/20150512-can-we-trust-forensic-science.
29. https://www.cnn.com/2018/06/29/us/casey-anthony-10-years-later/index.html.
30. Casey Anthony Trial. Transcript of the 911 call. https://sites.google.com/site/caseyanthonytrial280/transcript-of-911-call.
31. Ibid.
32. Kimberlianne Podlas, "The '*CSI* Effect,'" Criminology and Criminal Justice, Oxford Research Encyclopedias, August 22, 2017, https://doi.org/10.1093/acrefore/9780190264079.013.40.
33. https://albertmohler.com/the-briefing.
34. L-Tron. "What three types of photographs are taken at crime scenes?" Retrieved from https://www.l-tron.com/what-three-types-of-photographs-are-taken-at-crime-scenes.
35. "Principles of Crime Scene Photography." Retrieved from http://www.forensicsciencesimplified.org/photo/principles.html.
36. Ibid.
37. Eudie Pak, "O.J. Simpson Murder Case: A Timeline of the 'Trial of the Century,' " Biography, June 12, 2020, https://www.biography.com/news/oj-simpson-trial-timeline.
38. "The Trial of O.J. Simpson: The Incriminating Evidence," UMKC School of Law, http://law2.umkc.edu/faculty/projects/ftrials/Simpson/Evidence.html.
39. "Nicole Brown Simpson and Ron Goldman murdered," History, June 12, 1994, https://www.history.com/this-day-in-history/nicole-brown-simpson-and-ron-goldman-murdered.
40. Arthur Conan Doyle, "The Boscombe Valley Mystery," *The Strand Magazine*, 1891.
41. Dictionary.com. Retrieved from https://www.dictionary.com/browse/in--evidence.
42. David J. Shestokas, "Principles of Criminal Liability," October 25, 2012, http://www.shestokas.com/general-law/criminal-law/principles-of-criminal-liability/.
43. Ibid.
44. "What's the Rarest Blood Type?" Healthline, https://www.healthline.com/health/rarest-blood-type.
45. Stone (2006), in "The Forensic Analysis of Footwear Impression Evidence" by Michael B. Smith, Forensic Science Communications 11, no. 3 (July 2009), https://archives.fbi.gov/archives/about-us/lab/forensic-science-communications/fsc/july2009/review/2009_07_review02.htm.
46. Ashish Badiye, Neeti Kapoor, and Ritesh G. Menezes, "Chain of Custody," National Library of Medicine, February 17, 2022, https://www.ncbi.nlm.nih.gov/books/NBK551677/.
47. Arthur Conan Doyle, *A Study in Scarlet* (London: Ward, Lock & Co., 1888).
48. "Michael Jackson," World History Project, https://worldhistoryproject.org/topics/michael-jackson.
49. Erin Coulehan, "Michael Jackson Was a Drug Addict, AEG Expert Testifies," *Rolling Stone*, August 28, 2013, https://www.rollingstone.com/music/music-news/michael-jackson-was-a-drug-addict-aeg-expert-testifies-118882/.
50. Colin Bertram, "The Final Days of Michael Jackson," Biography, May 20, 2020, https://www.biography.com/news/michael-jackson-final-days.

51. Buddy T, "Drug Use Rates in America," Verywell Mind, June 10, 2022, https://www.verywellmind.com/rates-of-illicit-drug-abuse-in-the-us-67027.

52. "Depressants," Alcohol and Drug Foundation, June 29, 2022, https://adf.org.au/drug-facts/depressants/.

53. "Uber Coca: Freud's Cocaine Discoveries," *Journal of Substance Abuse Treatment 1* (1984): 205–217, https://www.sciencedirect.com/sdfe/pdf/download/eid/1-s2.0-0740547284900230/first-page-pdf.

54. "Cocaine: A Short History," Foundation for a Drug-Free World, https://www.drugfreeworld.org/drugfacts/cocaine/a-short-history.html.

55. Matt Gonzales, "Is Cocaine Addictive?" DrugRehab.com, February 27, 2020, https://www.drugrehab.com/addiction/drugs/cocaine/how-addictive/.

56. "What Are Opioids?" Johns Hopkins Medicine, https://www.hopkinsmedicine.org/opioids/what-are-opioids.html.

57. Psychology Today Staff, "Opioids," Psychology Today, March 28, 2019, https://www.psychologytoday.com/us/conditions/opioids.

58. "History of Heroin," United Nations, Office on Drugs and Crime, January 1, 1953, https://www.unodc.org/unodc/en/data-and-analysis/bulletin/bulletin_1953-01-01_2_page004.html.

59. Nora D. Volkow, "America's Addiction to Opioids: Heroin and Prescription Drug Abuse," National Institute on Drug Abuse, May 14, 2014, https://archives.drugabuse.gov/testimonies/2014/americas-addiction-to-opioids-heroin-prescription-drug-abuse.

60. "What Are Hallucinogens and Dissociative Drugs?" National Institute on Drug Abuse, April 9, 2020, https://www.drugabuse.gov/publications/research-reports/hallucinogens-dissociative-drugs/what-are-hallucinogens.

61. History.com editors, "LSD," History, August 21, 2018, https://www.history.com/topics/crime/history-of-lsd.

62. "What are cannabinoids? Where can cannabinoids be found?" Fundación Canna (n.d.), https://www.fundacion-canna.es/en/cannabinoids.

63. "Cannabinoids," Alcohol and Drug Foundation, June 28, 2022, https://adf.org.au/drug-facts/cannabinoids/.

64. "What You Should Know About Marijuana Concentrates/Honey Butane Oil," Get Smart About Drugs, March 19, 2022, https://www.getsmartaboutdrugs.gov/content/what-you-should-know-about-marijuana-concentrates-honey-butane-oil.

65. Aaron Cadena, "The History of CBD: A Brief Overview," *CBD Origin* (March 8, 2019), https://medium.com/cbd-origin/the-history-of-cbd-a-brief-overview-68545c05ccc9.

66. "Dr Raphael Mechoulam and his revolutionary cannabis research," Medical Cannabis Network, August 27, 2019, https://www.healtheuropa.eu/dr-raphael-mechoulam-revolutionary-cannabis-research/93049/.

67. Peter Grinspoon, "Cannabidiol (CBD): What we know and what we don't," Harvard Health Publishing, September 24, 2021, https://www.health.harvard.edu/blog/cannabidiol-cbd-what-we-know-and-what-we-dont-2018082414476.

68. "Medicinal cannabis," Alcohol and Drug Foundation, June 28, 2022, https://adf.org.au/drug-facts/medicinal-cannabis/.

69. Dennis Thompson, "CBD Oil: All the Rage, But Is It Safe & Effective?" WebMD, May 7, 2018, https://www.webmd.com/pain-management/news/20180507/cbd-oil-all-the-rage-but-is-it-safe-effective#1.

70. C. Michael White, "Synthetic Marijuana is Far More Dangerous Than Weed," Discover, August 29, 2018, https://www.discovermagazine.com/health/synthetic-marijuana-is-far-more-dangerous-than-weed.

71. "Controlled Substance Schedules," U.S. Department of Justice, Drug Enforcement Administration, Diversion Control Division, https://www.deadiversion.usdoj.gov/schedules/.

72. Jeremy Berke, Shayanne Gal, and Yeji Jesse Lee, "Marijuana legalization is sweeping the US. See every state where cannabis is legal," Insider, May 27, 2022, https://www.businessinsider.com/legal-marijuana-states-2018-1.

73. "Overdose Death Rates," National Institute on Drug Abuse, January 20, 2022, https://www.drugabuse.gov/related-topics/trends-statistics/overdose-death-rates.

74. "Janice Hartman," Forensic Files Wiki, n.d., https://forensicfiles.fandom.com/wiki/Janice_Hartman.

75. Paul Dowling, producer, *Forensic Files*, season 9, episode 19, "Deadly Matrimony," 2004.

76. Juan Ignacio Blanco, "John David Smith III," Murderpedia, n.d., https://murderpedia.org/male.S/s/smith-john-david.htm.

77. Arthur Conan Doyle, *The Complete Novels of Sherlock Holmes* (CA: Peachtree Press, 2021).

78. Sarah Pornaras and Rebecca Formosa, "History of Discovery," Forensics: Toolmark Analysis, n.d., https://toolmarkanalysis.weebly.com/history-of-discovery.html.

79. Ibid.

80. "Toolmarks," Missouri State Highway Patrol, n.d., https://www.mshp.dps.missouri.gov/MSHPWeb/PatrolDivisions/CLD/Firearms/toolmarks.html.

81. https://www.researchgate.net/figure/Tool-marks-in-database-Left-striation-mark-right-impression-mark_fig3_11454968.

82. "ToolScan R360," Laboratory Imaging, Forensic Examination Systems, n.d., https://www.forensic.cz/en/products/toolscan_r360.

83. http://www.bvda.com/en/silmark-gray.

84. "Beltway Snipers," Federal Bureau of Investigation, n.d., https://www.fbi.gov/history/famous-cases/beltway-snipers.

85. Ibid.

86. Marcia Slacum Greene, "Mother Warned Malvo of 'Demon,'" *The Washington Post*, June 24, 2003, https://www.washingtonpost.com/archive/local/2003/06/24/mother-warned-malvo-of-demon/64bddacd-7267-490f-a549-6ef9cb9c95cc/.

87. Doyle, *The Adventures of Sherlock Holmes*.

88. Mariel Alper and Lauren Glaze, "Source and Use of Firearms Involved in Crimes: Survey of Prison Inmates, 2016," *Bureau of Justice Statistics*, January 2019, https://www.bjs.gov/content/pub/pdf/suficspi16.pdf.

89. "Gun Timeline," History Detectives, PBS, n.d., https://www.pbs.org/opb/historydetectives/technique/gun-timeline/.

90. Samuel Florer, "The hand cannon: A very early (and heavy) firearm," National Museum of American History, November 12, 2014, https://americanhistory.si.edu/blog/1390s-german-hand-cannon.

91. "Gun Timeline," History Detectives, PBS.

92. NRA Staff, "3 Methods of Barrel Rifling: Pros vs. Cons," NRA Family, November 7, 2019, https://www.nrafamily.org/articles/2019/11/7/3-methods-of-barrel-rifling-pros-vs-cons/.

93. Jeffrey Scott Doyle, "Rifling," FirearmsID.com, 2019, http://www.firearmsid.com/A_bulletIDrifling.htm.

94. "Firearms & Ballistics," The Forensics Library, n.d., https://aboutforensics.co.uk/firearms-ballistics/.

95. "National Integrated Ballistic Information Network (NIBIN)," Bureau of Alcohol, Tobacco, Firearms and Explosives, December 6, 2021, https://www.atf.gov/firearms/national-integrated-ballistic-information-network-nibin.

96. "Fact Sheet – National Integrated Ballistic Information Network," Bureau of Alcohol, Tobacco, Firearms and Explosives, September 2021, https://www.atf.gov/resource-center/fact-sheet/fact-sheet-national-integrated-ballistic-information-network.

97. Indianapolis-Marion County Forensic Services Agency, "Evidence Submission Guideline," n.d., https://citybase-cms-prod.s3.amazonaws.com/cf34064de6594474877b0f1258ca614f.pdf.

98. Jeffrey Scott Doyle, "Gunshot Residue Test Results," FirearmsID.com, 2019, https://www.firearmsid.com/a_distanceresults.htm.

99. Steven Pearson, "Common Uses of Barium," Owlcation, January 11, 2018, https://owlcation.com/stem/Uses-of-Barium.

100. "Nitrite Residue Patterns," Firearm Examiner Training (2008), https://projects.nfstc.org/firearms/module12/fir_m12_t06_09.htm.

101. Flinn Scientific, Inc., "Bullet Trajectory Analysis," *Flinn Scientific Forensics Fax!* no. 11316 (2017), https://www.flinnsci.com/api/library/Download/274c70fa157f4e4b82b392846fabfc14.

102. History.com editors, "Unabomber (Ted Kaczynski)," History, August 21, 2018, https://www.history.com/topics/crime/unabomber-ted-kaczynski.

103. Jørgen Veisdal, "The Mathematics of Ted Kaczynski," Cantor's Paradise, March 16, 2020, https://medium.com/cantors-paradise/the-mathematics-of-ted-kaczynski-43eb6ca16633.

104. Biography.com editors, "Ted Kaczynski," Biography, May 3, 2021, https://www.biography.com/crime-figure/ted-kaczynski.

105. "The Unabomber," Federal Bureau of Investigation, n.d., https://www.fbi.gov/history/famous-cases/unabomber.

106. Dave Davies, "FBI Profiler Says Linguistic Work Was Pivotal In Capture Of Unabomber," Nhpr, August 22, 2017, https://www.nhpr.org/post/fbi-profiler-says-linguistic-work-was-pivotal-capture-unabomber#stream/0.

107. Ibid.

108. Arthur Conan Doyle, *The Return of Sherlock Holmes* (New York: McClure, Phillips & Co., 1905).

109. Carrie Hagen, "The Story Behind the First Ransom Note in American History," *Smithsonian Magazine*, December 9, 2013, https://www.smithsonianmag.com/history/the-story-behind-the-first-ransom-note-in-american-history-180948612/?no-ist.

110. Doug MacGowan, "The Kidnapping of Charley Ross," Historic Mysteries, n.d., https://www.historicmysteries.com/kidnapping-of-charley-ross/.

111. Ibid.

112. "Weinberger Kidnapping," Federal Bureau of Investigation, n.d., https://www.fbi.gov/history/famous-cases/weinberger-kidnapping.

113. Kieran Fogarty et al., "Hitler Diaries," Britannica, January 13, 2017, https://www.britannica.com/topic/Hitler-Diaries.

114. Dave Davies, "FBI Profiler Says Linguistic Work Was Pivotal In Capture Of Unabomber," SDPB, August 22, 2017, https://listen.sdpb.org/post/fbi-profiler-says-linguistic-work-was-pivotal-capture-unabomber.

115. Ibid.

116. Mark Songer, "Forensic Document Examination: Expert Overview," Robson Forensic, November 24, 2015, https://www.robsonforensic.com/articles/forensic-document-examination-expert-witness.

117. "JFK Assassination Records Processing Project – 2017 Update: NARA Commits to Processing the Withheld JFK Assassination Records by October 26, 2017," National Archives, December 15, 2021, https://www.archives.gov/research/jfk/processing-project.

118. "Morris Worm," Federal Bureau of Investigation, n.d., https://www.fbi.gov/history/famous-cases/morris-worm.

119. "Morris Worm," Radware, 2022, https://security.radware.com/ddos-knowledge-center/ddospedia/morris-worm/.

120. Editorial, "Lessons from the 1st Major Computer Virus," Intel Newsroom, October 25, 2013, https://newsroom.intel.com/editorials/lessons-from-the-first-computer-virus-the-Morris-worm/.

121. Arthur Conan Doyle, "The Adventure of the Dying Detective," *The Strand Magazine*, December 1913.

122. Statista Research Department, "U.S. consumers and cyber crime - Statistics & Facts," Statista, July 6, 2022, https://www.statista.com/topics/2588/us-consumers-and-cyber-crime/.

123. Chandrahas Halai, "How Pingala created the Binary Number System," Indica, June 24, 2020, https://www.indica.today/quick-reads/pingala-created-binary-number-system/.

124. Alane Lim, "Biography of Gottfried Wilhelm Leibniz, Philosopher and Mathematician," ThoughtCo., April 18, 2019, https://www.thoughtco.com/gottfried-wilhelm-leibniz-4588248.

125. Editors, "Charles Babbage," Britannica, December 22, 2021, https://www.britannica.com/biography/Charles-Babbage.

126. H.W. Buxton, *Memoir of the Life and Labours of the Late Charles Babbage Esq.*, unpublished, p. 1986. Cited in: J.M. Dubbey, *The Mathematical Work of Charles Babbage* (Cambridge: Cambridge University Press, 1978), 227.

127. "Hardware vs. Software," Diffen, n.d., https://www.diffen.com/difference/Hardware_vs_Software.

128. "Central Processing Unit," Learn Computer Science, 2022, https://www.learncomputerscienceonline.com/central-processing-unit/.

129. "Operating System," Learn Computer Science, 2022, https://www.learncomputerscienceonline.com/operating-system/.

130. "Why Use a Degausser/Hard Drive Eraser and Other FAQs," Data Security, Inc., 2021, https://datasecurityinc.com/security/degausser.html.

131. History.com editors, "The Invention of the Internet," History, October 28, 2019, https://www.history.com/topics/inventions/invention-of-the-internet.

132. Ibid.

133. Chris Woodford, "The Internet," Explain That Stuff!, July 6, 2021, https://www.explainthatstuff.com/internet.html.

134. Daily Mail reporter, "NatWest handed Al Qaeda terrorist 100% mortgage to buy £93,000 home he turned into a bomb factory," Daily Mail, December 16, 2009, https://www.dailymail.co.uk/news/article-1236301/Bank-blasted-giving-Al-Qaeda-terrorist-100-mortgage.html.

135. "Digital forensics," Infosec, 2022, https://resources.infosecinstitute.com/category/computerforensics/introduction/areas-of-study/application-forensics/web-email-and-messaging-forensics/.

136. Ibid.

137. "Communications Assistance for Law Enforcement Act," Federal Communications Commission, June 28, 2022, https://www.fcc.gov/public-safety-and-homeland-security/policy-and-licensing-division/general/communications-assistance.

138. Bradley Mitchell, "What Is a Server?" Lifewire, June 12, 2021, https://www.lifewire.com/servers-in-computer-networking-817380.

139. "CD/DVD Inspector," InfinaDyne, n.d., https://www.infinadyne.com/cddvd_inspector.html.

140. Sue Poremba, "The Future of Cybercrime: Where Are We Headed?" Security Intelligence, September 18, 2019, https://securityintelligence.com/articles/the-future-of-cybercrime-where-are-we-headed/.

141. "Digital forensics," Infosec, 2022.

142. Juan Ignacio Blanco, "Colin Pitchfork," Murderpedia, n.d., https://murderpedia.org/male.P/p/pitchfork-colin.htm.

143. "Colin Pitchfork: Double child killer denied parole," BBC, May 3, 2018, https://www.bbc.com/news/uk-england-leicestershire-43993232.

144. Juan Ignacio Blanco, "Colin Pitchfork," Murderpedia, n.d., http://www.murderpedia.org/male.P/p/pitchfork-colin.htm.

145. Doyle, *The Adventures of Sherlock Holmes*.

146. James W. Hazel and Ellen Wright Clayton, "Law Enforcement and Genetic Data," The Hastings Center, January 20, 2021, https://www.thehastingscenter.org/briefingbook/dna-and-law-enforcement/.

147. Natalie Angier, "Do Races Differ? Not Really, DNA Shows," *The New York Times*, August 22, 2000, http://partners.nytimes.com/library/national/science/082200sci-genetics-race.html.

148. "The Human Genome Project," National Human Genome Research Institute, December 22, 2020, https://www.genome.gov/human-genome-project.

149. Henry Harris, *The Birth of the Cell* (Connecticut and London: Yale University Press, 2001).

150. "The History of DNA Timeline," DNA Worldwide Group, 2014, https://www.dna-worldwide.com/resource/160/history-dna-timeline.

151. Kiona N. Smith, "Why Everyone Overlooked Gregor Mendel's Groundbreaking Paper," *Forbes*, February 8, 2018, https://www.forbes.com/sites/kionasmith/2018/02/08/why-everyone-overlooked-gregor-mendels-groundbreaking-paper/#753c65e7d761.

152. "The Human Genome Project," National Human Genome Research Institute.

153. "Combined DNA Index System (CODIS)," Federal Bureau of Investigation, n.d., https://www.fbi.gov/services/laboratory/biometric-analysis/codis.

154. "How Much DNA Does the Human Body Contain?" Wisegeek, 2022, https://www.wisegeek.com/how-much-dna-does-the-human-body-contain.htm.

155. Celia Henry Arnaud, "Thirty years of DNA forensics: How DNA has revolutionized criminal investigations," *Chemical & Engineering News*, September 18, 2017, https://cen.acs.org/articles/95/i37/Thirty-years-DNA-forensics-DNA.html.

156. JV Chamary, "How Genetic Genealogy Helped Catch The Golden State Killer," *Forbes*, June 30, 2020, https://www.forbes.com/sites/jvchamary/2020/06/30/genetic-genealogy-golden-state-killer/#6cf5b8315a6d.

157. "What Is Rapid DNA?" Ande, 2022, https://www.ande.com/what-is-rapid-dna/.

158. "Rapid DNA," Federal Bureau of Investigation, n.d., https://www.fbi.gov/services/laboratory/biometric-analysis/codis/rapid-dna.

159. Ibid.

160. Courtney Linder, "DNA Is Millions of Times More Efficient Than Your Computer's Hard Drive," *Popular Mechanics*, July 25, 2020, https://www.popularmechanics.com/science/a33327626/scientists-encoded-wizard-of-oz-in-dna/.

161. Ibid.

162. Dennis Murphy, "Death at the bottom of the stairs," NBC News, November 25, 2006, https://www.nbcnews.com/id/wbna15894727.

163. "Michael Peterson," Crime Museum, 2021, https://www.crimemuseum.org/crime-library/famous-murders/michael-peterson/.

164. Chege Karomo, "Where is Michael Peterson now? He lives in Durham in a house without a staircase," The Netline, May 6, 2022, https://thenetline.com/michael-peterson-now/.

165. Arthur Conan Doyle, "The Adventure of the Blue Carbuncle," *The Strand Magazine*, January 1892.

166. Dr. Alan L. Gillen and Jason Conrad, "Life Is in the Blood," Answers in Genesis, August 2, 2019, https://answersingenesis.org/biology/microbiology/life-is-in-the-blood/.

167. S. Hoole, *The Select Works of Antony van Leeuwenhoek, containing his Microscopical Discoveries in many of the Works of Nature*, 2 vols (London: G. Sidney, 1798; New York: ECCO Press, 2012 reprint), in "Life Is in the Blood" by Dr. Alan L. Gillen and Jason Conrad.

168. "History of Blood," Health.gov.mt, 2021, https://deputyprimeminister.gov.mt/en/nbts/Pages/About-Blood/History-of-Blood.aspx.

169. Lindsay M. Biga, Sierra Dawson, Amy Harwell, Robin Hopkins, Joel Kaufmann, Mike LeMaster, Philip Matern, Katie Morrison-Graham, Devon Quick, and Jon Runyeon, "Blood Typing," in *Anatomy & Physiology*, (Corvallis, OR: OpenStax/Oregon State University), https://open.oregonstate.education/aandp/chapter/18-6-blood-typing/.

170. "Composition of the Blood," National Cancer Institute, n.d., https://www.training.seer.cancer.gov/leukemia/anatomy/composition.html.

171. Biga et al., "Blood Typing."

172. "Phenolphthalein Blood Test Results Interpreted," Hrf, 2022, https://healthresearchfunding.org/phenolphthalein-blood-test-results-interpreted/.

173. Susmita Saxena and Sanjeev Kumar, "Saliva in forensic odontology: A comprehensive update," *Journal of Oral and Maxillofacial Pathology* 19, no. 2 (May-August 2015): 263–265, https://www.ncbi.nlm.nih.gov/pmc/articles/PMC4611940/.

174. "Blood and Bodily Fluids," Forensic Resources, 2022, https://forensicresources.org/forensic-disciplines/blood-bodily-fluids/.

175. Dr. Tim Sandle, "New saliva test helps with crime scene investigations," Digital Journal, January 22, 2017, https://www.digitaljournal.com/tech-science/new-salvia-test-helps-with-crime-scene-investigations/article/484184.

176. Maher Noureddine, "Forensic Tests for Semen: What you should know," Forensic Resources, October 19, 2011, https://ncforensics.wordpress.com/2011/10/19/forensic-tests-for-semen-what-you-should-know/.

177. Dr. Howard Markel, "How the Tylenol murders of 1982 changed the way we consume medication," PBS, September 29, 2014, https://www.pbs.org/newshour/health/tylenol-murders-1982.

178. Ibid.

179. "Chicago Tylenol Murders," Crime Museum, 2021, https://www.crimemuseum.org/crime-library/cold-cases/chicago-tylenol-murders/.

180. Cynthia Dizikes and Tribune Reporter, "Tylenol suspect's novel: 'Poison!'" *Chicago Tribune*, January 12, 2010, https://www.chicagotribune.com/news/ct-xpm-2010-01-12-1001110726-story.html.

181. Markel, "Tylenol murders of 1982."

182. "Chicago Tylenol Murders," Crime Museum.

183. Arthur Conan Doyle, *The Hound of the Baskervilles* (UK: George Newnes Ltd., 1902).

184. Mayo Clinic Staff, "Red wine and resveratrol: Good for your heart?" Mayo Clinic, January 14, 2022, https://www.mayoclinic.org/diseases-conditions/heart-disease/in-depth/red-wine/art-20048281.

185. "Alcohol Facts and Statistics," National Institute on Alcohol Abuse and Alcoholism, March 2022, https://www.niaaa.nih.gov/publications/brochures-and-fact-sheets/alcohol-facts-and-statistics.

186. "Underage Drinking," National Institute on Alcohol Abuse and Alcoholism, May 2021, https://www.niaaa.nih.gov/publications/brochures-and-fact-sheets/underage-drinking.

187. Carol Galbicsek, "Alcohol-Related Crimes," Alcohol Rehab Guide, March 21, 2019, https://www.alcoholrehabguide.org/alcohol/crimes/.

188. Ibid.

189. https://www.greatlakesdistillery.com/cms/wp-content/uploads/2014/02/standard-drink.jpg.

190. Joseph Raspolich, "How Long Does the Liver Take to Recover from Post-Alcohol Abuse?" The Palm Beach Institute, n.d., https://www.pbinstitute.com/alcohol/liver-recovery/.

191. "Alcohol's Damaging Effects on the Brain," National Institute on Alcohol Abuse and Alcoholism, October 2004, https://pubs.niaaa.nih.gov/publications/aa63/aa63.htm.

192. http://asklistenlearn.org/wp-content/uploads/brain.png.

193. Nena Messina, "The Risks of Underage Drinking," Addiction Resource, January 4, 2022, https://addictionresource.com/alcohol/resources/underage-drinking/.

194. Buddy T, "Field Sobriety Tests to Assess Drunk Driving," Verywell Mind, June 23, 2022, https://www.verywellmind.com/field-sobriety-test-67159.

195. Ibid.

196. Kailyn Champlin, Cyd Oldham, Paul Salvatoriello, Hui Zhao, and Zheng Fang, "Breathalyzer," Legal Dictionary, October 11, 2015, https://legaldictionary.net/breathalyzer/.

197. "Impaired Driving," Centers for Disease Control and Prevention, May 5, 2022, https://www.cdc.gov/motorvehiclesafety/impaired_driving/index.html.

198. Ashraf Al, ed., "Alcohol Impairment Chart," OnHealth, July 13, 2017, https://www.onhealth.com/content/1/alcohol_impairment_chart.

199. "Alcoholism," Healthline, August 23, 2017, https://www.healthline.com/health/alcoholism/basics.

200. Don Babwin, "Police identify another victim of serial killer John Wayne Gacy," abc10, October 25, 2021, https://www.abc10.com/article/news/nation-world/victim-serial-killer-john-wayne-gacy-identified/507-45be-1a4b-d88b-4c5f-948a-17de468b0d9d.

201. Cheish Merryweather, "10 Creepiest Facts About Killer Clown John Wayne Gacy," Listverse, July 6, 2019, https://listverse.com/2019/07/06/10-creepiest-facts-about-killer-clown-john-wayne-gacy/.

202. History.com editors, "John Wayne Gacy confesses to dozens of murders," History, December 22, 2020, https://www.history.com/this-day-in-history/john-wayne-gacy-confesses.

203. Arthur Conan Doyle, *The Case-Book of Sherlock Holmes* (London: John Murray, 1927).

204. "The FBI and the American Gangster, 1924-1938," Federal Bureau of Investigation, n.d., https://www.fbi.gov/history/brief-history/the-fbi-and-the-american-gangster.

205. "Forensic Anthropology," History Detectives, 2014, https://www.pbs.org/opb/historydetectives/technique/forensic-anthropology/.

206. Dr. David Menton, "Bones," Answers in Genesis, October 1, 2009, https://answersingenesis.org/human-body/bones/.

207. Ibid.

208. Warren Andrew, "human skeleton," Britannica, November 19, 2020, https://www.britannica.com/science/human-skeleton/The-spinal-cord.

209. Danny Rinehart, "Excavations of Skeletal Remains From an Anthropological Point of View," Crime Scene Investigator Network, 2020, https://www.crime-scene-investigator.net/excavation.html.

210. Tz'u, *The Washing Away of Wrongs*.

211. Le Thanh Minh, "Washing Away of Wrongs- the first forensic science book ever written in the World," Worldkings.org, August 29, 2016, http://worldkings.org/news/world-record-content-academy/washing-away-of-wrongs-the-first-forensic-science-book-ever-written-in-the-world.

212. Arthur Conan Doyle, "The Adventure of the Copper Beeches," *The Strand Magazine,* June 1892.

213. "Forensic Entomology," Crime Museum, 2021, https://www.crimemuseum.org/crime-library/forensic-investigation/forensic-entomology/.

214. Sara G. Miller, "9 Disgusting Things That the FDA Allows in Your Food," LiveScience, July 28, 2016, https://www.livescience.com/55459-fda-acceptable-food-defects.html.

215. Mark Benecke, "A brief history of forensic entomology," *Forensic Science International* 120, no. 1-2 (July 2013): 2–14.

216. Debbie Hadley, "Early History of Forensic Entomology, 1300-1900," ThoughtCo., February 1, 2020, https://www.thoughtco.com/forensic-entomology-early-history-1300-1901-1968325.

217. Benecke, "A brief history of forensic entomology," 2–14.

218. "Cheese Skipper," Everything About, 2009, https://www.everythingabout.net/articles/biology/animals/arthropods/insects/flies/cheese_skipper/.

219. "What are beetles?" Insects in the City, Texas A&M AgriLife Extension, n.d., https://citybugs.tamu.edu/factsheets/household/beetles-house/what-are-beetles/.

220. "Carrion Beetles (Burying Beetles)," Missouri Department of Conservation, n.d., https://nature.mdc.mo.gov/discover-nature/field-guide/carrion-beetles-burying-beetles.

221. "Forensic Entomology – Using Insects for Forensic Investigations," Incognito Forensic Foundation, 2021, https://ifflab.org/forensic-entomology-using-insects-for-forensic-investigations/.

222. Rebecca, "A New Tool for Forensic Scientists," Science Buzz, November 19, 2008, https://www.sciencebuzz.org/blog/new-tool-forensic-scientists.

223. John UpChurch, "Death's Cleanup Crew," Answers in Genesis, August 12, 2018, https://answersingenesis.org/sin/deaths-cleanup-crew/.

224. Sundance Now Exclusive, *Jonestown: Terror in the Jungle*, Sundance TV, 2018.

225. History.com editors, "Jonestown," History, April 19, 2022, https://www.history.com/topics/crime/jonestown.

226. Sundance Now Exclusive, *Jonestown: Terror in the Jungle*.

227. Ibid.

228. Ibid.

229. Ibid.

230. Ibid.

231. Author Conan Doyle, "His Last Bow. The War Service of Sherlock Holmes," *The Strand Magazine,* September 1917.

232. Bill Nye, "Hey Bill Nye! Do You Believe in Ghosts and the Afterlife?" Big Think, 2022, https://bigthink.com/videos/bill-nye-on-ghosts-and-the-afterlife.

233. "The Stages of Human Decomposition," Aftermath®, 2022, https://www.aftermath.com/content/human-decomposition/.

234. Ibid.

235. Jack Claridge, "Rigor Mortis and Lividity," Explore Forensics, 2022, http://www.exploreforensics.co.uk/rigor-mortis-and-lividity.html.

236. Francine Uenuma, "The First Criminal Trial That Used Fingerprints as Evidence," Smithsonian Magazine, December 5, 2018, https://www.smithsonianmag.com/history/first-case-where-fingerprints-were-used-evidence-180970883/.

237. "Hiller Suspect Is an Ex-Convict Identified by Bertillon Method," *Chicago Examiner*, September 20, 1910, cited in "First Fingerprint Murder Trial," Chicagology, 2022, https://chicagology.com/chicagopolice/firstfingerprinttrial/.

238. Doyle, *The Complete Novels of Sherlock Holmes*.

239. John Mark Hansen, "Flashback: How fingerprinting made Chicago famous: New technology led to 1910 murder conviction in a first for the nation," *Chicago Tribune*, April 3, 2020, https://www.chicagotribune.com/opinion/commentary/ct-opinion-flashback-fingerprinting-clarence-hiller-slaying-20200403-jgihdoi7xfdmra7jqs3zbq2bqq-story.html.

240. "Hiller Slayer Is Condemned to Be Hanged," *Chicago Examiner*, November 11, 1910, cited in "First Fingerprint Murder Trial," Chicagology, 2022, https://chicagology.com/chicagopolice/firstfingerprinttrial/.

241. Hansen, "How fingerprinting made Chicago famous."

242. Muin'iskw (Jean) and Crowfeather (Dan), "The Legacy of Muin'iskw - Records of a Historical Journey," Mikmaw Spirit, April 1, 2016, http://www.muiniskw.org/pgLegacy08_Journey.htm.

243. Ibid.

244. Francis Galton, *Finger Prints* (London: Macmillan and Co., 1892), http://galton.org/books/finger-prints/galton-1892-fingerprints-1up-lowres.pdf.

245. Julian Quinones and Arijeta Lajka, " 'What kind of society do you want to live in?': Inside the country where Down syndrome is disappearing," CBS News, August 15, 2017, https://www.cbsnews.com/news/down-syndrome-iceland/.

246. Harold Plotnick, and Hermann Pinkus, "The Epidermal vs. the Dermal Fingerprint: An Experimental and Anatomical Study," *AMA Arch Derm* 77, no. 1 (January 1958): 12–17, https://jamanetwork.com/journals/jamadermatology/article-abstract/525272.

247. Ian Curley, "Notable Events in Week Fortyeight," Herts Past Policing, November 24, 2020, https://www.hertspastpolicing.org.uk/content/police-history/this-week-in-hertfordshire-police-history/notable-events-in-week-fortyeight.

248. Ibid.

249. Ada McVean, "Koalas have fingerprints just like humans," McGill, July 19, 2019, https://www.mcgill.ca/oss/article/did-you-know-koalas-have-fingerprints-just-humans.

250. Doyle, *The Adventures of Sherlock Holmes*.

251. John Upchurch, "Convergent Evolution or Common Designer?" Answers in Genesis, October 1, 2016, https://answersingenesis.org/evidence-against-evolution/convergent-evolution-or-common-designer/.

252. Donald Chrisman, Richard S. MacNeish, Jamshed Mavalwala, and Howard Savage, "Late Pleistocene Human Friction Skin Prints from Pendejo Cave, New Mexico," *American Antiquity* 61, no. 2 (April 1996): 357–376, https://www.jstor.org/stable/282431.

253. Harold Cummins and Charles Midlo, *Finger Prints, Palms and Soles* (New York: Dover Publications, 1943); William D. Hopkins, Jamie L. Russell, Autumn Hostetter, Dawn Pilcher, and Jeremy F. Dahl, "Grip preference, dermatoglyphics, and hand use in captive chimpanzees," *American Journal of Physical Anthropology* 128, no. 1 (September 2005): 57–62, doi:10.1002/ajpa.20093.

254. A. Maceo, M. Carter, and B. Stromback, "Palm Prints," in *Encyclopedia of Forensic Sciences* by J.A. Siegel and P.J. Saukko, eds., Second Edition, vol. 4 (Waltham: Academic Press, 2013), 29–36, https://doi.org/10.1016/B978-0-12-382165-2.00277-4.

255. Ryn Gargulinski, "Human Vs. Primate Hands," Sciencing, March 13, 2018, https://sciencing.com/human-vs-primate-hands-6137415.html.

256. Harold Cummins and S.D. Shirley Spragg, "Dermatoglyphics in the Chimpanzee: Description and Comparison with Man," *Human Biology* 10, no. 4 (December 1938): 457–510, https://www.jstor.org/stable/41447376.

257. Gargulinski, "Human vs. Primate Hands."

258. Cummins and Spragg, "Dermatoglyphics in the Chimpanzee."

259. Maciej Henneberg, Kosette M. Lambert, and CM Leigh, "Fingerprinting a Chimpanzee and a Koala: Animal Dermatoglyphics Can Resemble Human Ones," ResearchGate, November 2012, https://www.researchgate.net/publication/233726390_1998_Fingerprinting_a_chimpanzee_and_a_koala/citations.

260. Yana G. Kamberov, Samantha M. Guhan, Alessandra DeMarchis, Judy Jiang, Sara Sherwood Wright, Bruce A. Morgan, Pardis C. Sabeti, Clifford J. Tabin, and Daniel E. Lieberman, "Comparative evidence for the independent evolution of hair and sweat gland traits in primates," *Journal of Human Evolution* 125 (December 2018): 99–105, http://dx.doi.org/10.1101/430454.

261. William Montagna, "The Skin of Nonhuman Primates," *American Zoologist* 12, no. 1 (February 1972): 109–124, https://doi.org/10.1093/icb/12.1.109.

262. Jason M. Organ, Magdalena N. Muchlinski, and Andrew S. Deane, "Mechanoreceptivity of Prehensile Tail Skin Varies Between Ateline and Cebine Primates," *The Anatomical Record* 294, no. 12 (December 2011): 2064–2072, https://doi.org/10.1002/ar.21505.

263. Henneberg, Lambert, and Leigh, "Fingerprinting a Chimpanzee and a Koala."

264. Ibid.

265. "Why do Koalas have Unique Fingerprints?" Uthinki, 2022, https://www.uthinki.com/articles/why-do-koalas-have-unique-fingerprints/.

266. Dr. Rys Farthing, "Tree kangaroos are real and awesome but are endangered and need help," MetroUK, October 13, 2015, https://metro.co.uk/2015/10/13/tree-kangaroos-are-real-and-awesome-but-are-endangered-and-need-help-5340535/.

267. Timothy Fridtjof Flannery, Roger Martin, and Alexandra Szalay, *Tree Kangaroos: A Curious Natural History* (Australia: Reed Books, 1996).

268. Renn Tumlison, "Our Only Marsupial Is Well-Adapted to Climb Trees," Henderson State University, 2022, https://hsu.edu/pages/academics/ellis-college-of-arts-and-sciences/biological-sciences/arkansas-nature-trivia/our-only-marsupial-is-well-adapted-to-climb-trees/.

269. Madeline Bodin, "Fingerprinting the Fisher," Northern Woodlands, March 1, 2008, https://northernwoodlands.org/knots_and_bolts/fingerprinting_the_fisher.

270. Peter H. Warman and A. Roland Ennos, "Fingerprints are unlikely to increase the friction of primate fingerpads," *The Journal of Experimental Biology* 212, no. 13 (July 2009): 2016–2022, https://doi.org/10.1242/jeb.028977.

271. Brad Kelechava, "Fingerprints: From the Trees to a Life of Crime," American National Standards Institute, July 27, 2018, https://blog.ansi.org/2018/07/why-we-have-fingerprints-history-crime/#gref.

272. Ken Ham, "What About Homology?" Answers in Genesis, July 2, 2018, https://answersingenesis.org/media/audio/answers-with-ken-ham/volume-130/what-about-homology/.

273. Richard F. Hall, "Latent Skin Print Identification Solves Homicide," FBI Law Enforcement Bulletin, October 1979.

274. One of the fingerprint experts on this case was the author's father.

275. Doyle, *A Study in Scarlet*.

276. Hall, "Latent Skin Print Identification Solves Homicide."

277. Gurvinder Singh Bumbrah, "Cyanoacrylate fuming method for detection of latent fingermarks: a review," *Egyptian Journal of Forensic Sciences* 7, no. 1 (July 2017), doi:10.1186/s41935-017-0009-7.

278. "Rhenium," Royal Society of Chemistry, 2022, https://www.rsc.org/periodic-table/element/75/Rhenium.

279. "Mendeleev's periodic table," BBC, 2022, https://www.bbc.co.uk/bitesize/guides/zxmmsrd/revision/1.

280. Brian Yamashita and Mike French, "Latent Print Development," in *The Fingerprint Sourcebook*, National Institute of Justice (July 2011), https://www.ncjrs.gov/pdffiles1/nij/225327.pdf.

281. Bumbrah, "Cyanoacrylate fuming method."

282. Yamashita and French, "Latent Print Development."

283. "Uses of 1,8-Diazafluoren-9-one," ChemicalBook, October 25, 2019, https://www.chemicalbook.com/Article/Uses-of-1-8-Diazafluoren-9-one.htm.

284. Allen Miller, "Choosing the Best Fingerprint Powder for Your Scene," *Evidence Technology Magazine* (September-October 2013), https://www.locifo-rensics.nl/images/Evidence_Technology_Magazine_-_SupraNano.pdf.

285. Yamashita and French, "Latent Print Development."

286. G.S. Sodhi and Jasjeet Kaur, "Physical developer method for detection of latent fingerprints: A review," *Egyptian Journal of Forensic Sciences* 6, no. 2 (June 2016): 44–47, https://doi.org/10.1016/j.ejfs.2015.05.001.

287. "Biometrics," Homeland Security, December 14, 2021, https://www.dhs.gov/biometrics.

288. "What is Electronic 'Live Scan' Fingerprinting Technology?" Accurate Biometrics, 2022, https://accuratebiometrics.com/what-is-livescan.

289. "Automated Fingerprint Identification System (AFIS) overview - A short history," Thales, January 27, 2022, https://www.thalesgroup.com/en/markets/digital-identity-and-security/government/biometrics/afis-history.

290. This is a personal account from Alex Tichy. In 1980, AFIS technology was sold to Thomas De La Rue (TDLR) of the United Kingdom. Since Mr. Tichy spoke multiple languages, he was hired by TDLR to promote the AFIS technology around the world. For over 25 years, he traveled to 90 countries, selling and installing the AFIS system.

291. "Automated Fingerprint Identification System (AFIS)," Thales.

292. Ibid.

293. "The Chance of Identical Fingerprints: 1 in 64 trillion," *Scientific American*, August 6, 2020 (originally published in June 1894), https://www.scientificamerican.com/article/the-chance-of-identical-fingerprints-1-in-64-trillion/.

294. University of Abertay Dundee, "Forensic breakthrough: Recovering fingerprints on fabrics could turn clothes into silent witnesses," ScienceDaily, February 2, 2011, https://www.sciencedaily.com/releases/2011/01/110131073141.htm.

295. Ibid.

296. University of Nottingham, "Cutting-edge fingerprint technology could help in the fight against knife crime," Phys.org, March 19, 2019, https://phys.org/news/2019-03-cutting-edge-fingerprint-technology-knife-crime.html.

297. Ibid.

298. C.L. Stallings and Dianne de Leon Stallings, *Death in a Red Desert* (PPC Book Publishing, 2011).

299. Bettina Boxall, "Proved Guilty by a Hair," *Los Angeles Times*, December 21, 2001, https://www.latimes.com/archives/la-xpm-2001-dec-21-mn-16999-story.html.

300. Stallings and Stallings, *Death in a Red Desert*.

301. Arthur Conan Doyle, "A Scandal in Bohemia," *The Strand Magazine*, June 25, 1891.

302. Kiierr International, "Hair Anatomy: Everything You Need to Know," Kiierr, November 9, 2020, https://kiierr.com/hair-anatomy-everything-you-need-to-know/.

303. Douglas W. Deedrick, "Part 1: Hair Evidence," *Forensic Science Communications* 2, no. 3 (July 2000), https://archives.fbi.gov/archives/about-us/lab/forensic-science-communications/fsc/july2000/deedric1.htm.

304. "Trace Evidence," Federal Bureau of Investigation, n.d., https://www.fbi.gov/services/laboratory/scientific-analysis/trace-evidence.

305. "Hair," Bureau of Criminal Apprehension, 2022, https://dps.mn.gov/divisions/bca/bca-divisions/forensic-science/Pages/trace-hair.aspx.

306. Dr. Georgia Purdom, "Variety Within Created Kinds," Answers in Genesis, April 1, 2010, https://answersingenesis.org/creation-science/baraminology/variety-within-created-kinds/.

307. Tz'u, *The Washing Away of Wrongs*.

308. Hans Sachs, "History of hair analysis," *Forensic Science International* 84 (1997): 7–16, https://www.sciencedirect.com/sdfe/pdf/download/eid/1-s2.0-S0379073896020439/first-page-pdf.

309. "Hair Analysis," Encyclopedia.com, May 14, 2018, https://www.encyclopedia.com/sports-and-everyday-life/food-and-drink/food-and-cooking/hair-analysis.

310. Deedrick, "Part 1: Hair Evidence."

311. Douglas W. Deedrick and Sandra L. Koch, "Microscopy of Hair Part II: A Practical Guide and Manual for Animal Hairs," *Forensic Science Communications* 6, no. 3 (July 2004), https://archives.fbi.gov/archives/about-us/lab/forensic-science-communications/fsc/july2004/research/2004_03_research02.htm.

312. Ibid.

313. National Forensic Science Technology Center, "A Simplified Guide to Trace Evidence," Forensic Science Simplified, 2013, http://www.forensicsciencesimplified.org/trace/TraceEvidence.pdf.

314. History.com editors, "Atlanta child murderer is traced using rare nylon fiber," History, May 20, 2020, https://www.history.com/this-day-in-history/atlanta-child-murderer-is-questioned.

315. "F.B.I. Fiber Expert Links Hairs to Wayne Williams," *The New York Times*, February 2, 1982, https://www.nytimes.com/1982/02/02/us/fbi-fiber-expert-links-hairs-to-wayne-williams.html.

316. Ibid.

317. William DeLong, "Wayne Williams And The Mystery Of The Atlanta Child Murders," All That's Interesting, August 19, 2021, https://allthatsinteresting.com/wayne-williams-atlanta-child-murders.

318. Doyle, *A Study in Scarlet*.

319. https://www.selectusa.gov/textiles-industry-united-states.

320. "National Overview: Facts and Figures on Materials, Wastes and Recycling," United States Environmental Protection Agency, June 29, 2022, https://www.epa.gov/facts-and-figures-about-materials-waste-and-recycling/national-overview-facts-and-figures-materials#Generation.

321. "Leading cotton producing countries worldwide in 2020/2021," Statista, 2022, https://www.statista.com/statistics/263055/cotton-production-worldwide-by-top-countries/.

322. Douglas W. Deedrick, "Hairs, Fibers, Crime, and Evidence Part 2: Fiber Evidence," *Forensic Science Communications* 2, no. 3 (July 2000), https://archives.fbi.gov/archives/about-us/lab/forensic-science-communications/fsc/july2000/deedric3.htm.

323. Bodie Hodge, "Why Were Eve's Eyes Not Opened Until Adam Ate?" Answers win Genesis, July 6, 2010, https://answersingenesis.org/adam-and-eve/why-were-eves-eyes-not-opened-until-adam-ate/.

324. "Why does the Bible speak against wearing clothing made of different types of fabric?" Got Questions, January 4, 2022, https://www.gotquestions.org/different-types-of-fabric.html.

325. Mohammad Zillane Patwary, "Silk Fiber: Physical And Chemical Properties Of Silk Fiber," Textile Fashion Study, June 27, 2012, https://textilefashionstudy.com/silk-fiber-physical-and-chemical-properties-of-silk/.

326. Steph Wright, "Top Cotton Producing Countries In The World," World Atlas, September 7, 2020, https://www.worldatlas.com/articles/top-cotton-producing-countries-in-the-world.html.

327. Deedrick, "Hairs, Fibers, Crime, and Evidence Part 2."

328. Mary Schimenz Hopkins, "About Rayon Fabric," Leaf, 2022, https://www.leaf.tv/articles/about-rayon-fabric/.

329. Hopkins, "About Rayon Fabric."

330. Sohanur Rahman Sobuj, "Crystalline and Amorphous Structure of Fiber," Textile Study Center, January 21, 2017, https://textilestudycenter.com/cry-str-fiber/.

331. Sobuj, "Crystalline and Amorphous Structure of Fiber."

332. Deedrick, "Hairs, Fibers, Crime, and Evidence Part 2."

333. Y. Li and X.-Q. Dai, "Fiber mechanics," *Biomechanical Engineering of Textiles and Clothing* (Cambridge: Woodhead Publishing, 2006), https://www.sciencedirect.com/topics/engineering/fibre-size.

334. Flinn Scientific, Inc., "Dyes and Dyeing," *Flinn Scientific Chem Fax!* no. 10153 (2016), https://www.flinnsci.com/api/library/Download/c46ad-9cfbff64e9cae7caf3aed645692.

335. Janet Wickell, "How to Do a Fabric Burn Test to Identify Fibers," The Spruce Crafts, June 26, 2020, https://www.thesprucecrafts.com/fabric-burn-test-to-identify-fibers-2821302.

336. Deedrick, "Hairs, Fibers, Crime, and Evidence Part 2."

337. Nick Poyntz, director, *Mind of a Monster*, season 1, episode 3, "Green River Killer," aired February 17, 2020.

338. Amy Tikkanen, "Gary Ridgway: American serial killer," Britannica, February 14, 2022, https://www.britannica.com/biography/Gary-Ridgway.

339. "Trace Evidence and Physical Evidence," The Green River Killer, n.d., https://greenriverkiller1.weebly.com/trace-evidence.html.

340. Ibid.

341. Doyle, *The Hound of the Baskervilles*.

342. The Editors of Encyclopaedia Britannica, "Glass," Britannica, August 3, 2021, https://www.britannica.com/technology/glass.

343. Maureen C. Bottrell, "Forensic Glass Comparison: Background Information Used in Data Interpretation," *Forensic Science Communications* 11, no. 2 (April 2009), https://archives.fbi.gov/archives/about-us/lab/forensic-science-communications/fsc/april2009/review/2009_04_review01.htm.

344. Ibid.

345. Mo-Sci Corp., "Changing Glass Properties with Glass Modifiers," AZO Materials, February 6, 2020, https://www.azom.com/article.aspx?ArticleID=18872.

346. The Editors of Encyclopaedia Britannica, "Soda-lime glass," Britannica, December 19, 2008, https://www.britannica.com/technology/soda-lime-glass.

347. National Forensic Science Technology Center, "A Simplified Guide to Trace Evidence."

348. Jakub Michał Milczarek, Grzegorz Zadora, Janina Zieba-Palus, and Paweł Kościelniak, "Forensic examination of car paints," ResearchGate, June 2008, https://www.researchgate.net/publication/294871293_Forensic_examination_of_car_paints.

349. Ibid.

350. https://www.researchgate.net/figure/Infrared-spectra-of-paint-samples-A-acrylic-resin-U-urethane-resin-S-styrene_fig1_200478636.

351. "Electrical Connections," The Nature of Physical Science, 1998, https://www.honolulu.hawaii.edu/instruct/natsci/science/brill/sci122/Programs/p27/p27.html.

352. "Forensic Palynology," The Forensics Library, n.d., http://aboutforensics.co.uk/forensic-palynology/.

353. Arthur Conan Doyle, *The Sign of Four* (London: Penguin Books, 1982).

354. "Forensics Lab 5.2: Examine The Physical Characteristics Of Soil," Make:, 2022, https://makezine.com/laboratory-52-examine-the-physical/.

355. Raymond C. Murray and John C.F. Tedrow, *Forensic Geology* (Upper Saddle River, NJ: Prentice Hall, 1992).

356. "Mineral Riches in the Soil," BYJU'S, 2022, https://byjus.com/biology/mineral-riches-in-the-soil/.

357. "Forensic Soil Analysis," Crime Museum, 2021, https://www.crimemuseum.org/crime-library/forensic-investigation/forensic-soil-analysis/.

358. "Forensics Lab 5.2," Make:.

359. "Daubert standard," Legal Information Institute, n.d., https://www.law.cornell.edu/wex/daubert_standard.

360. "5 Surprising Facts About Otzi the Iceman," National Geographic, October 18, 2013, https://www.nationalgeographic.com/history/article/131016-otzi-ice-man-mummy-five-facts.

361. Ibid.

362. Elon Green, "Fighting Crime, With Pollen," *The Atlantic*, November 17, 2015, https://www.theatlantic.com/science/archive/2015/11/fighting-crime-with-pollen/416259/.

363. Dallas Mildenhall, "Civil and criminal investigations: The use of spores and pollen," *Siak Journal* no. 4 (2008): 35–52, doi:10.7396/2008_4_E.

364. Vaughn Bryant and Gretchen Jones, "Pollen and Solving Crime," ASU - Ask A Biologist, December 21, 2009, https://askabiologist.asu.edu/pollen-and-solving-crime.

365. Sugandha G, "Forensic Palynology: Meaning, Analysis and Problems," Biology Discussion, n.d., https://www.biologydiscussion.com/palynology/forensic-palynology/forensic-palynology-meaning-analysis-and-problems/64740.

366. Ibid.

367. Bryant and Jones, "Pollen and Solving Crime."

368. Ibid.

369. Karen L. Bell, Berry Brosi, and Kevin Burgess, "Pollen genetics can help with forensic investigations," The Conversation, September 5, 2016, https://theconversation.com/pollen-genetics-can-help-with-forensic-investigations-53426.

370. Christianna Brand, *Heaven Knows Who: The Trial of Jessie M'Lachlan* (New York: Mysterious Press, 1960).

371. Doyle, *The Hound of the Baskervilles*.

372. "Pattern and Impression Evidence," NIST, January 9, 2017, https://www.nist.gov/oles/pattern-and-impression-evidence.

373. Jiaxin Zhu, Liangcheng Yi, Wenqian Ma, Ziyue Zhu, and Guillem Esquius, "The Reliability of Forensic Evidence: The Case of Curtis Flowers," Cornell University, 2010, https://courses2.cit.cornell.edu/sociallaw/FlowersCase/forensicevidence.html.

374. P. Smith, "U.S. footwear market – statistics & facts," Statista, January 12, 2022, https://www.statista.com/topics/4704/us-footwear-market/.

375. Michael B. Smith, "The Forensic Analysis of Footwear Impression Evidence," *Forensic Science Communications* 11, no. 3 (July 2009), https://archives.fbi.gov/archives/about-us/lab/forensic-science-communications/fsc/july2009/review/2009_07_review02.htm.

376. Smith, "The Forensic Analysis of Footwear Impression Evidence."

377. Scientific Working Group for Shoeprint and Tire Tread Evidence (SWGTREAD), "Standard for Terminology Used for Forensic Footwear and Tire Impression Evidence," Crime Scene Investigator Network, 2013, https://www.crime-scene-investigator.net/standard-for-terminology-used-for-forensic-footwear-and-tire-impression-evidence.html.

378. Smith, "The Forensic Analysis of Footwear Impression Evidence."

379. Ibid.

380. R.S. Stone, "Footwear examinations: Mathematical probabilities of Theoretical individual characteristics," *Journal of Forensic Identification* 56, no. 4 (2006): 577–599, https://www.researchgate.net/publication/285785802_Footwear_examinations_Mathematical_probabilities_of_Theoretical_individual_characteristics.

381. National Forensic Science Technology Center, "A Simplified Guide To Footwear & Tire Track Examination," Forensic Science Simplified, 2013, http://www.forensicsciencesimplified.org/fwtt/FootwearTireTracks.pdf.

382. R. H. Tuttle, 'Kinesiological inferences and evolutionary implications from Laetoli bipedal trails G-1, G-2/3 and A', Leakey and Harris, Ref. 1, Chapter 13.3, pp. 503–523.

383. Dr. Elizabeth Mitchell, "Laetoli Footprints Revisited," Answers in Genesis, November 12, 2011, https://answersingenesis.org/human-evolution/lucy/laetoli-footprints-revisited/.

384. SWGTREAD, "Standard for Terminology."

385. "Tire Construction Types: Cross Ply or Radial?" PresticeBDT, n.d., https://www.presticebdt.com/tire-construction-types-cross-ply-and-radial/.

386. "Vehicle Marks As Trace Evidence," GlobalSecurity.org, 2022, https://www.globalsecurity.org/military/library/policy/army/fm/19-25/CH11.htm.

387. Ibid.

388. G. Beauchamp, D. Hessel, N. Rose, Stephen J. Fenton, and Tilo Voitel, "Determining Vehicle Steering and Braking from Yaw Mark Striations," *SAE International Journal of Passenger Cars* (April 2009), doi:10.4271/2009-01-0092.

389. Stuart H. James and Jon J. Nordby, eds., *Forensic Science*, 3rd ed., (Boca Raton, FL: CRC Press, 2009).

390. Ibid.

391. https://www.njsp.org/division/investigations/trace-evidence.shtml.

392. Tuttle, 'Kinesiological inferences.'

393. Elizabeth Mitchell, "Clock in the Rock," Answers in Genesis, January 14, 2012, https://answersingenesis.org/geology/radiometric-dating/clock-in-the-rock/.

394. "Radiometric Dating," Answers in Genesis, 2023, https://answersingenesis.org/geology/radiometric-dating/.

395. Mike Wiser and Michael Kirk, "Transcript," Frontline, Death by Fire, 2014, https://www.pbs.org/wgbh/pages/frontline/death-by-fire/etc/transcript.html.

396. Ibid.

397. Ibid.

398. Ibid.

399. Doyle, *The Case-Book of Sherlock Holmes*.

400. I. Mitic, "The Fraudster Next Door: 30 Insurance Fraud Statistics," Fortunly, March 10, 2022, https://fortunly.com/statistics/insurance-fraud-statistics.

401. Richard Saferstein, *Forensic Science: From the Crime Scene to the Crime Lab*, 3rd ed. (New York: Pearson, 2016).

402. "Flammable range," Wärtsilä, 2022, https://www.wartsila.com/encyclopedia/term/flammable-range.

403. "Why does a flame burn upwards?" ScienceLet, August 18, 2013, http://www.sciencelet.com/2013/08/why-do-flames-burn-upwards.html.

404. Christine Hess Orthmann and Kären M. Hess, *Criminal Investigation*, 10th ed. (Independence, KY: Cengage Learning, 2013).

405. "Ignitable Liquids Reference Collection," National Center for Forensic Science, 2021, https://ilrc.ucf.edu/.

406. National Academies and the Department of Homeland Security, "IED Attack: Improvised Explosive Devices," *News & Terrorism: Communicating in a Crisis* (n.d.), https://www.dhs.gov/sites/default/files/publications/prep_ied_fact_sheet.pdf.

407. National Forensic Science Technology Center, "A Simplified Guide to Explosives Analysis," A Simplified Guide to Forensic Science, 2013, http://www.forensicsciencesimplified.org/explosives/Explosives.pdf.

408. A.D. Beveridge, "Improvised Explosive Devices," *Encyclopedia of Forensic Sciences* (2013): 59–63, https://doi.org/10.1016/B978-0-12-382165-2.00082-9.

409. "IED Attack Fact Sheet: Improvised Explosive Devices," Homeland Security, May 19, 2022, https://www.dhs.gov/publication/ied-attack-fact-sheet.

410. "United States Bomb Data Center (USBDC) Explosives Incident Report (EIR)," Bureau of Alcohol, Tobacco, Firearms and Explosives, 2017, https://www.atf.gov/file/128106/download.

411. "About IAAI," International Association of Arson Investigators, 2022, https://www.firearson.com/.

412. Douglas O. Linder, "The Dr. Sam Sheppard Trial," Famous Trials, 2006, http://law2.umkc.edu/faculty/projects/FTrials/sheppard/sheppardaccount.html.

413. Daniel Rennie, "The Trial Of Sam Sheppard: How A Media Frenzy Led To The Life Imprisonment Of A Young Doctor," All That's Interesting, February 22, 2019, https://allthatsinteresting.com/sam-sheppard.

414. Linder, "The Dr. Sam Sheppard Trial."

415. Douglas O. Linder, "Who Killed Marilyn?: Evidence Concerning Richard Eberling-- Was He 'the Bushy-Haired Man'?" Famous Trials, 2022, https://famous-trials.com/sam-sheppard/10-evidence.

416. Ibid.

417. Ibid.

418. Linder, "The Dr. Sam Sheppard Trial."

419. Ibid.

420. Doyle, *A Study in Scarlet*.

421. Dr. Dana Sneed, "Without God, Math Doesn't Make Sense," Answers in Genesis, March 14, 2021, https://answersingenesis.org/mathematics/without-god-math-doesnt-make-sense/.

422. Orrin Grey, "A Body and a Bloody Trunk: The Infamous Gouffé Case of 1889," The Lineup, August 24, 2016, https://the-line-up.com/gouffe-case-1889.

423. Douglas Starr, "Murder in the 19th Century France and the Birth of Forensic Science," Gizmodo, October 14, 2010, https://gizmodo.com/murder-in-19th-century-france-and-the-birth-of-forensic-5662454.

424. Arthur Conan Doyle, "The Adventure of the Abbey Grange," *The Strand Magazine*, September 1904.

425. Dr. Alan L. Gillen and Douglas Oliver, "Antony van Leeuwenhoek: Creation 'Magnified' Through His Magnificent Microscopes," Answers in Genesis, August 15, 2012, https://answersingenesis.org/creation-scientists/profiles/antony-van-leeuwenhoeks-microscopes-creation-magnified/.

426. Ibid.

427. David M. Menton, *Scope It Out! Microscope 101* (for private use at the Creation Museum).

428. Ibid.

429. Ibid.

430. Ibid.

431. "Microscope, Comparison," Encyclopedia.com, June 21, 2022, https://www.encyclopedia.com/science/encyclopedias-almanacs-transcripts-and-maps/microscope-comparison.

432. "Microscopy Polarization Explained," Microscope World, 2022, https://www.microscopeworld.com/p-3378-microscopy-polarization-explained.aspx.

433. "What is a Microspectrophotometer?" Craic, 2021, https://www.microspectra.com/support/learn/what-is-a-microspectrophotometer.

434. "VHA Diagnostic Electron Microscopy Program," U.S. Department of Veterans Affairs, August 1, 2017, https://www.va.gov/DIAGNOSTICEM/What_Is_Electron_Microscopy_and_How_Does_It_Work.asp.

435. Ibid.

436. History.com editors, "The Demise of the Mafia," History, February 22, 2019, https://www.history.com/topics/crime/the-demise-of-the-mafia.

437. History.com editors, "St. Valentine's Day Massacre," History, February 4, 2021, https://www.history.com/topics/crime/saint-valentines-day-massacre.

438. History.com editors, "The St. Valentine's Day Massacre," History, April 16, 2021, https://www.history.com/this-day-in-history/the-st-valentines-day-massacre.

439. "Goddard, Calvin Hooker," Encyclopedia.com, June 21, 2022, https://www.encyclopedia.com/science/encyclopedias-almanacs-transcripts-and-maps/goddard-calvin-hooker.

440. Arthur Conan Doyle, "The Boscombe Valley Mystery," *The Strand Magazine*, 1891.

441. Jay A. Siegel, "Crime laboratory," Britannica, February 7, 2019, https://www.britannica.com/science/crime-laboratory.

442. Steven Benner and Michael Sismour, "Synthetic Biology," *Nature Reviews Genetics* 6 (2005): 533–543.

443. Dr. Georgia Purdom, "Semi-Homemade Life," Answers in Genesis, September 5, 2007, https://answersingenesis.org/origin-of-life/synthetic-life/semi-homemade-life/.

444. Ibid.

445. Richard Saferstein, *Forensic Science: An Introduction*, 3rd ed. (New York: Pearson, 2016).

446. "Forensic Science and Technical Division," LAPD, 2022, https://www.lapdonline.org/office-of-the-chief-of-police/office-of-special-operations/detective-bureau/detective-services-group/forensic-science-and-technical-division/.

447. Kim Waggoner, "Research and Technology," *Forensic Science Communications* 9, no. 4 (October 2007), https://archives.fbi.gov/archives/about-us/lab/forensic-science-communications/fsc/oct2007/research.

448. Waggoner, "Research and Technology."

449. Siegel, "Crime laboratory."

450. Michael Ray, "London bombings of 2005," Britannica, June 30, 2022, https://www.britannica.com/event/London-bombings-of-2005.

451. Kevin J. Strom and Joe Eyerman, "Interagency Coordination: A Case Study of the 2005 London Train Bombings," *National Institute of Justice Journal*, no. 260 (July 2008), https://nij.ojp.gov/topics/articles/interagency-coordination-case-study-2005-london-train-bombings.

452. Ibid.

453. "Report of the Official Account of the Bombings in London on 7th July 2005," House of Commons, May 11, 2006, https://assets.publishing.service.gov.uk/government/uploads/system/uploads/attachment_data/file/228837/1087.pdf.

454. Arthur Conan Doyle, "The Adventure of Shoscombe Old Place," *The Strand Magazine*, April 1927.

455. Kristina Ericksen, "Cracking Cases with Digital Forensics," Rasmussen University, March 22, 2018, https://www.rasmussen.edu/degrees/justice-studies/blog/cracking-cases-with-digital-forensics/.

456. Dimitar Kostadinov, "The mobile forensics process: steps and types," Infosec, July 6, 2019, https://resources.infosecinstitute.com/topic/mobile-forensics-process-steps-types/.

457. "Fighting Crime with Mobile Technology," South University, August 10, 2016, https://www.southuniversity.edu/news-and-blogs/2016/08/fighting-crime-with-mobile-technology-137309.

458. Ivana Križanović, "Cell phone history: From the first phone to today's smartphone wonders," Versus, December 2, 2021, https://versus.com/en/news/cell-phone-history.

459. Ibid.
460. Meghan Tocci, "Smartphone History and Evolution," SimpleTexting, August 19, 2019, https://simpletexting.com/where-have-we-come-since-the-first-smartphone/.
461. Chris Stokel-Walker, "How smartphones and social media are changing Christianity," BBC, February 22, 2017, https://www.bbc.com/future/article/20170222-how-smartphones-and-social-media-are-changing-religion.
462. "Introduction to Mobile Forensics," eForensics Magazine, May 19, 2015, https://eforensicsmag.com/introduction-to-mobile-forensics/.
463. Ibid.
464. Kostadinov, "The mobile forensics process."
465. "Best Mobile Forensic Tools For iPhone & Android: 2022 Reviews," Cybericus, 2022, https://cybericus.com/best-mobile-forensic-tools/.
466. Reesha P. and Elizabeth Rose Lalson, "Forensics Analysis of Open Wifi Network," *International Research Journal of Engineering and Technology (IRJET)* 8, no. 2 (February 2021): 2253–2259, https://www.irjet.net/archives/V8/i2/IRJET-V8I2334.pdf.
467. Forensic Focus, "Mobile Phone Forensic Challenges," Forensic Focus For Digital Forensics & E-Discovery Professionals, May 17, 2012, https://www.forensicfocus.com/articles/mobile-phone-forensic-challenges/.
468. "Fighting Crime with Mobile Technology," South University.
469. Brendon Baxter, "File-based encryption vs full-disk encryption," Hexnode, January 24, 2022, https://www.hexnode.com/blogs/file-based-encryption-vs-full-disk-encryption/.
470. "Oklahoma City Bombing," Federal Bureau of Investigation, n.d., https://www.fbi.gov/history/famous-cases/oklahoma-city-bombing.
471. "The 'Art' of Solving Crime: There's More to the FBI Lab Than Science," Federal Bureau of Investigation, June 8, 2005, https://archives.fbi.gov/archives/news/stories/2005/june/ipgu060805.
472. "Oklahoma City Bombing," Federal Bureau of Investigation.
473. "FBI: McVeigh knew children would be killed in OKC blast," CNN, March 29, 2001, https://www.cnn.com/2001/US/03/29/mcveigh.book.01/index.html.
474. "Oklahoma City Bombing," Federal Bureau of Investigation.
475. History.com editors, "Timothy McVeigh convicted for Oklahoma City bombing," History, June 1, 2021, https://www.history.com/this-day-in-history/mcveigh-convicted-for-oklahoma-city-bombing.
476. Ibid.
477. Doyle, *The Hound of the Baskervilles*.
478. Dr. David Menton, "Did Humans Really Evolve from Apelike Creatures?" Answers in Genesis, February 25, 2010, https://answersingenesis.org/human-evolution/ape-man/did-humans-really-evolve-from-ape-like-creatures/.
479. Ibid.
480. Kate Bartlett, director, *Timewatch*, "Britain's Greatest Hoax," aired November 21, 2003, BBC Two.
481. Dr. Elizabeth Mitchell, "Piltdown Pals," Answers in Genesis, February 11, 2012, https://answersingenesis.org/human-evolution/piltdown-man/piltdown-pals/.
482. Heather Brinson Bruce, "The Making of a Caveman," Answers in Genesis, March 27, 2012, https://answersingenesis.org/human-evolution/cavemen/the-making-of-a-caveman/.
483. The University of Sheffield, "Preparation and tissue depth: A description of how to apply osteometric markers to determine the tissue depth of each facial muscle," Future Learn, n.d., https://www.futurelearn.com/info/courses/forensic-facial-reconstruction/0/steps/31185.
484. Ibid.
485. Heidi Kuivaniemi-Smith, "Facial reconstruction," Facial Depiction, n.d., http://facialdepiction.com/facial-reconstruction/.
486. Wesley Neville, "2D & Postmortem Reconstruction," Forensic Art World - Forensic Art Service LLC, n.d., https://forensicartist.com/new/2d-reconstruction/.
487. "Criminal Investigation Software – FACES for Law Enforcement," FACES, 2009, https://www.faces-id.com/products_faces_le.html.
488. Ron Alalouff, "Automatic Facial Recognition: authentication, identification and ethical use," Ifsec Global, November 26, 2020, https://www.ifsecglobal.com/critical-conversations/automatic-facial-recognition-authentication-identification-and-ethical-use/.
489. Thorin Klosowski, "Facial Recognition Is Everywhere. Here's What We Can Do About It," Wirecutter, July 15, 2020, https://www.nytimes.com/wirecutter/blog/how-facial-recognition-works/.
490. Ibid.
491. Alalouff, "Automatic Facial Recognition."
492. Biography.com editors, "Ted Bundy," September 15, 2021, Biography, https://www.biography.com/crime-figure/ted-bundy.
493. John Philip Jenkins, "Ted Bundy: American serial killer," Britannica, January 20, 2022, https://www.britannica.com/biography/Ted-Bundy.
494. Mike McPadden, "Crime History: Ted Bundy Dies Weeping in the Electric Chair, Crowds Cheer," Crimefeed, January 24, 2017, https://www.investigationdiscovery.com/crimefeed/crime-history/crime-history-ted-bundy-dies-weeping-in-the-electric-chair-crowds-cheer.
495. Doyle, *The Case-Book of Sherlock Holmes*.
496. ALF Animal Liberation Front, "Little Tyke: True Story of a Gentle Vegetarian Lioness," All-Creatures.org, April 2018, https://www.all-creatures.org/stories/a-tyke-veg-lion.html.
497. Ibid.
498. Ken Ham, "A Shark That Eats Its Veggies?" Answers in Genesis, September 14, 2018, https://answersingenesis.org/aquatic-animals/shark-eats-veggies/.
499. Rossella Lorenzi, "Oldest Dentistry Found in 14,000-Year-Old Tooth," Seeker, July 16, 2015, https://www.seeker.com/oldest-dentistry-found-in-14000-year-old-tooth-1770027700.html.
500. Reidar F. Sognnaes and Ferdinand Ström, "The odontological identification of Adolf Hitler: Definitive documentation by X-rays, interrogations and autopsy findings," *Acta Odontologica Scandinavica* 31 (1973): 43–69, https://www.dentalage.co.uk/wp-content/uploads/2014/09/sognnaes_rf__strom_f_1973_hitlers-dentition.pdf.
501. Ibid.
502. Ibid.
503. Dental Practice Management, "Forensic Dentistry: Identifying the Victims of 9/11," Oral Health, December 1, 2001, https://www.oralhealthgroup.com/features/forensic-dentistry-identifying-the-victims-of-9-11/.
504. Carlita Salazar, "Why Forensic Odontology Fails: An Ongoing Innocence Project Case," Elsevier SciTech Connect, January 28, 2014, http://scitechconnect.elsevier.com/forensic-odontology-fails-ongoing-innocence-project-case-2/.
505. G. Radford, J.A. Kieser, V. Bernal, J.N. Waddell, A. Forrest, "Biomechanical approach to human bitemark reconstruction," *J Forensic Odontostomatol* 27, no. 1 (June 2009): 33–36.
506. Swapna Jagadees Kuttikara, "Methods in bitemark analysis" (master's thesis, Universitetet I Oslo, 2017), https://www.duo.uio.no/bitstream/handle/10852/57560/Bitemark-analysis.pdf?sequence=1&isAllowed=y.
507. Shanna Freeman and Melanie Radzicki McManus, "How Forensic Dentistry Works," HowStuffWorks, January 27, 2022, https://science.howstuffworks.com/forensic-dentistry3.htm.
508. Sandeep Kaur, Kewal Krishan, Preetika M. Chatterjee, and Tanuj Kanchan, "Analysis and Identification of Bite Marks in Forensic Casework," *OHDM* 12, no. 3 (September 2013), https://oralhealth.ro/volumes/2013/volume-3/Paper500.pdf.
509. Ibid.

510. Dale Lezon and Peggy O'Hare, "Jurors hear Yates' chilling call to 911," Chron, June 26, 2006, https://www.chron.com/news/article/Jurors-hear-Yates-chilling-call-to-911-1866104.php.

511. "911 tape reveals unemotional Andrea Yates," CNN, January 6, 2002, https://edition.cnn.com/2001/US/12/10/yates.911/.

512. Lezon and O'Hare, "Jurors hear Yates' chilling call to 911."

513. Jan Martinet, producer, *American Justice*, season 12, episode 2, "The Andrea Yates Story," aired January 15, 2003.

514. Jessica Willey, "Andrea Yates: 20 years since the tragedy that shocked the nation," ABC13, June 17, 2021, https://abc13.com/andrea-yates-rusty-george-parnham-clear-lake-texas/10802560/.

515. Arthur Conan Doyle, "The Adventure of the Cardboard Box," *The Strand Magazine*, January 1893.

516. Emilee Green, "Mental Illness and Violence: Is there a Link?" Illinois Criminal Justice Information Authority, May 4, 2020, https://icjia.illinois.gov/researchhub/articles/mental-illness-and-violence-is-there-a-link.

517. National Center for Chronic Disease Prevention and Health Promotion (NCCDPHP) and Division of Population Health (DPH), "About Mental Health," Centers for Disease Control and Prevention (CDC), June 28, 2021, https://www.cdc.gov/mentalhealth/learn/index.htm.

518. Ibid.

519. National Academy of Sciences, "Violence and Mental Health: Opportunities for Prevention and Early Detection: Proceedings of a Workshop," National Library of Medicine, 2018, https://www.ncbi.nlm.nih.gov/books/NBK488196.

520. J. Bradford and G. Glancy, "Forensic Psychiatry," *International Encyclopedia of the Social & Behavioral Sciences* (2001): 5740–5745, cited in "Forensic Psychiatry," ScienceDirect, https://www.sciencedirect.com/topics/medicine-and-dentistry/forensic-psychiatry.

521. Florida National University, "The Role of Forensic Psychology in Criminal Justice," Florida National University, January 14, 2020, https://www.fnu.edu/role-forensic-psychology-criminal-justice/.

522. Payne Lindsey, "There's Our Guy," January 16, 2017, in *Up and Vanished*, podcast, https://season1.upandvanished.com/episode/episode-11/.

523. David Robertson, "Mental Health," Our Daily Bread, 2022, https://ourdailybread.org/christians-and-mental-illness/.

524. Michael B. First, "Routine Psychiatric Assessment," Merck Manual, May 2022, https://www.merckmanuals.com/professional/psychiatric-disorders/approach-to-the-patient-with-mental-symptoms/routine-psychiatric-assessment.

525. Katrina Kuzyszyn-Jones, "What Is A Forensic Psychological Evaluation?" KKJ Forensic Psychology, n.d., https://kkjforensicpsychology.com/psychological-forensic-evaluations/.

526. "What Does a Forensic Psychiatrist Do?" Learn.org, 2022, https://learn.org/articles/What_Does_a_Forensic_Psychiatrist_Do.html.

527. "What Is Criminal Psychology?" Online Psychology Degrees, 2018, https://www.online-psychology-degrees.org/study/criminal-psychology/.

528. Ibid.

529. Lisa Levy, "John Douglas on His Life's Work: Talking with Killers," Crime Reads, May 29, 2019, https://crimereads.com/john-douglas-on-his-lifes-work-talking-with-killers/.

530. Ibid.

531. "Criminal Profiling," Criminal Psychology, 2017, https://www.e-criminalpsychology.com/criminal-profiling/.

532. "Sample Questions for Expert Witnesses," Texas Department of Family and Protective Services, n.d., https://www.dfps.state.tx.us/Child_Protection/Attorneys_Guide/documents/Section_13_Tools/Evidence/Questions_Expert_Witness.pdf.

533. "Jack the Ripper: A Criminal Profile," The Jack the Ripper Tour, June 18, 2019, https://thejackthetrippertour.com/blog/jack-the-ripper-a-criminal-profile/.

534. David C. Hardy, "What are Miranda Rights and Who Was Ernesto Miranda?" The Hardy Law Firm, P.A., August 26, 2018, thehardylawfirm.com/blog/what-are-miranda-rights-and-who-was-ernesto-miranda/.

535. Joseph Petrocelli, "How It All Began: Miranda v. Arizona," *Police Magazine*, May 11, 2010, https://www.policemag.com/340315/how-it-all-began-imiranda-v-arizona-i.

536. Ibid.

537. Doyle, "The Adventure of the Blue Carbuncle."

538. Daniel E. Hall, *Criminal Law and Procedure*, 7th ed. (Clifton Park, NY: Cengage Learning, 2015).

539. Russel Fuller, "Is Capital Punishment for Today?" Answers in Genesis, December 28, 2014, https://answersingenesis.org/sanctity-of-life/capital-punishment-today/.

540. U.S. Const. art. III, § 1, https://constitution.congress.gov/constitution/article-3/.

541. "U.S. Supreme Court Research Guide: Overview," University of Michigan Law Library, June 10, 2022, https://libguides.law.umich.edu/scotus.

542. John Gramlich, "Only 2% of federal criminal defendants go to trial, and most who do are found guilty," Pew Research Center, June 11, 2019, https://www.pewresearch.org/fact-tank/2019/06/11/only-2-of-federal-criminal-defendants-go-to-trial-and-most-who-do-are-found-guilty/.

543. Ibid.

544. Hall, *Criminal Law and Procedure*.

545. "The Judicial Branch," The White House, n.d., https://www.whitehouse.gov/about-the-white-house/our-government/the-judicial-branch/.

546. Ibid.

547. American Bar Association, *Criminal Justice Standards: Prosecution Function*, 4th ed. (Washington, D.C.: American Bar Association, 2017), https://www.americanbar.org/groups/criminal_justice/standards/ProsecutionFunctionFourthEdition/.

548. Janet Portman, "The Prosecutor's Job," Lawyers.com, September 24, 2021, https://www.lawyers.com/legal-info/criminal/criminal-law-basics/keeping-law-and-order-the-prosecutor.html.

549. Tom Holland, "Why Do Prosecutors and Defense Lawyers Negotiate Plea Bargains?" Holland Law LLC, June 22, 2021, https://www.thollandlaw.com/blog/why-do-prosecutors-and-defense-lawyers-negotiate-plea-bargains/.

550. American Bar Association, *Criminal Justice Standards: Defense Function*, 4th ed. (Washington, D.C.: American Bar Association, 2017), https://www.americanbar.org/groups/criminal_justice/standards/DefenseFunctionFourthEdition/.

551. "What Is The Role Of A Defense Attorney?" The Law Dictionary, n.d., https://thelawdictionary.org/article/what-is-the-role-of-a-defense-attorney/.

552. STA Law Firm, "United States: Admissibility Of Forensic Evidence In Courts – USA Overview," Mondaq, February 26, 2020, https://www.mondaq.com/unitedstates/crime/897356/admissibility-of-forensic-evidence-in-courts-usa-overview.

553. Jess Scherman, "How Courtroom Technology has Revolutionized Criminal Cases," Rasmussen University, August 18, 2016, https://www.rasmussen.edu/degrees/justice-studies/blog/courtroom-technology-revolutionized-criminal-cases/.

554. U.S. Const. amend. IV.

555. Silverthorne Lumber Co. v. United States, 251 U.S. 385 (1920).

556. LawSchoolCaseBriefs.net, "Silverthorne Lumber Company v. United States case brief," Law School Case Briefs, November 3, 2013, https://www.lawschoolcasebriefs.net/2013/11/silverthorne-lumber-company-v-united.html.

557. Doyle, *A Study in Scarlet*.

558. Content Team, "Chain of Custody," Legal Dictionary, March 19, 2019, https://legaldictionary.net/chain-of-custody/.

559. J. Hampton Keathley, III, "Mark #16: Accountability," Bible.org, May 26, 2004, https://bible.org/seriespage/mark-16-accountability.

560. Ashish Badiye, Neeti Kapoor, and Ritesh G. Menezes, "Chain of Custody," National Library of Medicine, February 24, 2021, https://asomef.org.co/wp-content/uploads/2019/08/Chain-of-Custody.pdf.

561. Ibid.

562. Daniel Hall, *Criminal Law and Procedure*, 7th ed. (Stamford, CT: Cengage Learning, 2015).

563. Douglas O. Linder, "Testimony of Abbie Hoffman," Famous Trials, 2022, https://famous-trials.com/chicago8/1326-hoffman.

564. Leonard Kreicas, "Funny courtroom testimony," Daily Dose of Fun, June 3, 2014, https://ahumorsite.com/courtroom-testimony/.

565. Andy Simmons, "That's Outrageous! Funny Court Transcripts," *Reader's Digest*, April 16, 2016, https://preprod.rd.com/article/funny-court-transcripts/.

566. Doyle, *The Sign of Four*.

567. "What Is Criminal Psychology?" Online Psychology Degrees.

568. "DNA Exonerations in the United States," Innocence Project, 2022, https://innocenceproject.org/dna-exonerations-in-the-united-states/.

569. Greg Hurley, "The Trouble with Eyewitness Identification Testimony in Criminal Cases," ConstantReader, November 7, 2020, https://theconstantreader.com/es/the-trouble-with-eyewitness-identification-testimony-in-criminal-cases/.

570. Ron Smith, "Courtroom Testimony Techniques: 'Success Instead of Survival,'" Ron Smith & Associates, Inc., n.d., https://www.ronsmithandassociates.com/pdf/Ron%20Smith%20Courtroom%20Testimony%20112015.pdf.

571. "10 Etiquette Tips for Testifying in Court," Sweeney Merrigan Personal Injury Lawyers, 2022, https://www.sweeneymerrigan.com/blog/10-etiquette-tips-testifying-court/#.

572. Megan Wells, "6 tips for preparing yourself for courtroom testimony," Police1, November 15, 2016, https://www.police1.com/law-and-order/articles/6-tips-for-preparing-yourself-for-courtroom-testimony-aenP2IEFv49Iv8J8/.

573. Smith, "Courtroom Testimony Techniques."

574. The University of Sheffield, "Preparation and tissue depth: A description of how to apply osteometric markers to determine the tissue depth of each facial muscle," Future Learn, n.d., https://www.futurelearn.com/info/courses/forensic-facial-reconstruction/0/steps/31185.

575. Swapna Jagadees Kuttikara, "Methods in bitemark analysis" (master's thesis, Universitetet I Oslo, 2017), https://www.duo.uio.no/bitstream/handle/10852/57560/Bitemark-analysis.pdf?sequence=1&isAllowed=y.

576. Content Team, "Chain of Custody," Legal Dictionary, March 19, 2019, https://legaldictionary.net/chain-of-custody/.

577. American Bar Association, Criminal Justice Standards: Defense Function, 4th ed. (Washington, D.C.: American Bar Association, 2017), https://www.americanbar.org/groups/criminal_justice/standards/DefenseFunctionFourthEdition/.

578. J. Bradford and G. Glancy, "Forensic Psychiatry," International Encyclopedia of the Social & Behavioral Sciences (2001): 5740–5745, cited in "Forensic Psychiatry," ScienceDirect, https://www.sciencedirect.com/topics/medicine-and-dentistry/forensic-psychiatry.

579. Dr. Georgia Purdom, "Variety Within Created Kinds," Answers in Genesis, April 1, 2010, https://answersingenesis.org/creation-science/baraminology/variety-within-created-kinds/.

580. Heidi Kuivaniemi-Smith, "Facial reconstruction," Facial Depiction, n.d., http://facialdepiction.com/facial-reconstruction/.

581. Elizabeth Mitchell, "Clock in the Rock," Answers in Genesis, January 14, 2012, https://answersingenesis.org/geology/radiometric-dating/clock-in-therock/.

582. American Bar Association, *Criminal Justice Standards: Prosecution Function*, 4th ed. (Washington, D.C.: American Bar Association, 2017), https://www.americanbar.org/groups/criminal_justice/standards/ProsecutionFunctionFourthEdition/.

583. History.com editors, "The Invention of the Internet," History, October 28, 2019, https://www.history.com/topics/inventions/invention-of-the-internet.